The Semantic Conception of Theories
and Scientific Realism

The Semantic Conception of Theories and Scientific Realism

FREDERICK SUPPE

UNIVERSITY OF ILLINOIS PRESS

Urbana and Chicago

Publication of this work was supported in part by a grant from the
Office of Graduate Studies and Research, University of Maryland.

This book is printed on acid-free paper.

Library of Congress Cataloging-in-Publication Data

Suppe, Frederick.
    The semantic conception of theories and scientific
realism.

    Bibliography: p.
    Includes index.
    1. Science—Philosophy.   2. Science—Methodology.
3. Semantics (Philosophy).   4. Realism.   I. Title.
Q175.S9393   1989   501   88-27878
ISBN 0-252-01605-X (alk. paper)

To
Gertrude Cross Suppe
and
Jack Kingsley Suppe
(1910-1971)

Contents

PART III
Applications of the Semantic Conception

PART IV
Toward a Quasi-Realistic Theory of Scientific Knowledge

Preface

Although this book is based on some of my published and unpublished papers, it is no mere collection—none of the material here appears exactly as originally published or presented. Eight of the chapters have not appeared previously. The papers forming the basis for this volume have been selected and edited so as to produce a coherent work focusing on the Semantic Conception of Scientific Theories and scientific realism. I have edited out redundancies and overlapping discussions, altered terminology for consistency, adopted a unified reference style, augmented papers with passages from others, and in one case combined two articles into a single unit. In addition, various transitional sections and passages have been added for cohesiveness, and various passages have been edited to achieve a more concise prose style. For the most part, I have made such changes without comment. Where my alterations involve substantive changes in, or further development of, my published views or positions, I have indicated this by enclosing altered or additional material in brackets. (Such scruples were not adhered to in the case of papers previously presented but not published.) Thus none of the previously published articles presented here as chapters are exact reprintings of their original published versions, though unless noted, my views therein are essentially unchanged.

In writing the papers that appear here, I have incurred intellectual debts to a number of persons who read or commented on my work: Peter Achinstein, Nicholas Georgalis, Thomas Nickles, Robert Stalnaker, Arthur W. Burks, Anatol Rapoport, Keith Lehrer, Richard Boyd, Abraham Kaplan, Don F. Dulany, Bas C. van Fraassen, Wilfrid Sellars, Raymond Martin, Teddy Seidenfeld, Dudley Shapere, Ronald Giere, David Hull, Jaakko Hintikka, Fred Dretske, Clifford Hooker, Lars Svenonius, Kenneth Schaffner, George Estabrook, Hugh Chandler, J. L. Haller, H. Tristram Englehardt, Jr., Jack Meiland, Adolf Grünbaum, Ted McGuire, Thomas Kuhn, Alberto Cordero, Paul Thompson, Stephen G. Brush, Michael Gardner, Lindley Darden, Allen Stairs, Stephen

Stich, Ralph Kenat, Larry Laudan, Isaac Levi, Ernan McMullin, William Wimsatt, Nicholas Rescher, Michael Devitt, Michael Hooker, Hugh Petrie, and Patrick Suppes.

I especially thank Daniel Hausman who impressed upon me the need for a book on the Semantic Conception and repeatedly urged me to complete this volume. I apologize to those others whose contributions inadvertently have not been noted.

Some basic intellectual debts that were incurred in developing the Semantic Conception of Theories are detailed in chapter 1, section I. Patrick Suppes and Bas van Fraassen were most gracious in providing information and materials about the history of their versions of the Semantic Conception. I appreciate having had access to manuscript versions of Elisabeth Lloyd's and Paul Thompson's recent books on the Semantic Conception applied to biological theory and also Ronald Giere's new book, which utilizes the Semantic Conception and defends a form of realism.

I also wish to thank the many secretaries who have worked on various versions of the material in this volume over the last fifteen years, including Margaret Mary Ryan, Helen Wade, Mary Leutkemeyer, Susan Ragland, Anabelle Gregory, Karolyn Marshall, Sammy Ho, Jhana Bogan, and Lake Jagger. To these and others from the more distant past, I am grateful for their excellent work. David MacCallum read proof, and Richard Fyfe helped with the index.

Once again it is a pleasure to be publishing with the University of Illinois Press. I am especially grateful to my good friend, Richard Wentworth, Director of the Press, and my copyeditor, Beth Bower. I appreciate the good grace with which she handled my occasionally less than civil reactions to suggested revisions. Her conscientious efforts helped make this a better book, and the friendship that has emerged between us is highly valued.

Finally, some of the works appearing here have benefited from the support of the National Science Foundation, the National Endowment for the Humanities, the International Union for the History and Philosophy of Science, the American Council of Learned Societies, the University of Illinois Research Board, and the University of Maryland at College Park General Research Board. Their support is gratefully acknowledged. I also am indebted to other University of Maryland sources of support: A special research assignment by the Arts and Humanities Division gave me released time to complete this book. Michael Slote, Chairman of the Department of Philosophy, and Stephen G. Brush, Chairman of the Committee on the History and Philosophy of Science, made available special funds for secretarial assistance for the final preparation of the manuscript. Finally, the Office of Graduate Studies and Research paid for the preparation of diagrams and provided a generous publication subsidy which has helped to keep this volume affordable.

Frederick Suppe
Wethering Heights
Shenandoah County, Virginia
April 1988

Acknowledgments

Some of the material incorporated in this volume originally appeared elsewhere.

Chapter 2, section I. "On Partial Interpretation." *Journal of Philosophy* 68 (1971):57–76.

Chapter 2, sections II–IV. "What's Wrong with the Received View on the Structure of Scientific Theories?" *Philosophy of Science* 39 (1972):1–19.

Chapter 3. "Theories, Their Formulations, and the Operational Imperative." *Synthese* 25 (1973):129–64.

Chapters 3 and 4. "Theories and Phenomena." In *Developments in the Methodology of the Social Sciences*, ed. W. Leinfellner and E. Köhler, 45–92 (Dordrecht, Neth.: D. Reidel, 1974).

Chapter 5. "Theoretical Laws." In *Formal Methods in the Methodology of Empirical Sciences: Proceedings of the Conference for Formal Methods in the Methodology of Empirical Sciences*, Warsaw, June 17–21, 1974, ed. M. Przełecki, K. Szaniawski, and R. Wójcicki, 247–67 (Wrocklaw: Ossolineum, 1976).

Chapter 7. "Some Philosophy Problems in Biological Speciation and Taxonomy." In *Conceptual Basis of the Classification of Knowledge*, ed. J. Wojciechowski, 190–243 (Munich: Verlag Dokumentation, 1974).

Chapter 14. "Theory Structure." In *Current Research in the Philosophy of Science: Proceedings of the PSA Critical Research Problems Conference*, ed. P. Asquith and H. Kyburg, Jr., 317–38 (East Lansing, Mich.: Philosophy of Science Association, 1979).

Earlier versions of some material in the following chapters are being published elsewhere.

Chapters 1 and 11. "Nature and the Problem of Scientific Reason." To be published in *Review of Metaphysics,* May 1989.

Chapter 6. "A Nondeductivist Approach to Theoretical Explanation." In *The Limitations of Deductivism*, ed. A. Grünbaum and W. Salmon (Berkeley and Los Angeles: University of California Press, 1988), 128–66.

Chapter 13. "Is Science Really Inductive?" In *The Philosophy of Logical Mechanism: Essays in Honor of Arthur W. Burks, with his Responses,* ed. M. Salmon (Dordrecht, Neth.: D. Reidel), 1989.

Versions of the previously unpublished papers were presented as follows:

Chapter 8: "Interlevel Theories and the Semantic Conception of Theories." Conference on Methods in Philosophy and the Sciences, New School for Social Research, New York, May 1980.

Chapter 9. "Theoretical Perspectives on Closure." The Hastings Center Closure Project, The Hastings Center, June 1980.

Chapter 10. "Kuhn's and Feyerabend's Relativisms." The University of Delaware, 1976. The University of Maryland at College Park, 1977.

Chapter 11. "Scientific Realism." Originally prepared for the Pittsburgh Lecture Series in the Philosophy of Science, March 27, 1979. Versions were also presented at Indiana University and the University of Wisconsin at Milwaukee in 1979.

Chapter 12. "Conclusive Reasons, Causality, and the Objectivity of Scientific Knowledge." Georgetown University, Johns Hopkins University, and the University of Maryland at College Park, 1975.

Chapter 13. "Laudan on Meta-Methodology." Washington Philosophy Club, Washington, D.C., December 8, 1984.

PART I

From the Received View to the Semantic Conception

1

Prologue

The *Semantic Conception of Theories* is a philosophical analysis of the nature of scientific theories that has been undergoing development since at least 1948; anticipations as early as von Neumann 1932 and Birkhoff and von Neumann 1936 can be found. The Semantic Conception was offered as an alternative to the then-prevailing logical positivistic analysis of theories—the so-called Received View on Theories[1]—and proved to be one of many factors in the demise of the Received View. The Semantic Conception of Theories today probably is the philosophical analysis of the nature of theories most widely held among philosophers of science; it frequently is used to analyze or treat other philosophical problems including ones in the physical, biological, and social sciences,[2] and even has found its way into Ronald Giere's elementary philosophy of science textbook (1979), now in its second edition. Summarizing their discussion of the Semantic Conception, Lambert and Brittan (1987) write: "No clear objections, over and above those repetitions of their own positions that classicist and historicist defenders might urge, to the semantic view have yet emerged" (145–46). This acceptance and utilization have occurred despite the fact that the Semantic Conception's development is diffusely scattered throughout journals and edited volumes, and no single comprehensive work developing the Semantic Conception has been produced.

According to the Semantic Conception of Theories, scientific theories are not linguistic entities, but rather are set-theoretic entities.[3] This is in sharp contrast to many versions of the positivistic Received View on Theories, which construes theories as partially interpreted axiomatic systems, hence as linguistic entities. To say that something is a linguistic entity is to imply that changes in its linguistic features, including the formulation of its axiom system, produce a new entity. Thus on the Received View, change in the formulation of a theory is a change in theory. However, scientific theories have different individuation properties, and a given theory admits of a variety of different full and partial formulations. The Semantic Conception of Theories construes theories as extralinguistic entities which admit of different full and partial formulations. In this respect, theories are individuated on the Semantic Conception the same way science individuates them.

The Semantic Conception gets its name from the fact that it construes theories as what their formulations refer to when the formulations are given a (formal) *semantic* interpretation. Thus 'semantic' is used here in the sense of formal semantics or model theory in mathematical logic.

On the Semantic Conception, the heart of a theory is an extralinguistic *theory structure*. Theory structures variously are characterized as set-theoretic predicates (Suppes and Sneed), state spaces (Beth and van Fraassen), and relational systems (Suppe). Regardless which sort of mathematical entity the theory structures are identified with, they do pretty much the same thing—they specify the admissible behaviors of state transition systems. For example, in the case of classical particle mechanics, a system has n bodies, each characterized by three position and three momentum coordinate variables; the simultaneous values at time t of these $6n$ variables determine the state of the system, and the laws of the theory specify admissible change-of-state patterns. If one represents the states as points in $6n$-dimensional spaces, the theory structure is construed as a configurated state space (van Fraassen). One also can construe the state transition structure as a relational system consisting of the set of possible states as a domain on which various sequencing relations are imposed (Suppe). By defining set-theoretic predicates (Suppes, Sneed), one can specify either a state space, a relational system, or some other representing mathematical structure or class of structures.

When one propounds a theory, one specifies the theory structure and asserts a theoretical hypothesis claiming that real-world phenomena (or a particular real-world phenomenon) stand(s) in some mapping relationship to the theory structure whereby that structure models the dynamic behavior of the phenomena or phenomenon. The laws of the theory do not specify what that mapping relationship is. This is in sharp contrast to the Received View which construes theories as the conjunction of law statements and correspondence rules which specify how the laws manifest themselves in observable phenomena. Thus the Received View's linguistic analogues to the mapping relationships of the Semantic Conception are individuating proper parts of theories, and so any alteration in the correspondence rules produces a new theory. In particular, since the correspondence rules, inter alia, specify experimental methods and measurement procedures, on the Received View any improvements or breakthroughs in experimental design or measurement result in the replacement of the existing theory by an improved replacement theory.[4] In actual scientific practice, however, theories are not individuated that way. Improvements in experimental procedures, new measurement techniques, and the like, do not automatically alter the theory they are used with. On the Semantic Conception such experimental and measurement techniques are used to mediate or assess the mapping relationships asserted to hold between theory structure and phenomena, but are not specified by the theory structure and so are not individuating features of theories.[5] Thus, again, here is an instance where individuation of theories on the Semantic Conception corresponds to actual scientific practice, but individuation on the Received View does not.

Various versions of the Semantic Conception differ as to what is the strongest mapping relationship that can hold or be established between theory structures and their corresponding phenomena. Van Fraassen (1980) uses his version of the Semantic Conception to argue for what he calls an *antirealism* with respect to theories. In the chapters which follow I will develop a *quasi-realistic* version of the Semantic Conception. The differences here between van Fraassen and me concern the physical interpretation of theory structures on the Semantic Conception; and we take different stands on the issue of scientific realism — an issue which is highly controversial today. Thus the development of the Semantic Conception and the debates over scientific realism have become intertwined, and one cannot go very far developing the former without confronting the latter.

This book is concerned with developing a quasi-realistic version of the Semantic Conception of Theories. This requires taking positions on the contemporary scientific realism debates and also making progress in developing a quasi-realistic epistemology of science. These will be dealt with at length in subsequent chapters; the remainder of this chapter will provide a brief background to them and preview how later chapters contribute to the overall argument.

I. ORIGINS OF THE SEMANTIC CONCEPTION

Since this book focuses primarily on my own version of the Semantic Conception, it seems appropriate to say something about the other main versions of it and how my version relates to them. I think the most illuminating way to do this is to begin with a sketch of the history of the Semantic Conception's origins and the motivations behind its development.

During World War II, Evert Beth became increasingly dissatisfied with "the increasing discrepancy between science and philosophy, which is conspicuously demonstrated by the rejection, by well-known philosophers—such as H. Dingler, P. Hoenen, J. Maritain—, of fundamental conceptions quite unanimously accepted by men of science."[6] He viewed this as "one of the main causes of the downfall of contemporary philosophy which is manifest e.g. in existentialism, and which seriously menaces the future development of Western civilization" (Beth 1949, 178–79). In response to such developments and their antecedents in the history of philosophy which he traced back as far as Aristotle, Beth concluded that "a philosophy of science, instead of attempting to deal with speculations on the subject matter of the sciences, should rather attempt a logical analysis—in the broadest sense of this phrase—of the theories *which form the actual content of* the various sciences. The Semantic method, which was introduced by A. Tarski towards 1930 and which quite recently has been extensively studied by R. Carnap, is a very great help in the logical analysis of physical theories" (ibid., 180; italics added).

Combining the formal semantic techniques of Tarski and Carnap with von Neumann's (1932) work on the foundations of quantum mechanics and the work of Strauss (1938), Beth proposed a semantic analysis of Newtonian and quantum mechanics.[7] For Newtonian mechanics he postulated systems having states under the governance of Hamiltonian equations, introduced atomic statements of physical measurement, and defined how the state transition structure satisfies these atomic statements. He also gave the semantic interpretation for a consequence relationship as well as a similar Schrödinger equation treatment for quantum mechanics, which he used to provide a commentary on the Einstein-Podolsky-Rosen paradox. He characterized his analyses as not proposing new axioms of logic and said that it "only aims at clarifying and systematizing the methods by which physicists infer consequences from given or supposed observational data" (Beth 1949, 183–84). He was quite clear about the relevance of these structures to issues of quantum logic. So far as I know, the only subsequent work he produced on the Semantic Conception after his 1948 and 1949 publications was a very brief conference paper in 1961 containing nothing new.

The next important figure in the development of the Semantic Conception was Patrick Suppes. Suppes studied mathematics, physics, and meteorology as an undergraduate at the University of Chicago; he received a B.S. in the last subject in 1943 while in the activated army reserves. After the war he went to graduate school in philosophy at Columbia University, where he was influenced by Ernest Nagel more than anyone else. As a graduate student he continued to study mathematics and physics, including topology, group theory, and relativity theory. Of particular importance were the lectures in group theory and topology given by Samuel Eilenberg—a mathematician who came out of the same Polish logic school Tarski did. The elegance with which he used axiomatic methods throughout the course had a strong impact on Suppes. Equally important in impact was an informal graduate seminar on von Neumann and Morgenstern's theory of games. "Von Neumann's axiomatic approach, again, appealed to me, and I learned a great deal about how to think in axiomatic terms. Certainly there was little in my undergraduate education that taught me much about the axiomatic method" (Suppes, letter to author, May 21, 1987). Also influential was Ernest Nagel's excellent course on logic where everything was formulated with great care and rigor.

The axiomatic and foundational elegance Suppes enjoyed in these seminars was missing from the many physics courses he took as a graduate student. In these courses he found himself

> always searching for some way to put things in a completely organized, intellectually satisfactory way. . . .
>
> I can remember very well trying to organize the lectures in quantum mechanics I heard as a student. I typed the notes and made every effort to put them in as logically a coherent fashion as I could. I did not try to give them an axiomatic formulation. This was certainly much too difficult a task at this stage of my education and in terms of time I had available, but I was searching for some kind of foundational security. [ibid.]

Suppes enjoyed L. H. Thomas' course on general relativity, but nevertheless found it intellectually disturbing.

> Thomas was not a good lecturer but knew everything there was to know at the time about the subject. He distributed notes which were in one sense clear and detailed but also completely nonaxiomatic. I appreciated the clarity of the notes but also, in contrast to the lectures in mathematics I was attending, I very much wanted to see what an axiomatic formulation would look like. I think it was my dissatisfaction with the rather casual approach to foundations in a systematic way in physics that pushed me to want to do a dissertation on the axiomatic foundations of some branch of physics. [ibid.]

He decided to write a dissertation about the philosophy of physics, wanting to give an axiomatic treatment of some branch of physics.

Such a dissertation was not to be written:

> As I got deeper into the subject I realized that this was not the kind of dissertation that was considered appropriate in philosophy. The Department at that time was primarily historically oriented, and Nagel advised me to consider a more informal approach to the foundations of physics. What we finally agreed on was a study of the concept of action at a distance, and a good deal of the dissertation was devoted to an analytical study of this concept in the work of Descartes, Newton, Boscovich, and Kant. I was able to come closer to my original interest in a chapter on the special theory of relativity, but certainly what I had to say in that chapter was no contribution to the axiomatic foundations of the subject. [Suppes 1979, 6]

While not done in a serious axiomatic fashion, there was an attempt to state axioms in an informal way.

Arriving at Stanford to teach philosophy, Suppes "became acquainted with J. C. C. McKinsey, a logician who recently had joined the Department of Philosophy at Stanford. McKinsey served as my postdoctoral tutor. It was from him that I learned the set-theoretical methods that have been my stock in trade for much of my career." Suppes also attended Tarski's seminar at Berkeley. "It was from McKinsey and Tarski that I learned about the axiomatic method and what it means to give a set-theoretic analysis of a subject" (ibid., 8).

Soon after his arrival at Stanford, Suppes combined the set-theoretic methods of McKinsey and Tarski with his desire, stifled at Columbia University, to do axiomatic studies in the foundations of physics. With McKinsey, A. C. Sugar, and H. Rubin, he published a number of papers that tried to do rigorous set-theoretic axiomatizations of existing branches of physics that had minimal sets of independent axioms (e.g., McKinsey and Suppes 1953; McKinsey, Sugar, and Suppes 1953; Suppes 1957, 1959; Rubin and Suppes 1954). "I really felt what I wanted to do in the dissertation was completed with the publication of my 1959 paper 'Axiomatics for Relativistic Kinematics [with or] Without Parity,' [Suppes 1959] in which I derived from very simple assumptions the Lorenz transformations" (1987 letter). In 1957, Suppes, Tarski, and Leon Henkin organized a symposium on the axiomatic method with special reference to geometry and physics (Henkin, Suppes, and Tarski 1959); Suppes was especially responsible for organizing and suggesting the speakers on the axiomatic foundations of physics. He also did work on the foundations of quantum theory, initially working from the von Neumann 1932 and Mackey 1963 approach, but later moving away from it because he became conceptually dissatisfied with it from a probabilistic perspective (Suppes 1979, 12). By 1959 Suppes had begun to shift his attention away from the concentration on axiomatic foundations of physics because he had come to view the subject as too special to put all of his energies into it—physicists were not much interested in the subject, and "very few philosophers had the background, training, or interest to be enthralled by the subject" (1987 letter).

Around 1950 Suppes had become interested in learning theory. In 1955, while a fellow at the Center for Advanced Studies in the Behavioral Sciences, he began working with William K. Estes on mathematical learning theory. This led to a rather extended period of doing psychological research on learning theory with Estes and Richard C. Atkinson (Suppes 1979, 26–29). "My interest in axiomatic methods did not stop, as can be seen from some of my work in learning theory at the time, but I did swerve away from the concentration on the axiomatic foundations of physics" (1987 letter).

The combination of his set-theoretic work on axiomatic foundations and especially his hands-on experimental research in mathematical learning theory led Suppes to write several papers which generalized from this work to theses about the nature of models and theories. In Suppes 1961 he distinguished three types of models in the sciences—what I call metamathematical models, iconic models, and the "theory" sense of model—and illustrated their similarities and differences with examples from his own and others' work. The thrust of the paper "was to ask was it possible to have the same kind of foundational clarity about the use of the concept of model in science that is possible in mathematics, when one had adopted Tarski's viewpoint. I tried to say that fundamentally the answer is yes" (1987 letter).

Suppes 1962 is a generalized analysis of how the mathematical learning theories he was developing related to phenomena in the context of his own experimental designs and setups for testing his, Estes', and Atkinson's theories. Instead of following the correspondence rule approach of the positivists, he introduces a hierarchy of models and theories semantically related to each other. As Suppes later explained it,

> The models of data paper was an effort to combine my interest in axiomatic foundations with the problem of understanding how to think about analysis of experimental data in a more formal way. The thrust here was not to give an alternative to mathematical statistics as applied to experiments but rather to ask what is the

foundational framework within which one comes to experimental data ready to do appropriate statistical analysis. The models of data paper was an effort to show how much more is involved and what a high level of abstraction is required already at the level of data before any statistical analysis is appropriate. I also [tried] to bring out how issues of experimental design enter already . . . at an abstract level at the formulation of models. [1987 letter]

In a related paper, "What Is a Scientific Theory?" (1967), Suppes argued for the legitimacy of presenting theories via modeling rather than axiomatic methods and contrasted the approach emerging from his earlier papers with that of the Received View.

Joseph Sneed was a student of Suppes. Early in the 1960s he had decided not to complete a dissertation in physics at the University of Illinois but instead to get a doctorate in philosophy. After some graduate work in philosophy at Illinois he went to Stanford and worked with Suppes. His dissertation was a study of the structures of mathematical physics that exploited Suppes' axiomatic approach. He expanded his dissertation into his 1971 book. It had as one of its foci an attempt to characterize the nature of theoretical terms divorced from the positivistic observational/theoretical distinction—a problem posed by Putnam (1962). Sneed's solution utilizes correspondence rules, and so it seems to be far more positivistic in spirit than Suppes'.

The next work on the Semantic Conception to appear after Suppes' pieces and Sneed's dissertation was my dissertation (1967), which developed a version of the Semantic Conception. I now will try to sketch the main influences on my development of that version. Between high school and college, and during my undergraduate summers, I worked for General Electric Flight Test at Edwards Air Force Base on the research and development of jet engines. I began as an instrumentation technician, building, installing, and calibrating electronic and other data-gathering equipment. I witnessed the equipment progress from crude photo panels to fifty-channel oscillographs, from telemeters to airborne hundred-channel multiplexed pulse code–modulated digital tapes. Thus I was involved in state-of-the-art experimental research on military and civilian jet engines and aircraft, as well as playing a limited role in the work on Atlas missiles and the first flight of the NASA X-15 manned rocket.

Because I was in the later stages of obtaining a degree in mathematics, my last two summers at G.E. found me assigned to the new computer operation. Those were the very early days of using computers in military aircraft research and design, and we were pioneering experimental research uses for such machines as the IBM 650, the IBM 704, and the state-of-the-art IBM 709 and 7090. I worked on practical flight test data reduction problems and consulted on projects such as designing the control system for the LEM simulator, but I spent the bulk of my time doing exploratory and feasibility studies on three problems: (1) When we lost reference channels, could we use regression analysis to computer-generate dummy replacement data that would enable us to salvage our test data? (This involved fitting curves in up to one hundred-dimensional spaces, which was fairly ambitious for those days.) (2) Conversion of analog data (e.g., from flow meters) to digital involved electronic filtering, where the filters were chosen on a trial-and-error basis. Was it possible to develop an on-line, computer-generated dynamic filter which would exploit Norbert Wiener's "smoothing of time series" work (Wiener 1949) to produce a near-optimal transform function in a self-correcting manner? (3) Could we reduce the frequency of test flights by developing computer models that would simulate the operation of jet engines under a variety of circumstances and could be used as an alternative method of evaluating proposed design changes in, say, the core and annulus of a J-79 afterburner? The first problem involved representing dynamic systems as curves in hyperspace; the last two involved viewing phenomena as state transition systems. My colleague, who set me working on these problems, was Brandon Finney, a mathematician who had been a student of Reichenbach's; through him I learned a lot of Reichenbach's work. Thus, prior to graduate study in philosophy, I had already had an extensive background in engineering research—including instrumentation, measurement, and data reduction—and also had done a lot of work on dynamic computer modeling of physical phenomena. Through Wiener's work (1961, 1950) I had substantial exposure to the early developments in cybernetics, and they excited and influenced me a lot.

I was an undergraduate at the University of California at Riverside, which then was a small experimental honors campus. My degree was in mathematics, but I also studied physics, chemistry, biology, and philosophy. David Harrah had been my Western Civilization discussion leader, and I started taking courses in philosophy from him because he was a great teacher. I took a theory of knowledge course that paid a lot of critical attention to positivism (but not to philosophy of science), symbolic logic, an independent studies course on Toulmin 1953, and a course called "philosophy of science" from him. Harrah was a logician who had been an undergraduate student of Suppes at Stanford and a graduate student of Fitch at Yale. He was in the process of developing his erotetic logic and an associated formal model of information exchange and evaluation in the communication process (Harrah 1963). This work was introduced in some of his courses and had obvious links with my modeling interests at G.E.—it excited me very much. The philosophy of science course was actually a course in axiomatic set theory, taught out of the second part of Suppes 1957, and it presented Suppes' approach to the axiomatic foundations of theories. Before graduation I was fairly familiar with his approach and the papers he, McKinsey, Rubin, and Sugar had done, as well as the Henkin, Suppes, and Tarski (1959) volume resulting from their symposium on the axiomatic method.

Unable to decide whether to be a mathematician, philosopher, computer scientist, or marine biologist, I went to graduate school in philosophy because I liked it, it was fairly easy, and philosophy of science afforded me the opportunity to combine my interests—in effect, saving me from having to choose what I wanted to be. (Computer science departments did not really exist in 1962, though there were a few graduate programs.) I chose the University of Michigan at Ann Arbor because its philosophy department was top-rated and Arthur Burks was there. He was a philosopher of science and had been a co-inventor of the ENIAC (the first electronic computer) and, with von Neumann and Herman Goldstein, had designed the first stored-program computers and laid the basis for computer programming languages (Burks, Goldstein, and von Neumann 1946). He has continued to make important contributions to computer science and philosophy to the present.

It seemed I could combine my diverse interests rather well at Michigan. There I took about 40 percent of my course work outside philosophy. I was particularly influenced by work in metamathematics and recursive function theory, foundations of mathematics with Raymond Wilder, automata theory studies with Burks in computer science, and work with John Holland on adaptive systems theory. Both the adaptive systems theory and the automata theory added richness and abstract structure to my earlier state transition modeling ideas from G.E. I also began to look at the Fisher-Kimura natural selection theory in biology from the state transition perspective as incorporated in Holland's adaptive systems work. And, I studied more traditional philosophy as well; of particular importance were Abe Kaplan's Kant course and many other courses in the history of philosophy.

My philosophy of science graduate course work was limited. I took a course called "philosophy of science" from Burks, which was based on the then-current draft of what became the first half of his *Chance, Cause, Reason* (1977), and so was a course in the foundations of probability theory and inductive logic. (I later worked on the book as a research assistant.) I sat in on a seminar Abe Kaplan gave on his new book on the philosophy of social science (1964), and I assisted Arnold Kaufman in a philosophy of social sciences course that used Nagel against Skinner. But I never systematically studied the then-dominant positivistic philosophy of science.

When it came time to do a dissertation, my old interests at G.E. predominated, and I proposed a dissertation on models in science with Burks as director. The thesis was organized around Suppes' (1961) three kinds of models and was to characterize and compare metamathematical, iconic, and "theory" models. In the end it concentrated mostly on theories. I formed my committee: Burks as chairman, Abe Kaplan, the mathematical biologist and game theorist Anatol Rapoport, and Joe Sneed, who had just come from Stanford.[8] After the committee was appointed and the thesis prospectus approved, I devoted my time to taking courses covering more adaptive systems theory, more logic, some anthropology, linguistics, and Sanskrit; learning quantum theory on my own from various books including von Neumann 1955, Mackey 1963, and Messiah 1961 with Burt Moyer of the Berkeley physics department serving as tutor; studying on my own other things like relativity theory, works in the history of science, and game theory economics from von Neumann and Morgenstern 1953; working with Burks in editing von Neumann's self-reproducing automata material after von Neumann's death and accompanying Burks in 1965 to India, where I finally wrote my dissertation in 1966.

Despite these competing activities, I thought a lot about my dissertation, especially about theories. I recall going to see Rapoport to try out the idea that "theories are just Turing machines"—which, if one allows for a wide enough class of extended probabilistic and deterministic Turing machines, is not that far off the mark as an analysis of theory structures. I thought it was a daring idea. Rapoport responded, "Of course," and went to the board and showed me how to construe a number of physical and biological theories as automata. It was exhilarating, as Rapoport had wonderful intuitions on the mathematical modeling of phenomena of all sorts. I also bounced ideas off Harrah back in California one summer.

My discovery that von Neumann's cellular automata model of self-reproducing automata intuitively was similar to his quantum theory model (both involve viewing their phenomena as fluid flows through space) was very exciting. Indeed, Birkhoff and von Neumann's (1936) treatment of observation spaces and phase space models of quantum theory was of crucial importance in developing my dissertation version of the Semantic Conception. Many features of my version of the Semantic Conception find their seminal beginnings there. These include the notion of phase spaces, the idea that theories idealize their phenomena, the notion of the logic of a theory, the interpretation of propositions as corresponding to subsystems of phase and observation spaces, and the notion of a physical system (also influenced by Margenau [1950]). Formal semantics study with David Kaplan was another important influence. He stressed the importance of formal models being faithful to the phenomena being modeled, and I learned not to let formal wizardry mask poorly thought out philosophy.

In the initial development of my version of the Semantic Conception, the main influences on my analysis were von Neumann's and Birkhoff's work, my simulation modeling experiences and work at G.E., Suppes' set-theoretic approach, the sharp distinction between syntax and semantic structures in formal semantics and associated set-theoretic techniques, and the automata theory/adaptive systems perspective, including Holland's treatment of the genetic theory of natural selection. My views on the physical interpretation of theories were strongly influenced by Suppes 1962 and, I suspect, to an extent by Toulmin 1953, which I had studied as an undergraduate.

One very strong belief of mine was that philosophy of science had to reflect actual scientific practice and theories. I don't recall anyone telling me this, though Abraham Kaplan might have; he certainly believed it, and it shows in his 1964 book. It certainly shows in Suppes' work (e.g., Suppes 1962). David Kaplan's cautions on irresponsible formalization, Rapoport's critiques of Richardson's war models, and Burks' careful attempts to use modal logic to model subjunctive conditionals in drafts of his 1977 work also contributed to my belief. In any case, I do know that I didn't know much positivistic philosophy of science, with its reconstructive perspective. I looked at a little of it (e.g., Braithwaite 1953, Carnap 1956, and Nagel 1961), but quickly concluded that it didn't have much to do with real science as I knew it.[9] So I wrote an eight-page polemic against what I knew of the existing positivistic philosophical literature on theories, dismissing its relevance to my dissertation (1967), and proceeded to ignore it after page 46 of a 396-page thesis. Only later did I come to study and appreciate that body of literature. I hope my later treatment of it (1974b) atones for my early brashness, although I am grateful that my committee let me get away with the polemical dismissal in my dissertation. Had they not, I might have been distracted from developing the Semantic Conception. Had I been indoctrinated into positivism, I doubt I would have been able to develop the Semantic Conception.

Sneed introduced me to Kuhn (1962). The way his work rang true

to my scientific experiences, unlike positivistic accounts, excited me—
I became a Kuhnian. Kuhn wasn't very clear about his metaphysics,
but I read him as being in the tradition of C. I. Lewis (1929)—committed to a subjective idealism with intentional particulars being the
subject matter of science. An embryonic version of this view informed
the treatment of the physical interpretation of theory structures in my
dissertation, and I tried to work out the subjective idealism in fairly
fine detail in a series of lectures at Knox College in Galesburg, Illinois,
in 1969. My eventual dissatisfaction with that detailed attempt, reinforced by some critical comments by David Schwayder, convinced me
that subjective idealism was wrongheaded. I began to explore a realistic
approach. In an extended series of weekly discussions with Wilfrid
Sellars when he visited at Illinois, I began developing a correspondence
theory of truth (Suppe 1973), a realistic approach to natural classification
(see ch. 7 below), and a quasi-realistic physical interpretation for theories
on the Semantic Conception (see chs. 3–5 below).

Bas van Fraassen is the final main developer of the Semantic Conception, and his version was initially stimulated by Beth. Van Fraassen
had encountered Beth's 1959 book as an undergraduate at the University
of Alberta and had become quite enamored with Beth. Over the next
several years he read everything of Beth's he could get his hands on.
He requested a copy of Beth's 1948 book and received it as a present
on his birthday, April 5, 1965. During the academic year 1965–66, his
last year as a graduate student at Pittsburgh, he taught a course at West
Virginia University where he first wrote down a summary and explication of Beth's semantic view of theories.

In a letter (February 19, 1985), van Fraassen wrote me,

> I had read his *Synthese* article before, about the Einstein Podolsky
> Rosen Paradox, and had not properly understood it. It was I think
> after the book that I suddenly saw how his ideas actually worked
> and how they could be used to provide a semantics for quantum
> logic. During my last years of graduate school in Pittsburgh I
> presented a paper on Quantum Logic, which concentrated on the
> paper by Birkhoff and von Neumann. That paper I had already
> read and . . . [been] thinking about when I was an undergraduate,
> but had understood very imperfectly. I think probably that the
> main problem which exercised me and for which the semantic
> conception showed me the way out, was his question of how to
> provide a semantic analysis of quantum logic. There was a second
> factor, besides Beth's work that motivated me. I was writing my
> dissertation on the causal theory of time, and as part of that de-

veloped a theory of events (I started with Reichenbach's theory, especially as given in his *Elements of Symbolic Logic*, but developed [a] somewhat different theory). Developing a theory of events when you're not allowed to use any spatio-temporal terms has special difficulties, and it was in connection with this that I mobilized the notion of logical space; reading that I then saw my views about logical space and its connection with modal logic (as developed in my "Meaning Relations among Predicates" *Nôus*, 1967) could be identified with the state space idea that was mobilized by Beth.

In that *Nôus* article, van Fraassen (1967) introduced the idea of a semi-interpreted language and announced that he intended to exploit those developments in the analysis of scientific theories in a subsequent paper. I read this, saw the relevance to my own work, and wrote to him. We corresponded, he read my dissertation, and then I visited him in New Haven, and we had extended discussions about the Semantic Conception of Theories. He then published his 1970 work, in which he put forth his extension and generalization of Beth's approach. In a footnote (325) he expressed his debt to me "for stimulating discussion" and said that my dissertation developed "a point of view closely related to Beth's." My recollection of those early exchanges is that they were exciting and stimulating, and that we both profited greatly from them, but that each of us had pretty well worked out his basic position prior to initiating contact. It was through van Fraassen that I first learned of Beth (1948, 1949) and saw the significance of his work.[10] In a number of subsequent works van Fraassen has made important further contributions to the Semantic Conception (e.g., 1972, 1974, 1980).

As I look over the foregoing history, I am struck by how heavily intertwined the lines of influence are and the extent to which the influences of von Neumann, Tarski, and set-theoretic approaches have dominated us. I am also struck by how little attention we paid to positivistic views during the formative stages of developing our views and the extent to which a concern with actual science predominates. For the most part, we did not pay much attention to the Received View until our own views were fairly well developed.

New developments along the lines of the Semantic Conception have continued. For example, the Kimura multiple-locus, multiple-allele generalization of Fisher's genetic theory of natural selection in evolutionary biology was one of my paradigm cases in developing my version of the Semantic Conception. A number of other philosophers have been active in utilizing and further developing the Semantic Conception in biological contexts; most of these efforts have focused on evolutionary theory, especially population genetics. For example, a long-standing issue in philosophy of biology has been whether evolutionary theory has genuine laws, for it is claimed that scientific laws must hold universally over all space and time, but that evolutionary laws seem to be specific to our planet or similar planets in similar solar systems.

John Beatty wrote a doctoral dissertation (1979), directed by Ronald Giere, which turned to the Semantic Conception to help resolve that issue. As an outgrowth of his dissertation, he published his 1981 work on the universality (or generality) issue and his 1980 work on the issue of the cognitive status of optimal design models in evolutionary biology. Central to his treatment of both issues is his claim that according to the Semantic Conception, "[t]heories do not consist of empirical claims, much less general, empirical laws of nature. . . .[The] empirical claims of science are not considered to be components of theories" (1980, 542–43). By my lights, this constitutes a serious misconstrual of the Semantic Conception (certainly I would deny these claims under my version of it), and so I have not found Beatty's efforts terribly convincing. (See Sloep and van der Steen 1987 for other criticisms of Beatty and see Beatty's 1987 reply.) Nevertheless, Beatty is correct that the Semantic Conception is capable of shedding light on both issues. In chapter 8, I show how my version of the Semantic Conception handles the generality issue so as to render evolutionary and other "local" biological theories genuine scientific theories with scientific laws. And developments in subsequent chapters allow me to use the Semantic Conception to characterize optimal design models as conceptual devices—which yields a superior defense of much the same account of optimal design models as the one Beatty attempted to defend on questionable grounds. The sort of account I would give is sketched briefly in the Epilogue.

Elisabeth Lloyd defended a dissertation at Princeton in October 1984 entitled, "A Semantic Approach to the Structure of Evolutionary Theory," which was directed by Bas van Fraassen. In it Lloyd looked at the special case modern evolutionary theory presents for questions about scientific explanation and theory structure, utilizing the semantic view of theories (as developed by Suppes, myself, and van Fraassen). In particular, she used it as a framework for analyzing some major topics in evolutionary theory, including population genetics, group selection, and species selection models. After publishing articles containing material from her dissertation (1984, 1987, 1988), Lloyd revised it and expanded it into book form (1988a).

Lloyd tends to use van Fraassen's state space, antirealist version. She shows how closely Semantic Conception state space models conform to the way evolutionary biologists such as Lewontin actually formulate population genetics. She also provides classifications for population genetics models, discusses the confirmation of ecological and evolutionary models, and analyzes the "unit of selection" controversy (whether the gene, the entire phenotype, or something else should be considered the unit of selection). Her book focuses especially on the structure of evolutionary theory, concentrating on population genetics, and contains chapters on group, kin, and organismic selection models, and other chapters on species selection and genic selection, the "unit of selection" controversy, and the confirmation of evolutionary theory. One merit of her treatment is the detailed attention paid to specific theories and models: Lloyd's book does not merely use the Semantic Conception, it furthers its development.

Sloep and van der Steen (1987) mount some rather bizarre criticisms of some of Lloyd's work which are rooted in part in the misguided supposition that the only function of a philosophical analysis of theories is to help scientists solve the scientists' own problems, and hence an analysis which coheres well with actual scientific practice has no philosophical contribution to make. Although there is little substance or merit to their objections, Lloyd's rejoinder (1987a) is not terribly effective.

While a graduate student in philosophy at the University of Toronto, Paul Thompson studied with van Fraassen and became familiar with his work on semi-interpreted languages (van Fraassen 1967), but not his exploitation of those ideas in his 1970 paper on the Semantic Conception. Around 1977, as Thompson began to work toward a dissertation in philosophy of biology directed by Thomas Goudge, he learned of the Semantic Conception from John Beatty, who was then writing his dissertation using the Semantic Conception. Around the same time, Thompson encountered some of Giere's work with the Semantic Conception of Theories and the brief description of it in my 1974b. This initial exposure led him to work through the literature, including van Fraassen's work, my dissertation, and my published writings (incorporated into the present volume). Thompson's work exploits details of my quasi-realistic version of the Semantic Conception to a greater degree than Lloyd's or Beatty's work does. His 1983 paper defends the superiority of the Semantic Conception over the Received View for foundational research in evolutionary biology and presents an analysis of Hardy-Weinberg law–based population genetics theories. Of particular note in his account is his view that laws of coexistence specify the sets of states of which a system is capable, and then laws of quasi-succession are used to specify state transition behavior or histories of members of a population. His defense of the superiority of the Semantic Conception includes the claim that it naturally corresponds "to the way in which biologists expand, employ, and explore the theory" (227). Further, it also provides a particularly clarifying perspective for approaching the debate between the classical and balance theories of population structure in evolutionary theory.

In his 1985 work, Thompson addresses controversies surrounding the testability of sociobiological theories, arguing that "a semantic conception of theories provides a more thoroughgoing analysis of this problem" than the Received View, because the Semantic Conception "more accurately represents the relation between a theory and phenomena" (201). In his 1986 work he discusses the roles of laws of interaction in evolutionary theory from the perspective of the Semantic Conception. Many of these themes are developed further in other works of his (1988, 1988a, n.d.) especially in his new book (1989).

Thompson's defense of the superiority of the Semantic Conception for foundational studies of evolutionary theory is criticized in Sloep and van der Steen 1987. His rejoinder (1987) is very much to the point in showing how seriously confused their understanding of the Semantic Conception is; it provides a convincing defense of Thompson's views— Sloep and van der Steen's reply (1987a) notwithstanding.

Kenneth Schaffner (1980) is of the opinion that evolutionary theory is quite untypical of biological theory, and thus philosophy of biology's focus on evolutionary theory as the paradigmatic biological theory is misleading and distorts our understanding of biological science. He argues that biological theories more typically resemble what he calls interlevel theories of the middle range. He has attempted to look at such theories from a number of perspectives including the Semantic Conception (see my treatment of them in chapter 8, where I argue that the Semantic Conception straightforwardly accommodates and illuminates such middle-range interlevel theories).

A number of other philosophers have attempted to analyze theories as set-theoretic predicates or structures; the best-known analysis is Sneed 1971. Moulines 1975 exploits Sneed's approach, and Stegmüller 1976 is an exposition of Sneed 1971 together with an attempt to exploit Sneed's analysis to provide an improved analysis of Kuhn's notion of incommensurability. (Sneed was involved in the development of Stegmüller's attempt.) This attempt seems to me somewhat bizarre, since a key idea of Kuhn's is the rejection of correspondence rules, and Sneed's analysis of theories retains certain explicit correspondence rules in the form of Ramsey sentences (used in Sneed's analysis of theoretical terms). By retaining some explicit correspondence rules, Sneed seems to concede far too much to positivism—indeed, far more than Kuhn would, or should, be happy with. Further, Stegmüller 1976 displays a cavalier disrespect for actual scientific practice—which, I'm afraid, is all too characteristic of this general approach. The problems Sneed and Stegmüller choose to address all too frequently seem to me to be philosophical impositions on the science rather than arising out of it. Sneed, Moulines, and Stegmüller have collaborated on various works relating to their semantic analysis of theories.

In Europe one finds other philosophers who are attempting to wed a set-theoretic structure approach to analyzing theories with a neopositivistic approach that employs explicit correspondence rules. Prominent among these are M. L. Dalla Chiara, G. Toraldo di Francia, Marian Przełecki, and Ryszard Wójcicki.[11] While I am uncertain of the historical background behind these attempts, my impression is that they essentially try to employ Tarski semantic techniques within a positivistic approach to theories. These approaches, like those of Sneed, Stegmüller, and Moulines, are sufficiently different in their treatment of the physical interpretation of theories from the approaches of Beth, Suppes, van Fraassen, and myself that it is appropriate to construe them as advancing a different analysis. For one of the key distinguishing features of the Semantic Conception of Theories, as developed by Beth, van Fraassen, Suppes, and myself, is the absence of anything like correspondence rules—and this absence is crucial to the way the individuation of theories is handled. Subsequently throughout this book, I will confine my attention to semantic conceptions which eschew correspondence rules as integral components of theories.

This concludes the historical account of the origins of the Semantic Conception of Theories. To follow the subsequent development of views of the main developers of the Semantic Conception who have been featured here, one may consult the philosophical literature. I now turn to other matters of background.

II. SCIENTIFIC REALISM

The first known scientific revolution arose over the replacement of Eudoxus' theory of celestial movements with Aristotle's. Aristotle objected to Eudoxus' account on the grounds that it did not make mechanical sense—that his mechanisms could not be the actual mechanisms producing the celestial motions. Aristotle figured out how to combine Eudoxus' various mechanisms for the specific planets (as reworked by Callippus) to produce a single mechanism responsible for all celestial mechanisms. The resulting mechanism had fifty-six nested crystalline spheres concentric on the earth, whose motions were driven by the outermost spheres (see Aristotle's *De Caelo* and *Physica*). Aristotle's theory replaced Eudoxus' and Callippus' despite the fact that the two theories were *provably* equivalent in their accounts of the apparent motions of the planets and stars.[12] Aristotle's theory won out because it was a realistic theory, whereas Eudoxus' was an instrumentalistic theory, and Aristotle had convinced people that adequate scientific theories had to be realistic.

The dispute between Eudoxus and Aristotle marks the beginning of the realism-versus-instrumentalism disputes that have surfaced repeatedly in the history of science. Such disputes were at the heart of Copernicus' rejection of Ptolemaic astronomy—Osiander's preface to *De Revolutionibus Orbium Coelestium* notwithstanding. And they played a central role in the atomism debates of the nineteenth century (see Gardner 1979), as well as issues surrounding the Copenhagen interpretation of quantum mechanics during this century. Even within logical positivism and the Received View, one finds realism-versus-instrumentalism disputes between, for example, Gustav Bergmann and allied behaviorists such as B. F. Skinner on the instrumentalist side, and Hempel and the later Carnap (1937 and onward) on the realist side. Hempel's "Theoreticians' Dilemma" (1958) is the classic positivistic statement of scientific realism.

Modern post-positivistic debates over scientific realism surround the work of W. V. Quine and Wilfrid Sellars and the ontic realisms they championed. Although Cornman ultimately came out in support of what he called "compatible common-sense realism," he challenged Sellars' brand of scientific realism (Sellars 1959, chs. 7, 12, 14, 15; 1963, chs. 2, 3; 1965) and in the process took instrumentalism seriously and gave it a good run for its money (see, e.g., Cornman 1975). The two of them had a number of go-arounds over scientific realism, and later (e.g., at the 1976 Philosophy of Science Association meetings) van Fraassen joined in championing an "antirealism" as opposed to an instrumentalism (Sellars 1977; Cornman 1977; van Fraassen 1977). Van Fraassen summarized his objections to Sellars' scientific realism in his 1975.

Van Fraassen's antirealism took on a life of its own and was challenged by Glymour and Boyd, among others (see Glymour 1976; Boyd 1973, 1976; van Fraassen 1976, 1980). Hesse (1977), Laudan (1981), and others have joined in the fray. The results are what MacKinnon (1979) calls "the New Debates" on scientific realism. MacKinnon's 1979 article and his earlier book (1972, 3–71), provide an excellent introduction to, and survey of, the older and newer modern debates over scientific realism (see also Leplin 1984).

It is not my purpose in this volume to attempt any systematic or comprehensive survey or critique of the recent or current controversies over scientific realism. My concern is limited to their impact upon the development of the Semantic Conception of Theories. Thus I am concerned primarily with van Fraassen's incorporation of his antirealism into his version of the Semantic Conception and with my own quasi-realistic version. In effect, my concerns with the scientific realism issue are twofold: I am interested in how theory structures are to be interpreted on the Semantic Conception and in learning what sorts of mapping relationships between theory structures and phenomena are epistemologically knowable. To my knowledge, Suppes has not taken a position on the scientific realism issue. MacKinnon (1979) considers the implications of Sneed's and Stegmüller's program of using Sneed's work on theories to rework Kuhn's view of science (Sneed 1971, 1976; Stegmüller 1976), and concludes

> the Sneed program, so interpreted, is neutral with respect to the problem of scientific realism. It can either accept or disregard the pre-critical realism implicit in functioning science. In neither case does the new method really treat the philosophical problems [concerning scientific realism] considered earlier. If this S-type formulation were to be generally accepted, however, it would certainly favor instrumentalism over realism. There remain, as I see it, serious obstacles in the way of such general acceptance: practical problems, stemming from the difficulties involved in reading Sneed and Stegmüller; theoretical problems concerning the use of Ramsey-reduction sentences and the instrumentalist interpretation of theories; and, perhaps, the most formidable difficulty of all, the Sneed-Stegmüller acceptance of Kuhn's descriptive account as an empirically adequate basis for the dynamics of theory development.[13]

Since I already have decided to exclude Sneed's and Stegmüller's approach from my consideration of the Semantic Conception, I will not pursue its possible implications for the scientific realism controversy any further.

An antirealism essentially involves the claim that there are epistemological limits to what can be known, and the physical interpretation of theories ought to be restricted to those which make theories knowable. Thus the mapping relations which constitute the physical interpretations of theories on the Semantic Conception should be restricted to ones that can be known. Actually, a realist can accept this line of reasoning, too, as the primary difference between a realist and an antirealist is over how much can be known. Van Fraassen's antirealism is based on the adoption of the following empirical adequacy condition for theory acceptance: All of the measurement reports of phenomena are to be isomorphic to one of the models of the structure (van Fraassen 1976).

Van Fraassen (1980) characterizes scientific realism as follows:

> Scientific realism is the position that scientific theory construction aims to give us a literally true story of what the world is like, and that acceptance of a scientific theory involves the belief that it is true. Accordingly, antirealism is a position according to which the aim of science can be well served without giving such a literally true story, and acceptance of a theory may properly involve something less (or other) than belief that it is true. [9]

Expanding on this, he says

> The idea of a literally true account has two aspects: the language is to be literally construed; and so construed, the account is true. This divides the antirealists into two sorts. The first sort holds that science is or aims to be true, properly (but not literally) construed. The second holds that the language of science should be literally construed, but its theories need not be true to be good. The antirealism I shall advocate belongs to the second sort. [10]

Van Fraassen's above adequacy conditions for theory acceptance are a reflection of his antirealism. If one accepts his characterizations of realism and antirealism,[14] then the position I defend in this book is an antirealism of the first sort he mentions. Theories typically are formulated in formulae or sentences that are in the indicative mood, but on my version of the Semantic Conception they are interpreted as giving a counterfactual (subjunctive) characterization of phenomena. (This is done via the mapping relationship between theory structure and phenomena, which is counterfactual.) Thus theories are not literally true. Further, although science can and does aim to accept theories as non-literally but counterfactually true, often theories are propounded as conceptual devices whose epistemic claims are weaker—for example, that the theory is a simplification or a promising first approximation worth pursuing, and the like.

While my position thus fails to qualify as a scientific realism, instead qualifying as an antirealism on van Fraassen's characterizations, it seems to me that the spirit of my enterprise is decidedly realistic and that what I am defending is a slightly attenuated kind of realism. Thus I call the position I defend a *quasi-realism*. Since my quasi-realism is for van Fraassen an antirealism and since his arguments against scientific realism do not favor his second sort of antirealism to the exclusion of the first sort, which I support, I will not rehearse or critique his arguments. Rather, I will concentrate on the positive development of his *constructive empiricism* form of antirealism. The plausibility of this strategy is enhanced when one notes that while van Fraassen argues against scientific realism and in favor of his antirealism, he virtually ignores the first sort of antirealism (including the sort of quasi-realism I will develop and defend here) and does not give it serious consideration in his arguments. For example, in discussing the "conjunction of theories" objection to antirealism, he maintains that "if one believes both T and T' to be true, then of course (on pain of inconsistency) one believes their conjunction to be true" (1980, 83). Granting that this is true for realists,[15] it generally will be false for antirealists of the first sort: It is not generally true that the conjunction of two nonliterally true theories is itself a nonliterally true theory.[16]

In barest outline, van Fraassen's antirealism maintains that

> *[s]cience aims to give us theories which are empirically adequate; and acceptance of a theory involves a belief only that it is empirically adequate.* This is the statement of the anti-realist position I advocate; I shall call it *constructive empiricism.* . . . In addition it requires an explication of 'empirically adequate'. For now, I shall leave that with the preliminary explication that a theory is empirically adequate exactly if what it says about the observable things and events in this world, is true — exactly if it 'saves the phenomena'. A little more precisely: such a theory has at least one model that all the actual phenomena fit inside. I must emphasize that this refers to *all* the phenomena; these are not exhausted by all those actually observed nor even by those observed at some time, whether past, present, or future. [van Fraassen 1980, 12, italics original]

This adequacy condition determines the strongest mapping relation between theories and phenomena allowed by his version of the Semantic Conception and thus delimits the extent of theoretical scientific knowledge. For "what the antirealist decides to believe about the world will depend in part on what he believes to be his, or rather the epistemic community's, accessible range of evidence" (18).

The persuasiveness of van Fraassen's attack on scientific realism ultimately depends in large part on the cogency of his constructive empiricism. At the very heart of the latter is his observable/nonobservable distinction (van Fraassen 1980). The burdens this distinction carries are great indeed:

> To accept the theory involves no more belief therefore than what it says about observable phenomena is correct. [57]

To the antirealist, all scientific knowledge is ultimately aimed at greater knowledge of what is observable. [31]

To be an empiricist is to withhold belief on anything that goes beyond the actual, observable phenomena, and to recognize no objective modality in nature. To develop an empiricist account of science is to depict it as involving a search for truth only about the empirical world, about what is actual and observable. . . . [I]t must involve throughout a resolute rejection of the demand for an explanation of the regularities in the observable course of nature by means of truths concerning a reality beyond what is actual and observable, as a demand which plays no role in the scientific enterprise. [202–03]

. . . according to constructive empiricism, the only belief involved in accepting a scientific theory is belief that it is empirically adequate: all that is both actual and observable finds a place in some model of the theory. So far as empirical adequacy is concerned, the theory would be just as good if there existed nothing at all that was either unobservable or not actual. Acceptance of the theory does not commit us to belief in the reality of either sort of thing. [157]

These quotations pretty well exhaust what van Fraassen has to say about the import of the observable/nonobservable distinction for constructive empiricism.

Van Fraassen has surprisingly little to say when it comes to precisely characterizing what it means to be observable, perhaps because he believes that "if there are limits to observation, these are a subject for empirical science, and not for philosophical analysis" (1980, 57). He does tell us that

[a] look through a telescope at the moons of Jupiter seems to me a clear case of observation, since astronauts will no doubt be able to see them as well from close up. But the purported observation of micro-particles in a cloud chamber seems to me a clearly different case—if our theory about what happens there is right. . . . [W]hile the particle is detected by means of the cloud chamber, and the detection is based on observation, it is clearly not a case of the [p]article's being observed. [16–17]

And in discussing the hermeneutic circle, he says:

To delineate what is observable, however, we must look to science—

and possibly to that same theory—for that is also an empirical question. This might produce a vicious circle if what is observable were itself not simply a fact disclosed by theory, but rather theory-relative or theory-dependent. It will already be quite clear that I deny this; I regard what is observable as a theory-independent question. It is a function of facts about us *qua* organisms in the world, and these facts may include facts about the psychological states that involve contemplation of theories—but there is not the sort of theory dependence or relativity that could cause a logical catastrophe here. [57–58]

Van Fraassen's statements suggest that what is observable is what can be seen with unaided vision; this is how most critics and commentators in Churchland and Hooker 1985 interpret his position. For van Fraassen this observable/nonobservable distinction is supposed to mark a fundamental epistemological distinction. In chapter 11 I will establish that, so drawn, the observable and the nonobservable are equally problematic epistemically, and so they mark no fundamental epistemological distinction. Churchland (1985), Glymour (1985), and Gutting (1985) urge the same conclusion. Given the deep affinities between my arguments in chapter 11 and the criticisms that Churchland (1985) raises on the basis of a thought experiment concerning a man for whom absolutely nothing is observable (42–43), it is clear that none of the rejoinders van Fraassen (1985) offers in rebuttal to these various objections constitutes an effective rejoinder to the criticism that will be raised later in chapter 11. Thus if the "unaided vision" reading is the proper interpretation of van Fraassen's position, we have every reason to reject his constructive empiricism—hence his antirealism.

We thus turn to the consideration of other possible interpretations of van Fraassen's observable/nonobservable distinction that might enable him to salvage his constructive empiricism. Despite the claims of the passage last quoted, a considerable amount of text by van Fraassen (1980) suggests that his observable/nonobservable distinction *is* a theory-dependent one:

[1] Nor can the limits [of what is observable] be described once and for all. . . . To find the limits of what is observable in the world described by theory T we must inquire into T itself, and the theories used as auxiliaries in the testing and application of T. [57]

[2] . . . the empirical import of a theory now is defined within

science, by means of a distinction between what is observable and what is not observable drawn by science itself. [81]

[3] ... what counts as an observable phenomenon is a function of what the epistemic community is (that *observable* is *observable-to-us*). [19; italics original]

[4] Not only objectivity, however, but also observability, is an intrascientific distinction, if the science is taken wide enough. [82]

[5] For science itself delineates, at least to some extent, the observable parts of the world it describes. Measurement interactions are a special subclass of physical interactions in general. The structures definable from measurement data are a subclass of the physical structures described. It is in this way that science itself distinguishes the observable which it postulates from the whole it postulates. The distinction, being in part a function of the limits science discloses on human observation, is an anthropocentric one. But since science places human observers among the physical systems it means to describe, it also gives itself the task of describing anthropocentric distinctions. It is in this way that even the scientific realist must observe a distinction between phenomena and the transphenomenal in the scientific world picture. [59]

These five claims by van Fraassen virtually exhaust what he has to say by way of characterizing observability; typically these claims are asserted rather than defended. Based on such statements, Wilson (1985) interprets van Fraassen as holding an "internalist" theory-laden view of observation. Van Fraassen (1985) rejects this interpretation, saying that he wants "to draw a sharp distinction between the use of science to help delineate what is observable, and Wilson's program, which can issue only... in a theory-relative notion of observability" (304–05). Unfortunately, his rejoinder leaves unclear what sense we are to make of the passages above.

I did not find a coherent viewpoint in the above five quotations. The first quotation suggests two distinct interpretations:[17] (1) What is observable is theory-dependent and is determined by a given theory T alone, and (2) What is observable is theory-dependent and is determined by a given theory T and any auxiliary theories used to test and apply T. Although the third quotation suggests that this combination of T

and its auxiliaries might be construed as the body of accepted theory and background knowledge accepted by a scientific community, the fourth quotation (among others) suggests a third interpretation: (3) What is observable is determined by science in some quite broad but unspecified sense of the term 'science'.

The first interpretation regarding the observable/nonobservable distinction is just false, since many theories have nothing to say about what is observable—especially in the anthropocentric ways outlined in the fifth quotation. The second interpretation is more plausible, but it is incompatible with a key doctrine of van Fraassen's antirealism—namely, that anything nonobservable is a gratuitous metaphysical addition. In other words, "there is no general physical difference to which it corresponds," and recourse to such nonobservables is to be avoided. On the contrary, in a very straightforward sense, it plausibly can be maintained that there are components of theories that correspond to nothing observable which nevertheless affect the sorts of auxiliary hypotheses that can be used in conjunction with the theory. For example, Ralph Kenat has argued that Planck's and Einstein's different stances with respect to Planck's blackbody radiation "permitted different auxiliary hypotheses to be employed; only if we accept the corpuscular nature of light does it make any sense to employ the conservation of momentum in analyzing the interaction of light and electrons."[18] Now, if the auxiliary hypotheses are part of what determines what is observable, as the second interpretation indicates, then one can get different observability boundaries depending on what nonobservable components one tacks onto one's theories. Van Fraassen has no basis for objecting to tacking on such nonobservable components, so long as one does not believe in them. This leaves open, then, the possibility that what is observable, hence what is empirically adequate, depends on nonobservables incorporated into one's theories. This surely is unacceptable to van Fraassen.

The way to block this possibility is to modify (2) to restrict the auxiliary hypotheses which determine observability to those that depend only on observable theory constituents for their applicability. However, doing so would seem to be incompatible with the ways in which the boundaries of observability in fact are expanded in science. For example, in the Planck-versus-Einstein blackbody radiation case, Einstein's assumption that light is in fact propagated in individual particles was about nonobservables originally, but it allowed the use of auxiliary hypotheses, which led to predictions that Compton could then experimentally test. Compton's experiments established the truth of Einstein's hypothesis and thereby expanded the range of what was observable to include light being propagated in individual particles.[19] To restrict auxiliary hypotheses to observables alone would preclude such developments and thus is incompatible with the ways science in fact does determine what is observable. Therefore, the second interpretation is unacceptable.

The third interpretation (expressed in the fourth quotation) is unacceptably vague. What constitutes this science "taken wide enough"? Van Fraassen gives us no idea, and so this interpretation is difficult to assess. Moreover, van Fraassen gives no arguments in support of the notion that science decides what is observable.

Shapere (1982), however, has provided arguments in support of this claim, if observability is construed as direct observation. On the other hand, he also argues that current notions of direct observation in astrophysics make observation involving human receptors be a special case of the more general analysis. Indeed, observation generally involves interactions between the observable phenomena and suitable detectors, with a given branch of science defining what a suitable detector is. Such a view enjoys some affinity with van Fraassen's anthropocentric interpretation (in the fifth quotation), but if this is what van Fraassen has in mind, note that much of what empiricists and antirealists have objected to as unreal fictions now qualify as observable. His notion of observability is indeed extremely wide now, seemingly designed primarily to exclude entities such as the space-time manifold in relativity theory from the class of observables.

More generally, van Fraassen's observability notion seems to become the idea that what is observable is simply a function of the measurable interactions. Let us distinguish between (a) those measurable interactions that in fact are possible in the world and (b) those that are believed to be measurable interactions by, say, a scientific discipline. Under the third interpretation, (b) seems to represent his position, but elsewhere he has made such claims as "observation is a special species of measurement" (1980, 59), which suggests that not all measurable interactions are observations. More importantly, he claims,

When the hypothesis is solely about what is observable, the two procedures [acceptance as true and empirical adequacy] amount to the same thing. For in that case, empirical adequacy coincides with truth. [72]

I would still identify truth of a theory with the condition that there is an exact correspondence between reality and one of its models. [197]

Van Fraassen thus seems to be claiming under (b) that what is observable is what is true in a correspondence sense, and thus that what is true in a correspondence sense depends on what are *believed* to be measurable interactions by a scientific discipline. This is incoherent, though, for what is true in a correspondence theory does not depend on scientific belief. What a scientific discipline believes to be true in a correspondence sense is a doxastic, not a correspondence, matter; and what is believed may be constrained by what the discipline believes to be measurable interactions or to be observable. But this is a position quite unlike (b); indeed, it is compatible with (a). In a fundamental sense, what is *observable* is determined by the actual real-world measurable interactions which enable observers to detect effects of things or processes.

This fundamental limitation imposes an ultimate boundary on scientific knowledge. One cannot know what one is incapable of interacting with, even in torturously remote and involved ways. I can, and do, accept something like this as a fundamental limitation on scientific knowledge, which my quasi-realism must accept—call this *ultimate observability*. By contrast, on the present reading, van Fraassen tries to limit science not to knowledge of the ultimately observable, but rather to what presently is believed to be observable—to the *doxastically observable*. However, the boundaries of the doxastically observable are variable, changing, and expanding over much of the history of science. The Planck-Einstein–Compton case sketched earlier is fairly typical: By taking seriously what is not doxastically observable, we thereby expand the limits of what is doxastically observable. Thus the doxastically observable is not a fundamental epistemic limit on science—contrary to van Fraassen's antirealistic position. Moreover, although it does strongly constrain what a scientific discipline will accept as empirically true, it does so in ways that allow one to test the correctness of statements about the doxastically nonobservable. Without this, the limits of doxastic observability cannot expand; thus van Fraassen's position makes the limits imposed by doxastic observability too severe.

I conclude that van Fraassen has not coherently presented his observable/nonobservable distinction. None of the plausible readings is satisfactory for his purposes and capable of escaping my arguments in chapter 11, while being faithful to actual scientific practice—thus the case for his constructive empiricism and antirealism is far from convincing. The world imposes limits of ultimate observability, which do constitute limits on what science can know. Science, of course, does not presently know, and may never fully know, what these limits are, but at a given time a scientific discipline's body of accepted belief defines a range of phenomena that it is confident its methods do enable it to know. Whatever the limits of science are, they probably are at least as broad as that. By seriously countenancing the reality of things that presently do not qualify as knowable, a scientific discipline is capable of expanding its ranges of doxastic observability and of phenomena it confidently claims to know. I think something very like this is a correct picture — it is a more plausible picture than van Fraassen's antirealistic one, and it allows for a more robust science than his constructive empiricism does. Indeed, it is a picture that my quasi-realism embellishes and enriches. In the chapters that follow I will develop it as an alternative to van Fraassen's antirealistic version of the Semantic Conception of Theories.

Finally, there is an important point to be made about philosophical method. Suppose van Fraassen were correct that empirical science need not countenance or pay attention to the doxastically nonobservable in theorizing about or explaining phenomena, or in any of its other characteristic activities, and suppose that empirical adequacy is the closest approximation to truth that science need concern itself with. From this it does not follow that an antirealism is correct. While it is the case that philosophical analyses are empirical in the sense that actual scientific theories or practices can refute them, it does not follow that scientific realism and the antirealisms are themselves empirical scientific theories. Indeed, the problems philosophical analyses attempt to solve typically are not scientific problems; thus there is no guarantee that what is adequate for doing science is adequate for doing philosophy of science.

To provide an adequate philosophical analysis of science — to explain and provide an understanding of what science does and why it has the epistemic or other philosophical attributes claimed for it — may require philosophical theorizing about things that science itself need not countenance. For example, let us grant that scientific realism concerns what is ultimately observable and that this typically is distinct from what a branch of science deems doxastically observable and is typically more expansive in scope. In order to defend a realism or antirealism, the issue of ultimate observability must be addressed, as it was, for example, in the discussion of the Einstein-Planck–Compton case. Or, granting that empirical adequacy is sufficient for science to do its job, defending that claim may require recourse to a stronger correspondence notion of truth that relates to ultimate observability.

The specifics of these examples are not important. What is important is the point that the ontic commitments of working science may be different than — indeed may be weaker than — the ontic commitments that philosophy of science must make in providing *its* analyses and answering *its* questions. And the issues of scientific realism really concern what sorts of ontic commitments are essential to a *philosophical* understanding of science, not what sorts of ontic commitments are essential to the scientists in going about the business of science. Thus, for example, the argument that a correspondence notion of truth is of no help to working scientists, since they can only assess truth on the basis of coherence with data and a body of background belief and theory accepted by their scientific discipline — hence that working scientists can eschew a correspondence notion of truth — says nothing whatsoever about whether a correspondence notion of truth has a substantive role to play in a philosophical analysis from the perspective of scientific realism or quasi-realism. To think otherwise is simply to confuse philosophy of science with science.

III. PLAN OF THE BOOK

My quasi-realistic version of the Semantic Conception employs no observational/theoretical or observable/nonobservable distinction (though it does respect the limits of ultimate observability). In chapter 2 I use a consideration of the Received View as a foil to argue that anything like the positivistic observational/theoretical distinction is unnecessary. I do so under the guise of evaluating how successful Achinstein's and Putnam's attacks on the Received View have been. The chapter, inter alia, argues that their attacks on partial interpretation miss the mark. The model-theoretic analysis of partial interpretation I give there (sec. I) is divorceable from the positivistic observational/theoretical distinction, and when so divorced it has a minor technical role to play in the developments of chapters 4 and 5. Chapter 2, section III, introduces a heuristic version of the Semantic Conception which is intended to be fairly intuitive.

That intuitive version of the Semantic Conception is developed in the next three chapters (chs. 3–5). Chapter 3 introduces the basic components of theories and explores the semantic relations between the linguistic formulation of theories and theory structures, physical systems, and phenomena. In the process, the chapter also argues against the operational imperative. Chapter 4 explores more fully the relations between theories and phenomena, including the roles of observation, measurement, experimental design, and standard inductive confirmation techniques. Chapter 5 investigates a number of different kinds of theoretical laws, including laws of succession, interaction, and coexistence; teleological and functional laws; and laws of quasi-succession. In the process, it is argued that approximate truth notions are unnecessary for understanding the truth status of laws and theories on the Semantic Conception.

An important test of a philosophical analysis is its ability to deal successfully with problems and issues that were not key to its development — that is, its robustness. The robustness of the Semantic Conception is extensively explored throughout the book. Chapters 3 and 5 consider the implications of the Semantic Conception for the operational imperative and Scriven's view that laws are fundamentally inaccurate. Chapters 6 through 9 further test the power of the Semantic Conception by examining its implications for a range of other issues. Chapter 6 focuses on theoretical explanation. Chapter 7 takes on issues about what makes a biological taxonomy natural instead of artificial, presents a solution, and explores the relationships between theories and taxonomies on the Semantic Conception. Chapter 8 explores the robustness of the Semantic Conception by showing how it can accommodate what Schaffner calls interlevel theories of the middle range in the biomedical sciences — theories which appear to be quite different in structure than what philosophy of science typically has considered. Chapter 9 shows how the Semantic Conception's treatment of teleological laws (in ch. 5) enables one to better understand public scientific controversies (such as the one concerning nuclear power) which become entangled in moral and public policy disputes, and it also sheds light on engineering applications of scientific theories. The ability of the Semantic Conception to deal productively with all these issues adds to the evidence supporting it. Since its treatment of each of these issues turns centrally on features of its quasi-realistic treatment of the physical interpretation of theory structures, these chapters provide considerable support for adopting that quasi-realistic version rather than some weaker antirealist or instrumentalist one.

In developing his antirealist version of the Semantic Conception, van Fraassen (1980) maintains that "philosophy of science is not metaphysics" (82) and that "we cannot settle the major questions of epistemology *en passant*" (19). In passing, no — but the quasi-realistic version of the Semantic Conception developed in chapters 2 through 5, and elaborated and applied in chapters 6 though 9, has taken a number of stands that have significant metaphysical and epistemological implications. In particular, it imposes rather strong constraints on what sort of epistemology of science one can adopt in conjunction with it. There are two main approaches one can take here: One can develop a realist or quasi-realist view that has such implications and then try to finesse them — as Glymour tries to do in his *Theory and Evidence* (1980). Alternatively, one can view these implications as incurring an obligation to develop and defend an epistemology/metaphysics that must be met. I prefer the latter approach.

Many years ago Carnap commuted once a week by train from Chicago to a university some hours away to guest-teach a graduate seminar. A young faculty member sat in on Carnap's seminar and soon sought him out. He told Carnap that he was very interested in the problem of induction and hoped it would be possible to meet with Carnap some time during the semester and discuss it. Carnap listened, then asked, "Tell me, Mr. _____, do you have your own theory of inductive logic?" The young professor answered, "No, but I'm very interested in induction and would like very much to discuss it with you." Carnap replied, "Well, Mr. _____, when you have your own theory of inductive logic, I'd be more than happy to discuss induction with you." Carnap's reply to the young professor simply was that it was pointless to discuss induction if you don't have a position. And for him, to have or defend a position was to develop a theory of inductive logic.

My quasi-realistic version of the Semantic Conception commits me to a kind of position on some basic epistemological issues. Carnap's view on having a position on induction is generalizable to the issue of scientific realism: To take a position on scientific realism, especially to defend a realism or quasi-realism, is to make some fairly strong metaphysical and epistemological commitments. To defend them adequately requires developing an epistemology and associated metaphysics in fair detail. Chapters 3 and 7, inter alia, present key metaphysical and ontological assumptions which underlie my quasi-realism and use these to sketch a correspondence account of factual truth and empirical truth for theories (based on my 1973 article). The treatment of natural versus artificial biological taxonomies in chapter 7 provides a general quasi-realistic construal of the difference between natural and merely artificial classification. Thus it provides the *antinominalism* which van Fraassen (1989) so rightly insists must underlie any plausible realistic construal of science. Chapters 10 through 13 are intended to be a fairly detailed prolegomenon to such a fully developed epistemology, and the issues taken up there should give a good idea of the epistemological lines I wish to take in defending my quasi-realistic version of the Semantic Conception. The introductory section to part IV provides an overview of the specific contents and objectives of each of those chapters.

To me, the question of scientific realism is how strong an epistemology can be and still be defensible. I do not believe much progress can be made by the recently fashionable practice of delimiting an ever-growing variety of realisms, antirealisms, instrumentalisms, and so on, characterizing them in a few sentences or paragraphs, and then mounting abstract arguments for or against each. Far more appropriate, it seems to me, is for the various proponents to attempt to develop in fine detail epistemologies that are faithful to their realist, quasi-realist, antirealist, or instrumentalist beliefs.

The strongest defense I know of for a scientific realism or quasi-realism is to develop a realistic or quasi-realistic epistemology that works in fine detail and proves robust in solving problems other epistemologies and philosophies of science have floundered on. This is precisely the strategy I take in chapters 10 through 13 where I develop an underlying epistemology for my quasi-realistic version of the Semantic Conception of Theories. I welcome criticisms from those who do not have their own competing epistemologies, but, like Carnap on induction, I think the most productive debates will be with those who have developed their own epistemologies. For the viability of a realism or a quasi-realism, or any other approach, ultimately depends on the *details* of how knowledge is analyzed and handled. And it is precisely those sorts of details that contemporary debates over scientific realism too often ignore — and must ignore if the protagonists do not have their own detailed theories of knowledge.

The Epilogue attempts to place the development of the Semantic Conception into the larger picture of scientific theorizing and explores the connection between developments here and other issues in the philosophy of science. Problems about scientific theories and theorizing needing further research are indicated.

NOTES

1. For an extensive discussion of the Received View, see Suppe 1974b, 3–118, and Suppe 1977a, 619–32. See also ch. 2 below.

2. For example, Beatty 1979, 1980, 1981, 1982; da Costa and French n.d.; Edelson 1984; Giere 1988; Hardegree 1976; Hausman 1981; Horan 1986; Lloyd 1984, 1987a, 1988, 1988a; Moulines 1975; Sneed 1971; Schaffner n.d.; Stegmüller 1976; Thompson 1983, 1985, 1986, 1988, 1988a, 1989, n.d.; Wessels 1976; as well as various writings of its main developers (e.g., Beth, Suppes, van Fraassen, and myself).

3. For the distinction, see Suppes 1957, 232.

4. A few versions of the Received View do not identify theories with their linguistic formulations, instead requiring that theories be such that they can be given canonical linguistic formulations meeting the requirements of the Received View (see Suppe 1974b, 57–62). On such versions it still remains the case that the content of the correspondence rules are individuating components of the theory, and so substantive changes in correspondence rules produce new theories.

5. Sneed (1971) and Stegmüller (1976) maintain that in some instances such measurement procedures are individuating characteristics of theories and in others they are not. Specifying when they are is a central task of their analysis and is offered as a solution to the "problem of theoretical terms" (theoretical terms, roughly, being those terms or variables whose measurement presupposes the very theory in question). Their theoretical terms exclude most of what the positivists counted as theoretical terms. Later I exclude such approaches from the Semantic Conception.

6. Beth 1949, 178. Beth 1949 is a journal article in English summarizing his 1948 book, which has never been translated from the Dutch.

7. He also cites Destouches 1942 as influential.

8. By the time I had done much work on my thesis, Sneed had left Michigan for Stanford. He was replaced by Richard Boyd on my committee. I vaguely knew about Sneed's thesis, though I never looked at it then, and I do not think his thesis had much influence on my development of the Semantic Conception. In particular, I was not in residence at Michigan in the winter of 1966 when he gave a course of lectures on his dissertation, and did not learn of that series of lectures until recently. But Sneed *was* influential in turning me on to Kuhn 1962—which he still is high on—and in bringing Mackey 1963 and Messiah 1961 to my attention. Around the summer of 1964 he arranged for me to meet Suppes at Stanford; from that contact I gained access to a prepublication version of Suppes 1967, which influenced my dissertation a lot.

John Holland was not on my committee (the philosophy department objected to the number of nonphilosophers I wanted on it, just as it objected to the amount of course work I wanted to do outside philosophy), but he served unofficially and was extremely helpful to me.

9. Specifically, its treatment of correspondence rules bore no resemblance to my experience at G.E. with how theories related to phenomena.

10. I had seen Beth's 1961 work previously, but it hadn't said much to me then.

11. See Dalla Chiara 1976; Dalla Chiara Scabia and Toraldo di Francia 1973; Przełecki 1969 and 1976; Wójcicki 1974, 1974a, and 1976.

12. Aristotle preferred Callippus' version but actually provided his replacement versions for both Eudoxus' and Callippus' theories. See Aristotle *Metaphysics* Λ, 8. Since Callippus' versions were refinements of Eudoxus', it is standard to refer to it as Eudoxus' theory.

13. MacKinnon 1979, 518. See also Feyerabend 1978.

14. In ch. 11 I will argue for a reconstrual of the scientific realism issue that implicitly rejects these characterizations of van Fraassen.

15. Since on a realistic construal of quantum theory, such a principle does not hold for statements in general, it is not clear that it holds for theories on a scientific realism.

16. These difficulties are discussed in chs. 4 and 5.

17. The following analysis and line of objection is based in part on the ideas of my student Ralph Kenat.

18. Ralph Kenat, unpublished paper, "Some Critical Problems with van Fraassen's *Scientific Image*," written for a seminar I gave on the Semantic Conception.

19. It certainly made light being propagated in individual particles part of the phenomena, and for van Fraassen the phenomena are just the observables (1980, 56). Thus it follows that it is observable. Michael Friedman (1983a) has argued that assessing the reality of the space-time manifold in general relativity theory allows for a richer range of inductive inference that affects the testability of the theory. It appears that his line constitutes another example that could pose problems for the second theory-dependent interpretation of van Fraassen's account of observability.

2

What's Wrong with the Received View on the Structure of Scientific Theories?

For many years the *Received View on Scientific Theories* has been that theories are to be construed as axiomatic calculi in which theoretical terms are given a partial observational interpretation by means of correspondence rules. Underlying this analysis is a strict bifurcation of the nonlogical terms of the theory into an observational vocabulary and a theoretical vocabulary. Putnam, Achinstein, and others have urged the rejection of the Received View because (i) the notion of partial interpretation it employs cannot be given a precise formulation adequate for the purposes of the Received View, and (ii) the observational/theoretical distinction cannot be drawn satisfactorily.[1] It is my contention that the Received View is unsatisfactory and ought to have been rejected, but not for these reasons. Section I of this chapter (based on my 1971 article, "On Partial Interpretation") argues that reason (i) is false. Section II goes on to argue that it is virtually impossible to establish reason (ii). Section III attempts to show that the Received View nonetheless ought to be rejected because its reliance on the observational/theoretical distinction causes it to obscure a number of epistemologically important and revealing features of the structure of scientific theories. In the process of arguing for this latter claim, a more adequate account of the epistemological structure of scientific theories is presented—it is a version of the *Semantic Conception of Theories*.

I. ON PARTIAL INTERPRETATION

Achinstein and Putnam argue in support of reason (i) for rejecting the Received View by observing that its advocates have not made the notion of partial interpretation clear. They consider a number of possible explications of the notion, then show that they are inadequate for the purposes of the Received View (Achinstein 1968, 85–91; Putnam 1962, 244–48).

In this section I attempt to present an analysis of partial interpretation compatible with the rest of the Received View. My interests in presenting this analysis do not lie in the direction of attempting to rescue the Received View from its critics—for I am convinced that ultimately it must be rejected as unsatisfactory—but rather are grounded in the belief that a clear understanding of the notion of partial interpretation employed by the Received View will bring to light a number of important characteristics about scientific theories and scientific meaning.

A. An Explication of the Received View

Explication of the notion of partial interpretation requires a precise formulation of the Received View, and since Carnap and Hempel have given its most extensive and sophisticated development, their formulation will be used.[2] Since their position has undergone considerable revision over the years, and because they have published no single comprehensive account of their ultimate formulation, I have reconstructed it from their various recent writings on the subject.

The reconstruction is as follows: Scientific theories are such that they can be given a canonical reformulation which satisfies the following conditions:

(1) There is a first-order language L in terms of which the theory is formulated, and a calculus K defined in terms of L.

(2) The nonlogical or descriptive primitive constants (i.e., the "terms") of L are bifurcated into two disjoint classes:
   (a) V_O, which contains just the observation terms, and
   (b) V_T, which contains the nonobservation or theoretical terms.
   V_O must contain at least one individual constant.

(3) The language L is divided into the following sublanguages, and the calculus K is divided into the following subcalculi:
   (a) The *observation language, L_O,* is a sublanguage of L which contains no quantifiers or modalities and contains the terms of V_O, but none from V_T. The associated calculus K_O is the restriction of K to L_O and must be such that any non-V_O-terms (i.e., nonprimitive terms) in L_O are explicitly defined in K_O. Furthermore, K_O must admit of at least one finite model.

(b) The *logically extended observation language, L'_o*, contains no V_T-terms. It may be regarded as being formed from L_o by adding the quantifiers, modalities, etc., of L to L_o. Its associated calculus, K'_o, is the restriction of K to L'_o.

(c) The *theoretical language, L_T*, is that sublanguage of L which does not contain V_o-terms; its associated calculus, K_T, is the restriction of K to L_T.

These sublanguages together do not exhaust L, for L also contains *mixed sentences*, i.e., those in which at least one V_T- and one V_o-term occur. In addition, it is assumed that each of the sublanguages above has its own stock of predicate or functional variables and the L_o and L'_o have the same stock, which is distinct from that of L_T.

(4) L_o and its associated calculi are given a *semantic interpretation* which meets the following conditions:

(a) The domain of interpretation consists of concrete observable entities such as observable events, things, or thing-moments; the relations and properties of the interpretation must be directly observable.

(b) Every value of any variable in L_o must be designated by an expression in L_o.

It follows that any such interpretation of L_o and K_o, when augmented by appropriate additional rules of truth, will become an interpretation of L'_o and K'_o. We may construe interpretations of L_o and K_o as being *partial semantic interpretations of L and K*, and we require that L and K be given no empirical semantic interpretation other than that provided by such partial semantic interpretations.

(5) A *partial interpretation* of the theoretical terms and of the sentences of L containing them is provided by the following two kinds of postulates: the *theoretical postulates T* (i.e., the axioms of the theory) in which only terms of V_T occur, and the *correspondence rules* or postulates C which are mixed sentences. The correspondence rules C must satisfy the following conditions:

(a) The set of rules C must be finite.

(b) The set of rules C must be logically compatible with T.

(c) C contains no extralogical term that does not belong to V_o or V_T.

(d) Each rule in C must contain at least one V_o-term and at least one V_T-term essentially or nonvacuously.[3]

Let T be the conjunction of the theoretical postulates and C be the conjunction of the correspondence rules. Then the scientific theory based on L, T, and C consists of the conjunction of T and C and is designated by 'TC'.

Note that condition (4) allows the possibility of alternative semantical systems (or interpretations) for L_O which may differ in the designata of V_O-terms. The Received View intends, however, that there be a fixed set of designata for the terms of V_O, and so restrictions must be imposed on the class of admissible interpretations. Let us assume that a fixed set of rules of designation has been specified for these V_O-terms; then let us say that the class of semantical systems that use these rules are *permissible semantical systems* for L_O, and the class of interpretations they specify are *permissible interpretations* for L_O and K_O. Notice that different permissible interpretations are possible, since the rules of designation for predicate variables may differ. The classes of permissible semantical systems and interpretations for L_O' and K_O' are defined analogously.

B. A Formal Analysis of Partial Interpretation

A central claim of the Received View is that TC together with the specification of a permissible semantical system for L_O and L_O' provides L (and hence the V_T-terms and L_T-sentences) with a partial interpretation. As Carnap puts it:

> All the interpretation (in the strict sense of this term, i.e., observational interpretation) that can be given for L_T is given in the C-rules, and their function is essentially the interpretation of certain sentences containing descriptive terms, and thereby the descriptive terms of V_T. . . .
>
> For L_T we do not claim to have a complete interpretation, but only the indirect and partial interpretation given by the correspondence rules. . . .
>
> . . . Before the C-rules are given, L_T, with the postulates T and the rules of deduction, is an uninterpreted calculus. . . . Then the C-rules are added. All they do is, in effect, to permit the derivation of certain sentences of L_O from certain sentences of L_T or vice versa. They serve indirectly for derivations of conclusions in L_O, e.g. predictions of observable events, from given premises in L_O, e.g. reports of results found by observation, or the determination of the probability of a conclusion in L_O on the basis of given premises in L_O. [1956, 46–47]

The crucial notion here, partial interpretation, plays a central role in the Received View analysis, and as many authors have pointed out, the notion is far from clear.[4] For, as Putnam points out, nowhere have Carnap, Hempel, and the other proponents of the Received View defined what they mean by partial interpretation.

Hempel (1963) has given what is perhaps the most detailed explication of partial interpretation advanced by any proponent of the Received View. He raises the following question: In what sense and to what extent does an interpretative system (rules of correspondence) specify an interpretation for L_T? He points out that for a given term in V_T, the interpretative system C "may establish a necessary and sufficient condition" in terms of V_O, which he illustrates with an explicit definition. But he adds that this need not be the case, since for some terms, C will establish (1) "only a necessary and a different sufficient condition" in terms of V_O, (2) just a necessary condition, (3) a sufficient condition, or (4) "neither a necessary nor a sufficient condition" in terms of V_O (693). This, however, tells us little, since he never stipulates what these conditions are necessary or sufficient for—are they truth conditions, derivability conditions, or what?

Although Hempel doesn't explicitly address these questions, it is possible to construe his subsequent discussion, which focuses on possible ways in which partially interpreted theoretical sentences are significant, as constituting a somewhat oblique partial answer to this question (694–95). He distinguishes three concepts of significance: (a) pragmatic intelligibility, (b) empirical significance, in the sense of being relevant to potential empirical evidence expressible in terms of V_O, and (c) semantical significance, in the sense of being true or false. Further, he claims that partially interpreted theoretical sentences are significant in all three senses. With respect to (a) he says that scientists understand how to employ partially interpreted theoretical sentences in the sense that they know how "to use" them correctly, and that in the Received View reconstruction, this is, in essential respects, equivalent to knowing the rules of TC. As to (b), this condition is met, since TC has derivable sentences of L_O that may be used for prediction and are subject to empirical test. Thus a necessary condition for the existence of a partial interpretation seems to be that the C-rules must enable one to derive sentences in L_O from T that could not be derived otherwise. Hempel's argument that theoretical statements are semantically significant in the sense of being true or false, simply put, is that they can be stated in a suitable metalanguage, and so it is possible to specify truth criteria for theoretical statements. Although this tells us nothing about the way C-rules provide a partial interpretation, it does provide a certain indirect support for my analysis, which follows.

Although Hempel's discussion of significance sheds some light on what is meant by partial interpretation—telling us, at most, that partial interpretations must supply theories with observational or testable consequences—it does not provide an adequate analysis. Since it would appear that little more can be said syntactically in the way of characterizing partial interpretation, if we are to find an adequate analysis of the concept, we must turn to semantic considerations. As a first step, let us consider the semantics of explicit definition.

Consider a language L^* which is that sublangauge of L'_0 whose only nonlogical symbols are the individual variables and the symbols in V_0, and let K^* be the restriction of K to L^*. Let S be a true interpretation of K^*—that is, a semantical system S for L^* such that every sentence of L^* that is a theorem of K^* is true under S. Suppose now that we augment the alphabet of L^* with the one-place predicate constant 'P', and we introduce a definition of 'P' in terms of V_0 as an additional axiom for K^*. Call this new language and this new calculus L^{**} and K^{**} respectively. Under what circumstances will this definition qualify as an explicit definition?

Suppose that our definition is of the form

(1) $$(x)(Px \equiv \phi(x))$$

where ϕ is a formula whose only predicates are from V_0, and 'x' is the only free variable in ϕ. Then, for (1) to qualify as an explicit definition of 'P', for any formula θ such that 'P' occurs in θ, if θ is a theorem of K^{**}, then the result ψ of replacing all occurrences of 'P' in θ by ϕ (with appropriate changes of variables) must be a theorem of K^*. That is, for 'P' to be explicitly definable, the introduction of 'P' must be noncreative and theoretically eliminable.[5] But this, in essence, is nothing other than the requirement that 'P' be definable in accord with the modern theory of definition in logic as developed by Padoa and Beth.[6] The key semantic features of this theory are summarized in Padoa's principle and its converse, the Beth definability theorem. Stated heuristically, for 'P' to be *explictily definable in terms of V_0 in K^{**}*, it is necessary and sufficient that the following conditions be met: Let S_1 and S_2 be any two true interpretations of L^{**} such that S_1 and S_2 have the some domain and assign the same designata to terms in V_0. Let P_1 be the designatum of 'P' under S_1 and let P_2 be its designatum under S_2. Then 'P' is explicitly definable in terms of V_0 in K^{**} if and only if for each member a of the domain (of both S_1 and S_2), a has property P_1 if and only if a has property P_2.[7]

This result admits of the following interpretation: Let S' be a true permissible interpretation of L'_0. Call the result S^* of deleting all relations, properties, functions, and so on, in S' that are not the designata of terms in V_O *the restriction of S′ to L**. The class of *permissible interpretations for L** is the class of restrictions of $S′$ to L^*, where $S′$ is an arbitrary permissible interpretation for L'_O. Let S be a permissible interpretation for L^*. The result of adding a new property P to S and a new rule of designation that 'P' designates P is said to be a *permissible extension of S from L* to L***. Then the Beth-Padoa result says that 'P' must have the same extension (be "true of" the same entities) in every true interpretation of K^{**} that is a permissible extension of S from L^* to L^{**}. This simply means that whenever one explicitly defines a term 'P' on the basis of V_O, if one assumes both that all the theorems of K^* are true and that the sentence defining 'P' is true, then the property designated by 'P' in any given permissible extension of a true interpretation will be extensionally equivalent to the property designated by 'P' under any other such interpretation. Taken in conjunction with the various assumptions made about permissible interpretations for L'_O, this result essentially says that the assumed truth of the definition of 'P' and K^{**} necessitates that the true permissible extensions to K^{**} of true permissible interpretations of K^* be indistinguishable on extensional grounds.

Now recall from Hempel's discussion, referred to earlier, that terms introduced by interpretative systems of C-rules generally fail to meet all the requirements imposed on explicit definitions. Thus, such terms generally will *not* be explicitly definable on the basis of V_O in the Beth-Padoa sense of definability. Since Padoa's principle and the Beth definability theorem supply us with necessary and sufficient conditions for the explicit definability of terms on the basis of V_O, they yield the following characteristic of partial interpretations: The designata of 'P' in true permissible extensions to K^{**} of true permissible interpretations of K^* will *not* be extensionally equivalent.

Despite this fact, however, the assumed truth of the sentence partially defining 'P' does in general impose considerable restrictions upon the class of true permissible extensions. For example, suppose the definition sentence is of the form

$$(2) \qquad (\exists x)(Px \lor (\phi x \ \& \ \psi x))$$

where ϕ and ψ are different one-place predicates in V_O. Then any permissible semantical system for L'_O whose restriction to L^* is a true interpretation of K^* such that '$(\exists x)Px$' or '$(\exists x)(\phi x \ \& \ \psi x)$' are also true, will qualify as a true permissible extension to K^{**} of a true permissible interpretation of K^*. But suppose that the definition sentence is of the form

$$(3) \qquad (x)(Px \lor (\phi x \ \& \ \psi x))$$

Then only those extensions to K^{**} such that every individual either has P or else has both ϕ and ψ will be true, and the class of such extensions will be a proper subclass of those such that '$(\exists x)Px$' is true or '$(\exists x)(\phi x\ \&\ \psi x)$' is true. Accordingly, the class of defining sentences will impose differing restrictions on the class of true permissible extensions to K^{**} of true permissible interpretations of K^*.

Thus far this discussion has considered what happens under partial and explicit definition when a single-place predicate constant from L_o' is defined. The same basic treatment will generalize to the case where a finite set of predicate symbols is defined sequentially via introductive chains,[8] provided the following assumption is made (which has been tacit in the discussion thus far): the only permissible definitions are those which do not make K^{**} inconsistent. This treatment also extends more or less straightforwardly to the case where terms of V_T are given either explicit or partial definitions via C-rules on the basis of V_O. Here we consider those permissible extensions of K^* to K, where we treat the conjunction TC (of the sentences in the set T of theoretical postulates and the set C of sentences in the interpretative system, or C-rules) as being the defining sentence. The primary difference is that the entire set of terms in V_T is being defined simultaneously by TC.

For permissible extensions S of S^* for K^* to K we do not require that S and S^* have the same domain, but rather only that the domain of S contain the domain of S^*. This allows the possibility that the domain of S may contain both theoretical entities and observable entities. As long as K (whose nonlogical axioms are the sentences in T and C) is consistent, the assumed truth of TC will impose restrictions upon the class of true permissible extensions to K of true permissible interpretations of K^*. This in turn will impose restrictions on the class of relations, and so on, which qualify as designata for terms in V_T in such extensions. But from a different perspective, this simply means that the assumption that TC is true imposes restrictions on the class of permissible models of K. This, then, suggests that the sense in which the interpretative system C supplies L_T (and its associated calculus) with a partial interpretation is that it imposes restrictions on the class of permissible models for it. Furthermore, the C-rules must enable sentences of L_O (or possible L_o') to be derivable in K.

C. The Analysis Evaluated and Defended

How adequate an analysis of partial interpretation is this? Since Carnap and Hempel have not revealed sufficiently what they mean by partial interpretation, one cannot be sure whether this is what they have in mind, but as far as I have been able to determine, the analysis just suggested is wholly compatible with what they have to say on the matter. However, Achinstein and Putnam have considered possible analyses of partial interpretation that are somewhat similar to this and have rejected them as inadequate for the purposes of the Received View. It will be illustrative to consider these to see whether the objections to them present a challenge to my own analysis and also to display further features of partial interpretation.

Achinstein (1968) suggests the following analysis which, so far as it goes, has some affinity with mine: "To speak of a term 'X' as partially interpreted might be to say that although the term has a meaning, in the sense of a semantical rule or explicit observational definition, only part of that meaning has been given."[9] This suggested analysis is rejected by Achinstein as not being consistent with the Received View, since it presupposes that the term in question has a meaning, in the sense that there is either an explicit semantical rule or explicit observational definition for it, and for theoretical terms this is denied. If the only kind of meaning a theoretical term can have is that supplied by explicit semantical rules or explicit observational definitions, then Achinstein is correct in rejecting this interpretation. But why can't the meaning partially given or captured by the C-rules be the pre-analytic meaning for the theoretical term or its translation in the ordinary or metalanguage of science (of which the C-rules provide a partial explication)? Viewed in this manner, the analysis Achinstein considers becomes the claim that the partial interpretation captures a part, but not all, of the pre-analytic meaning.

Now it might be objected that the proponents of the Received View would reject this suggestion on the grounds that it presupposes the sorts of meanings their program has tried to eschew—and once they would have made such an objection. Later it became unlikely that they would so object, for consider what Hempel (1963) has written:

To turn, finally, to the question of semantic significance: Let T be interpreted by a system C which does not furnish every V_T-sentence an equivalent in terms of V_O. Then it is nevertheless quite possible to provide a necessary and sufficient condition of truth for every sentence expressible in terms of the theoretical vocabulary. All that is needed for the purpose is a suitable metalanguage. If we are willing to use a metalanguage which contains V_O, V_T, and C, or translations thereof, then indeed each V_T-sentence has a truth criterion in it, namely simply its restatement in, or its translation into, that metalanguage.[10]

Thus it would appear that my suggestion is quite compatible with Carnap's and Hempel's published views.

Achinstein's proposal is of considerable value, because when altered and taken in conjunction with Hempel's statement just quoted, it will allow a more perspicuous treatment of partial interpretation. But first we must consider Hempel's statement further. At first blush it is an extremely surprising statement which seems to go contrary to the basic tenets of the Received View. For does it not seem to give ontological status to the very abstract entities the Received View regards with such suspicion that it wishes to avoid them? Indeed, one doubts that the assertion is even consistent with the remainder of the Received View analysis.

This first-blush reaction is, I think, quite understandable but cannot be sustained under analysis. To see this we need to remember that the Received View is offered as a reconstructive account of scientific theories and, in particular, that its notion of partial interpretation is intended to provide a reconstructive account of the *empirical* or *observational meaning* of theoretical terms. If we look at theoretical terms such as 'electron' in the ordinary scientific language, we find that much of the content of the concepts these terms embody is related in no explicitly discernible manner to the observational or empirical manifestations of, say, electrons, but does concern extra-empirical associations. For electrons, these might include various features of the billiard-ball model, various classical intuitions about macroscopic point-masses, and so on.

Such associations contribute to the meanings of the theoretical terms in ordinary scientific language, and it is quite likely that without them little scientific progress would be made. But despite their legitimate place as meaning constituents of theoretical terms, they need not — and usually do not — have empirical or observable or testable consequences. The proponents of the Received View do not deny this point, and they need not, for all they are committed to doing is presenting a reconstructive analysis of theoretical terms so as to explicate the ways in which they have empirical content, and the ways in which the empirical aspects of their meanings interrelate with observation reports or statements and with empirical laws. They need not be committed to the position that their analysis exhausts all the conceptual or meaning content of the corresponding ordinary scientific-language terms, or to the position that statements about electrons, for example, are neither true nor false. They certainly are not committed to the position that when scientists talk about electrons, they are speaking metaphysical gibberish, but only to the position that when scientists talk about electrons, only part of the meaning of 'electron' is empirical.[11]

Accordingly, although committed to including only the empirical aspects of meaning of these theoretical terms in their treatment of meaning specification for theoretical terms via C-rules or interpretative systems, the Received View can tolerate nonempirical meaning components. The resolution of the seemingly paradoxical or contradictory claims made in the Hempel quotation thus lies in the fact that by using the ordinary scientific-language meanings of theoretical terms, we can specify a semantic interpretation for TC—stipulating that, for example, the domain includes neutrons, electrons, protons, and so on, and that the term in V_T that corresponds to 'is an electron' denotes the class of objects in the domain that are electrons. At the same time we can refuse to allow the terms of V_T that are partially interpreted to be given an independent empirical semantic interpretation. That is, the semantic interpretations allowed in the Hempel quotation are allowed simply because they are not empirical interpretations.

But does not Hempel's claim now reduce to the trivial assertion that it is possible to give an unofficial extra-empirical semantic interpretation of the terms of V_T, but that officially such interpretations are banned? If so, have we not misinterpreted Hempel's claim? Possibly, but I think not—for Hempel continues by saying:

> Let us note here with Carnap that the semantical criteria of truth and references which can be given for the sentences and for the terms, or "constructs," of a partially interpreted theory offer little help towards an understanding of these expressions. For the criteria will be intelligible only to those who understand the metalanguage in which they are expressed; and the metalanguage must contain either the theoretical expressions themselves or their translations; hence, the latter must be antecedently understood if the semantical criteria are to be intelligible. [1963, 696]

Although this passage seems to me to contribute something to the plausibility of the interpretation I have advanced, it still is quite possible that I am misinterpreting Hempel. But if so, I find it impossible to see a reading of his position which does not deviate fundamentally from what I have just suggested and which does not at the same time make Hempel's assertions violently contradict the prohibition against providing TC with a direct empirical semantic interpretation (condition [4] of sec. I-A).

Assuming that my interpretation of Hempel is more or less accurate, does it not follow that Hempel's claim that partially interpreted theoretical statements are significant in the sense of being true or false is now beside the point? For is not the real question whether partially interpreted theoretical sentences are true or false when reconstructed in accord with the defining conditions (1) through (5) of the Received View (sec. I-A)? In deciding this it will be helpful to recall the restatement made earlier of Achinstein's possible analysis of partial interpretation: For a term in V_T, the C-rules specify part, but not all, of the meaning of the corresponding theoretical term in ordinary scientific language. Thus advocates of the Received View refuse to commit themselves to the existence of entities that have *all* the attributes specified by the meanings of ordinary scientific-language theoretical terms. However, so long as any TC in which the corresponding terms in V_T occur has some observable consequences, it seems highly unlikely that they would want to maintain that one can simultaneously assert TC and refuse to be committed to the existence of *some* entities that have the properties specified by TC and also lead to these observational consequences.[12] Admittedly, even then they would likely refuse to say anything more about these entities other than that they have these observable consequences. If this is the case, and if we accept—as I think we must— this analysis of partial interpretation as telling at least an important part of the story about partial interpretation, then the obvious conclusion is that in ordinary scientific discourse about electrons, and so on, ontological commitments are being made that commit one to terms such as 'electron' having referents. But this commitment is limited to the extent determined by the partial interpretation supplied for the V_T-terms by TC; that is, one is committed to the existence of *something* that has the specified observational consequences.

This last observation provides a basis for supplying Hempel's quoted assertion with an interesting and nontrivial construal. To assert TC and then give it a semantic interpretation in the manner he specifies is to commit oneself to the existence of a true permissible interpretation of TC; that is, to the assertion that one of the interpretations within the class circumscribed by the partial interpretation of TC is in fact true. But at the same time, one is *not* thereby committed to being able to specify on empirical grounds which of these interpretations one is committed to. Differently put, this commitment requires that one be able to specify empirically a semantic interpretation modulo-equivalence by virtue of being within the class of true permissible interpretations, but does not commit one to being able to specify it further on empirical grounds (except possibly by the addition of further C-rules). Viewed in this way, I do not find Hempel's assertion trivial, since it illuminates the way in which ordinary scientific language carries ontological commitment and the extent to which it can be used to specify an empirical semantic interpretation for the sentences of TC, and further, it illustrates how it is that partial interpretation via the observational consequences of a theory modulates the extent and specificity of that ontological commitment.

Putnam considers a suggested analysis of partial interpretation which is a less specific version of mine and claims that it is inadequate for the purposes of the Received View. This serious challenge to my analysis is worth looking at in detail. Putnam suggests that to partially interpret L_T is to specify a nonempty class of intended models and that if the class contains just one member, the interpretation is complete; otherwise it is partial (1962, 245). He then rejects this analysis as inadequate, arguing roughly as follows: To specify the class of intended models, one will have to employ theoretical terms (presumably from the metalanguage), and to rule out flagrantly unintended interpretations, one must use such notions as 'physical object' and 'physical magnitude' to specify the domains and designata of V_T-terms. For example, to interpret 'mass' as a real-valued function, the function's values must be restricted to physical magnitudes if those interpretations which a realistically minded scientist would reject are to be ruled out. And terms such as 'physical magnitude' are neither theoretical nor observational terms, but rather "broad-spectrum terms" which are *not* defined in advance, science itself telling us what "physical magnitudes" are. In short, although these are not theoretical terms, they eventually tend to acquire technical senses via theoretical definitions (Putnam 1962, 246).

Although Putnam takes these observations as demonstrating that his proposal is inadequate for the Received View's purposes, he never explains how it is that they bear upon the adequacy of his proposal—and it is neither clear nor immediately obvious that they do demonstrate its inadequacy. Presumably the inadequacy lies in the fact that terms such as 'physical magnitude' are broad-spectrum terms not defined in advance, their scope determined by science, with many changes of opinion along the way. But if science can tell us at a given time what the scope of such a term is, why cannot science use these terms to specify the intended class of models or interpretations for a theory? Surely not because the scope of a term may later change, for presumably such a change will be reflected in a change in theory which may alter the class of intended interpretations. Perhaps Putnam's point here is that what is meant by, for example, 'physical magnitude' will be determined in part by the theory itself, and so if we specify the models for L_T in terms of such notions, this will be rather unenlightening to anyone who does not understand the theory beforehand. But if this is so, it will not be taken as a telling criticism by proponents of the

Received View, for as evidenced by the Hempel quotation interpreted earlier, this is precisely what they themselves claim.

In what way might Putnam's observation lead to a telling objection against his proposed analysis? It will be helpful to use my own suggested analysis of partial interpretation as a foil, for Putnam's comments do suggest a way in which it may be inadequate. Recall that any possible extension of an S for L^* such that TC is true under it is allowed as a true permissible interpretation. Putnam's discussion suggests that this will allow the inclusion of flagrantly unintended interpretations that any realistically minded scientist would reject. Should we not impose restrictions on this class of permissible interpretations so as to exclude these? Perhaps, but it is not clear that this actually can be done—for although we (who understand the theory) have some idea of what we would count as reasonable and unreasonable interpretations, often we have no idea whether the interpretation in question is reasonable or not. Furthermore, in that case we are unwilling to decide by fiat whether it is or not, perhaps basing our refusal on the grounds that this is an open question, and so we must remain undecided. It follows, then, that we cannot appeal to the theory or the scientific metalanguage in order to specify what will count as a reasonable interpretation in any way that will make the class of intended interpretations well defined. Accordingly, it is impossible to characterize the class of intended interpretations in any acceptable way that rules out the flagrantly unintended interpretations, since we never will be certain which they are.

These observations suggest what may be the brunt of Putnam's observations: The reason we are not always able to specify whether certain interpretations are intended or not is that any specification of intended interpretations must employ broad-spectrum terms that are open-textured. If this is so, then presumably Putnam's charge is that the Received View cannot adequately specify the class of intended interpretations; hence the proponents of the Received View cannot mean by partial interpretation the analysis he has suggested. Read in this fashion, I think that Putnam's objections tell.

If Putnam's objections against his suggested analysis are telling in this way, what consequences do they have for my own proposed analysis of partial interpretation? First, my analysis differs from Putnam's in one crucial respect: It does not demand that all the permissible interpretations be reasonable in the sense of capturing what realistically minded scientists would intend. It purports to specify only a class of interpretations which, while it includes the class of intended interpretations, also includes any interpretation that is empirically compatible with the assumed truth of *TC;* and it is quite likely that some of these interpretations will be flagrantly unintended. Or, differently put, my analysis purports to specify the class of intended interpretations only insofar as they can be specified in terms of empirical or observational consequences—and of course, this is all that partial interpretation is supposed to do.[13] What Putnam's analysis (under my construal of it) shows is *not* that my analysis is inadequate; but rather, given the limited interpretative objectives of partial interpretation, my analysis would be inadequate if partial interpretation were to be analyzed so as to completely specify the class of intended interpretations, since such a precise specification is impossible. Thus, it partially vindicates my analysis by showing that it is as strong as possible.

Nevertheless, does it not seem that Putnam's objections show that the notion of partial interpretation is bankrupt? I think not, for as I suggested earlier, the Received View is concerned only with using partial interpretation to specify the extent to which theoretical terms have empirical meaning content and the ways this content relates to L_O-statements. Given this limited objective, there is no reason why partial interpretation should do any more than specify how empirical meaning content imposes restrictions on the class of possible interpretations; in particular, these restrictions need not rule out all the unintended interpretations, since whether an interpretation is intended or not depends in part on considerations that are not of an empirical sort.[14]

Putnam raises one further objection to his analysis of partial interpretation which requires consideration. He makes the claim that theories with false observation consequences have *no* model "standard" with respect to the observation terms. This difficulty is unacceptable, since we normally would say under such circumstances that such a theory is wrong, not senseless (1962, 247).

This objection is serious but can be avoided. In general, we do not have sufficient observational data to give a completely explicit semantic interpretation to L_O. Rather, we proceed roughly as follows: First we specify rules of designation by stating that the predicate constant ψ will designate, say, the property of being red. Second, we specify the rules of truth for sentences ϕ of L_O as follows: The sentence ϕ is true under the interpretation if and only if the situation, event, or whatever, that ϕ describes under the specified rules of designation actually obtains. No more precise a statement of the rules of truth can be given, since in general we do not have sufficient information abut what situations do or do not obtain. But notice that, employing the same rules of designation, we could specify other interpretations where situations obtain that are different from those in the real world. For example, we could specify a world in which objects that are red in the real world are green. In particular, given the specified rules of designation, we could specify a world such that a situation obtains in that world if and only if it is described under the rules of designation by a provable L_o-sentence of TC. Then we can use this interpretation to obtain the interpretation of K^* and, hence, to define the class of true permissible interpretations of TC. So the set of permissible models specified by partial interpretation will always be nonempty, and so the possibility Putnam considers can never occur.[15]

Under this proposal we employ the following characterization of what it is for a theory TC to be *empirically true*. The L_o-theorems are interpreted as being true statements about some possible world which is similar to the real world, and this world is specified jointly by TC and the rules of designation. Using the same rules of designation, the sentences of L_o are interpreted in terms of the real world, and the truth conditions are specified in terms of what situations actually obtain there. Thus we have two interpretations of L_o: one, determined by the theory TC, and the other, determined empirically. Then TC is empirically true if and only if these two worlds are identical — that is, TC is empirically true just in case the following condition is met: For each wff ϕ of L_o, ϕ is true under the one interpretation if and only if ϕ is true under the other interpretation.

This characterization of empirical truth for theories seems to me to be in close accord with what actually happens in the exact or formalized sciences, and so I find it an acceptable formulation of the notion. (A more sophisticated version of it will be developed in chapter 3.) This construal in turn points out some important differences between semantic truth and empirical truth for formalized theories. Since it is possible that TC can be semantically true without being empirically true, it follows that the theory TC can have empirically false consequences, yet be meaningful under my analysis of partial interpretation. In such cases, the possible state of affairs truly described by TC will not be the state of affairs that actually will be observed. Putnam's objection thus fails to show that my analysis is unsatisfactory.

One might object to the way I have avoided Putnam's objection with the argument that since TC in general will be undecidable, my specification of the interpretation determined by TC will be nonconstructive. This is, of course, true; but I think it is an unsatisfactory objection, since in practice, the specification of the interpretation of L_o in terms of situations that actually obtain will be equally nonconstructive. In general, the specification of truth conditions will cover situations where we do not yet know what actually obtains, and since the truth conditions are specified in terms of what in fact does obtain there, the specification will be no more constructive than that determined by TC.

D. Partial Interpretation Summarized

This discussion of partial interpretation concludes with a summarization of my main lines of argument and my findings. First, recall that the C-rules together with T partially interpret L_T in the sense that their assumed truth imposes restrictions on the class of permissible extensions of true interpretations of K^* by imposing extensional restrictions on the relations, and so forth, that are admissible designata for V_T-terms. These restrictions are not sufficient to circumscribe the class of intended interpretations for TC; rather, they only specify the class of intended interpretations to the extent possible on the basis of empirical or observational considerations. The complete specification of the class of intended interpretations would require an appeal to extra-empirical considerations, and in general, a complete specification cannot be given, since many of these additional considerations constitute open questions for science. In addition, although the specification of permissible interpretations for TC captures the empirical meaning components of theoretical concepts, these concepts also involve extra-empirical meaning components.

Further, partial interpretations also reveal the extent of one's ontological commitment to theoretical entities: that entities exist that have the observable manifestations specified by TC. Although in asserting a theory one is committed to some permissible interpretations being true, one is not committed to being able to specify which ones they are. One must only be able to specify which are true to the extent made possible by TC and perhaps also on the basis of the extra-empirical meaning components. Even if recourse is made to such extra-empirical considerations, it will not be possible to specify the true interpretation of the theory to the exclusion of all other permissible interpretations.

This construal of partial interpretation suffices to refute Achinstein's and Putnam's reason (i) for rejecting the Received View (stated at the outset of this chapter): that the notion of partial interpretation cannot be given an adequately precise formulation.

II. THE OBSERVATIONAL/THEORETICAL DISTINCTION

Achinstein's and Putnam's second main reason (ii) for rejecting the Received View is that the observational/theoretical distinction cannot be drawn satisfactorily. The arguments Achinstein (1968, chs. 5 and 6) and Putnam (1962, 240–44) advance in support of reason (ii) attempt to show that

> (a) the observational/theoretical distinction cannot be drawn on the basis of the ordinary usage of scientific terms.

Of course, (ii) follows from (a) only if the further assumption is made that

> (b) to be tenable for the purposes of the Received View, the observational/theoretical distinction must be drawn on the basis of the ordinary usage of scientific terms.

This latter assumption is neither made explicit nor argued for in either work; as such, Achinstein and Putnam have not made their case. But I wish to establish something stronger—namely, that (a) is true, whereas it is virtually impossible to establish (b). However, I do not want to base my claim that (a) is true on their arguments, for I do not find them wholly satisfactory: Achinstein's arguments only show that the observational/theoretical distinction cannot be drawn on the basis of ordinary usage in the ways Carnap and others have suggested, and so they establish a conclusion that is weaker than (a); Putnam's arguments contain numerous lacunae. Rather, I will refine the sorts of considerations they raise into a much tighter and stronger argument for (a); then I will use features of that argument to argue that (b) is virtually impossible to establish.

Condition (2) of my reconstruction of the Received View stipulates that the nonlogical terms of L be bifurcated into two disjoint classes—observation terms and theoretical terms. Since this distinction lies at the heart of the Received View analysis, one would expect that in advancing the Received View, its proponents would have extensively discussed the nature of this bifurcation and the basis upon which it is drawn. In fact, however, all one usually finds in the literature is discussion of a very few examples of what would count as observation terms and what would count as theoretical terms. The most extensive discussion I have found of the observational/theoretical distinction by a proponent of the Received View is in Carnap's *Philosophical Foundations of Physics* (1966).

Carnap begins by stating that "the term 'observable' is often used for any phenomenon that can be *directly observed*" (225, emphasis added). He then observes that this use of 'observable' is not that of the scientist, and that he intends to use the term in a very narrow sense "to apply to such properties as 'blue', 'hard', 'hot','" and so on, which are "properties directly perceived by the senses" (ibid.). In defending his somewhat special sense of 'observable' he says:

> There is no question of who [the philosopher or the scientist] is using the term "observable" in a right or proper way. There is a continuum which starts with direct sensory observations and proceeds to enormously complex, indirect methods of observation. Obviously no sharp line can be drawn across this continuum; it is a matter of degree. . . . In general the physicist speaks of observables in a very wide sense compared with the narrow sense of the philosopher, but, in both cases, the line separating observables from non-observables is highly arbitrary. [ibid., 226]

Thus far Carnap is discussing the use of the term 'observable' and its application to attributes, things, events, objects, and so on. He claims that he is using the terms to apply to those such attributes and entities that can be directly perceived by the senses. From this it follows that attributes, entities, events, objects, and so on, are to be divided into two classes—the observable and the nonobservable. In terms of this distinction Carnap bifurcates the nonlogical constants of L: "The terms of V_O are predicates designating observable properties of events or things (e.g. 'blue,' 'hot,' 'large,' etc.) or observable relationships between them (e.g. 'x is warmer than y,' 'x is contiguous to y,' etc.)" (1956, 40). On the other hand V_T contains theoretical terms often called 'theoretical constructs' or 'hypothetical constructs', which are intended to refer to such entities as electrons and their attributes. The vocabularies V_O and V_T constitute an exhaustive bifurcation of the nonlogical constants of L into the class of those which refer to observable attributes or entities, and the class of those which refer to nonobservable or theoretical entities or attributes.

Carnap apparently believes that the bifurcation into V_O and V_T can be drawn on the basis of the standard usages of nonlogical terms in, e.g., scientific English. For example, Carnap (1966) writes:

> For many years it has been found useful to divide *the terms of a scientific language* into three main groups.
>
> 1. Logical terms, including all of mathematics.
> 2. Observational terms, or O-terms.
> 3. Theoretical terms, or T-terms (sometimes called "constructs").
>
> It is true, of course, . . . that no sharp boundary separates the O-terms from the T-terms. The choice of an exact line is somewhat arbitrary. From a practical point of view, however, the distinction

is usually evident. Everyone would agree that words for properties, such as "blue," "hard," "cold," and words for relations, such as "warmer, "heavier," "brighter," are O-terms, whereas "electric charge," "proton," "electromagnetic field" are T-terms referring to entities that cannot be observed in a relatively simple, direct way. [259; emphasis added]

Thus V_O will contain all those terms of a natural scientific language, such as scientific English, which in their normal usage refer to observables, and V_T will contain all the nonlogical terms of that language which refer to nonobservables in their normal usage; moreover, V_O and V_T are jointly exhaustive of the nonlogical terms of the language L (see condition [2] in sec. I-A).[16] The Received View thus seems to presuppose that a bifurcation of the nonlogical terms of a natural scientific language (such as scientific English) into theoretical and observational terms can be drawn on the basis of ordinary usage. Of course, it remains to be seen whether it is necessary for the Received View to make that presupposition.

Although Carnap usually does not make it explicit, it is obvious from this discussion that the observational/theoretical bifurcation is a dual dichotomy. First, there is a bifurcation of entities, properties, and so on, into those which are capable of direct observation and those which are not. Second, the terms in natural languages of science (such as scientific English) are bifurcated into two disjoint classes—the observational terms and the theoretical terms. These two bifurcations must parallel each other in the sense that a term may be included among the observational terms just in case it is used only in reference to directly observable attributes or entities. Or, differently put, the bifurcation of terms is drawn on the basis of the bifurcation of attributes and entities into the directly observable and the nondirectly observable. (In case an artificial language L is used, in setting up L we divide the nonlogical constants of L into those terms which are allowed to stand for, abbreviate, or correspond to observational terms of, say, scientific English, and those which are not.)

Is the observational/theoretical dichotomy a viable one? The answer to this question turns on what answers can be given to the following three subsidiary questions: (A) Is it possible to dichotomize entities and attributes on the basis of whether they are directly observable or not, and if so, what will be the nature of the dichotomy? (B) Is it the case that terms of, for example, scientific English under normal scientific usage can be bifurcated into the observational and the theoretical? (C) If the answers to the first two questions are affirmative, then are the two bifurcations coextensive?

A. The Entity and Attribute Dichotomy

Question (A). Carnap suggests that the property of being blue is a paradigmatic observable property, in the sense that its presence is directly ascertainable without recourse to complicated apparatus. But this is too imprecise. Is he claiming that a property is observable if its presence *sometimes* is ascertainable by direct observation? Or must it *always* be so ascertainable?

If he intends the latter, then the property of being blue is not directly observable: Although in some cases I can directly ascertain whether things are blue, when objects are too small it becomes impossible. Similarly, consider another of Carnap's paradigm examples, 'being warmer than'. While in some circumstances I can directly ascertain that something is warmer than something else (e.g., the water in the shower before and after adjusting it), there are numerous other circumstances in which I cannot because my sensory apparatus will not function at the temperatures involved (e.g., for an object at −250°C, which is warmer than an object at −273°C).

To take another example, I cannot directly observe that one part of the sun is warmer than another. Since direct observation precludes recourse to elaborate instrumentation, reliance on spectrographic evidence, and so on, in order to directly observe that one part of the sun is warmer than another I would have to be at those parts of the sun and compare their warmth. But this is humanly impossible in the following sense: Minimally, I would have to wear protective clothing, but in that case I would be directly observing that the air inside my space suit was warmer when I was at one part of the sun than when I was at another—not that one part of the sun is warmer than another. The latter could be determined only indirectly—for example, by using known heat transfer properties of my protective dress. To conclude: Even though it may be possible to determine by direct observation whether a particular attribute obtains under certain circumstances, the same attribute often will obtain in circumstances where it is impossible in principle to determine whether it does or does not obtain.

Since Carnap takes attributes such as being blue and being warmer than as paradigmatic examples of directly observable attributes, it follows that it is not necessary that one should be able in principle to ascertain by direct observation whether a directly observable attribute obtains in *every* circumstance in which it could obtain; rather, it is required that there be *some* circumstances in which it is possible in principle to ascertain by direct observation whether the attribute obtains. Since there is a strict bifurcation of attributes into the directly observable and the nondirectly observable (which for convenience we call nonobservables), it follows that an attribute is nonobservable if for every circumstance in which it could obtain, it is in principle impossible to ascertain by direct observation whether it obtains. Thus, for example, the property of being a gas must be directly observable, since it is possible to directly observe the presence of certain gases under certain circumstances (e.g., I can smell sulfur gas). And being electrically charged is directly observable, since by sticking my finger into a socket I can directly observe the presence of the electrical charge. Similarly, static electricity, forces, acceleration, gravitational attractions, and so on, would qualify as directly observable since we sometimes can directly observe their presence.[17] But this is clearly unsatisfactory, since we now are forced to count as directly observable various attributes which, according to Carnap, clearly should count as nonobservable.

To summarize: If we require that an attribute's presence *always* must be ascertainable in principle by direct observation in order for it to qualify as directly observable, then the paradigmatic ones (such as the property of being blue) fail to qualify. Further, if we require only that their presence *sometimes* be so ascertainable, then paradigmatic non-directly observables (such as the property of being a gas) become directly observables.

The problems encountered in attempting to draw a line between observable and nonobservable properties, and so forth, stem from the fact that many attributes of scientific relevance have both directly observable and nondirectly observable occurrences, which makes any natural division into the observable and the nonobservable impossible. If an observational/nonobservational distinction is to be drawn, perhaps it ought to be drawn on the basis of occurrences of attributes rather than on the basis of attributes simpliciter. Then, perhaps on the basis of the limits in discrimination of human sensory apparatus, we could count this or that attribute-occurrence observable or not. For example, we might say that for objects between such and such dimensions, the attribute of one being longer than the other is a directly observable attribute-occurrence; but if the objects are of larger or smaller size, then in that instance the attribute of being longer than is not a directly observable attribute-occurrence. Assuming this can be done in a sufficiently precise and general manner (which is by no means obvious), it would then be possible to distinguish observable occurrences and nonobservable occurrences of attributes and entities.

What we are doing here, in effect, is defining two new attributes (e.g., *observable-red* and *nonobservable-red* in terms of the old attribute (e.g., *red*) and replacing the old one with the two new ones. Thus we would say that the barn has the property of being *O*-red (observable-red), whereas the microscopic blood speck is *N*-red (nonobservable red). This, of course, has rather unusual consequences. If I take an *O*-red object of minimal area and smash it to pieces, the pieces will not be *O*-red, but rather *N*-red. And if I combine together a number of *N*-red blood specks, I will obtain an *O*-red blood patch. More complicated situations are encountered in the case of relations. If I heat an object at *t'* to a certain degree, it will be *O*-warmer than it was at time *t*, but if I heat the object still more at *t"*, it may be that the object is too hot for '*O*-warmer than' to apply. In such a case the object presumably will be *N*-warmer at *t"* than it was at *t*. These examples show why some provision will have to be made for allowing comparisons between nonobservable and observable occurrences of properties and also for comparative relations whose applications straddle the observable/nonobservable boundaries.

It is not clear whether this proposal is workable, but it is clear that it will be rather complicated if it is. It is equally clear from the considerations raised above that some such division of attribute-occurrences into the observable and the nonobservable is required if we are to obtain an observational/nonobservational dichotomy for attributes which at all resembles the one Carnap requires.

B. The Term Dichotomy

Question (B). Since the observational/theoretical bifurcation of terms can be drawn along Carnap's lines only if a bifurcation of properties, and so on, into the observable and nonobservable can be drawn satisfactorily, let us assume that the dichotomy has been drawn along the rough lines previously suggested. Is it then the case that a natural bifurcation of terms can be drawn on this basis?

The linguistic analogues to the problems raised above now confront us. For we can use paradigmatic observation terms such as 'blue' or 'is warmer than' to refer to both observable and nonobservable occurrences of properties. (In the previous section's discussion [sec. II-A] we used such terms in precisely this way.) Thus we are faced with two choices: We may employ the terms in their natural uses (in which case observational terms sometimes have nonobservable referents and theoretical terms sometimes have observable referents) or we may adopt special uses (say 'red$_O$' and 'red$_T$') together with the rule of usage that the former may be used to refer only to observable occurrences of red and the latter only to nonobservable occurrences. The latter option will require introducing rather complicated semantic rules into the language, including rules which enable us to use 'red$_O$' and 'red$_T$'

comparatively. Whether sufficiently precise and general rules can be specified is not clear.

C. Are the Dichotomies Coextensive?

Question (C). Turning to the question whether the two bifurcations discussed in sections II-A and II-B are coextensive, the previous discussions lead immediately to the following conclusion: On the basis of ordinary linguistic usage, there is no natural bifurcation of terms into the observational and the theoretical which is coextensive with any reasonable distinction between either observable and nonobservable attributes and entities, or observable and nonobservable occurrences of attributes and entities. Only in an artificial or reconstructed language *L* could the distinction be drawn naturally. Hence the truth of claim (a) (see above) follows, that the observational/theoretical distinction cannot be drawn on the basis of the ordinary usage of scientific terms.

It is notorious that Carnap and most other proponents of the Received View have had little respect for ordinary usage as an instrument of precision in philosophical analysis, and so it would seem that the truth of claim (a) should not bother them, so long as a viable observational/theoretical distinction can be drawn in some other way. For if this is possible, their mistake in supposing that it could be drawn on the basis of ordinary usage does not in itself seriously jeopardize the tenability of the Received View. Can the observational/theoretical distinction be drawn in some other way? That is, what is the status of claim (b) (i.e., that to be tenable for the purposes of the Received View, this distinction must be drawn on the basis of the ordinary usage of scientific terms)?

The underlying motivation for the observational/theoretical distinction is the idea that statements which describe what can be directly observed are relatively nonproblematic as to truth, whereas those which describe what cannot be directly observed are more problematic as to truth. Moreover, the verification of scientific theories must ultimately rest on the nonproblematic evidence supplied by the senses. Accordingly, any observational/theoretical distinction which reflects the division of nonlogical statements into those which can be directly verified on the basis of the senses and those which cannot should be acceptable to proponents of the Received View. In particular, a dichotomy of terms which parallels what we intuitively would accept as a bifurcation of occurrences of attributes and entities into the observable and the nonobservable should be satisfactory for the purposes of the Received View. The discussion so far makes it clear that such a distinction will have to proceed roughly along the lines sketched earlier in sections II-A and II-B. Thus, demonstrating the falsity of claim (b) amounts to showing that no such distinction can be drawn on the basis of occurrences of attributes and entities. This in turn amounts to showing that the sort of division of occurrences of attributes and entities proposed in section II-A is impossible.

How would one show that such a division is impossible? To show that any such division will be an "artificial" convention will not do, since Carnap and others admit this. To discuss problems about borderline cases also will not do, since someone like Carnap could admit these and make conventional conservative decisions about how to handle these cases. And to consider various proposed divisions and attack them does not demonstrate the impossibility of drawing such a distinction. In fact, it seems that the only way to show that such a division is impossible is to demonstrate either that no finite characterization of the division is possible, or else that any possible division which clearly makes observable occurrences directly observable will result in such an impoverished stock of observable occurrences that most of science could not be confirmed.

The chances of successfully demonstrating either of these contentions seems quite remote. Accordingly, it appears virtually impossible to establish claim (b). And since claim (a) leads to reason (ii) (that the observational/theoretical distinction cannot be drawn satisfactorily) only if claim (b) can be established, it follows that reason (ii) for rejecting the Received View has not been established. This, together with the fact that reason (i) (that partial interpretation cannot be formulated adequately) is false, is sufficient warrant to conclude that Achinstein and Putnam are urging the rejection of the Received View for the wrong reasons.

III. THE RECEIVED VIEW VERSUS THE SEMANTIC CONCEPTION

Our consideration of the observational/theoretical distinction makes it clear that if the distinction can be drawn in a manner satisfactory for the purposes of the Received View, things will be exceedingly complex. The fact that science manages to go about its business without involving itself in such complexities suggests that the distinction is not really required or presupposed by science, and so is extraneous to an adequate analysis of scientific theories. The question, then, is whether the observational/theoretical distinction is required for an adequate analysis of the epistemological structure of theories. More specifically, is it possible to give an analysis of the structure of theories which does not employ the observational/theoretical distinction, yet is epistemologically more revealing than the Received View? If such an analysis can be shown possible, then I think we have sufficient reason for rejecting the Received View.

Those who claim that the observational/theoretical distinction is an essential ingredient of an adequate analysis of scientific theories apparently justify their contention with the following implicit line of argument:

Scientific theories are developed to explain or predict events which can be observed; however, for reasons of simplicity, scope, and economy, such theories typically must employ theoretical entities or constructs in providing these explanations or predictions; these theoretical constructs are not directly observable. Accordingly, in any theoretical explanation or prediction one finds two sorts of sentences: (a) various premises the truth of which is nonproblematic in virtue of their being confirmed by direct observation; (b) various laws the truth of which is problematic since they cannot be confirmed by direct observation. And the observational-theoretical distinction is needed to keep distinct the different statuses of these two kinds of sentences.[18]

This picture is partially correct. Evidently it is the case that in theoretical explanation and prediction the truth of the laws used often is problematic, (especially when predictions are made in order to test the theory), whereas the truth of the evidential premises used in conjunction with the laws is assumed to be nonproblematic. Thus far the dichotomist's argument is satisfactory; but to infer from this that the premises are nonproblematic by virtue of being observational statements and that the laws are problematic by virtue of being nonobservational is unwarranted, for it amounts to assuming an additional premise in the argument—that to be nonproblematic is to be an observational statement.

Not only does this premise beg the question, it also seems false. For the purposes of explanation and prediction all that is required is that the data premises used with the theory be considered nonproblematic relative to the theory or law which provides the prediction or explanation. This is, in applying a theory (or law) to phenomena, what we do is collect data about phenomena; the process of collecting the data often involves recourse to rather sophisticated bodies of theory. If accepted standards of experimental design, control, instrumentation—and possibly involved reliability checks—are carried out, a body of "hard" data is obtained from experimentation and is taken to be relatively nonproblematic; sometimes generally accepted laws or theories are also employed in obtaining these "hard" data.[19] It is to this body of "hard" data that the theory is applied.

If the purpose of the application of a theory is explanation, then the theory explains the event under the description provided by this "hard" data by relating it to other "hard" data which function as descriptions of other features which were the cause of the event so described.[20] If the point of the application of the theory is prediction, then the initial "hard" data are used as premises from which to obtain predictions as to the "hard" data one subsequently would obtain. And these "hard" data may be quite theory-laden, hence nondirectly observable. In addition, what counts as "hard" or nonproblematic data is relative — for should the theory's predictions fail, we may come to treat the data as problematic again.[21] Thus the relevant distinction is between "hard" data and the more problematic theories, and not between the directly observable and the nondirectly observable. Accordingly, the correspondence rules for a theory should not correlate direct-observation statements with theoretical statements, but rather should correlate "hard" data with theoretical statements. Thus it seems that the observational/theoretical distinction is not essential to an adequate analysis of the structure of scientific theories.

Suggestive as this may be, this line of argument does not establish the inadequacy of the Received View. For an advocate of it could accept such an argument and still deny the conclusion, arguing as follows: "It is true that in actual scientific practice theories are pitted against 'hard' data. But what makes them 'hard' is that they ultimately rest on directly observable evidence; and in the Received View reconstruction of theories, that dependence of 'hard' data on the direct evidence of the senses is reflected in the correspondence rules. In fact, even the relativity of 'hard' data can be accommodated in terms of changes in the correspondence rules." There is little doubt that this can be built into the correspondence rules, but the relevant question is whether this can be done without obscuring important epistemological features of scientific theorizing. However, when one reflects that the theory's reliance on the results and procedures of related branches of science, the design of experiments, the interpretation of theories, calibration procedures, and so on, are all being lumped into the correspondence rules, there is reason to suspect that a number of epistemologically important and revealing aspects of scientific theorizing are being obscured.

I maintain that this is indeed so: Because of its reliance on the observational/theoretical distinction, the Received View's account of correspondence rules must combine together a number of widely disparate aspects of the scientific enterprise in such a manner as to obscure a number of epistemologically important and revealing aspects of scientific theorizing. To support this contention it will be necessary to sketch a more adequate alternative account of scientific theories, the Semantic Conception, which reveals what the Received View's treatment of correspondence rules obscures.

The notion of a *physical system* provides us with a convenient starting point for sketching and motivating this alternative account. A science does not deal with phenomena in all of their complexity; rather, it is concerned with certain kinds of phenomena only insofar as their behavior is determined by, or characteristic of, a small number of parameters abstracted from those phenomena.[22] Thus in characterizing falling bodies, classical particle mechanics is concerned with only those aspects of falling-body behavior which depend upon mass, velocity, distance traveled over time, and so on. The color of the object and such are aspects of the phenomena that are ignored; but the process of abstraction from the phenomena goes one step further: We are not concerned with, say, actual velocities, but with velocity under idealized conditions (e.g., in a frictionless environment, with the mass the object would have if it were concentrated at an extensionless point). Thus, for example, classical particle mechanics is concerned with the behavior of isolated systems of extensionless point-masses which interact in a vacuum, where the behavior of these point-masses depends only on their positions and momenta at a given time. A physical system for classical particle mechanics consists of such a system of point-masses undergoing a particular behavior over time. Physical systems, then, are highly abstract and idealized replicas of phenomena, being character-izations of how the phenomena *would have* behaved *had* the idealized conditions been met. Looking at classical particle mechanics again for an illustration, the phenomena within its scope are characterized in terms of the physical systems corresponding to the phenomena.

In arguing that scientific theories are concerned with characterizing the behavior of physical systems, and not phenomena, I may seem to be making the case too easy for myself by using the example of classical particle mechanics—which is what Quine has called a "limit myth" and thus is particularly susceptible of my treatment. However, a brief consideration of some examples will indicate that this is not so and will display the generality of my treatment.

First, consider classical thermodynamics, statistical mechanics, and quantum mechanics. These embody essentially the same "limit myth" and easily can be shown susceptible of my treatment (see Suppe 1967, ch. 3, for details). Second, observe that the gas laws (e.g., Boyle's law and Charles' law) describe the behavior of ideal gases, not real gases; yet they are used in work with actual gases. Here, the ideal gases described by the laws are the physical systems. Subject to appropriate experimental design, and so on, they correspond to actual gases as idealized replicas.

The third example, the valence theory of chemical reactions, is similar. It describes the way theoretically pure chemical substances react together. However, such pure substances are fictional ideals, and the substances in actual chemical reactions are always only approximations of them. The theory describes physical systems, which are chemical reactions theoretically pure substances undergo in this case, and with appropriate experimental and quality controls we can approximate the fiction that our actual substances are pure substances and thereby treat the actual chemical reactions (phenomena) as if they were idealized reactions between pure substances (physical systems).

The fourth example concerns the genetic theory of natural selection which characterizes evolutionary phenomena in terms of changes in the distributions of genotypes in populations as a function of reproductive rates, reproductive barriers, crossover frequencies, and so on. As such, the theory treats populations of individuals (phenomena) as if they were idealized populations of genotypes (physical systems) whose changes in genotypic distributions are functions of only a few selected factors.[23]

A fifth example is the body of stimulus-response behavioral theories which attempts to characterize various kinds of behavior as functions of selected stimulus and response parameters. Such theories describe the behavior of populations of idealized individuals whose behavior is only a function of the specified stimulus and response patterns, reinforcement schedules, and so on (physical systems). On the contrary, the behavior of individuals in actual populations of, say, rats or humans (phenomena) is not simply a function of these selected parameters, and only under the most strictly controlled laboratory conditions can this fiction be approximated. The stimulus and response theories thus describe the behavior of physical systems, not phenomena.

In addition to the above examples, one may include grammatical theories of linguistic competence, kinship system theories, theories in animal physiology, and so on, which also describe the behavior of idealized systems or mechanisms, whose actual systems or mechanisms are, to varying degrees, only idealized approximations. Although brief and sketchy, the examples suffice to illustrate the variety of theories susceptible of my treatment. Further, their variety strongly suggests that scientific theories in general describe the behavior of physical systems, which are idealized replicas of actual phenomena. I will defend this stronger claim in chapter 11.

In general, a scientific theory has the task of describing, predicting, and (possibly) explaining a class of phenomena. It does so by selecting and abstracting certain idealized parameters from the phenomena, then characterizing a class of abstract replicas of the phenomena which are characterized in terms of the selected idealized parameters (see note 22). These abstract replicas are physical systems. The theory thus provides a comprehensive characterization of the behavior of phenomena under the idealized conditions characteristic of the physical systems corresponding to the phenomena; typically, this characterization enables one to predict the behavior of physical systems over time.[24] When coupled with an appropriate experimental methodology, the theory can also predict or explain phenomena which do not meet these idealized conditions by displaying how these phenomena *would have* behaved *had* the idealized conditions been met.

A central task of a theory, then, is to present descriptive, predictive, and possibly explanatory accounts of the behavior of physical systems which correspond to phenomena. The theory is not concerned merely with providing such an account for just the phenomena we do in fact observe, but also with providing one for any phenomena of the sort we *might* encounter in *any* causally possible universe.[25] Further, it must provide a predictive, and possibly explanatory, characterization of all those physical systems which correspond (as abstract replicas) to phenomena of the latter sort. Let us call this class of physical systems the class of *causally possible physical systems*. A central task of any scientific theory is to provide a precise characterization of the set of causally possible physical systems for the theory.

How does the theory provide such a characterization? Once the relevant parameters for the theory have been abstracted and selected from the phenomena, the physical systems for the theory can be specified in terms of these parameters (a physical system being a possible behavior pattern specifiable in terms of these parameters). For example, in classical particle mechanics we might specify a particular state of a physical system in terms of the values of position and momentum parameters at a given time, and then characterize a physical system as a possible sequence of states over time. Of all logically possible physical systems capable of being specified in terms of the chosen parameters, only some will be empirically possible. For example, some of them will not be compatible with accepted existing bodies of theory. Of those which are, only some will be causally possible—in the sense that they correspond (as abstract idealized replicas) to phenomena which could be observed in some causally possible universe.

The theory, then, must specify which logically possible physical systems are causally possible—typically, by providing general laws which are claimed to describe the behavior patterns characteristic of just the causally possible physical systems. These laws are designed to yield predictions of subsequent system states when used together with specifications of initial states and boundary conditions. For example, in classical particle mechanics the equations of motion provide a general description of the class of causally possible physical systems. The characterization of a particular causally possible physical system can be obtained by solving the equations of motion relative to specified boundary conditions and an initial state; the solution can then be manipulated to yield predictions of subsequent system states.[26]

The account of theories just sketched seems to cohere closely with the actual formulations of many theories in the physical sciences. If it is substantially correct, then an observational/theoretical distinction is not required in an adequate analysis of the structure of scientific theories; this is so because theories are not concerned primarily with applying laws directly to phenomena, but rather with using laws to predict and explain the behavior of physical systems abstracted from phenomena in such a manner that their behavior can be correlated with phenomena. These conclusions obviously have important implications for the Received View's notion of a correspondence rule.

We now explore these implications, beginning with a look at how the "hard" data relate to physical systems and their corresponding phenomena. The observation reports or "hard" data to which the theory is applied are partial descriptions of the behavior of some physical system, the physical system being an abstract replica of the phenomena from which the data were collected. Data collection not only involves performing measurements upon the phenomena, which determine the "actual" values of the chosen parameters at different times, but it also involves employing various correction procedures (such as using friction coefficients, and the like) to alter the observed data into data representing the measurement results which *would have been* obtained *had* the defining features of the idealized parameters of the physical system been met by the phenomena.

Thus, in classical particle mechanics our data do not represent, for example, the velocity with which the milk bottle actually fell, but rather the velocity with which it *would have* fallen *had* it fallen in a vacuum, *had* it been a point-mass, and so on. That is, in a typical predictive or explanatory application of a theory, the "hard" data employed are data about the behavior of a physical system at certain times rather than about the actual behavior of the corresponding phenomena. As such, the "hard" data will be expressed in terms of the basic parameters common to the physical system and the theory—which is to say, in terms of what might be called the "theoretical" vocabulary.

Once these "hard" data are obtained, perhaps together with "hard" data about boundary conditions, and so forth, they are used in conjunction with the laws of the theory to deduce various predictions or explanations about the physical system. These deductions typically are "calculational" in nature. For example, in classical particle mechanics they might encompass solving the basic equations of motion for special case solutions, and then "plugging in" values of the parameters to calculate subsequent states of the physical system. Typically the predicted data about these subsequent states of the physical system are then converted into data about the corresponding phenomena by reversing the procedures used originally to convert the data about the phenomena to data about their corresponding physical system.

What we have here, then, is a two-stage move from raw phenomena to statements of the theory—first a move from phenomena to "hard" data about the physical system in question, and then a second move from the physical system to the postulates, and so on, of the theory.[27] The two sorts of moves are qualitatively quite different, the former being essentially empirical or experimental (being, in effect, a "translation" from the phenomena to an idealized description of it in the vocabulary of the theory's formalism), and the latter being essentially mathematical or computational in nature.

This perspective—together with the observation that theories have "hard"-data reports as their primary subject matter rather than direct-observation reports—invites reassessment of the Received View's account of the correspondence rules. For the rules of correspondence lump together the two sorts of moves just discussed so as to eliminate the physical system. It is tempting to reject the Received View's treatment of correspondence rules on the ground that most paradigmatic exact theories in physics and chemistry do work in terms of physical systems in the manner just explained, and then conclude that the Received View is inadequate since it fails to take them into account. While this is a somewhat appealing line, given the explicative character of the Received View analysis, it is not clear how far the criticism cuts. However, if important epistemological features of scientific theorizing are obscured by the failure to countenance physical systems, then it is justifiable to insist that the Received View is defective and epistemologically misleading by failing to include them.

The second-stage movement from data about the physical system to the theory (e.g., the various predictions, etc., about subsequent behavior of the physical system calculated on the basis of these data and the laws or postulates of the theory) is essentially computational in nature. If the theory is quantitative, the theory will be essentially mathematical, involving the solution of equations of motion, various auxiliary definitions and hypotheses, and so on;[28] and at no time are counterfactual inferences involved. On the other hand, the transition from phenomena to a physical system (or vice versa) involves processes of measurement, equipment design, experimental techniques, interpretation and correction of raw data, the employment of theory from other branches of science, inter alia. And the transition from phenomena to physical system is, as I said before, fundamentally counterfactual—being a characterization of what the phenomena *would have been* under idealized circumstances.

From these characteristics it follows that the ways a transition from a physical system to theory can go wrong will be quite different from the ways that the transition from phenomena to a physical system can go wrong. And in the case of a disconfirming experiment, if the source of the difficulty can be isolated as occurring in the transition from phenomena to physical system (i.e., the data proved to be less "hard" than thought), the resolution of the disconfirmation does not require alteration of the theory. In this case, the theory was not at fault; rather, poor experimental procedure was followed (e.g., the instrumentation was miscalibrated, the wrong corrective factors were applied to the raw data, etc.). Only when the disconfirmation cannot be attributed to the transition from the phenomena to a physical system (i.e., the data are as "hard" as we had first supposed), will resolution of the defects require alteration or modification of the theory itself.[29]

It seems amply clear from these observations that there is considerable epistemic difference between the two transitions, and that attention to these differences exposes some rather characteristic features of the relations holding between theory and phenomena. The correspondence rules of the Received View obscure these differences by agglomerating all these various aspects of the relations holding between theory and phenomena into the one correspondence-rule transition. This, in particular, means that experimental errors, and so on, which result in disconfirming instances of a theory will require modification of the correspondence rules and hence of the theory itself, for the correspondence rules are part of the theory and embody a complete specification of all allowable experimental procedures. Another related problem is that the Received View's treatment of correspondence rules gives one little reason to suppose that an exhaustive explicit specification of allowable experimental procedures of the sort required can be given for most theories.[30]

It seems quite obvious, then, that the Received View's characterization of the correspondence rules gives a quite misleading account of the ways in which theories correlate with phenomena, thus obscuring a number of characteristic and important epistemic features of scientific theorizing. Using my characterization of physical systems and the two- (or more) stage transition between phenomena and theory, we obtain an epistemologically more revealing picture of scientific theorizing. Indeed, the need for an observational/theoretical dichotomy disappears, for at no point in that picture is such a dichotomy needed. Replacing it is the distinction between nonproblematic "hard" data about physical systems and boundary conditions, and so on, and the more problematic theoretically obtained assertions about these systems.[31]

And in place of the correspondence rules providing a bridge between theory and phenomena, we now have a two-stage transition: (a) the transition from phenomena to physical systems (which reduces to problems of measurement, experimental design, counterfactuals, and the like) and (b) the connection between the theory and physical systems, which are deductively determined by the (often mathematical) apparatus of the theory without requiring additional correspondence rules or postulates other than boundary conditions and data about the initial state of the physical system. The former transition is not part of the theoretical apparatus of the theory, but rather belongs to the experimental procedures used in applying the theory to phenomena; the latter transition is essentially computational in nature.

This suggested alternative account of the structure of scientific theories enables us to see another flaw in the Received View. If it is correct that the subject matter of a theory is the behavior of physical systems and that the "hard" data include experimental data about the behavior of physical systems, then the central distinction between the nonproblematic "hard" data and the more problematic theoretical assertions about physical systems cannot be drawn on the basis of language. This is because the defining parameters of the physical systems (e.g., position and momentum coordinates in classical particle mechanics) are the basic parameters of the theory, and so the same "theoretical" terms will be used to provide linguistic characterizations of both the theory and the "hard" data. That is, the relevant distinction here is not a linguistic one, but rather an epistemological one. The fact that the key distinction here is not a linguistic one indicates that a number of epistemologically revealing features of the structure of scientific theories are not reflected in their linguistic formulations, and so they cannot be characterized adequately by an analysis of the language of theories—herein lies the ultimate inadequacy of the Received View.

IV. SUMMARY AND CONCLUSION

To summarize, in section I of this chapter my primary aim has been to make the nature of partial interpretation as employed in the Received View reasonably precise for two reasons. First, I feel that this analysis can lead to a number of interesting criticisms of the Received View. In particular, it would appear that the sort of semantic interpretation provided by partial interpretation is insufficient to make Carnap's treatment of inductive logic and degree of confirmation applicable to *TC*. Second, although ultimately the Received View is unsatisfactory and must be rejected, a number of facts about the meaning of scientific terms revealed in the discussion of partial interpretation will prove useful in developing an alternative analysis to the Received View. In particular I suggest that an adequate analysis of theories in the exact or formalized sciences will have to treat the relationships between ordinary scientific language and mathematical formalism along the lines presented here, albeit in a manner that does not make recourse to an observable/theoretical distinction.

I also have tried to show that the sort of criticisms against the Received View raised by Achinstein and Putnam do not succeed in showing its inadequacy. Nonetheless, the Received View is unsatisfactory, since its reliance on the observational/theoretical distinction obscures much that is epistemologically important and revealing about how theories relate to, or connect with, phenomena. To demonstrate this, I have sketched an alternative analysis of the structure of theories and used it to show the following: how the Received View obscures the role of physical systems, the way in which extratheoretical postulates provide nonexhaustive characterizations of the admissible transitions between phenomena and physical systems, and wherein lies the role of counterfactuals in connecting theories with phenomena. These epistemic revelations do not exhaust the potential of this alternative account. To indicate just some of its potential, further development of the analysis (e.g., along the lines of Suppes 1962) will reveal much more about the experimental relations holding between phenomena and physical systems. In addition, the isolation of the counterfactual component of scientific theorizing in the transition between phenomena and physical systems provides a perspective which conceivably could advance us toward a breakthrough on the problem of laws and counterfactuals. For the exact sciences, there is ample evidence that this sort of account can be expanded and developed so as to give a particularly revealing account of exact theories (e.g., the sorts of revelations about phase spaces, the connection between deterministic and indeterministic theories, and so on, found in van Fraassen 1970; Suppe 1967, ch. 2; and parts II and III of this volume).

What's wrong with the Received View? It obscures much of epistemic importance other analyses can reveal. For this reason it should be rejected in favor of such an alternative analysis, which I have tried to sketch. In part II of this volume, the Semantic Conception analysis will be developed in much further detail.

NOTES

1. Cf. Putnam 1962 and Achinstein 1968, 85–91, 157–58, 197–202. Achinstein's 1968 book incorporates his earlier writings on the subject with minor changes. Putnam 1962 also urges that the observational/theoretical distinction is untenable. He argues that it is misleading both to label the class of nonobservational terms 'theoretical terms' and to characterize sentences formulated solely in terms of the observational vocabulary as observational sentences, and those formulated solely in terms of the theoretical vocabulary as theoretical sentences. However, while this is true, it hardly necessitates rejection of the Received View.

Although Achinstein (1968, 199–201) suggests that it would be epistemologically more revealing if we avoided reliance on an observational/theoretical distinction in our analysis of theories, this is only a corollary to his main arguments against the observational/theoretical distinction. The strength of Putnam's and Achinstein's contention that the Received View should be rejected lies in the establishment of (i) and (ii), and I shall confine my attention to those arguments.

2. Versions of the Received View have been advanced by a number of authors, including Braithwaite (1953, 22 ff.), Campbell (1920, ch. 6), Carnap, (e.g., 1956, 43), Duhem (1954, 19), Hempel (1952, 1958), Hesse (1962, 1966), Kaplan (1964, 298–99), Margenau (1950), Nagel (1961, 90), Northrop (1947), Ramsay (1931, 212–36), and Reichenbach (1962, ch. 8). Although a number of differences exist (some significant) between these various versions of the Received View, there is a substantial core of agreement among them.

The primary disagreements among them are about the form of the correspondence rules: Various authors refer to the rules as coordinating definitions, dictionaries, interpretative systems, operational definitions, epistemic correlations, and rules of interpretation. Campbell, Nagel, Hesse, and Kaplan maintain that (in addition to satisfying conditions [1] through [6] of my reformulation of Carnap's and Hempel's version) the theory also must possess realizable or concrete models. Kaplan deviates from the others in that he claims that the analysis only works for one type of theory. Hempel (1974) no longer adheres to the Received View and later adopted a similar position in which the observational/theoretical distinction was replaced by a different bifurcation of terms.

My discussion of the Received View and of partial interpretation will require recourse to a fair amount of symbolic logic. I assume that the reader is familiar with first-order languages, their alphabets, predicate calculi based on first-order languages, theories formulated in a first-order predicate calculus, semantical systems for languages, rules of designation, rules of truth, interpretation of first-order theories via semantical systems, true interpretations or models of first-order theories, and validity. Those readers requiring further details on these notions may skip the more technical portions of section I-B, relying on the informational summaries of their technical results. For further comprehension, one can consult Carnap 1942 and also the relevant portions of Mates 1965.

3. This formulation of the Received View is extracted from Carnap 1956, 1959, 1963, and 1966 and Hempel 1958 and 1963. Conditions (2), (3), and (4) are more explicit in certain respects than either Carnap or Hempel specifically requires, but this is necessary if Carnap's restrictions on the sublanguages L_O and L'_O (Carnap 1956, 41–42) are to be satisfied. To meet these restrictions different additional conditions could have been imposed, but I have selected the most conservative ones. My particular choice in no way affects the analysis of partial interpretation given here.

Carnap and Hempel disagree as to the requirements to be imposed on the rules of correspondence. Hempel would replace clause (5)(d) with the following: "C contains every element V_O and V_T essentially—i.e., C is not logically equivalent to some set of sentences in which at least one term of V_O or V_T does not occur at all" (1963, 692). His version thus is more restrictive than Carnap's. Carnap also would require that the theory be cognitively significant, whereas Hempel doubts that a satisfactory criterion of cognitive significance can be given. These minor differences between Carnap's and Hempel's formulations need not concern us here.

4. Cf., e.g., Achinstein 1968, 85 ff., and 1963, and Putnam 1962.

5. See Hempel's (1952) discussion of explicit definition for such a characterization.

6. See Suppes 1957, ch. VIII, for a very lucid and not excessively technical discussion of this theory.

7. Selected for the sake of simplicity and intelligibility, this formulation is only a very special case of the Beth-Padoa result and takes a number of heuristic liberties that are of no consequence here. For a rigorous treatment of the result in general form, see Shoenfield 1968, 81.

8. For a discussion and characterization of introductive chains, see Carnap 1936–37, sec. 6. The characterization there is for terms partially interpreted

via reduction sentences, but extends straightforwardly to C-rules as formulated here.

9. See pages 85–86. Achinstein also considers two other possible interpretations which need not concern us here (despite the fact that the second one, on p. 86, at first seems quite similar to mine and thus possibly relevant to my proposal). This is because his criticism turns on various features of the peculiar semantical rules he introduces, and since my rules do not have these features, his discussion in no way affects my proposal.

10. See p. 695. (Minor notational changes have been made in this and other quotations to bring the notation into agreement with that adopted in this chapter.) Carnap makes essentially the same observations (1939, 62).

11. Such a position was, of course, not theirs initially, but seems to have gradually developed since Carnap (1936–37); most adherents of the Received View were slow in coming to such a realization, however, and some (e.g., Bergmann) apparently never did. But the position seems to be either implicit or semi-explicit in the more recent writings of Hempel and Carnap.

12. See, e.g., Carnap 1966, 256, for a statement in this vein.

13. This seems to be the point of Carnap's (1956) claim that "all the interpretation *(in the strict sense of this term, i.e., observational interpretation)* that can be given for L_T is given in the C-rules" (46; emphasis added).

14. These are, e.g., the sort of considerations Kuhn's (1962) paradigms are supposed to handle.

15. This last set of claims may be overstated; it may be that for a certain TC no such interpretation is conceivable given the specified rules of designation. Whether this is possible requires further investigation, and I leave it as an open question. I would conjecture, however, that if such a situation did occur, the TC in question would be so bizarre that a good case could be made for treating the theory as being meaningless, given the observational phenomena to which it was supposed to be applied. Unfortunately, I don't know how to demonstrate this.

16. In case the L used in the Received View canonical formulation is a symbolic language of the sort used by Carnap (1956), then V_O would contain predicates which correspond to, for example, English observational terms, and V_T would contain predicates which correspond to, e.g., English theoretical terms. Regardless of whether the L used in the Received View is a natural or an artificial language, then, the V_O-V_T distinction apparently would be drawn on the basis of standard usages in some natural language.

17. I can imagine that some proponents of the Received View would protest here that I do not directly observe, for example, that something is a gas, but rather that I observe certain manifestations of the presence of the gas; accordingly, the property of being a gas never can be directly observed. But this argument fails; for if it is legitimate, then it seems equally fair to argue that I do not directly observe that something is hard, but instead merely observe certain manifestations of the thing being hard. In this sense one can never directly observe the property of being hard, and so it is not a directly observable property—contrary to the fact that Carnap advances it as a

paradigmatic example of a directly observable property. It should also be noted that the Received View does not limit direct observation to visual perception; direct observation can be made by any sense, as Carnap's own examples in the quotations above make clear. Finally, although the argument here proceeds in terms of attributes, it is clear that analogous arguments could be given, and similar conclusions drawn, for entities. For simplicity of exposition I present the arguments just for attributes.

18. At one time proponents of the Received View also might have justified introducing the dichotomy by appealing to considerations of cognitive significance and using a thesis about language acquisition. The apparent failure of the positivistic account of cognitive significance and the falsity of the thesis about language acquisition make it both unlikely and undesirable that Received View advocates would argue it on these grounds.

19. This discussion has benefited from my conversations with Professor Don E. Dulany. See Suppe 1974, 424–33, for Putnam's treatment of the use of such auxiliary hypotheses; see also van Fraassen 1970 for a related discussion.

20. This rough characterization of the role of data in explanation turns on an observation—insufficiently considered in the literature on explanation—that explanations do not explain events simpliciter, but rather explain *events under a particular description* (see p. 189). While it is beyond the scope of this chapter to argue it, this observation apparently can be exploited to show that the alleged symmetry between explanation and prediction collapses.

21. See the introduction to Quine 1959 for a discussion of this point.

22. I use the term 'parameter' rather than 'variable' to mark the fact that the state "variables" need not be measurable on my quasi-realistic version of the Semantic Conception. This fact will be crucial in my treatment of measurement in ch. 4. I am not using 'parameter' in the statistical sense, where it means a variable set to a fixed or constant value.

23. In sec. XI of ch. 7, the applicability of the analysis of theories presented here to the genetic theory of natural selection is worked out in some detail. See also sec. III-C of ch. 6. In ch. 5, sec. II, microeconomic examples are considered.

24. For brevity, I confine my attention here only to theories which describe the behavior of physical systems in terms of changes in state over time. In addition to working for such theories with laws of succession, the analysis also will work for theories with laws of coexistence, laws of interaction, functional laws, and laws of quasi-succession. Also, it makes no difference whether the laws are deterministic or statistical. See chapter 5.

25. The problems of characterizing causally possible universes are many, but they can be viewed roughly as the class of universes in which all the laws assumed nonproblematic relative to the theory in question hold. For a detailed characterization of the notion of a causally possible universe, see Burks 1977, ch. 10. My purpose in employing the notion is to use it to introduce the concept of a causally possible physical system later on. Since the rough characterization given meets the limited purposes set for it here, the difficult

problem of providing an adequate characterization of causally possible universes can be avoided for the time being. I offer a detailed analysis of the notion in a book in progress, *Facts, Theories, and Scientific Observation* (see also p. 300 below).

26. On this account, a theory may be construed as defining a class of theoretically possible physical systems; the theory will be empirically true just in case this class is identical with the class of causally possible physical systems. The account of empirical truth just specified is essentially a generalization of that introduced in section I of this chapter. In both cases the idea is that there exists a class of systems determined theoretically and a class determined empirically, the theory being empirically true just in case the classes are coextensive. Thus, intuitively, the class of causally possible physical systems is the class of physical systems which are empirically possible. Further consideration of this key notion of a causally possible physical system can be found in my dissertation (1967, chs. 1, 2) and in ch. 3 below.

27. Actually this is still an oversimplification, the former move involving many more steps. (See ch. 4 and also Suppes' discussion in his 1962 and 1967 works.)

28. For an illuminating discussion of what is involved in this sort of move, see Putnam's discussion in Suppe, 1974, 424–33.

29. For a detailed discussion of this point, see Suppe 1967, ch. 3.

30. For a more detailed discussion of this last point, see Kuhn 1974, where he discusses the role of exemplars in the application of theories to phenomena; see also my commentary (1974a) on Kuhn 1974.

31. Hempel now rejects the Received View, and in his 1969, 1970, and 1974 works he advances an analysis based on a distinction similar to this. He distinguishes between a *theoretical vocabulary* and *an antecedently available vocabulary*, where the latter may include theoretical terms from generally accepted theories. His proposal differs from mine in that he thinks the relevant distinction can be drawn on linguistic grounds, whereas I explicitly deny that it can. His analysis differs in other respects as well—especially on the nature of the transition between the "hard" data and the theory (his so-called *bridge principles*).

The "hard" data notion proves to be an overly simple heuristic notion. It will be supplanted by the analysis of experimental methodology in ch. 3, sec. VIII, and ch. 4 below.

PART II
The Semantic Conception
of Theories

Section III of chapter 2 presented a heuristic account of the Semantic Conception of Theories. The next three chapters provide a detailed development of a quasi-realistic version of the Semantic Conception. Chapter 3 sets forth the basic structural account and examines the various relations holding between theories and their linguistic formulations. Chapter 4 focuses on the physical interpretation of theories, their empirical truth conditions, and the ways observation, measurement, and experimental design relate theories to actual phenomena. Chapter 5 explores the structure of scientific laws on the Semantic Conception.

In addition to helping to flesh out the development of the Semantic Conception, these chapters also use the quasi-realism of the Semantic Conception to contribute to the resolution of other philosophical issues. Chapter 3 addresses positivistic instrumentalism-versus-realism debates and argues against the operational imperative (and it provides background for the discussion of scientific realism in chapter 11). Chapter 4 develops a realistic approach to measurement and argues that so construed, measurement is a species of observation. Chapter 5 argues against Scriven's claim that theories are inaccurate and against the associated idea that approximate truth notions must be invoked in interpreting laws or theories.

3
Theories, Their Formulations, and the Operational Imperative

The *operational imperative* demands that all theoretical concepts be defined or introduced into theories operationally.[1] Its tenability can be judged only relative to an analysis of the nature or structure of scientific theories. For the most part, philosophical assessment of the operational imperative has been relative to the positivistic Received View. When viewed from this perspective, the operational imperative is interpreted as the requirement that theoretical terms be defined as explicit definitions (or possibly as reduction sentences) in terms of an observation vocabulary which specifies various operations and possible outcomes resulting from such operations being performed: "An operational definition of a term is conceived as a rule to the effect that the term is to apply to a particular case if the performance of specified operations in that case yields a certain characteristic result. . . . The operations are to be intersubjective in the sense that different observers must be able to perform 'the same operations' with reasonable agreement in their results."[2]

So interpreted, the operational imperative becomes the requirement that the correspondence rules in the Received View be restricted to a species of explicit definition (or, possibly, reduction sentences). Since the positivistic account of theories is untenable when correspondence rules are restricted to explicit definitions or reduction sentences,[3] it follows that the operational imperative is untenable.[4] On the basis of such arguments most philosophers of science rejected the operational imperative, although a number of working scientists (especially in the social and biological sciences) continued to swear by it.

It is the contention of this chapter that these arguments do not settle the philosophical question of the operational imperative's tenability. Strictly speaking, such arguments only show that the operational imperative is incompatible with the Received View, and the untenability of the operational imperative follows only if the Received View of theories is itself an adequate analysis. However, the arguments of the previous chapter and a number of other papers make it clear that the Received View is untenable and must be rejected,[5] so the incompatibility of the operational imperative with the positivistic analysis of theories does not show that the operational imperative is untenable. Accordingly, the operational imperative deserves a new philosophical hearing. It is one task of this chapter to provide that hearing.

I. THEORIES

In order to reassess the operational imperative it will be necessary to presuppose some analysis of the nature of scientific theories. To my mind the most plausible and developed analysis currently available is the Semantic Conception, introduced in the previous chapter. This chapter will develop in further detail some of its main features.

As actually employed by working scientists, theories admit of a number of alternative linguistic formulations—for example, classical particle mechanics sometimes is given a Lagrangian formulation and other times a Hamiltonian formulation—but it is the same theory regardless which formulation is employed. As such, scientific theories cannot be identified with their linguistic formulations; rather, they are extralinguistic entities which are referred to and described by their various linguistic formulations. This suggests that theories be construed as propounded abstract *structures* serving as models for sets of interpreted sentences that constitute the linguistic formulations. These structures are *metamathematical models* of their linguistic formulations, where the same structure may be the model for a number of different, and possibly nonequivalent, sets of sentences or linguistic formulations of the theory.[6]

Theories are formulated to characterize a class of phenomena known as the *intended scope of the theory*, perhaps, say, the class of all mechanical phenomena of interacting bodies. The theory does not attempt to characterize the phenomena in all their complexity, but only attempts to do so in terms of a few parameters abstracted from the phenomena. For example, classical particle mechanics attempts to characterize mechanical phenomena *as if* they depended only on the abstracted position and momentum parameters.[7] In point of fact, however, other unselected parameters usually do influence the phenomena; so the theory does not characterize the actual phenomena, but rather characterizes the contribution of the selected parameters to the actual phenomena, describing what the phenomena *would have been had* the abstracted parameters been the only parameters influencing them. For example, classical particle mechanics does not describe actual inclined plane phenomena, but instead describes what inclined plane phenomena *would be* in frictionless environments. In effect, then, what the theory does is directly describe the behavior of abstract systems, known as *physical systems*, whose behaviors depend only on the selected parameters. However, these physical systems are abstract replicas of actual phenomena, being what the phenomena *would have been* if no other parameters exerted an influence. Thus by describing the physical systems, the theory indirectly gives a counterfactual characterization of the actual phenomena.

In abstracting from the phenomena, the physical systems also may idealize the phenomena in various ways. For example, in classical particle mechanics physical systems are isolated systems of dimensionless point-masses interacting in a vacuum. Such physical systems are abstract replicas of phenomena on which certain idealized conditions (e.g., being isolated systems of dimensionless point-masses) are imposed, which actual phenomena cannot ever meet. In such cases, the physical systems still are characterizations of what the phenomena would be were certain conditions met—only some of these conditions cannot possibly be met by any actual phenomenon.

The behavior of physical systems can be described wholly in terms of the selected parameters abstracted from the phenomena; these are the *defining parameters of the physical system*. The values of these parameters are *physical quantities*, which may be determinate or statistical.[8] A set of simultaneous values for the parameters of a physical system is a possible *state* of the physical system. At any given time, a physical system is in exactly one of its possible states, though the state it is in may change over time. The *behavior* of a physical system is its change in states over time, and this can be viewed as its history. Just as each phenomenon has a unique history, each physical system has a unique sequence of states it assumes over time.[9] Each physical system, then, can be characterized fully by a specification of the possible states it can assume (as a function of the defining parameters) and the sequence of states it assumes over time. The defining parameters of a physical system will be *basic parameters* of its associated theory, and so physical systems will be described in "theoretical language."

Corresponding to any *causally possible phenomenon* P within the theory's intended scope will be a physical system S such that S is what P *would have been were* the idealized conditions (if any) imposed by the theory met and the phenomenon P were influenced *only* by the selected parameters. Let the class of *causally possible physical systems for a theory* be the class of physical systems which correspond in the manner just indicated to causally possible phenomena within the theory's intended scope. Inter alia, it is the job of a scientific theory to exactly circumscribe the class of causally possible physical systems for the theory.[10] The theory does so by determining a class of physical systems known as *theory-induced physical systems.* In propounding the theory we are claiming that the class of theory-induced physical systems is identical with the class of causally possible physical systems for the theory. If the theory is *empirically true*, then these two classes are identical;[11] and if they are not identical, the theory is *empirically false.* In testing a theory it is the job of the experimental methodology to determine which physical systems correspond to which phenomena;[12] and if one subscribes to an inductive logic approach to confirmation, the confirmation of a theory essentially involves determining through (nonparametric) goodness-of-fit statistics or their informal analogues whether the class of theory-induced physical systems is identical with the class of causally possible physical systems for the theory.[13]

Our discussion thus far has indicated two important features of theories: (1) they are propounded extralinguistic structures which qualify as metamathematical models of their linguistic formulations, and (2) they determine a class of theory-induced physical systems. These features can most easily be accommodated if we analyze theories as *relational systems* (Tarski and Vaught 1957) consisting of a domain containing all (logically) possible states of all (logically) possible physical systems for the theory together with various attributes defined over that domain. These attributes, in effect, are the *laws* of the theory.[14]

If the theory has *laws of succession*, then the attributes will be relations of succession indicating which sequences of states various physical systems will assume over time; these relations may be such that the sequences are deterministic or statistically determined, continuous or discrete. Deterministic laws of succession are exemplified by the laws of classical particle mechanics, and statistical ones by the transition matrix for a finite Markov process. If the theory has *laws of coexistence*, then the attributes will be equivalence relations indicating which states are equivalent (if it is a deterministic law) or which states are equiprobable (if it is a statistical law). Deterministic laws of coexistence are exemplified by the ideal gas law, and statistical ones by the Boltzmann hypothesis that each microstate of a gas has equal probability. Finally, if a theory has *laws of interaction* (deterministic or statistical), the attributes will determine which states result from the interaction of several systems and will be composites of the kinds of attributes mentioned previously.[15]

Regardless which forms of laws a theory has, the laws do two things. First, they indicate which states are *physically possible* (these being the states which enter into the satisfaction of the theory's attributes). Second, they indicate which sequences of states a physical system can assume; as such, the laws determine the class of theory-induced physical systems. Deterministic laws of coexistence sanction all sequences whose constituent states belong to the same equivalence class; statistical laws of coexistence sanction those whose constituent states have an assigned probability measure; and laws of interaction sanction sequences analogously to the above cases or their admixture. Finally, sequences sanctioned by statistical laws have a probability measure assigned to them by the sanctioning laws; these measures determine the probability that a physical system in state s at time t will be in state s' at time t' ($> t$). The class of sequences so sanctioned constitutes the class of theory-induced physical systems. Usually this class is a proper subclass of the class of all logically possible sequences.[16]

Some states may enter into no sequence, and so are not physically possible. And certain logically possible sequences of states do not satisfy the relations determining sequences of states, and so do not qualify as behaviors of physical systems in the class of theory-induced physical systems. On the other hand, every sequence of states determined by the theory's relations will be the behavior of a physical system in the class of theory-induced physical systems. Thus the relations of the theory determine all and only those sequences which are the behaviors of physical systems in the class of theory-induced physical systems.

Although theories directly determine only the class of theory-induced physical systems, they can be used to predict phenomena in the following manner: Suppose the theory is one whose laws are deterministic laws of succession and that we wish to predict the subsequent behavior of some phenomenon at t'. By means of one's experimental methodology it is determined what physical system state corresponds to the phenomenon at some prior time t. Then, using some formulation of the theory, one determines which theory-induced physical system characterizes the behavior of a physical system in state s at time t; this may be done, for example, by solving the equations in the theory formulation to obtain special case equations. Determining the physical system in question indicates a sequence of states the physical system subsequently will assume, and from that sequence one determines (e.g., by solving the special case solution relative to initial, boundary, and time conditions) what state s' the physical system will be in at t'. If the theory is empirically true, then s' will correspond to the phenomenon in question at t' — that is, s' indicates what the phenomenon *would be* at t', if its parameters *were* the only ones affecting the phenomenon and the phenomenon *were* to meet the idealized conditions imposed by the theory. Then by the experimental methodology, one determines the actual phenomenon p' which should correspond to s', yielding the theory's predictions about the phenomenon at t'. If T has statistical laws of succession or laws of coexistence, the procedure is analogous except that we are only able to determine from the theory that one member of some restricted class of physical systems corresponds to P. Hence we are limited to predicting that P will be in a state at time t' which corresponds to one of a number of physical system states s'; if the laws in question are statistical, our predictions can assign a probability to each of these states s'.[17]

II. THE OPERATIONAL IMPERATIVE REFORMULATED

Viewed from the perspective of this analysis, it becomes clear that the operational imperative is about theory formulations and in effect stipulates that certain relationships do or should hold between theories and their linguistic formulations. This, together with the fact that theories admit of alternative and nonequivalent linguistic formulations, reveals that the operational imperative could be making either of the following demands:

(1) *Weak Operational Imperative.* Every scientific theory must admit of a full linguistic formulation in which theoretical terms are operationally defined.

(2) *Strong Operational Imperative.* The only theory formulations which may be employed are those in which theoretical terms are operationally defined.

The strong imperative clearly presupposes the weak imperative. The weak imperative can be construed either as a descriptive claim supposedly true of all possible theories or else as a prescription for how scientific research should be conducted. As a descriptive claim, the weak imperative is not obviously true of all theories (e.g., there is good reason to doubt whether it is true of quantum theory's ψ function), and it is difficult to see how one would show it true. Most likely the weak imperative is intended as a prescriptive claim. The strong imperative clearly is prescriptive.

Why should anyone insist on either the weak or the strong imperative as a prescription for doing science? Historically, the operational imperative was introduced to explain how theories legitimately could employ parameters which could not be directly observed or measured, and how theories describing phenomena in terms of such parameters could be tested and confirmed observationally. Following the operational imperative not only explained the legitimacy of such procedures, but it also afforded a method for testing such theories and also guaranteed that they did not invoke ad hoc fictitious theoretical entities in explaining phenomena.

Bridgman (1927) clearly had these ends in mind when he introduced the operational imperative. Underlying the operational imperative was the idea that what could be directly observed was epistemologically secure, whereas nonobservable parameters and assertions about nonobservable entities lacked this surety. However, if theoretical parameters could be specified (wholly or partially) in terms of observable conditions and operations whose performance could be observationally checked for correct execution, then the epistemic surety of observation could be passed on to theories. The point, then, of following the operational imperative was to put one's scientific theorizing on an epistemologically sound footing, and to explain how theories employing nonobservable parameters could be tested by observing phenomena.

If the operational imperative does not adequately capture the relations holding between observable phenomena and theoretical parameters which make the empirical testing of theories possible, and if the claimed epistemic advantages of following the operational imperative do not accrue, then there is little point to insisting on it. As such, we can evaluate the weak and strong operational imperatives by considering whether there is any epistemic advantage to following them and whether they adequately characterize the ways in which theories are empirically testable. In order to do so it will be necessary to consider in some detail the semantic relations which hold between theories and their formulations, between physical systems and theory formulations, and between phenomena and theory formulations. It also will be necessary to consider the epistemological or structural relations holding between phenomena, their corresponding physical systems, and theories. These relations will be investigated in the next five sections and then in section VIII, we will use our findings to assess the operational imperative.

III. SEMANTIC RELATIONS

A *formulation of a theory* is a collection of propositions which are true of the theory.[18] Typically, a formulation of a theory consists of a few specified propositions together with all of their deductive consequences under some logic. A *full formulation* of a theory is one which describes all the characteristic features of the theory, whereas a *partial formulation* of a theory describes some, but not all, of the theory's characteristic features. The propositions constituting a theory formulation are of some language, known as the *theory formulation language*, and typically constitute a proper subset of the propositions in that language. Propositions in a theory formulation language may be used not only to describe the theory, but also with reference to physical systems and phenomena within the theory's intended scope. We need to consider the semantic relations holding between theory-formulation-language propositions and theories, physical systems, and phenomena.

At this point it will be useful to introduce a distinction between *strict usage* and *amplified usage* of propositions, which originated with Evert Beth.[19] Often descriptive propositions are such that they can be asserted about any of a number of different systems. Under strict usage, one intends to describe a particular one of these systems and uses the proposition solely with reference to that intended system. Under amplified usage, the proposition is used indifferently to describe any or all of the different possible systems. Any proposition admitting of amplified usage also admits of strict usage, but the converse is not true.

The propositions in theory formulation languages must admit of amplified usage. For the same propositions of a theory formulation language may be used to describe the theory, physical systems, or phenomena. For example, 'the force of the entity is equal to the product of its mass and acceleration', a proposition in a formulation of classical particle mechanics, can be used to describe a characteristic feature of the theory, a particular physical system in the class of theory-induced physical systems, and a particular phenomenon within the theory's intended scope. The amplified usage of such propositions must be such that the proposition can be used *simultaneously* with reference to the theory, one or more physical systems, and phenomena within the theory's intended scope.

For example, suppose we are predicting the velocity of a block on an inclined plane at t' whose friction is negligible, and we experimentally determine that at t ($< t'$) the velocity is 32 ft./s. This yields the proposition 'the body has velocity 32 ft./s at t', which describes the phenomenon. But in carrying out the procedure for prediction given at the end of section I, this proposition also must be taken as describing the initial state of the physical system corresponding to the phenomenon and as describing a state in the theory structure itself; otherwise the process of prediction given in section I would involve an equivocation fallacy. Hence amplified usage is necessary for predicting phenomena with theories.[20] Also, propositions in the theory formulation language may be used strictly with reference to the theory, physical systems, or phenomena. Key features of propositions in a theory formulation language can be discerned by investigating the strict usages of such propositions with reference to theories, physical systems, and phenomena—for the amplified usage of a proposition must be consistent with its various strict usages.

We begin by looking at the strict usage of propositions in a theory formulation language with reference to theories. Regardless whether a theory formulation is full or partial, it has the following basic features. First, there is a set of elementary propositions in the theory formulation language to the effect that a certain physical parameter p has a physical quantity q at time t. An elementary proposition ϕ will be true of a state s in the theory's domain if s has q as the value of parameter p at time t. For each elementary proposition ϕ there will be a maximal subset $h(\phi)$ of the theory's domain such that ϕ is true of all states in that subset; the function h from elementary propositions to subsets of the theory is known as the *satisfaction function* for the set of elementary propositions. Second, elementary propositions can be compounded together in accordance with some logic or other known as the *logic of the theory*. The logic must be such that every compound proposition is *empirically significant;* that is, it is true of at least one state which, according to the theory, is physically possible.[21] Thus the logic of the theory is determined by the theory, and different theories may impose different logics. For example, classical particle mechanics imposes a Boolean algebra mod-2 and quantum theory imposes a nondistributive lattice. The set of elementary propositions, the theory, the satisfaction function h, and the logic of the theory determine a *language of physical description*, which is a sublanguage of the theory formulation language. This language is capable of describing physically possible individual states, or collections of states, in the theory and thus is able to describe any physically possible state of affairs in a physical system. The logic of the theory enables one to deduce logical consequences of propositions in the language of physical description. In most circumstances, however, the logic of the theory is too impoverished to deduce changes in state over time (because these usually are nonlogical consequences of the propositions in the language of physical description). In order to do so, the language of physical description must be incorporated into a more comprehensive language, using an augmented logic able to express the laws of the theory and deduce various predictions, and so on, from these laws. For example, in classical particle mechanics the additional logic might include the vocabulary and mechanisms of differential equations, and in quantum theory the additional logic might be the algebraic theory of Hilbert spaces or matrix algebra. This expanded logic and language is the *theory formulation language*. The truth conditions for this expanded language (used strictly with reference to the theory) are specified in terms of the attributes of the theory and the truth conditions for the language of physical description. Third, a *formulation* (full or partial) *of a theory* is a set of propositions deductively closed under the logic of the theory formulation language such that every proposition in the set is true of the theory. For example, a formulation of the theory might be a set of *law statements* together with all their deductive consequences. The theory formulation language may be a natural or an artificial language, though typically it is a natural language such as scientific English.

We next turn to a consideration of the semantic relations holding between propositions in the theory formulation language and theory-induced physical systems. A physical system, it will be recalled, is a relational system consisting of a domain of states and a sequence defined over that domain; the sequence is the behavior of the physical system. If the physical system is in the class of theory-induced physical systems, then the domain of the physical system will be a subset of the domain of the theory, and the sequence will be one of the sequences determined by the theory's attributes. Thus a physical system in the class of theory-induced physical systems may be construed as the restriction of the theory to a single sequence. For example, the theory of ideal gases defines various equivalence classes of states in terms of the relation $PV = nRT$ and determines the set of all sequences of states such that the states in the sequence are equivalent. Each of these sequences is the behavior of some physical system in the class of theory-induced physical systems, and so the restrictions of the theory to individual sequences are physical systems.

Since physical systems are restrictions of the theory, propositions in the theory formulation language can be used to refer to and describe physical systems. The truth conditions for these propositions will be the restriction to the physical systems of the truth conditions for the propositions when they are used with reference to the theory. Only some of the propositions which are true of the theory will be true of a particular physical system in the class of theory-induced physical systems, but every proposition true of a physical system in that class will be true of the theory. Some propositions in the theory formulation language cannot meaningfully be used with reference to a particular physical system in the class of theory-induced physical systems (e.g., a true proposition about a four-body system in a formulation of classical particle mechanics cannot be meaningfully asserted about a two-body physical system). However, every proposition in the language of physical description will be true of some physical system in the class of theory-induced physical systems.

If the class of theory-induced physical systems is identical with the class of causally possible physical systems for the theory, then the semantic relations holding between propositions in the theory formulation language and the latter class of physical systems will be exactly the same as for theory-induced physical systems; and every proposition in the theory formulation language which is true of a causally possible physical system will be true of the theory. Suppose, however, that the theory is empirically false—hence that the class of causally possible physical systems is not identical with the class of theory-induced physical systems. In this case, the semantic relations holding between propositions in the theory formulation language and causally possible physical systems will be of exactly the same sort as those holding between such propositions and theory-induced physical systems. But in this case there is no guarantee that propositions true of a causally possible system will be true of the theory, or that any propositions true of the theory will be true of some causally possible physical system.

At this point, a further complication needs to be considered: The logic of the theory restricts the ways in which elementary propositions may be compounded together in the theory formulation language. If the theory is empirically false, then the logic of the theory may prevent certain compoundings of elementary propositions which are true of causally possible physical systems. As such, there may be propositions excluded from the theory formulation language which can be truly asserted of casually possible physical systems. Moreover, one way of falsifying a theory is to show that there are causally possible physical systems which do assume states the theory counts as physically impossible. If the theory is falsified in this way, propositions in the language of a physical description needed to describe the falsifying causally possible physical systems will not be propositions in the theory formulation language, and so the counterinstance to the theory is unstatable in that language.

This indicates that in order to describe and characterize all causally possible physical systems we must use an *expanded theory formulation language* which allows all truth-functional combinations of elementary propositions to be propositions. This language also must have a descriptive mechanism adequate to describe any logically possible behavior of any logically possible physical system (a feature not necessarily possessed by the theory formulation language). As a result, the deductive logical apparatus of this expanded theory formulation language may also have to be expanded. The theory formulation language is a sublanguage of the expanded theory formulation language, and the semantical relations holding between propositions in this expanded language and causally possible physical systems, or the theory, will be generalizations of those holding for propositions in the theory formulation language.

Finally, we turn to a consideration of the strict use of propositions in the expanded theory formulation language with reference to phenomena in the theory's intended scope; for such propositions employing theoretical vocabulary can be, and often are, used with reference to actual phenomena. When so used the propositions are making statements of putative fact and will be true if and only if the propositions are factually true. Thus to analyze the semantic relations holding between propositions in the expanded theory formulation language and phenomena, we will need to employ some account of factual truth.

For brevity I will assume an analysis of factual truth I have developed and used elsewhere.[22] In this analysis, empirical propositions are used to assert that certain states of affairs hold in the world, and if the asserted states obtain, the proposition is true. The world is assumed to consist of particulars having intrinsic properties together with various intrinsic relations particulars may enter into. Particulars may be simple or complex, with a complex particular being the continuous instantiation of an intrinsic relation by particulars.[23] For the purposes of the natural sciences, these particulars are assumed to be nonintentional, and the properties of particulars and the intrinsic attributes they enter into in principle can be specified in an extensional language containing the class abstraction operator, infinite disjunctions, and temporal names for particulars.[24]

When a proposition 'S is P' is used to make a putative factual assertion, its sense determines ostensible referents for S and P; the ostensible referent for S will be a possible particular, and the ostensible referent for P will be a possible intrinsic property (an extensional property a particular could possess). Then

'S is P' is factually true if and only if
  (i) the ostensible referent of S is an actual particular in the world, and
  (ii) the ostensible referent of S has an intrinsic property which has the same extension as does the ostensible referent of the predicate P.

Factual truth conditions for simple relational propositions are defined analogously, and the analysis can be extended to compound proposi-tions, universal and existential propositions, and so on, in standard ways.

Since, on this account of factual truth, the world consists of particulars which possess intrinsic properties and enter into various intrinsic re-lations, the phenomena within a theory's intended scope will be systems of particulars in the world which possess certain kinds of properties and enter into certain types of relations; these particulars, their properties, and the relations they enter into need not be observable, though they may be. Such systems will be known as *phenomenal systems*, and each causally possible phenomenon is a *causally possible phenomenal system.* From our previous discussion, there will be at least one causally possible physical system corresponding to each causally possible phenomenal system for a given theory.

Can elementary propositions be used to describe phenomenal sys-tems? Elementary propositions, it will be recalled, make assertions to the effect that a certain physical parameter p has a physical quantity q at time t. But these physical parameters are nothing other than *kinds of attributes* which physical particulars may possess, and physical quan-tities are attributes of the requisite kinds which the particulars may possess. For example, in classical particle mechanics the physical pa-rameters are the position and momentum coordinates of bodies, and so the elementary propositions of that theory each specify a position or a momentum coordinate of a body; that is, an attribute of a particular (a body) in the phenomenal system at time t. As such, elementary propositions can be used to refer to particulars in phenomenal systems and predicate attributes of them. When so used, the propositions will be factually true of the phenomenal system if and only if the particulars referred to have the attributes indicated. In a manner analogous to that for physical systems, nonelementary propositions in the expanded the-ory formulation language may be used with reference to phenomenal systems. Here the truth conditions are defined analogously relative to the truth or falsity of elementary propositions. If the theory is empirically false, there may be propositions true of causally possible phenomenal systems that are false of all theory-induced physical systems and also false of the theory.

If a theory is empirically true, does it follow that all propositions true of causally possible phenomenal systems in the theory's intended scope are true of some theory-induced physical system, hence true of the theory? To answer this we will have to investigate the relations holding between phenomenal systems and their corresponding physical systems (for the answer, see the end of sec. V).

IV. STRUCTURAL RELATIONS

Physical systems and phenomenal systems are relational systems. A physical system is a relational system having a domain of states and attributes defined over these states. A phenomenal system is a relational system having a domain of particulars and attributes defined over these particulars; these attributes include properties the particulars possess at various times and relations they enter into at various times. Collectively they are the behavior of the phenomenal system. Let S be a physical system corresponding to a phenomenal system P. S is characterized in terms of various parameters abstracted from P; these parameters are *kinds of attributes* the particulars in P may possess. A state in S is a simultaneous set of values for these parameters; but the value of parameters are physical quantities, which is to say that the values are attributes which particulars could possess.[25] Thus a state of S is a possible state of affairs P could assume (being a possible set of simultaneous attributes the particulars in P could possess). An important consequence follows from this discussion: Since states in S are possible simultaneous attributes of particulars in P, the states are not themselves particulars even though they are theoretical entities. Theories and physical systems have sets of theoretical entities (the states) as their domains, but do not contain any particulars in their domains. Phenomenal systems, on the other hand, do not have theoretical entities in their domains, having particulars instead.

The attributes in S determine a sequence of states over time and thus indicate a possible behavior of P (i.e., a sequence of changing attributes the particulars in P could have at various times). Accordingly, S is a kind of *replica* of P; however, it need not replicate P in any straightforward manner. For the state of S at t does not indicate what attributes the particulars in P possess at t; rather, it indicates what attributes they *would have* at t *were* the abstracted parameters the only ones influencing the behavior of P and were certain idealized conditions met. In order to see how S replicates P we need to investigate these abstractive and idealizing relations holding between them.

Begin by considering *abstraction*. Scientific theories do not describe the behavior of phenomenal systems in all their complexity, but rather attempt to characterize the phenomena in terms of a few selected parameters. For example, in classical particle mechanics, one treats mechanical phenomena involving interacting bodies *as if* the phenomena *only* involved certain specified bodies and *only* involved the positions and momenta of these bodies. As such, a mechanical phenomenon is treated as an n-body system whose behavior is wholly specified in terms of $6n$ position and momentum coordinates (parameters). In effect, one assumes the fiction that no other bodies and no other parameters exert an influence on these n bodies' behaviors.

Under certain circumstances this fiction can be approximately realized—if, for example, the experimental setup is such that other bodies and other parameters exert a negligible influence. In such special cases, we have abstracted certain aspects of the systems' behavior and duplicated them with a physical system. And any difference between the actual behavior of the phenomenal system and the corresponding states in the physical system will be negligible. In most circumstances, however, the fiction is not realized—other bodies or other parameters do exert a nonnegligible influence on the behavior of the physical system. For example, the density of the medium in which the bodies act is such that they retard motion, or the system is not frictionless, or other massive bodies are present altering the motion of the specified bodies. In such cases, the values of the parameters characteristic of the state s that the physical system S is in at t are *not* the actual parameter values characteristic of the phenomenal system P at t. Rather, they stand in the following *replicating relation* to the values in P:

If P were an isolated phenomenal system in which all other parameters exerted a negligible influence, then the physical quantities characteristic of those parameters abstracted from P would be identical with those values characteristic of the state at t of the physical system S corresponding to P.

In this case, any proposition in the expanded theory formulation language true of S would be counterfactually true of P (being an assertion about what P's behavior would be were certain conditions met).

There are two ways this counterfactual could be true of P, and the difference between the two cases marks the difference between pure abstraction and idealization. First, it may be causally possible for P to realize the conditions such that P's behavior would be as S indicates. For example, an electrically charged sphere phenomenon might be such that, through experimental controls, the phenomenon could have occurred in circumstances where it in effect was isolated from other influences. Second, it may be such that it is causally impossible for P to realize the conditions such that P's behavior would be as S indicates. For example, in classical particle mechanics (as opposed to rigid body mechanics) spatial location (position) is a parameter, and the possible values for the parameter are the coordinates of points in space. This in effect imposes the requirement that at each time a body must have a unique point in space as its spatial location, which in turn requires that the body be extensionless or dimensionless. But this condition is causally impossible, since it would require that bodies have an infinite gravitational potential, which is impossible if classical particle mechanics is true.[26] As such, it is causally impossible, then, to put the physical system P in circumstances that would meet the conditions required to make statements about S (noncounterfactually) true of P. The reason why these conditions cannot be met is that they require that parameters characteristic of phenomenal systems have physical quantities as values which are causally impossible for any phenomenal system to possess.

The former case (causally possible) is an example of *pure abstraction,* and the latter case (causally impossible) is one of *idealization.* Roughly put, the difference between the two cases is this: In cases of pure abstraction, the theory simply ignores a number of parameters and other factors which in most cases exert a nonnegligible influence on the phenomena within the theory's intended scope, but it is causally possible that there could be phenomena within the theory's intended scope on which only the abstracted parameters exert nonnegligible influences. Cases of idealization also involve abstraction, but in a way that imposes conditions on the phenomena which are causally impossible for any phenomena to meet.

A physical system S corresponding to a phenomenal system P must be such that the above counterfactual condition is met. This condition can be met either by S being an abstract replica of P, or else by S being an idealized replica of P—depending on the circumstances in which it is causally possible that phenomena within the theory's intended scope can be realized.

V. THE EMPIRICAL TRUTH OF THEORIES

The next step in our investigation of the relations between phenomena, physical systems, theories, and linguistic formulations of theories is to consider what it is for a theory to be empirically true. As stated previously, there are two empirical truth conditions for theories:

(1) If the theory is empirically true, then the class of theory-induced physical systems is identical with the class of causally possible physical systems for the theory.

(2) If the class of theory-induced physical systems is not identical with the class of causally possible physical systems for the theory, then the theory is empirically false.

The first condition is a necessary condition for the empirical truth of a theory, but is it a sufficient condition? The second condition is a sufficient condition for a theory being empirically false, but is it a necessary condition? These questions must be answered if we are to know what it is for a theory to be empirically true or false.

First, let us see what is involved in asserting a theory. A theory has as its intended scope a natural kind class of phenomenal systems. In propounding a theory, one commits oneself to the existence of the phenomenal systems within the theory's intended scope.[27] Further, one presents a theory structure and asserts that the class of theory-induced physical systems is identical with the class of causally possible physical systems. This in turn commits one to the existence of a class of causally possible physical systems which *are* abstract and/or idealized replicas of the phenomena within the theory's intended scope.

A physical system is an abstract replica of a phenomenal system if for each t, its state stands in the counterfactual replicating relation to its corresponding phenomenal system. This replicating relation obtains only if the defining parameters of the physical system are parameters abstracted from phenomenal systems in the theory's intended scope or else are idealizations of them. Recall (from sec. III) that these defining parameters must be kinds of attributes characteristic of the particulars in phenomenal systems; hence the existence of the class of causally possible physical systems for a theory presupposes the existence of particulars having the kinds of attributes selected as defining parameters of physical systems for the theory.

Further, if the physical systems in the class of causally possible physical systems are pure abstractions of phenomenal systems, one also commits oneself to the notion that the physical quantities that are values of parameters in casually possible physical systems must also be attributes of causally possible phenomenal systems within the theory's scope. However, if the physical systems in the class of causally possible physical systems are idealized replicas of causally possible phenomenal systems, one does not commit oneself to the values of parameters in the causally possible physical systems being attributes of particulars in causally possible phenomenal systems. Rather, one commits oneself to their being idealizations of attributes which particulars in causally possible phenomenal systems do possess.

In order for a theory to be empirically true, all the commitments made in propounding the theory must be satisfied. Based on the previous discussion, these are the requirements for a theory to be empirically true:

Let T be a theory with intended scope I whose defining parameters are $p_1, \ldots, p_n$. Then T is *empirically true* if and only if

(a) I is a natural kind set of causally possible phenomenal systems whose domains contain particulars of which $p_1, \ldots, p_n$ are characteristic kinds of attributes.

(b) The possible values of the parameters $p_1, \ldots, p_n$ allowed by T are attributes which particulars in the phenomenal systems in I do possess or else are idealizations of such attributes.[28]

(c) The set of theory-induced physical systems for I is identical with the class of causally possible physical systems for T.

If any of these three conditions fail to be met by T, then T is *empirically false*.

The requirement that I be a natural kind set in effect commits my version of the Semantic Conception to an antinominalism (to a view that some classes correspond to real divisions of nature and others do not) that van Fraassen would reject. I must postpone defense of that condition until chapter 7, where I develop and defend a specific version of the antinominalistic thesis.

Whenever a theory is propounded as *being empirically true*, a commitment to requirements (a) through (c) being satisfied is made. However, it is possible to propound a theory without propounding it as being empirically true; one may propound it instead as being some kind of *conceptual device*. For example, the theory may be known to be empirically false but approximately correct for certain types of phenomena within the theory's intended scope, and then used to make approximate predictions within that range of phenomena. For example, the ideal gas laws are known to be empirically false, yet they are used in this way. In such a case, the theory is propounded as *being approximately true for a restricted scope $I' \subset I$*, which carries the commitment that the restrictions of (a) through (c) to I' are satisfied.

A theory also can be propounded as *a simplification*. For example, for certain purposes it may prove convenient to employ an astronomical theory which considers planetary orbits to be circular rather than elliptical, even though the theory is known to be empirically false. Here there is no question whether the theory is empirically true—it is known to be empirically false since it fails to satisfy truth condition (c). And unlike the approximation case, the theory is not even true for a restricted scope I' contained in the intended scope I of the theory. Rather, it is used because it conveniently yields incorrect predictions which are close enough for the purposes at hand.[29]

Let T be a theory which is empirically true, and let ϕ be a proposition in the theory formulation language which is true of some physical system in the class of theory-induced physical systems for the theory. Since the theory is empirically true, ϕ will be true of some causally possible physical system for T; hence by the replicating relation, ϕ will be counterfactually true of some causally possible phenomenal system. And if the counterfactual conditions imposed on the physical system were true of the phenomenal system, then ϕ would be factually true of the phenomenal system. A proposition ψ factually true of a causally possible phenomenal system usually will not be noncounterfactually true of its corresponding physical system; whether it is counterfactually true of the physical system is an open question.[30]

VI. INSTRUMENTALIST VERSUS REALIST CONSTRUALS OF THEORIES

Our findings on the empirical truth conditions just discussed yield certain consequences for the issue whether theories are to be construed instrumentally or realistically which will be helpful in assessing the operational imperative. In its classic formulation, the instrumentalist-realist controversy has centered on the question whether statements of laws or theories incorporating nonobservable theoretical entities are factually true or false, or whether they are merely calculating devices for predicting observable phenomena. The realist answers the question as follows:

> Scientific theories are factually true or false; hence if true, the theoretical (i.e., nonobservable) entities postulated by the theory do exist.

The Instrumentalist answers the question this way:

> Insofar as scientific theories employ theoretical terms (i.e., non-logical terms which do not designate observable entities or attributes), they are not factually true or false. Only if the theory makes no reference to theoretical entities is it factually true or false. Theories incorporating theoretical terms are mere calculating devices for predicting and controlling observable phenomena.

Typically both realists and instrumentalists identify theories with their linguistic formulations, though it is possible to divorce the main tenets of realism and instrumentalism from that identification.

The realist claims that theoretical assertions are factually true or false. Under the analysis of theories being considered here, the realist in effect is claiming that propositions in the theory formulation language which are true of the theory will be factually true of the phenomena within the theory's intended scope if the theory is empirically true. Our findings have shown that this generally will not be so; rather, it will be the case that such propositions will be counterfactually true of the phenomena. The realist also claims that the theoretical (i.e., nonobservable) entities postulated by the theory do exist if the theory is empirically true. Construed in terms of our analysis of theories, this becomes the claim that (a) that the particulars (both observable and nonobservable) in the phenomenal systems within the theory's intended scope do exist and have the kinds of properties (both observable and nonobservable) which are the theory's defining parameters, and (b) that the physical quantities which may be values of the theory's parameters are properties possessed by particulars in causally possible phenomenal systems. This in effect requires that the class of causally possible physical systems for a theory not be idealizations of phenomenal systems. We have seen, however, that there are theories (e.g., classical particle mechanics) which do incorporate idealizations, and so realism is descriptively false of the theories science actually uses.

Realism's mistake rests, I think, in the common but mistaken suppositions that all theoretical entities are particulars and that if a realistic theory is to be empirically true, the theoretical entities must exist. But, as Wilfrid Sellars has shown (1956, sec. 61), not all theoretical entities need be particulars; indeed, the states of theories and physical systems employed here are examples of theoretical entities that are not particulars. And as Dudley Shapere has shown (1969, Part II), theoretical entities can be invoked in a theory without committing oneself to their existence; idealizations typically are theoretical entities used nonexistentially. Thus idealizations can be employed in theories without committing oneself to their existence.

In particular, when the physical system *S* corresponding to a phenomenal system *P* is an idealized replica of *P*, one need not commit oneself to the idealized values of parameters being properties possessed by particulars in causally possible phenomenal systems. And using such idealized values does not preclude the theory from being empirically true or false, for by the empirical truth conditions of the previous section, theories are *counterfactually* true or false of the phenomena within their intended scopes, regardless whether causally possible physical systems are purely abstractive or idealized replicas of phenomena. The realists are correct, then, in supposing that theories are empirically true or false and may commit one to the existence of nonobservable particulars or attributes, but they are wrong in identifying empirical truth or falsity with factual truth or falsity and in supposing that to invoke theoretical entities in a theory *always* is to commit oneself to their existence as particulars. When these errors are eliminated from realism, a modified or *quasi-realism* emerges which is defensible and therefore is built into my empirical truth conditions for theories.

Viewed as a descriptive account of theories, instrumentalism fares worse: It becomes the claim that there are no scientific theories which deal with phenomena involving nonobservable particulars. For if theories did, then properties of these particulars would have to be parameters of the theory, which in turn means (by the empirical truth conditions) that the theory is empirically true or false—contrary to instrumentalism's claims. Since scientific theories dealing with phenomena of nonobservable particulars do exist, instrumentalism is descriptively false of actual science. If instrumentalism is to be viable, then, it must be viewed as a prescriptive thesis—saying that the only theories which should be used are those which presuppose only observable particulars and attributes. From the foregoing analysis of theories and from the empirical truth conditions for such theories it follows that such theories may employ no parameters of particulars *whose values* are not (in some cases at least) observable. If followed, prescriptive instrumentalism would rule out most present-day scientific theories.

To summarize, classical realism is untenable if my analysis of theories is correct; but modified or quasi-realism not only is tenable, but in effect is built into the analysis.[31] In addition, instrumentalism appears to be a conservative doctrine, demanding that science should restrict its attention just to observable phenomena; in effect, it is a modified realism restricted to a limited class of phenomena.

[Recall from chapter 1 that the classical realism-versus-instrumentalism debates have been replaced by what MacKinnon (1979) terms "the new debates" over scientific realism.[32] The Semantic Conception proves to be a particularly effective vehicle for displaying some fundamental oppositions within the new debates. For example, van Fraassen and I agree on nearly all aspects of the Semantic Conception except that he champions an antirealistic approach to the physical interpretation of theories, whereas I embrace a quasi-realistic one. The heart of my quasi-realism is the empirical truth analysis of theories expounded in section V and the replicating relation of section IV above. Van Fraassen rejects this quasi-realism, denying that theories are empirically true or false either in some literal sense or in accordance with my counterfactual ("nonliteral") empirical truth analysis. Instead he says we evaluate theories as to their "empirical adequacy":

> To present a theory is to specify a family of structures, its *models*; and secondly, to specify certain parts of those models (the *empirical substructures*) as candidates for the direct representation of ob-

servable phenomena. The structures which can be described in experimental and measurement reports we can call *appearances*: The theory is empirically adequate if it has some model such that all appearances are isomorphic to empirical substructures of that model. [1980, 64; italics original]

Further, van Fraassen requires that "empirical adequacy concerns actual phenomena: what does happen, and not what would happen under different circumstances" (ibid., 60). By virtue of his antirealism's reliance on an observational/nonobservational distinction, it also is a modified realism restricted to a limited class (or aspect) of phenomena; this feature of his view is criticized in chapters 1 and 11.

The preceding discussion of the physical interpretation of theories provides another line of objection: My arguments in sections IV and V strongly support the contention that theories virtually always abstract their phenomena—which is to say, treat them as if they were isolated from outside influences. Moreover, this claim is separable from my quasi-realistic account of the empirical truth of theories. Such a process of abstraction carries no guarantee that any of the theory's models or substructures will be isomorphic to any actual phenomenal systems; hence there is no guarantee that there will be any models such that all appearances are isomorphic to empirical substructures of the model.

Empirical adequacy minimally would require that every phenomenal system within the theory's scope actually occur in isolated circumstances—which is a huge philosophical assumption (by no means obvious, but possibly defensible) that requires argument and defense. But even this is insufficient to establish that "*all* appearances are isomorphic to empirical substructures of that model," for in paradigmatic cases such as Newton's theory (an example van Fraassen uses [1980, 46]), appearances more often than not are at odds with the models of the theory, hence are not isomorphic. For example, real inclined planes usually are neither frictionless nor have constant coefficients of friction. In short, to the extent that empirical adequacy concerns "what does happen, and not what would happen under different circumstances" for *all* appearances, virtually no real-life scientific theory ever meets van Fraassen's empirical adequacy conditions. Differently put, van Fraassen's antirealism is a literal realism when it comes to appearances; my quasi-realism, with rare exceptions, is the most that is defensible—even for appearances.

The only way I can see to salvage van Fraassen's empirical adequacy conditions is to allow the idea that empirical adequacy concerns what would happen under isolated conditions, as well as what sometimes may happen under actual circumstances—which is to adopt something like the replicating relationship of section IV. Of course, this would be tantamount to abandoning his antirealism in favor of some sort of quasi-realism.]

VII. EXPERIMENTAL METHODOLOGY

Before turning to an assessment of the operational imperative, there is one last aspect of the relations holding between theory and phenomena which should be explored—how experimental methodology enables us to determine the states of a causally possible physical system by observing and measuring, and so on, the corresponding phenomenal system.

The most basic feature of the relation holding between a casually possible phenomenal system P and its corresponding physical system S is that S is a (possibly idealized) counterfactual replica of P satisfying the replicating relation discussed in section IV. This condition must be met regardless whether the particulars in P, their attributes, and the defining parameters of the theory are observable or not. For all empirically true theories stand in a counterfactual relationship to their phenomena regardless what the nature of the phenomenal system is (even if an occasional causally possible physical system is a noncounterfactual replica of its corresponding phenomenal system).[33]

In applying a theory to specific phenomena, it is the task of the experimental methodology to convert data about a phenomenal system P into data about the corresponding physical system S in such a way as to satisfy the replicating relation. Suppose, for example, that we wish to use the theory to predict the subsequent behavior of a phenomenal system P. In accordance with the discussion at the end of section I, we first determine the actual values of various parameters in P at t—we determine the physical quantities (attributes) of the various particulars in P at t. Then, in accordance with some experimental design, we convert this data about P into data about the corresponding physical system S—that is, we convert the data about P into data about what P would have been had P been isolated, dependent only on the defining parameters of S and the various idealized conditions met.

The *experimental design* governing this process is not part of the theory; rather, it is based on various extratheoretical regularities, other theories, laws, known regularities about the kind of phenomena involved, and so on. For example, for inclined planes we may employ various other theories which enable one to determine friction coefficients; for bodies falling in viscous media, we use various hydrodynamic laws to determine the retarding effects of the medium; for falling bodies we idealize the fiction that the position of the body is its center of gravity. These various laws, theories, and assumptions in effect are putative regularities which hold between the theory's parameters and other factors affecting them, and if the regularities do obtain for P (if the laws, theories, and assumptions are empirically true of P), then their use (together with experimental controls which succeed in keeping any other factors from influencing the phenomena) enables one to determine what states S is in at t. The truth of these then guarantees that the replicating relation is satisfied.[34] In different circumstances, and for different Ps, different laws and theories will be used to determine that state of S at t. And there may be Ps or circumstances in which no laws or theories exist which enable one to determine what state the S corresponding to P will be in at t.

Although the above discussion is exceedingly crude and does not even suggest the full complexity of the way experimental methodology enables us to determine the state of S at t from data about P at t,[35] it does enable us to draw several conclusions relevant to our assessment of the operational imperative.

(1) In order to apply a theory to a phenomenal system P, data about P must be converted into data about the corresponding physical system S; this must be done regardless whether the defining parameters in S and the particulars in P are observable or nonobservable.

(2) The conversion of data about P to data about S requires the employment of laws, theories, known regularities, and so on, which are not a part of the theory in question, as well as whatever idealizing conventions are associated with the theory. These are applied to data about P.

(3) Different phenomenal systems P within the theory's intended scope may require different laws, theories, and so on, to effect the conversion of data about P to data about S, and there may be Ps such that we do not know how to effect the conversion.

These conclusions hold for all theories regardless whether the physical quantities which are values of the defining parameters of states in S are qualitative or measurable.

When the physical quantities involved in applying a theory to phenomena are measurable, certain complications result. The process of measurement consists of attaching numbers to physical quantities which describe the physical quantities. *Quantitative theories* are ones in which all of the defining parameters of the theory are measurable. These theories admit of *mathematic models,* and typically these models are employed in lieu of the theory.

I will briefly characterize them as follows: Let T be a theory with $p_1, \ldots, p_n$ having determinate attributes as values[36] and assume that $p_1, \ldots, p_n$ are measurable. Since states of physical systems are n-tuples of physical quantities $q_1, \ldots, q_n$, which are possible values of $p_1, \ldots, p_n$, we can represent or characterize states by numbers which are measures of $q_1, \ldots, q_n$. Such measures are determined relative to a *frame of reference,* and different frames of reference typically will assign different numbers to the same physical quantities. The various measures assigned to a given physical quantity under different frames of reference must be equivalent under some *system of transformations* (e.g., the Galilean system of transformations in classical particle mechanics or the Lorentz system of transformations in the special theory of relativity). For to say that a physical quantity is measurable is to say, inter alia, that it can be described by numbers up to some system of transformations.[37] These systems of transformations in effect are putative laws stating that certain physical quantities remain invariant under certain changes in frames of reference, measurement techniques, and so on. And the system of transformations is included among the laws, theories, and so forth, (mentioned in point [2] regarding methodology) used in converting data about P into data about S.

When a theory employs measurable parameters, formulations of the theory typically employ a mathematic vocabulary, and states of S are represented by n-tuples of numbers (or functions over numbers) which describe the physical quantities characteristic of the state in question. In such cases S often is represented by an *arithmetic model* describing S relative to some frame of reference, where the domain of the model consists of n-tuples of numbers which describe the states relative to the frame of reference, and where the behavior of S is represented by a sequence of these n-tuples of numbers. Similarly, the theory will be represented by a *phase space* model, which is an n-dimensional space whose points represent the states whose physical quantities are described by the coordinates of the point under the frame of reference in question. The laws of the theory are represented by trajectories directed through the space against time, subspaces, and the like.

Admissible frames of reference for a theory must be such that every possible physical system state can be represented by an n-tuple of numbers assigned to physical quantities relative to that frame of reference.[38] This enables us to construe each n-tuple of numbers representing states relative to a frame of reference as being coordinates of points in some n-dimensional vector space. And various configurations can be imposed on that space, such as trajectories, subspaces, probability measures, and the like. In particular, we can impose configurations on the points of such a space which correspond to laws of succession, laws of coexistence, and laws of interaction. When such a space, obtained relative to a frame of reference, has such configurations imposed on it corresponding to the attributes of the theory, we say the space is a *phase space model of the theory*.

Phase space models can be given linguistic formulations which are analogous to theory formulations as characterized in section I. Such formulations are called *model formulations* and are given in an (expanded) *model formulation language*, which is a mathematical *language* having the same structural properties as the (expanded) theory formulation language. In particular, it will have elementary propositions, a logic of the model, and a language of physical description. Deductions in this language are undertaken by solving equations.

An appropriately chosen phase space model will be isomorphic to the theory, and propositions will be true of the model if and only if their analogues in the theory formulation language are true of the theory. Likewise, the quasi-realistic interpretation of propositions in the model formulation language and the model will be analogous to that for propositions in the theory formulation language and the theory. As such, whenever a theory admits of phase space models, these models may be employed in lieu of the theory and model formulation languages may be employed in lieu of theory formulation languages. In actual scientific practice this is what invariably is done.[39]

VIII. TENABILITY OF THE OPERATIONAL IMPERATIVE

We now have discussed enough about the relations holding between theories, physical systems, phenomena, and theory formulations to assess the operational imperative. We concentrate our attention on the weak operational imperative, which says that every scientific theory must admit of a full linguistic formulation in which theoretical terms are operationally defined. Suppose we have a full formulation F of a theory T meeting the operational imperative. Then it must be possible to divide the nonlogical terms of the theory formulation language for F into *observation terms* which designate observable particulars or attributes and *theoretical terms* which designate nonobservable particulars or attributes.[40] And the formulation F must include propositions of the following form for each theoretical term Q:

X is Q if and only if [or, only if] performing operations O in circumstances C would yield results R, where O, C, and R do not involve theoretical terms. These are the *operational definitions*. For simplicity of argument we will assume that the theoretical terms Q designate defining parameters of the theory's physical system or physical quantities thereof, and we also will assume that physical systems are *not* idealized replicas of phenomenal systems.[41] The observational terms used to define O, C, and R may or may not designate defining parameters of the theory or attributes thereof, but they clearly must designate attributes or kinds of attributes possessed by particulars in phenomenal systems within the theory's intended scope.

Suppose T is empirically true of the phenomena within its intended scope. Then by the results of section V the sorts of particulars asserted to exist by the theory do exist in causally possible systems, and the defining parameters of the theory and physical quantities thereof are kinds of attributes and attributes possessed by these particulars. Hence the Q in the operational definitions designate attributes or kinds of attributes possessed by particulars in the phenomenal systems. Since T is empirically true, the propositions in F are counterfactually true of the phenomenal systems if they meaningfully can be asserted of these phenomenal systems (secs. III, V). But the Q, O, C, and R do designate attributes or kinds of attributes which can be possessed by particulars in these phenomenal systems, so the operational definitions are counterfactually true of the phenomenal systems. But then, the operational definitions specify that certain regularities hold between particulars being Q and particulars being R when operations O are performed on them in circumstances C. As such, operational definitions are true or false statements of empirical regularities holding between particulars in phenomenal systems. This precludes operational definitions from being definitions in the usual stipulative sense; for empirical regularities cannot be defined into existence, and definitions are analytically true whereas statements of empirical regularity cannot be analytically true.

The discovery that operational definitions are contingent statements of empirical regularity enables us to see the operational imperative in its true color. For we now see that the operational imperative in effect prohibits the employment of nonobservable parameters (or values thereof) in theories unless it is possible to state empirical regularities holding between these parameters (or values) and other observable parameters (or values). In a word, one cannot incorporate parameters (or values thereof) into testable theories unless one knows some of their observable manifestations. On the other hand, any observable parameters (or values thereof) are admissible. This makes the question whether operational definitions should be explicit definitions or reduction sentences rather silly; for to demand that operational definitions be explicit definitions is nothing other than a refusal to theorize with parameters which do not manifest themselves observationally the same way in all phenomenal systems within the theory's intended scope.

As we saw in section II, the operational imperative, inter alia, is supposed to explain how theories with nonobservable defining parameters can be tested and confirmed observationally. To see whether it does, first consider what happens if the strong operational imperative holds. To test a theory with nonobservable parameters it is not sufficient merely that the operational definitions in F be true if the theory is empirically true. For one tests a theory by comparing the theory's predictions (obtained in accordance with the procedures of sections I and VII) about P with P's actual behavior. And this requires knowing the actual values in P of T's defining parameters independently of the theory's empirical truth or falsity. When these parameters or values are nonobservable, the operational definitions are supposed to enable one to determine the actual values of the parameters in P, but they can do so with reliability only if the operational definitions are known to be true of the phenomenal systems prior to testing the theory T.[42] But the operational definitions—being empirical statements of regularities holding between observable and nonobservable parameters or values thereof (when all other parameters exert a negligible influence on the regularities)—are themselves formulations of (simpler) theories. And since the operational definitions must be known to be true, by the discussion of sections III through V, the theories they formulate must be known to be empirically true prior to the testing of T. How do we determine that this is so? By testing the theories, it seems. But under standard accounts this requires testing their predictions against the actual attributes of particulars in the phenomenal systems within their intended scope, and as before, to do this one must know in advance the actual attributes of those particulars. However, some of these attributes are nonobservable (namely, those designated by the term being operationally defined), and if the testing is to be noncircular, one must have some other theory (incorporating the laws, theories, and so on, of section VII) specifying empirical regularities holding between the nonobservable attributes and other observable attributes under various causally possible circumstances. Moreover, this theory would have to be known to be empirically true prior to the testing. The catch is that the same arguments apply to *this* theory, showing the need for still another prior theory—and so on into an infinite regress. Since this is a vicious regress, it follows that no theory embodying nonobservable parameters or values thereof can be tested. *Thus the strong operational imperative is untenable.* Rather than explaining how testable theories can employ nonobservable parameters or values thereof, the strong operational imperative in effect precludes the employment of such parameters or values, which in turn forces one to adopt the instrumentalist account of theories as characterized in section VI.

Next, consider whether the weak operational imperative does any better in explaining how theories employing nonobservable parameters or attributes thereof are observationally tested. Unlike the strong imperative, the weak operational imperative does not require that one only employ formulations of a theory in which theoretical terms are operationally defined. Indeed, it does not even require that users of a theory *possess* a formulation of the theory in which all theoretical terms are operationally defined; it only requires that the theory *admit* of such formulations. It follows from the previous arguments, then, that if an empirically true theory admits of such a formulation, the operational definitions will be counterfactually true statements of regularities holding between particulars — that is, that the nonobservable parameters or values thereof employed in the theory do admit of observable manifestations which can be operationally discerned. It is this fact that explains how it is that theories employing nonobservable parameters or values thereof can be observationally tested; it is surely true that one cannot observationally test a theory about phenomena which do not have observable manifestations. If this is all there is to the weak observational imperative, then it is defensible.

Few proponents of the operational imperative would be willing to say that this is all there is to the operational imperative, though, for the operational imperative is intimately connected with the following epistemological doctrine: Determining the truth or falsity of propositions about observables is straightforward and nonproblematic, but knowledge about nonobservables is problematic and ultimately must rest on our knowledge about observables. It is operational definitions which enable us to expand our knowledge of the observable to knowledge of the nonobservable: From our observable knowledge and operational definitions we are able to deductively gain knowledge of nonobservables.

There is some plausibility to this thesis *if* operational definitions are thought to be definitions, hence, analytically true. For then, from our sure knowledge of observables and our operational definitions which are nonproblematic as to truth, whatever we deduce about nonobservables must be true; hence operational definitions yield knowledge of the unobservable. However, we have seen that operational definitions are not really definitions and are not analytically true. Rather, they are counterfactual empirical truths about particulars and their attributes, some of which are nonobservable.[43] Hence if operational definitions are to enable us to deductively expand our observational knowledge to knowledge of the unobservable, the operational definitions must be known to be empirically true.

But this requirement gets the weak imperative into the same regress as the strong operational imperative does; hence, it does not explain how we come to have theoretical knowledge about the nonobservable. And if the only way we have of obtaining knowledge of the nonobservable is by using operational definitions to deductively expand our knowledge of the observable, then there can be no knowledge of the nonobservable. The epistemology of the operational imperative thus is a skeptical one which ultimately forces science into an instrumentalism.

The fact that science does yield knowledge of nonobservable particulars and attributes indicates that there is something drastically wrong with the operational imperative's associated epistemology. Part of the difficulty clearly rests in the operational imperative's embrace of the observational-theoretical term distinction which, as argued in chapter 2, is untenable in that it cannot be drawn on the basis of natural language usage. Indeed, without that distinction it is very hard to give a coherent formulation of the operational imperative. However, I suggest that the difficulty with the operational imperative rests with deeper problems with its associated epistemology—in its suppositions that one can *only* have observational knowledge of attributes of particulars which can be directly seen, and that knowledge of attributes and particulars which cannot be directly seen must be obtained *inferentially* from observational knowledge of what can be directly seen.

This thesis, I suggest, is fundamentally mistaken. While it is true that our sensations are essential to having observational knowledge, the sensations we have in various circumstances of observation are the product of empirical regularities involving both "observable" and "nonobservable" particulars (particulars we can see and ones we cannot see). What we observationally are able to determine to be the case depends on these regularities regardless whether the objects of our observational knowledge themselves can be seen or not. In fact, several recent philosophical analyses of perceptual and observational knowledge strongly suggest that these regularities enable us to have noninferential observational knowledge of particulars and attributes of particulars which we are unable to directly see; also, this knowledge can be had without knowing what those regularities are, provided that we know how to use language to describe them.[44] (For example, while looking at a bubble chamber I may be able to observe that or see that an α particle has been emitted even though I cannot see the α particle, and I thereby gain *observational*—not inferential—knowledge that an α particle has been emitted). Furthermore, it is possible to know how to use language to describe particulars which cannot be directly seen and their attributes without possessing operational definitions of them. (Consider, e.g., descriptions of men "too little to be seen" in children's stories.)

If these claims are philosophically defensible (and there is good reason to suppose they are), then the operational imperative is pointless, for then we can have observational knowledge of particulars and attributes which cannot be directly seen. Such knowledge enables us to test and confirm theories about such particulars and attributes; these theories can then be used to test and confirm other theories in accordance with the procedures of section VII. As such, the operational imperative seems plausible only if certain questionable epistemological suppositions are made about the nature of observation.

IX. CONCLUSION

We have seen that the operational imperative is a prescriptive thesis about formulations of theories, which imposes restrictions on the sorts of theories science may employ. We assessed the operational imperative by investigating a number of relationships holding between theory formulations, theories, physical systems, and phenomena and then applying our findings to the operational imperative. These applications showed that the operational definitions required by the operational imperative were not definitions at all, but rather statements of putative empirical regularities holding between particulars, which in effect are formulations of empirically true or false theories. From this fact it followed that the supposed epistemic advantages of following the operational imperative fail to obtain: Operational definitions do not enable one to go deductively from knowledge of observables to knowledge of nonobservables, and operational definitions do not provide a means for testing theories about unobservable phenomena. As such, the operational imperative should be rejected in both its weak and strong versions. However, we did discover a grain of truth in the operational imperative; namely, that theories with nonobservable parameters are testable only if these parameters have observable manifestations. But that grain of truth does not lead to the operational imperative as typically advanced, unless one embraces certain epistemological theories about observation which recent work on observation makes highly doubtful.

NOTES

1. The operational imperative apparently was first introduced by Bridgman in 1927 and elaborated in a number of his subsequent works. However, earlier anticipations of the operational imperative are found in C. S. Pierce's pragmatic theory of meaning (see Burks [1977] for discussion).

2. See Hempel (1954, reprint, 1965, 126). He imposes the observation language requirement on the specification of operations and results.

3. For arguments that this is so, cf. Hempel 1952, secs. 5–7; and Suppe 1974b, sec. II–B.

4. For an explicit statement of this argument, see Hempel 1952, 41. Hempel 1954 is largely devoted to developing the same line of argument. In it, Hempel also raises other objections against specific versions of the operational imperative which are not based explicitly on the Received View; these objections do not constitute an attack on the operational imperative in general.

5. Cf. Achinstein 1968, chs. 3–6; Putnam 1962; Suppe 1974b, sec. IV. A critical assessment of Achinstein's and Putnam's attacks is found in ch. 2 above.

6. That the alternative linguistic formulations need not be equivalent follows from the fact that one can have partial formulations of theories (e.g., the difference equation formulations of classical mechanics found in high school physics texts). See section III for a characterization of partial formulations.

7. For simplicity of exposition my examples are taken from the physical sciences, which are particularly susceptible of the analysis. For examples showing the applicability of the analysis to theories in other branches of science, see chs. 2, 7, and 8.

8. Physical quantities need not be measurable quantities. For example, if color were a parameter, then the physical quantities which were possible values of the parameters might be colors as differentiated in a Munsell color table. Physical quantities also might be probability distribution functions, as in quantum theory.

9. The sequence may have a wide variety of different ordinal properties depending on whether, for example, time is viewed as discrete or continuous by the theory. Even though each physical system has a unique sequence of states, the theory may be unable to predict that sequence to the exclusion of all others.

10. Other requirements imposed on the theory, related to this basic one, might ask that it yield certain kinds of predictions, be compatible with certain other theories, or yield answers to certain types of questions, and so on.

11. This is a generalization of the analysis of empirical truth for theories introduced in ch. 2. Note that it only states a necessary condition for the empirical truth of theories. In sec. V, a set of necessary and sufficient conditions is given.

12. See sec. VII for an elaboration.

13. For a detailed discussion of how this works and for arguments sup-

porting the contention that confirmation of theories is reducible to goodness-of-fit problems, see Suppe 1967, sec. 3.4 and ch. 4 below. The inductive logic approach to confirmation as a vehicle for obtaining general or theoretical knowledge in science is rejected in ch. 13.

14. Laws are being construed as extralinguistic entities here; for a defense of the legitimacy of doing so, cf. Achinstein 1971, ch. 1; and Bunge 1959, ch. 10. Here and elsewhere in this chapter, short passages from my 1974c work have been interpolated.

15. The precise properties of these different kinds of laws are explained in ch. 5.

16. If the states are numerically specifiable, or if unique sets of n-tuples of numbers are assigned to each state, then the theory can be construed as a space upon which certain configurations (e.g., trajectories, branching trees, subspaces) have been imposed by the laws of the theory. Beth (1949) and van Fraassen (1970) identify theories with such phase spaces, whereas I tend to view them as canonical iconic models of theories. For a discussion of the relative merits of the two approaches, see Suppe (1974b, 227, n. 565). Phase space models of theories are discussed in sec. VII below.

17. This account only applies to theories with deterministic and indeterministic laws of succession and coexistence. How theories with other sorts of laws can be used to make predictions is discussed in chs. 5 and 6.

18. I am using 'proposition' here in the medieval sense—not the modern sense—as a linguistic entity which can be propounded but need not be asserted. Propositions contain sentences as components, but the sentences do not completely determine the proposition, since the same sentence can be used to express more than one proposition. Roughly speaking, when a proposition is asserted with reference to some subject matter, it becomes a statement. As such, propositions are interpreted declarative sentences which may be propounded with reference to one or more situations, states of affairs, things, and so on. See Geach (1962, 25) for a fuller characterization of this sense of 'proposition'.

19. Beth introduced this distinction (1963, 479–80). My formulation of it is somewhat different.

20. If the friction of the inclined plane were significant, then the proposition would describe only the phenomenon, and a different proposition, embodying a corrected value specifying the corresponding frictionless velocity, would be used with reference to the physical system and the theory. The general conclusion about the necessity of amplified usage still follows.

21. This requirement is rather significant, since not all states in the domain of the theory need be physically possible states. For example, in quantum theory the only physically possible states are those which satisfy the Heisenberg uncertainty principle, and so not all truth-functional combinations of elementary propositions satisfy this empirical significance requirement; as such, quantum theory requires a special quantum logic. My formulation of the empirical significance requirement is one of several possible ones.

22. See my 1973 article where the basic analysis is developed. The same analysis is partially developed and employed in ch. 7 below.

23. This characterization of complex particulars is not the only possible one. This formulation, though, yields individuation characteristics for complex particulars which allow Leibniz' law and the principle of absoluteness of identity to hold, and it also enables one to solve various problems concerning identity and spatio-temporal continuity. See my 1973 article for a discussion of these issues.

24. Cf. ch. 7 and especially Suppe 1973 for details and a discussion of the necessity of so construing the scientific world.

25. Note that physical quantities *never* are numbers. Rather, as J. von Neumann and O. Morgenstein so aptly put it, "[Measurable] physical quantities ... are described by numbers up to [some] ... system of transformations" (1953, 22). As we are using 'physical quantity', the term includes differentiable qualities such as colors, preferences, and so on. (See n. 8 above.)

26. For a discussion of this case, see Shapere 1969, 147–49.

27. More precisely, one commits oneself to the existence of some of the phenomenal systems in the intended scope (past, present, or future), and to the assumption that it is causally possible for the remaining phenomenal systems to exist.

28. [A case can be made for the contention that theories with idealizations really cannot be empirically true, but rather are another sort of conceptual device. My own inclination is that whether one wishes to make this move or employ the definition given in the text probably will hinge on the physical interpretation one makes of the causal modalities implicitly contained in the notion of "causally possible physical system." Presently I believe that the more restrictive definition of truth (where "or else idealizations thereof" is deleted from clause [ii]) probably will prove to be preferable on such metaphysical and related epistemological grounds. If this is done, minor but obvious adjustments will have to be made in the discussion that follows. If the more restrictive empirical truth definition is adopted, one can avoid the counterintuitive conclusion that it is impossible that classical particle mechanics *(CP)* could be empirically true by distinguishing it from *CP**, which is *CP* augmented by the principle that the position of a particular is the point at which its center of gravity is located. Thus, although *CP* could not possibly be empirically true, *CP** possibly could be. In actual practice, physicists employ CP* in most circumstances.] (Recall that brackets indicate new material.)

29. There are other ways in which approximations, simplifications, and idealizations occur in working with theories. Often in manipulating a theory, in using some theory formulation, one makes idealized assumptions, employs approximations, or simplifies the statements of problems to facilitate calculations; these approximations, simplifications, and idealizations may be inconsistent with the theory in question, yet are employed for convenience. Such cases need to be distinguished from the ones we have been considering where the theories themselves are propounded *as* idealizations, approximations, or simplifications.

A pioneering discussion of idealization, approximation, and the like, with respect to theories is to be found in part II of Shapere 1969. In writing this chapter, I have relied heavily on Shapere's work, which contains a number of useful detailed case studies. Shapere's 1969 discussion is marred, however, by his failure to clearly distinguish theories as idealizations, approximations, or simplifications from idealized, approximate, or simplified manipulations of theories; his discussion is concerned largely, but not exclusively, with the latter case. [Cartwright (1983) shares much of my concern with ceteris paribus conditions, idealizations, simplifications, etc., but takes her analysis in a more instrumentalistic direction. See also Hacking (1983).]

30. The answer to the question turns on the following question: Suppose that

If P which is A were C, then P would be B

is true. Under what circumstances does it follow that

If P which is B were C, then P would be A

is true?

31. The fact that a quasi-realism is built into my analysis of theories may lead philosophers, such as Feyerabend (1962a), who are of the opinion that no realistic interpretation has been given and/or can be given for quantum theory to suppose quantum theory is a counterexample to the analysis. Although I do not have enough space to give detailed consideration to the matter here, quantum theory is not a counterexample. However, the following comments may help to dispel the illusion that it is.

Under quasi-realism, a realistic interpretation of quantum theory requires a commitment (1) that the subatomic particles to which the theory is applied exist and (2) that they have the kinds of attributes (with the sorts of physical quantities as values) the theory postulates. Only commitment (2) is problematic, as all proponents of quantum theory accept (1). Physical system states for quantum theory have position and momentum coordinates as parameters, and unlike classical mechanics, the possible values of these are probability distribution functions (characteristic of the Borel subspaces which are projections of wave packets in the von Neumann model), specifying the probabilities with which various measured values can be obtained. To mention just two possibilities, these probability distribution functions can be interpreted as specifying statistical dispositional attributes of the subatomic particles or (following von Neumann) attributes of interacting systems of subatomic particles and measurement apparatus. In either case, one is committed to the functions designating attributes which can be possessed by systems of interacting particulars. Thus under quasi-realism, quantum theory receives a realistic interpretation.

Note also that quasi-realism does not require that, e.g., the ψ function designate any particular or attributes. Its function, like most of the apparatus of quantum theory, is to determine sequences of states—which requires that the ψ function be a theoretical term, but does not require that it be used existentially or designate a particular or an attribute of particulars.

32. The bracketed material beginning here constitutes a substantive addition to the original text.

33. This reflects the fact that it is the task of a theory to characterize all phenomena of a given sort which are causally possible (not just to characterize those phenomena of the sort which happen to occur) and the fact that all theories necessarily must abstract from their phenomena.

34. If the replica is an idealization, then, of course, the satisfaction of the idealization conventions is not met just by following laws or theories. For example, there is no empirically true law or theory which says that if a massive body were extensionless, then its location would be that of its center of gravity. Rather, this is a convention built into the idealization itself. This is not to say, however, that the convention is arbitrary. In the case of classical particle mechanics, it is a convention which must be imposed if rigid body mechanics is to be reducible to classical particle mechanics.

35. For further discussion of what is involved, see Suppes (1962, 1967), Suppe (1974b, secs. IV–E, and V–C) and ch. 4 of the present book.

36. By doing so we are excluding theories, such as quantum theory, which have statistical attributes from our discussion of models. Such theories also admit of mathematical models, though of a quite complicated sort (usually being configurated, infinite-dimensional spaces). Nothing in this chapter involves the details of these complexities, so they will be ignored here. For discussions of models for such theories, cf. Suppe 1967, sec. 2.3, and van Fraassen 1974a.

37. See note 25 above. [These systems of transformations determine symmetry relationships (of which invariances are a species). For an illuminating discussion of symmetry relationships, see van Fraassen 1989, part II.]

38. If, as in classical particle mechanics, varying numbers of defining parameters are required to completely specify the states of physical systems (e.g., in classical particle mechanics an n-body system requires $6n$ defining parameters), then this requirement and the discussion which follows is to be restricted to the class of physical system states having the same number of defining parameters as the dimensionality of the frame of reference. (See ch. IV, sec. 2, for a precise characterization of frames of reference.)

39. For a detailed discussion of how these models relate to the theory and how employment of theories with measurable parameters can be accomplished by working just with these models, see Suppe 1967, secs. 2.3–2.4. A fuller discussion of how these models are employed in experimental measurement is found in ch. 3 of the same work.

When these models are employed in lieu of the theory, one often formulates the theory by specifying the model and system of transformations rather than giving a linguistic formulation of the theory itself (see Suppes 1967 for a discussion of this practice).

Since he has been concerned exclusively with quantitative theories, van Fraassen (1970) identifies the theory with (one of) its phase space models.

While legitimate for his purposes there, the Semantic Conception of Theories must distinguish the theory from its phase space models if its account of theories is to apply to qualitative theories as well.

40. The possibility of such an observational/theoretical distinction being drawn has been seriously challenged, and most philosophers of science deny that it can be drawn. (See ch. 2 for an assessment of these challenges.) Despite the evidence against it, I will grant the distinction to the operational imperative for the moment.

41. There is no guarantee that these assumptions will be met by all theories or their formulations under the foregoing analysis. However, theories meeting this assumption provide the most favorable cases for the operational imperative, and so it will suffice to consider just them.

42. For simplicity of exposition I am presenting the argument in terms of knowledge that they are true; in point of fact, however, on most epistemologies, it would suffice for them to be inductively highly confirmed. Either way, the same sort of argument leads to the same conclusions.

43. In ch. 7, I examine in detail species definitions which also are thought to be operational definitions and argue for a similar conclusion: In natural taxonomies, species definitions are not definitional; rather they are counterfactually true or false statements of putative laws and theories.

44. Cf., for example, Dretske 1969 and Sellars 1956. Chapters 4 and 11 through 13 below further develop these ideas and suggest the outlines of such an approach to epistemology in science.

—— 4 ——
Theories and Phenomena

This chapter explores how, according to the Semantic Conception, theories are experimentally related to phenomena in the experimental testing and confirmation of theories. The Semantic Conception's viability ultimately depends on the extent to which the counterfactual relation of chapter 3 holding between phenomenal systems and their corresponding physical systems can be analyzed. In any experimental application of a theory to phenomena, it is the experimental methodology which must mediate this counterfactual relation. The most promising way to analyze this counterfactual relation, then, is through an examination of the experimental methodology which relates theories to particular phenomena.

Sections I through IV of this chapter develop an analysis of experimental testing for the Semantic Conception: Section I outlines a theory of scientific observation which is compatible with the Semantic Conception. Since theories are given a quasi-realistic physical interpretation on the Semantic Conception, measurement must be construed realistically if it is to play a role in the testing and confirmation of theories; as measurement theory usually is developed conventionalistically, it is necessary to present a realistic theory of measurement. Section II presents such a theory and then argues that measurement is a species of scientific observation. Sections III and IV are concerned with analyzing experimental design and data reduction techniques and present a general account of experimental testing. Finally, in section V, the results of the previous sections are exploited to show how experimental testing can contribute to the confirmation of theories under the Semantic Conception if one accepts a traditional probabilistic-based inductive confirmation theory.

I. OBSERVATION

Observation plays an essential role in any experimental relation of theory to phenomena, whether in the testing or confirmation of the theory, or in the measurement, prediction, or explanation of phenomena. This being the case, various characteristic features of observation must play an essential role in the discussion which follows. Since the full development of an analysis of scientific observation obviously is beyond the scope of this chapter, the content of this section will be admittedly somewhat dogmatic, though I will try to motivate the position I take, which will be developed further in chapters 11 and 12. To further simplify matters, I will restrict my attention to visual scientific observation.

In science, visual observation involves attending to something, in a manner which essentially involves seeing, so as to obtain information that something is the case: One must *see that* something is the case. But it is not merely a case of seeing that, for inference sometimes enjoys a place in visual observation. Consider the following example: Through the use of a Wheatstone bridge apparatus I am trying to determine what the unknown resistance is of a resistor X. I adjust the knobs of the Wheatstone bridge until I see the galvanometer balance, than look at the dial attached to the appropriate potentiometer and thereby see that the dial reads 32.5Ω. However, my Wheatstone bridge is calibrated, so I consult the calibration data and find that when the dial reads 32.5Ω, the true resistance of resistor X is not 32.5Ω, but rather 32.7Ω. From this data and from the fact that the dial read 32.5Ω, I infer that resistor X has a resistance of 32.7Ω. I thereby have *observed that* X has a resistance of 32.7Ω, and my observation has essentially involved both seeing that *and* inference.

Inferences are not allowed to intrude into observation without restriction, however; for whenever it is the case that one has *observed that* ϕ, one thereby *knows that* ϕ.[1] Further, since knowing that ϕ entails that 'ϕ' is true, one can observe that ϕ only if 'ϕ' is true. As such, the inferences allowed in observing that ϕ must be restricted to inferences from ψ to ϕ, where one sees that ψ and where ψ and *known* collateral information χ entail that ϕ. This restriction, together with the fact that seeing that ψ entails knowing that ψ, guarantees that whenever one observes that ϕ, one thereby knows that ϕ. Nevertheless, resort to inferences, while allowed, is not essential to observing that; for one can observe that ϕ just by seeing that ϕ. But not every case of seeing that ϕ is a case of observing that ϕ, for observation must also meet certain requirements of relevance and reliability.

Not all information about the world is scientifically relevant, and seeing that φ is observing that φ only if φ is relevant information. But relevance is not absolute, since information relevant in one area of science may be utterly irrelevant in other areas. Thus, in order to specify the relevance conditions for observation, we must determine what an *area* of scientific investigation is.

Some of Dudley Shapere's work provides a helpful approach to the matter.[2] Through detailed consideration of historical examples, Shapere convincingly argues that scientific research is undertaken with respect to a *scientific domain*, which is a number of items of *information* that come to be associated together as a *body of information* having the following characteristics: The association is based on some well-grounded, significant relationships between the items of information which are suggestive of deeper unities among the items; there is something problematic about the body so related; the problems are important; and (usually) science is "ready" to deal with them. In primitive science, the similarities or relationships which cause items of information to be viewed as a body constituting an object for investigation usually are sensory similarities, but as science progresses the basis often becomes deeper relationships which hold in the face of sensory dissimilarities.

In order to have a scientific domain, it is not enough to have a number of related items of information; rather, it must be the case that the bodies of information, related in certain ways, raise problems or pose questions of various sorts, where the problems or questions are considered significant and are such that some of the questions are reasonably capable of being answered given the current resources of a particular science. These problems can include problems calling for clarification of the limits of the domain, for more precise determination of information in the domain, or for a deeper account or explanation of the relationships among the items of information in the domain, problems concerning the testing of theories designed to account for the domain, and so on. Thus a scientific domain rationally gives rise to a set of questions (statements of problems) which we will call the set of *domain questions*.

In all but the most primitive sciences, theory, experimental canons, and information other than that comprising the scientific domain are involved in the generation of domain questions and in attempts to answer such questions. Let us call these theories, experimental canons, and other information *background information*. If one opts to work in a certain domain, one thereby normally is committed to accepting all the information in that domain and all background information that is not challenged by the domain questions; collectively this information constitutes what we call the *background to a scientific domain*.[3]

In terms of scientific domains, we can now specify the relevance and reliability requirements imposed on observation. A case of seeing that ϕ is a case of observing that ϕ only if one sees that ϕ in the process of investigating a scientific domain, and ϕ is a partial answer to one or more questions in the set of domain questions for that domain.[4] Similarly, if an observation that ϕ involves inferring ϕ from some ψ (which is seen that) and from collateral knowledge, ϕ must be a partial answer to one or more domain questions (though ψ need not be). This is our relevance condition.

The results of scientific observation must be *reliable* as well as relevant. One mark of reliability is *replicability*—whether other observers in the scientific community could in principle recreate the conditions of observation and obtain the same experimental results. If observation that B is D were restricted only to cases in which one sees the B being D without recourse to instruments (if all observation were the direct observation of the positivists),[5] then there would be nothing more to observational reliability than mere replicability. But observation typically involves recourse to instrumentation of varying degrees of complexity and elaborateness, and in many cases one *observes* that B is D without ever *seeing* the B or its being D.[6] For example, one observes that an α particle is emitted by looking at a light flash on a scintillation counter. These features of observation make the reliability of observation in this case depend on something more than mere replicability.

One might argue that there is no real problem of reliability other than mere replicability here, for in the scintillation counter case one sees that the light is flashing and then *infers* from that information that an α particle has been emitted, thereby observing that it has. So long as the inference is sanctioned by accepted laws, there is no question of reliability other than mere replicability. This case is typical, but the argument will not do; for in the scintillation counter case, I can *noninferentially* observe that an α particle has been emitted by *seeing that* an α particle has been emitted: It is possible to see that B is D without ever seeing B or its being D.[7]

More generally, unless an observation involves data reduction (as in the case of the Wheatstone bridge example), whenever it is possible to observe that ϕ, it is possible to do so by seeing that ϕ. And when one observes that B is D by seeing that B is D under circumstances where one cannot see either B or its being D, then we have problems of reliability which are more than mere questions of replicability. In such cases (assuming them to be noninferential), our ability to see that ϕ consists in our having a visual sensory experience such that, given what we already know about the objects referred to in 'ϕ', we could not be having that experience unless ϕ were the case. And whenever I do see that ϕ, I thereby know that ϕ. For example, sitting in the car, I see the gas gauge reading 'empty'; since the gas gauge works, the ignition is on, and so forth, I could not be having this visual experience unless the gas tank were empty. By virtue of that fact I am able to see that, hence know that, the gas tank is empty. My seeing that and knowledge are noninferential and do not require that I know the empirical regularities by virtue of which what I saw enabled me to see that ϕ.[8]

Whenever 'observing that' involves this sort of 'seeing that', unreliability in the observation usually will stem from the possibility that the visual sensory experience one is having might not be such that ϕ *must* be the case under the circumstances. The same possibility occurs whenever apparatus is involved in the observation. However, if the background to the domain enables one to explain how it is that a normal observer could not have the sort of visual experience under the circumstances, given all he knows about the objects referred to by 'ϕ', unless ϕ were the case, then the reliability of the observation is guaranteed, given replicability. For example, in the scintillation counter case, for any scientific domain wherein use of the scintillation counter would produce relevant information, the background to the domain will contain the resources necessary to explain how it is that one could not see the light on the scintillation counter flash unless it were the case that an α particle is being emitted. Thus I can meet the reliability requirement for observation and thereby observe that an α particle is being emitted, even though I only see a light flash. Of course, no such explanation is required for cases where one can see that B is D by seeing B being D without recourse to instruments; for in such cases replicability guarantees reliability.

If an observation involves inferences, to be reliable these inferences must be sanctioned by the background to the domain (see sec. V for a discussion of "sanctioning"). Putting together all these considerations, we obtain the following account of visually observing that in science:

With respect to a given scientific domain, one *visually observes that B is D* if and only if

(i) Either

    (a) one sees that B is D by seeing B being D without resort to apparatus; or

(b) one sees that B is D, either by seeing something other than B being D or by resort to apparatus, but one can explain in terms of the background to the domain how one could not have seen what one did see under the circumstances unless B, possessing all the attributes (other than D) you know it to have, were D; or

(c) one sees that ϕ in satisfaction of either (a) or (b), where ϕ asserts something other than that B is D, and one infers that B is D from the fact that ϕ together with known collateral information (including theories) sanctioned by the domain, its background, and details of the experimental design;

and

(ii) 'B is D' is a partial answer to one or more questions in the set of domain questions for the domain.

It follows that whenever one visually observes that ϕ, one thereby knows that ϕ. For simplicity of exposition, I have stated the condition in terms of propositions of the form 'B is D', but the analysis just indicated can be extended straightforwardly to other forms of propositions. Although this section's discussion hardly constitutes a full defense of this account of scientific observation, I think it does render it plausible; ultimately, it is defensible, so I will assume it in what follows.[9] With this account of observation, we now are in a position to investigate the ways theories are applied experimentally to phenomena.

II. MEASUREMENT

Theories are applied to phenomenal systems within their intended scopes for a variety of purposes, including the testing of the theory, prediction of phenomena, and the explanation of phenomena. Basic to any application of a theory to a phenomenal system P is the observational determination which physical system S stands in the replicating relation set forth in chapter 3 to P. When the defining parameters of the theory are measurable, this observational determination usually is made through measurement. We now turn to a consideration of measurement, including the way it functions in observation and the application of theories to phenomena.

Roughly speaking, a parameter is *measurable* when it is a kind of attribute which admits of gradation, its various gradations being the physical quantities which the parameter can have as values. *Measure-*

ment of a parameter essentially involves two steps: (1) the attachment of different numbers to different physical quantities for the parameter, where the number attached to a physical quantity is called the *measure* of the physical quantity (this amounts to determining the measurement *scale* for the parameter) and (2) the experimental determination of a physical quantity by determining its measure on a given scale. Most treatments combine these two steps so as to make the first step parasitic upon the second: The operational procedures for determining the measure of a physical quantity also define which numbers are to be the measures of which physical quantities. To do so is to let the measurement procedures determine the scales—which commits one to a *conventionalistic* view of measurement. For example, Brian Ellis tells us that we have a measurement scale if and only if we have an appropriate operational procedure for assigning numbers to different physical quantities, where two procedures are procedures for measuring on the same scale if, whenever they are deemed to be applicable, they lead to the same numerical assignments being made to the same physical quantities.[10] But this seems to me undesirable, for it in effect restricts a measurement scale to that range of values for parameters which at a given time we are able to assign measures to using *existing* measurement procedures; this means that the measurement scales are not defined for any physical quantities outside that range. In actual practice (e.g., in *Gedanken* experiments), however, we do work with measures for quantities for which we have no experimental procedures for determining their measures. Under Ellis' account, the measurement scales involved are undefined, making such practices impossible. This strongly suggests that it is undesirable to *identify* the specification of a measurement scale with available measurement procedures. Accordingly, in what follows I will treat the two as separate but related issues.

My first concern is to characterize scales of measurement. Since my account must explain the use of measurement in conjunction with theories, and since theories are interpreted quasi-realistically on the Semantic Conception, my account of measurement scales must be realistic, not conventionalistic. The quasi-realism of the Semantic Conception rests on the observation that phenomenal systems are systems of particulars having *intrinsic attributes*—that is, possessing properties and entering into relations independently of how we conceptualize things. To obtain a realistic account of measurement scales, then, I must make the order properties of my measurement scales reflect orders determined by the intrinsic attributes of particulars.

What sorts of orders can the intrinsic attributes impose on particulars? In chapter 2 we saw that the kinds of attributes particulars can possess are parameters, and the different attributes of the kind particulars can have are physical quantities; physical quantities thus are possible values of the parameters. Let Q be the set of all possible physical quantities which can be values for a parameter p—that is, let Q be the set of all those physical quantities of kind p which particulars could possess.[11] Now, let A be a particular of kind p; then A will have a number of other intrinsic attributes including intrinsic relations it enters into at various times. If the intrinsic relations A and the other particulars of kind p enter into are such that they impose a *linear order* on the particulars of kind p, then p is measurable. More precisely:

Let p be a parameter and let Q be the set of possible physical quantities for p. Then p is *measurable* if and only if there are intrinsic relationships $R_<$, $R_>$, and $R_=$ such that for any two different particulars, A and B, having physical quantities q_A and q_B of kind p respectively, either $A\,R_<\,B$, $A\,R_>\,B$, or $A\,R_=\,B$, where
(1) $R_=$ is symmetric and transitive;
(2) $R_>$ and $R_<$ are assymmetrical and transitive; and
(3) $R_=$, $R_>$, and $R_<$ are mutually exclusive alternatives in the sense that if one in fact holds, neither of the others in fact can, but if one in fact holds, it is logically possible that the others could hold.[12]

Collectively $R_<$, $R_>$, and $R_=$ constitute a *quasi-serial ordering* of particulars of kind p.[13] Derivatively, that quasi-serial ordering of particulars of kind p imposes a *linear ordering* on Q, namely:

For any q_1, $q_2 \in Q$,
$q_1 <_p q_2$ if and only if $A\,R_<\,B$,
$q_1 >_p q_2$ if and only if $A\,R_>\,B$, and
$q_1 =_p q_2$ if and only if $A\,R_=\,B$,
where A is any particular of kind p having q_1 and B is any particular of kind p having q_2.

(The subscripts on the equality and inequality signs indicate equality or inequality with respect to p.)

Thus p is measurable if and only if the intrinsic relationships into which particulars of kind p enter impose a linear ordering on Q in the above manner. Since it is possible that the particulars of kind p may enter into different sets of intrinsic relationships $R_>$, $R_<$, and $R_=$ which satisfy the above conditions, it is possible that Q may be linearly ordered in a variety of ways.[14] Since intrinsic relationships impose the orderings, they are natural orderings of Q. When we wish to refer to Q under a particular linear ordering, we will use '**Q**'.

A measurement *scale* is a function which assigns numbers to the members of **Q** for a measurable parameter p in such a way that the ordinal properties of the numbers mirror the linear ordering of **Q**. More precisely,

> Let **N** be an ordered set of numbers having ordinal properties such that '<', '>', and '=' hold under their standard definitions. (That is, **N** must have an ordering which satisfies all the conditions for being a linear ordering; other ordinal properties may be imposed as well.) Then a function f from **Q** *into* **N** is a *complete scale* for Q if and only if the following conditions are satisfied for arbitrary q_1, q_2:
>
> If q_1, $q_2 \in \mathbf{Q}$ and $q_1 =_p q_2$, then $f(q_1) = f(q_2)$;
> if q_1, $q_2 \in \mathbf{Q}$ and $q_1 <_p q_2$, then $f(q_1) < f(q_2)$; and
> if q_1, $q_2 \in \mathbf{Q}$ and $q_1 >_p q_2$, then $f(q_1) > f(q_2)$.

Note that this definition requires that the domain of f be **Q**, but does not require that **N** be the range of f—that is, it does not require that every number in **N** be assigned to a physical quantity in **Q** (thus, f is *into*, not *onto* **N**).

If there is a function f with domain $\mathbf{D} \subseteq \mathbf{Q}$ such that it satisfies the restriction of the above conditions to **D**, we say f is a *partial scale* for **Q**. Recall that when one asserts a theory T, one commits oneself to a set R being the possible physical quantities which can be values for a parameter p (ch. 3, sec. V). If according to T, R is linearly ordered and a scale s for p meets the conditions for being a complete scale for R (where it is possible that $R \neq Q$), we say that f is a *complete scale relative to* T. Similarly, we define what it is for f to be a *partial scale relative to* T. From this point on we use 'scale' to refer indifferently to complete and partial scales and scales which are complete or partial relative to T.

For a given scale f, $f(q)$ is called the *measure* of q relative to f. The choice of **N** determines what sorts of arithmetic operations can be performed on the measures for $q \in \mathbf{Q}$. It may be the case that some arithmetic operations allowed by **N** will not yield physically significant results, since the result of performing the operation may not be the measure of any $q \in \mathbf{Q}$. For example, suppose that our parameter is length and that f is a partial scale for length restricted to ordinary-sized physical objects. Measurements of such lengths usually are significant only to three decimal places, so let us suppose that f assigns, as measures to lengths, numbers having at most the first three decimal places nonzero. Now, suppose we measure a square table, having sides of lengths q_1 and q_2, where $f(q_1) = 1.000$ and $f(q_2) = 1.000$. Then we solve the equation $f^2(q_1) + f^2(q_2) = x^2$ for x, getting $\sqrt{2}$, in an attempt to find the length of the diagonal of the table top. But $\sqrt{2}$ has more than the first three decimal places nonzero, so it fails to be $f(q)$ for any length q. As such, $\sqrt{2}$ fails to be the measure of any length, so $\sqrt{3}$ is not an empirically significant operation relative to f.

In order for an arithmetic operation o defined on N to be *empirically significant*, the following condition must be met.

For every $q_1, \ldots, q_n$ in the domain of f,
$$o(f(q_1), \ldots, f(q_n)) = f(r)$$
for some r in the domain of f.

Thus, for example, if in our table case the operation o had been to find the solution x of $f^2(q_1) + f^2(q_2) = x^2$ truncated to three decimal places, then the number obtained by this operation would have been a measure of the diagonal of the table. Only empirically significant operations for a given scale yield measures of physical quantities.

We can now characterize frames of reference in terms of the notion of a measurement scale. Let T be a theory with measurable defining parameters $p_1, \ldots, p_n$. Then $\langle f_1, \ldots, f_n \rangle$ is a *frame of reference* for T if and only if each of the f_i is a complete scale for p_i and at the same time a complete scale relative to T for p_i.[15] The frame-of-reference transformation group for a model of a theory (see ch. 3, sec. VII) does three things: (1) it specifies what admissible frames of reference the theory will countenance; (2) it indicates which measures in different frames of reference F_1 and F_2 are measures of the same physical quantity; and (3) it indicates which physical quantities are invariant under changes in frame of reference. As such, formulations of frame-of-reference transformations are true or false.

Measurement is an indirect process whereby scales are employed to determine what physical quantities particulars possess: Rather than directly ascertain which q is the value of p for a particular, one adopts a scale f for p, employs some measurement procedure to determine $f(q)$, and thereby indirectly determines q.

We now investigate the various types of measurement procedures possible for determining the measures of physical quantities. Procedures for measuring physical quantities of kind p can be distinguished on the basis of whether they involve the measurement of any other physical quantities of kinds other than p. Those which do not are called *direct* measurement procedures.

Direct measurement procedures often are referred to as *fundamental measurement* procedures.[16] Suppose a is a particular of kind p, where p is measurable and q (a property of a of kind p) is the value of p for a.[17] A direct or fundamental measurement procedure for determining the measure of q relative to scale f for p in essence is a procedure C for the direct comparison of a with respect to p against a system of standards for f, and whenever $a =_p b$ (where b is in the system of standards), assigning to a whatever measure $f(q)$ is assigned to b. A number of technical notions will need to be introduced in order to make this precise. Since fundamental measurement procedures for p relative to f usually apply only to the values of p for some range $R \subseteq Q$, we will relativize these notions to some range R.

By a procedure C for the *direct comparison* of a against a system of standards for f in range R, we mean some general procedure involving a and the b in the system of standards wherein one observes that $a <_p b$, $a >_p b$, or $a =_p b$. Further, a *system of standards* for p with respect to f in range R is a finite collection of objects of kind p, each object possessing some q as value of p, with $f(q)$ assigned to a standard as value when it possesses q. If a system of standards is such that for every q in R, there is an object in the system of standards which is q, we say that the system of standards is *complete for R;* otherwise the system is *incomplete for R*. Whenever a system of standards is incomplete for range R, an extended system of standards E for p in range R must be resorted to; such extended systems of standards are generated by a fundamental operation:

> A binary operation O is a *fundamental operation* for p in range R if and only if, for every $a_1, a_2, \ldots$; b_1, b_2, c_1 of kind p in range R,
> (1) $O(a_1, b_1) =_p O(a_2, b_2) =_p O(b_2, a_2)$,
>   where $a_1 =_p a_2$, $b_1 =_p b_2$;
> (2) $O(a_1, b_1) >_p b_1$;
> (3) $O(O(a_1, b_1), c_1) =_p O(a_1, O(b_1, c_1))$; and
> (4) if $a_1 =_p a_2 =_p a_3 =_p \ldots$, and $a_1 <_p b_1$,
>   then there is a positive integer N such that for all $n > N$,
> $O(O(\ldots O(a_1, a_2), \ldots), a_n) >_p b_1$.

An example of such an operation O, *where p is length*, would be the operation of placing objects end to end. Whenever an iterated sequence of applications of operation O to $a_1, \ldots, a_n$ produces an object b in E such that $b =_p O(O(\ldots O(a_1, a_2), \ldots), a_n)$, we will use '$O(a_1, \ldots, a_n)$' to designate the result of performing that iterated sequence of operations on $a_1, \ldots, a_n$.

An *extended system of standards* E for range R of p, relative to scale f generated by O from set S of standards, is a set A of objects of kind p which satisfies the following conditions:

(1) Every object in A is q for some q in R;
(2) O is a fundamental operation for p in range R;
(3) A is generated from a set of standards S for range R of p relative to scale f according to the following rules:
  (a) If a is in the set of standards S, then a is in A;
  (b) if a is in A and $b =_p a$, then b may be added to A;
  (c) if $a_1, \ldots, a_n$ $(n \geq 2)$ are objects of kind p such that
    $a_1 =_p a_2 =_p \ldots =_p a_n,$
    and $O(a_1, \ldots, a_n) =_p b$ for some b in A,
    then $a_1, \ldots, a_n$ may be added to A;
  (d) if $a_1, \ldots, a_n (n \geq 2)$ are objects in A,
    and $b =_p O(a_1, \ldots, a_n)$, then b may be added to A; and
(4) For every object a in A, if a is q, then its measure f(q) is known.

Notice that an extended system of standards E may be such that for some q in R, there is no object in E which is q. Also note that every system of standards is an extended system of standards.

We are now in a position to define precisely what a fundamental measurement procedure is:

A *fundamental measurement procedure*, $\langle C, S, O, E, R \rangle$, is a procedure C for the direct comparison of objects a of kind p in range R with members of an extended system of standards E for p in range R (which has been generated by the fundamental operation O from the set of standards S) so as to determine equality or inequality with respect to p, which assigns to such an object a the measure of a member b of E whenever C determines that $a =_p b$.

We will illustrate this definition with a very simple example of a fundamental measurement. Suppose we have a resistor X and we wish to determine its resistance r' (see fig. 1). Our procedure C is to put it into the following circuit (which is a primitive Wheatstone bridge), where R_1 and R_2 have the same resistance, P_1 is a variable resistor which has been calibrated, and G is a galvanometer. P_1 adjusted to its various different resistances constitutes our extended system of standards, and its dial reading together with its calibration enables us to know its value on scale f for each different adjustment. Then we adjust P_1 until we obtain zero deflection on the galvanometer, at which time

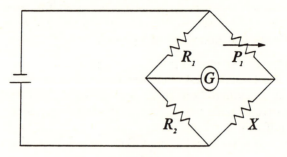

Figure 1

we observe that the adjusted resistance of P_1 is identical to that of X, and we assign the known value of P_1 so adjusted to X.

This example of fundamental measurement is particularly revealing, because it displays the extent to which fundamental measurement may involve the use of an apparatus; in such a case, fundamental measurement involves "theory-laden" observation. In the example, all that we saw was that when the resistor X was put in the apparatus and P_1 was adjusted a certain way, the galvanometer showed no deflection. This enabled us to *see that* X and P_1, so adjusted to reading r, had the same resistance *only* because given the circumstances, there would not have been zero-deflection unless this were the case. Then, inferring the true resistance r' from r and the known calibration information, we were able to observe that (hence came to know that) the resistance of X was r'; to do so we had to be able to explain the fact that, under the circumstances, there would not be zero-deflection unless the resistance of X were r' in terms of the electrical theory and the design of the apparatus. The basis for that explanation was part of our domain background. Thus our observation that the resistance of X was r' depended essentially on our theory. More generally given the account of observation in section I, whenever fundamental measurement involves an apparatus, some theory must be assumed in order to make the observations required in performing the fundamental measurement.

Next we turn to *derived measurement* procedures, wherein the measurement of p essentially involves measuring some other parameter. Let $p_1, \ldots, p_n$ be parameters and let $Q_i (1 \leq i \leq n)$ be the sets of possible values for the p_i. Suppose we determine (usually by measurement) that p_2 has q_2 as value $, \ldots,$ and that p_n has value q_n in some situation. Suppose further that we have scales $f_1, \ldots, f_n$ for these parameters and that these scales constitute the frame of reference for some phase space model M of some theory T, and that the laws in the model's formulation together with various boundary conditions, and so on, entail that $f_1(q_1) = g(f_2(q_2), \ldots, f_n(q_n))$ for some numerical function g. Then we determine (by direct or indirect measurement) what the measures $f_2(q_2), \ldots, f_n(q_n)$ are, and then use the function g to determine what $f_1(q_1)$ is. This process is known as the *derived measurement* of p_1 relative to scale f_1.

An example of derived measurement would be determining the height (on scale f_2) of a mercury column of known diameter (on scale f_3), and then using a numerical law relating these physical quantities (on scales f_2 and f_3) to the temperature of the mercury (on scale f_1) and another law relating the temperature of the mercury (on scale f_1) relative to a known coefficient of heat transmission (on scale f_4) to determine the measure of the temperature of the surrounding medium (on scale f_1). Notice that all derived measurement is "theory-laden" in that bodies of theory must be assumed in order to carry it out. When we work in a given domain, these bodies of theory must be sanctioned by the domain's background.

Our account of measurement is realistic in that on our account measures always are measures of physical quantities possessed by causally possible particulars. Now, in actual practice a given measurement procedure is often used to set up a scale,[18] but there is no guarantee that the resulting scale will meet our scale definition. For the operational definition of a parameter does not guarantee that any objects do possess values of that parameter.[19] And if (as is done when proceeding operationally) we operationally define a scale in terms of a measurement procedure, we may obtain a *pseudoscale*, in the sense that the scale fails to measure any parameter actually possessed by the objects being measured; such pseudoscales fail to qualify under our definition.[20] I suspect that many "scales" used in the behavioral sciences may be pseudoscales. Let us call any procedures involving a pseudoscale, which would otherwise qualify as direct or indirect measurement under our account were the scale a (partial) scale rather than a pseudoscale, *pseudomeasurement*.

For the purposes of explaining how experimental testing contributes to the confirmation of theories (see sec. V), it is essential that we not count pseudomeasurement as measurement. This is not to say, however, that pseudomeasurement is worthless and scientifically illegitimate if it is recognized for what it is. So recognized, it is just as scientifically legitimate and valuable as artificial taxonomies.[21] For example, as an admissions officer for my department's graduate program, I operationally define a "scale" for "potential as a graduate student" in terms of test scores, grade point averages, strength and reliability measures of letters of recommendation, and so on; then I use it to assign a measure of potential as a graduate student to each candidate and fill our entrance quota with the applicants whose measures are highest. Now, suppose that "potential as a graduate student" is not a parameter that has intrinsic physical or mental quantities possessed by humans as values. Then my scale is a pseudoscale, and my measurement is a pseudomeasurement. But if my decision procedure succeeds in selecting highly successful students (i.e., has high predictive validity), then my use of pseudomeasurement is thoroughly justified. What would be unjustified is to suppose that potential as a graduate student is an intrinsic attribute possessed by students, or to maintain that I have discovered an empirically true theory relating potential as a graduate student to other properties of individuals.

In discussing the Wheatstone bridge example above, it was tacitly assumed that the experimental determination that the resistor had resistance r' was a case of observing that the resistor had resistance r'. To evaluate that assumption, we need to ask: What are the circumstances in which measurement qualifies as observation?

We saw in section I that in order to observe that ϕ, ϕ must be factually or counterfactually true. Can measurement propositions be factually true? Consider the proposition 'the resistor has resistance 35Ω'. This proposition asserts that the resistor has an intrinsic attribute which (on the ohm scale of measurement) carries the measure of 35 ohms. In effect, it asserts that the resistor has a certain intrinsic attribute, using '35 Ω' to specify what that attribute is. The proposition would be factually true, then, if the resistor had the attribute designated by '35 Ω'.[22] What this example shows is that measurement scales are systematic linguistic procedures for designating intrinsic attributes of objects, and that measurement procedures are systematic ways of determining which attributes particulars have. Although scales and measurement procedures are somewhat arbitrary human fabrications, this in no way prevents measurement statements from being factually or counterfactually true or false. On the other hand, it clearly follows that propositions stating the results of pseudomeasurements can never be factually true.

Since measurement propositions can be factually true, it is possible to observe that ϕ, where ϕ is a measurement proposition. In particular, it is possible to see that ϕ when ϕ is a measurement proposition; for if it is the case that, given what you know about an object B, you would not be having the visual experience you are having unless B possessed a particular attribute D and '$f(D)$' is the measure of D on some scale f, then it will be the case that 'B is $f(D)$' must be true, and you thereby are able to see that B is $f(D)$, hence know that B is $f(D)$. If inferences are involved in determining that B is $f(D)$, the epistemic situation is not appreciably changed. Since any resort to instrumentation or derived measurement (which involves inference) requires the possession of theory sanctioned by the background to the domain adequate to explain why it is the case that you could not be having the experiences you are having unless B were $f(D)$; you thereby can observe that B is $f(D)$, providing B being $f(D)$ is relevant and you know those portions of the background to the domain used to make the inference. Thus measurement can be observation. In practice, our visual experiences will be unable to distinguish between $f(D)$ and $f(D')$ where $D' \in [D-\epsilon, D+\epsilon]$ for some ϵ which is a measure of the reliability of the measurement apparatus issue. Thus what observation via measurement establishes is not that B is $f(D)$, but rather that B is $f(D) \pm \epsilon$. This corresponds to actual scientific practice and causes no particular problems for the quasi-realistic construal of the Semantic Conception. (These qualifications will be tacitly assumed from this point on.)

Not only can measurement be observation, but legitimate measurement *must be* observation. For our account of fundamental measurement requires observing that $a =_p b$, where b is in the extended system of standards and a is the particular being measured, and requires assigning b's measure to a; hence fundamental measurement will be a case of observing that. Derived measurement requires inferring the measure of a from known measures of $b_1, \ldots, b_n$ by recourse to known theories. These measures are obtained fundamentally or derived from still other measures which ultimately depend solely on fundamentally measured quantities; thus any derived measurement will be inferentially obtained from observationally obtained measures; hence derived measurements are cases of observing that when the inferences are on the basis of known theories sanctioned by the background to the domain and known collateral information. To conclude, measurement is a species of observation wherein whatever inferences are involved are sanctioned by our background knowledge.[23] By virtue of this fact we may confine our attention to observation, treating measurement as a special case.

III. EXPERIMENTAL TESTING

Physical systems are abstract, possibly idealized replicas of phenomenal systems, representing how the phenomenal system *would have behaved were it the case* that only the basic defining parameters of the theory exerted an influence and the idealized conditions were met. In applying the theory to phenomena, data about the phenomenal system must be converted into data about the corresponding physical system. This can be accomplished in two ways. First, we can observe the phenomena in highly controlled experimental situations in which we can closely approximate the fiction that only the defining parameters for the theory exert an influence on the behavior of the phenomenal system (the controls being such that all other parameters exert a negligible influence). Second, the phenomenal system can be observed under less controlled circumstances wherein we know what "outside" factors (other than the defining parameters) influencing its behavior are present, and we are able to isolate their influence on the values of the defining parameters. Then we can convert data about the actual behavior of the physical system to data characteristic of what the behavior of the phenomenal system *would be, were* it the case that only the abstracted parameters were exerting an influence. In both cases, if the theory idealizes phenomena, further conversion of data is required; data about the phenomenal system must be converted into data about the corresponding physical system. These two methods of obtaining data about phenomenal systems constitute the main approaches to applying theories to phenomena.

Both approaches require an *experimental design* in order to apply theory T to phenomena; it is comprised of the experimental setup, the instrumentation, and measurement or data-gathering procedures, and so on, to be employed. A statement of these general design principles, and so on, specifies a theory called the *theory of experimental design.* Not all considerations involved in the experiment are made explicit in this theory; in particular, various ceteris paribus conditions (unstated experimental control conditions) are tacitly presumed.

One also must take into account that running the experiment in accordance with the theory of experimental design will yield *raw data* about the actual values of the parameters of the phenomenal system. If the experiment involves measurement, the experimental design must be compatible with the basic measurement conditions (set forth in sec. II). Accordingly, the theory of experimental design must include a theoretical explanation about how the measurement operations in question enable one to observe that a is $f(q)$ (raw data) under the experimental circumstances. If the experiment does not involve measurement, the theory of experimental design must be such that if the theory is empirically true, one could not perceive (e.g., see) what one does under the experimental circumstances, unless the raw data statements were true. The theory of experimental design explains how this is possible relative to the ceteris paribus conditions being met.

Once the experiment has been run in accordance with the theory of experimental design, the resulting raw data may not be in a form compatible with T. In particular, if parameters other than the defining parameters exert a nonnegligible influence on the phenomenal system, the raw data must be corrected so as to obtain *reduced data* about what the phenomenon would have been had the "outside" influences not been present. In addition, if the theory idealized the phenomena, the idealization conventions involved must be used to further alter the data. Also, calibration corrections of raw data may be required. It is the *theory of the data* which determines how the raw experimental data are to be converted into canonical-form data about the behavior of the corresponding physical system.

Finally, once the data have been reduced via the theory of the data, they describe a physical system, and now the theory can be directly applied to the data—for example, to make predictions (see ch. 3, sec. I). To summarize, an application of the theory T to a phenomenon depends upon appropriate ceteris paribus conditions, a theory of experimental design, and a theory of data; together they constitute the *theory of the experiment.*[24]

Suppose that we experiment with a phenomenal system in circumstances for which we have a theory of the experiment which is applicable relative to certain ceteris paribus conditions being met, and we then perform the experiment in accordance with the theory of the experiment and thereby obtain reduced data about the corresponding physical system. Regardless of whether measurement is involved in the theory of the experiment, observation is involved in obtaining this data whenever the theory of the experiment is known. Given the simplifying assumptions of section I, we may assume it is visual observation. Does it follow that we have observed that ψ, where ψ is a relevant statement of the reduced data?

Suppose that the reduced data proposition ψ is counterfactually true of the phenomenal system and is relevant (in the sense of sec. I). Further suppose that the theory of the experiment is empirically true (in accordance with ch. 3, sec. V), that it is known and sanctioned by the background to the domain, and that the ceteris paribus conditions are met. Then it will be the case that the theory of experimental design is empirically true and that if it has been correctly followed, the raw data statements obtained will be factually true. Moreover, from this chapter's discussion thus far, it follows that one has observed that ϕ, where ϕ is a raw data statement. Furthermore, the theory of data also will be empirically true, so any data statement ψ correctly obtained from such raw data statements ϕ will be counterfactually true. According to the account of inference-aided observation in section I, it follows that we have observed that ψ (the reliability condition on observation having been met by virtue of the theory of the experiment). Thus we may conclude that if one obtains counterfactually (or factually) true reduced data propositions ψ in accordance with an empirically true theory of the experiment which is known and sanctioned by the domain in question, and if the ceteris paribus conditions are met, then one has observed that ψ. (Of course, if the theory of the experiment is empirically false, or not known, or if the experiment is not carried out in accordance with it, or if the ceteris paribus conditions are not met, one fails to observe that ψ.) These findings indicate how theory-laden observation can be and how wide the range of observable phenomena is. Only when an observation yielding reduced data about a physical system involves neither apparatus nor inference is a theory of the experiment not required.

An *experimental test* of a theory consists in the comparison of a theory's predictions against observed data obtained via a theory of experiment (when one is required). Whether a theory is *testable* against a given phenomenal system will depend upon what theories of the experiment are sanctioned by the background to the domain. In light of this fact, there is little point in attempting to discover some absolute sense in which theories are or are not testable (as the positivists tried to do).

IV. THEORIES OF THE EXPERIMENT AND BACKGROUNDS TO DOMAINS

Whenever observation involves apparatus or inference, a known theory of the experiment is an essential part of the observation; thus theories of the experiment occupy a central place in scientific observation. This section explores the theoretical properties of theories of the experiment. Since apparatus are involved in all but the most primitive scientific observations, we will confine our attention primarily to cases of observation involving apparatus.

Suppose we are experimentally applying a theory T to a phenomenal system P by observing P using apparatus G. In this observation, the following parameters are of interest: (1) the defining parameters $p_1, \ldots, p_n (n \geq 1)$ of the theory T; (2) parameters $v_1, \ldots, v_m (m \geq 0)$, characteristic of particulars in P, other than $p_1, \ldots, p_n$, which under the experimental circumstances exert a nonnegligible influence on some of the $p_1, \ldots, p_n$; (3) those parameters $g_1, \ldots, g_k (k \geq 1)$ of the apparatus G which are relevant to the observation (e.g., positions of switches, dial readings, hookups of wires, refractory indices of telescopes, etc.); (4) parameters $e_1, \ldots, e_l (l \geq 0)$ which, under the experimental circumstances, exert a nonnegligible influence on some of the $g_1, \ldots, g_k$; and (5) various parameters involved in ceteris paribus conditions. Note that some of these parameters may occur on more than one list—as will be the case, for example, if the apparatus affects the values of any of the $p_1, \ldots, p_n$, in which case some of the parameters of type (2) also will be type (3) parameters. The apparatus G itself is a phenomenal system, and in order for the apparatus to play any significant role in the observation, there must be some correlation between the state s_P of the phenomenal system P and the state s_G of the apparatus G at various times during the course of the experiment; for it is by determining the state of the apparatus that we are able to determine the state of P at the same time. In order for this sort of correlation of states of P and G to occur, it must be the case that P and G *interact* in such a way that what state G is in is influenced by the state P is in. The theory of experimental design must account for this interaction; thus it requires laws of interaction.

The theory of experimental design in question will have the parameters $p_1, \ldots, p_n, v_1, \ldots, v_m, g_1, \ldots, g_k$, and $e_1, \ldots, e_l$, and inter alia, it will specify that P and G interact under the circumstances in such a way that the values of (at least some of the) $p_1, \ldots, p_n$ are functions of the values of the remaining parameters.[25] A possible set of simultaneous values for $p_1, \ldots, p_n, v_1, \ldots, v_m, g_1, \ldots, g_k$ and $e_1, \ldots, e_l$ will be a state of the theory of experimental design physical system that corresponds to the phenomenal system consisting of P and G interacting. Using laws of interaction from the theory of experimental design, from a determination of the values of $v_1, \ldots, v_m, g_1, \ldots, g_k$, and $e_1, \ldots, e_l$ we then determine the values for one or more of the $p_1, \ldots, p_n$ characteristic of the interaction of P and G under the circumstances. Although these values are characteristic of the theory of the correspondence of experimental design state s' to the phenomenal system consisting of P and G interacting, if $m > 0$, the values of $p_1, \ldots, p_n$ are *not* characteristic of the theory T physical system state s corresponding to the phenomenal system P; for the values of $p_1, \ldots, p_n$ so obtained are influenced nonnegligibly by $v_1, \ldots, v_m$. The theory of the data then describes how to convert the values of $p_1, \ldots, p_n$ obtained via the theory of the experimental design into values of $p_1, \ldots, p_n$ characteristic of what P *would have been* were it the case the $v_1, \ldots,$

v_m were not influencing $p_1, \ldots, p_n$ (i.e., to determine the theory T physical system state s). Putting these observations together with the fact that the theories of experimental design and data are components of the theory of the experiment, we obtain the following general result: Whenever an observation involves significant recourse to apparatus, the theory of the experiment contains laws of interaction. It is this fact which explains why apparatus can augment our observational abilities.

Two sorts of laws of interaction can be distinguished. First, there are *noninterfering laws of interaction;* under these, P would be in the same state, under the circumstances, were the apparatus G not present. In this case none of the $g_1, \ldots, g_k$ occur among the $v_1, \ldots, v_m$. Second, there are *interfering laws of interaction*, under which the interaction of P and G alters or affects the values of one or more of the $p_1, \ldots, p_n$. In this case some of the $g_1, \ldots, g_k$ will be among the $v_1, \ldots, v_m$. If the theory of experimental design involves interfering laws of interaction, the theory of the data must enable one to determine what the values of $p_1, \ldots, p_n$ would have been if P and G had not interacted; otherwise the theory of the experiment will be incapable of determining what the values of $p_1, \ldots, p_n$ would have been were p's behavior dependent only on those values—which is what is required to obtain reduced data about the physical system corresponding to P.

Sometimes no known theory of data sanctioned by the domain is able to "undo" G's interference with P, in which case data about the physical system corresponding to P cannot be obtained. In extreme cases, this always will happen with a certain class of phenomena; for example, according to the Copenhagen interpretation of quantum theory, this will always be the case of any physical system of subatomic particles. In such a case, apparatus-aided observation still may be possible; for if the interaction of P and G is itself a phenomenal system $P*$ within the scope of the theory T, one can make observations of $P*$, and if the theory of the data enables one to convert raw data about $P*$ into reduced data about what $P*$ *would have been were* it only influenced by $p_1, \ldots, p_n$ and $g_1, \ldots, g_k$, then we do obtain data characteristic of the physical system corresponding to $P*$. Thus we are able to observe the states of physical systems corresponding to $P*$ even though we cannot observe the states of physical systems corresponding to P. This is the situation characteristic of quantum-theoretic observation (measurement), and the peculiar features of quantum measurement theory are reflections of this fact. Thus we see that the Semantic Conception of Theories can make intelligible sense of the peculiarities of quantum theoretic measurement.[26] For it is the case that the theories of the experiment sanctioned by the background to the domain in question only allow this sort of measurement.[27]

It is reasonable to suppose that backgrounds to domains can be delimited somewhat precisely, in the sense that persons working in a given domain generally can agree on what belongs to the background to the domain. This suggests that the number of theories in the background to a domain should be finite. Accepting this suggestion poses a problem, however; for any experimental application of a theory to phenomena which involves apparatus or inference must be in accordance with a theory of the experiment sanctioned by the domain. And since for theories of any complexity, the number of different sorts of experimental applications of a theory to phenomena is potentially unlimited, the number of theories of the experiment sanctioned by the domain must be potentially unlimited. Moreover, many "interesting" experimental applications of theory to phenomena involve experimental breakthroughs where the application is not covered by any previously employed theory of the experiment; nonetheless, persons working in the domain often readily accept such new, and often ingenious, theories of the experiment, because they are sanctioned by the domain.

Our account of observation and the experimental application of theories to phenomena must explain how this is possible.[28] As a starting point, I assume that the number of theories in the background to the domain is finite. Then I present a general procedure for generating theories of the experiment from the theories in the background to the domain and argue that they are sanctioned by the domain.

An example (borrowed from Clifford Hooker)[29] will help motivate the procedure for generating theories of the experiment. The example concerns the generation of a theory of experimental design for a cloud chamber experiment. A cloud chamber is a box in which air can be supersaturated with water vapor in such a way that a charged particle (an electron or a proton) traveling fast enough can ionize gas atoms which disturb the supersaturated air and cause water droplets to form around the gas atoms. Thus an observer sees a cloudy vapor trail in the chamber along the particle's path. Since the particles in question are electrically charged, they can experience forces in the presence of electric fields; so if an electric field is applied to the chamber, electrons and protons will have different characteristic paths through the chamber. These paths will be observed as differently shaped vapor trails in the cloud chamber. By putting in a source of particles (e.g., a filament for electrons), we can observe the presence of protons and electrons by seeing the various vapor trails.

In actual practice such observations would be explained with a theory of experimental design obtained as follows: Taking various formulations of theories in the background to domain, together with statements of facts about the experimental setup and collateral information, we would deduce and/or induce propositions stating that whenever, while observing with such an apparatus, a vapor trail of such and such shape is observed, an electron (proton) is traveling along the path of that vapor trail. In this case the theories used would be the atomic theory, electromagnetic theory, heat theory, the theory of gases, and the theory of mechanics.[30] When such a special case generalization is obtained covering the particular observation, the scientist will accept the experimental design as being sanctioned by the background to the domain. But this sanctioned generalization is a proposition, a linguistic entity, so it cannot be the theory of experimental design (since theories are extralinguistic structures); moreover, the generalization so obtained may not provide the explanation of the experimental setup required by observation. The generalization is, however, a proposition in a formulation of the theory of experimental design.

How, then, do we obtain the theory of experimental design? In cases such as the cloud chamber observation, formulations $\mathcal{T}_1, \ldots, \mathcal{T}_n$ of a number of theories $T_1, \ldots, T_n$ are used together with statements $\mathcal{T}$ of facts and collateral information $\mathcal{I}$ to obtain the special generalization $\mathcal{E}$ covering the cloud chamber experiment. In order to do so, $\mathcal{T}_1, \ldots,$ $\mathcal{T}_n, \mathcal{T}$, and $\mathcal{I}$ must be compatible in the sense that they use the same terms to refer to any parameters common to several theories, the facts, or the collateral information. Let $\mathcal{T}^*$ be the set of propositions from compatible $\mathcal{T}_1, \ldots, \mathcal{T}_n, \mathcal{T}$, and $\mathcal{I}$ used to obtain $\mathcal{E}$ in the sort of derivation described earlier; such a derivation requires that $\mathcal{T}^*$ contain statements of laws from $\mathcal{T}_1, \ldots, \mathcal{T}_n$. If $T_1, \ldots, T_n$ are empirically true, and if $\mathcal{T}$ and $\mathcal{I}$ are factually true, then it follows that the propositions in $\mathcal{T}^*$ are consistent; as such, $\mathcal{T}^*$ will have a model.[31] In particular, $\mathcal{T}^*$ will have a model whose domain of discourse contains states whose defining parameters are all those parameters designated by parameter terms in the propositions in $\mathcal{T}^*$. Since the propositions in $\mathcal{T}^*$ typically do not include complete formulations of $T_1, \ldots, T_n, \mathcal{T}^*$ can have a number of different but nonequivalent models with the same domain of discourse indicated above. The set of all such models with the same domain of discourse constitutes a partial interpretation of $\mathcal{T}^*$. From the results concerning partial interpretation presented in chapter 2,[32] it follows that one of the models with that domain of discourse will be an empirically true theory if $T_1, \ldots, T_n$ are empirically true and $\mathcal{T}$ and $\mathcal{I}$ are factually true. Thus $\mathcal{T}^*$ is a partial formulation of an empirically true theory (though we are not sure what a complete formulation would be), and $\mathcal{T}^*$ is true of that theory.

The theory so obtained is the required theory of experimental design and will suffice to provide the explanations of the experimental setup required for observation to occur, and if we know that $\mathcal{T}_1, \ldots, \mathcal{T}_n, \mathcal{T}$, and $\mathcal{I}$, then we know that $\mathcal{T}^*$ and $\mathcal{E}$. Essentially the same procedure can be used to obtain the theory of the data, hence used to obtain the theory of the experiment. It amounts to a generalized procedure for obtaining a potentially unlimited number of different theories of the experiment from a finite number of empirically true theories in the background to the domain which enables us to know the theories so obtained. Thus the variety of observations required by the discussions of the previous sections is possible. Notice that this procedure is a little-noticed form of theory reduction wherein a number of more global theories $(T_1, \ldots, T_n)$ are reduced to a special case theory (partially formulated by $\mathcal{T}^*$) of relatively limited scope.

V. EXPERIMENTAL TESTING AND THE CONFIRMATION OF THEORIES

Although experimental testing is undertaken to provide or contribute to answers to a wide variety of domain questions, one of its chief functions is to enable the confirmation or disconfirmation of a given theory. A standard characterization of the confirmatory process normally employed by science is as follows: The theory is subjected to a number of experimental tests; these tests consist in comparing predictions made by the theory with the observed behaviors of physical systems. If the theory passes an appropriate variety of such tests, we conclude that it is highly probable that the theory is empirically true. A *confirmation theory* is a philosophical explanation why such confirmatory processes are legitimate—assuming that they are. Although the entire development of a confirmation theory is beyond the scope of this chapter, one will be sufficiently outlined for the Semantic Conception to display how experimental testing contributes to the confirmation of theories on traditional inductive theories regarding the confirmation of theories.[33]

In section III we saw that a theory T with intended scope I and defining parameters $p_1, \ldots, p_n$ is empirically true if and only if (i) I is a set of causally possible phenomenal systems whose domains of discourse contain particulars of which $p_1, \ldots, p_n$ are characteristic kinds of attributes; (ii) the possible values of the parameters $p_1, \ldots, p_n$ allowed by T are attributes possessed by particulars in the phenomenal systems in I, or else are idealizations of these; and (iii) the set of theory-induced physical systems for T is identical with the class of causally possible physical systems. A confirmation theory must explain how the experimental testing procedure can lead to a determination that these three conditions are met.

In chapter 3 we said that the defining parameters $p_1, \ldots, p_n$ of T are parameters abstracted from the phenomenal systems in I and that every phenomenal system in I stands in the replicating relation set forth in that chapter to some causally possible physical system. It follows from these two conditions that $p_1, \ldots, p_n$ are characteristic of all causally possible phenomenal systems comprising I. As such, empirical truth condition (a) of chapter 3, section V is met.[34] We also saw that whenever a phenomenal system P in I stands in the replicating relation to some physical system S, the values of the parameters $p_1, \ldots,$ p_n occurring in the states of S are attributes possessed by particulars in P or else idealizations thereof. Accordingly, every attribute which occurs in any state of any causally possible physical system will be an attribute (or an idealization thereof) possessed by particulars in some physical system in I. Suppose, now, that empirical truth condition (c) (ch. 3, sec. V) is met; then the class of theory-induced physical systems is identical with the class of causally possible physical systems. This means that every attribute deemed physically possible by T will occur in the state of some causally possible physical system; hence, by the foregoing discussion, the attribute (or an idealization thereof) will be possessed by some particulars in some physical system in I. In other words, empirical truth condition (b) is met whenever (c) is. Accordingly, it is sufficient for the confirmation of a theory T to establish that condition (c) is met, and for the disconfirmation of T it is sufficient to establish that either condition (b) or condition (c) fails to be met.

How does experimental testing enable us to determine that condition (c) is met or that conditions (b) or (c) fail to be met? Recall from section III that empirical testing consists in (i) the observational determination of physical system states corresponding to observed phenomenal systems in I—the determination that the physical system S corresponding to the observed phenomenal system P is in the state s_0 at time t_0, is in state s_1 at time $t_1, \ldots,$ and is in state s_k at time t_k. Then, (ii) these observations are compared with the theory's predictions as to what states S will be in at times $t_0, \ldots, t_k$; this amounts to determining whether the physical system S is in the class of theory-induced physical systems for T. In order to see how experimental testing contributes to the confirmation of theories, we need to explore both aspects of testing further.

(i) Suppose we subject a physical system P to experiemental testing and observe that the physical system S corresponding to P is in states $s_0, \ldots, s_k$ respectively at time $t_0, \ldots, t_k$. By virtue of the results of chapter 3 and section II through V of this chapter, it must be the case that S is in states $s_0, \ldots, s_k$ respectively at times $t_0, \ldots, t_k$ (or some variation along the lines of note 22). Hence a proposition to this effect is true of S and counterfactually true of P, and we have observational *knowledge* of the causally possible physical system S.

(ii) We use T to predict what states S will be in at times $t_0, \ldots, t_k$ (following ch. 3, sec. I). If the laws of the theory are deterministic laws of succession, this will yield states $s_0', \ldots, s_k'$ respectively for $t_0, \ldots, t_k$. And if s_i is s_i' for $i = 0, \ldots, k$, then we say that S is a *confirming instance* of the theory; if for any i, s_i and s_i' are different, we say that S is a *disconfirming instance*.[35] If the theory has deterministic laws of coexistence, for each t_i ($i > 0$) we will obtain some range of possible states $s_i', \ldots, s_i'' \cdots {}'$. And if s_i is among the $s_i', \ldots, s_i'' \cdots {}'$ for $i = 1, \ldots, k$, then we say S is a *confirming instance* of T; if for some i, s_i is not among the $s_i', \ldots, s_i'' \cdots {}'$, we say S is a *disconfirming instance* of T.[36]

If T has statistical laws of succession or coexistence, the predictions will be as with deterministic laws of coexistence except that a probability measure will be assigned to each of the $s_i', \ldots, s_i'' \cdots {}'$. The $s_i', \ldots, s_i'' \cdots {}'$ for each i determine a class of possible sequences S^* of states beginning with s_0 at time t_0, and the probability measures assigned to the various $s_i', \ldots, s_i'' \cdots {}'$ ($i = 1, \ldots, k$) assign a probability to each of these sequences in S^*. In order to obtain a confirming instance of T in these cases, it is necessary to repeatedly observe phenomenal systems $P_1, P_2, \ldots$ whose corresponding physical systems $S_1, S_2, \ldots$ are in state s_0 at t_0, determining their states at $t_1, \ldots, t_k$. Doing so gives us a sample distribution of such physical systems. If all the $S_1, S_2, \ldots$ observed are in S^*, and if enough have been observed that we can determine, using some appropriate statistical goodness-of-fit test, that the probability that $S_1, S_2, \ldots$ is a random sample from S^* exceeds a predetermined confidence level, we then say that $S_1, S_2, \ldots$ constitute a *confirming instance* of T. If one or more of the $S_1, S_2 \ldots$ fail to be in S^*, or else enough phenomenal systems have been observed that (using some appropriate statistical goodness-of-fit test) we are entitled to reject the hypothesis that $S_1, S_2, \ldots$ is a random sample from S^* at a predetermined confidence level, we say $S_1, S_2, \ldots$ constitute a *disconfirming instance* of T. The notions of confirming and disconfirming instances of T, when T contains laws of interaction, will be some admixture of the ones just described.

We now can turn directly to the confirmation and disconfirmation of T. If, as a result of experimental testing of T, we obtain a disconfirming instance of T, either T is false or there is a probability P that T is false (which depends on the notion of disconfirming instance appropriate according to the above discussion). In such a case, the falsity of T may be by virtue of the failure of clause (b) or clause (c) of the definition of empirical truth. Turning to confirmation, recall that to confirm T as being empirically true it suffices to show that empirical truth condition (c) is satisfied; however, a number of problems complicate this task. Since I typically will be infinite, and since the current state of technology may preclude observing certain types of phenomenal systems in I, it usually is the case that we cannot examine all the physical systems in I, and so we cannot completely determine what the class of causally possible physical systems for T is; indeed, as a matter of practical economy, only a tiny number of phenomenal systems in I can be examined. As a result, [according to conventional epistemological wisdom] we usually cannot determine with certainty that condition (c)—hence condition (b)—is satisfied.

In this sense, *absolute confirmation* of T typically is impossible [on conventional epistemologies]. The most experimental testing can enable us to determine, then, is that it is highly probable that conditions (c), hence (b), are satisfied; hence that it is highly probably that T is empirically true. That is, [conventional epistemological wisdom tells us] we typically must settle for the *relative confirmation of T*.

The relative confirmation of T must be determined on the basis of confirming instances of T. In some way or another, from observing a variety of phenomenal systems in I, we obtain a number of confirming instances of T. When a sufficient variety of confirming instances is obtained, with no (or relatively few) disconfirming instances, we *inductively* conclude that T is empirically true. In light of the foregoing discussion, this amounts to concluding that condition (c) is met.

It is beyond the scope of this chapter to attempt an account of the logic of such inductive inferences, especially given the primitive level of our current understanding of inductive logic. Nonetheless, a few suggestions about the nature of this inductive inference are in order. On the Semantic Conception, the problem of confirming a theory T reduces to the question whether the class of theory-induced physical systems and the class of causally possible physical systems for T are coextensive (i.e., whether [c] is satisfied), making it an "identity of population" question. The class of theory-induced physical systems is, in principle at least, knowable, whereas the class of causally possible physical systems is not. Experimental testing yields scattered knowledge about members of the class of causally possible physical systems (e.g., the confirming instances), and from that knowledge we try to determine if the two classes of physical systems are identical. It would seem, then, that the determination that condition (c) is met is a species of goodness-of-fit problem concerning the identity of two populations and that the inductive inference required to confirm T will be sanctioned by some goodness-of-fit statistic.

We conclude our discussion of confirmation with an epistemic observation. If we accept the common thesis that knowledge is justified true belief, and further allow that the determination that T is highly confirmed (along the lines of this section's discussion) constitutes sufficient justification, then the confirmation of a theory T is a means of obtaining knowledge. For by the discussion earlier in this section, our confirming instances of T are known; so if on the basis of these confirming instances, the application of our confirmation procedure determines that it is highly probable that T is empirically true, we know that T. In such cases, resort to T can enable us to obtain theoretical knowledge about the world and various unexamined phenomenal systems. Moreover, as indicated in section I, this theoretical knowledge can be used to enhance our observational capabilities. [Such an approach, embodying conventional epistemological wisdom, is not without its own difficulties, however. Allowing that T is highly confirmed and constitutes sufficient justification for knowledge on a justified true belief analysis renders the approach liable to Gettier paradox difficulties. It also involves imposing a weaker evidential requirement on theoretical knowledge than that built into the account of perceptual knowledge embedded in section I's treatment of observation. For these and related concerns (discussed in Suppe 1977a, 716–28) one may want to impose a stronger evidential requirement that precludes inductive confirmation from yielding knowledge. This possibility will be explored seriously in chapters 11 through 13. If this possibility is embraced, as I do in chapter 13, then the above "goodness-of-fit" confirmation strategy still may have a role to play in the fallible evaluation of theoretical knowledge claims even though it is incapable of yielding theoretical knowledge.]

VI. SUMMARY

This chapter further developed the Semantic Conception by exploring the ways theories relate to phenomena in experimental testing (secs. I–IV). We argued that measurement can be construed realistically (sec. II) and that when so construed, adoption of a plausible account of observation (sec. I) yields the result that measurement is a species of observation which yields objective knowledge about the world (sec. II).

We then turned to a consideration of the nature of experimental design and its role in prediction and experimental testing. We argued that such applications of theory to phenomena required auxiliary theories of the experiment (sec. III) and explored the epistemic properties of such theories of the experiment (sec. IV). Then we marshalled our findings on these topics to explain how, assuming standard epistemological views on probabilisitic inductive logic, empirical testing can lead to the relative confirmation of theories and yield theoretical knowledge of the world (sec. V). In doing so we made speculative comments about the nature of such a confirmation theory [and raised some doubts about the viability of such an inductive apporach. These doubts will be explored in later chapters.]

NOTES

1. See Dretske 1969, ch. 6, for defense of this claim. There is a certain arbitrariness in the claim, since ordinary usage does sanction talk of erroneous observation and so on. My preference in handling such cases is to stick to a strong sense of observation meeting the condition just stipulated and to treat erroneous observations that ϕ as cases of failing to observe that ϕ.

2. See Shapere 1974b. My treatment of observation here has been influenced by, and in some respects resembles, his 1982 article. See his more recent 1984 book for further developments.

3. It is possible to approach a scientific domain from the perspectives of different backgrounds to the domain; this characteristically occurs when there are competing schools working on the same scientific domain. In such cases, the alternative backgrounds generate different but overlapping sets of domain questions. Such alternative backgrounds are possible because each one contains theories, and so on, which may contribute to the generation of domain questions but do not properly belong to the domain. Domain questions include what Shapere calls domain problems, theoretical problems, and theoretical inadequacies (1974b, Part II). For simplicity of exposition, I will ignore the possibility of alternative backgrounds to scientific domains.

4. For a discussion of the notion of a partial answer to various types of questions, see Belnap 1963, Harrah 1963, Belnap and Steel 1976, and Bromberger 1966.

5. For a discussion of direct observation, see ch. 2, sec. II.

6. See Achinstein 1968, 160–65, for a defense of these claims about observation and for a useful discussion of other key features of observation.

7. For a very strong defense of this claim see Dretske 1969, ch. 4. Although there are features of his analysis that I do not accept, I think his defense of *this* claim is thoroughly correct. He has since repudiated much of this approach, however, and replaced it with an "information-theoretic approach" (see his

1981 book). In ch. 12 I will argue that his repudiation is a mistake and that his new analysis does not constitute an improvement.

8. See Dretske 1969, for a defense of these claims; the example is his. Although I do not accept his account (in terms of his seeing$_n$) of the nature of the sensory experience which enables on to see that ϕ, his arguments given in support of the claims just made still are convincing, since they do not depend essentially on any of his questionable views about seeing$_n$.

9. My account of visual observation will be further developed and defended in chs. 10 through 13.

10. Cf. Ellis 1966, 40-42. Note that on pp. 41-42 he conflates having a rule with having an operational measurement procedure. For expository purposes I have restated his view in the terminology of this paper and restricted his claims so as to exclude nominal measurement scales. My reason for ignoring nominal scales here is that nominal measurement is a procedure for *naming* particulars with numbers rather than determining physical quantities.

11. Some clarification about this assertion is required for cases, such as quantum theory, wherein the parameters for physical system states are position and momentum coordinates which have as possible values probability distribution functions specifying the probabilities with which various measured values can be obtained. (See n. 33 of ch. 3 for further discussion of this point.) Accordingly, the physical quantities which are attributes of particulars in physical systems will be statistical dispositional attributes—that is, stochastic dispositions to manifest different classical physical quantities (e.g., positions and momenta) when interacting with other (measurement) systems. In such cases we can measure the classical physical quantities manifested in a given interaction; strictly speaking, it is only classical physical quantities manifest under conditions of interaction to which measurement scales apply. Accordingly, in such cases as quantum theory we take Q to be the set of all the classical quantities which can so be manifested, not the set of different stochastic dispositional attributes.

12. See Ellis 1966, 25–32, for a defense of these conditions. Unlike Ellis, here we give a realistic interpretation to the relations $R_>$, $R_<$, and $R_=$.

13. See Hempel 1952, sec. 11, for a characterization of quasi-serial orderings of particulars.

14. Cf. Ellis 1966, 32. Unlike Ellis's definition, ours allows, but does not require, that measurable quantities be relations.

15. The requirement that each of the f_i be complete scales which are also complete scales relative to T (not partial scales) is imposed to guarantee (1) that every state deemed physically possible by the theory will be represented by an n-tuple of points in the phase space determined by the frame of reference, and (2) that every possible state of every causally possible physical system will be representable by an n-tuple of points in the phase space. These two conditions are necessary to guarantee that the theory is fully testable in principle. The reasons these conditions are required are strictly analogous to the reasons why full testability of the theory requires an expanded theory formulation language (see ch. 3, sec. III).

16. Although this is true under most accounts of measurement, Ellis (1966) disputes it and distinguishes two types of direct measurement procedures—fundamental measurement and elemental measurement (55–57). Paradigmatic of elemental measurement procedures is the determination of which of two minerals is harder than the other by using the scratch test. But such a test is *not* a measurement in the sense adopted by my analysis, since it does not assign measures to the substances but rather only determines that for a given "scratch" scale of hardness, the measure of one mineral is higher than the other. In order to use a scratch test to determine the measure of a given mineral, one would have to determine that the sample in question could scratch all such minerals and that it could be scratched by all the same minerals as some standard mineral to which a given numerical measurement of hardness had been assigned. But this process is itself a fundamental measurement. Thus the statement just made in the body of the text holds.

17. For simplicity of exposition I am supposing the q which are values of p are properties; in fact, however, they could be relations. If so, a similar statement in terms of $a_1, \ldots, a_n$ entering into the relationship q holds; formulation of the relational case is straightforward and so will be omitted here.

18. Although we have treated the determination of a scale and measurement procedures as being logically distinct, this does not prevent the practice of using a particular measurement procedure *in* the establishment of a scale; all it does is make such a practice optional, not mandatory.

19. See ch. 3, sec. VIII, for an extended discussion of this point.

20. Rather than attempt a precise definition, let us simply observe that a pseudoscale is anything which qualifies as a scale under Ellis's definition of a scale but fails to be a scale under our account.

21. See ch. 7 for a realistic account of the natural-artificial taxonomy distinction which is compatible with the quasi-realistic interpretation of theories adopted in ch. 3. The connection between pseudomeasurement and artificial taxonomies is not superficial; for from the results of the present chapter and ch. 7, it follows that a measure for a parameter is a pseudomeasure if the parameter is characteristic of an artificial taxon. In ch. 7, sec. VII, I discuss the legitimate uses of artificial taxonomies.

22. For simplicity, we have been ignoring the problem of measurement error. A measuring apparatus is able to determine the measures of physical quantities only with a limited degree of precision. Often its level of precision is lower than that of the measurement scale in question (e.g., my measurement scale for length is accurate to three decimal places, but my yardstick is only significant to one decimal place). In such cases, to report one's measurement result as, for example, 3.100 inches is to treat the last two digits as significant when they are not. In such a case, the proper report is $m \pm b$, where m is the measured value and b indicates the range of error inherent in the measurement. The measurement report 'the object has measure $m \pm b$' says that the object has a certain intrinsic attribute whose measure on the scale in question falls within the range $[m - b, m + b]$. If the measurement has

been obtained correctly, the measurement report will be factually true even though 'the object has measure m' may not be. As such, even imprecise measurement propositions can be factually true.

23. This is a bit stronger than what our arguments actually establish, since we have limited ourselves to visual observation, and nonvisual measurement is possible; however, if our account of observation were extended to cover nonvisual cases, the considerations just raised would establish the result for all measurement.

24. The account just given how theories apply to phenomena is based on Suppes 1962. (For a discussion of his views on the matter, see Suppe 1974b, sec. IV–E.) In relating his views to the foregoing discussion, it is important to note that I use 'theory of the experiment' to mean something quite different than he does; the function of *his* theory of the experiment is performed by the theory T on the Semantic Conception, and so it does not figure in my account. What I call the theory of the experiment is what he calls the *hierarchy of models* or theories, roughly speaking.

25. For simplicity, if measurement is involved, we assume that all the measurable parameters other than $p_1, \ldots, p_n$ are parameters whose values are determined by fundamental measurement procedures, and that the apparatus G is completely able to carry all of them out. This assumption is reasonable even if derived measurement procedures are involved, since derived measurements ultimately depend on fundamentally measured quantities.

26. For an excellent and extended discussion of the peculiar nature of quantum-theoretic measurement from the perspective of the Semantic Conception of Theories, cf. van Fraassen 1972, Part II.

27. This suggests that part of the dispute between advocates of the Copenhagen interpretation of quantum theory and advocates of the hidden variable hypothesis can be attributed to differences in the backgrounds to the domain adopted by these two camps; they even may be dealing with different (albeit overlapping) domains.

28. Much of Kuhn's 1974 paper is concerned with attempting to solve much the same problem from the perspective of his own view of the scientific enterprise. I have severely criticized his treatment elsewhere (1974a). The discussion which follows can be construed as my counterpart to his treatment of the problem, as suggested by the Semantic Conception of Theories.

29 See Hooker 1975, appendix. He develops the example in far greater detail.

30. See ibid., for a detailed account of the derivations from these theories.

31. An assumption, tacitly made in the cloud chamber example and our generalization from it, is crucial to the procedure being presented and thus needs to be made explicit. We tacitly have assumed that the relevant statements from $\mathcal{I}_1, \ldots, \mathcal{I}_n$ which are incorporated into $\mathcal{I}^*$ all are factually (as opposed to counterfactually) true of the experimental situation. Without this assumption, there is no guarantee that $\mathcal{I}^*$ will have a model of the required sort. This is because the counterfactual nature of the physical interpretation of theories makes the empirical truth of theories a counterfactual matter, which

complicates the model theory of their formulations. In cases where the relevant laws of $T_1, \ldots, T_n$ relate to the experimental situation counterfactually, formulations of special case versions of the laws (obtained via auxiliary hypotheses) which *are* factually true of the experimental situation enables the procedure being presented to be employed.

32. See ch. 2, Sec. I-B, for a precise formulation of the partial interpretation notion. The term 'partial interpretation' was coined by the positivists. Although, following the positivists, I formulate the notion in terms of an observational/theoretical term distinction, nothing in my basic account requires tying partial interpretation to an observational/theoretical term distinction. In the present context, my basic account of partial interpretation is assumed to be divorced from such a distinction.

33. [In ch. 13 the traditional notion that science (including the confirmation of theories) is inductive will be challenged. The position developed there potentially downgrades the importance of the sort of testing and confirmation developed here.]

34. Some readers will be bothered that condition (1) is met virtually by definition. Such worries are unfounded, however, for in general we do not have prior knowledge of the extension of I (one job of the theory being to yield such knowledge). To specify I prior to development of the theory we must resort to some implicit characterization which typically is in terms of $p_1, \ldots, p_n$. For example, we indicate the scope I of classical particle mechanics by referring to the class of mechanical phenomena involving a finite number of bodies, where by a body we mean massive objects having positions and momenta, and by mechanical phenomena we mean the phenomena consisting in changes of position and momentum of such bodies; by doing so we use the defining parameters of classical particle mechanics to indicate its scope and thereby automatically satisfy empirical truth condition (a). Accordingly, the fact that condition (a) is met virtually by definition on the Semantic Conception is acceptable, since it is a reflection of actual scientific practice.

35. If our determination of $s_0, \ldots, s_k$ is subject to measurement error (cf. n. 22), we will have to submit the decision whether the s_i and s_i' are the same to statistical arbitration; statistically, the problem is a goodness-of-fit question concerning whether s_i and s_i' are possible error-laden measurements from the same phenomenal system. Since the distribution of measurement errors typically are approximately normal, a χ^2 or student's t test often can be used; in other cases, various other statistics such as nonparametric goodness-of-fit statistics may be required. (For further details, cf. Suppe 1967, sec. 3.4).

Note that a disconfirming instance may occur in either of two ways. First, it may be that one of the s_i may be deemed physically impossible by T; here we have a failure of condition (b). Second, all the s_i may be physically possible according to T, but $s_0, \ldots, s_k$ are not characteristic of any causally possible physical system; here we can have the failure of (c) in the face of the satisfaction of (b). It was to display these two different types of disconfirming instances that we elected to distinguish conditions (b) and (c) despite the fact that they are redundant.

36. For theories such as quantum theory, where $p_1, \ldots, p_n$ have probability distribution functions as values, the above account must be complicated to include repeated testing to determine which causally possible physical system corresponds to the phenomenal systems involved. This type of case is not unlike the sorts of cases considered subsequently in this section.

5

Theoretical Laws

Just as the computer who wants his calculations to deal with sugar, silk, and wool must discount the boxes, bales, and other packings, so the mathematical scientist, when he wants to recognize in the concrete the effects which he has proved in the abstract, must deduct the material hindrances, and if he is able to do so, I assure you that things are in no less agreement than arithmetical computations. The errors, then, lie not in the abstractness or concreteness, not in geometry or physics, but in a calculator who does not know how to make a true accounting.

Galileo Galilei
Dialogue Concerning Two Chief World Systems

I. INTRODUCTION

Michael Scriven (1961) has argued plausibly that the various standard attempts to characterize laws of nature are inadequate—in part because they fail to recognize that the key property of physical laws is their inaccuracy.[1] He then suggests that this insight can be accommodated by an analysis along the following lines: "Typical physical laws express a relationship between quantities or a property of systems which is the *simplest useful approximation* to the true physical behavior and which appears to be theoretically tractable."[2] More generally, recognition of the pervasive inaccuracy of physical laws has suggested to a number of philosophers that an adequate analysis of theories might involve recourse to some notion of *approximate truth*. In particular, the German G. Ludwig (1981) has argued that imprecisions of measurement require construing theories as imprecise, and in response he has developed a formal analysis in terms of imprecise sets which he has incorporated into his analysis of theories. (See also the various papers in Hartkämper and Schmidt 1981.) While the approximate truth approach has plausibility, my suspicion is that it is not the most promising way to deal with the inaccuracy of laws; for I suspect that the inaccuracy of physical laws is a manifestation of relatively deep structural and epistemological properties of laws and theories which will be obscured or missed if one attempts to analyze laws as approximately true generalizations (or other sorts of propositions). Accordingly, in this chapter I explore the nature of physical laws in a manner that avoids recourse to the notion of approximate truth.

Exploiting the fact that laws often, if not always, are components of scientific theories, I will investigate the properties of laws occurring in a scientific theory; as such, my concern here is restricted to *theoretical laws*. Whether there are nontheoretical laws and if so how they differ from theoretical laws are issues which will not be considered here. The Semantic Conception of Theories will be assumed in the analysis of theoretical laws. In section III I will look at various types of theoretical laws and determine a number of their more significant properties. Section IV considers the nature of teleological and functional laws. Section V summarizes the findings of this chapter and indicates in what sense it is true that a key feature of (theoretical) physical laws is their inaccuracy.

II. LAWS ON THE SEMANTIC CONCEPTION OF THEORIES

Although the term 'law' can be used in science to refer to the most elementary isolated empirical generalizations (e.g., "Ducks have webbed feet"), clearly its most central use is with reference to entities occurring within theories—to *theoretical laws*. It is reasonable to expect, then, that considerable light can be shed on the nature of laws by investigating the nature and function of theoretical laws within theories. We will assume the Semantic Conception of Theories, exploiting the following key features from developments in previous chapters: A theory models the behaviors of the possible systems in its intended scope by determining sequences of state occurrences which correspond to the behaviors of all possible such systems. However, as is the case generally with such models,[3] this correspondence need not be one of identity. For in specifying possible changes in state, the theory tacitly assumes that the only factors influencing the behavior of a system are those which show up as state parameters in the theory, whereas in fact the values of these parameters often are influenced by outside factors which do not show up as parameters of the theory. As such, the nature of the correspondence is as follows: The sequences of states determined by the theory indicate what the behaviors of the possible systems within the theory's scope would be were it the case that only the parameters of the theory exerted a nonnegligible influence on those behaviors.[4] That is, the theory characterizes what the possible behaviors of systems are under idealized circumstances wherein the values of the parameters do not depend on any outside influences, and thus relates counterfactually to many actual systems within its intended scope.

An example will help here. Consider a microeconomic theory concerning the interplay of supply and demand schedules for goods. According to this theory, goods will be priced at an equilibrium price wherein supply equals demand; supply, demand, and price may change over time, but according to the theory these changes will always be such that there is an equilibrium of supply and demand at a given price. As such, the theory is one whose variables are price, quantity of supply, and quantity of demand, with deterministic laws of coexistence such that for a given price, supply quantity equals demand quantity. The theory in effect says that the behavior of supply-demand-price market system will be such that the system always will be in a state where supply equals demand at the given price.

But this is a highly *idealized* picture of the market which assumes that there is perfect competition, that cobweb situations do not occur, that there is no time lag in the reaction of prices to changes in supply or demand situations, and so on—it is an idealized situation wherein the behavior of the system depends *only* on supply, demand, and price. Although this idealized situation often fails to obtain in the market, such failures do not show the theory to be wrong; for the theory here *only* purports to describe what the supply-demand-price behavior *would be* for that market *were it the case that these idealized conditions were met*.[5] When the idealized conditions are met, the theory directly can predict what will happen; when the idealized conditions are not met, it still may be possible to use the theory to predict what will happen by using *auxiliary theories*. For example, suppose we have a supply-demand-price system which does not satisfy the idealized conditions, but we have an auxiliary theory which tells us how the other factors operant in the system (e.g., cartels) influence the supply quantity, demand quantity, and price. Then, using our supply-demand-price theory, we can predict what *would be* the subsequent state of the system *were* the idealized conditions met, then use the auxiliary theory to determine how the actual situation will deviate from the idealized situation. The two theories together yield an accurate prediction of what the actual behavior will be.[6]

According to the Semantic Conception of Theories, then, scientific theories are relational systems functioning as iconic models which characterize all the possible changes of state the systems within its scope could undergo under idealized circumstances. And the theory will be *empirically true* if and only if the class of possible sequences of state occurrences determined by the theory is identical with the possible behaviors of systems within its intended scope under idealized conditions. Whenever a system within the theory's intended scope meets the idealized conditions, the theory can predict the subsequent behavior of the system (the preciseness of the prediction depending on what sorts of laws the theory has); and when the idealized conditions are not met, the theory can predict the behavior of the system if used in conjuction with a suitable auxiliary theory.[7]

III. LAWS OF SUCCESSION, COEXISTENCE, AND INTERACTION

On the Semantic Conception of Theories, laws are relations which determine possible sequences of state occurrences over time that a system within the law's intended scope may assume. We now investigate a number of types of such laws which commonly are encountered in scientific theories and establish various theorems about them. We begin by considering the types of laws most commonly discussed in the scientific theories literature—deterministic and statistical laws of succession, coexistence, and interaction.[8]

Depending on the theory, time is construed as being either *discrete* or *continuous*. In discrete time theories, time usually is construed as having the order properties of the natural numbers (i.e., as an ω sequence) or the integers (i.e., as an $\omega^* + \omega$ sequence).[9] Continuous time theories construe time as having the order properties of the real numbers (i.e., as a λ sequence). Let α be a variable whose only values are ω, $\omega^* + \omega$, or λ; any simple ordering of times having the order properties of ω, $\omega^* + \omega$, or λ order type will be known as an α *time sequence*. The laws of a theory are relations which determine possible simple orderings of states having the order properties of an α time sequence.

The defining parameters $p_1, \ldots, p_n$ ($n \geq 1$) of a theory are variables ranging over attributes and/or probability distribution functions over attributes; time, t, may or may not be a defining parameter of the theory. Let $p_i(t)$ be the value of parameter p_i at time t. Then the *state* s of a system at time t is $\langle p_1(t), \ldots, p_n(t) \rangle$. (Where needed, $q_i(t)$ and $r_i(t)$—with or without primes or subscripts—will be construed analogously.) Since the same state s may occur at more than one time (i.e., in distinct state occurrences), we will use '$s(t)$' to designate the occurrence of state s at time t. D will be the set of all logically possible state occurrences for a theory.[10]

At each time t a physical system within the intended scope of a theory assumes some particular state, and the *behavior* of that system consists in its changes in states over time. That behavior is represented by a simply ordered set of state occurrences wherein $s(t) < s'(t')$ if and only if $t < t'$ (t and t' ranging over some α time sequence). It is the job of the laws of the theory to characterize all (and only) those possible behaviors of systems within the theory's intended scope by determining those simple orderings of state occurrences which represent the idealized behaviors of systems within that intended scope; the class of simple orderings so determined is known as the class of *theory-induced simple orderings*. The *laws* of a theory T are relations $R(s(t), s'(t'))$ {or $R(s(t),$ $s'(t'), p)$} holding between state occurrences {or between state occurrences and real numbers p}. Suppose T is a theory with only one law, R, and let O be a simple ordering of state occurrences for T of order type α, and let t, t' range over the α time sequence associated with T; then O is a theory-induced simple ordering of state occurrences if and only if for every $s(t), s'(t')$: (1) $s(t) < s'(t')$ under O if and only if $t < t'$ under the α time sequence, and (2) either $\langle s(t), s'(t') \rangle \in R$ or $\langle s(t),$ $s'(t'), p \rangle \in R$ for some real number p such that $O \leq p \leq 1$. If T has more than one law, condition (2) must be satisfied for each law R.

The foregoing preliminaries out of the way, we now define a variety of different kinds of laws.

Definition 1. Let t, t' be variables ranging over an α time sequence. Then a *classical deterministic law of succession* is a relation $R(s(t),$ $s'(t'))$ meeting the following condition for every t and t' such that $t < t'$:

If $\langle s(t), s'(t') \rangle \in R$ and $\langle s(t), s''(t') \rangle \in R$, then $s' = s''$.[11]

An example of such a classical deterministic law is that specified by the equations of motion for classical particle mechanics.

Definition 2. Let t, t' be variables ranging over an α time sequence. Then a *classical statistical law of succession* is a relation $R(s(t), s'(t'),$ $p)$ meeting the following conditions for each t and t' such that $t < t'$:

$\langle s(t), s'(t'), p \rangle \in R$ *iff* $P(s'(t'), s(t)) = p$,

where P satisfies the axioms for the conditional probability operator, and for each $s(t)$,

$$\sum_{s'(t')\in D} P(s'(t'), s(t)) = 1.$$

An example of such a classical statistical law of coexistence is that determined by a finite Markov process. Intuitively, a classical deterministic law of succession is one where the current state determines unique subsequent states; a classical statistical law of succession is one where for a given current state, the law allows that the system may assume a number of different subsequent states and assigns conditional probabilities that these various subsequent states will be assumed.

Other laws of succession are possible, too. In particular, there could be *nonclassical* deterministic laws of succession where the present state does not determine unique subsequent states, but the states assumed over some time interval do determine unique subsequent states. History sometimes is alleged (e.g., by Thucydides) to be deterministic in this nonclassical way.[12]

Next we define two types of laws of coexistence:

Definition 3. Let t, t', and t'' be variables ranging over an α time sequence. Then a *deterministic law of coexistence* is a relation $R(s(t), s'(t'))$ meeting the following conditions for any t, t', t'' such that $t < t'$ and $t' < t''$:

For every s, $\langle s(t), s(t')\rangle \in R$;
For every s, s', if $\langle s(t), s'(t')\rangle \in R$, then $\langle s'(t), s(t')\rangle \in R$;
For every s, s', and s'', if $\langle s(t), s'(t')\rangle \in R$ and $\langle s'(t'), s''(t'')\rangle \in R$, then $\langle s(t), s''(t'')\rangle \in R$.

The Boyle-Charles gas laws are examples of such laws. It would be more accurate but less traditional to call these *nonstatistical laws of coexistence*.

Definition 4. Let t, t' be variables ranging over an α time sequence. Then a *statistical law of coexistence* is a relation $R(s(t), s'(t'), p)$ meeting the following condition for every t and t' such that $t < t'$:

$$\langle s(t), s'(t'), p\rangle \in R \text{ iff } P(s(t)) = P(s'(t')) = p,$$

where P satisfies the axioms for the unconditional probability operator; and for any t,

$$\sum_{s(t)\in D} P(s(t)) = 1.$$

A special case example of such a law where for any t, $P(s(t)) = P(s'(t))$ for all $s'(t) \in D$ is the Boltzmann hypothesis that all states of a gas are equiprobable. More generally, statistical laws of coexistence say that a system is such that it subsequently may assume only equiprobable states.

Although such statistical laws of coexistence typically are cited in the literature as a distinct type of law,[13] in fact they are a special variety of statistical laws of succession.

Theorem 1. Every statistical law of coexistence is a classical statistical law of succession.

Proof. Let $R(s(t), s'(t'), p)$ be a statistical law of coexistence.
(i) Then for every t, t' such that $t < t'$, $\langle s(t), s'(t'), p \rangle \in R$ iff $P(s(t)) = P(s'(t')) = p$. But, then, for any $s(t), s'(t')$, and p such that $\langle s(t), s'(t'), p \rangle \in R$, $P(s'(t'), s(t)) = P(s(t)) = p$. So, $\langle s(t), s'(t'), p \rangle \in R$ iff there is some real number p such that $P(s'(t'), s(t)) = p$.
(ii) Since R is a statistical law of coexistence, for any t,

$$\sum_{s(t) \in D} P(s(t)) = 1.$$

But via (i), $P(s(t)) = p = P(s'(t'), s(t))$ for any $s'(t')$ such that $\langle s(t), s'(t'), p \rangle \in R$, so

$$\sum_{s'(t') \in D} P(s'(t'), s(t)) = 1.$$

It should be noted that the nonstatistical analogues to statistical laws of succession are just deterministic laws of coexistence. Hence the laws defined by Definitions 1, 2, and 3 (together with their various expansions described above) are exhaustive of the actual laws of succession and coexistence.

Given the usual taxonomy of laws, it would seem reasonable next to consider laws of interaction. However, it will prove expedient if instead we consider two types of laws which apparently have not been identified in the literature: deterministic and statistical *laws of quasi-succession.*[14] The so-called teleological and functional laws are special cases of such laws.

Definition 5. Let t and t' be variables ranging over an α time sequence, let $p_1, \ldots, p_n$ be the basic parameters of the theory, and let $i_1, \ldots, i_k$ ($k \leq n$) be a nonredundant listing of parameters among $p_1, \ldots, p_n$. For simplicity, suppose that $s(t) = \langle i_1(t), \ldots, i_k(t), p_{k+1}(t), \ldots, p_n(t) \rangle$. Then $R(s(t), s'(t'))$ is a *classical deterministic law of quasi-succession* iff the following condition is met for any t, t' such that $t < t'$ and $p_{k+1}, \ldots, p_n$ remain unchanged over time internal $[t, t']$:

if $\langle s(t), s'(t') \rangle \in R$ and $\langle s(t), s''(t') \rangle \in R$, then $s' = s''$.[15]

Similar expansions to nonclassical deterministic laws of quasi-succession can be made as they were for deterministic laws of succession. Such expansions being made, it is obvious that a deterministic law of succession is a deterministic law of quasi-succession where $k = n$. Hence,

Theorem 2. Every deterministic law of succession is a deterministic law of quasi-succession.

A statistical analogue to deterministic laws of quasi-succession is also possible.

Definition 6. Let t and t' be variables ranging over an α time sequence, let $p_1, \ldots, p_n$ be the basic parameters of the theory, and let $i_1, \ldots, i_k$ ($k \leq n$) be a nonredundant listing of the parameters among $p_1, \ldots, p_n$. For simplicity, suppose that

$$s(t) = \langle i_1(t), \ldots, i_k(t), p_{k+1}(t), \ldots, p_n(t) \rangle.$$

Then a *classical statistical law of quasi-succession* is a relation $R(s(t), s'(t'), p)$ meeting the following condition for each t and t' such that $t < t'$ and $p_{k+1}, \ldots, p_n$ remain unchanged over the time interval [t, t']:

$$\langle s(t), s'(t'), p \rangle \in R \text{ iff } P(s'(t'), s(t)) = p$$

where P satisfies the axioms for the conditional probability operator, and for each $s(t)$,

$$\sum_{s'(t') \in D} P(s'(t'), s(t)) = 1.$$

Clearly, a statistical law of quasi-succession is a statistical law of succession where $k = n$. Hence,

Theorem 3. Every statistical law of succession is a statistical law of quasi-succession.

In Definitions 5 and 6, let us call $s(t)$ the *complete state* of the system at t, $\langle i_1(t), \ldots, i_k(t) \rangle$ the *internal substate* of the system at t, and $\langle p_{k+1}(t), \ldots, p_n(t) \rangle$ the *external substate* of the system at t. Thus what is characteristic of systems with laws of quasi-succession is that subsequent internal substates, but not subsequent external substates, are a function of the prior complete states of the system.

Laws of interaction concern the behavior resulting from the interaction of two physical systems. Perhaps one of the methodologically most significant sorts of interaction is that in which one of the interacting systems is a measurement device allowed to interact with a system, where the outcome of the measurement system is indicative of the value of one or more parameters characteristic of the measured system (see ch. 4, sec. IV). But interactions are of wider interest, since the auxiliary theories which enable the application of theories to nonisolated systems within their intended scopes often are governed by laws of interaction.

We begin by considering deterministic laws of interaction.

Definition 7. Let t and t' be variables ranging over an α time sequence, let $s_1(t) = \langle p_1(t), \ldots, p_m(t)\rangle$, $s_2(t) = \langle q_1(t), \ldots, q_n(t)\rangle$. Let $s_{12}(t) = \langle p_1(t), \ldots, p_m(t), q_1(t), \ldots, q_n(t)\rangle$. Let the $i_1, \ldots, i_k$ ($k \leq m + n$) be distinct elements of the list $p_1, \ldots, p_m, q_1, \ldots, q_n$, and let $j_1, \ldots, j_{m+n-k}$ be the remaining elements on the list. Then a *classical deterministic law of interaction* is a relation $R(s_{12}(t), s'_{12}(t'))$ satisfying the following condition for every t, t' such that $t < t'$ and $j_1, \ldots, j_{m+n-k}$ remain unchanged over the interval $[t, t']$:

if $\langle s_{12}(t), s'_{12}(t')\rangle \in R$ and $\langle s_{12}(t), s''_{12}(t')\rangle \in R$, then
$s'_{12}(t')$ and $s''_{12}(t')$ have the same value for the $i_j(t')$ ($1 \leq j \leq k$).

An example of such a law of interaction is that governing a Wheatstone bridge when it is used to test the unknown resistance of a resistor (see ch. 4, sec. II).

From Definitions 5 and 7 we immediately obtain:

Theorem 4. Every classical deterministic law of interaction is a classical deterministic law of quasi-succession.

It is obvious that Definition 7 can be extended to nonclassical cases in the manner discussed earlier, and when so extended the nonclassical extension of Theorem 4 will be obtained.

A restricted class of deterministic laws of interaction underlies classical measurement processes involving apparatus.[16] For in such cases we typically have a system s in state $s_1(t)$, and we bring it into "contact" with a measurement apparatus in state $s_2(t)$ in order to ascertain the value of some parameter $i_1(t)$. As a result of that interaction, the system assumes some state $s_{12}(t')$ where $t' = t + \Delta t$, such that the combined systems will be in a state $s'_{12}(t')$ having $i'_2(t'), \ldots, i'_k(t')$ as parameter values only if $i_1(t)$ was a specific unique value. Thus, via the law of interaction governing the combined systems, the determination of $i'_2(t'), \ldots, i'_k(t')$ enables one to determine $i_1(t)$. If S is governed by a classical deterministic law of succession R, the interacting combined systems are governed by a classical deterministic law of interaction R', and R and R' are such that for a given $s_1(t)$ and $s_{12}(t)$,

R and R' determine $s_1'(t')$ and $s_{12}'(t')$ such that i_1 was the same value in both states for all $t' > t$, then the measurement process is *non-disturbing with respect to* i_1. Similarly, if this condition is met for all the parameters characteristic of states in S, then the measurement process is *nondisturbing*. When these conditions are not met for i_1 or all the parameters characteristic of states in S, then the measurement process is, respectively, *disturbing with respect to* i_1 or *disturbing*.[17] Definition 7 is sufficiently general as to encompass all these types of interacting and noninteracting measurement procedures, as well as other sorts of interactions. Finally, we note the possibility that the measured system could be one governed by statistical laws of quasi-succession and the measurement apparatus could be such that their interaction is governed by a classical deterministic law of interaction.

In many cases the interaction of a system governed by a statistical law of succession and a measurement system (governed either by statistical or deterministic laws) will result in a combined system governed by a statistical law of interaction.

Definition 8. Let t and t' be variables ranging over an α time sequence and let $s_1(t) = \langle p_1(t), \ldots, p_m(t) \rangle$, $s_2(t) = \langle q_1(t), \ldots, q_n(t) \rangle$, and $s_{12}(t) = \langle p_1(t), \ldots, p_m(t), q_1(t), \ldots, q_n(t) \rangle$, and let $i_1, \ldots, i_k$ ($k \leq m + n$) be distinct elements of the list $p_1, \ldots, p_m, q_1, \ldots, q_n$ and let $j_1, \ldots, j_{m+n-k}$ be the remaining elements on the list. Then a *classical statistical law of interaction* is a relation $R(s_{12}(t), s_{12}'(t'), p)$ satisfying the following condition for every t, t' such that $t < t'$ and $j_1, \ldots, j_{m+n-k}$ remain unchanged over the interval $[t, t']$:

$$\langle s_{12}(t), s_{12}'(t'), p \rangle \in R \text{ iff } P(s'(t'), s(t)) = p$$

where P satisfies the axioms for the conditional probability operator, and for each $s(t)$

$$\sum_{s'(t') \in D} P(s'(t'), s(t)) = 1.$$

From Definitions 6 and 8 it immediately follows that

Theorem 5. Every classical statistical law of interaction is a classical statistical law of quasi-succession.

Obviously Definition 8 and Theorem 5 admit of the sorts of nonclassical extensions mentioned above.

In manners analogous to those discussed for classical deterministic laws of interaction, a system S and an interacting measurement apparatus M such that the interacting system SM is governed by a classical statistical law of interaction can be used to obtain measurements of a parameter i characteristic of S—provided that the statistical law of interaction is such that from selected parameters in $s_2(t)$ and $s_{12}'(t')$ one is able to determine a conditional probability p that $i(t)$. Repeated measurement interactions with type S systems and recourse to stochastic techniques may allow further data about the behavior of S-type systems to be obtained.

Our survey of the standard classification of laws (including even their nonclassical extensions) has determined that there are only three basic types of laws—deterministic laws of quasi-succession, statistical laws of quasi-succession, and deterministic laws of coexistence. Other sorts of laws may be possible; in particular, we need to consider the perennial question whether the teleological and functional laws found in the social sciences and in biology constitute new and additional sorts of laws. This will be considered in section IV.

Before we address these specific questions, we need to consider another possible source of additional varieties of laws: Nothing in the Semantic Conception of Theories restricts a theory to the possession of just one law. However, if a theory possesses more than one law, the theory will sanction only those sequences satisfying *all* the laws. Since laws are state-occurrence simple-ordering relations, the conjunctive combination of several laws in effect is the intersection of several relations; and the result of such an intersection is itself a relation. Accordingly, theories generated by multiple laws will be theories governed by a single law. This raises the possibility that combinations of the basic three types of laws we have discovered thus far may yield laws of new sorts. Whether they do is an open question to which we have no answer—though our conjecture is that they do not. Regardless of the closure properties on the combination of laws, the use of such combinations to characterize local regularities is a commonplace in science which plays a central and possibly essential role in the scientific enterprise.[18]

IV. TELEOLOGICAL AND FUNCTIONAL LAWS

Teleological and functional laws are often claimed to constitute a distinct variety of laws differing from those found in physics (this is the so-called *separatist analysis*). We now investigate whether this is so.

By a *teleological system* we mean a system governed by a *teleological law*. What is characteristic of teleological systems is that they *tend toward some goal state or set of states.*[19] Crucial to analyzing teleological systems, hence teleological laws, is understanding what 'tends' means.

We begin our investigation of 'tends' by considering an example of an archetypal teleological system—a servomechanism. Our servomechanism will be a simplified TV antenna rotor, which can move the antenna to one of four positions, labeled 1, 2, 3, and 4 (see fig. 2).

The servomechanism has an input device consisting of a dial which can be turned to one of four numbers: 1, 2, 3, or 4. If the antenna is at the location indicated on the dial, then the antenna remains in its current position. If the antenna is in a location other than that indicated on the dial, the antenna moves toward the position indicated on the dial, passing through intermediate positions in ascending or descending numerical order (thus it cannot pass directly from position 1 to 4 or from 4 to 1). It moves to an adjacent location each time step until the dialed location is reached. The law governing this system, $R(s(t), s'(t'))$, uses an ω time sequence and is such that $s(t) = \langle d(t), l(t) \rangle$, where $d(t)$ is the number indicated on the dial at time t and $l(t)$ is the location of the antenna at time t. Sixteen different $s(t)$ are possible, and R is such that

$$\langle s(t), s'(t{+}1) \rangle \in R \text{ if and only if}$$

$$l(t{+}1) = \begin{cases} l(t) \text{ if } d(t) - l(t) = 0 \\ 1 + l(t) \text{ if } l(t) < d(t) \\ l(t) - 1 \text{ if } l(t) > d(t) \end{cases}$$

regardless what $d(t{+}1)$ is.

Several observations are in order. First, R is a deterministic law of quasi-succession. Second, the set of goal states are those such that $d(t) = l(t)$.

We can now see the way in which this system is such that it 'tends' toward a set of goal states. So long as the goal state d remains unchanged over a time interval $[t, t']$, its behavior will be such that $|d(t) - l(t)|$

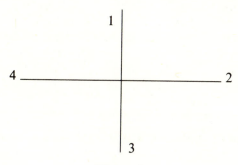

Figure 2

will be progressively reduced over time until it is minimized—which will be the case only if a goal state is reached. However, if $d(t) \neq d(t+1)$, then the behavior may be such that $|d(t) - l(t)| < |d(t+1) - l(t+1)|$. The crucial general point here is that teleological systems typically are systems whose behavior is in part a function of their interaction with an environment (here d) outside their control; and the tendency toward a goal state is an essential characteristic of their behavior only when reacting with a stable environment. If the environment is unstable, the goal state may never be reached or even closely approached.

The foregoing example is fairly typical of a deterministic teleological system[20] and can be generalized. For simplicity, we will restrict our generalization to the case where the state parameters of the system all are measurable.

Definition 9. Let $R(s(t), s'(t'))$ be a classical deterministic law of quasi-succession where $s(t) = \langle i_1(t), \ldots, i_k(t), p_{k+1}(t), \ldots, p_n(t) \rangle$, where the $p_i(t)$ and $i_j(t)$ are as in Definition 5 and are all measurable. Let $f(i_1(t), \ldots, i_k(t), p_{k+1}(t), \ldots, p_n(t))$ be a function whose values are real numbers. Let $G = \{s(t) \mid f(s(t)) = \max(f(s(t)))\}$. Then R is a *classical deterministic teleological law with respect to goal G* just in case the following condition is satisfied for every $s(t)$ whenever each $p_j(t')$, $(k+1 \leq j \leq n)$ is constant for all $t' > t$:

$$\lim_{t' \to \infty} f(s'(t')) = \max(f(s(t))).[21]$$

The statistical analogue to the notion of deterministic 'tending toward a goal state' intuitively is that in a stable environment the probability of the system being in a goal state will approach unity in the limit.

Definition 10. Let $R(s(t), s'(t'), p)$ be a classical statistical law of quasi-succession where $s(t) = \langle i_1(t), \ldots, i_k(t), p_{k+1}(t), \ldots, p_n(t) \rangle$, where the $p_i(t)$ and $i_j(t)$ are as in Definition 6 and are all measurable. Let $f(i_1(t), \ldots, i_k(t), p_{k+1}(t), \ldots, p_n(t))$ be a function whose values are real numbers. Let $G = \{s(t) \mid f(s(t)) = \max(f(s(t)))\}$. Then R is a *classical statistical teleological law with respect to goal G* just in case the following condition is satisfied for every $s(t)$ whenever each $p_j(t')$ $(k+1 \leq j \leq n)$ is constant for all $t' > t$:

$$\lim_{t' \to \infty} \left(\sum_{s'(t')} P(s'(t'), s(t)) f(s'(t')) \right) = \max(f(s(t))).$$

An R which determines an absorbing Markov chain with set G of absorbing states is an example of such a classical statistical teleological law (where $k = n$) with respect to G.

The notion of a boundary condition[22] provides an interesting perspective on teleological laws: For a given goal determined by a function f, a teleological law relative to that goal is nothing other than a law of quasi-succession such that the imposition of a boundary condition to the effect that the non-i parameters remain constant yields a new law satisfying the tendency conditions given in Definition 9 or Definition 10. Inter alia, this indicates that teleological laws do not constitute some new form of law irreducible to the traditional sorts of laws encountered in physics. Since it is well known that functional laws are just a species of teleological law,[23] it follows that functional laws are also not some new form of law irreducible to the traditional sorts of laws encountered in physics. The separatist analysis is false.

V. CONCLUSION

In this chapter, we have investigated the nature of theoretical laws on the Semantic Conception of Theories. On that view, laws are just relations which determine temporal simple orderings of state occurrences of systems. We characterized the standard sorts of laws found in science: deterministic and statistical laws of succession, coexistence, and interaction, and teleological laws. We also introduced two new sorts of laws: deterministic and statistical laws of quasi-succession. We showed that deterministic and statistical laws of quasi-succession and deterministic laws of coexistence are more basic than the others in the sense that all the other standard sorts of laws turn out to be reducible to one of these three sorts. We also showed that teleological and functional laws are special sorts of laws of quasi-succession; to that extent, the separatist thesis is false.

Before concluding our discussion, though, a possible objection to our analysis of theoretical laws needs to be anticipated and answered. It is a philosophical commonplace that laws must support counterfactual inferences. From this it usually has been concluded that in order to analyze or characterize laws, essential resort to the counterfactual conditional must be taken, and that in the absence of an adequate analysis of the counterfactual conditional, little in the way of analyzing laws is possible. Our analysis of various types of theoretical laws here has been set-theoretical, and at no place has the counterfactual conditional been resorted to. To many this is sufficient to render the analysis suspect. Such suspicions deserve serious but brief consideration.

The reason we have been able to proceed set-theoretically and avoid the counterfactual conditional is that we have confined our attention to theoretical laws—that is, to laws which occur within theories. On the Semantic Conception of Theories, the laws of a theory describe what the behavior of the systems within its intended scope *would be were* the systems isolated and/or certain idealized conditions met. It does so by *noncounterfactually* describing the behavior of systems under these idealized and isolated conditions and asserting that these idealized systems stand in a counterfactual relation to most actual systems within its scope. As such, a theory does support counterfactual inferences, and by extension so do its laws; but the counterfactual element in a theory is localized not in the actual statement of the laws, but rather in the *physical interpretation* of the theory—that is, in the relation between the idealized systems described by the laws and the actual typically nonidealized circumstances obtaining in the world.[24] Differently put: To be lawlike is to support counterfactual inferences. And on the Semantic Conception of Theories, this amounts to being a state-sequencing relation occurring in a theory that simple-orders state occurrences, and that theory must relate counterfactually to the physical systems in its intended scope. But such simple-ordering relations themselves (as opposed to their counterfactual interpretation) can be characterized set-theoretically without recourse to the counterfactual conditional. In this way the line of objection sketched fails.

This discussion of how the counterfactual component enters into theories and their laws also indicates in what sense it is true that a fundamental characteristic of (theoretical) laws is their inaccuracy: Theoretical laws precisely characterize the behavior of systems under isolated and/or idealized conditions which usually do not obtain in actual systems within the theory's intended scope. As such, the behavior of real-world systems within a theory's intended scope often will deviate from that specified by the theory. But that deviation does not make the theory or its laws inaccurate: For if the theory is empirically true, its laws are a totally accurate description of what the behaviors of the real-world systems within its scope *would be were* the systems isolated and/or various idealized conditions met. And given that this is the descriptive function of a theory and its laws, the characterizations provided by an empirically true theory are totally accurate. Thus a fundamental feature of theoretical laws is that they abstract and/or idealize their phenomena—but doing so does not make them ipso facto inaccurate. Indeed, on the Semantic Conception of Theories, the only inaccurate laws are those characteristic of empirically false theories. This finding vindicates the suspicion mentioned at the outset, that resort to a notion of approximate truth is not required for an adequate analysis of theoretical laws.[25]

NOTES

1. A commentary on this work by Henryk Mehlberg and a rejoinder by Scriven follow after it in Feigl and Maxwell 1961, 102–04.

2. See Scriven 1961, 100. Defects in this proposal are presented in Mehlberg's commentary.

3. The word 'model' must be used with extreme care, since it can mean a number of different things in science. Here we are using 'model' to mean *iconic model*—an entity which is structurally similar to the entities in some class (as, e.g., a model airplane is a model of the real planes in the class of F-4H fighters). For good discussions of the various meanings 'model' can take on in science, cf. Suppes 1961 and ch. 7 of Achinstein 1968; our discussion follows Suppe 1967, 80–107.

4. This correspondence is the heart of the physical interpretation of theories on the Semantic Conception. For a full and detailed discussion of the physical interpretation of theories, see ch. 3. In the discussion that follows, for simplicity of exposition we will ignore the distinction between abstraction and idealization drawn in ch. 3, sec. IV; we will use 'idealization' to refer indifferently to the two operations, since nothing in the present context turns on that distinction.

5. For a discussion of applications of the Semantic Conception to analyze the status of generalized equilibrium theory in microeconomics, see Hausman 1981.

6. The auxiliary theory must be such that in the particular circumstances *its* idealized conditions are met. Auxiliary theories can be "local theories" applying only to a very limited variety of circumstances (see ch. 4 for a detailed discussion of the foregoing claims).

7. See ch. 4 for a discussion of suitable auxiliary theories. For additional discussion of the empirical truth conditions for theories, see ch. 3. In case the theory contains statistical laws, the various probabilities with which state changes occur in the sequences determined by the theory also must be empirical probabilities characteristic of such changes for corresponding phenomena under idealized conditions.

8. Such a classification is used by van Fraassen 1970, by myself (in previous chapters), and partially by Hempel (1965a, 352).

9. Other discrete orderings of time are possible (e.g., time having the order properties of the rational numbers) but they will be ignored here, as science does not seem to have resorted to them.

10. The notation, $s(t)$, for the occurrence of s at t is somewhat misleading in that it suggests that s is a function of t, which it is not; rather, state occurrences are ordered pairs, $\langle s, t \rangle$. The use of ordered pairs $\langle s, t \rangle$ to indicate

state occurrences in the developments which follow proves to be notationally quite messy, and so I have opted for the (somewhat nonstandard) $s(t)$ notation.

11. Note that this definition employs a cut procedure when $\alpha = \lambda$; since laws are extralinguistic entities, this definition is not liable to the sorts of defects in defining 'deterministic laws' that Montague (1962) points out. [See also Earman 1986, 20–21. Laws are being construed as expressing regularities in phenomena rather than some metaphysically more loaded construal. For defenses of such an approach, see Earman, ibid., ch. V, Swartz 1985, and van Fraassen 1989.]

12. The deterministic laws of succession (including both classical and nonclassical ones such as those just discussed) intuitively seem to include the so-called causal laws. Whether they do in fact depends upon whether Hume, Reichenbach, and others are correct that cause must precede effect, or whether Kant was correct that cause and effect can be simultaneous. If Hume is correct, then Definition 1 and the expansion to nonclassical cases would encompass all causal laws; if Kant is correct, they do not. For a defense of Kant's position, see Melnick 1974.

If Kant and Melnick are correct, Definition 1 is adequate for those cases where cause precedes effect; the extension to cases where cause and effect are simultaneous involves major difficulties which we will not go into here. Whether they are correct or not is, to my mind, an open question, the resolution of which will have a crucial bearing on the problem of explanation and deserves serious investigation.

13. Cf. the sources cited in note 8 above.

14. [Definitions 5, 6, 7, and 8 are improved replacements for the definitions published in the original version of this paper. I thank Ronald Giere for help with the improvements.]

15. For appropriate caveats, see notes 11 and 12 above.

16. For a discussion of the role of laws of interaction in the design of a realistic (vs. conventionalistic) theory of measurement, see ch. 4, sec. II.

17. For simplicity I have confined the characterization of interfering and noninterfering measurements to systems S governed by classical deterministic laws of succession; analogues to these notions for S governed by deterministic or statistical laws of quasi-succession and/or statistical measurement apparatus are possible (see ch. 4, sec. IV).

18. See ch. 4, sec. IV for further discussion.

19. Cf. Rudner 1966, ch. 5, esp. 94–95.

20. There are respects in which it is atypical in that the goal state d is part of the environment (in many cases this will not be so), and no hysteresis occurs in the tending toward relation under a stable environment. Our formal definitions allow for these possibilities.

21. Notice that this definition allows considerable hysteresis in the "tending toward" relation, as does the next definition.

22. The phrase 'boundary condition' tends to be used with two different meanings in science: (1) conditions concerning the extent to which the system in question meets the abstraction or idealization conditions of the theory,

and (2) local regularities characteristic of a system within the scope of a theory which further restrict the possible behaviors allowed by the laws of the theory (as, e.g., when a parameter in a theory whose only law is a deterministic law of coexistence is allowed variable values, but outside constraints on system S are such that the parameter maintains a constant value). I am using 'boundary condition' in the second sense here.

23. See Rudner 1966, sec. 19.

24. For further discussion of this localization of the counterfactual element, see Suppe 1974b, 42–45.

25. Approximate truth may play a role, however, in assessing whether measured data (error-laden as all such data must be due to the limitations in accuracy of measurement apparatus) are in agreement with the predictions afforded by the theory. Differently put, although approximate truth plays no role in determining the empirical truth or falsity of a theory (hence its laws), it may figure centrally in deciding which theories to accept as true. Also, work on the growth of scientific knowledge indicates that in assessing theories one often is less concerned with the empirical truth of a theory than with its *promise* for subsequent development into a true theory; here approximate truth sometimes plays a role. For discussion of this latter point, see Suppe 1977a, sec. III-C, and ch. 11, sec. II, below.

PART III
Applications of the Semantic Conception

The Semantic Conception of Theories is offered as an explanatory philosophical analysis. Its abilities to contribute to the solution, or at least to the enhanced philosophical comprehension, of important problems about the nature of science and scientific knowledge constitute significant evidence for evaluating its adequacy as a philosophical analysis. Chapter 6 explores the implications of the Semantic Conception for philosophical problems in the area of scientific explanation, arguing (inter alia) that an account of theoretical explanation based on the Semantic Conception avoids the major difficulties encountered by the earlier covering law and statistical relevance approaches, and at the same time affords a deeper understanding of explanations based on theories.

Chapter 7 focuses on long-standing controversies over the relations between phenotypic classification schemes and evolutionary theory and (from the time of Aristotle) over natural versus artificial taxonomies in biology. While the latter issue does not explicitly concern the development of the Semantic Conception, it is absolutely crucial to the development and defense of a quasi-realistic version of that conception. Van Fraassen (1989, ch. 8) makes it clear that central to the defense of any scientific realism must be an adherence to an *antinominalism* that provides a fundamental distinction between natural groupings and merely arbitrary classifications.

In presenting my quasi-realistic version of the Semantic Conception thus far, I have already had to embrace an antinominalism—in chapter 3 I imposed the requirement that the intended scope *I* for an empirically true theory must be a natural kind set of causally possible phenomenal systems. The central business of chapter 7 is to develop an antinom-inalism by presenting an account of natural versus artificial classification schemes or taxonomies in biology and then to generalize that account to all classifications. The resulting antinominalism is a central meta-physical component of my quasi-realism and underlies the quasi-realistic epistemology developed in chapters 10 through 13. In sections V and IX the Semantic Conception is used to explore the relationships between scientific theories and taxonomies—both in general and with specific reference to the genetic theory of natural selection in evolutionary biology.

Chapter 9 exploits the Semantic Conception to explore the ways moral, social, political, and other extrascientific values legitimately and illegitimately influence scientific controversies and how they might be brought to closure. It also explores implications of the Semantic Conception for engineering contexts. In the process, it further enhances our understanding of teleological theories on the Semantic Conception.

Another way of testing the adequacy of the Semantic Conception is to explore its robustness—its ability to accommodate, without signif-icant alteration, newly discovered types of scientific theories which were not considered at the time the Semantic Conception underwent its basic development. Schaffner (1980) has argued that biomedical theories for the most part are rather different in structure than theories in evolu-tionary biology, being what he calls "Inter-level Theories of the Middle Range." Since such theories were not taken into account in developing the Semantic Conception, they provide a good test of its robustness. In chapter 8 I argue that the Semantic Conception accommodates these interlevel theories without alteration. That chapter also sheds further light on some characteristic features of theories on the Semantic Con-ception—features such as "universality" of laws. Although not discussed in any great detail, it obviously follows from the discussions in chapters 6 through 8 that the types of theories Shapere (1974a) has identified as compositional and evolutionary theories readily fall within the scope of the Semantic Conception, further testifying to its robustness.

6

Theoretical Explanation

Whereas most philosophical analyses of explanation focus on the use of laws to explain specific events, in actual scientific practice *theoretical explanations* are far more important and central. Wesley Salmon (1975) makes the point as follows:

> Arguments by Greeno and others have convinced me that explanations of particular events seldom, if ever, have genuine scientific import (as opposed to practical value), and that explanations which are scientifically interesting are almost always explanations of classes of events. This leads to the suggestion . . . that the goodness or utility of a scientific explanation should be assessed with respect to its ability to account for entire classes of phenomena, rather than by its ability to deal with any particular event in isolation. [119–20]

In fact there are two distinct sorts of theoretical explanations which explain entire classes of phenomena. One sort involves the use of a theory to explain another law or theory, as, for example, when Newtonian theory is used to explain Kepler's laws. This sort has been discussed by Hempel and others and is closely associated with intertheoretic reduction. The other sort, which I am solely concerned with here, involves the use of theories to explain events; we will see that such theoretical explanations invariably account for entire classes of phenomena.

Theories possess rich structural properties, which we investigated in chapters 2 through 5. One would expect them to bear a major burden in any philosophical analysis of theoretical explanation. Yet in his "Theoretical Explanation," Salmon exploits nothing more about theories than that they contain laws and theoretical entities, and nowhere in Hempel's discussions of explanation does Hempel exploit any of the detailed structural characteristics of theories provided by the Received View or its later incarnations which he helped develop. Similarly, theory structure plays no important role in other analyses of explanation such as those offered by Bromberger (1966) or Toulmin (1961). It is a central contention of this chapter that only by exploiting the structural properties of theories can we come to an adequate philosophical understanding of scientific explanation. The focus of my efforts here will be to explore the implications of the Semantic Conception of Theories for the understanding of theoretical explanation.

I. PHILOSOPHICAL ANALYSES OF EXPLANATION

Although the account which follows is most strongly influenced by the Semantic Conception, it also is influenced by the philosophical debates about explanation of the last several decades and what I take to be the lessons to be learned from those controversies. I begin with a selective and compact discussion of those points of agreement and disagreement which have influenced my account. Doing so hopefully will help locate the place of my treatment of theoretical explanation in the broader context of philosophical discussions of explanation.

Modern discussions of scientific explanation begin with the covering law model developed by Hempel in a series of papers.[1] On this model an explanation of some event (the explanandum) consists of a suitable argument wherein the explanandum follows deductively (D-N model) or with high probability (I-S model) from premises, consisting of laws and factual conditions (the explanans). The explanans must contain at least one lawful generalization and must be true or highly confirmed. In addition, a maximal specificity condition is imposed.

A number of criticisms have been raised against this covering law model. First, a number of counterexamples have been advanced against the D-N model by Bromberger, Salmon, and others. Bromberger's (1966) flagpole example is typical: The D-N model allows a law of coexistence relating the angle of the sun, the height of a flagpole, and the length of its shadow to be used to explain not only the length of the shadow, but also the height of the flagpole. The former he sees as legitimate; the latter illegitimate. This is typical of the D-N counterexamples in that it involves laws of coexistence. For reasons that will be developed in section IV-E, I do not find such objections compelling and believe they can be blocked by disallowing genuine laws of coexistence from being the only laws in D-N explanations.

Second, counterexamples have been advanced by Salmon (1970) and Jeffrey (1970) against the I-S model. These typically involve statistical laws which are causally irrelevant. For example, the I-S model allows the law "Persons who regularly take birth control pills have a low probability of getting pregnant" and the fact Mr. Jones regularly takes birth control pills to explain why Mr. Jones is not pregnant. And the generalization "People who wear high-heeled pumps have a high probability of wearing lipstick" and the fact Willard Scott showed up in drag wearing a Carmen Miranda outfit including high-heeled pumps, according to the I-S model, explains why Willard was wearing lipstick. What these counterexamples point to is that Hempel never gave (nor claimed to give) an adequate characterization of what a statistical law is, and that not all statistical generalizations (including those in the examples) constitute explanatory statistical laws. While this is a serious defect in the I-S model, it fails to establish that, given an adequate characterization of statistical laws, the I-S model would be unsatisfactory.[2]

Third, Hempel himself has argued that D-N explanations cannot meet the requirement of being deductively valid, since laws always are relative to unstated ceteris paribus conditions which violate deductive validity for the argument.[3] I did not find this convincing, since I see no reason why the laws cannot be stated in the form "Ceteris paribus all A are B" and "the ceteris paribus conditions are satisfied" be added to the factual conditions in the explanans, thus rendering the argument deductively valid.

There is, however, one objection to the covering law model that I do find convincing: Salmon (1970) and Jeffrey (1970) claim that explanations are not arguments at all. They argue the case as follows: The I-S model requires that the explanandum follow from the explanans with high probability. Thus on the I-S model only high probability events can be explained statistically. But in fact, extremely low probability events admit of statistical explanations (they give compelling examples), and such explanations cannot be inductively sound arguments. Hence the I-S model is defective, and statistical explanations are not arguments. Moreover, the D-N model also is defective in this respect: Causal explanations are limiting cases of statistical explanations, and if statistical explanations are not arguments, neither are causal ones. I am in basic agreement with Salmon and Jeffrey on this point. However, while we often give arguments in presenting explanations in order to be convincing, I do not believe that casting explanations as arguments adequately captures the structure of explanations. Thus I reject the D-N and I-S covering law models as seriously flawed.

Others who reject the covering law model have tried to present alternatives. Bromberger (1966) and Toulmin (1961) present models of explanation which resemble Hempel's model in many respects but introduce new ingredients designed to avoid deficiencies in his account. At the heart of both their accounts is the idea that the scientific laws employable in explanations are highly idealized and do not directly describe, and are not directly applicable to, most actual circumstances where explanations are needed. Bromberger calls such laws *general rules,* and Toulmin calls them *ideals of natural order.*

Bromberger maintains that, because of cases such as the flagpole one, Hempel's D-N model provides necessary conditions, but not sufficient conditions, for causal explanations; and he attempts to augment the D-N model with additional requirements. At the heart of these proposals is the idea that explanations are required only when there are deviations from the idealized circumstances of the general rule. At the core of an explanation is the expansion of the general rule to an *abnormic law* which contains a finite list of all the possible deviations from the general rule and effects of each such deviation. Bromberger's account is fundamentally defective for three main reasons: (a) all deviations from the idealized circumstances (hence all ceteris paribus conditions) are presumed to be finitely specifiable, and this generally is not the case; (b) in many cases where we do know how to give explanations (e.g., using classical particle mechanics), we do not know how to specify all the deviations from the idealized conditions or what their effects are, hence cannot supply the abnormic law his account requires; and (c) it appears that the only reason that cases such as the flagpole one are disallowed is because they are in accordance with the general rule, and Bromberger maintains that explanations cannot be given in such cases (a point I will dispute in a moment). Thus I find Bromberger's account seriously defective.

Toulmin's account does not adhere as closely to Hempel's D-N model as Bromberger's does, but it nevertheless shares a number of Bromberger's key insights. For him, events in accordance with ideals of natural order are self-explanatory and thus require no explanation—but no phenomena ever are in accord with the ideal (e.g., Newton's first law concerning inertia). Therefore, to explain such deviations one must use other laws which account for deviations from the ideal of natural order. Unlike Bromberger, Toulmin does not attempt to give a formal analysis of this procedure, and he does not commit himself to the finite specificity of all deviations from the ideal. My main complaints are that the account is inadequately precise, and unlike both Toulmin and Bromberger, I *do* think that events in accordance with the idealized conditions of laws do admit of explanations via the laws; they are explainable, and their explanation rests in the fact that they are in, or they approximate, the idealized circumstances of an empirically true or validated law and behave in conformity with that law. On the other hand, I agree with Toulmin and Bromberger that an important aspect of explanation is the use of laws to explain events which do not meet the idealized conditions of the laws and hence are not in conformity with them. Unlike Bromberger, I do not believe these deviations can be handled by anything like a finitely specified abnormic law, but I do agree with Toulmin that in explaining such deviations we do have recourse to other laws or theories. How this is accomplished in theoretical explanations will be discussed later.

A much more radical response to Hempel is found in Salmon's *Statistical Explanation and Statistical Relevance* (1970). At the heart of his treatment there are the ideas that (a) statistical explanations are more basic (causal explanations being a limiting case) and (b) that the essence of statistical explanation consists in citing factors which are statistically relevant to the explanandum event. Roughly, the idea is this: Suppose we wish to statistically explain the event B of kind A. We partition A into a set of homogeneous classes $AC_1 \ldots AC_n$. (The AC_i are homogeneous if none of its various subdivisions—called place selections—are statistically relevant to the occurrence of B.) Further, the partition must be such that

$$P(B,AC_1) = p_1$$

$$\cdot$$
$$\cdot$$
$$\cdot$$
$$\cdot$$

$$P(B,AC_n) = p_n$$

where $p_i \neq p_j$ ($i \neq j$). Then to explain why $x \in A$ is B, we determine which AC_k ($1 \leq k \leq n$) x is in, and the explanation why x is B would be "$x \in AC_k$." That is, among the As, the statistically relevant property responsible for x being B is C_k. To avoid various statistical paradoxes two further rules are required: The *reference class* rule requires one to choose the broadest homogeneous reference classes to which x belongs, and the *screening off* rule says that if one has a choice of properties with which to make a statistically relevant partition of a reference class, and one screens off the other (where D *screens off* C from B in reference class A iff $P(B, ACD) = P(B, AD) \neq P(B, AC)$), then the property that does the screening off is to be used in preference to the screened-off property.[4] The point of this rule is to eliminate cases such as Scriven's barometer case, wherein two effects (barometer change and storm) of a common cause (certain atmospheric conditions) are statistically relevant to each other and so, if allowed, would yield spurious explanations (e.g., the barometer change caused the storm).

There are a number of difficulties with this statistical relevance (S-R) account. First, the net effect of the homogeneity and screening-off requirements is fundamentally at odds with capturing everyday explanations of a practical sort, having the effect of sanctioning as legitimate explanations only those which are expressed in the very deepest physical terms.[5] Second, on Salmon's account, causal explanations are supposed to be limiting cases of statistical explanations—cases where $P(B,A) = 1$. Let A = "The flagpole is α feet tall," let B = "The shadow is β feet long," and let C = "The sun is at angle θ over level terrain." The law involved in the flagpole case is such that A & C implies B and B & C implies A. Thus we have

$$P(B,AC) = 1$$
$$P(B,A \sim C) = 0$$

meeting the conditions of Salmon's analysis. But we also have

$$P(A,BC) = 1$$
$$P(A,B \sim C) = 0$$

meeting the conditions of Salmon's analysis. Furthermore, because the probabilities of $P(B,AC) = 1 = P(A,BC)$, there is no way the screening-off rule is applicable; AC and BC are homogeneous classes, and broadening the reference class will not help.[6] Thus we have the flagpole counterexample all over again. The point here is that in the causal explanation cases a temporal asymmetry is crucial to explanatory capability—AC explains B because there is a tiny time lag between a light ray hitting the flagpole and the resulting shadow being cast, but BC does not explain A because that temporal asymmetry is violated. If Salmon's account cannot capture this crucial causal asymmetry in the limiting case, there is reason to doubt that it can in other genuinely statistical cases.

Third, on somewhat different grounds (involving various counterexamples), Salmon has come to the conclusion that statistical relevance cannot capture the asymmetries required for explanations and now sees causal notions as having a most fundamental role to play:

Although we believe that the S-R model of explanation has certain virtues, we do not believe it can provide a fully adequate account of scientific explanation. In order to have any hope of

achieving a satisfactory treatment of this notion, we must supple-
ment the concept of statistical relevance with some kinds of causal
considerations. . . . The relation of cause to effect has a distinct
temporal asymmetry; causes come before effects, not after them.
The relation of explanatory facts to the fact-to-be-explained has a
similar asymmetry. In the D-N and I-S models, there is no demand
that the explanatory relation be any kind of causal relation. . . .
The same is true of S-R explanations; they are not explicitly causal,
and it is not clear that they embody any temporal asymmetry
requirements. . . . Only by introducing causal considerations explicitly, it appears, can we impose the appropriate asymmetry conditions upon our scientific explanations.[7]

To the end of imposing such conditions, Salmon (1984) has been developing an account based on continuity and the use of "marks."

I am sympathetic to Salmon's earlier view that statistical explanations
are more fundamental than causal ones—though I would claim that
it is indeterministic explanations which are more fundamental than
deterministic ones. Further, he is absolutely correct that there is a fundamental temporal asymmetry in explanation—and I concur in the
opinion that "screening off" and "statistical relevance" conditions do
not capture that asymmetry. I am, however, far less sanguine about the
prospects for his "marks" and "continuity" criteria capturing that asymmetry, partly for reasons that overlap qualms L. Jonathan Cohen (1975)
has registered. More fundamentally, many scientific theories that employ
discrete, not continuous, time parameters (e.g., the genetic theory of
natural selection, which measures time in "generations") seem quite
capable of providing explanations but do not meet Salmon's "continuity" requirements; thus I doubt that the requirements will capture
the essential asymmetry of explanation except perhaps for certain special
cases. Further, I am convinced that the structure of theories revealed
by the Semantic Conception of Theories has all that is needed to capture
that asymmetry without recourse to specific analyses of causality or
hypotheses about the role of "marks" therein.

II. ARE ALL EXPLANATIONS EXPLANATIONS WHY?

Virtually all the philosophical literature on explanation assumes tacitly,
if not explicitly, that explanations are explanations *why* or responses to
explanation-seeking *why* questions. While Salmon and others assume
this, to my knowledge only Hempel has attempted to defend this view,
and then only briefly:

A scientific explanation may be regarded as an answer to a why question, such as: 'Why do the planets move in elliptical orbits with the sun at one focus?' 'Why does the moon look much larger when it is near the horizon than when it is high in the sky?' 'Why did the television apparatus on Ranger VI fail?' 'Why are children of blue-eyed parents always blue-eyed?' 'Why did Hitler go to war against Russia?' There are other modes of formulating what we will call *explanation-seeking* questions: We might ask what caused the failure of the television apparatus on Ranger VI, or what led Hitler to his fateful decision. *But a why-question always provides an adequate, if perhaps sometimes awkward, standard phrasing.*[8]

Is it really the case that every explanation-seeking question is equivalent to a why question, hence that all explanations are equivalent to answers to such why questions?

Consider a partial list of possible erotetic descriptions of explanations:

(1) The anthropologist explained *who* slept in the village longhouse.
(2) The technician explained *what* the significance of the peaks in the oscilloscope pattern was.
(3) The biologist explained *where* to look for sea urchins.
(4) The man explained *why* the event *did* happen.
(5) The man explained *why* the event *was possible,* though improbable.
(6) The biologist explained *what* hemoglobin does.
(7) The biologist explained *when* the grunion run.
(8) The physician explained *how* the multiple birth *did* occur.
(9) The physician explained *how* the multiple birth *could have* [might have] occurred.
(10) The economist explained *which* product's production *would* maximize marginal cost.

Some of these questions (e.g., [2]) are such that there is a corresponding why question that could have been asked, and such that an answer to the indicated question would contain the ingredients of an answer to the corresponding why question. But erotetic logic today is sufficiently advanced that we know that different sorts of questions have different presuppositions and that what counts as an answer to a question is dependent upon the answer standing in the appropriate logical or empirical relationship to the question's presupposition.[9] In particular, answers to who, where, what, whether, and so on, questions generally entail their presuppositions, whereas the answers to why and how questions generally do not.[10] Since why, how, who, where, what, and so on, questions have different presuppositions, it is not clear that the answer to an explanation-seeking non-*why* question automatically qualifies as an answer to any corresponding *why* question. Thus, for example, some answers to the *who* question of (1) above may answer the corresponding *why* questions, while others may not. Hempel's thesis thus seems suspect at best—and certainly in need of more sustained defense than he has offered.

My concern is with theoretical explanation, for which the explanation of isolated events is not central; thus it may seem that such qualms over the why-explanation equivalences of, for example, questions (1), (2), (6), (7), and (10) may be beside the point (though I remain unconvinced). However, I would maintain that there are types of theories which afford a variety of *explanations how* but are incapable of providing *explanations why,* in which case the point of the objection is fundamental. There is a variety of known classes of systems which, in the ideal at least, appropriately are characterized as a finite Markov process or chain. For the sake of quick illustration, suppose that we have such a class of systems characterized by four states governed by the state transition matrix shown in figure 3. This matrix, of course, determines a probabilistic state transition branching tree, where all paths are equiprobable. Suppose that at t we know what state s a particular such system is in and that at $t + 34$ the system is in state s'. Since the number of paths from s to s' is exceedingly large, and since each path is equiprobable, I claim this Markov theory is incapable of explaining on the basis of being in state s at time t *why* the system is in state s' at time $t + 34$. I do claim, though, that it could explain *how* the system in state s at t *could have* come to be in state s' at $t + 34$—namely, that there is a *possible* state transition path from s to s' in 34 state transitions. Indeed, there will be an inordinately large number of such *how could* explanations which are equiprobable. If I had, in addition, *full* knowledge of each of the state transitions at intermediate times from t to $t + 34$, I would be able to explain via the above matrix (law) *how did* a system in state s at t come to be in state s' at $t + 34$; but I would not be able to explain *why* the system in state s at t was in state s' at $t +$

Figure 3

		State at $t + 1$			
		1	2	3	4
	1	¼	¼	¼	¼
State at t	2	¼	¼	¼	¼
	3	¼	¼	¼	¼
	4	¼	¼	¼	¼

34, for I cannot explain *why* the various state transitions at intermediate times that occurred did occur (as opposed to other possible and equiprobable ones).

The situation would not be significantly different if one had larger matrixes or ones with radically unequal probabilities in the various cells. Indeed, even the existence of absorbing states would not appreciably alter the situation. Crudely overstated: If a theory generally allows at least one theoretically possible state transition path from state s at t to state s' at t' ($> t$), then a *how could* explanation for being in state s' at t', given that the system previously was in state s at t, is possible. If one also knows the state transition history between s and s', one can give an explanation *how did* the system previously in s at t come to be in s' at t'; but only if one can show, via the theory and its laws, that a system in state s at t *had* to go into state s' at t' ($> t$) can one give an *explanation why* that system in state s at t is/was in state s' at t'. In short, an *explanation why* is an explanation *how could* coupled with the uniqueness claim "and that is the *only* thing that could have happened."

Not only do I deny that all explanation-seeking questions are reducible to equivalent explanation-seeking *why* questions, but I am convinced that explanation-seeking *how could* questions are explanatorily more basic. Thus I believe Hempel, and also Salmon and others, are mistaken in their assimilation of *explanation* into explanation why. More importantly, I believe that full appreciation of this point leads one to treat indeterministic (as opposed to deterministic) theoretical explanations as the basic case—and that doing so ultimately displays in part why Salmon's recent retreat to causality, continuity, and marking conditions misses the mark.

My bottom-line conclusion is that *explanations how could*, not *explanations why*, are the basis for an adequate philosophical analysis/ understanding of theoretical explanation. Further, I believe that the Semantic Conception of Theories has the resources to provide an adequate understanding of such explanations. In showing that this is so I will confine my attention to the question how empirically true theories can provide, or function in, explanations.

III. THEORETICAL EXPLANATION ON THE SEMANTIC CONCEPTION

Although it is common to formulate theories using multiple laws (e.g., Newton's Three Laws) on the Semantic Conception, theories with multiple laws are always equivalent to ones with single laws.[11] We may assume, then, that theories have only one law as we investigate the explanatory capabilities of the main sorts of laws. (We also assume the notation and detailed analyses of these forms of laws from ch. 5.) We now analyze the sorts of explanations that different kinds of laws can provide via theories construed in accordance with the Semantic Conception.

A. How Could *Explanations with Statistical Laws of Succession*

Let us first consider statistical laws of succession. The key feature of such laws is that for a given current state, the law allows that the system may assume a number of different subsequent states and assigns conditional probabilities that these various subsequent states will be assumed. The Mendelian laws of genetics and finite Markov processes are paradigmatic examples.

Suppose we are concerned with the way molecules of a gas behave when put in a compartment in which there is a thin semipermeable membrane that divides the compartment into equal-sized cells (see fig. 4).

Suppose further that we know there are $2n$ molecules of gas (for some n) and that we have the following empirically true theory T about such systems: The possible states are $\langle j, k \rangle$, where j is the number of molecules in compartment 1 and k is the number in compartment 2, and the state transition law governing the behavior of this system is characterized by

$$k = 2n-j$$
$$P(j-1, j) = j/2n$$
$$P(j+1, j) = (2n-j)/2n$$
$$P(m,j) = 0 \quad \text{otherwise.}$$

(In this theory it is assumed that exactly one molecule crosses the membrane each time step.)[12]

Suppose I walk into my lab, examine the contents of cell 2 and find it empty, then count $2n$ molecules in cell 1 (i.e., it is in state $\langle 2n, 0 \rangle$). Perplexed, I seek an explanation. I ask the lab assistant what he has

Figure 4

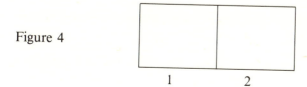

1   2

done recently to the apparatus, and he replies that two hours ago he cleaned the apparatus, then introduced n molecules of gas into each compartment, and that he has not touched a thing since.

Drawing on my theory (above), I now am able to explain how state $\langle 2n, 0 \rangle$ could have happened: I use the theory to draw a branching tree, which begins as depicted in figure 5 below. (Note that the p_i labeling branches are probabilities, not necessarily distinct). I calculate the number of time steps that have elapsed from the time the apparatus was filled until I observed state $\langle 2n, 0 \rangle$ at t', then determine that, yes, state $\langle 2n, 0 \rangle$ is on several of the nodes for the t' column of the tree. Then I see that (since $t' = t + 2$ hours $>> 2n + t$) there are multiple paths down the tree from the root to each of those nodes. I now have an explanation *how could* the apparatus be in state $\langle 2n, 0 \rangle$ at t': There are one or more possible paths from known state $\langle n, n \rangle$ at $t = 0$ to observed state $\langle 2n, 0 \rangle$ at time t'.

The foregoing example involves a case where the actual situation approximates the fiction that only the defining parameters of the system affect the system's state transition behavior—the fiction that the system is isolated from outside influences. Suppose, however, that when I examined the compartment contents I found not state $\langle 2n, 0 \rangle$, but instead state $\langle 2n-16, 0 \rangle$. The above theory does not allow this as even a possible state, so by itself T affords no explanation. Knowing this, I suspect the

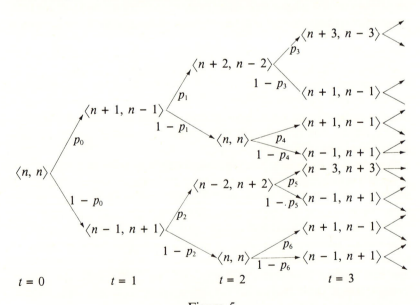

Figure 5

apparatus does not meet the isolation conditions of the theory. On careful inspection I discover there are several microscopic breaks in the welded corners of compartment 1 large enough for a gas molecule to escape; then I experimentally determine the likelihood that a molecule will escape over a time step. I combine this new "local law" with the original theory (relativizing its equations to a variable number of molecules in the system) to get a new special case theory that covers the situation. I again construct my (revised) state transition tree, determine the existence of one or more paths from known prior state $\langle n, n \rangle$ at $t = 0$ to state $\langle 2n-16, 0 \rangle$ at t' and thereby explain *how could* the system be in state $\langle 2n-16, 0 \rangle$ at t'.

Some comparison of these two cases is in order: In the second case the isolation conditions presupposed by our basic theory T were not met. But once we found what the nonisolation circumstances were, we established a local law governing them and combined these with the basic theory T, producing a new local theory T'. This T' imposes its own conditions of isolation from outside influences, and relative to these our apparatus was isolated from outside influences. This case points out that theories are capable of providing *how could* (and other) explanations *only* of systems which are isolated from outside influences not taken into explicit account by the theory—and that in actual practice we sometimes can use local laws in conjunction with quite general theories to produce explanations of systems that fail to meet the isolation conditions of the general theory. In either case our explanation of the singular event is an explanation *how could* for such events in *all* systems meeting the isolation conditions of the theory providing the explanation, and so it accounts for entire classes of phenomena.

It is noteworthy that this account of statistical *how could* explanations does not directly resort to any notions such as statistical relevance, requirements of "maximal specificity," or causal notions. Some comments on this are in order. First, consider the indeterministic nonstatistical analogue to statistical *how could* explanations: That is, consider a theory which indicates possible state transitions without assigning any probabilities to them. Examples of such theories include certain grammatical theories with optional transformation rules, as well as a number of anthropological theories about social structure such as those concerning the circumstances where in certain tribes some young boys are selected to become *berdache shaman* (transvestite medicine men or priests) while most are selected to become warriors. From such theories one can explain how certain phenomena *could be*—even though one cannot assign probabilities to the explanandum states. This strongly suggests that statistical considerations are not essential to *how could* explanations, but rather greatly enhance the predictive capabilities of a theory.

Second, in the case of statistical theories it might seem that statistical relevance conditions are necessary to avoid conjunctive forks, the introduction of superfluous parameters, and so on. I do not agree: The requirement that the theory be empirically true is strong enough. If a theory can meet the empirical truth requirements for theories imposed in chapter 3 (which are quite strong), it is virtually certain that none of its defining parameters are superfluous or artificially included. However, although such statistical relevance considerations may have a legitimate place in the confirmation/testing theory utilized to determine whether a theory is empirically true, that fact does not require its inclusion in any analysis of theoretical explanation.

Third, statistical laws of succession have built in the sort of temporal asymmetry required for explanation, without explicit recourse to any causal notions.[13] Moreover, it is unclear that any causal notions—even statistical ones—truly are built into statistical laws of succession. It may be that under some statistical theories of causation, statistical laws of succession are causal—but if so, it is not obvious to me that they are causal in the sense required to give explanations why. Nevertheless, we will see in the next section that there are rather peculiar circumstances in which statistical laws of succession do provide explanations why. In my opinion, the discussion there lays the basis for doubting that there is any simple connection between cause and the ability to provide *why* explanations.

B. Why *Explanations with Deterministic Laws of Succession*

Why explanations typically (but not inevitably) are supplied by theories with deterministic laws of succession. Intuitively, the characteristic feature of such laws is that the current state of a system determines unique subsequent states. If we view laws of succession as specifying state transition trees, the main difference between deterministic and indeterministic laws is that whereas the latter allow multiple paths to branch off from each node, the former allow only one state transition path to emit from each node.[14] Consequently, in indeterministic theories there may be multiple paths from a prior state at t to the explanandum state at t', and it is possible that the system might have been in some other state at t'. In contrast, both possibilities are precluded by deterministic laws of succession. Thus if we know that a system was in state $s(t)$ and we want to explain its being in state $s'(t')$, we are able to explain *how* the system *could be* in state $s'(t')$: We have an empirically true theory with a deterministic law of succession that applies to the system, the system meets the law's isolation conditions, and the theory specifies a state transition path from $s(t)$ to $s'(t')$. But the theory tells us more: It tells us that this is the *only* state that the system could be in at t' and that there is a *unique* path whereby it came to be in $s'(t')$—given that it previously was in $s(t)$. In short, the theory tells us not just how the system could be in $s'(t')$, but *that is how it had to be:* It provides an *explanation why* it is in $s'(t')$.

This suggests that an explanation *why* is an explanation *how could* such that there is a unique state the system could be in at the time of the explanandum event/state and a unique path to that state from a known prior state. The analysis following will evaluate this suggestion.

We now can say something more about the relations between explanations afforded by statistical laws of succession and explanations *why.* First, consider our examples from the previous section. Suppose that we augmented our explanation how the apparatus could be in the explanandum state with detailed knowledge of each state transition between t and t'. In this case we would have an explanation *how did* the system come to be in the explanandum state; but we would *not* have an explanation *why* it came to be in that state at t, since it could come to be in that state by a different path and it could have been in a different state at time t'. There are, however, circumstances in which a theory with a statistical law of succession can provide explanations *why.* Consider, for example, the following portion of the state transition tree defined by a statistical law of succession shown in figure 6. Such a law could only explain *how* a system in state s_0 at t could be in state s_8 at $t + 5$: It could not explain *why* it was, but it could explain *why* the system in state s_2 at t was in s_8 at $t + 3$.

Consider, now, a system such as a pinball machine which is governed by a finite Markov process with an absorbing state such that all paths lead to a terminal state (in that the play ball leaves the playing area

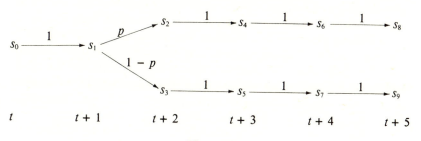

Figure 6

through a single slot). Let s_I be the initial state and s_A be the terminal absorbing state. To visualize this, take a simplified pinball system with three states having the state transition matrix depicted in figure 7. A portion of its state transition tree is shown in figure 8. The characteristic features of this tree are that multiple state transition paths are possible, but all paths eventually lead from s_I to s_A. Can the correct theory for this sort of system provide explanations why? Initially I thought not — my intuition being that the unique terminus, unique path requirement (suggested above) was essential for explanations why. However, a number of persons have pressed intuitions that in cases such as this the theory does enable one to explain why the system initially in state s_I ended up in s_A. For a long time I resisted such an intuition, construing the explanation why request as requiring that we answer the question why the system initially in s_I (at t) *now* is in state s_A (at time t'). I believed that the unique path, as well as the unique terminus, requirement was needed to do this. (In the simplified example in fig. 8, which path is taken uniquely determines at which time the system goes into s_A.) But the contrasting intuition seems to construe the explanation why request differently — as why the system *eventually* will come to be in state s_A.

Figure 7

State at $t + 1$

	s_I	s_1	s_A
s_I	0	½	½
s_1	0	½	½
s_A	0	0	1

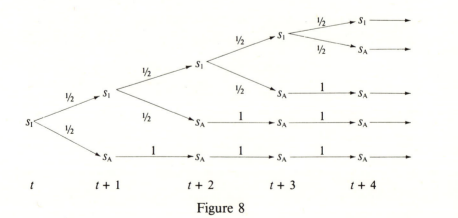

Figure 8

This time-unspecified explanation does not seem to require the unique path condition, though it does require the unique terminus one.

This suggests that there are two sorts of requests for explanations why: one sort asking *why* something had to happen and another sort asking *why* something had to happen *when* it did. Thus we should distinguish two sorts of explanations why: *Strong explanations why* explain why a system in state s at t had to be in state s' at t' and thus are explanations *how could* that meet the originally proposed unique path and unique terminus requirements. *Weak explanations why* explain why a system in state s at t eventually had to end up in state s' (but not why it did at a particular time), and thus are explanations *how could* that meet the unique terminus, but not the unique path, requirement.

Is this suggestion viable? Let us reconsider our simplified pinball machine example. It clearly does not allow a strong explanation why, since there is not a unique path to state s_A; but it also does not meet the requirements of a weak explanation why, since it is not the case that the system eventually *has* to end up in state s_A—for at every time t' there is some finite probability $(\frac{1}{2})^{r-t}$ that it will be in s_1 (despite the fact that $\underset{t'-t\to\infty}{\text{Limit}} (\frac{1}{2})^{r-t} = 0$). By contrast, consider a system governed by a statistical law of succession with the tree portion shown in figure 9. It would enable one to give a weak explanation why the system in s_1 (or $s_1 - s_6$) had to be in state s_7 at time $t + 4$; but since it does not meet the unique path condition, it does not afford us a strong explanation why. Nevertheless, it does explain why the system in s_0 at t had to be in state s_7 at $t + 4$. This indicates that the unique path requirement of strong explanation why is not necessary: Although it is a condition met only by deterministic explanations why an event had to happen at t', indeterministic explanations why an event had to happen at t' are also possible. What is essential for explanations why an event happened at time t' is that there be only one state the system could be in at time

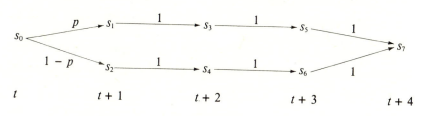

Figure 9

t', not how many paths lead there in the same time. In other words, what counts in explaining why Caesar got to Rome when he did is not that all paths lead to Rome, but that all paths lead to Rome and are of the same length.

We conclude, then, that our proposed weak and strong explanation why distinction is unsatisfactory. Rather, in order to explain why a system in state s at t was in state s' at t', the applicable theory must be such that s' is the only state the system could be in at t'. Deterministic theories in addition are such that there will be a unique path whereby the system in s at t came to be in state s' at t', but such unique paths are not essential to explanations why. Our discussion thus indicates how very subtle and complex are the relations between deterministic laws, indeterministic laws, and the ability to provide explanations why. It should be noted that although explanations why automatically provide explanations *how could,* only explanations why based on deterministic laws of succession automatically provide explanations *how did.*

I should stress that, as was the case with indeterministic theories, deterministic theories can provide explanations only for systems that meet the isolation conditions for the theory, although, even in cases of nonisolation, given suitable auxiliary laws or theories we frequently can produce special-purpose theories for which our explanandum systems do meet the isolation conditions. Thus, for example, for classical particle mechanics we can produce terminal velocity or frictional inclined plane, special case theories which are applicable to some sky diving and loading dock situations by virtue of their isolation conditions being met.

Finally, I note in passing that I allow that the defining parameters for states in a theory with a deterministic law of succession may be probability distribution functions, as in the case of quantum theory. In such cases one can explain why a system *was* in a particular quantum state at time t', but one can *only* explain (statistically) *how* a particle of the system *could have* a particular observed position or momentum.

C. Why *Explanations with Laws of Quasi-Succession*

Among the more prominent laws, besides those of succession, are laws of interaction and teleological and functional laws.[15] We have shown in chapter 5 that these are special cases (as are laws of succession) of a more basic sort of theoretical law—*laws of quasi-succession.* To use terminology introduced in chapter 5, section III, what is characteristic of systems with laws of quasi-succession is that subsequent internal substates, but not subsequent external substates, are a function of the prior complete states of the system.

One of the most interesting examples of a theory with a law of quasi-succession is the genetic theory of natural selection. On this theory, the internal states are genotypic makeups of an interbreeding biological population. The basic law of the theory involves various rules of chromosomal recombination during cell meiosis and recombination. These rules determine the next generational makeup of the population (at $t + 1$) as a function of not only the population distribution at t (the internal substate), but also the birth/death/reproduction ratios of the various genotypes (which are the external substate parameters). The theory and knowledge of just a prior complete state at t provides absolutely no means for predicting subsequent internal substates beyond $t + 1$.[16]

This latter fact complicates the giving of explanations. Take a simple special case: Suppose I know the genotypic makeup of a population at time t, have monitored the birth/death/reproduction ratios of the various genotypes from t to $t + 3$ (measured in generations), and have determined that genotype G is becoming extinct (i.e., at t it was α-proportion of the population and at $t + 3$ it is $\alpha/100$ths of the population). From the data I have I can determine how it is *possible* that the population is in internal substate $s'(t')$ such that G has $\alpha/100$ths proportionate representation in the population, but the way I do so is rather different from that used with laws of succession. To see this, consider a portion of the simplified tree representation of the theory (shown in fig. 10), where E and I represent the external and internal substates of the complete state $\langle E, I \rangle$ at t. (Asterisks indicate the state actually assumed at each time, and time is measured in generations.) Note that at any time, given the complete state, the theory enables us to predict a unique I for the next generation; but it does not enable us to predict the next or subsequent complete states. However, since we know the external states for each time, we can in fact predict, generation by generation, subsequent internal states and, combining that with our knowledge of the external states, determine what the subsequent complete states will be. Indeed, the theory together with prior knowledge of the external states at $t + 1$, $t + 2$, $t + 3$ yields a unique path from $\langle E_0, I_0 \rangle^*$ to $\langle E_3'', I_3^9 \rangle^*$; given those external states, $\langle E_3'', I_3^9 \rangle$ is the unique terminus allowed by the theory, and so we explain *how could* the system in $\langle E_0, I_0 \rangle$ at t be in state $\langle E_3'', I_3^9 \rangle$ at $t + 3$. Further, we can give an explanation how the system in state $\langle E_0, I_0 \rangle$ at t could be in internal state I_3^9 at $t + 3$: there is a path (indeed, three of them) from $\langle E_0, I_0 \rangle$ to I_3^9 at $t + 3$. Thus if $\alpha/100$ths is G's representation in I_3^9, we can

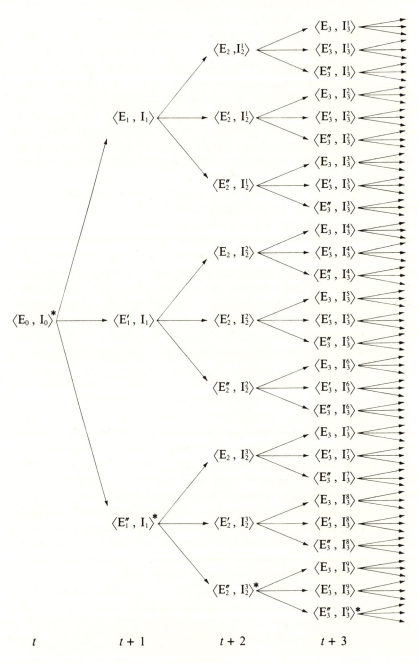

t $t + 1$ $t + 2$ $t + 3$

Figure 10

explain how it could be that G's representation has dropped so drastically as to risk extinction.

How did and *why* explanations are more problematic in this case. Given knowledge of the external states the system was in at $t + 1$ and $t + 2$, we know how the system in $\langle E_0, I_0 \rangle$ at t came to be in I_3^0 at $t + 3$. It also seems plausible to say that we can explain *how did* the system come to be in I_3^0 at $t + 3$: "The system was in $\langle E_0, I_0 \rangle$ at t, E_1 and E_2 occurred, and so the system went into I_3^0 at $t + 3$." In the case of G's extinction, the explanation would be "At t, G had α-proportion of the population, but its reproduction rates at t, $t + 1$, and $t + 2$ were relatively low compared to others in the population, so via the laws of natural selection theory it only had $\alpha/100$ths of the population at $t + 3$." On the other hand, we would want to say that we could not explain *how did* the system in $\langle E_0, I_0 \rangle$ at t come to be in $\langle E_3'', I_3^0 \rangle$ at $t + 3$; for the explanation would have to be the *how did* explanation of its being in I_3^0 at $t + 3$ coupled with the fact that the external state at $t + 3$ was E_3, and it seems illegitimate to include part of the explanandum in the explanans. This example illustrates that in explanations *how did,* only knowledge of prior states and the theory may figure in the explanans.

Are any *why* explantions possible in this case? Consider G's nearing extinction. The birth/death/reproduction ratios essentially are a summary of the effects of environmental, ecological, and other factors which affect the reproductive success of a genotype. Our path tree indicates that given birth/death/reproduction ratios (external states) E_1'' and E_2'' at $t + 1$ and $t + 2$, there is a unique internal state I_3^0 that the system can be in at $t + 3$. Thus the theory, augmented by knowledge of E_1'' and E_2'', enables us to explain why the system in $\langle E_0, I_0 \rangle$ at t was in internal state I_3^0 at $t + 3$. And since G having $\alpha/100$ths representation is part of I_3^0, we can explain why it has gone into near extinction since t: The population was in state $\langle E_0, I_0 \rangle$ at t, the various genotypes at times $t + 1$ and $t + 2$ were E_1'' and E_2'', and given the laws of natural selection theory, the system had to be in internal state I_3^0 at $t + 3$; under I_3^0 G's representation is $\alpha/100$ths. Note that the explanation why here requires taking into account the reproduction ratios of all genotypes of the population, and not just G's. Theories with deterministic laws of quasi-succession together with knowledge of the external states at t' ($t < t' < t''$) can provide explanations why a system in complete state s at t is in internal state i at t'' just in case there is a unique state i the system could be in at t'' given the external state history between t and t''.[17]

Compare the previous case with the following one: Our theory is natural selection theory, but instead of knowledge of the intermediate external states, we have an empirically true ecological theory with a deterministic law of succession which enables us to predict (inter alia) the birth/death/reproduction ratios for a population. Then we can combine this ecological theory with natural selection theory to produce a new evolutionary theory which will have a deterministic law of succession. And of course, the new theory could explain (in a deeper or fuller fashion) why G was undergoing extinction. Lacking such a theory of the external state transitions, we still can explain why the system came into internal state i by resorting to detailed specific information about the external state history.

In the former case, where we used the ecological theory as well, we were using it to impose boundary conditions on the deterministic law of quasi-succession so as to make natural selection theory act as if it were governed by a deterministic law of succession. In the latter case we used knowledge of the external state history to impose local boundary conditions (for a short time span and for a specific population) to essentially reach the same explanatory effect. Note that in this case, while we can explain why the system is in internal state i, we cannot explain why it is in complete state s'; for that would require part of the explanandum figuring crucially in the explanans. On the other hand, in our combined ecological and natural selection theory, we could explain why the system was in complete state s' at t' given that it was in s at t, for that theory can predict subsequent birth/death/reproduction ratios.

The same process of using another theory or external state histories to impose boundary conditions is applicable to theories with statistical laws of quasi-succession. Thus, drawing from earlier results, we conclude that when the statistical law of quasi-succession and boundary conditions require the explanandum state to be the unique possible outcome, an explanation why is possible. We conclude, therefore, that an empirically true theory with laws of quasi-succession augmented with boundary conditions specifying an external state history over (t, t') can provide an explanation *why* a system in complete state s at t is in internal state i at t' just in case there is a unique internal state i at t' allowed by the law and the boundary conditions.

D. Why *Explanations Reconsidered*

In my discussions of statistical explanations why, I tacitly was maintaining that theories with statistical laws can give theoretical explanations why a system in state s at t is in state s' (or i) at t' only when the specified unique terminus conditions have been met. In science, however, we frequently encounter statistical explanations why where a unique terminus does not obtain. For example, in the 1950s, the American Cancer Society ran a study whose conclusion was that smoking causes cancer. From the statistical generalizations produced by that study one can give statistical explanations why Jones developed cancer (because he smokes three packs a day), even though not everybody who smokes three packs a day gets cancer.[18] Since there is no unique terminus in such cases, does this show that our requirements are too stringent?

There are a number of important differences between the cancer case and theoretical explanations why: First, in the cancer case we do not have an empirically true theory with a theoretical law. Rather, we have various empirical statistics about the relative incidence of cancer among smokers and nonsmokers which are not equivalently recast as a theory.[19] Thus it is not a case of theoretical explanation at all. Second, the notion of causality involved in such studies is a statistical one which essentially measures causal influence, whereas our account is concerned with "complete causes."[20] Third, our account is concerned with explaining why events happen *at the time they do* and why they happen instead of some alternative event. The cancer study does neither; it does not provide explanations of why individuals got cancer when they did, or why they got it as opposed to not getting it. Fourth, what the cancer studies allow is explanations *why it was more likely* Jones would get cancer than some other people. Thus, at best, it enables us to explain how Jones could get cancer and to predict the likelihood of his getting it. If (contrary to our first point) the study resulted in an empirically true theory about cancer (with a statistical law), it would enable precisely the sorts of *how could* explanations which our account already allows, but would not yield an explanation why.

Collectively these considerations show that *why* explanations based on statistical notions of causality constitute no challenge to our analysis of theoretical explanations why. The discussion further demonstrates how important it is in philosophical discussions of explanation to be clear and precise as to what explanation requests the analysis is concerned with: 'why did,' 'why did at *t*,' 'why is it likely that,' 'why is it possible that' are responses to different explanation requests, and require different analyses. Failure to specify precisely what is the explanation request is commonplace in the explanation literature and at times has hindered our understanding of scientific explanation.[21] Our discussion here also lays the basis for further doubting the claim that all explanation requests equivalently can be recast as requests for explanations why, for it reveals that not all requests for explanations why are equivalent.

Our discussion of theoretical explanations also lays a basis for further assessing the adequacy of treatments of explanation by Hempel, Salmon, and others. Such discussions typically employ laws of the forms

$$\text{If } C_1, \ldots, C_n \text{ then } E$$

(*)

$$P(E, C_1 \ldots C_n) = r$$

These laws (or as I prefer, "law statements") are *highly unrepresentative* of the sorts of theories science typically produces. Other than in the design of measurement apparatus (generally "local" as opposed to "global" theories) or occasional exceptions such as the genetic theory of natural selection, scientific theories tend to characterize their phenomena as "closed," rather than "open" systems—which is to say that they present theories with laws of succession or coexistence. But philosophical discussions of explanation largely ignore theories, looking at laws of the forms (*) above. These essentially describe transducers from an input/output perspective and amount to laws of quasi-succession with degenerate internal substates. It is natural to construe such laws as (deterministically or statistically) causal, hence affording explanations why.

Here it is important to remember, and take seriously, the Salmon quotation that began this chapter, which asserted the relative scientific importance of theoretical explanations of *general* classes of events and the relative unimportance of explanations of isolated events. Scientific theories generally are about closed systems governed by laws of succession, and the explanations they afford are of classes of phenomena.[22] And to these, laws of forms (*) are utterly irrelevant. Other than in the design of measurement apparatus or special-case solutions/versions of more "global" theories, theories with laws of quasi-succession are relatively rare—although one of our most impressive global theories, the genetic theory of natural selection, fundamentally employs such laws. As we saw in the previous section, however, such theories can yield explanations beyond $t + 1$ only when augmented by boundary conditions which make them act as if they had laws of succession. Further, since laws such as those of forms (*) ignore the crucial importance of internal substates in laws of quasi-succession, they are theoretically impoverished and highly unrepresentative. By ignoring the rich structural properties of theories, earlier accounts of explanation have missed much of what is most central to the ability of theories to give explanations.

E. The Problem of Laws of Coexistence

If one carefully peruses the various counterexamples of Bromberger (1966), Salmon (1970), and some others to Hempel's D-N model of explanation, one finds that they frequently involve "laws of coexistence"—of which the "ideal gas laws," such as

$$(**) \qquad PV = nRT$$

are typical and, as Salmon notes, are noncausal.[23] The flagpole case we considered in section I is generally presented as employing a law of coexistence. These laws commonly are *not* stated as state transition laws. They merely assert that such equilibria will hold, "come what may," without any specification *how* alterations in any of the state parameters may occur. In a certain sense they are *degenerate* statistical laws of succession in that they say "any equilibrium state as defined by an equation such as (**) is equiprobable." But as actually formulated, they say nothing explicitly about state transitions. However, it is not difficult to reformulate such laws to be explicitly state-transitional (as in Defs. 3 and 4 of ch. 5). So long as they are in reformulated form and are empirically true, I have no qualms about allowing them to be the basis for *how could* or (if augmented) *how did* explanations. Still, they are a cause for worry, since they are at the mercy of factors not reflected in the law for state transitions and ultimately are quite non-deterministic: They are explanatorily tepid. Even so, such a reformulation minimally gives a weak *how could* explanation. With respect to *explanations why* it is totally impotent, for such laws never can meet the unique terminus requirement.

Still, it might seem that I have allowed too much. Consider the notorious flagpole counterexample to Hempel's D-N model wherein laws of coexistence allow the shadow cast by a flagpole to "explain" the angle of the sun to the horizon. Do I not allow such cases? No! The most I allow is a degenerate explanation of how the collective angles, height of the flagpole, and length of the flagpole shadow lawfully covary—without any imputation of cause. The troublesome causal influence abnormalities occur only when one illegitimately attempts to convert laws of coexistence into laws of succession or quasi-succession, and to do so is to radically transform the laws in ways that do violence to the time variables and temporal asymmetry. For example, in the flagpole example, when stated in a form analogous to (**) (as it generally is stated in the explanation literature), it would appear that the length of the shadow, the height of the flagpole, and the angle of incidence of the sun to the ground are simultaneous variables. But given an appropriately discriminative time scale, what we actually have (given fixed height for the flagpole), is that the angle of incidence of the sun at t determines the length of the shadow at time $t + \epsilon$; in short, we have a law which fails to be a type (**) law of coexistence—rather, it is a deterministic law of quasi-succession which incorporates precisely the sorts of temporal asymmetries needed to block the standard counterexamples pertaining to explaining *why*. Once this clarifying move is made, I believe not only can we explain away such troublesome cases but also that (depending upon the form of the laws) they can be assimilated into the prior accounts of theoretical explanation.

The foregoing prompts me to advance the following hypothesis: Insofar as we confine our attention to explaining subsequent complete system states as functions of prior ones, where such state transitions are mediated by empirically true theories, laws of coexistence raise no special problems for *how could* explanations. They afford no *why* explanations since they cannot meet the unique terminus requirements on *why* explanations introduced variously above. Standard counterexamples are pseudo ones we can explain away because of their inadequate care to the details, especially ones of temporal asymmetry, or else because they represent an attempt to push theories beyond their explanatory capabilities—which, hopefully, have been better articulated in this chapter.

IV. CONCLUSION

This chapter has been very much a prolegomenon: While I remain impressed by the profound intellectual efforts of Hempel, Bromberger, Salmon, and others to fathom the profundities of scientific explanation, I do believe that they have been seriously misled by assimilating *theories* into *laws* and that they have failed to adequately appreciate the extent to which the structure of scientific theories radically affects the nature of scientific explanation. I do not claim to have solved all the philosophical problems concerning scientific explanation, but I do hope to have mounted an enticing case that these problems need to be rethought—and that seriously treating the structure of theories is key to a productive rethinking of these mainstream explanatory issues in philosophy of science.

One last caveat: For all my discussion, I have not offered a "standard" philosophical analysis of "theoretical explanation." Specifically, I have not offered *necessary* or *sufficient* conditions for being a *theoretical explanation,* although I have given necessary conditions for various kinds of laws being able to yield explanations *how could, how did,* and *why.* Since I cannot prove that the sorts of laws I have considered are exhaustive of the laws which can figure in theories,[24] it is premature to claim to have found necessary conditions for being a theoretical explanation. As to sufficient conditions, I doubt any exhaustive set of sufficient conditions is or can be forthcoming, for any conclusive account of what a theoretical explanation is must be parasitic upon an account of what it is to be a *scientific* theory.

While I believe the Semantic Conception provides a defensible account of what it is to be *a* theory, I do not believe it is, or potentially can become, an adequate account of what a *scientific* theory is. The issue of what theories are scientific ultimately is based upon the domain a science deals with and the science's evolving standards as to what is scientific, and thus ultimately it is not a matter for philosophical fiat or decision. However, one can present, as I have tried to here, a philosophical account of what it is about theories that *enables* them to provide scientific explanations, and to explain how—and what sorts—of explanations they afford. I believe that doing so can be philosophically and scientifically illuminating—but I do not believe that either I or philosophers of science can have the last word on the subject.

NOTES

1. The most important are Hempel and Oppenheim 1948 and Hempel 1965a.

2. A number of other counterexamples have been raised in the literature by Scriven (1958, 1962), Toulmin (1961), and others. Hempel has responded to these in Hempel 1965a. Given his rejoinders there, I do not find these other counterexamples as plausibly convincing as the ones I consider here. I have discussed some of the others elsewhere (1977a, 619–23).

3. For example, Hempel's lecture at Johns Hopkins University, Spring, 1974.

4. Note 14 of Meixner 1979 points out that this rule is superfluous whenever the reference classes are homogeneous (as Salmon's analysis requires).

5. Ibid.

6. Even if *BC* and *AC* were not homogeneous, that would not affect things, for we could break them down into homogeneous reference classes. But that would not alter things, since the event we are concerned with belongs to *AC* and to *BC*.

7. M. Salmon and W. Salmon 1979; W. Salmon 1975, 1977, 1978, 1984.

8. Hempel 1965a, 334; some italics added.

9. See, e.g., Harrah 1963; Belnap 1963; Belnap and Steel 1976. Bromberger 1966 also is relevant.

10. See Bromberger 1966 and Belnap and Steel 1976, for related discussion. Presently there is no satisfactory treatment of the relationships between answers to *why* and *how* questions and their presuppositions.

11. See ch. 5, sec. III, for supporting arguments.

12. This example is adapted from Kemeny, Mirkil, Snell, and Thompson 1959, 416–17. That the example is an oversimplification and not really an empirically true theory does not affect my argument.

13. I will have more to say about this when we consider laws of coexistence in sec. E. For the moment it will suffice to note that the state transition paths are time-directed graphs.

14. I am assuming, for simplicity of illustration, that time is discrete here.

15. Another important sort of laws, laws of coexistence, will be discussed in sec. E.

16. In its standard formulation, this theory has a deterministic law of quasi-succession with statistical state parameters (probabilistic population distribution functions.) Presumably (and with great complexity) it could be presented as a theory with a statistical law of quasi-succession. That it is not probably reflects the facts that (a) every theory with statistical laws can be formulated equivalently as a theory with a deterministic law over probabilistic states, and (b) the latter tend to be more compact, manageable, and mathematically tractable (Suppe 1967, 144–49). The genetic theory of natural selection will be discussed further from the perspective of the Semantic Conception in ch. 7.

17. I intend this formulation to allow the possibility that if only partial knowledge of the external state history enables one to determine a unique terminus, an explanation *why* can be given.

18. Salmon's S-R model will sanction such explanations. Hempel's I-S model would not allow them, since the probabilities are too low.

19. A theory must have a notion of state, and the law must be one of state transition. Given the data the American Cancer Society collected, states would have to be something like the following

⟨years smoked, amt. smoked per day, age, cancer—yes or no⟩.

Then given some appropriate time scale (say, year intervals), one would have to have a law specifying state transitions (via either a statistical law of succession or of quasi-succession). The actual data of the study (or all other cancer studies for that matter) are not adequate to specify or even validate such a law. For a description and philosophical analysis of the study, see Giere 1979, sec. 12.3, 14.5.

20. For discussions of statistical notions of causality, see Giere 1979, ch. 12; 1980; and Suppes 1970.

21. For example, I believe it to play an important role in the inconclusive controversy between Scriven (1958, 1959, 1962) and Hempel (1965a) over the adequacy of the D-N model.

22. The complications due to laws of coexistence will be considered in sec. E.

23. See ch. 5, sec. III, for discussion and conjectures on this issue.

7

Some Philosophical Problems in Biological Speciation and Taxonomy

In this chapter I am concerned with a body of problems arising in biological taxonomy: What is a species? How are taxa defined? What is the difference between a natural and an artificial taxonomy? Are taxonomies true or false? What theoretical properties do taxonomic systems possess? My interests in these problems are primarily philosophical, not biological. Although these problems arise most dramatically in biological taxonomy, they are by no means peculiar to biology; indeed, similar problems can be raised for most branches of science as well as for common garden varieties of knowledge.

Ultimately, the issues are those of developing an antinominalism which is an essential ingredient of the full defense of a scientific realism or quasi-realism. Although my treatment will proceed in terms of the biological versions of these problems, my investigation has as its aim the establishment of a number of general epistemological and metaphysical results about taxonomic systems and classification—results which will lay the foundation for a general philosophical analysis of taxonomic and classificatory systems in science, generalize to an anti-nominalism, and thus contribute to the development of a quasi-realistic account of scientific knowledge. As such, my interests here are different from most of the recent philosophical treatments of biological speciation and taxonomy which have as their focus such questions as, How is 'species' to be defined in biological taxonomy?, What is a natural biological taxonomy?, and What sorts of definitions are or ought to be given for biological taxa?[1] Whereas those treatments attempt to provide philosophical solutions to biological problems, my purpose is to exploit the biological problems in an attempt to provide antinominalist solutions to some quite general philosophical problems about classification. The fact that my concern with investigating these issues comes from the perspective of defending a scientific quasi-realism further distinguishes my discussion from most of the literature on taxonomy and classification. The resulting antinominalism will be used to enhance our understanding of the empirical truth conditions for theories adopted in chapter 3 and will provide a basic ontological underpinning for the quasi-realistic epistemology for science developed in chapters 10 through 13.

I. KEY PROBLEMS IN TAXONOMIC THEORY:
A HISTORICAL SURVEY

By way of providing background for my investigation, I want to begin by characterizing what a taxonomic system is, introducing some key terminology and indicating more precisely the problems concerning taxonomy and classification that I intend to consider. In doing the latter, my approach will be largely historical.

By a *taxonomy* (or *taxonomic system*) I mean a system of categories for classifying individuals on the basis of similarities; these similarities may be morphological, functional, social, or whatever. A *standard taxonomy for domain D* is a finite collection of *taxa* (classes of individuals in D) such that each taxon is assigned to a unique category in a hierarchial ordering of categories, and each individual in D belongs to exactly one taxon of each category. More precisely, a standard taxonomy must meet the following conditions:

(1) There is a finite, serially ordered sequence of *taxonomic categories, $C_1, \ldots, C_n$*;
(2) each taxonomic category C_i ($1 \leq i \leq n$) contains m_i taxa, $T_{i,1}, T_{i,2}, \ldots, T_{i,m_i}$;
(3) The $T_{i,1}, \ldots, T_{i,m_i}$ are each collections of individuals in D such that each member of D is a member of exactly one $T_{i,j}$ ($1 \leq j \leq m_i$);
(4) all individuals in a given $T_{i,j}$ ($1 \leq i < n$; $1 \leq j \leq m_i$) must be members of the same $T_{i+1,k}$ ($1 < i \leq n$; $1 \leq k \leq m_{i+1}$).[2]

Most biological taxonomies are standard taxonomies of this sort. For example, the usual phylogenetic taxonomies are of this sort, where D is the class of living organisms. In such taxonomies, the taxonomic categories $C_1, C_2, C_3, \ldots$, respectively, will be the classes of species, genera, families, and so on, where, for example, the category *species* is the set consisting of all those taxa (classes of organisms) which qualify as species. As such, individual organisms are members of taxa but not of taxonomic categories; and taxa are members of taxonomic categories, whereas the individuals belonging to the taxa are not. For example, a man is a member of the taxon *Homo sapiens* (a species) but is not a member of the category *species;* and the taxon *Homo sapiens,* being a species, is a member of the category *species.*

[Recently, Hull (1976) and others have suggested that species are individuals, not classes. Such a view violates the requirements for standard taxonomies in that the $T_{1,j}$ taxa are replaced by individuals or particulars (sometimes called "superorganisms"). This nonstandard view will be discussed later in several places.]

Certain features of standard taxonomies need to be emphasized. A given taxon of whatever taxonomic category will always be a collection of individuals in D. Thus a species is a collection of living organisms, a genus is a collection of living organisms, a family is a collection of living organisms, and so on. When we say that the species *Rosa multiflora* is of genus *Rosa,* which in turn is of family *Rosaceae,* we are saying that every living organism which is a member of the taxon *Rosa multiflora* is also a member of the taxon *Rosa* and of the taxon *Rosaceae;* we are *not* saying that the species *Rosa* is a member of the genus *Rosa multiflora.*

Taxa of whatever taxonomic category are collections of individuals grouped on the basis of some "similarity." A given taxon (e.g., species *Rosa multiflora*) is defined by specifying the similarity characteristic of its members, the similarity by virtue of which they are classed together.[3] The hierarchical nature of standard taxonomies simplifies the definition of a given taxon. If an individual a is a member of taxon T_{1,i_1} of category C_1, it follows that a also must be a member of a taxon T_{2,i_2} of category C_2, a member of taxon T_{3,i_3} of category $C_3, \ldots$, and a member of taxon T_{n,i_n} of category C_n (where $1 \leq i_j \leq m_j$ for $j = 1, \ldots, n$). Since T_{1,i_1} and $, \ldots, T_{n,i_n}$ each are collections of individuals having certain similarities, to specify a taxon T_{j,i_j} of category C_j all that need be done is to specify that an individual is a member of T_{j,i_j} if and only if it is a member of $T_{j+1,i_{j+1}}, \ldots, T_{n,i_n}$, and has similarity characteristics c which are characteristic of T_{j,i_j} but of no other taxon of category C_j. That is, we need not specify all the similarities by virtue of which individuals are grouped together in T_{j,i_j}, but rather only those not common to all members of $T_{j+1,i_{j+1}}$. Thus to define the taxon Class *Mammalia* (T_{j,i_j}) we need only specify that its members are those living organisms of Subphylum *Vertebrata* ($T_{j+1,i_{j+1}}$), Phylum *Chordata* ($T_{j+2,i_{j+2}}$), and Kingdom *Animalia* (T_{n,i_n}) which have hairy skin, the transverse division of the body cavity by a diaphram, the nonnucleated condition of mature red blood corpuscles, and milk-producing mammary glands used to nurse the young. To define the Subclass *Prototheria* ($T_{j-1,i_{j-1}}$) all that need be said is that it consists of those individuals of Class *Mammalia* (T_{j,i_j}) which are egg-laying.

Depending upon what sorts of similarities are chosen to define taxa, a number of different standard taxonomies may be defined for a given domain, *D*. For example, one may define plant species on the basis of morphological similarity, genetic similarity, similarity of sexual parts, affinity by common ancestry, size, and so on. Some choices (e.g., length of body) may result in highly arbitrary taxonomies. Since the recorded beginnings of taxonomy (Aristotle and Theophrastus), the attempt has been made to distinguish such artificial from "natural" taxonomies, and throughout the history of taxonomy much theoretical dispute has centered on the issue of what makes a taxonomy natural. Most accounts accept the intuitive idea that *natural taxonomies are those which classify in accord with the objective reality confronting us in nature,* but differ in what is required to do so.

Dispute over this question often has become intertwined with dispute over three other questions: (1) What form of definition should be used in defining the various taxa (e.g., What definitional form is to be given for *Rosa multiflora*?)?, (2) How are the taxonomic categories to be defined (e.g., What is a species?)?, and (3) Should taxonomic systems be natural? These three subsidiary questions obviously are interconnected with the basic question about natural taxonomies. For if one denies taxonomies should be natural, the choice of definitional form for taxa and taxonomic categories will be restricted only by what makes the taxonomy useful for its intended purposes. And if one maintains that taxonomies ought to be natural, then what is taken as being natural must be reflected in the way one defines taxonomic categories and how one may define the individual taxa. It is a useful oversimplification to view differing theoretical views on taxonomy as constituting differing answers to these four questions.[4]

The earliest recorded theoretical position on the nature of taxonomy is to be found in Aristotle's writings.[5] According to Aristotle, systems of classes can be formed in a number of ways, but only certain classes are *natural*. Natural classes are those which have a *form* or an essential nature (*essence*); artificial classes lack a form. This form is immutable and eternal, being the secondary substance of things with being (individual existents, or primary substances). A natural taxonomy is one comprised wholly of natural classes; an artificial taxonomy is one comprised, at least partially, of artificial classes.[6]

Aristotle's notion of natural taxonomies, which he maintains ought to be adopted, strongly influences the account he gives of taxonomic categories. According to him, species are the essences of natural classes which are indivisible in the sense that none of their parts are essences or forms of primary substances; derivatively, the individuals which possess that species' essence are of the species. Two individuals are of the same genus if their forms differ only in the quality of their parts, but have the same parts. This characterization of the taxonomic categories largely determines the admissible definitional form for the individual taxa. For the parts of a form or essence are, according to Aristotle, characters. And the form of a species thus is determined by its combination of parts and their qualities — that is, by the combination of characteristics of specified qualities. The form of a genus will be determined by the combination of parts without regard to quality — that is, by the combination of characteristics without regard to quality. For example, men are of the same species, since their essences have the same parts with the same qualities (e.g., eyes are similar, as are noses, etc.) whereas not all fishes are of the same species, but are of the same genus, since their parts are the same, but differ in quality (e.g., fins are located differently, etc.). Thus the appropriate form of definition for a taxon is the specification of those characteristics (with regard to kind and, possibly, quality) which constitute its essence. That is, the definition of the individual's species and genus is to be given by listing a set of necessary and sufficient characteristics which constitute its essence. Insofar as Aristotle deals with the higher taxonomic categories, it is on the basis of parts common to the essences of genera. Thus Aristotle's basic theory of taxonomy is one wherein natural taxonomies classify on the basis of the essences of individuals (on the species level) and their similarities (in the higher taxonomic categories), where essences can be specified in terms of the necessary and sufficient characteristics of the essence or forms of the individuals. These essential characteristics, which collectively constitute the form of an individual, are largely (but apparently not exclusively) morphological.[7]

Through the Dark and Middle Ages, taxonomy remained essentially Aristotelian, with insignificant changes. By the sixteenth century, biologists (e.g., Cesalpino, Harvey, and De Graaff) were beginning to discover more and more morphological characters, which were added as "essential" characters to the Aristotelian definitions of essences, and by the seventeenth century (with the work of Malpighi and Grew), plant anatomy had come into being. The net effect of this increase in "essential" characters for classifying organisms was that the doctrine of essential natures was eroded until Aristotle's doctrine of species as essences was rejected. The influential John Ray (1627–1705) maintained that all parts of the plant should be used in classification, and not just selected essential ones. For Ray, species were natural and immutable but not determined by essences.

The changes in taxonomic theory begun under Ray find fairly full articulation in Linnaeus' (1707–1778) work. According to Linnaeus, a natural taxonomy is one which serves to teach the "nature" of plants and animals, rather than merely distinguishing them one from another; natural taxonomies do so by being based on "the simple symmetry of all the parts." Linnaeus differs from Aristotle on what it is to be a natural taxonomy, though not as radically as it might seem. For according to him, species are fixed, being stable and timeless classes of organisms which are to be defined in terms of the symmetry of all parts, including physiological as well as morphological characters.[8] In a word, species are like Aristotle's except that all characters are essential. And the form of definition is exactly the same as Aristotle's — in terms of necessary and sufficient characteristics. Although Linnaeus did succeed in developing a very good artificial taxonomy (based on sexual organs) for plants, he never succeeded in developing a natural taxonomy.

And it is no wonder that Linnaeus failed; for if his dictum that natural species are to be defined in terms of *all* characteristics of the organism, where these become necessary and sufficient characteristics for species membership, is taken at face value, there will be far too many species (e.g., males and females, varieties, deformities, etc., will end up as different species). If species are to be defined in terms of necessary and sufficient characteristics, and such proliferation of species is to be avoided, of necessity only certain characteristics of an organism may be used to define species. Two obvious ways of resolving this dilemma present themselves: either reintroduce essentialism or maintain that species are arbitrary.

The latter approach was taken by Buffon (1707–1788), who initially rejected Linnaeus' fixity of species but accepted the idea that species are not essences. Noting the variations and diversity of characteristics within a species, he concluded that species are arbitrary and can only be defined arbitrarily. Later he changed his position and maintained that while genera, orders, classes, and so on, are arbitrary and unreal, species are real, being nonarbitrary and defined on the basis of interfertile breeding and the production of fertile offspring. Buffon's taxonomic theory thus is that only on the species level are taxonomic categories real, and they are to be defined solely in terms of an interbreeding criterion. There is no place for diagnostic characteristics in defining species. On the higher levels, no taxonomy can be natural: taxonomic categories are to be defined arbitrarily in terms of necessary and sufficient characteristics.

Similar positions, which nonetheless retreat from Buffon's nominalism, were advanced by Adanson (1727–1806) and others. Adanson maintained that natural taxa are based on affinity, which is to be measured by taking all characters into consideration, taxa being separated from each other by means of correlated features. This notion was further developed by Vicq-d'Azyr (ca. 1792), who treats a natural class as the result of assembling species which have the greatest number of resemblances to each other, where these resemblances are greater than those they have to specimens in other classes. Here we find a genuinely different approach to taxonomic theory. As with Linnaeus, a natural taxonomy is based on all characteristics, but it does so in terms of resemblances, allowing speciation in the face of divergence; it is a crude approximation of the modern numerical taxonomic approach of defining taxa via clusters of characteristics which do not provide necessary conditions for inclusion in the species. The upshot of doing things this way is that one can obtain a kind of natural taxonomy which admits intraspecies variation.

Closely related to this approach to handling variations is the neo-Platonist account developed by Louis Daubenton (1716–1800) and Cuvier (1769–1832), wherein classification is on the basis of prototypical organisms—basic plans inherent in nature—of which individual organisms were descendant variations. Here, a natural taxonomy would be one which classified on the basis of these prototypes with the species definition giving the prototypical ancestor's necessary and sufficient conditions. Thus, like Buffon, breeding true (but with variations allowed) is the mark of a species. This is the ancestor of typological classification.

Lamarck (1748–1829) was a staunch opponent of Cuvier's neo-Platonism. In 1812 he had discovered geographical variation among species, which prompted him to develop a theory of evolution. With his theory of evolution, the doctrine of fixity of species (which Linnaeus, Cuvier, et al., had defended) was rejected, for, following de Candolle (ca. 1819), he maintained that physiological (functional) characteristics were useless in classification, the only legitimate basis being comparative morphology. A species, then, is a group of individuals with the same or similar morphological characters, and as these morphological characters change as a result of evolution, species, too, must evolve. Species at best can be construed as sufficiently similar collections of organisms *at the moment,* and such a collection of organisms can only be called a species for the time being. Species, classes, genera, et al., thus are unreal. All taxonomy is artificial. The form of definition in an artificial taxonomy still is the Aristotelian one of necessary and sufficient characteristics. Although Darwin's (1809–1882) evolutionary theory was quite different than Lamarck's, his basic positions on these taxonomic issues were much the same as Lamarck's.

In these seventeenth-, eighteenth-, and nineteenth-century positions, we find the seeds of most commonly contemporary theoretical positions on taxonomy. First, there is the school of taxonomy known as *typology*. Its chief tenets are that species are natural groups by virtue of an ideal type of which individual specimens are variants, that the task of taxonomy is to discern the essences of these ideal types, and that these ideal types are to be defined in terms of necessary and sufficient characteristics. While this approach is not widely held today, it is the dominant method in many branches of paleontology (Mayr 1964, 109). It also finds widespread employment in the social sciences.[9] This position obviously is heir to the tradition associated with Cuvier.

The widespread acceptance of evolution has had the effect of most taxonomists abandoning anything like an Aristotelian essentialism or typology. Some taxonomists admit evolution, but maintain that there are fixed species which can be defined in Aristotelian fashion in terms of necessary and sufficient characteristics; holders of this position, however, have found it virtually impossible to define species accordingly.[10] Other taxonomists admit evolution and genetic continuity, yet adhere to Aristotelian definitions, and thereby deny species reality. This position is heir to Lamarck's position. Neither of these positions is particularly satisfactory, however,[11] and various different approaches have been tried to avoid these problems.

One of these approaches stems from Buffon's later position, maintaining that there is some sort of functional characteristic in terms of which natural species are to be defined. In its modern guise, this position, known as the New Systematics, takes as its basic position the idea that natural species represent phylogeny. Various attempts have been made to provide a definition of the species category under this approach. The more important definitions proposed for the species category are: (1) the *genetic definition:* "A species is a group of genetically identical individuals"; (2) the *interfertility definition:* "A species is a group of interfertile individuals"; (3) the *biological definition:* "Species are actual or potentially interbreeding natural populations which are reproductively isolated from other such groups"; (4) the *evolutionary definition:* "An evolutionary species is a lineage (an ancestral descendant sequence of populations) evolving separately from others and with its own unitary role and tendencies." Unfortunately, none of these definitions proves satisfactory.[12] Buffon's taxonomy was similar in that he attempted to define the species category along the lines of the biological definition, but to do so he had to eliminate the use of morphological characteristics in defining taxa names because of the intraspecies morphological variation which occurs under the biological definition.

To avoid this defect, the New Systematics has replaced the Aristotelian form of definition by a disjunctive *polytypic definitional form.* Simply put, this form of definition consists of clusters of sufficient characteristics which are characteristic of each variety of subspecies of a species, these clusters being disjunctively joined together. Unlike the Aristotelian definition, it usually will be the case that no member of a species will have all the characteristics used to define a species, but rather will have only some of them. As originally proposed, polytypic definitions are limited to a finite number of clusters disjoined together.[13] But Hull has shown that such polytypic definitions are inadequate (1964, 71–83). Rather, taxa are cluster concepts because they are definable only disjunctively and because the number of disjuncts is indefinite.[14] That is, they are polytypic definitions with an indefinite number of disjuncts.

The reason an indefinite number of disjuncts is required is that: "A definition of a species name is sufficient if it distinguishes the population of that species from all other known species. As evolution proceeds or as new species are discovered, the list of defining properties must be changed and expanded. A definition that was once sufficient is no longer sufficient . . . but the definition of the name of a taxon need not be prepared in advance for all possible contingencies. But it must be modified as new contingencies arise" (Hull 1964, 116). That is, the definition must have an indefinite number of disjuncts since, as evolution progresses, new varieties of a species will emerge, and their defining clusters must be included as defining disjuncts; since we don't know what these clusters will be, these disjuncts cannot be specified in advance. The advantage of this approach is that a species definition remains fixed throughout the species' evolutionary course. This is done by only partially specifying the definition; many taxonomists (and also philosophers) find this definitional form unacceptable qua definition because of its incompleteness, and so reject the proposal.

The failure of the New Systematics to provide a phylogenetic criterion of species (what they view as a failure to supply an adequate means for defining taxa under a phylogenetic account of the species category) and the extremely loose correlation between genotypic and phenotypic characteristics, have prompted another group of taxonomists to reject the idea that species definitions should have a phylogenetic basis. More precisely, they accept the notion that species do have a phylogenetic basis, but deny that it can be employed practically to define species (cf. Sokal and Sneath 1963, 21). Instead, they take their lead from Adanson and maintain that in a practical taxonomy, species are those classes of organisms which have the greatest affinity to each other, where affinities are determined on the basis of as many characters as possible.[15] This position, known as *numerical taxonomy,* takes such a taxonomy as being a natural one in the sense that it is adequate for general use by all scientists; an artificial taxonomy is one designed for restricted use for a special purpose (Sokal and Sneath 1963, 12). On the basis of a number of rather naive and questionable arguments, they maintain that there is a practical incompatibility between being natural in this way and defining species names phylogenetically.[16]

In the survey just given, we have seen a number of different answers given to the four questions we asked about taxonomy. It will help if we summarize the various sorts of answers we have seen, for much of what follows in this chapter consists in the philosophical evaluation and examination of these answers and their consequences:

(1) Should taxonomies be natural?
   (a) Yes, they have an objective basis in nature.
   (b) No, they are arbitrary groupings made for convenience in achieving some goal.
(2) What is the objective basis in nature which makes a taxonomy natural?
   (a) Organisms have an essential nature or form, and a natural taxonomy classifies on the basis of common essential forms.
   (b) Organisms are variations of one ideal type or another; a natural taxonomy is one which establishes taxa on the basis of these ideal types.
   (c) Organisms stand in some phylogenetic relationship to some organisms but fail to be phylogenetically related to others; a natural taxonomy is one which classifies on the basis of shared phylogenetic relationships.
   (d) Organisms are to be classified on the basis of affinity in their characteristics; a natural taxonomy is one which classifies on the basis of affinity in the totality of characteristics of organisms.
(3) How are taxa to be defined?[17]
   (a) By listing a set of necessary and sufficient characteristics.
   (b) By a polytypic finite disjunction of clusters of sufficient characteristics.

    (c) By a polytypic disjunction of clusters of sufficient characteristics, where there is an indefinite number of disjuncts.
    (d) On the basis of some statistical measure of affinity which proceeds in terms of a large number of characteristics.
(4) How are taxonomic categories to be defined?
    (a) So as to yield a natural taxonomy.
    (b) So as to be the most useful for the intended purposes of the taxonomy.

In the remainder of this chapter, I try to investigate and evaluate philosophically these various answers to these questions. Doing so will lead me to examine some more general problems about taxonomic systems, their theoretical properties, and their epistemological status. Although my treatment thus stems from the biological considerations just sketched, my investigation will be much more general and will give some insight into taxonomic systems in general. Dominating my discussion will be various concerns essential to defending a scientific realism or quasi-realism. In particular I will be concerned with a quasi-realistic construal of natural taxonomies.

II. NATURAL TAXONOMIES AS FACTUAL DESCRIPTIONS OF NATURE

For a while I want to confine my attention to natural taxonomies. Common to answers (a) through (d) for question (2) is a core of agreement: natural taxonomies have an objective basis in nature, which artificial ones lack. What is this objective basis? A plausible answer, which is implicitly contained in several of the answers to questions (2) and is quite congenial to scientific realism, is that natural taxonomies, if correct, are factually true, whereas artificial ones are not factually true or false. Presumably, the underlying idea here is that artificial taxonomies are essentially conventional, whereas natural ones are factual descriptions of nature. This suggestion is an attractive one; for if it is correct, then natural taxonomies apparently are nothing other than a variety of true or false realistic scientific theories, and presumably they have the general properties characteristic of scientific theories.
    In order to assess this suggestion, it is necessary to know what it is to be factually true. Elsewhere I have developed a philosophical model of factual truth which I want to assume here.[18] As Strawson (1964) says, facts are what statements (when true) state or assert about the world. As such, any detailed account of facts and empirical truth must be in terms of the world and its characteristics. The world is composed

of *particulars* which have *intrinsic characteristics*—that is, properties they possess and relationships which they enter into with other particulars independently of how anybody characterizes, conceptualizes, or conceives of them. There are two sorts of particulars—*simple particulars* and *complex particulars*. A complex particular is formed by the continuous instantiation of an intrinsic relationship by particulars; these instantiating particulars may be either simple or complex. Simple particulars are those particulars which would remain if all intrinsic relationships were eliminated from the world. Depending upon one's ontology, intrinsic characteristics may or may not themselves have characteristics, and these characteristics of characteristics themselves may or may not have characteristics, and so on. It should be emphasized that whereas all objects are particulars, there are particulars which are not objects.

Intrinsic characteristics are extensional in the sense that in principle, they could be specified in an extensional language having infinite disjunctions and distinct temporal names for each particular. For intrinsic properties, the specification would be as follows:

$$p = \hat{x}(x = a \lor x = b \lor \ldots)$$

where '*a*', '*b*', etc., are temporal names for particulars or else characteristics which have intrinsic properties; intrinsic relationships are specified analogously.[19] It has been shown that the following principles of individuation hold for a world of the sort just sketched:

Leibniz' law: If *a* and *b* are identical particulars or characteristics, then for every intrinsic property *f*, *a* is *f* if and only if *b* is *f*.

Absoluteness of Identity: If *a* and *b* are particulars which are the same *f*, and *a* is *g*, then *a* and *b* are the same *g* (here *f* and *g* are sortal intrinsic characteristics).[20]

We now are in a position to characterize factual truth. When an empirical predicative proposition of the form '*S* is *P*' is asserted, where '*S*' is the logical subject and '*P*' is the logical predicate of the proposition, its sense determines definite ostensible referents for '*S*' and '*P*'. The ostensible referent for '*S*' is a possible particular or a possible characteristic capable of having characteristics; the ostensible referent of '*P*' is a possible intrinsic property—that is, an extensional property which particulars or characteristics in the world could possess. Analogously, relational propositions determine ostensible subject and predicate referents. A proposition 'S is P' is *factually true* if and only if (i) the ostensible referent of 'S' is a particular or a characteristic capable of having characteristics which exists in the world, and (ii) the ostensible referent of 'P' has an intrinsic property which has the same extension as the ostensible referent of the predicate 'P'. 'S is P' is *factually false* if it is not empirically true but refers to ostensible particulars. Whenever a proposition 'S is P' is factually true, then it is a fact that the referent of 'S' has an intrinsic property whose extension is identical with that of the predicate 'P'. Factual truth and facts can be defined analogously for relational propositions, and these definitions can be extended in the usual fashion to include compound and general propositions. To summarize: put crudely, this analysis says that the factual truth of 'S is P' depends on whether 'S' refers to a particular in the world possessing the intrinsic property specified by the predicate 'P'; and if it does, then it is a fact that S is P. Whether that particular has the intrinsic property specified by 'P' is in no way dependent upon how anyone conceptualizes the world.

If natural taxonomies are factually true, how are they to be analyzed under this account of facts and factual truth? Several possibilities present themselves:

> (A) Whether an individual belongs to a particular taxon T is a matter of empirical fact; hence in a correct natural taxonomy, *being a T* is an intrinsic characteristic.

A second possibility is

> (B) The definitions given for taxa, if correct, will be factually true.

This in effect means that taxa definitions will be universal generalizations which qualify as scientific laws. This would make a taxonomic system a kind of scientific theory. A third possibility is

> (C) The definitions of taxonomic categories, if correct, are factually true.

This admits of at least two different interpretations:

> (C') Being of _____ taxonomic category is a characteristic of the intrinsic characteristics which determine taxa.
>
> (C") The definition of a taxonomic category, if true, specifies intrinsic characteristics common to each of the taxa it comprehends.

These possible explications of what it is to be a natural taxonomy in the sense of being factually true or false are, of course, not mutually exclusive; indeed, it is logically possible that a taxonomy could be factually true in all four of these senses. The next several sections are devoted to the systematic development of these suggestions and an examination of how they relate to the various answers which have been given to the four main theoretical questions about taxonomy given at the end of the previous section. The account of the world, facts, and factual truth just outlined is assumed throughout the discussion.

However, before we begin that analysis, a word needs to be said about my use of the locutions *'is a T'* and *'being a T.'* In presenting my analysis, it is necessary to distinguish sharply between predicates used to attribute intrinsic characteristics and the characteristics attributed by them. The predicate expression 'is a chair' is used to attribute a characteristic to an object; the characteristic (property) attributed is that of *being a chair* or *chairness.* Whenever I am talking about the predicate expression (or predicate), I enclose the predicate expression in single quotation marks. Whenever I am talking about a characteristic I use such expressions as

   being a chair

or

   is a chair.

And when speaking generally or abstractly of predicates and characteristics I will use

   'is a *T*'

and

   being a T

analogously to refer respectively to the predicate expression and the characteristic it attributes. Thus my use of single quotation marks here (as throughout the book) is in accordance with Quine's notion of quasi-quotation, where I am using single quotation marks in lieu of his "corners." These conventions for marking the distinction between predicate expressions and the intrinsic characteristics they attribute are used throughout the chapter, and its central argument can be understood only in light of them.

It is also important to realize that there is no necessary or intrinsic connection between the use of the word 'chair' and the intrinsic characteristic *being a chair,* and that with a change in meaning, 'is a chair' could be used to attribute a characteristic other than that of *being a chair.* It is also possible that the predicate 'is a *T*' in a language may attribute a complex characteristic (i.e., the joint occurrence of C_1 and C_2, where 'C_1 & C_2' is an intrinsic characteristic). These observations enable us to forestall a possible source of confusion. Requirement (A) requires that to belong to a taxon T, an individual must possess the intrinsic characteristic *being a T*. All this requires is that there be a single intrinsic characteristic (simple or complex) possessed by all those and only those individuals belonging to the taxon T. From the fact that I employ '*being a T*' to designate the characteristic it does not follow that the characteristic can only be specified using taxon name 'T'. It is perfectly possible that the characteristic *being a T* can be specified using some other (possibly more common garden) predicate expression—so long as that expression, whatever it is, designates a single characteristic common to all those and only those individuals in the taxon.

III. TAXA, NATURAL KINDS, AND ATTRIBUTES

Interpretation (A) of what it is for a taxonomy to be natural was that belonging to a particular taxon was a matter of empirical fact. More precisely, (A) says that if an individual a is correctly classified as belonging to taxon T in a natural taxonomy, then the characteristic *is a T* (or *being a T*) is an intrinsic characteristic of a. Differently put, interpretation (A) requires that in a natural taxonomy, membership of an individual in a taxon be by virtue of possessing an intrinsic characteristic common to all members of the taxon which is possessed by no individuals which are not members of the taxon. Thus for example, under (A), being a *Homo sapiens* would be an intrinsic characteristic of humans, and nothing correctly could be classified as a *Homo sapiens* without having this characteristic; and the only flowers which correctly could be classified as *Rosa multiflora* would be those having the intrinsic characteristic *being a Rosa multiflora*. Thus interpretation (A) postulates that *being a Rosa multiflora* is just as genuine a property as *being a desk, being red, being a Thompson gazelle, being a dog,* or *being an electron;* and a natural taxonomy will be one in which species membership will be by virtue of a single shared common intrinsic characteristic such as *being a Homo sapiens* or *being a Rosa multiflora.*

As such, (A) takes extremely seriously a doctrine on the problem of universals attributed to the later Wittgenstein by Renford Bambrough (1966). In *Philosophical Investigations* (1953), Wittgenstein raises the question, What is common to all games? He then considers a number of characteristic features of games such as requiring skill, having a winner, and so on. But Wittgenstein observes that none of these are common to all games and concludes that "if you look at them you will not see something that is common to all [games], but similarities, relationships, and a whole series of them at that." That is, all we see is "a complicated network of similarities overlapping and crisscrossing: sometimes overall similarities, sometimes similarities of details" (1953, sec. 66). Such similarities he calls *family resemblances,* and he concludes that while there are no distinguishing characteristics common to all games, they all are games by virtue of standing in a family resemblance to each other. Concepts designating family resemblance classes have come to be known as *cluster concepts,* and biological taxa concepts often are alleged to be such cluster concepts. Bambrough inteprets Wittgenstein's treatment of family resemblances as not denying that, for example, games have anything in common, but rather as maintaining that "games have nothing in common except that they are games" (1966, 199).

The problem of universals can be formulated as the question, What must all the referents of a general term have in common?, and Bambrough generalizes his interpretation of Wittgenstein's discussion of family resemblances to the following solution to the problem of universals: General terms in a language are nonarbitrary in that the class of individuals they designate is not a closed class. All the referents of a general term must have in common the possession of the characteristic specified by the general term. In addition, there may be other characteristics common to all of them, but there need not be. What is required, however, is that there be objective similarities between the members of the class. These objective similarities sometimes will be such that there is only a family resemblance between the members of the class, but in other cases it may consist in the possession of certain other characteristics common to the members of the class but not to other individuals (1966, 200–04).

If taxa are family resemblance classes and taxa names are cluster concepts, as is often suggested, then (A) together with Bambrough's interpretation of Wittgenstein has the following consequences for taxonomy: (1) In a nonarbitrary natural taxonomy, an individual belongs to a taxon T by virtue of possessing a characteristic common to all members of the taxon; (2) the common characteristic will be that of *being a T;* (3) wherever taxa are family resemblance classes, *being a T* will be the only characteristic common to all members of the taxon T; (4) in any natural taxonomy, there will be some objective similarities common to all members of the taxon. Thus in the ordinary language classification scheme, the individuals in the taxon *chair* all possess the common characteristic of *being a chair* and possess no other common characteristics, but do evidence various similarities to each other. And the common characteristic, *being a chair,* is an intrinsic characteristic in the sense of the previous section. Viewed from the perspective of Bambrough's interpretation, (A) stipulates that in a natural or nonarbitrary taxonomy, there is a single objective or intrinsic property characteristic of all and only those individuals which are members of the taxon T; this is the property normally designed by the predicates 'being a T' or 'is a T', but may be designated by other predicates as well. (A) leaves open the question whether there are any other characteristics common to all members of T. Crudely put, then, (A) amounts to nothing more than the requirement that in a natural taxonomy there must be a single intrinsic property characteristic of all and only those individuals belonging to a given taxon.

Many biological taxonomists are not of the opinion that *being a T*, where T is a taxon, is an intrinsic or objective characteristic of the organisms placed in biological taxon T, and so would not be inclined to accept (A).[21] Other than to a commitment to a conventionalist theory of taxonomy, I think much of the resistance to accepting *being a T* as an intrinsic characteristic can be traced to the fact that if *being a T* is an intrinsic characteristic of organisms, it does not have the same status as other intrinsic characteristics of organisms; in particular, it is not a diagnostic characteristic, and it is not as readily recognized as a diagnostic or other characteristic.[22]

That *being a T* is not as readily recognized as a diagnostic characteristic does not, of course, mean that it is not an intrinsic characteristic—any more than the difficulty in recognizing electrons means that *is an electron* is not an intrinsic characteristic (though it certainly makes it ineligible for being a diagnostic characteristic). When this difficulty of recognizing *being a T* is coupled with taxonomy's typical insistence on operational definition, it becomes clear why taxonomists are reluctant to view *being a T* as an intrinsic characteristic. Recall from chapter 3 that according to operationalism, the descriptive terms a science uses are of two sorts—those which refer to directly observable entities of attributes and those which do not; the former are called *observational terms* and the latter are called *theoretical terms*. The presence or absence of the characteristics referred to by observational terms can be checked readily; but since the presence of characteristics referred to by theoretical terms cannot be so readily checked, the only theoretical terms allowed are those which are fully "operationally" defined in terms of observation terms. In biological taxonomy this becomes the requirement that taxa names (being theoretical terms) must be defined in Aristotelian or polytypic fashion in terms of diagnostic characteristics specified by observational terms. This requirement, in effect, requires that taxa names be nothing other than abbreviations for the combined occurrences of certain diagnostic characteristics — for example, if Aristotelian definition is required, then the definition becomes "x is a T if and only if x has characteristics c_1 & c_2 & ... & c_n," and 'is a T' designates the combined occurrence of the characteristics $c_1, \ldots, c_n$. Thus 'is a T' does not designate any distinct characteristic of the organism. This in turn prompts a denial of (A) and requires embracing a conventionalistic position wherein taxa names are nothing other than conventional abbreviations for the combined occurrence of certain diagnostic characteristics.

It has been amply demonstrated, however, that the above picture of theoretical terms and how they function in science generally is untenable.[23] In particular, most theoretical terms in science do not admit of full specification and cannot be reduced to abbreviations for combinations of observational terms. The reasons leading to this conclusion, coupled with the notable lack of success in developing theoretically viable taxonomies in accordance with the dictates of operationalism, suggests there is little basis for hoping that taxonomy will prove to be an exception.

If the claim is rejected that taxa names are merely abbreviated descriptions of clusters of diagnostic characteristics, then it becomes plausible to suppose that 'is a T' does refer to or designate a characteristic possessed by some organisms. But then, *being a T* becomes an intrinsic characteristic of organisms. Once this is accepted, it is plausible to suppose that natural taxonomies are those whose taxa are such that *being a T* is an intrinsic characteristic of all and only those organisms which are in taxon T — but this is nothing other than maintaining (A). Thus developments in philosophy of science strongly suggest that the operational imperative is nonsense, which in turn suggests that (A) plausibly might hold for taxonomic theory; in any case, the denial of (A) commits one inextricably to a pure conventionalistic theory of taxonomy. Such a commitment is incompatible with a scientific realism or quasi-realism.

The acceptance of (A) suggests a new perspective for viewing taxa definitions. Consider the following Aristotelian definition of a taxon:

$$'x \text{ is a } T' \text{ if and only if}$$
$$x \text{ is } c_1 \text{ \& } x \text{ is } c_2 \text{ \& } \ldots \text{ \& } x \text{ is } c_n,$$

where $c_1, \ldots, c_n$ are diagnostic characteristics. By the rejection of operationalism, 'is a T' does not mean the same thing as 'is c_1 & c_2 & ... & c_n'; rather, the definition asserts a *correlation* between the occurrence of the characteristic *being a T* and the combined occurrence of characteristics $c_1, \ldots, c_n$ in organisms, stating that whenever *being* *a T* occurs, $c_1, \ldots, c_n$ also jointly occur, and vice versa. This asserted correlation is a factual matter, and so the definition takes on the status of being a factually true or false generalization about correlations of occurrences of characteristics in organisms. Thus if (A) holds, then (B)—that taxa definitions must be factually true or false in a natural taxonomy—follows naturally. This in turn indicates that if (A)—hence (B)—holds, question (3), How are taxa to be defined in a natural taxonomy?, becomes an empirical issue. If (A) holds, *being a T* is an intrinsic property of organisms, and by (B), taxa definitions must be factually true or false. If there is no set of characteristics $c_1, \ldots, c_n$ such that the Aristotelian definitional form is factually true, then there can be no factually true taxonomy which includes *T* as a taxon if the Aristotelian definition is insisted on. Similarly, whether *T* can be defined by polytypic definition in a factually true taxonomic system depends upon what sorts of correlations occur between occurrences of *being a T* and diagnostic characteristics.

These last observations bring us back to Bambrough's interpretation of Wittgenstein. It is often alleged that taxa names are cluster concepts, and that there are no diagnostic characteristics common to, and characteristic of, all members of a taxon. Whether this is so is a matter of contingent fact. If it is so and (A) is accepted, then on Bambrough's account, *being a T* will be a common characteristic of all and only those organisms in *T;* and new "definitional" forms will be required for taxa membership in a factually true taxonomy. But regardless what form is required, Bambrough's account provides a means for still providing natural taxonomies with an objective factual basis in such cases and thereby escaping from the unsatisfying conventionalistic account of taxonomic systems. Doing so requires, however, acceptance of both (A) and (B). And that acceptance amounts to taking quite seriously the idea that natural taxonomic systems are a species of scientific theory and that they are factually true or false—an idea which must be taken seriously if the operational imperative is rejected for biological taxonomy. It is an idea that a scientific realism or quasi-realism should take very seriously.

Having seen the rationale underlying both (A) and (B), we can return to a detailed consideration of (A). As stated, (A) is ambiguous, since it is not clear whether *is a T* must be an intrinsic property or relationship. Suppose an individual *a* is a *T* and *is a T* is an intrinsic relationship *T*. Presumably *a* will then be a complex particular, and so consists of the continuous instantiation of some intrinsic relationship *R* by particulars. This relationship *R* will have to be the *T* relationship. That this is so follows from the individuation properties of complex particulars, which are such that if the same particulars instantiate two different intrinsic relationships R_1 and R_2, two different particulars result—one from the instantiation of R_1, and the other from the instantiation of R_2 (Suppe 1973, sec. III). From this it follows that if a is a T and T is an intrinsic relationship, then T must be the particularizing relationship R whose continuous instantiation comprises a. Thus if a is a flower of species *Rosa multiflora,* under this proposal a would be comprised of particulars (e.g., perhaps cells, organs, or parts of the plant) standing in the *Rosa multiflora* relationship to each other; then it would be an empirical fact that a is *Rosa multiflora,* but it would not be an intrinsic property of a that it is a *Rosa multiflora.* Since *is a T* is an intrinsic relationship, *is a Rosa* is also an intrinsic relationship; it is obvious that being *Rosa multiflora* and being *Rosa* have different extensions, and so are different intrinsic relationships. As complex particulars are individuated on the basis of the intrinsic relationships which are continuously instantiated, it is impossible for the same particular to be both a *Rosa multiflora* and a *Rosa* (Suppe, ibid.). But under a standard taxonomy, anything which is a *Rosa multiflora* automatically is a *Rosa;* hence *is a T* cannot be an intrinsic relationship, and thus must be an intrinsic property.[24]

Under (A), then, *is a T* must be an intrinsic property. Hence if a is correctly classified as a T in a natural taxonomy, a must have an intrinsic property whose extension is identical with that of 'is a T.' Thus, if a is a *Rosa multiflora,* it is factually true that a is a *Rosa multiflora,* which is to say that a has an intrinsic property whose extension is identical with that of 'is a *Rosa multiflora*'—just as my desk is a desk, since it has an intrinsic property whose extension is identical with that of 'is a desk.' Since every individual of species *Rosa multiflora* is also of genus *Rosa,* it also follows that a has an intrinsic property whose extension is identical with that of 'is a *Rosa.*' To summarize, (A) is to be interpreted thus:

(A-1) In a natural taxonomy, whether an individual belongs to a particular taxon is a matter of empirical fact in the sense that *being of taxon T (being a T, is a T)* is an intrinsic property the individual does or does not have.

We mentioned above that if interpretation (A-1) is adopted, question (3), How are taxa to be defined?, becomes primarily an empirical issue. Suppose, for example, that answer (a) were correct—that taxa are to be defined in terms of necessary and sufficient conditions, then it would be the case that for appropriate intrinsic characteristics $c_1, \ldots, c_n,$

x is a T if and only if

x is c_1 & x is c_2 & ... & x is c_n.

This implies that there is a constant correlation between the intrinsic property *is a T* and the combined occurrences of the intrinsic characteristics $c_1, \ldots, c_n$. Whether such a correlation of intrinsic characteristics occurs is, of course, a contingent empirical matter, and if no such correlation occurs for any $c_1, \ldots, c_n$, then such a form of definition is impossible.

Moreover, if such a correlation does occur, there may be more than one such correlation—for example, *is a T* may be additionally correlated with the combined occurrence of $b_1, \ldots, b_m$, where $b_1, \ldots, b_m$ are not all the same as $c_1, \ldots, c_n$. Should this eventuality occur, then more than one natural taxonomy using the same taxa would be possible for D, where the taxonomies differ on what characteristics are to be used to define D. These taxonomies, if natural in the sense of (A-1), would not disagree on which species an individual will be (except in cases of misapplication of definition). Thus there is the possibility that different but equivalent natural taxonomic systems could be adopted for different purposes. There is also the possibility that natural taxonomies could be formed for D which select different taxa; this would result in different and inequivalent taxonomies.

These considerations indicate that the question whether answer (a) to question (3) is acceptable and the question whether more than one characterization is possible for a given taxon will be factual, empirical questions. And their answers will consist in establishing empirical generalizations about characteristic correlations within the taxon. Similarly, answers (b) through (d) to question (3) are empirical claims about characteristic correlations within the taxon. Actually, (a) through (d) are more generalized than this suggests. In their typical versions, these answers state that all taxa within the taxonomic system admit of the same form of generalization and, sometimes, that the same kinds of diagnostic characteristics are to be used in all such definitions. Again, these are empirical generalizations which will be factually true or false. Thus, if (A-1) is accepted, then the issue of definitional form is empirical, not philosophical.

Before going on to consider interpretation (B), interpretation (A-1) should be distinguished sharply from a significantly weakened version of (A) which is satisfied by every plausible taxonomic system, whether artificial or natural:

(A-2) In a taxonomy where taxa are defined in terms of diagnostic characteristics, the specified diagnostic characteristics must be intrinsic characteristics of any individual belonging to a species defined in terms of them.

That is, whether natural or artificial, a taxonomic system must define its taxa and taxonomic categories in terms of the intrinsic characteristics which members of the domain D may or may not possess. That (A-2) is significantly weaker than (A-1) indicates that (A-1) is a nontrivial notion of what it is to be a natural taxonomy.[25]

[(A) and (A-1) tell us that natural taxa must be natural kinds. This suggests that we can extend our account of natural versus artificial taxa to a general antinominalism. That is, we can use it to provide a general account of the distinction between natural groupings or classes and merely arbitrary classifications. What would such an extension look like? The first thing to note is that the arguments above which led us to restrict natural taxa-making attributes to properties—hence to adopt (A-1) instead of (A)—turned critically on considerations specific to standard (biological) taxonomies. It is not incumbent that antinominalist classifications conform to the requirements of standard classifications, so we ought to generalize (A) rather than (A-1). Differently put, natural kind-making intrinsic attributes can be properties or relations.

While our intuitions are that mice and humans are natural kinds, their sum (the mouse-or-human kind) is not. What about the products of natural kind classes? Do we, for example, wish to say that the mouse-and-human class is a natural kind? Here we do not, since the constituent natural kind classes are disjoint. But we have no problem accepting the class of blue-eyed humans as a natural kind, since the class of blue-eyed creatures and the class of humans are natural kinds. The difference in the two cases seems to rest on the fact that there are no mouse-and-humans, but there are blue-eyed humans. We adopt the following conditions, then, which exhaustively characterize *natural kind classes:*

(i) The class of all and only those entities possessing an intrinsic attribute *being a T* is a natural kind class.

(ii) If A and B are natural kind classes, then so is $A \cap B$, provided $A \cap B \neq \varnothing$.

One further complication needs to be considered. Cladistic and other lineage taxonomies are becoming increasingly popular in biology. Consider the class of all descendants of a particular mating pair. That is, if a and b are the pair and R is the intrinsic relation _____ *is a descendant of* _ _ _ _ *and* . . . . , then is

$$\{x \mid Rxab\}$$

a natural kind class? Note that by generalizing (A), rather than (A-1), we already have allowed that

$$\{x \mid Rxyz \text{ for some } y \text{ and } z\}$$

is a natural kind class. Thus the question is whether the restriction of such natural kind classes via setting certain placeholders to specific individuals (or groups) is itself a natural kind class. My intuitions are that the class of all descendants of John and Elizabeth Tilley (ancestors of mine who came over on the Mayflower) quite possibly might be a natural kind class. On the other hand, I am quite certain that the class of all M & M's in my hand right now is not; I am less clear whether the class of all M & M's I ever eat is or is not a natural kind class. If we were to allow the contemplated restrictions of natural kind classes to be natural kind classes, it seems that we would have to develop completely independent criteria for distinguishing natural kind classes from other classes. This in effect amounts to abandoning the idea that (A) can be generalized to provide an account of natural kind classes. This in turn would call into question our account of natural taxonomies and my account of explanatory laws in chapter 6. I conclude, then, that we should reject the idea that natural kind classes can be extended beyond what (i) and (ii) allow. Having made this decision, we have completed the fleshing out of requirement (a) for the empirical truth of theories given in chapter 3, section V.

Returning to biological classification, so far our discussion has been restricted to standard classifications wherein taxa are classes of particulars, individuals, or organisms. Recently, Ghiselin (1974) and Hull (1976) seriously have advanced the hypothesis that species are individuals or particulars, not classes of individuals. In Hull's words,

> The units of organic evolution, both units of selection and units of evolution, are spatio-temporal individuals integrated by certain causal processes which do not require similarity. . . . Genes produce new genes, organisms new organisms and populations new populations. Sometimes the entities concerned are similar to each other, sometimes not. It does not matter. What matters is evolutionary unity and continuity over time. At any one time the organisms which make up the population can be extremely heterogeneous. When traced through time, this heterogeneity only increases. [Hull 1979, 429]

The plausibility of their position rests in large part on the emergence of cladistic approaches to evolutionary theory that construe taxa as lineages. On this species-as-individuals approach, taxa definitions are singular factual statements, not generalizations. To say that x is a *Rosa multiflora* is simply to say that the organism x is a constituent particular of the complex particular *Rosa multiflora*—a claim which is or is not factually true. On this proposal, only species (and possibly lower-level taxa) are individuals. Taxa at levels higher than species are classes.

As Hull (1976, 174–75) puts it, the traditional view has been that

> the relation between organisms, species, and the species category is membership. An organism is a member of the species category. On the view being urged in this paper, both particular species and the species category itself must be moved down one category level. Organisms remain individuals, but they are no longer members of their species. Instead an organism is part of a more inclusive individual, its species, and the names of both particular organisms (like Gargantua) and particular species (like *Gorilla gorilla)* become proper names. The species category itself no longer is a class of classes, but merely a class.

It follows that our treatment of natural versus artificial taxonomies will continue to hold for all taxa above the species level on this account. Species and lower taxa are natural if and only if they are complex particulars. Thus the species-as-individuals proposal does not cause any problem for our account of natural versus artificial taxonomies, hence for our antinominalism, provided we allow that taxa can be individuals rather than classes.

Hull claims that "if species are individuals, no law of nature can refer to a particular species. Such statements as 'All swans are white', even if true, would not be scientific laws" (1976, 189). He bases this claim on neo-positivistic views he holds about theories (see Thompson's forthcoming work, n.d., for a characterization), especially the claim that genuine laws must be spatio-temporally universal. In chapter 8 I will argue that this view is false if one accepts my version of the Semantic Conception. I maintain that the universality of scientific laws in theories consists in their having natural kind classes as the intended scope of the theory. Thus on my version of the Semantic Conception, the issue whether there can be scientific theories (hence theoretical laws) about particular species turns on whether the class of organisms which are the parts (*not* members) of a natural species (as individual) can constitute a natural kind class.

Consider the class of organisms which are constituent parts of a natural species individual s. Each of these organisms stands in a part-whole intrinsic relation Rxy to the species. The class of all particulars standing in the part-whole relation Rxy to some particular would be a natural kind class on our account. Would not, then, treating the class of constituent organisms amount to forming a class by restricting Rxy to Rxs? And did we not already decide not to count such classes as natural kinds? Not quite. We decided not to allow such classes to be natural kinds *merely* by virtue of being so constituted. But if

$$\{x \mid Rxs\} = \{x \mid x \text{ is } T\}$$

for some intrinsic attribute T, then the class *will* be a natural kind class. Thus it is possible that even if species are individuals, the class of organisms which are members of that species can be a natural kind class. Moreover, given my general account about natural taxa being constituted as natural kinds by the shared attribute *being a T*, such a possibility does not seem particularly outlandish. Indeed, my intuitions are that this is a pretty common occurrence.

Call the class of constituent organisms in a species individual *the species' corresponding constituent class*. Such a class can be a natural kind class, hence can be the intended scope of an empirically true scientific theory in accordance with the analysis in chapter 3 as further developed above. Technically, Hull may be correct that when species are individuals there can be no laws about *species*. But it does not follow that there cannot be any empirically true laws and theories about the *species' corresponding constituent class*. For it is entirely possible that such a class will be a natural kind class. When it is, the class of empirically true theories and laws will be exactly the same whether species are viewed as classes or individuals. Indeed, a stronger claim is forthcoming: Consider two worlds W_1 and W_2, identical in all respects except that species are natural kind classes in W_1 and are individuals in W_2. Suppose s is a species in W_1. Then

$$s = \{x \mid x \text{ is a } T \text{ for some intrinsic attribute } T\}.$$

But s is just the corresponding constituent class c for the species individual in W_2. Since W_1 and W_2 are identical except for the status accorded species, *is a T* is an intrinsic attribute in W_2. Hence c is a natural kind class. Now suppose c is the corresponding constituent class for some species and c is a natural kind class in W_2. Then

$$c = \{x \mid x \text{ is a } T \text{ for some intrinsic attribute } T\}.$$

Then c qualifies as a species class in W_1. It follows that precisely the same stock of laws about the individuals in species obtain regardless whether species are classes or individuals. Thus whether there are laws about species depends on how the world is, and not on the methodological decision whether to view species as individuals (which is how Hull would have it). This is precisely the antinominalistic conclusion one needs for a quasi-realism.

In our subsequent discussion we will assume species are classes unless otherwise indicated. We now turn to a consideration of thesis (B).]

IV. FIXED TAXA DEFINITIONS AND EMPIRICAL TRUTH

Recall interpretation (B) from the previous section—that in a natural taxonomy the definitions given for taxa, if correct, will be empirically true. We saw that (B) follows from the acceptance of (A-1); in this section we will see that (B) presupposes (A-1); and it of course presupposes (A-2). In this section I want to consider (B) for cases where fixed taxa (in the sense that diagnostic characteristics for membership in the taxa are immutable) are assumed.

If (A-1) is assumed and taxa are fixed, two basic sorts of taxonomic systems are possible: essentialist and nonessentialist systems. *Essentialism* is the doctrine that of the intrinsic properties an individual has, certain of these, the essential characteristics, are necessary for the individual being the thing it is, whereas others, the accidental characteristics, could be different than they are without changing the thing the individual is. To take an example of Aristotle's, man is a rational animal; if an individual is not rational or is not an animal, then it cannot be a man. Thus *being rational* and *being an animal* are essential characteristics for being a man. Men also either are or are not pugnosed; but whether an individual is pug-nosed or not is of no relevance to whether it is a man. Thus, *being pug-nosed* is an accidental characteristic for men.

As a taxonomic theory, essentialism maintains that taxa are to be defined in terms of essential characteristics (in the above sense). Two versions of essentialism can be distinguished, which I call *invariance essentialism* and *nomic essentialism*. Invariance essentialism takes the position that for each kind of individual there are certain intrinsic characteristics possessed by every individual of the kind. Thus, if something is a *Homo sapiens*, then there are certain intrinsic characteristics common to all *Homo sapiens*. And the taxon *Homo sapiens* is to be defined in terms of these essential characteristics. A variation on invariance essentialism, which I call *polytypic invariance essentialism*, allows that for a given kind (taxon) there may not be any single set of essential characteristics, but requires that there be a finite number of sets of sufficient characteristics such that each individual of a given kind will always possess one of these sufficient sets of characteristics.

Both versions of invariance essentialism implicitly assume that (A-1) is met; for they assume that certain characteristics must be possessed to be of a given kind, and so being of that kind must be an intrinsic characteristic. Then invariance essentialisms are nothing other than versions of (A-1), wherein the definitions of taxa are in keeping with answers (a), (c), or (d) to question (2). By the discussion of (A-1) we thus see that taxa definitions are empirically true or false, depending on whether or not the diagnostic intrinsic characteristics correlate with the intrinsic characteristic *is a T.*

It should be apparent that invariance essentialism makes a taxonomic system relative to an initial choice of taxa. In effect, essentialism assumes that there is a set of intrinsic characteristics (namely, *being a T*) such that every individual in the system's domain possesses one or more of them,[26] and then views its problem as how to define the taxa corresponding to these intrinsic characteristics (e.g., the taxon T determined by possession of *being a T*). A set of definitions constitutes a solution to its problem, and this solution will be factually true or false in exactly the way specified in the above discussion of (A-1). Thus, we obtain the following version of (B):

(B-1) A taxonomy is natural if it is an invariance essentialism, meets condition (A-1), and its taxa definitions, if correct, are factually true empirical generalizations about the members of its taxa.

Notice that, depending upon the initial choice of taxa-determining characteristics, a number of different and nonequivalent invariance essentialist taxonomic systems may be possible for a given domain D. Whether more than one is possible will depend upon the kinds of correlations which do obtain between intrinsic characteristics. And if more than one is possible, to argue that one is more natural than another requires a premise to the effect that one is more natural than the other; that is, in this sense of natural, all taxonomies meeting (B-1) are equally natural, and so if any is more natural, it is in some other sense of 'natural'; most post-Aristotelian and pre-Linnaean taxonomies seem to have been invariance essentialisms.[27]

Whereas invariance essentialism holds that for each kind of individual there are certain intrinsic characteristics possessed by every individual of the kind, nomic essentialism maintains that for each kind of individual there are certain characteristics which *must* be possessed by all individuals of the kind. These are the essential characteristics for taxon membership. Thus, according to nomic essentialism, whether intrinsic characteristics are essential for taxon membership is a function of the laws of nature holding in the world.

An intrinsic characteristic possessed by an individual is an essential characteristic for membership in taxon T under a nomic essentialism if and only if any individual in the taxon has the characteristic in every possible world containing it which is consistent with the laws of nature. Thus the essential characteristics of an individual in taxon T are intrinsic characteristics which it is *causally necessary* that the individual must possess if it is to remain in T; moreover, the essential characteristics for each taxon must be such that no organism not of taxon T possesses all of them.[28] Nomic essentialism clearly assumes that (A-1) holds; for it amounts to the requirement that the definitions in a taxonomy stipulate a lawlike correlation which holds between taxa membership and the possession of diagnostic characteristics in all causally possible worlds. In effect, then, nomic essentialism is an invariance essentialism which has had imposed upon it the requirement that the same correlations between taxa membership and diagnostic characteristics will hold in all other worlds compatible with the laws of nature. As such, (B) clearly is assumed in a nomic essentialism, though more stringent truth conditions are imposed on taxa definitions. We obtain the following version of (B):

> (B-2) A taxonomy is natural if it is a nomic essentialism, meets condition (A-1), and its taxa definitions, if correct, are factually true lawlike generalizations about the members of its taxa.

Are alternative natural taxonomic systems possible for a given domain under (B-2)? There are two possible ways alternative taxonomic systems could be possible. First, it may be that there is more than one selection of taxa-determining properties which, given appropriate definitional forms for taxa and selection of diagnostic characteristics, will result in true nomic essentialisms. This, of course, will result in nonequivalent taxonomic systems. Second, relative to a choice of taxa-determining properties, hence taxa, the correlations between possession of the characteristic *being a T* and diagnostic characteristics may be such that different choices of diagnostic characteristics will result in different but equivalent taxonomic systems for domain D. Whether such alternative taxonomies are possible for a given domain D depends, of course, on the lawlike correlations which obtain, and so is a matter of empirical fact. As such, what the possible definitional forms for taxa are is a factual matter.

In discussing both versions of essentialisms, we have assumed tacitly that species are fixed in the sense that criteria for taxa membership are invariant over time. For essentialism this amounts to the assumption that the essential characteristics are invariant over time. Certain possible versions of evolution are compatible with this assumption—namely, any version of evolution in which the variation in intrinsic characteristics of members of a given species is limited to accidental characteristics of individuals. No existing evolutionary theories other than ad hoc creationist ones meet this condition, but, as a matter of empirical fact, some such theory might be true.

Other than essentialist views, only two other views seem plausible for fixed species. First, one may deny that any characteristics are essential and maintain that all that is required is that taxa definitions be empirically true correlations (possibly polytypic) of intrinsic characteristics with taxa membership. This position is nothing other than invariance essentialism minus the appellation 'essentialism' and it differs in no significant way from invariance essentialism. Mentioning it does serve, however, to emphasize how little weight 'essentialism' bears in invariance essentialism. Second, one can maintain what I call an *affinity taxonomy.* According to an affinity taxonomy, taxa are not defined in either Aristotelian or polytypic fashion. Rather, taxa are groupings of individuals who have a mutual affinity. This affinity typically need not be in all characteristics, and this allows some divergence in shared characteristics. Typically, it proceeds by looking at a large variety of intrinsic characteristics for a group of individuals, then applying a measure of affinity and grouping the individuals on the basis of greatest affinity. Numerical taxonomy is a paradigm example of an affinity taxonomy, though nonstatistical versions of affinity taxonomies are possible.

Now suppose (A-1) holds; then there are two possibilities. First, the affinity relationship may be such that it is an intrinsic relationship; if so, then we obtain the following version of (B):

> (B-3) A taxonomy is natural if it is an affinity taxonomy, meets condition (A-1), and, if correct, it is factually true that all members of a taxon T stand in an intrinsic affinity relationship to each other and also have the intrinsic characteristic *being a T.*

In such a theory, the definition of a taxon T will be that x is a member of taxon T if and only if x is in the largest class of individuals which stand in such and such intrinsic relationship of affinity to each other. Taxa definitions thus are empirical generalizations and are factually true or false. It is also obvious that depending on the constitution of the world, more than one taxonomy meeting (B-3) may be possible for a given domain D; relative to a given choice of taxa-determining characteristics, these alternatives all would be equivalent.

The second possibility is that (A-1) is met, but the affinity relationship is not an intrinsic relationship. At first blush it boggles the mind to conceive of an affinity taxonomy where the affinity relationship is not an intrinsic relationship but (A-1) is met. Yet with some thought and ingenuity, it emerges that this possibility is highly plausible, though making it so will require a somewhat extended discussion. Doing so is worthwhile, however, because it yields what seems to me a highly plausible taxonomic theory.

As a starting point, I want to consider an account of scientific definition presented by Peter Achinstein in chapters 1 and 2 of his book *Concepts of Science*.[29] He observes that in actual scientific practice the definitions given for terms such as 'copper', 'electron', 'oxygen', 'insect', and so on, rarely provide necessary and sufficient conditions (i.e., they are non-Aristotelian definitions). Rather, the characteristics listed are cited as being *relevant*—either in the sense that their presence tends to count in and of themselves, to some extent, *toward* classifying something as being, for example, copper, or in the sense that their absence tends to count, to some extent, *against* classifying something as copper. Such properties are said to be *semantically relevant* to being copper. But for a thing to be copper, it need not possess all of the semantically relevant properties, as the semantically relevant properties are neither necessary nor sufficient. For example, having atomic number 29 is semantically relevant to 'copper'; in many contexts it is required if something is to be correctly classified as copper, but in other contexts, it is not required.

After presenting detailed and careful arguments in support of the above claims, Achinstein concludes that scientific definitions often are definitions meeting the following conditions:

Suppose that as the term "X" is used by a speaker or group of speakers, $P_1, \ldots, P_n$ are properties semantically relevant . . . for X, though not logically necessary or sufficient; suppose also that they are among the most central ones for X. Then we might have:

D_2: As the term "X" is normally used by . . . , items (both actual and hypothetical) are correctly classifiable as X's if and only if they have most, or at least many of properties $P_1, \ldots, P_n$ among others. [1968, 25]

Achinstein's discussion makes it quite clear that much of actual scientific definition does proceed in terms of D_2, and that this form of definition cannot be assimilated to polytypic definition.[30]

It is clear that Achinstein's "cluster" definitions do require that there be a certain affinity between all the members of a given class—namely, that they stand in the relationship to each other of having a goodly number of the characteristics $P_1, \ldots, P_n$ in common. Now it is entirely plausible to suppose that this affinity relationship might not be an intrinsic relationship the members of a taxon enter into. At the same time, it may be possible that the assertion 'x is a T if and only if x has a goodly number of the intrinsic characteristics $P_1, \ldots, P_n$' is empirically true or false.[31]

If so, then Achinstein's definitions establish an affinity between members of a taxon which is not an intrinsic relationship of affinity holding between members of the taxon. At the same time, it does require that (A-1) and (B) hold. Since (A-1) holds, *being a* T is an intrinsic property; and the semantically relevant $P_1, \ldots, P_n$ must be intrinsic properties—by virtue of (A-2). Thus the definition that a is a T if and only if a possesses a goodly number of the intrinsic characteristics $P_1, \ldots, P_n$ asserts a factually true or false correlation between the occurrence of *being a* T and the joint occurrence of a goodly number of $P_1, \ldots, P_n$, wherein not every one of the P_i always must be possessed by a T for the correlation to obtain. Thus we have the following version of (B):

> (B-4) A taxonomy is natural if (A-1) is met, taxa are defined in terms of semantically relevant properties $P_1, \ldots, P_n$ (for a given taxon T) in such a way that an individual is of taxon T if and only if it has most, or at least many, of the intrinsic characteristics $P_1, \ldots, P_n$, and this correlation of *being a* T and having most or many of $P_1, \ldots, P_n$, if correct, is a factually true generalization.

Since Achinstein's definitional form has received little attention in the taxonomic literature, it is worth making a few comments about its potential applications in taxonomy. One such application is to incorporate it into modified versions of polytypic and indefinite polytypic definitions. Taxonomies actually employed in biology, of whatever sort, in effect define the conditions for being *ideal* or *perfect* specimens of a taxon; they do not take into consideration damaged, deformed, or other such specimens. Accordingly, it is possible that there may be specimens of a given species and variety who lack certain of the defining characteristics which show up in the disjunct for the variety in the species' polytypic, or indefinite polytypic, definition.[32] In such a case, the lack of these characteristics by the specimen need not falsify the definition, require the introduction of a new variety, or necessitate any other revision of the taxonomic system. Rather, it is just an organism belonging to the taxon which lacks some of the defining characteristics.

However, if it is the case that unmodified polytypic or indefinite polytypic definitions are employed in the system, the above interpretation becomes impossible, since the definitions are exhaustive exceptionless biconditionals: Strictly speaking, the organism cannot be of the species if it lacks any of the conjoined diagnostic characteristics specified in the appropriate disjunct of the definition, unless the definition is false. This indicates that, contrary to what is claimed, in actual practice polytypic definitions rarely meet the official criterion, wherein to belong to a taxon an organism *must* have *all* of the characteristics occurring in one of the disjuncts; rather, these disjuncts really specify semantically relevant characteristics, of which a goodly number must be present in an organism for it to qualify the organism as belonging to the taxon.[33] It might be objected here that deformed specimens in actual practice do not falsify taxa definitions and can be disregarded—perhaps with the explanation that, for example, it is a crab which has lost a foot. I grant that this is what is done, but the question here is, How is this practice legitimate? If taxa are classes of actual organisms and the definition in question is of the form *x is a T* if and only if *x* is c_1 & ... & *x* is c_n (or the polytypic analogue), and a deformed specimen of taxon *T* lacks, say, c_1, then the specimen either cannot be of the taxon, or else the definition is false. If the definition is not falsified and the specimen is of taxon *T,* it follows that the definition does not have the claimed form. Rather, it is a misleading way of stating, say, that *ceteris paribus, x* is a *T* if it has all of the characteristics $c_1, \ldots, c_n$, or most of them, or that if *x* were normal, it would—or some such hedge clause. That is, in actual practice, something like Achinstein's definitional form is used in biological taxonomy.[34]

I can see only two ways of avoiding this conclusion. One is to adopt an essentialism (most likely, a nomic one). Historically, this problem was one of the reasons for adopting an essentialism, the idea being that deformities which did not affect taxa membership were deformities in accidental characteristics. Of course, the difficulty encountered in finding such essential characteristics make the possibility of such an essentialist taxonomy highly unlikely. The second way is to deny that taxa are collections of organisms and construe the members in taxa as abstracted replicas of organisms. For example one could construe taxa as collections of phenotypes of which actual specimens are imperfect realizations; then a deformed specimen would just be an imperfect specimen of phenotype P, and hence its phenotype explicitly satisfies the definition (having $c_1, \ldots, c_n$) even though the specimen does not. Thus unless this latter proposal is accepted,[35] something like Achinstein's definitional form will be required; and if the proposal is accepted, something like Achinstein's definitional form may be required to specify the condition for specimens being of a given phenotype.[36]

It is also possible to have affinity taxonomies in which (A-1) is denied. In such taxonomies, taxa will be classes of individuals standing in some relation of affinity to each other. This affinity relationship may or may not be an intrinsic relationship. But since (A-1) is denied, being of a given taxon is not an intrinsic property; hence, either way the taxon definition cannot be factually true. Rather, the definition does nothing more than to establish the convention that taxon name 'T' will be used to refer to the largest class of individuals in domain D which stand in such and such an affinity to each other. (B) clearly does not hold for such taxonomies, and it is quite clear that such taxonomies will be artificial in any reasonable sense of the term. Given appropriate choices of affinity relationships, such artificial taxonomies may be of considerable scientific use (see sec. VII).

So far in this section I have concentrated my attention on various versions of (B) and the ways they render taxonomies natural. Now I want to consider systematically what happens if (B) does not hold; (A-2) is assumed to hold.[37] Let us suppose that (B) does not hold for a taxonomic system. There are two ways in which (B) could fail to hold, depending whether *is a T* is an intrinsic characteristic or not. If it is an intrinsic characteristic, then the failure of (B) must be by virtue of the fact that the correlation between the intrinsic characteristic *is a T* and the diagnostic intrinsic characteristics specified by the definition fails to be realized—that is, if the definition is factually false. In other words, the taxonomy is a putative natural taxonomy, but fails to actually be one because it asserts false generalizations about the world in its taxa definitions. Strictly speaking, this sort of taxonomy is incompatible with a denial of (B); for (B) says only that the taxa definitions, *if correct,* will be empirically true. Thus if (B) fails, (A-1) also must fail. Suppose then, that (A-1) does not hold. Then (B) could not be met, since the definition fails to establish an empirically true or false correlation between diagnostic characteristics and *being a T.* The affinity taxonomies where (A-1) fails (discussed earlier) constitute a species of this sort of taxonomy, and the same considerations that were raised with respect to such affinity taxonomies apply equally well here. The conclusion also applies: If both (B) and (A-1) do not hold for a taxonomy, then the taxonomy is artificial and conventional. The above, of course, is an insufficient discussion of conventional taxonomies; they will be given more extended treatment in section VII below.

V. VARIABLE TAXA DEFINITIONS AND EMPIRICAL TRUTH

In examining (B) so far, I have confined my attention to taxonomic systems with fixed taxa in the sense that the criteria for membership in a taxa are invariant over time. I now want to remove that restriction and consider cases where taxa are not so fixed. The considerations raised at the end of the previous section in effect establish that whenever (B) holds, (A-1) also must hold; since they in no way depended on the assumption that taxa were fixed, the result is completely general. Thus we may assume (A-1) holds whenever (B) holds.

If a taxonomic system has reasons for not assuming fixed taxa, it is because there is reason to suppose that the diagnostic characteristics which could be used to define taxa vary over time; often the motivation underlying this assumption is some sort of evolutionary theory. If (B) holds for a taxonomic system, (A-1) also must. Hence we obtain the following:

> *Principle of limited variation:* There is a limit to the variation an organism of taxon *T* may undergo—namely, it cannot lose the intrinsic characteristic *being a T* and still remain in the taxon.

This is a double-edged principle. One edge allows unlimited variation in an organism's characteristics; the other edge puts limits on the variation the organism can undergo and still remain in the taxon. It is the task of the taxa definitions to specify the latter edge, by stating the extent of allowable variation.

In our survey of taxonomic history only two main approaches to specifying this limit were found—the ideal-type, or topological, approach and the phylogenetic approach. I will begin by considering the ideal-type approach.

An *ideal-type taxonomy* asserts that for each taxon there is an ideal specimen of the taxon, and that all members of the taxon must stand in some relationship to that ideal specimen. Presumably, the taxon is to be defined by means of an Aristotelian-form definition of the ideal specimen and a specification of the relationship which must hold between the ideal specimen and the remaining members of the taxon. For example, in Cuvier's version of an ideal-type taxonomy, the relationship is one of ancestral descendance. This much is clear about such taxonomies if (B) is to hold: (i) all the members of a taxon *T* must possess the intrinsic characteristic *being a T;* (ii) the relationship relating the ideal specimen to other members of *T* must be an intrinsic relationship which holds between the ideal specimen and all and only those individuals which have the intrinsic characteristic *being a T;* and (iii) the ideal specimen must be a particular. Should any of (i) through (iii) fail, the taxon definition could not be factually true or false, and so (B) would fail.

Depending on the way (iii) is satisfied, different versions of ideal-type taxonomies are obtained. First, (iii) could be satisfied because the ideal specimen is an actual specimen (e.g., a fossil). On this version, which might be called a *non-Platonic ideal-type taxonomy,* a number of different and nonequivalent taxonomies may be obtained for a given *D,* since there will be different specimens which could be chosen as the ideal specimen for a given taxon. Since it is unrealistic to suppose that a single specimen could be, for example, ancestor to all members of a taxon, this approach to taxonomy is unlikely to be acceptable for biological organisms. Second, (iii) could be satisfied by virtue of the ideal specimen existing not as an organism, but as an ideal abstraction which also is a particular. The paradigm of this case is Plato's metaphysics, wherein physical chairs were distinct from the *form* chair (the ideal specimen) itself, and all physical chairs stood in a *mimetic* (resemblance) and *methexic* (participatory) relationship to the form chair. The ideal specimen could be an independent existent, as were Plato's *forms,* or it could exist as an intentional particular.[38] Such a position is generally viewed as metaphysically excessive and is repugnant to most contemporary philosophers. Nonetheless, if such a position, which might be called a *neo-Platonic ideal-type taxonomy,* were viable, condition (B) obviously would be met. If the ideal type is an independent existent, presumably only one correct taxonomic system would be possible for a given domain *D;* under the intentional particular version a number of different taxonomic systems could be correct for a given domain, depending on what ideal specimens were conceived.

Thus, for ideal-type taxonomies, we obtain the following version of (B):

> (B-5) A taxonomic system is natural if it is an ideal-type taxonomy wherein each taxon has an ideal specimen with specified intrinsic characteristics, (A-1) holds, and the taxon definition, if correct, specifies a factually true relationship which holds between each member of the taxon and the ideal specimen.

The shortcomings mentioned above for both sorts of ideal-type taxonomies are sufficient to render such taxonomies implausible in virtually every biological application as well as in many other areas of investigation.[39]

If an ideal-type taxonomy fails to meet (i) through (iii), then (B) is not met. Such a taxonomy will be a version of one of the sorts of taxonomies considered in section IV; for example, if (A-1) holds, it will be one where no matter how much variation there is among members of taxon T, the members of T are similar to the ideal type (an affinity taxonomy); or if (A-1) fails to hold, one where 'is a T' is conventionally reserved to apply to those individuals who show a certain affinity to the ideal specimen. Some versions of numerical taxonomy seem to be of this latter, conventional, sort.

The second approach to meeting the principle of limited variation in biological taxonomy is that of the phylogenetic approach. Several different possible versions can be distinguished. The first, which might be called a *population-descendance taxonomy*, is quite similar to the ideal-type approach. On this theory, one recursively defines a taxon thus: An initial natural population T_1, consisting of all of the individuals which have the characteristic *being a T* at time t_0, is defined so as to meet (B-1), (B-2), (B-3), or (B-4). Then the taxon T is defined as the class of individuals which either belongs to T_1 or else stands in a stated intrinsic relationship to one or more individuals in T_1. For example, T_1 might be the class of all *Rosa multiflora* at a given time (or evolutionary stage), and then T might be the class of all organisms which either are in that initial class or else are descendants of members of that initial class. Buffon's taxonomy (sec. I) seems to have been of this sort; also a phylogenetic taxonomy which requires that species be defined in accord with the evolutionary definition (see sec. I) could be of this sort. The taxa definitions for such taxonomies will be factually true or false. Thus the following version of (B) is obtained:

(B-6) A taxonomic system is natural if it is a population-descendance taxonomy wherein (A-1) holds, each member of a taxon T is either a member of a subclass T_1 of T whose definition meets (B-1), (B-2), (B-3), or (B-4), or else stands in a specified intrinsic relationship to one or more members of T_1.

It should be noted that a number of different and nonequivalent taxonomic systems which meet (B-6) may be possible for a given domain D, depending upon the choice of T_1 and the intrinsic (descendance) relationship chosen. [The "species-as-individuals" approach discussed earlier in section III provides an alternative analysis of population-descendance, or lineage, taxonomies which will not be considered in the present discussion.]

Most phylogenetic taxonomic systems are not population-descendance taxonomies. Typically, a phylogenetic taxonomy begins by stipulating a criterion for being a taxon of a given taxonomic category—for example, the biological definition of species might be adopted, which requires that species be classes of individuals which are actual or potentially interbreeding natural populations reproductively isolated from other such groups. This defines what it is to be a taxon in the taxonomic category *species*. Then the individual taxa must be defined in terms of diagnostic characteristics so as to meet the condition that the class so defined also qualifies as a taxon of the requisite taxonomic category. For example, a specimen of *Rosa multiflora* must belong to exactly one species taxon. The definition of that taxon must be such that the class of all and only those individuals which satisfy that definition qualifies as a species—for example, if the biological definition is adopted, the class defined must be a population of actual or potentially interbreeding natural populations reproductively isolated from other groups. For (B) to be satisfied, it is clear that the taxa definition, if correct, must be factually true, and also that the criterion for a class being a taxon of the specified taxonomic category must be factually true of the class defined by the taxa definition. Thus the following version of (B) is obtained:

(B-7) A taxonomic system is natural if (A-1) is met, it is a phylogenetic taxonomy, the definition for each taxon T, if correct, is factually true, and the definition of what it is for a taxon to be of the appropriate taxonomic category C, if correct, is factually true of the class determined by the definition of taxon T.

Since the majority of contemporary biological taxonomic systems (those advocated by adherents to the New Systematics) are phylogenetic taxonomies which are supposed to meet (B-7), some extended discussion of such systems is in order.[40] Depending on the form of taxa definition and the choice of criterion for being of a taxonomic category, a number of different taxonomies meeting (B-7) could be possible for a given domain D.

The many attempts to produce a taxonomy meeting (B-7) have not been particularly successful. Two different and distinct sorts of difficulties have been experienced. First, it has proved extremely difficult to produce an adequate criterion even for being a taxon on the species category. None of the definitions (biological, genetic, etc.) considered in section I are satisfactory,[41] though a polytypic definition has been suggested which may prove adequate.[42] Second, there has been a problem defining the individual taxa in terms of diagnostic character-istics. The problem, simply put, is that all the plausible criteria for being a taxon of a given taxonomic category allow extensive and seemingly unpredictable evolutionary variations in the phenotypic characteristics of organisms in the taxon. Thus while it is possible to disjunctively specify (using polytypic definitions) the known variations in the diagnostic characteristics, the subsequent variations resulting from evolution cannot be fully anticipated. The most that can be explicitly given in a definition of a taxon is a polytypic definition which covers all the known varieties of the taxon, but does not cover the unknown later members of the species, which may have different phenotypic characteristics because of evolutionary changes. The result is that if standard polytypic definitions are used, the class of organisms defined will be a proper subclass of the taxon in question if the taxon is still evolving, and this proper subclass generally will not meet the criterion for being a taxon of the taxonomic category: (B-7) thus is violated. Hence polytypic definitions generally cannot be employed for still-evolving taxa in a taxonomy natural by virtue of meeting (B-7).

As was mentioned in section I, David Hull has suggested that the problem can be overcome by adopting indefinite polytypic definitions for still-evolving taxa. For example, one would define species T by saying

x is of species T if and only if
$$x \text{ is } C_1 \lor \ldots \lor x \text{ is } C_n \lor \ldots ,$$

where $C_1, \ldots, C_n$ are clusters of diagnostic characteristics which con-stitute sufficient conditions for being of each of the *known* varieties of organisms of taxon T, where it is necessary that specimens of any of the known varieties of T must meet one of the $C_1, \ldots, C_n$. In addition to $C_1, \ldots, C_n$, an indefinite number of additional *unspecified* clusters are included in the definition to cover unknown varieties that evolution will subsequently bring into existence. Without quibbling over whether a partially specified definition is a definition, it should be noted that if such indefinite polytypic definitions are used to specify taxa in a phylogenetic taxonomic system, the system cannot meet condition (B-7). That it cannot is easily shown. For (B-7) to be met the definition of the taxa must be factually true. But as stated, an indefinite polytypic definition is not factually true or false: For if indefinite polytypic definitions are required, then it will be false that every individual of domain D which has the intrinsic property *being a T* (all the members of taxon T, since [A-1] is presumed to hold) will have the intrinsic characteristics in one of the specified clusters $C_1, \ldots, C_n$—some varieties to emerge later will not. Whether the definition is empirically true will depend upon the unspecified clusters in the definition. Hence the most that can be said of indefinite polytypic definitions is that *when made fully explicit they will be factually true or false.* But an indefinite polytypic definition made fully explicit is nothing other than a polytypic definition. So if indefinite polytypic definitions actually are required in a taxonomic system, (B-7) fails for that system. Insofar as such systems are supposed to be natural in virtue of (B-7), the suggestion that indefinite polytypic definitions be adopted is unsatisfactory.

Since polytypic and indefinite polytypic definitions alike fail to yield phylogenetic taxonomies in biology which are natural by virtue of meeting (B-7), is it to be concluded that natural phylogenetic taxonomies are impossible? Since (B-7) seems the obvious sense in which phylogenetic taxonomies are supposed to be natural, this may seem the only reasonable conclusion. [The thesis that species are individuals constitutes a radical solution to this problem. Hull (1976, 180) writes

> If species are conceptualized as classes, then at best the names of species can be defined only polytypically, but there is another way of accounting for the phenomenon in question. Species names cannot be defined in the traditional manner because they cannot be defined at all. They are proper names introduced by a baptismal act denoting particular chunks of the geneological nexus (Ghiselin, 1974). The list of traits which taxonomists include in their diagnoses and descriptions do not perform the function of definitions but are, at most, definite descriptions.

When the diversity of traits is such that indefinite polytypic "definitions" are required, species names cannot function as definite descriptions. For the criticisms we raised against indefinite polytypic definitions on construal (B) carry over *mutatis mutandis* to the thesis that they are definite descriptions. The fact that the "species-as-individuals" proposal does not succeed in providing a general resolution of this problem seriously undercuts some of the advantages Hull claims for the proposal.

The Semantic Conception provides a general-form solution to the problem of natural phylogenetic taxonomies. It yields a plausible analysis whereby] taxa can be defined in phylogenetic taxonomies so as to meet (B-7). This proposal does involve a form of definition whose acceptance will require rather drastic alteration in the way taxonomies currently are conceived.

If a taxonomic system rationally denies the fixity of taxa, it must assume there is some underlying mechanism which brings about the alteration in taxa characteristics; for without the regularities of some such mechanism bringing order to the variation in taxa characteristics, it will be impossible to specify the varying taxa. And if taxa with varying characteristics cannot be specified for a given domain, the taxonomic system must be replaced by one with fixed taxa.[43] Thus, if a phylogenetic taxonomy is feasible for a given domain, there must be some underlying mechanism which determines the variation in the possible diagnostic characteristics for taxa. This underlying mechanism, in principle at least, can be characterized by a scientific theory.

Suppose we do have a theory which describes the variation in at least some of the possible diagnostic characteristics for taxa. This theory obviously must be relative to a set of definitions of taxonomic categories and a specified set of possible diagnostic characteristics. It is clear that such a theory can be used to define taxa in terms of the specified diagnostic characteristics—namely, by the definition of taxonomic category we have a criterion for being a taxon of category C. For each taxon T of a category C, the theory describes the possible variations in the specified diagnostic characteristics. Thus the theory specifies for each taxon all of the various possible combinations of the selected diagnostic characteristics which may be manifested by members of the taxon. Accordingly, whenever phylogenetic taxonomies are feasible for a domain D, it is possible to have a phylogenetic taxonomy consisting of a theory describing the variation in a set of diagnostic characteristics together with definitions of the taxonomic categories.[44]

An example will help clarify this. For biological speciation, a phylogenetic taxonomy apparently is required (although some taxonomists would deny it). The reason for this is that taxonomy typically works in terms of morphological diagnostic characteristics, and if evolutionary theory is correct, these morphological characteristics will vary over time for a species. But these morphological characteristics are phenotypic reflections of genotypic variations in the species: The variation in morphological characteristics is a result of alteration in the genotypes of members of the species. Moreover, evolutionary theory (together with natural selection theory) characterizes the mechanism which brings about the genotypic variations. Thus following the discussion of the previous paragraph, from the coupling of evolutionary theory together with a definition of the taxonomic category *species*, a taxonomic *system* results which defines species genotypically. I have emphasized the systematic character of the resulting taxonomy to underscore the point that the resulting taxonomy is systematic in a way the taxonomies heretofore employed by biologists are not. For the resulting taxonomic system does not by itself explicitly specify the various species. Rather, it is a system of taxonomic laws applying to biological organisms.

To see clearly what this means, a comparison with physical theory is illuminating. Classical particle mechanics is a system of laws characterizing the behavior of systems of interacting particles. When it is applied to a physical system through use of auxiliary hypotheses, it does yield a description of the system in question. Specifically, when various auxiliary hypotheses specifying the initial state of the physical system (its configuration at some time *t*) and various boundary conditions, and so on, are specified, then the laws of the theory (the "equations of motion") can be solved to obtain a special case solution of the theory which is a law describing the behavior of the system in question.[45] The special case law *does* describe a particular system of interacting participles.

An analogous situation prevails for evolutionary theory: The laws of the theory describe the sorts of genotypic variation which are possible for populations. Relative to the genotypic profile of a population at a given time, the theory describes the possible genotypic variations in that population over time.[46] This class of possible genotypic variations in that population is not itself the species. Rather, the species is that portion of this class which additionally meets the definition of being a *species* taxon—for example, if the definition for sexually reproducing taxa were that a species is a population whose members consistently interbreed producing a reasonably large proportion of reasonably fertile offspring, then the species would consist of that temporal sequence of populations of genotypes such that the genotypes of the population do consistently interbreed producing a reasonably large proportion of reasonably fertile offspring. But this is just a sequence of populations of genotypes which have certain reproduction rates,[47] and so the species will be the class of genotypes within the class of possible genotypic variations which have appropriate reproduction rates for a given time.[48] Thus evolutionary theory together with the definition of taxonomic categories provides us with a systematic definition of taxa, wherein definitions of a particular taxon can be obtained by use of auxiliary hypotheses specifying the genotypic distribution of the taxon at some time together with other boundary conditions.[49]

I imagine that many taxonomists may be willing to grant that such an evolutionary genotypic taxonomy is, in principle, possible but would deny that it has any relevance to phylogenetic taxonomy. The most important reason given for this position probably would be the following: From the phylogenetic perspective, taxonomy is an ordering of phenotypes, not genotypes, and since the slip between genotype and phenotype is loose, the sort of genotypic taxonomic system proposed will not translate into a phenotypic classification. To quote Simpson, "genetic evolution and somatic evolution are not identical or precisely parallel and . . . it is somatic evolution that is directly pertinent in taxonomy" (1961, 91). While what Simpson says is true, the objection is misguided and turns on a failure to understand the nature of scientific systems. An illustration from physics will help indicate what the confusion inherent in the objection is. In classical particle mechanics the theory describes and provides a taxonomy of mechanical systems in terms of an underlying mechanism; these systems are described by the theory in terms of abstract, idealized parameters such as position and momentum under idealized conditions. For many purposes, these descriptions are inadequate. For example, in engineering applications, it is desirable to describe and classify these systems as being inclined planes of such and such dimension, angle of inclination, and friction coefficients, and so on. For such systems, there are local laws which describe connections between these applied descriptions and the theoretical descriptions of the systems. These laws in effect say that if a mechanical system has such and such characteristics, then it corresponds to such and such system of particles whose current positions and momenta are . . . . These local laws are not operational definitions of the theoretical parameters; they are not definitions at all.[50] They are laws describing sufficient conditions for being such and such a sort of system; they are procedures for applying the theory to the phenomena and have no definitional status whatsoever.

The situation is similar in phylogenetic taxonomy. Taxa are sets of organisms; each of these organisms has a specific genotype and a specific phenotype. The phenotypic variations due to evolution in practice preclude giving an exhaustive phenotypic definition of a taxon, but it is possible to give an exhaustive genotypic characterization of taxa by specifying the taxonomic categories and the evolutionary laws at work. The portion of a taxon extant at any given time can be investigated with respect to phenotypic characteristics, and general phenotypic laws can be determined of the form

If x has phenotypic characteristics C, then x is of taxon T,

where C is a cluster of phenotypic characteristics. These laws in effect will be laws correlating phenotypic characteristics with genotypes, and they will be factually true or false. On the basis of these, one is able to classify organisms on the basis of phenotypic characteristics; this in no way requires knowing what the evolutionary future of the taxon is. At a subsequent point in the taxon's evolutionary history, these laws will still be true, even though there may be no individuals which manifest the specified phenotypic characteristics. For new characteristic phenotypic combinations introduced by evolution, new laws may be discovered which are empirically true; and these may be used to classify organisms by taxon. Thus all the practical advantages of phenotypic classification are obtained, even though taxa are genotypically defined; and doing so in no way requires knowing the general mechanisms whereby phenotypic characteristics are manifestations of genotypic characteristics.

It is worth comparing this proposal with Hull's indefinite polytypic definitional form of phylogenetic taxonomy. Hull's account defines a taxon in terms of an indefinite disjunction of clusters of phenotype characteristics; if fully specified, this will specify a class of organisms. Since these individuals have genotypes, it also indirectly specifies a class of genotypes which meets the taxonomic category definition and is consistent with evolutionary law. But the evolutionary law is not definitive of the taxon—the indefinite disjunction is. And we have seen that this makes the taxonomy nonnatural by virtue of violating (B-7). In my suggested alternative, the evolutionary laws together with the taxonomic category definition specify the taxon by establishing laws which describe the variations in genotype possible for organisms of a given taxon. Since (A-1) holds, if correct, these laws will be factually true; hence the taxon definition is. The various *specified* clusters which occur in Hull's indefinite disjunctive definition now function as the clusters C of phenotypic characteristics which occur in the above-mentioned laws specifying *sufficient* phenotypic conditions for membership of an organism in the taxon. These laws, if correct, are factually true; they are not definitional. A moral is to be learned from the comparison: Whereas taxonomy has proceeded on the assumption that the definitions of taxa had to be in terms of the diagnostic characteristics used to classify the organism, this is not necessary. Rather, the criteria for definition need not be the same as those for its employment so long as laws are possible which guarantee that the criteria for its employment necessitate that the definitional requirements are met.

One last possible objection to this alternative requires consideration. I can imagine some taxonomists objecting to my alternative account of phenotypic taxonomies as follows: "We are willing to grant that for some areas, taxonomies of the sort you suggest are feasible, but they do not work in the biological realm. For in the absence of full knowledge of the subsequent reproductive isolations which a species will encounter, it is impossible for even the special case taxonomic laws to give a characterization of the genotypes actually occurring in the species population at different times. The most that these laws can yield is a characterization of the potential genotypes which, given appropriately favorable environmental conditions, could be manifested in species organisms. But this is not identical with the class of genotypes which actually will be manifested by organisms of the species in subsequent evolutionary history of the species, and so the laws do not define the species, but rather only define a class of organisms (by genotypes) which contains the species as a proper subclass.[51] Thus, in the biological realm, your proposal does not define species."

This criticism is not without substance. It is true that the special case taxonomic laws, by themselves, do not directly specify the class of genotypes actually manifested by organisms present in the species; rather, they specify which genotypes will be present as a function of other parameters such as reproduction rate and satisfaction of the species category criterion. For any given time this gives the actual makeup when the appropriate values for these other parameters are supplied. However, this is sufficient, for all that is required to define a particular species is that necessary and sufficient conditions for membership in the species be given, and the special case taxonomic laws do this. They stipulate, for example, that an organism is of the species T if and only if its genotype is in set G, that the genotype has reproduction rate r, and that organisms of that genotype consistently interbreed with other genotypes, producing offspring whose genotypes have an average reproduction rate greater than r'. Thus the species itself *is* defined, only the definition is such that it cannot yield a test condition for species membership at time t unless augmented by some additional empirical data about the population at t. That is, the objection misses the point, because it confuses the definition of a species with a test condition for membership in the species.[52] On my proposal, the two are relatively distinct, with the empirical generalizations stating that organisms with phenotypic characteristics C belong to taxon T serving as the test conditions for membership (but not for nonmembership) in the taxon. Again, the moral to be drawn here is similar to the one drawn from the discussion comparing classicle particle mechanics theory to evolutionary theory: Although taxonomists traditionally have proceeded on the assumption that taxa definitions must be capable of functioning as test conditions for taxon membership, they need not do so. And if the taxonomy is a reflection or manifestation of the workings of deep mechanisms operating over the taxonomy's domain (as taxonomy *is* for the New Systematics), it probably is a mistake to insist that the taxa definitions also function, by themselves, as practical test conditions for taxon membership.

It is clear from the above discussion that if the underlying theory is factually true, the combination of it with an appropriate definition for taxonomic categories yields a factually true set of empirical generalizations about the range of possible variations in organisms of a given taxonomic category. Thus such taxonomic systems meet the following version of (B):

(B-8) A taxonomy is natural if (A-1) is met and it yields (relative to appropriate boundary conditions, etc.) a set of laws characterizing the range of variations in combinations of a specified set of characteristics which members of a given taxon may manifest; if correct, these laws will be factually true. The actual classification of individuals may be done on the basis of characteristics not occurring in these laws so long as there are factually true laws established to the effect that any individual having these characteristics also has a combination of characteristics within the variation allowed for the taxon in question.

With a little reflection it easily is seen that whenever a taxonomic system satisfies any of (B-1) through (B-7), it also satisfies (B-8). (B-1) through (B-4) are cases where the laws state that there is no (or virtually no) variation in the specified set of diagnostic characteristics; (B-5) through (B-7) allow variation, but require, in effect, that the taxa definitions be laws describing the allowable variation. Thus (B-8) constitutes the substance of (B): Any taxonomy which fails to satisfy (B-8) is conventional and, in an important sense, artificial.

Finally, the results of this section and the previous sections can be applied to the answers to question (2) in section I: Any taxonomy committed to answers (a) through (c)—and some taxonomies committed to answer (d) to question 2—thereby are committed to (B-8), and hence to (A-1) and (A-2).

VI. ARE CATEGORY DEFINITIONS EMPIRICALLY TRUE OR FALSE?

Interpretation (C) requires that definitions of taxonomic categories be factually true. Clearly, this requires that *being of taxonomic category C* be an intrinsic characteristic entering into the definition. As indicated in section II, (C) admits of two plausible interpretations.

Interpretation (C') states that being of taxonomic category C is a characteristic of the intrinsic characteristic *being a T* which determines the various taxa T in the taxonomic category. (C') thus presupposes (A-1); in practice, it also presupposes (B-8). Such a taxonomy will assign a taxon T to taxonomic category C only if *being of taxonomic category* C is an intrinsic characteristic of the intrinsic characteristic *being a T.* In such a case, the appropriate form of definition for taxonomic categories will be an empirical issue, being the question, What regularities govern taxa characteristics having the intrinsic characteristic *being of taxonomic category C?* If one holds this position in answer to question (4), the issue is not wholly empirical, since it requires commitment to the metaphysical claim that characteristics can have characteristics; this metaphysical commitment would be unacceptable to a nominalist.

Interpretation (C″) states that the definitions of the taxonomic categories, if true, specify intrinsic characteristics common to all of the taxa each comprehends. If taxa are themselves complex particulars, then taxa (as opposed to their members or the intrinsic characteristics *being a T*) will have intrinsic characteristics. (C″) then requires that *being of taxonomic category C* be one of these intrinsic characteristics. (A-1) and (B) clearly must hold, so the definition will be that

x is a taxon of taxonomic category *C* if and only if
x has intrinsic characteristics . . . ;

thus the definition will state an empirically true or false correlation between the occurrence of *being of taxonomic category C* and other intrinsic properties of taxa. The exact form of definition to be used (Aristotelian, polytypic, etc.) will be an empirical matter.

This interpretation is able to accommodate the biological, evolutionary, etc., definitions of species, where these definitions are interpreted as stating the intrinsic relationship by virtue of which the taxon is the compound particular it is. Its viability depends primarily on whether taxa are particulars.[53] If taxa are not particulars, it appears (C″) is impossible, since *being of taxonomic category C* cannot be an intrinsic characteristic of the individuals in the taxon (the taxa are the members of taxonomic category *C,* not the individuals in the taxa, and it must be an intrinsic characteristic of some particular). If taxa are particulars, the taxonomic category definitions will be empirically true or false, and the exact definitional form is an empirical issue.

Thus if (C) is viable, it must be either as (C′) or (C″). I would hazard a guess that (C″) is the more likely version, since if (C) holds, it most likely will be in terms of the taxa being constituted by their members standing in certain relationships to each other, and if these relationships are intrinsic, the taxa will be complex particulars. Whether (C′) or (C″) are viable depends on the way the world is. If (C) does hold, there may be more than one taxonomic system for a domain in *D* which meets it. If neither is viable for a taxonomic system, (C) fails, and so the definitions of the taxonomic categories will be conventional, being nothing more than a decision to reserve certain terms to discuss collectively certain taxa. Even though (A-1) and (B) hold, (C) may fail for a taxonomic system. If the system is a standard taxonomy, this will diminish the usefulness and empirical significance of the hierarchical ordering. But so long as (B) holds, the taxa will be empirically significant, and thus not wholly arbitrary; the taxonomic system will be artificial only with respect to its hierarchical ordering.

VII. ARTIFICIAL TAXONOMIES ARE NOT FACTUALLY TRUE OR FALSE

So far we have considered three main different ways taxonomies can be natural in the sense of being factually true: (A), (B), and (C). It follows from our discussion that they are successively stronger requirements in the sense that (B) presupposes (A), and (C) presupposes (A) and (B); (B) is compatible with the denial of (C). Clearly any taxonomy which denies (A), (B), and (C) must, in a very basic sense, be construed as an artificial taxonomy; for such a taxonomy does nothing more than establish conventional names for referring to classes of individuals which share certain features in common. This is not to say that such artificial taxonomies are wholly without use; for they are based on a kind of affinity, and for some purposes may be adequate. For example, I might introduce a taxonomy with a taxon comprised of all humans born since 1946 in Italy who emigrated to the U.S. at age 16 or older, play the concertina, are 6'4" or more tall, and are glabrous. Such a taxonomy presumably will be artificial by virtue of (A) not holding; still, if I were a scholarship director at a large university, it conceivably might be a useful taxon for classifying applicants as to scholarship eligibility. A less bizarre possibility would be classification by statistical profile or statistical covariance—for example, the sorts of taxonomies numerical taxonomists produce. Such taxonomies may or may not satisfy (A), and it is possible that useful taxonomies which do not will result. Useful as they are, in a certain basic sense such taxonomies are artificial.

Taxonomies which do not satisfy (B) by virtue of satisfying (B-8) or one of its stronger versions—(B-1) through (B-7)—also will fail to satisfy (A-1). The plausible taxonomies which fail to satisfy (B) invariably will be of the affinity type and have the same sort of plausibility mentioned above in the discussion of taxonomies which fail to satisfy (A).[54] Again, these are artificial in the sense of being mere conventions for usage of classificatory terms.

It seems to me quite clear from the discussion in section I that as used throughout most of the history of taxonomy the notion of a natural taxonomy tacitly has required that (A) and (B) be met. In most cases, (C) probably has been incorporated in the notion. For phylogenetic taxonomies, it is absolutely crucial for the species category, and probably necessary for higher taxa. In any case, a very plausible notion of naturalness for taxonomies is that (A), (B), and (C) must be met. However, if a taxonomy fails to meet (C) but meets (A) and (B), it does not seem reasonable to defame it as being artificial; for it is artificial in a much weaker sense than those taxonomies which are purely conventional. I do not think much more can be said in the abstract than the following in deciding which of these two senses of 'natural' is to be preferred in taxonomy: If a taxonomy's intended applications are such that which taxonomic category a taxon is in is to be empirically significant and not just a matter of convenience, then (C) must be met; otherwise it is sufficient for just (A) and (B) to be met. Any taxonomy which fails to meet (A) and (B) clearly is artificial.

At this point it may prove helpful if the discussion thus far is summarized briefly. Through a consideration of the history of taxonomic theory, it was found that throughout most of taxonomic history natural taxonomies have been understood as having an objective basis in nature. As such, natural taxonomies are neither stipulative nor conventional systems for classifying organisms. To say that natural taxonomies have an objective basis in nature is excessively vague, and I have urged that this most plausibly can be construed as stating that natural taxonomies are factually true or false of the organisms or individuals in their domains—that is, that the "definitions" of taxa are factually true or false assertions about the characteristics distinctive of members of the various taxa. Having suggested this interpretation, I then turned to an investigation of a number of kinds of taxonomic systems which historically have been advanced and tried to determine what conditions must be met by each of these sorts of taxonomies if they are to be natural in this sense. It was determined that conditions (A-1), (A-2), (B-8), and possibly some of (B-1) through (B-7) or (C) must be met if the taxonomy is to be natural. In general, it was seen that whether a given kind of natural taxonomy was viable for a given domain was an empirical matter depending on the sorts of correlations holding between the various characteristics of the individuals. In particular, the question of the appropriate taxa definitional form for given taxa in a domain is a question of empirical fact—just as the question of the appropriate law form for a given domain is a question of empirical fact. Indeed, we saw that under this interpretation of what it is for a taxonomy to be natural, taxonomies turn out to be a kind of scientific theory which must be confirmed much like any other theory.

That natural taxonomies are empirically true or false opens the possibility that none of the sorts of taxonomic theory proposed ever could be empirically true; however, if the interpretation of phylogenetic taxonomies given in (B-8) is accepted, this is highly unlikely.[55] Nonetheless, there is a definite possibility that this is so. Such a possibility could be realized in two ways. First, it could be that for the taxa chosen (e.g., those used in the usual biological taxonomies), (A) fails—that is, that *being a T* is not an intrinsic property of organisms. Second, it may be that any taxonomic system using standard taxa is such that no allowed definitional form results in an empirically true taxonomic system. Should either of these possibilities occur, the only taxonomic systems of the desired sort will be artificial or conventional in the sense discussed above. As many taxonomists today are convinced that only conventional taxonomies are possible, somewhat more systematic consideration should be given to conventional taxonomies than has been given above.

Suppose a taxonomic system employing taxa $T_1, \ldots, T_n$ is desired and (A-1) is denied for the taxa. Such a taxonomy clearly will be conventional in the following sense. If a membership in a taxon T is defined, say, as

> For all organisms x (x belongs to T if and only if
> x is C_1 or . . . or x is C_n),

where $C_1, \ldots, C_n$ are combinations of diagnostic characteristics, the definition cannot be empirically true or false; for if it were, (B) would hold, which is impossible since (B) presupposes (A-1) and the latter has been denied. Rather, the definition can be nothing other than a decision to define any individual having C_1 or . . . C_n as being in taxon T, and vice versa. Thus to say a is a T is to say nothing more than that a is C_1 or a is C_2 or . . . or a is C_n. The fact that the definition of T is just a convention for naming does not mean that the taxonomy will not have interesting theoretical properties. For suppose that the $C_1, \ldots, C_n$ have been chosen in such a way that there are a number of significant correlations between things which are C_1 or . . . or C_n and other organisms, genetic characteristics, etc. Then a number of significant laws may be established about the members of taxon T. For example, it might be possible to establish various genetic novelties or traits which are characteristic of, or distinctive to, members of taxon T. In such a case, the taxonomy will be nontrivial and scientifically valuable. This indicates that being an artificial or conventional taxonomy need not be demeaning. Indeed, it may be that only such conventional taxonomies are viable for a given domain.

VIII. NATURAL TAXONOMIES AS UNIVERSAL SYSTEMS OF TAXONOMY

So far I have interpreted the thesis that natural taxonomies are those which have an objective basis in nature as the requirement that natural taxonomies be factually true or false. Our historical survey suggests a second interpretation which needs to be considered. Since Linnaeus, many taxonomists have maintained that natural taxonomies are those which take into consideration *all* characteristics; presumably the idea is that when one looks at organisms in all their characteristics, one finds that they naturally fall into similarity groups in such a way that all the organisms in a given group are much more similar to each other than they are to organisms in other groups, and that the similarity groups are noticeably distinct from each other.

Such taxonomies which take into consideration all characteristics and classify taxa on the basis of greatest affinity are claimed to be natural. Their naturalness is attributed to the alleged fact that by taking into consideration all characteristics, the resulting taxonomy is a universal one useful for all branches of science; on the other hand, it is alleged that those which take into consideration only selected characteristics are useful only for special purposes and hence are artificial. This interpretation of what it is for a taxonomy to be natural seriously challenges the interpretation I have given in preceding sections, and so deserves serious consideration. As this interpretation has been advanced recently by numerical taxonomists, I now turn to a consideration of their development of the thesis.

According to numerical taxonomists, "a 'natural' taxonomy is a general arrangement intended for general use by all scientists" (Sokal and Sneath 1963, 12). As such, natural taxonomies convey more information than arbitrary or special classifications, in the sense that "a system of classification is the more natural the more propositions there are that can be made regarding its constituent classes" (ibid., 19). Because of this, "a classification serving a large number of purposes will be more natural than one which is more specialized and that the most useful and generally applicable classification will be the most natural one" (ibid.). Thus in a natural taxonomy, "many generalizations can be made regarding a natural family of plants (e.g., with reference to distribution, chemical properties, wood structure, etc.), whereas regarding an artificial group very few of such generalizations are possible."[56] Thus, "a natural classification is that grouping which endeavors to utilize *all* the attributes of the individuals under consideration, and is hence useful for a very wide range of purposes" (Gilmour 1940, 472).

As stated, this characterization of what it is for a taxonomy to be natural is compatible with condition (B), hence with (A-1). But it is clear that many numerical taxonomists take this to involve a denial of (A-1), hence a denial of (B): taxa are just conventional classes.[57] So far as this definition of naturalness entails a denial of (B) and (A-1), it is just nonsense. First, it is not at all clear that the more similarities there are between individuals in a class, the more generalizations can be made. Suppose my class consists of two extremely similar individuals, for example, identical twins. Does it follow that more generalizations can be made? At best, it is true in a very trivial sense: Since virtually all their characteristics are similar, it is possible to generalize "all members of the class S have character C" for a large number of characters; and I certainly can make many more generalizations about specific characteristics for this class than I could for the class of all human beings. Does this make classification on the basis of being identical siblings more natural than to classify on the basis of being human beings? By the criterion of "the more generalizations, the more natural it is," it apparently is. The point here is that if one measures on the basis of the number of different characteristics about which generalizations can be made for a class, then the smaller the class, the more similarities possible, and the more generalizations possible. The natural taxonomy, then, would be one which puts each individual into a separate taxon.

This clearly is not a reasonable criterion of naturalness in classification. At the very least, if this is to be the criterion of naturalness, then it cannot be reasonable to demand that *all* characteristics be taken into account in determining affinity; rather, the criterion must be that those organisms which share the greatest affinity in terms of a selected set of characteristics are to be classified together. But this is, in effect, to give up the whole program. For once selection of characteristics is allowed, there is no way to prevent different characteristics from being selected for different purposes, and naturalness will be relative to the intended application; but the greatest affinity definition is supposed to be one that is neutral with respect to intended application—which was the reason for requiring that *all* characteristics be taken into account.

It may be held that I am trivializing their claim. This may be. Numerical taxonomists nowhere give any indication how generalizations are to be counted or under what measure the number of generalizations is to be measured. There is no standard measure of the number of generalizations forthcoming from a system; indeed, there is a fairly extensive literature on the subject, with a notable lack of success in developing measures of the number of generalizations or systematic import of scientific systems.[58] As such, it seems to me that the burden of proof is on the numerical taxonomists to specify a reasonable measure of the number of generalizations which supports their claim. For other than the above sense of 'number of generalizations', there are no obvious measures which give one any reason to believe that taxonomies which take into consideration all characteristics yield more generalizations.

Furthermore, even if a plausible measure could be found which did yield the result that such taxonomies yield more generalizations, it would provide no good reason for taking the classification as natural—even if we grant that natural taxonomies are those most useful to the scientific community as a whole. For what counts in science is not the number of generalizations, but rather the sorts of generalizations which are afforded. To use a terminology which is less popular than it once was, what counts is not the number of generalizations, but the systematic import of the generalizations yielded (see Kemeny and Oppenheim 1955).

Aristotle's dynamics employed a classification of dynamical systems which took into account a large number of low-level generalizations about various kinds of systems. Thus Aristotle's classification of dynamics was natural in the sense under consideration. On the other hand, Newton's dynamics classified dynamical systems merely on the number of bodies involved, their relative positions, and their respective momentums. The taxonomy itself afforded significantly fewer generalizations than Aristotle's; but the generalizations it did afford had great systematic import, and were ultimately much more important, much more useful, to a wider range of scientific disciplines than Aristotle's larger number ever were. To turn the definition of naturalness under question back on its proponents, what historically has proven the most useful in science for a wide range of purposes has been generalization having high systematic import; thus, if to be natural is to be useful for a wide range of scientific purposes, then the natural taxonomy is the one which yields generalizations with highest systematic import. If any one lesson is to be learned from the history of science, it is that the classifications which yield such generalizations are ones which use relatively few characteristics to classify. The issue, then, is not how many characteristics should be used to classify, but *which* few.

The difference between scientific classification and common garden classification is that the latter takes everything into account, whereas scientific classification works on the assumption that in nature different aspects of phenomena are "orthogonal" and hence can be treated independently from the rest of reality. Taxonomies which are natural in the numerical taxonomists' sense are so only in virtue of being pristine; to claim they are natural in any stronger or scientifically relevant sense is self-indulgent.[59] I conclude that this interpretation of 'natural taxonomy' offers us no viable alternative to the account developed in preceding sections.

IX. TAXONOMIC SYSTEMS AND SCIENTIFIC THEORIES

The thrust of sections III through VII has been that whether a taxonomic system is natural or not is a function of whether it is factually true or not. In section VIII, I considered a current account of naturalness which tries to equate naturalness with scientific usefulness. While this attempt fails, it does make (albeit confusedly) a rather important point: The adequacy of a taxonomic system must be judged not only on its naturalness and truth, but also on its scientific usefulness. This is particularly important when one recalls that, depending on the world's makeup, we have shown that there may be a number of factually true, different, and nonequivalent taxonomies which are natural by virtue of meeting conditions (A-1) and (B)—and possibly (C). In deciding between such competing taxonomies, some assessment of their relative merits must be made on a basis other than their naturalness. In the last section, and obliquely toward the end of section V, I have suggested that the criterion should be their usefulness—the scientific fecundity of the theories they can be incorporated into. On this criterion, I find the phylogenetic approach headed in a more promising direction than numerical taxonomy. At least the former is not trying to convert taxonomy into plant and animal sociology.

It should be obvious from this that I see a very close connection between taxonomy and scientific theories; in this section I want to sketch briefly and systematically what the connection is on the Semantic Conception. For an example, let us take the genetic theory of natural selection, which is concerned with evolutionary phenomena. It does so by considering populations of organisms as if they were populations of genotypes with various reproduction rates, crossover frequencies, and so on, and ignores all other characteristics (including phenotypic ones) of the organisms. These idealized populations are the physical systems of the theory. In the genetic theory of natural selection, the laws of the theory are deterministic laws whose states are statistically specific. The laws define genotypic distributions for the population over time as a function of reproduction rate functions for the genotypes, crossover frequency functions, and so on. The laws are stated as differential equations, and when the reproduction rate and other functions are specified for a population, a special case solution can be obtained by solving the differential equations. This solution together with the specification of the population's genotypic distribution, and so on, at time t (the physical system's state at t) can be used to predict what state (genotypic distribution, etc.) the population will assume at any subsequent time t'. As such, the various special case solutions describe a class of possible physical systems; if this class is identical with the set of physical systems corresponding to phenomena (biological populations) which in principle could occur in the world, then the theory is empirically true; otherwise it is empirically false.

The abstracted parameters in terms of which physical systems are specified rarely are amenable to direct observation; thus, in the genetic theory of natural selection they are genotypes, crossover frequencies, reproduction rates, and so forth. Accordingly, to apply the theory to actual phenomena, it is necessary to adopt experimental procedures, which often are complicated and involve sophisticated apparatus, to determine the values of the physical system's parameters. These experimental procedures, in essence, are methods for converting observations and measurements on the observed phenomena into specifications of the values for the parameters which are used to specify physical systems. For example, in the genetic theory of natural selection, births and deaths of various genotypes, morphological characteristics, and so on, are measured and then converted into characterizations of the genotypic makeup of the population, their reproduction rates, and so on, thereby determining the physical system's current state and boundary conditions.[60] The experimental procedures for determining the values of the parameters specifying the physical system generally apply only to relatively homogeneous classes of phenomena; they are laws of rather limited generality applying only to restricted classes of phenomena. For example, in the natural selection case, they might only specify that classes of organisms which have morphological characteristics C will have such and such genotypic distribution. The theory, then, has as its subject matter the characterization of a class of physical systems of which the phenomena experienced and observed are manifestations, and the application of the theory to phenomena is by means of local laws describing the correlations between physical systems and their phenomenal manifestations. (See ch. 6, sec. III-C, for further discussion of the genetic theory of natural selection from the Semantic Conception's perspective.)

Given this picture of theories, what implications does it have for taxonomy? First, it should be noted that the theory itself (if augmented by definitions of taxonomic categories) embodies a classification of physical systems. (The special case solutions of the theoretical laws in effect define classes of physical systems; the definitions of taxonomic categories specify which classes are to count as taxa of what category). This taxonomy typically is highly abstract, classification being carried out in terms of a few abstract characteristics (namely, the parameters of the physical systems and boundary conditions). Since the physical systems manifest themselves as phenomena, this taxonomy thereby imposes a taxonomy on the phenomenal manifestations of these physical systems—a taxonomy which is in terms of the underlying physical systems, not their phenomenal manifestations. Thus the genetic theory of natural selection together with boundary conditions and a definition of taxonomic categories imposes a taxonomy on organisms in terms of their phylogenetic properties, not their morphological characteristics. This taxonomy is wholly natural. The application of the theory to phenomena is in terms of local laws or experimental procedures of physical systems; implicit in these laws is a classification scheme, since the laws are to the effect that such and such kinds of phenomena correspond to and are manifestations of such and such physical systems. Thus a taxonomy of phenomena is also needed. This taxonomy, however, is likely to be fragmentary and nonsystematic, with overlapping taxa, and so on, due to technological limitations, inaccessibility of phenomena, and ignorance. Thus the phenomenal taxonomy, in practice, is likely to have relatively few of the nice properties taxonomists have demanded.

What implications are to be drawn from this for biological taxonomy? Insofar as it is the function of the scientific enterprise to generate comprehensive theories, the taxonomists, by their insistence that taxonomy must be morphological, have offered little of value to biological science.[61] The problems they are working on and the solutions they find acceptable are of little use to theoretical biology. I would like to suggest that this is not so much the case because taxonomists do not wish their work to be of value to theoretical biology,[62] but rather because taxonomists have had a very unclear and distorted idea about the nature of scientific theorizing and taxonomy's role and function in it.[63] The above discussion hopefully sheds some light on that role.

This is not to say, however, that the work of taxonomists has been without scientific merit. For the generation of comprehensive theories certainly is not the only legitimate function of science, and so there is no reason why taxonomy should concern itself exclusively with the production of taxonomies which can be incorporated into, or defined in terms of, comprehensive theories. There are several reasons why morphological taxonomies (as well as other sorts, e.g., cytological taxonomies) are needed. First, for many practical applications (e.g., agricultural ones), even if a highly abstract theory-embedded taxonomy existed, it would be too cumbersome to employ; simpler, less abstract taxonomies will be needed (much as classical physics continues to be used in most practical applications just because quantum theory is too complicated).

An analogy is useful at this point. Chemistry initially was a kind of taxonomy of reactions (qualitative analysis). As physical and atomic chemistry developed, new taxonomies of a more abstract and theoretical nature were required (e.g., the periodic table); but this did not obviate the need for qualitative chemical analysis, and it still continues to be a respectable branch of chemistry. Indeed, in practical applications it is among the most used. Similarly, while more abstract taxonomies are needed for incorporation into evolutionary theory, morphological taxonomies are also needed for many applications. An important point must not be overlooked here: The practical usefulness of qualitative chemical analysis is not sufficient to account for its continued survival. Essential to its continued use is the fact that it is compatible with (and in the main yields the same classifications as) the more abstract taxonomies incorporated into physical and atomic chemistry, for example. Analogously, to the extent that biology has comprehensive theories (such as evolutionary and natural selection theories) which embody nonmorphological taxonomies, the morphological taxonomies which will be of general biological use will be those which are compatible with, and in substantial agreement with, the taxonomies incorporated into the accepted, more comprehensive theories. Thus the instincts of phylogenetic taxonomy are sound; those of the numerical taxonomists are not—except to the extent that they are concerned with producing taxonomies which meet these requirements of compatibility.

A second reason why morphological taxonomies are needed and are useful is that in a number of areas of biology there are no accepted comprehensive generalized theories. Any attempt to develop highly abstract taxonomies in the absence of such comprehensive theories would be premature and mistaken. This point can be made clearer in the following way: Although it involves a fair amount of oversimplification, a scientific theory consists in generalized laws holding between the taxa of a taxonomic system which uses the theory's parameters as diagnostic characteristics for defining taxa. Where the only existing theories or laws known are in terms of morphological features, morphological taxonomies are needed. But where more generalized (cytological, evolutionary, genetic, etc.) laws or theories exist, taxonomies are required which are formulated in terms of the theories' parameters. For the practical reasons mentioned above, morphological taxonomies are required as well. If the further assumption is made that these various theories in different branches of science, if true, are mutually consistent and form a coherent whole, then the taxonomies they embody also must be consistent with each other, not merely self-consistent; accordingly, there should be a morphological taxonomy which is consistent with all these more abstract taxonomies. Such a morphological taxonomy should be the goal of morphological taxonomy, for it will provide a biological lingua franca which can be used to relate the theoretical results of these various branches of biology on the organism level. This means, of course, that new theoretical developments in theoretical biology may require modifications in morphological taxonomy.

X. SUMMARY AND CONCLUSION

This has been a long, complicated, and involved chapter, and so a short summary and conclusion is in order. I began historically by tracing a number of themes in the history of biological taxonomic theory. From this I extracted four basic questions, to which differing answers yield different positions on the nature of biological taxonomy (sec. I). These questions and the answers given to them make it clear that the pivotal issue is the nature of the distinction between natural and artificial taxonomies, so I turned my attention to the natural/ artificial distinction. Although there is general agreement that natural taxonomies have an objective basis in nature which artificial taxonomies lack, two basic different opinions prevail about what that objective basis is. One opinion is that natural taxonomies are factually true or false; the other is that natural taxonomies are those based on the largest number of affinities in all characteristics between organisms, and hence the most useful for science.

Prima facie, a scientific realism or quasi-realism should embrace the thesis that natural taxonomies are factually true or false. Sections II through VIII considered that thesis in detail. In section II, I presented an analysis of facts and empirical truth and then used it to isolate three different ways in which taxonomies could be factually true; these were conditions (A), (B), and (C). Then in sections III through VII, I considered these conditions in detail, looking at a fairly exhaustive selection of the various ways in which these conditions could be met. In the process, careful consideration was given to the various proposed definitional forms for taxa and for taxonomic categories. From this investigation, some quite general results were obtained [assuming taxa are classes of organisms]: (i) Condition (A-2) must be met by every taxonomy, whether natural or not; (ii) a more specific version of (A), namely (A-1), was obtained, and it was determined that this must be met by any natural taxonomy in this factual sense; (iii) condition (B) in its various versions was shown to presuppose a basic condition (B-8), and to be natural, taxonomies must meet (B-8); and (iv) it was shown that questions regarding the appropriate sort of natural taxonomic system for a domain D, and issues about the definitional form to be adopted, are primarily empirical, though in certain cases metaphysical commitments are required. In section VII, it was argued that taxonomies which fail to meet (A) and (B) clearly are artificial in the very basic sense that they are nothing more than conventions to reserve certain terminology for referring to collections of individuals sharing a certain affinity. The theoretical employment of such conventional taxonomies was briefly considered. Collectively, sections II through VII provide the sort of realistic analysis of classification and taxonomy our scientific quasi-realism requires.

Section VIII considered the second opinion on what it was for a taxonomy to be natural—that it was a taxonomy which classified on the basis of greatest affinity in all characteristics. It was argued that as developed by numerical taxonomists, this criterion failed to guarantee that taxonomies meeting it are natural in any scientifically relevant sense. It was granted, however, that the general usefulness of a taxonomy in a wide range of scientific enterprises is a legitimate and important factor in assessing the adequacy of a taxonomy. Consideration was given to the way taxonomies can have a wide range of scientific usefulness, and it was concluded that this was largely a matter of compatibility with generalized theories having a high degree of systematic import. Since such theories generally employ a very few highly abstract characteristics for classifying organisms, the thrust of the numerical taxonomists' notion of naturalness and usefulness is at odds with what is required for a wide range of scientific utilization. Phylogenetic taxonomy's orientation is sounder. Section IX considered the role of taxonomy in scientific theorizing and made certain generalizations about the contributions taxonomy can make to scientific theorizing, and it indicated what changes in biological taxonomy are required if these contributions are made. This discussion shows the applicability of the Semantic Conception to some difficult problems in the foundations of phylogenetic taxonomy.

Although the discussion here has been of taxonomic problems arising *in* biological taxonomy, it has proceeded in terms of general epistemological and metaphysical considerations, and the vast majority of my conclusions are independent of any specifically biological considerations. In particular, in Section II we showed how our discussion generalizes to an antinominalistic account of natural kinds. As such, my conclusions are general philosophical conclusions about the nature and role of taxonomy and classification in science in general, not just in biological science. In particular, they tell us how a scientific realism or quasi-realism must interpret or construe (natural) taxonomies and classifications. Thus our discussion not only indicates theoretical properties of taxonomies, and the relationships between taxonomies and scientific theories, it also contributes substantially to our development and defense of a quasi-realistic account of scientific knowledge by providing an antinominalistic account of natural kind classes. In fact, many of the considerations raised in this chapter will figure centrally in the developments in part IV of this book.

NOTES

1. Cf., e.g., Beckner 1959; Buck and Hull 1966; Gilmour 1940; Hull 1967, 1967a, and Hull's other works cited later. I do not mean to suggest that because these authors limit themelves to peculiarly biological problems that their work is not of philosophical interest—for they are philosophically interesting, and my own discussion is heavily indebted to them.

2. Although phrased differently, this definition of standard taxonomy is equivalent to that given for taxonomies elsewhere in the literature—e.g., by Beckner (1959, 55) and by Hull and Buck (1966). I call such taxonomies standard taxonomies to distinguish them from other taxonomies or classification systems which do not share this hierarchical character.

3. This sort of definition is often referred to (somewhat incorrectly) as the definition of taxa names.

4. This list, of course, is not exhaustive of the theoretical issues which have been raised with respect to what it is for a taxonomy to be natural. For example, the question whether different weightings should be given to diagnostic characteristics in taxa definitions often is raised in conjunction with "cluster" analysis approaches to taxonomy (e.g., the approaches of Adanson and the numerical taxonomists). Nothing I do here turns on such questions, and so they will be ignored here.

5. Strictly speaking, this is not correct, as Aristotle sketches features of earlier systems (e.g., Empedocles' and Democratis' in *De Partibus Animalium* I), but the accounts extant of these are very fragmentary, and so will be

ignored here. All references to Aristotle here and in the rest of the chapter are to Aristotle (1928–52).

6. To my knowledge, Aristotle never explicitly uses terminology corresponding to 'natural taxonomy' and 'artificial taxonomy'; but he clearly has the distinction, since he warns against adopting artificial or nonnatural taxonomies, e.g., in *De Partibus Animalium* 643a-b, where he discusses how classifications ought not to be made.

7. Most of Aristotle's taxonomic theory can be found in *De Partibus Animalium; Historica Animalium* contains some theoretical discussion (bk. I) without the metaphysics, together with an extensive classification of animals. The metaphysical principles employed are to be found scattered through his writings—e.g., *Posterior Analytics* bk. I, ch. 4, and bk. II; *Metaphysica* bk. IV (Γ); and *Topica* 101b, 39 ff. Good historical treatments of Aristotle's theory of taxonomy can be found in Hopwood 1950, Hull 1955, and Hull 1967a. Aristotle's plant taxonomies have been lost, but Theophrastus' work (1916) seems to embody much of Aristotle's own observations and to be based on the same theoretical principles. For a good discussion of his taxonomy, see Sprague 1950. These articles by Hull, Sprague, and Hopwood provide good historical discussions of the various developments subsequent to Aristotle, mentioned below, as do Wilmott 1950, Hopwood 1950a, Shaw 1950, and J. Smart 1950. A somewhat biased discussion can be found in Sokal and Sneath 1963, 11–30, which has an extremely good bibliography. Another excellent source is Whewell 1859.

8. There is some dispute over whether species are fixed; e.g., Wilmott (1950) and Hopwood (1950a) disagree on whether this is so.

9. See Hempel 1965b for further discussion and examples from the social sciences.

10. Modern adherents to this position would include those who adhere to the *morphological definition* of species ("a species is a group of individuals or populations with the same or similar morphological characters").

11. That this is so is indicated by the fact that there seem to be few adherents to either position today; however, Mayr (1964) devotes several pages (103ff) to their discussion, which indicates that these positions still had many adherents in the 1930s and 40s.

12. For detailed discussion of the shortcomings of each of these definitions, see Hull 1964, 37–70. In his 1955 article Hull attempts to get around these difficulties with a disjunctive definition.

13. The notion of polytypic definition apparently was first introduced by Beckner 1959, 21 ff.

14. Hull 1964, 115. It should be noted that this is not a cluster concept in the sense of Gasking 1960; see Hull 1964, 83–105, for Hull's discussion of why they are not.

15. Perhaps the best philosophical defense of this analysis of what it is for a taxonomy to be natural is by J. S. Mill (1965, bk. I, ch. vii, and esp., bk. IV, ch. vii.)

16. Sokal and Sneath 1963, ch. 2. A discussion of some of these problems in their arguments can be found in Hull 1955, sec. 5A.

17. The answers to this question are somewhat vague. Answer (a) encompasses the range of answers given by those who give the various answers listed for question (2). Another form of the question is, What definitional form is appropriate for taxonomic categories? In the recent literature, this question has been dealt with only on the lower taxonomic levels—especially the species and variety, or subspecies, levels. Modern taxonomic theory has given relatively scant attention to the higher taxonomic categories.

18. See Suppe 1973. For brevity, the arguments used in developing and supporting this model will not be presented. Indeed, the entire model will not be presented, as a number of its features are not relevant to the issues under consideration. It should be mentioned that this model is heavily indebted to a number of suggestions made by Wilfrid Sellars in a stimulating series of conversations on facts. A very much expanded treatment of the model will be presented in my *Facts, Theories, and Scientific Observation* (in progress).

19. If one is committed to intentional particulars, then this account must be revised (see Suppe 1973, sec. IV). Since biological taxonomy, for the most part, is not concerned with intentional particulars, this complication is ignored here. Some terminology needs to be clarified, though. By the *extension* of a proposition I mean that portion of its meaning or propositional content which can be specified by giving its logical form and specifying the references of its subject and predicate terms; by the *intension* of a proposition I mean its sense (in Frege's sense). A language is *extensional* if the meanings of its propositions consist in their extensions; a language is *intensional* if the intensions of at least some of its propositions are parts of their meanings.

20. Suppe 1973, sec. III. A sortal characteristic is an intrinsic characteristic whose extension is identical with that of some sortal concept or predicate of some language; a sortal concept or predicate, roughly, is one which specifies a *kind* of entity.

21. I am grateful to Professor George Estabrook for pointing this out to me.

22. It is the case, however, that taxonomists who disagree on taxa definitions can agree on what taxon a specimen belongs to; and taxonomists come to be able to recognize that a specimen is of, e.g., species *Rosa multiflora* without checking any list of diagnostic characteristics. These phenomena suggest that *being a T* sometimes is and can be easily and directly recognized by competent taxonomists.

23. See Suppe 1974b, esp. secs. II-A, II-B, and IV-B-2, for a comprehensive discussion of the results leading to this conclusion. See also chs. 2 and 3 above. For a particularly good critique of operationalism with specific reference to biology, see Hull 1968.

24. [This argument presupposes that taxa are classes of particulars and that our taxonomy is standard. We will explore below what happens when these conditions are not met.]

25. To see that it is weaker, suppose, e.g., that one is committed to the Aristotelian definition for taxa. Then x *is a* T if and only if x is $c_1, c_2, \ldots,$ c_n for some intrinsic characteristics; this does not guarantee satisfaction of (A-1) although (A-2) is satisfied. To see this, suppose that the taxonomy is artificial in the sense that (A-1) fails. Then *is a* T is not an intrinsic property. One might object that this is impossible, viz.: if x is a T, then x is $c_1, \ldots,$ c_n, and so x has the intrinsic property *is* c_1 & ... & *is* c_n; so (A-1) is satisfied. But this is not generally true, since there is no guarantee that the conjunction of intrinsic properties is itself an intrinsic property. Whether it is depends on the constitution of the world. See Suppe 1973, sec. I. [If the species as individual approach to taxonomy is taken, then (A-2) will not be satisfied for species-level taxa.]

26. The exact number individuals must (or can) possess depends on the nature of the taxonomic system—whether it is standard, how many levels there are in the hierarchy, whether taxa may be overlapping in a given taxonomic category, etc.

27. Aristotle's own taxonomy was not, however, since his position was that the intrinsic characteristics which were taxa were a combination of other intrinsic characteristics, which were the essential characteristics. Any individual who possessed a taxon intrinsic characteristic thus had the essential characteristics; it also had various other accidental intrinsic characteristics. The metaphysics of this version of essentialism seem unacceptable to taxonomists today, and so this view of essentialism will not be considered further.

28. For a discussion of the notion of causal necessity in the sense it is used here, see Burks 1977, ch. 6. Note that being an essential property is a modal characteristic in a nomic essentialism.

29. Achinstein's work has been anticipated in some respects by Chandler 1966 and works by Dugold Stewart, J. S. Mill, William L. Davidson, and others from the nineteenth century.

30. See Achinstein 1968, ch. 1, for arguments that D_2 cannot be assimilated to polytypic definition (27–28) and to other forms as well (28–31).

31. Whether this is possible is a difficult question, being part and parcel of the problem of specifying truth conditions for vague generalizations. The problem is akin to that of specifying the logic of semi-universal generalizations—i.e., the logic of the quantifier "for most x." It seems clear, however, that assertions involving semi-universal quantifiers are empirically true or false, even though their logic is not understood. [Another plausible approach is to resort to factually true-or-false assertions of statistical correlation or covariance.]

32. Aristotelian definitions can be construed as degenerate polytypic definitions; the discussion thus applies to Aristotelian definitions as well.

33. In fact, a major practical problem facing taxonomists is determining whether an organism is an anomalous specimen of an established taxon or is a new variety, species, or whatever. That this is a practical problem constitutes confirmation of the claims just made. Cuppy (1983) satirically

exploits the difficulty when he writes, "By counting the dorsal scales and the labial, ventral, and subcaudal scutes, studying the stripes and measuring the tails of thousands and thousands of Garter Snakes, they have succeeded in dividing the little fellows into a number of species and subspecies; more, to be candid, than actually exist. For each new species he discovers, the herpetologist receives a bonus. Would that explain it?" (50).

34. However, it should be noted that in those cases where polytypic definitions are required (even with fixed taxa), Achinstein's form of definition cannot replace disjunctive definitions, since his form of definition is incapable of separating the varieties in the required way. (See Achinstein 1968, 27–28, for related discussion.) Where varieties or subspecies occur, disjunctive definitions still are required—but with the disjuncts each being of Achinstein's definitional form.

35. Although it is beyond the scope of this discussion to argue it fully here, I am of the opinion that this last alternative is essentially correct. Indeed, it is a natural corollary to the analysis presented below in secs. V and IX.

36. If, however, the proposal in sec. IX below is accepted, recourse to this quasi-universal form of definition will not be required.

[Embracing the proposal of secs. V and IX together with an eschewal of a quasi-universal form of definitions is a move reminiscent of my rejection in ch. 5 of Scriven's idea that a key feature of scientific laws is their inaccuracy. Indeed, precisely the same kind of reasons invoked there apply *mutatis mutandis* to the proposal of sec. IX below. Thus the considerations of ch. 5 commit me much more strongly to rejecting Achinstein's quasi-universal form of definition than the originally published, somewhat equivocal discussion in this chapter would suggest. However, that commitment will be mitigated to the extent that factually true-or-false assertions of statistical correlation or covariance can capture Achinstein's insights.]

37. Some of the possible cases where (B) does not hold already have been considered.

38. Intentional particulars are particulars which exist in virtue of being thought about, believed, or conceptualized; many philosophers deny the existence of intentional particulars.

39. This is not to say that there are not areas where it might be plausible to adopt such taxonomies; e.g., a case can be made that kinship systems and other social taxonomies are of this sort.

40. Whatever the merits of operationalism are (see ch. 3 for my opinion), it is clear that no operationalist taxonomy is compatible with the claim that taxa should have a philogenetic basis which is reflected in taxa definitions. As such, the philogenetic approach entails a rejection of operationalism and an acceptance of (B-7).

41. See Hull 1964, 22–70, for a detailed consideration of their failures.

42. See Hull 1955, sec. 5-E. Section 5 also contains a discussion of the failures of the various definitions mentioned in sec. I of this chapter.

43. Indeed, some of the arguments in support of numerical taxonomy are exactly of this sort: it is impossible (in practice) to specify phylogenetic taxa,

so a nonphylogenetic taxonomy must be adopted. Cf. Sokal and Sneath 1963, sec. 2.3.

44. This strongly suggests that *every* scientific theory either presupposes or contains (implicitly or explicitly) a taxonomic system as a subtheory.

45. For discussion of auxiliary hypothesis, cf. Putnam 1971, Suppe 1974, 424–33, and ch. 4 above. Boundary conditions are discussed in ch. 6 above.

46. In its present form, evolutionary theory probably cannot actually do this since it is not known, e.g., how to predict the range of possible nonlethal mutations which can occur in a given population. This does not count against the feasibility of the proposal—it only indicates that current evolutionary theory itself may be inadequate to do the job. For related discussion, see ch. 6, sec. III-C.

47. For a discussion of reproduction rates, see Fisher 1958, ch. II.

48. This suggestion may prove inadequate; whether it does is of no concern to the point I want to make here, which is to illustrate how evolutionary theory plausibly can be used to define phylogenetic taxa.

49. These boundary conditions might include, e.g., reproductive barriers at subsequent times.

50. For a discussion of the literature showing why they are not definitions of any sort, see Suppe 1974b; see also Hull 1968. For a discussion of what they are, cf. Suppe 1974b, sec. IV-E, and ch. 2 above, wherein they are what enables one to translate between phenomena and physical systems.

51. This line of objection turns essentially on the fact that the genetic theory of natural selection employs a deterministic law of quasi-succession. See ch. 6, sec. III-C for a related discussion.

52. Such confusion has been characteristic of philosophy of science the first half of this century. Cf. Suppe 1974b (esp. secs. II-A, II-B, IV-B-1, IV-C, IV-E) and the Epilogue below).

53. Recall here from sec. II above that particulars need not be objects.

54. It is important to note that the various versions of (B) do *not* require that the taxa definitions be factually true, but rather only that they be capable of being factually true and are advanced as being putatively true. Thus the falsity of a taxa definition does not render it unnatural.

55. See sec. IX, where the analysis given there reinforces this judgment.

56. Gilmour 1940, 466–67. It is fashionable among numerical taxonomists to attribute their account of natural taxonomy to Gilmour (see, e.g., Sokal and Sneath 1963).

57. For example, Gilmour (1940) is often cited approvingly as the source of this doctrine, and he makes it quite explicit that classes are conventional.

58. For a sampling of the problems, see Kemeny and Oppenheim 1955.

59. This is not to say that there will not be any scientifically reputable applications where a special-purpose taxonomy working in terms of greatest affinity would not be useful.

60. More specifically, to determine the genotypic makeup, a random sample of organisms of different morphological types might be examined as to genetic

makeup; the distribution of genotypes in the sample then is projected onto the population as a whole to determine its genotypic distribution.

61. This is underscored by the relatively low repute taxonomy often is held in by biologists working in other areas of biology.

62. Indeed, there is ample evidence that they are concerned with its relevance. Certainly the whole program of the New Systematics and phylogenetic taxonomy is aimed at making taxonomy useful to theoretical biology. And it is very clear in the writings of the numerical taxonomists that they take its presumed usefulness to biologists working in other areas to be one of its chief merits.

63. Witness all the concern among taxonomists that taxonomy must be operational. No scientific theories of any substance exist (or ever did) which meet the requirements of operationalism. The adherence to operationalism is symptomatic of the gross misunderstanding of science and scientific knowledge which impeded progress in psychology for several decades earlier this century. Cf. Suppe 1984, 1984a, and Hull 1968.

—— 8 ——
Interlevel Theories and the
Semantic Conception

Kenneth Schaffner (1980) has noted that philosophical discussions about the nature of biological theory structure have taken place in isolation from major recent changes in the philosophy of science — especially ones concerning the structure of scientific theories — and that "a focus on evolutionary theory as the main paradigm in biology has led to an overly parochial notion of theory structure in the biomedical sciences" (58, 63–64). In support of the latter charge he has identified what he calls "Interlevel Theories of the Middle Range," which he argues are more typical of theories in the biomedical sciences than evolutionary theory (ibid.). Prompted by correspondence with me, Schaffner subsequently has attempted to explore the extent to which the Semantic Conception of Theories can provide a suitable analysis of these interlevel middle-range theories. His tentative answer has been that the Semantic Conception can accommodate many characteristic features of these theories but requires modifications to accommodate others. His attempts at modification initially involved use of "fuzzy sets"[1] and more recently, the use of cluster analysis techniques from numerical taxonomy.[2]

Schaffner's identification of interlevel middle-range theories is a valuable contribution to the philosophy of biology. While I am sympathetic to his use of the Semantic Conception to analyze them, it is my contention that his recourse to fuzzy sets or cluster analysis is wrongheaded and unnecessary. For, as I shall argue, the Semantic Conception needs no alteration to accommodate interlevel middle-range theories.

I. INTERLEVEL BIOMEDICAL THEORIES OF
THE MIDDLE RANGE

According to Schaffner (1980), "The bulk of biomedical theories can be . . . best characterized as a series of overlapping interlevel temporal models . . . [which] fall into what I term the 'middle range' " (83). Such theories are nonuniversal in the sense that while they do not hold unexceptionally over the universe or even over all organisms in the world, they support counterfactuals, organize their subject matter, are testable, and are technologically significant (1980, 83, 89–90). I will discuss some of these features of interlevel middle-range theories in turn, focusing on how they relate to the Semantic Conception of Theories.[3]

A. Nonuniversality

Philosophers of science have debated whether biological laws are "universal," focusing on whether they hold over all the universe or for all species in the world. One of Schaffner's main theses is that biological laws need not be universal in either of these senses (1980, 89–90). The Semantic Conception of Theories has a lot to say on this issue. Under the Semantic Conception, the subject matter of a theory—its *scope of intended application*—is a natural kind class of causally possible phenomenal systems. For example, classical particle mechanics has as its scope the class of systems of massive objects possessing position and momentum attributes. The theory characterizes how the states of such systems change over time when such systems are isolated from outside influences. If classical particle mechanics were empirically true, it would characterize the behavior of *any* such isolated systems *anywhere* in the universe. Thus it would meet the strong universality condition that J. J. C. Smart (1963, 52ff) has insisted on. One reason it would is because position and momentum are spatio-temporal characteristics, and so the class of causally possible physical systems includes all massive body systems in space-time. But this is just a peculiar characteristic of this class of systems. For if true, classical particle mechanics also would be universal in a *more fundamental sense*—it would correctly describe the state transition behavior of *all* causally possible systems within its scope. And this latter condition is the only condition of universality the Semantic Conception imposes on theories.

This fundamental point deserves elaboration. Classes of causally possible systems constituting the scope of an empirically true theory must be natural kinds on the Semantic Conception. This means they can be specified in terms of attributes possessed, without recourse to proper names. Some natural kinds are distributed over the universe, others over the whole of the earth, and still others enjoy very local distribution. Regardless of the distribution of such systems, an empirically true theory about them is universal in the very strong sense that it covers all such systems. (In a sense, this makes them universal in Smart's strong sense—that it will be true of any such system found in the universe, even if most of the universe does not and never will contain such systems.)

It might be argued that all this is irrelevant to the biomedical case at hand, since on Schaffner's view the models comprising theories often characterize systems of a particular species; and since species names are presumed to be proper names, we do not have natural kinds of systems here. In chapter 7 I argued that an organism's species is a natural attribute of the organism, and thus species "names" are not really names but denote attributes of the sort which can form natural kinds.[4] Accordingly, classes of systems comprising all (causally) possible organisms (or all causally possible organisms possessing certain other attributes) of a species constitute natural kinds of the sort the Semantic Conception requires; thus theories about such systems can be universal.

The Semantic Conception of Theories, therefore, can accommodate Schaffner's middle-range theories even though they lack the kinds of universality Smart and others have insisted on. For the philosophically significant sense in which empirically true theories *must* be universal is quite a different condition—universality over natural kind classes of causally possible phenomenal systems. The Semantic Conception not only identifies what that universality is, but it provides a deeper explanation for, and defense of, Schaffner's contention that his middle-range theories are not deficient in the respect that it lacks Smart's strong universality.

B. The "Interlevel" Condition

Fleshing out his characterization of interlevel middle-range theories, Schaffner (1980) writes, "The term 'interlevel'. . . is being used to refer to entities grouped within a theory (or model) which are at different levels of aggregation" (84). Roughly speaking, they stand in a part-whole relation involving additional organizing relations. Schaffner (n.d.) has argued that the Semantic Conception can accommodate this interlevel feature: "In connection with the Semantic Conception of Theories . . . I do not see any difficulties with extending it to encompass interlevel theories. All that is required is that the appropriate interlevel parameters be utilized in defining the state space." This certainly is most of what is required; in addition, the state transition laws of the theory will need to embody or reflect the aggregative organizing relations (roughly, as internalized boundary conditions).

However, I do quibble with the suggestion that doing so is an *extension* of the Semantic Conception. From the very beginning, in my development of the Semantic Conception I have examined and discussed interlevel theories. Examples include the laws of chemical composition, which involve atoms and molecules (and thus are interlevel). I have discussed how the Semantic Conception accommodates the multiple-allele version of the genetic theory of natural selection, which—by virtue of involving alleles, linked genes, gene pools, various crossover and inversion mechanisms, epistatic effects, and so on—is interlevel.[5] The sorts of compositional theories Dudley Shapere has investigated provide further examples (1974b, 534–42; 1974a), as do various psychosocial theories in nursing (Suppe and Jacox 1985).

C. Theories as Series of Overlapping Models

On Schaffner's (1980) account of interlevel theories, 'model' refers to "rather specific systems found in particular strains of organisms. Thus the *lac* operon in inducible (z^+) K12 *E. coli* with 'wild type' β-galactosidase (z^+) and galactoside permease (y^+) is a model . . ." (83). According to Schaffner, these models vary by mutation in closely related strains, and overlapping collections of them constitute a *theory.* He then explains what he means by 'a series of overlapping models': "I intend that the subtle variation encountered in organisms in a specific strain is presented as part of the theory, or at least part of the textual elaboration of the theory. . . . It is this variation which 'smears out' the models and makes them more a family of overlapping models . . . which as a collective theory is related by similarity" (84–85).

Why does Schaffner think theories are overlapping collections of models? One source for this view is R. Levins' views on the nature of evolutionary population biology theory—a theory which Schaffner denies is middle-range, although he admits that "some of the significant features of middle-range theories such as polytypy and interlevel elaboration can be found" in it.[6] Levins' view of evolutionary population biology theory includes natural selection theory, classical population genetics, developmental biology, ecological components, and the like—it is a very broad theory, indeed. However, unlike a number of these constituent types of theory, it is not the sort of theory that either the Semantic Conception or Schaffner is concerned with analyzing.

Bromberger (1963) sketches two main uses of 'theory' in science. First, he notes, theories such as the kinetic theory of heat or the electromagnetic theory of light "can be accepted, rejected, believed, remembered, stated, granted, confirmed, refuted, have authors." By contrast, theories such as the theory of heat or the theory of systems in stable equilibrium do not possess these characteristics, though they may encompass many things which do possess these attributes. Rather, "they can include contributions from many sources; they have founders and perhaps foundations; they are academic subjects; they can be and they have subdivisions [which are theories of the first sort]" (83). The Semantic Conception is an analysis of—and Schaffner's middle-range theories are examples of—Bromberger's first sort of theory, whereas Levins' conception of evolutionary population biology theory more closely resembles the latter sort.

Levins' sort of theory is one of those supratheoretical entities (theoretical in the first sense) that philosophers of science increasingly have been concerned with, but it is not the sort of "theory" the Semantic Conception is concerned with. Moreover, recent suggestions regarding the nature of such supratheoretical entities (e.g., Shapere's domains, Toulmin's disciplines, Darden and Maull's fields, Lakatos' research programmes, Kuhn's disciplinary matrixes, and Laudan's research traditions)[7] do nothing to suggest that modifying the Semantic Conception via recourse to fuzzy set or cluster analysis notions is particularly promising. In short, Levins' views on evolutionary population theory do not provide compelling reasons for construing middle-range theories as overlapping collections of models, since that construal seems to be based on an analogy to quite different and dissimilar notions of (supra) theory.

Another of Schaffner's reasons for construing middle-range theories as overlapping collections of models is "that biological theories are usually given in the form of a series of temporal models" (1980, 71) rather than axiomatizations. Also, such models not only describe basic or "pure type" models, but also variations and patterns of deviation due to mutations and other factors (n.d.; 1980, 85–90). Several points need to be sorted out here. First, when theories are concerned with highly complex systems, Suppes (1967, 58) has noted, it is not unusual to forego axiomatization and instead introduce theories via descriptions of their models. This is commonly done in diverse areas of science including quantum mechanics, classical thermodynamics, and modern quantitative versions of learning theory. Thus recourse to models in order to present theories is not a peculiar distinguishing feature of middle-range interlevel theories in the biomedical sciences. Moreover, since the Semantic Conception sharply distinguishes theories from their linguistic formulations, diagrammatic specifications, and so on (see ch. 3), the mode of presentation used to describe the theory is not terribly significant, for a central theme of the Semantic Conception is that scientific theories are extralinguistic entities which admit of alternative and even nonequivalent (linguistic and other) formulations.

The foregoing comments may not get at what Schaffner (1980) has in mind when he talks of middle-range theories being given as a series of models. Recall his statement that "the subtle variation encountered in a specific strain is presented as part of the theory, or at least part of the textual elaboration of the theory" (84). Specifically, he notes that in research articles and advanced textbooks, theories such as the operon theory are introduced not only with a description of a basic (or pure type) process, but also with a characterization of the variations in it when various mutations are involved (n.d., ms. pp. 13–14). A crucial question is at issue here: whether such variations are integral components of the theory or whether they are just "part of the textual elaboration of the theory," and if the latter is the case, what this means.

In an initial attempt to answer this question, it will be useful to look at the theory of classical particle mechanics. Recall that this theory provides equations of motion (state transitions) for isolated systems of n-bodies characterized by position and momentum coordinates. But no such isolated n-body systems actually exist, although with suitable experimental controls, real instances of such systems can be approximated to within experimental error. (That is, in the laboratory we can set up controls so that influences from bodies "outside" the systems are held negligible.) The theory thus provides a description of how such n-body systems *would* behave *were* they isolated from outside influences.

In abstract theoretical formulations of classical particle mechanics (e.g., as a preliminary foil for introducing quantum mechanics), this is the extent to which classical particle mechanics would be presented.[8] However, in textbook discussions, and even in advanced treatises concerned with the application of classical particle mechanics to real (phenomenal) systems, one would find not only the basic theory (often in abbreviated form), but also a whole host of variant solutions for standard circumstances where the isolation condition is breached or compromised. For example, in inclined plane problems, the significant friction of the plane (and also the existence of the plane) violates the isolation condition. And for a number of standard conditions where uniform friction coefficients can be calculated, textbooks typically present "special case solutions" based on delineable influences which, while violating isolation assumptions, do so in ways that enable *local laws* about such violations to be exploited in conjunction with the basic theory to provide "special case solutions" for specific kinds of nonisolation; that is, they provide accounts of specific patterns of deviation from the basic "pure case" account provided by the theory. And in textbook treatments of classical particle mechanics such textual elaborations of the basic theory constitute the bulk of the text.

I suggest that presentation of, for example, the operon theory via introduction of the "pure types" plus discussion of variations[9] is nothing other than a repetition of the "special case" pattern encountered in physics and evolutionary theory (especially population genetics, including the genetic theory of natural selection)—a pattern which lies at the heart of the physical interpretation of my version of the Semantic Conception of Theories, as has been stressed repeatedly in earlier chapters. Specifically, the operon theory describes what will happen in *lac* systems when they are isolated from any gene mutations and other modifying influences. The special case "textual elaborations," then, are derivative descriptions of what happens in standard circumstances when the "isolation" condition is violated.

If one recalls from our prior discussion (sec. I-A) that theories about particular species (or subgroups of species sharing other attributes) enjoy the universality necessary to qualify as theories, then it appears that the standard textual presentations of middle-range biological theories are not significantly different from physics theories—at least as construed by the Semantic Conception. The mutation effects modify "pure cases" analogously to the way friction, the atmosphere, other bodies, and so on modify "pure cases" of classical particle mechanics. It also follows that such special case theories inherit the same isolation caveats (ceteris paribus conditions) as the more general theories do; a theory of a specific pattern of nonisolation due to, for example, a type of gene mutation in the operon context still is a "universal" theory about operon processes when isolated from any *other* sorts of influence. Thus this much more "local" theory still provides the basic account of how a system *would* behave *were* it isolated, which lies at the heart of my version of the Semantic Conception.

The foregoing construal of Schaffner's middle-range theories apparently is able to accommodate such theories with no extension or revision of my version of the Semantic Conception—hence it is an account that renders recourse to fuzzy sets or cluster analysis unnecessary. The fact that my quasi-realistic version of the Semantic Conception accommodates interlevel theories of the middle range, such as the operon theory, in exactly the same way that it accommodates natural selection theory in evolutionary theory strongly suggests that Schaffner is mistaken in supposing that interlevel theories are more typical of theories in the biomedical sciences than is evolutionary theory. This conclusion is reinforced by the fact that operons are bacterial examples of supergenes (Ayala 1982, 140). Since the theory of supergenes is a part of population genetics (a paradigm case for the Semantic Conception), one would expect that the operon theory should have the same general structure.

My responses here to Schaffner have been based on the textually supported assumption that a series of overlapping models consists of a basic (or pure-type) model and models representing various variations on that basic model. Schaffner's approach would seem more plausible if one were to deny that the series contains a basic or pure-type model. For then it would seem that the series is constituted by some family resemblance notion, and cluster analysis and fuzzy sets are promising vehicles for analyzing family resemblances. Moreover, in such cases my treatment does not avail.

Such an eventuality does not seem to me to require significant alteration of the Semantic Conception, however. For it seems to me the situation is one in which we have a family of individual theories (models), each of which will involve the above pattern of textual elaboration in application to nonisolated cases. Such, for example, was the case in the early stages of electricity and magnetism theory prior to Maxwell's (1891) unified treatment. To the extent such "overlapping" models are considered established by a science, they tend to comprise what Shapere (1974b) calls a scientific domain—items of information so related as to suggest there is a deeper underlying unity, where an account of that underlying unity would be a theory (525–28). Key to such a theory on the Semantic Conception would be the basic, or pure, case model, of which the extant models (or a portion thereof) would be the "textual elaboration." Thus reference to the now-overlapping series of models, minus the basic or pure case, signals the expectation that a unifying basic or pure case will be found so as to produce a full-fledged theory satisfying the account given above in rejoinder to Schaffner. Should subsequent events in the particular science involved prove this rational expectation of underlying unity wrong, the science would cease referring to the series of overlapping models as a theory. Thus even when the basic or pure-case model is missing from the series of overlapping models, modification of the Semantic Conception by recourse to cluster analysis, fuzzy sets, or the like is unnecessary.

Schaffner's attempts to use such "smearing" techniques as fuzzy sets or cluster analysis is reminiscent of Michael Scriven's (1961) earlier claim that the key property of physical laws is their inaccuracy and also of the oft-inferred conclusion thereupon that laws must be approached via some notion of approximate truth or verisimilitude. In chapter 5 I argued that the Semantic Conception's treatment of variations from isolated systems along the lines just sketched precludes the necessity of recourse to such approximate truth notions. A similar position was suggested with respect to Achinstein's quasi-universal "cluster" definitions in the context of biological taxonomy in chapter 7, section IV.[10] My present discussion has been another argument to the same general effect—that Schaffner's recent attempts are equally unnecessary.

Actually, my response to Scriven raises the prospect of an even more powerful and instructive response to Schaffner, although I do not know if it will survive sustained scientific and philosophical scrutiny. In chapter 5 I introduced a class of theoretical laws known as *laws of quasi-succession*. (The canonical example is the genetic theory of natural selection where environmental, gene pool, and recombinatory operations in a biological population only determine the subsequent genotype proportions but do not determine environmental features including birth/death ratios [see ch. 6, sec. III-C, and ch. 7, secs. V and IX].) The variation, for example, in the operon theory, which Schaffner imposes such a burden on, may be such that with proper state specification, the mutant influences resulting in variation on the "pure case" (e.g., *lac* transfer) state transitions may prove to be parameters characteristic of a theory with a law of quasi-succession, where such characteristics are *not predictable* by the theory alone but nevertheless play a crucial determining role—one that is analogous to the role that reproduction rates and birth/death rates play in the genetic theory of natural selection. If so, the Semantic Conception *without alteration* provides an even more powerful accommodation of Schaffner's interlevel middle-range theories than what he has argued for.

II. CONCLUDING COMMENTS

Schaffner has delineated a class of interlevel middle-range theories in the biomedical sciences. Acknowledging the potential of the Semantic Conception of Theories to account for them, but misperceiving the extent of that potential, he has made several attempts to extend or modify the Semantic Conception to accommodate them. I have mounted arguments to the effect that *without modification* the Semantic Conception readily *does* accommodate and provide significant philosophical understanding of such theories.[11]

To amplify these claims, one other consideration needs to be addressed. A clearly underlying motivation for Schaffner's "overlapping collection of models" view is the extent to which he sees theories as *reticulate* (Schaffner 1980, 89–91). This is to say that the articulation (i.e., the specification of variant forms of the "pure case") of middle-range theories depends heavily on a broad spectrum of biological theory, and that various such middle-range theories (as well as global evolutionary theory) draw heavily from each other in producing their special case "solutions" for particular nonisolated types of systems. Schaffner apparently sees such reticulateness as a distinguishing feature of the biomedical sciences. The implied suggestion that physics lacks this reticulateness seems to me unwarranted. In chapter 4, section IV, we discussed Hooker's (1975) treatment of the reticulate combination of elements in physical theory required to obtain a theory of the operation of a cloud chamber for detecting charged subatomic particles. In the face of such experimental design and other examples, the biological sciences appear to be no more reticulate than the physical sciences.

In the fundamental sense of universality defended in section I-A, middle-level biomedical theories are just as significantly universal as classical physical theories. The only plausible source of difference between theories in the physical and biological sciences is that, possibly, the most significant natural kinds of classes of systems crying for study and investigation within biology are radically more complex than those on which physics and chemistry have concentrated their attention — hence biology may require radically different sorts of theories than those encountered in physics and chemistry. But nothing Schaffner has adduced gives great weight to such a suggestion; if such a suggestion is vindicated, it will reflect more the inherent complexity of biological systems as opposed to physical ones (and possibly an attendant deviation from physical science techniques necessary to render theories of such systems manageable and theorizable) than it will any fundamental difference in the kind of phenomena within systems or admissible theoretical approaches to them. Complexity introduces its own problems, but it does not radically alter the philosphical dimensions of scientific theorizing.[12] Indeed, the Semantic Conception of Theories indicates that "middle-range interlevel" biomedical theories are quite typical of theories in the natural sciences, suitably understood and philosophically analyzed, and thus that special pleading for their scientific legitimacy is quite unnecessary.

NOTES

1. Schaffner (n.d., ch. 3) and also in a talk at the University of Maryland, November 5, 1979.

2. Schaffner, in a talk for the Conference on Methods in Philosophy and

the Sciences at the New School for Social Research, New York, May 1980. The present chapter originally was written as a commentary on that talk.

3. The middle-range feature will not be dwelt on. Schaffner obtained the terminology from the sociologist Robert Merton (1949). Merton defines middle-range theories as ones from which directly testable consequences can be deduced. His account amounts to the requirement that middle-range theories contain correspondence rules, as required by the Received View. It is unclear whether his middle-range/grand theory distinction satisfactorily can be divorced from the now widely rejected Received View. Despite his official characterization of middle-range theories in terms of testable consequences, Merton sometimes writes as if the primary difference between middle-range and grand theories were their intended scopes, with the former having a somewhat limited scope (as, e.g., role theory does). Schaffner appears to be using 'middle range' in this latter sense, rather than following Merton's official positivistic definition.

4. This assumes that species are classes, not individuals. If species are individuals, the same conclusions will be forthcoming, provided that the species' corresponding constituent class is a natural kind class (see ch. 7, sec. III for details). If it is not a natural kind class, there can be no empirically true theories about the species. My hunch is that this is an unlikely outcome.

5. See Suppe 1967 and ch. 6, sec. III-C, and ch. 7, secs. V and IX, above for the latter. Specifically, I have used the version of this theory developed by Fisher (1958) and generalized by Moran (1962), which includes much of Kimura's sophisticated development of the theory. Other interlevel examples are considered in Suppe 1967.

6. See Schaffner 1980, 89, also 84–86. For Levins' views, see his 1966 article and 1968 book.

7. Shapere 1974b; Toulmin 1972; Darden and Maull 1977; Lakatos 1970; Kuhn 1962 and 1974; and Laudan 1977.

8. Cf., e.g., Pauling and Wilson 1935 or Mackey 1963.

9. See Schaffner 1980, 84, and Schaffner's discussion of Strindberger's admirable presentation of the operon theory (n.d.).

10. At the same time, in Suppe 1977a, 706–16, and in ch. 11 and the Epilogue below, I have noted that although the construal of theories as putatively true under the interpretation previously given sometimes occurs, nonmoribund scientific theories typically are put forward as "conceptual devices" purporting claimed relations to actual causally possible phenomenal systems weaker than those I have been discussing thus far in this chapter. A defensible integration of Schaffner's work on analyzing interlevel middle-range theories with more general issues of discovery and the development of biomedical science eventually will have to take this fact into account.

11. However, as this chapter evidences, the need to further develop the implications of, and articulate the details of, application of the Semantic Conception to newly identified kinds of theory is important and sometimes illuminating.

12. Complications of issues of scientific theorizing due to complexity have

not been adequately explored by philosophers. Less than successful feints have been made in the symposium on "Complex Fuzzy Systems" (with H. A. Simon, R. J. Nelson, and P. Suppes) in Suppe and Asquith 1977 (507–47), and in my own work (1985, 1985a).

—9—

Theoretical Perspectives on Closure

This chapter is concerned with scientific disputes which cease to be purely scientific matters rationally resolved by ordinary scientific means, and become public controversies as well. These controversies often take on ethical, political, or social dimensions that alter not only the nature of such disputes, but also the ways in which they are brought to closure. Examples include the nuclear power controversy, the laetrile controversy, and the decision by the American Psychiatric Association to remove homosexuality per se from its catalogue of mental disorders.[1] Of particular concern are the genesis and dynamics of such controversies; for it appears that only through understanding these will we be able to understand why and how attempts to bring such controversies to effective closure succeed or fail.

Simplistic explanations of such controversies are easy to come by: "They are the result of irrational behavior by scientists who have let emotional involvement destroy their scientific detachment and objectivity," or "They are the result of nonscientific outsiders violating the sanctity of science, attempting to manipulate the outcome of a scientific dispute to serve personal or vested interests," and so on. While such explanations often are advanced by opponents as charges against each other in such controversies (sometimes with some plausibility), they do little to further our understanding of these controversies, let alone provide any insight as to how to bring such disputes to more effective closure. That will require more searching, penetrating examinations of the genesis and dynamics of such disputes, involving such questions as: Is it really the case that when such scientific disputes become embroiled in public controversy, it always is a mark of being "unscientific"—a confusion of empirical scientific issues with moral and social ones? If so, are there characteristics of theoretical or applied science which invite such confusion? Or might it be the case that there are characteristics of theoretical or applied science which legitimately invite, or even require, the inclusion of extrascientific ethical or social policy considerations in the resolution of at least some scientific disputes?

It is the purpose of this chapter to contribute to the search for answers to such questions. My aim is to explore the implications of the Semantic Conception for problems of closure in scientific controversies. My discussion will exploit the counterfactual mappings that constitute the physical interpretation of theories developed previously:

(*) The sequences of states (behaviors) determined by the theory indicate what the behaviors of the possible (phenomenal) systems within the theory's scope *would be were it the case* that only the defining parameters of the theory exerted a nonneglible influence on those behaviors.

Recall that a theory is empirically true just in case this counterfactual mapping holds. For purposes of understanding closure, this yields a very important finding: Empirically true theories provide highly idealized pictures of the world in ways that themselves do not translate straightforwardly into accurate characterizations of how real-world phenomenal systems actually behave. Nevertheless, when the theory is augmented by suitable auxiliary hypotheses that specify effects of outside influences on the defining parameters of the theory, it may be possible to make accurate predictions of, and describe, the actual behavior of a system. However, typically we have such auxiliary hypotheses only for a few straightforward simple cases: For most cases of nonisolation we lack the requisite auxiliary hypotheses needed to enable precise theoretical predictions and descriptions of the actual behavior of phenomenal systems.

The mapping relation (*) is the strongest we can establish. Often theories do not purport to be empirically true (hence do not assert mapping relation [*]), but instead are introduced as conceptual devices; or one may have a theory in a particular stage of development such that one does not know what its status is—whether it is empirically true or whether it is some conceptual device standing in a different mapping relationship (see ch. 11). In short, it is important to note that theories admit of a variety of uses, and depending on the use, a theory may be advanced as standing in any one of a variety of mapping relations to physically possible phenomenal systems—of which (*) is the strongest that generally can be satisfied. Failure to discern whether a theory is advanced as empirically true or as some other conceptual device—what sort of mapping is being asserted between theory structure and phenomenal systems—can be a great source of confusion and lead to unproductive arguments at cross-purposes in debates over the adequacy of a theory.

I. COUNTERFACTUAL CONFUSIONS

The mapping relations employed in asserting theories are *counterfactual.* Thus theories do not purport to describe how phenomenal systems *actually* behave, but rather how they *ought* to behave under certain conditions, which typically do not obtain. Moral and social policy pronouncements also are concerned with how the world *ought* to be. Once it is realized that both theoretical science and moral and social deliberations are concerned with *how the world ought to be* and that both are making counterfactual assertions about the world, the propensity for scientific and moral/social debates to intertwine becomes more understandable.

Nevertheless, the counterfactual 'ought' of mapping relation (*) for putatively true theories and the 'ought' of moral and social policy pronouncements are different, and these differences need to be sorted out.[2] Recent philosophical work on counterfactuals will help. Counterfactual conditionals typically are analyzed via modal logic and possible-worlds semantics. For example, scientific laws, as well as mapping relation (*), are interpreted as containing a *causal necessity* operator—as asserting that it is causally necessary that certain patterns of regularity hold. This in turn is interpreted either as asserting that the pattern of regularity holds for all causally or physically possible worlds, or else for all such worlds that are suitably similar to the actual world. In this chapter, I will assume the latter approach.[3] That is, the laws of nature determine which logically possible worlds are physically possible and also, which of these most closely resemble (are similar to) the actual world; and a counterfactual assertion will be true of the actual world if it is true of suitably similar physically possible other worlds (Lewis 1973, ch. 1, esp. 9). Thus the *ought* of physical laws and mapping relation (*) fundamentally is rooted in the laws of nature, which determine physical possibility and the attendant similarity of other physically possible worlds to the actual world. The ought of moral and social pronouncements have a different basis. While *deontic* (e.g., moral or social) 'ought' implies 'can' (hence what morally or socially ought to be done must be physically possible), the laws of nature do not determine truth conditions for such deontic ought assertions.

Deontic ought statements, like mapping relation (*), implicitly involve the modality of necessity—but it is moral (or social justice) necessity.

Possible-worlds semantics can be used to analyze that necessity and deontic counterfactuals. The procedure is essentially the same as sketched above, except that we replace the similarity of worlds with a ranking of the comparative goodness of possible worlds, or else a ranking based on a preference ordering of *values* that are realized at worlds. Roughly speaking, a deontic counterfactual is true of this world if it is true of the best worlds which resemble the actual world in relevant respects (ibid., ch 5, sec. 1).

The basic difference, then, between the 'ought' of mapping relation (*) and the deontic 'ought' of moral or social pronouncements is that laws of nature determine which alternative possible worlds have a bearing on the truth of both, whereas only in the case of the deontic 'ought' does the relative goodness, or value, of the alternative worlds have a bearing on truth. This displays how easy it is for moral or evaluative considerations to intrude into scientific debates. And at first blush, it would seem to follow that in debates about the truth of a theory, such intrusions are illegitimate.

Such a conclusion seems to me justified when the issue is ascertaining the empirical truth of a theory—ascertaining whether mapping relation (*) holds[4]—and so such evaluative considerations have no legitimate place in determining whether a theory is empirically true. However, it can have a legitimate place in deciding whether to do the experimentation necessary to ascertain the empirical truth of a theory or to develop such a true theory, for such experimentation can have the effect of modifying the actual world. The actual world is not fixed in its specific characteristics; and changes in the actual world, while constrained by physical possibility and the laws of nature, are not the purely passive effect of such laws.[5] We *do* routinely influence and alter what is characteristic of the actual world—in introducing experimental controls in the laboratory, in making engineering and technological developments, and at social and other levels. And the result of such manipulation may convert our world to one which is better or worse than it was. When scientific experimentation necessary to investigate the truth of a theory requires techniques that will affect the goodness of our world, it is a legitimate question whether the scientific investigation deontically ought to be undertaken in ways that involve no confusion of the 'ought' of scientific assertions and deontic 'ought'.

But assessing the deontic ought in such cases is far from straightforward. For the debate involves claims about what the altered world will be like if the experimentation is done and whether such a world deontically ought to be created. What the world will be like as a result of the experimentation fundamentally is a factual issue, but it is one that our present scientific knowledge and body of established theory typically are incapable of mediating.

Recall that empirically true theories provide highly idealized accounts of the behavior of isolated systems, and only in a few cases do we have the auxiliary hypotheses necessary to make accurate predictions of precisely what will happen in nonisolated systems. The more avant-garde, the more pioneering the research, the less that established results of science enable us to predict precisely what the effects of experimental manipulation will be. Thus in evaluating what the risks are of pursuing a piece of experimental research, we have to rely on informed conjectures rather than accurate prediction. And in such risk assessment circumstances, there is plenty of room for disagreement on whether a piece of research deontically ought to be undertaken.

When some feel that the risks of the research necessary to develop and test pure scientific theories are high in that they might result in a world which is less good, the situation becomes ripe for the scientific issue to become intertwined with larger public policy disputes. Joining such disputes need not be unscientific or antiscientific, but there clearly is potential for the public debate to be far less rational than our present state of scientific knowledge affords. A paradigmatic example of a recent scientific controversy exemplifying the general pattern indicated here is the recombinant DNA controversy (see Jackson and Stich 1979).

If one turns to applied science and science-based engineering efforts, the problems are exacerbated. Whereas in pure science, modifying the world is not the point of the enterprise but is instead an incidental by-product of basic research, in engineering, modifying the world *is* the point of the enterprise. To the extent possible, engineering draws upon the results of pure science to design its products; but scientific theories concern how things will behave in nice isolated circumstances, whereas the engineer's job is to build systems that reliably function in routine nonisolated circumstances. The variability and complexity of possible circumstances of nonisolation in which the systems may actually have to operate are such that engineering almost never possesses well-established auxiliary hypotheses which can be used in conjunction with the more basic scientific theories to predict accurately how an engineering device as designed will behave in the range of possible real-world circumstances it will encounter.

What engineering tries to do, then, is first determine a worst-case (nonisolated) circumstance the device might have to operate in, where this worst case is sufficiently simple that auxiliary hypotheses can be developed which will predict how a particular design will fare in it.

One then theoretically overdesigns one's prototype to work reliably in this worst-case circumstance and tests the prototype with relatively low risk of failure. But such overdesigns are expensive and inefficient, so one then experimentally tries a cumulative series of design modifications that gradually eliminates the "overdesign," subjecting the modifications to testing in a variety of normal-use situations, until one comes up with a sufficiently modified design that is both reliable and economical. Such "trial and error" design improvement is at the heart of engineering research and development, and it is guided more by the intuitions and experience of designers than by accurate predictions rooted in established scientific theory.[6]

The success of such an approach depends centrally on accurately anticipating the range of nonisolated conditions the design will have to operate in (a factual issue), as well as assessments as to the likelihood of being in extreme conditions, the likelihood of failure in ordinary and extraordinary circumstances (factual issues), and what failure likelihoods are acceptable in ordinary and extraordinary circumstances (an evaluative issue). Sometimes this last issue is primarily an economic or business decision—as in deciding what is sufficient reliability for a refrigerator design. But in other cases, failure may substantially alter the world, in which case what counts as an acceptable risk of failure will involve considerations of what the consequences of failure for the future of the world might be, what the benefits of implementing the design would be if failure does not occur, and how to balance the effects of possible failure and success. And the severe limits of idealized scientific theories in predicting real-world performance, which underlie the design process mentioned above, make it virtually impossible to come up with precise estimates of the likelihood of failure, hence precise estimates of risk—even if there are shared agreements on how to measure risks and what are acceptable risks. When there is the possibility that failure of an engineering design would negatively affect how good the world is, the intrusion of moral, social, and other evaluative considerations and the involvement of informed persons outside the scientific and engineering communities into the debate does seem legitimate; for in such cases the issue is not a purely scientific or technological one. The nuclear power controversy appears to be a paradigmatic example of this sort of controversy.

The foregoing discussion displays two things: (1) The ways in which questions of what deontically ought to be the case legitimately can enter into scientific and technological debates; but (2) the close similarities between the 'ought' of scientific theories and deontic 'ought' also indicate there is great potential for the confusion of what is being disputed—whether the issue is what scientifically is correct or whether the issue is what deontically ought to be the case. To the extent such confusions occur, the issues become clouded, arguments will be at cross-purposes, and closure will be more difficult to obtain.

II. GOAL-DIRECTED THEORIES

In the biological and behavioral sciences one frequently encounters teleological or functional laws and theories. Debates over such theories are particularly susceptible to becoming embroiled in normative controversies. To see why, we draw on our account of them given in chapter 5, section IV. The crucial features of that analysis are that a teleological system typically is a system whose behavior is in part a function of its interaction with an environment outside its control, and the tendency toward a goal state is an essential characteristic of its behavior only when interacting with a stable environment. If the environment is unstable, the goal state may never be reached or even closely approached.

A teleological theory involves a law of quasi-succession such that systems governed by it tend toward some specified set of goal states. For any given set G of goal states, it is a factual matter whether such systems *do* tend toward goal states G—whether all such systems interacting with stable environments in the limit end up in G. Since systems of genuine scientific interest rarely enjoy such stable environments it is extremely difficult to determine observationally or experimentally whether the systems tend toward any particular G. However, to the extent that the theory is precisely articulate and well established as empirically true, we may be able to deduce, as a consequence of the theory itself, what set G of states systems do tend toward. For example, this has been done for the genetic theory of natural selection using plausible fitness measures. Things are much more difficult when the theory is not established as true—in that case one must hypothesize what the goal states are (based on background knowledge, beliefs, and informed expectations), and in such a case there is a danger that normative considerations may bias the assessment.

Although the term 'goal' ordinarily has a normative connotation, we have been using the term 'goal state' in a nonnormative sense. But sometimes normative goal states[7] are imposed on theories with laws of quasi-succession. For example, we may know that the goal states are not likely to be attainable, because a stable environment is impossible; but we would like to approximate them to a reasonable degree by partially controlling (exerting a stabilizing influence on) the environment. Such a decision typically involves playing off a consideration of the feasibility of manipulating the environment against an assessment of what constitutes a desirable approximation of the goal states. These normative considerations result in the specification of a broader class of normative goal states.

In other cases, we wish to prevent certain goal states from being achieved when there is a fairly stable environment. For example, in the genetic theory of natural selection a stable environment consists in fixed reproduction rates (a function of birth/death ratios), and an endangered species may have a fixed reproduction rate that tends to move toward an extinction goal state (see ch. 6, sec. III-C). If we value the preservation of all species, we may decide on a normative set of goal states which excludes the extinction of any species and try to modify the environment so as to preclude achieving any extinction goal states—by artificially producing reproduction rates for endangered species that are favorable to survival. Unlike the first sort of normative sets of goal states, this sort of normative set of goal states does not contain the "natural" goal states as a proper subset.

Broadly conceived, then, we can have natural goal states and normative goal states which we associate with laws of quasi-succession, thus producing nonnormative and normative teleological theories—where in both cases, achievement of the (normative or nonnormative) goal states depends on environmental influences—which we may try to manipulate in order to achieve goal states. Thus specification of goal states may or may not involve normative considerations, but whether to attempt to achieve such goal states inevitably involves normative considerations. Thus the deontic ought has plenty of potential for intrusion into disputes involving teleological theories, and the confusions between scientific ought and deontic ought discussed in section I are liable to occur. Indeed, it often is extremely difficult to determine whether a proffered set of goal states is normative or nonnormative and, if normative, in what ways. This can exacerbate inconclusive scientific debates and make closure problematic.

III. A PSYCHIATRIC EXAMPLE

A somewhat detailed example will illustrate the above points and thus help clarify matters. Freudian psychoanalysis, and many other psychoanalytic theories, essentially are theories with laws of quasi-succession.[8] These laws typically specify a "normal" pattern of psychological development that stresses typical patterns of interaction with one's environment, as well as various patterns of "abnormal" psychological development or influence. Such theories typically also include accounts of how to manipulate the environment so as to affect the state of psychological adjustment a person enjoys. In short, the theory views a patient at time *t* as having a particular psychological/behavioral substate and being in a particular environmental substate. A psychotherapeutic theory is concerned with systems whose *composite states* are comprised of an individual's psychological/behavioral state and environmental state, and the theory characterizes subsequent psychological/behavioral states as a function of prior composite states. Certain psychological/behavioral states are goal states[9] characteristic of "normal," "well-adjusted," or at least nonpathological individuals. Thus the theory provides an account of the interaction between psychological/behavioral states of persons and the environments they interact with, the intention being that the theory will provide an account of the aetiology of normal and deviant behavior and psychological adjustment as well as lay a basis for manipulating a pathological patient's environment (e.g., via therapy) so as to facilitate achievement of goal states (i.e., being cured, becoming mentally healthy).

Psychotherapy is not a monolithic enterprise: There is a plethora of different theories (and associated schools) ranging from the classical (earlier and later) Freudian theories to the neo-Freudian theories of the ego-analysts, and from the social-interactionist theories of Harry Stack Sullivan to the "adaptive systems" views of Carl Rogers; and among psychiatrists there is considerable disagreement as to what are appropriate goal states—that is, over what constitutes mental health. Some therapists, such as Thomas Szasz (1964, 1970), doubt whether there is any objective notion of mental health (goal states). Psychological and psychiatric notions of mental health, according to Szasz, are just social mores and prejudices masquerading as objective notions. Other practitioners follow a medical model and posit an ideal type of psychological adjustment wherein mental health consists in a suitable approximation of that ideal. Still others, such as Maslow and Rogers, posit various adaptional or interactionist views wherein mental health consists in being able to cope productively with one's environment. Note that all of these apparently involve normative goal states, although there is considerable disagreement as to what ought to be characteristic of them.[10]

It is because mental health notions appear to employ normative goal states in their teleological theories that the mental health area is ripe for becoming embroiled in public controversies. Such was the case when the American Psychiatric Association (APA) decided to declassify homosexuality per se as a mental disorder. We now explore this case.

Homosexuality long has been thought by psychotherapy to be a paradigmatic mental disorder. However, psychotherapeutic theories tend to be evaluated primarily on the basis of clinical case studies, and only rarely have psychotherapists attempted to engage in controlled empirical tests of their theories.[11] One of the few exceptions was a study by a group of psychoanalysts headed by Irving Bieber (Bieber et al. 1962). Viewing homosexuality as "a key problem in psychoanalytic theory and a clearly defined behavioral pattern which would not present any diagnostic difficulties" (vii), beginning in 1952 his group developed a lengthy 500-item questionnaire which was used to collect data on 106 male homosexuals and 100 comparison patients in psychotherapy, the questionnaire being filled out by the patients' therapists. The findings were claimed to substantiate not only the psychopathology of homosexuals but also the aetiological view that homosexuality was caused by close-binding mothers, distant fathers, and various aberrations in the "triangular system" of parents and offspring.[12] In short, it was claimed that the psychopathology of homosexuals was confirmed, and its aetiology fairly well established.

While this study was going on, and prior to its publication, in 1957 Evelyn Hooker published a study, based on a sample of homosexuals not in therapy and a control group, which found that homosexuals and heterosexual controls could not be distinguished in terms of psychopathology using projective psychometric techniques such as the Rorschach — from which she concluded homosexuality per se was not a clinical (i.e., psychopathic) entity.[13]

These findings, coupled with criticisms of the Bieber study's methodology (viz., the use of purely clinical samples and the use of therapists' responses rather than patient responses), prompted a plethora of subsequent studies of the psychological adjustment of homosexuals. Some of these attempted to rectify defects in Bieber's study by using self-report versions of Bieber's questionnaire and (biased) nonclinical populations (e.g., service men in danger of being separated from the military on grounds of homosexual activity) and obtained results that tended to replicate Bieber's findings. Others attempted to use standard psychometric instruments such as the clinical scales of the MMPI (Minnesota Multiphasic Personality Inventory), the MMPI *Mf* (masculinity/femininity) scale, the 16 PF, Gough's Adjective Checklist, and various projective tests. There is considerable disagreement between the claims of these studies; some find homosexuals less well adjusted, and others find them no different from heterosexual controls. These studies generally are methodologically flawed by poor sample selection, the use of inadequately validated psychometric instruments and the misuse of better-validated ones, and so on. Little confidence can be placed in their findings.[14]

For example, at least five studies between 1959 and 1972 use the MMPI *Mf* scale with various samples, three of them finding that male homosexuals scored significantly higher than heterosexual controls. From this, one informed and careful commentator concluded, "In general, it appears that homosexuals do obtain higher femininity scores than heterosexuals"—the implication being that male homosexuals are effeminate and possess inappropriate gender identities symptomatic of serious maladjustment and psychopathology. However, such conclusions are inappropriate since the MMPI *Mf* scale is known to be seriously flawed and unreliable: It originally was intended to be a diagnostic instrument for measuring degree of heterosexual adjustment in males, but it had such a high false-positive rate in distinguishing heterosexuals from homosexuals that this interpretation was abandoned and the scale was reinterpreted as a masculinity/femininity scale. This failure probably is due to the fact that standard procedures for empirically generating MMPI scales were not adhered to, and the normal group for the scale was not the broad-spectrum sample used for most other MMPI scales. Instead, the normal group was a separate group of 54 male soldiers and 67 female airline employees; the number of homosexuals was only 13. Thus it is not surprising that the normalized scores on the *Mf* scale for males strongly correlate with educational level; college undergraduates across the country typically score one to one-half standard deviations above the norm. In fact, factor analysis indicates that the *Mf* scale loads on six different nondemographic factors, only one having anything to do with sexual matters, and "masculine interests" and "feminine interests" are separate orthogonal factors. In what probably is the best designed and executed study using the *Mf* scale, Braaten and Darling (1965) found that heterosexual and homosexual males did not differ in feminine interests, but the male homosexual subjects had lower masculine interest scores. Careful examination of their data indicates that higher scores on the *Mf* scale for the homosexuals were primarily attributable to the homosexuals being less interested in athletics and hunting. Overall, the *Mf* scale is completely unreliable as a psychometric measure of masculinity versus femininity or of psychological adjustment, and studies relying on it establish nothing about the psychological adjustment of homosexuals—although it may be a valid measure of sterotypically male interests in athletics and sporting events. The flaws of the MMPI *Mf* scale studies are not untypical of most of the research on the psychological adjustment of homosexuals, although they may be more documentably blatant.

Nevertheless, bolstered by studies such as Hooker's—which claimed to establish that homosexuality per se did not evidence mental illness or psychological maladjustment (and apparently dismissing conflicting studies, including Bieber's)—by 1970, homosexual activists began to actively challenge the psychiatric orthodoxy that homosexuality per se was a mental disorder. By 1973, their efforts resulted in the opportunity to present evidence (based on the above-mentioned studies) before the American Psychiatric Association's Committee on Nomenclature challenging the continued inclusion of "Homosexuality" per se as a disorder in the APA's 1968 *Diagnostic and Statistical Manual of Psychiatric Disorders* (DSM-II). Following this, the committee (under Robert Spitzer's leadership) removed homosexuality per se from DSM-II, provoking considerable opposition from Bieber and others. A referendum was forced to allow the members of the APA to vote on the removal, and gay activist groups became involved in influencing the outcome of the referendum. The removal was supported in the referendum, and the acrimonious controversy surrounding it continued. The objectivity of the removal became a matter of contention and dispute—in ways that have affected the drafting of DSM-III (1980).[15]

We now have enough background on the APA decision and the rather dreadful state of research on homosexuality at the time (1973) to return to our prior discussion of teleological theories and normative goal states. What we have in the APA case is a dispute among psychotherapists and psychologists over the relationship between homosexual behavior and mentally healthy goal states. The dispute ostensibly appears to be an empirical issue, in which the claims of competing research projects are pitted against each other in the attempt to objectively resolve the dispute on the basis of empirical findings. And given the methodological inadequacy of most of the pertinent studies (on both sides of the debate), it is easy to believe that the lack of closure in the dispute was due to uncritical reliance on questionable and unreliable research studies.

Such a conclusion is suspect for two reasons. First, we have already seen good reason to suspect that the goal states in psychiatric theory (and related mental health notions) are normative—in which case there is no prospect for resolving such disputes on purely factual grounds.[16] Second, if the issue was a nonnormative, factual one, then one is hard-pressed to explain why there were so few attempts to evaluate or refute conflicting empirical claims in the debate: The statistical means used by Bieber and his group are totally incapable of establishing their close-binding mother, distant father, and aberrant "triangular system" claims,[17] but nowhere in the debates are such criticisms raised. Similarly, criticisms of psychometric studies were rare, and penetrating ones (e.g., showing the extreme inadequacy of the MMPI *Mf* scale used in many studies) were virtually absent from the debate, even when there was ample evidence in the literature (as was the case then for the MMPI *Mf* scale). In short, although factual claims were bandied about in the debate over the APA decision, the record suggests that the veracity of empirical research claims was not a major focus in the debate whether to remove homosexuality as a mental disorder from DSM-II. Indeed many psychoanalysts denied the relevancy of nonpsychoanalytic data.[18] It is clear, then, that the question whether homosexuality is a mental disorder—hence whether a homosexual can possess a mentally healthy goal state—is a normative, not a factual, issue.

This conclusion is reinforced by subsequent retrospective statements on the APA decision prepared by the two chief protagonists in the dispute—Irving Bieber and Robert Spitzer.[19] Spitzer relates:

> When I first was given the job of considering the claims . . . that homosexuality should not be regarded as a mental disorder, I was confronted with the absence of any generally accepted definition of mental disorder. I therefore reviewed the characteristics of the various mental disorders and concluded that, with the exception of homosexuality and perhaps some of the other "sexual deviations," they all regularly cause subjective distress or were associated with generalized impairment in social effectiveness or functioning. It became clear to me that the *consequences* of a condition, and not its *etiology* determined whether or not the condition should be considered a disorder. Therefore, it seemed irrelevant to me then (and still does now) whether a condition is a result of childhood conflicts and intrapsychic anxieties, since many desirable conditions that no one would suggest are disorders, such as ambition and self-discipline, may also result from conflict. . . . I therefore proposed that the criterion for a mental disorder was either subjective distress or generalized impairment of social effectiveness.[20]

In contrast, Bieber disputes the contention that the absence of both subjective distress and generalized impairment in social effectiveness or functioning are sufficient conditions for mental health:

> A so-called "well-adjusted" individual is not necessarily free of

psychopathology. Despite the ability to function adequately, have satisfactory social relationships and be free of incapacitating feelings of anxiety or suffering, major psychopathology, including psychosis may, nonetheless be present.

... Psychopathology can be ego syntonic and not cause distress; ... social effectiveness, that is, the ability to maintain positive social relations and perform work effectively, may coexist with psychopathology even of a psychotic order.[21]

Specifically, Bieber maintains that homosexuals who lack subjective distress or generalized impairment in social effectiveness or functioning nevertheless display psychopathology.

Behavior is abnormal when it is based on irrational or unrealistic fears. In the case of homosexuality ... the fears are of lethal attack by other men should heterosexuality be attempted or contemplated. Such fears may have been realistic during early life ... [b]ut in adult life, the expectation of injury from other men for heterosexual activity is not rational. Homosexuality first develops as a consequence of such fear and is maintained in adult life, usually unconsciously, by the continuity of such fear.[22]

Bieber's contention, then, is that practicing homosexuals are haunted by fears of lethal attack by other men should heterosexuality be attempted or contemplated, and that the presence of such fears *alone* is sufficient to make homosexuality a mental disorder (a non–goal state) regardless whether the homosexual experiences subjective distress or generalized impairment in social effectiveness or functioning.[23]
What we have here is a clear dispute as to what the characteristics of mental health goal states are—Spitzer maintaining that absence of subjective distress or generalized impairment in social effectiveness or functioning are necessary and sufficient, and Bieber denying their necessity, maintaining that behavior based on irrational or unrealistic fears is sufficient. And Bieber further maintains that homosexual behavior *inevitably* is based in such irrational unrealistic fears—ergo is pathological and indicative of mental disorder. The dispute thus appears to be a purely normative dispute over what the criteria are for being a mental health goal state.
So construed, the logic of the dispute becomes complicated: If Bieber is correct in his aetiological/nosological claim that homosexual behavior is based on fear, then the issue is a purely normative one whether such (usually unconscious) fear overrides lack of subjective distress and demonstrable functional effectiveness in assessing whether one is in a

mental health goal state. If such fears are admitted into the goal state criteria, grounds still exist for normative dispute over whether such fears are "irrational or unrealistic." However, the question needs to be raised whether the factual claim that homosexual behavior inevitably is rooted in such "irrational or unrealistic" fears is correct. For if it is not, the normative contention can be refuted on grounds that such fears are not a necessary concomitant of homosexuality, hence homosexuality per se is not a mental disorder on Bieber's *own* criteria. If such fears are an inevitable concomitant of homosexuality, the factual veracity of the claim does not resolve the normative issue—since *is* does not imply deontic *ought*. The fact is that despite the impression promulgated by Bieber, he has advanced no convincing evidence that such fears are an omnipresent concomitant of homosexual behavior (see note 23). So construed, the dispute between Bieber and Spitzer over what are appropriate mental health goal states becomes a normative issue by empirical default.

But the dispute appears to be deeper, and more theoretical. For Bieber and Spitzer disagree whether aetiological considerations are to be included as state parameters in psychological adjustment substates relevant to assessing mental health. Spitzer maintains that "the *consequences* of a condition, and not its *etiology* determined whether or not the condition [e.g., homosexual behavior] should be considered a disorder,"[24] whereas Bieber maintains that aetiology does determine whether such behavior is a disorder, since it inevitably is a manifestation of irrational or unrealistic fears.[25] But Bieber is maintaining that aetiologically based fears *still* are present and that they are *proximate causes* of homosexual behavior. Thus the dispute simply is whether such "fear" parameters are relevant state parameters and whether they are significant factors in determining mental health goal states, so the issues are essentially no different than have been discussed above.

The APA dispute case not only evidences the ways normative and purely scientific/factual issues can become intertwined when teleological theories are involved, but it also displays the extent to which such teleological disputes inherit the more general potential for "scientific/ factual" and "deontic" issues to become intimately and confusedly intertwined.

IV. CONCLUSION

A tacit restriction on the discussion in this chapter has been the consideration of scientific disputes which become embroiled in moral or social disputes *insofar as* these disputes are conducted *rationally*.

Once such disputes enter the lay and public arenas, there is no guarantee that they will be conducted in manners that are either informed or rational. Nevertheless, I have focused my attention on such disputes insofar as they are rational, informed, and focus on reasonably well-articulated scientific theories. I have drawn on the Semantic Conception to argue that even under such restrictive ground rules, there are characteristics of theoretical and theory-based applied science that not only invite, but in some cases legitimize, the intertwining of scientific and various deontic considerations in resolving controversies surrounding scientific pronouncements.

I hope that the abstract considerations presented here will provide some deep insight into the *rational* basis for the genesis of such controversies, which may advance their understanding and help contribute to their more effective and objective resolution—to bring them to reasonable closure. I hope the discussion of the APA homosexuality case reveals the extent to which the purely rational attempt to debate such issues enjoys complexities that work against such closure. While I know no way to ensure that scientifically oriented debates in the public arena can be constrained to even approximate rational assessment, I hope that what I have presented here makes some contribution to the understanding of such debates insofar as they are rational—even if it is the minimal one of contributing to our understanding of the extent to which science, in its very nature, rationally or legitimately encourages such free-wheeling controversies. Finally, I hope this chapter has added to our understanding of teleological theories on the Semantic Conception.

NOTES

1. An earlier version of this chapter originally was written for the NEH-sponsored Hastings Center Closure Project which explored general issues of closure in scientific disputes and also made a detailed examination of several real-life case studies, including the three just mentioned. Most of my examples are taken from the case studies that this project examined in detail.

2. It is my expectation that the differences will become blurred, hence more difficult to sort out, when one considers theories propounded as conceptual devices.

3. An example of the former approach is Burks 1977, chs. 6, 7, 9. For the latter, see Lewis 1973. On any possible-worlds approach, one must avoid various problems of vacuity, and so on, and these two works enjoy quite different strategies for doing so. I will follow Lewis' approach here, since it is more transparently relatable to deontic logic; but I believe the same points could be made using Burks' approach.

Both approaches involve postulating possible worlds other than the actual world. Antirealists such as van Fraassen view such postulations with suspicion and horror. In my forthcoming *Facts, Theories, and Scientific Observation,* I will offer an analysis of causal necessity which grounds such necessity in actual-world regularities and does not involve ontological commitments beyond the constituents of the actual world. (Thus such an analysis should not be ontologically objectionable to someone like van Fraassen.) The resulting analysis of causal necessity suffices for the Semantic Conception's empirical truth condition (ch. 3) including replication relation (*) above, but not for those counterfactuals which involve suspending laws of nature or postulating nonactual particulars. Analysis of the latter and deontic 'ought' statements apparently requires postulating nonactual alternative possible worlds. Thus the analysis of controversies in the present chapter may incur ontological commitments that go beyond those incurred by my quasi-realistic version of the Semantic Conception.

4. One might dispute this on the grounds that we can alter the nature of our world (as discussed below) in ways that might affect which other possible worlds are similar to ours in ways that affect the truth status of such scientific counterfactuals; however, since mapping relation (*) concerns all physically possible phenomenal systems of a certain kind, this seems impossible.

5. Unless, possibly, one maintains a strict determinism that includes the actions of humans.

6. The original overdesign, for the most part, has exhausted the possibilities for such prediction.

7. Whenever goal states are normative I will use the phrase 'normative goal state'; 'goal state' simpliciter will be reserved for the nonnormative ones discussed previously—unless the context makes it clear that I am using it to encompass both normative and nonnormative goal states.

8. The psychotherapeutic theories under discussion here are qualitative theories. For a good comparative account of a number of the main competing psychotherapeutic theories, see Ford and Urban 1963.

9. Whether they are normative or not for the present will be left an open question. The issue will be taken up later in this section.

10. For a good philosophical discussion of various approaches to obtaining an objective notion of mental health and the ways deontic considerations compromise such efforts, see Macklin 1972.

11. Alisdair MacIntyre explores some of the reasons for this in his "Post-Skinner and Post-Freud: Metaphysical Causes of Scientific Disagreements," an unpublished working paper for the Hastings Closure Project, 1980. Some psychoanalysts (e.g., Socarides [1970]) deny the relevance of such controlled tests (see note 18 below).

12. The Bieber study also claimed a substantial "cure" rate for homosexuals. For discussion of that claim and serious problems with it that challenges Bieber's contention that homosexuality does "not present any diagnostic difficulties," see Suppe 1984b.

13. Hooker 1957. Hooker published several other related studies around the same time.

14. Lester (1975, ch. 13) summarizes these studies. See Suppe 1981 and n.d. for critical discussion of this literature.

15. For details, see Bayer 1981. The suffix on 'DSM' indicates the edition.

16. Robert Spitzer, chairman of the APA Task Force on Nomenclature and Statistics, maintains that the decision whether to classify homosexuality as a disorder "is a value judgment and not a factual matter" ("Homosexuality and Mental Disorder: A Reformulation of the Issues," Hastings Center Closure Project, unpublished working paper, 1979-80, 10–11).

17. See Suppe n.d. for the problems.

18. See, e.g., Socarides 1970. His position is philosophically evaluated and refuted in Suppe 1986 and n.d.. Grünbaum 1984 also is highly relevant.

19. Bieber, "On Arrival at the APA Decision," Hastings Center Closure Project, unpublished working paper, 1979–80, and Spitzer, working paper.

20. Spitzer, 5–6. His views subsequently were altered, and he now embraces the stance taken in the introduction to DSM-III: "In DSM-III each of the mental disorders is conceptualized as a clinically significant behavioral or psychological syndrome or pattern that occurs in an individual and that is typically associated with either a painful symptom (distress) or impairment in one or more important areas of functioning (disability). In addition, there is an inference that there is a behavioral, psychological, or biological dysfunction, and that the disturbance is not only in the relationship between the individual and society. (When the disturbance is *limited* to a conflict between an individual and society, this may represent social deviance, which may or may not be commendable, but is not by itself a mental disorder.)" (American Psychiatric Association 1980, 6.)

It should be noted that within medical nosology, "diseases" ideally are classified on the basis of symptoms with a known aetiology or pharmacological response; within psychiatry these standards are reflected in the fact that psychiatric syndromes which respond to chemotherapy (e.g., schizophrenia, which responds to phenothiazenes, and manic syndromes, which respond to lithium carbonate therapies) are viewed as nosologically the most secure, objective, and established. This is despite the fact that, as a matter of policy, DSM-III rejects aetiological or pharmacological-response considerations as diagnostic criteria.

21. Bieber, working paper, 14 and 22–23.

22. Ibid., 11–12.

23. It should be noted that these sweeping claims of "fear of lethal attack by other men should hetrosexuality be attempted or contemplated" are completely unsupported by the findings of Bieber et al. 1962. An examination of the questionnaire used in that study (321–48) reveals *no* questions that directly address the existence of such *present* fears on the part of homosexuals—either in the patient's or the therapist's opinion, and those few that are even tangentially relevant make the claim highly tenuous at best. We must assume that these claims are based on Bieber's other interviews of more

than one thousand homosexuals (working paper, 1)—for which his diagnosis and interpretation have not been subjected to any nonclinical empirical testing or attempts at validation.

24. Spitzer, working paper, 5.
25. Bieber, working paper, 11–12, 14, 22–23.

PART IV
Toward a Quasi-Realistic Theory of Scientific Knowledge

My version of the Semantic Conception gives theory structures a quasi-realistic physical interpretation: Theories characterize how phenomenal systems would behave if they were isolated from outside influences. This quasi-realism is pointless, though, unless theories so interpreted can be known. Thus the full defense of my quasi-realistic version of the Semantic Conception depends upon the development of an appropriate quasi-realistic epistemology of science.

For over a decade now, I have been developing a causal theory of knowledge that would provide such a full defense (to be set forth in a book in progress entitled *Facts, Theories, and Scientific Observation*.) The satisfactory resolution of two issues has long eluded me and slowed completion: how to handle the physical interpretation of the causal modalities and how to develop an interpretation for probabilistic and statistical claims (such as claims used in factor and multivariate analysis) that would enable such stochastic empirical claims to be known under my causal theory of knowledge. Although I have finally reached the basic breakthroughs that allow me to resolve these issues, unfortunately they have arrived too recently to be included in the present volume. For a deep ultimate epistemological defense of my quasi-realistic version of the Semantic Conception, the reader will have to await the completion of *Facts, Theories, and Scientific Observation*.

Thus the next four chapters (augmented by the antinominalism of ch. 7, the account of empirical truth in ch. 3, and pp. 716–28 of my afterword to *The Structure of Scientific Theories* [1977a]) constitute only a prolegomenon to my ultimate epistemological analysis. My goal here is to introduce a number of the main motivations behind my ultimate forthcoming approach and to present preliminary accounts of some of its key moves and developments.

I take the sort of relativistic epistemology built into Kuhn's and Feyerabend's work to be incompatible with the sort of quasi-realism built into my Semantic Conception of Theories. As a first step toward my quasi-realistic epistemology, in chapter 10 I try to identify precisely what it is about Kuhn's and Feyerabend's epistemologies that traps them into the unacceptable extreme relativisms I need to avoid. Doing so requires careful exegesis of their work that, inter alia, corrects a number of misinterpretations of their work that commentators (myself included) have made. I also attempt to place their epistemological views in a larger historical context, arguing that their epistemologies essentially are the final skeptical responses after Hume to Locke's empiricism. I argue that commitment to the K-K thesis ('S knows that P' entails 'S knows that S knows that P') ultimately is responsible for both the collapse of the eighteenth-century empiricist program and the unacceptable relativism in Kuhn's and Feyerabend's positions. Thus I conclude that a viable epistemology for science should reject the K-K thesis.

Chapter 11 claims that traditional debates over realism versus instrumentalism, as well as contemporary debates, mistakenly rest on the assumption that direct perceptual experiences are in some sense epistemically privileged. In arguing against this assumption, I not only offer a new perspective on the issue of scientific realism, but I also attempt to delineate the role of sensory experiences in perceptual knowledge. I argue that perceptual knowledge does not rest upon any knowledge of our sensory experiences (including sense data); rather, such knowledge exploits causal or empirical regularities between attributes of physical objects (or other particulars) and the sensory, doxastic, and other cognitive *states* of perceivers without requiring knowledge of such regularities. This chapter thus rejects empiricist and latter-day sense-datum approaches to the epistemology of perception.

Chapter 12 gathers up various threads that have been emerging in prior chapters and attempts to develop an epistemology that (1) rejects the K-K thesis, (2) eschews knowledge of sensations as a source of perceptual knowledge, and (3) exploits empirical regularities between objects (or particulars) and the various doxastic, cognitive, and sensory states of perceivers without requiring knowledge of these regularities. In developing this view, I use Dretske 1969 and various objections to Dretske's analysis as foils to my arguments, and I indicate revisions that would avoid most objections. One sort of objection, from Raymond Martin (1975), cannot be avoided by tinkering with the analysis. Dretske's response ultimately was to capitulate to Martin's attack, abandon much of his 1969 analysis, and develop his 1981, 1983, and 1983a works as a substantially modified replacement analysis. I argue that his response was mistaken and that, instead, had he fully understood the implications of his own earlier position, he would have seen that his sort of position can be defended against Martin's attack. In the process of providing such a defense, a general epistomology of a posteriori knowledge is developed and defended in chapter 12. Critical consideration also is given to other strategies for avoiding Martin-like problems that are suggested by the recent epistemological writings of Nozick, Millikin, Goldman, and others. At the end of the chapter further development of my epistemological views is sketched, including the claim that observation can yield knowledge of causal generalizations in theories.

Chapter 13 focuses on general scientific knowledge and challenges the traditional role of induction. Earlier in chapter 4 I showed how, upon taking a conventional inductive confirmation view, theories could be confirmed under the Semantic Conception. However, probabilistic induction does not meet the stringent evidential or justification standards built into the epistemology of observation developed in chapter 12. If that standard is insisted on for all a posteriori knowledge, then induction has no role to play in the knowledge of theories; if induction is given its traditional role and can provide knowledge of theories (as scientific realisms demand), then an epistemic double standard will have to be invoked to preserve inductive general knowledge. Chapter 13 argues that probabilistic inductive inferences must rest on logically prior plausibility assessments that are not reducible to probabilistic notions and that standard inductive logic is a poor descriptive model for scientific reasoning. Given these conclusions—and the fact that on the epistemology of chapter 12, single observations can provide knowledge of causal generalizations, hence theories—I am led to further conclude that probabilistic induction is not a basis for general or theoretical scientific knowledge. However, invoking a distinction between knowledge and claims to know, I do argue that probabilistic induction has a role to play in the rational evaluation of *claims* to know. Finally, I also discuss the role of probabilistic induction in methodological deliberations and possible problems facing my approach.

Collectively these four chapters (together with the empirical and factual truth analysis of chapter 3 and the antinominalism of chapter 7) should give a fairly good idea of the sort of epistemology I am developing in support of my quasi-realistic Semantic Conception of Theories. The four epistemological chapters here also should give some idea of the considerations that prompt me to approach the epistemology the way I do and why I see it as an improvement over the sorts of epistemologies that have dominated philosophical thought about science since early in the Copernican Revolution.

The main ingredients missing from this prolegomenon to my quasi-realistic epistemology are the treatments of the physical interpretation of causal modalities and empirical probabilities mentioned earlier. These will be provided in my *Facts, Theories, and Scientific Observation* (in progress), where I will argue that the sort of causal necessity required by my quasi-realistic version of the Semantic Conception and its associated epistemology can be analyzed in terms of (usually) nonrecursive actual-world regularities without making ontological commitments that extend beyond the actual world. Empirical probabilities sufficient for doing science will be analyzed in terms of relative frequencies over the actual world history, observational knowledge of samples enhanced by the logic of statistical estimation procedures, and a nontheoretical analogue for statistical claims to chapter 3's empirical truth conditions for theories on the Semantic Conception.

Finally, the developments in this prolegomenon reflect my belief that the reason why traditional debates over realism versus instrumentalism and contemporary debates over scientific realism versus antirealism are so inconclusive is because they are wrongheaded. As I argued in the Prologue, it seems to me that the best way to argue for a scientific realism or quasi-realism is to develop in some detail an epistemology that embodies it and then see how well it accommodates the sort of knowledge we do in fact have and how well it resolves, dissolves, or avoids traditional problems prior epistemologies have floundered on. A full epistemology for my version of the Semantic Conception is yet to come — still, the "Ur" version presented here seems sufficient to meet the spirit of Carnap's challenge in another context: "Well, Mr. _____, when you have your own theory of inductive logic, I'll be happy to discuss induction with you."

10

Kuhn's and Feyerabend's Relativisms

A central function of science is to provide systematic general knowledge of the world, and the ultimate task of philosophy of science is to investigate the nature of such knowledge. Although neither enjoys widespread acceptance today, recent philosophy of science has been dominated by two opposing views on the nature of scientific knowledge — the neo-empiricist views of logical positivism and the highly relativistic "subjective" views of Kuhn, Feyerabend, and others. According to logical positivism, observation yields factual knowledge which can be used inductively to confirm or disconfirm laws or theories and provides a neutral factual basis for assessing the relative merits of competing theories. Kuhn and Feyerabend rejected this view, maintaining that observation is "theory-laden" in such a way that adherents to different competing theories cannot observationally obtain knowledge of the same facts, hence there is no neutral body of facts against which the relative merits of competing theories can be assessed. They argue further that theories are incapable of empirical testing in the sense that they cannot be inductively confirmed or disconfirmed by observation. Clearly, a central point of contention between these two schools of thought concerns the question of how relativistic scientific knowledge is, and they seem to mark two extremes on this issue.

Both these views of scientific knowledge have been the subject of intense and devastating criticisms,[1] and within philosophy of science today, neither enjoys significant acceptance — both being influential relics of the history of the philosophy of science. Rather, a central focus of contemporary philosophy of science seems to be on developing an account of scientific knowledge which accommodates the sound insights of both perspectives while avoiding the known defects of either.[2] It is the intent of this chapter to contribute to such a development.

Specifically, it is my thesis that despite the appearance of nearly total opposition between the positivistic and "subjectivist" views of scientific knowledge, these two views uncritically share key epistemic doctrines inherited from eighteenth-century British empiricism, and the defects of these two views are traceable to these shared doctrines. More strongly put, both are last-ditch attempts to salvage remnants of a moribund eighteenth-century empiricism. Through the delineation of these shared doctrines, and a consideration of their defects, I hope not only to indicate why these two views of scientific knowledge are defective, but also to point philosophy of science toward a viable post-empiricist treatment of scientific knowledge. By examining these relics from the recent history of the philosophy of science, I hope to clarify the nature of epistemic and metaphysical relativisms characteristic of scientific knowledge.

Examining the relativisms inherent in the views of Feyerabend, Kuhn, and their positivistic and empiricist predecessor-foes will be a central theme of my analysis. To avoid confusion, let us clarify the notion of "relativism" at the onset. Several important types of relativism can be delineated and should be kept relatively distinct in what follows. First, there is *epistemological relativism*, which is concerned with the extent to which differences in background beliefs, conceptual apparatus, experience, and so on, lead to differences in what can be *known*. Second, one can inquire into the extent to which the above differences in background beliefs, and so on, affect what is *regarded, claimed,* or (rationally) *accepted as being known* (regardless whether it is in fact known or only claimed to be known). This might be termed *epistemic-avowal relativism*. These two types of *epistemic relativism* usually are not distinguished, reflecting the common practice of identifying *knowledge* with reasonable or justified *knowledge claims*. An underlying theme of this chapter is that such an identification is illegitimate, hence that such types of epistemic relativism need to be distinguished. Third, there is *metaphysical relativism*, which is concerned with the extent to which the particulars and kinds of particulars that exist depend upon the above background beliefs, conceptual apparatus, and so on, of knowers. The extent of metaphysical relativism allowed tends to be conditioned on the extent of the first two sorts of epistemic relativism claimed. Because our interest in Kuhn's and Feyerabend's views focuses on these three sorts of relativism, in considering their views we will concentrate only on selected metaphysical and epistemological doctrines found in their views of science. This means that we will tend not to discuss a number of aspects of their views which often figure centrally in many discussions of their philosophies of science and which I have discussed in *The Structure of Scientific Theories* (1974, 1977).

I. EMPIRICIST VIEWS OF SCIENTIFIC KNOWLEDGE

Kuhn's and Feyerabend's epistemologies of science were advanced in response to key features in the neo-empiricism of logical positivism, and so they are best understood relative to that background. Although our initial focus is logical positivism's views of scientific knowledge, since logical positivism's brand of empiricism is a twentieth-century reworking of earlier empiricisms, it is desirable to begin with those earlier doctrines and show how they lead to the logical positivist view. Obviously, a detailed history of empiricism would be inappropriate and impossible here, so I will content myself with sketching certain leitmotifs which are particularly relevant to the dispute between positivism and Kuhn and Feyerabend over how relativistic scientific knowledge is.

The empiricist philosophy of science conveniently can be construed as beginning with Francis Bacon's *Novum Organum* (1620). Responding to the failure of Aristotelian science occasioned by developments in heliocentric astronomy (the Copernican Revolution), Bacon traced that failure to the reliance on philosophical presuppositions, such as Aristotle's first principles, which have no experiential basis, and other false notions which he called *idols*. Thus the appropriate method for doing science was to confine one's attention to principles (laws) which could be established experientially. Bacon sought to develop a method for doing science which, if followed, on the one hand, would preclude the introduction of false notions, and on the other hand, would yield true empirical generalizations or laws. This was his *first method of induction*, which consisted in the comprehensive observation of a wide variety of phenomena without any presuppositions as to what data will be obtained, subjecting such data to preliminary classification and arrangement into tables, and then determining those correlations which invariably hold among the data.

It is important to note that this method of induction is a procedure for the *discovery* of generalizations, where it is claimed that the method will yield only true generalizations; hence any generalizations obtained by following this method qualify as knowledge. Thus Bacon's first method of induction is both a procedure for *discovery* and a method for *justifying* knowledge. As Bacon himself notes (*Novum Organum* II, 19), this method generally is impractical and useless, since we will be unable to obtain the comprehensive range of data required for the method to be accurate. To overcome this difficulty, he introduces a *second,* more powerful, *inductive method* which only yields tentative results: (1) the available observational data, however incomplete, are organized into tables as in the first method; (2) then a preliminary hypothesis or guess is made as to what the causal factors in question are; (3) the hypothesis then is tested via comparison with the tables; and (4) if there are no contrary instances, it is tentatively accepted. This second method does not provide a procedure for the discovery of hypotheses but, rather, only provides a means for the inductive justification of hypotheses, where the justification does not guarantee the truth of the hypothesis.

Thus in Bacon's two inductive methods we find two quite different views of induction: one, in which induction provides a "logic of discovery" for obtaining knowledge; and the other, in which induction is a means for verifying or justifying knowledge—a "logic of justification."[3] Both views of induction are encountered in the subsequent history of empiricism; for example, Hume and the logical positivists were concerned with induction construed as just a "logic of justification," Whewell was concerned with induction more as a "logic of discovery," and Mill was concerned with both sorts of induction.

Key to Bacon's empiricism was the notion that observation could yield knowledge of the world and that such observational knowledge could be exploited through induction to obtain general knowledge of the world of the sort post-Renaissance astronomy and physics was yielding. Subsequent developments of empiricism in the seventeenth and eighteenth centuries by Hobbes, Locke, Berkeley, Hume, and others had as their focus the detailed development of this view. This focus was to show how observation (sense perception) could yield particular knowledge of the world and how that knowledge could be exploited so as to obtain general knowledge of the world; a key motive was to vindicate the knowledge being yielded by the physics and astronomy of the time.[4] Insofar as such empiricists were concerned with induction, it was with respect to induction as a "logic of justification."

The development of such an empiricist epistemology required (a) showing how observation or sensory experience could provide singular knowledge about the world and (b) showing how that knowledge could be exploited via reasoning to obtain additional knowledge. Induction was the reasoning method whereby general knowledge was so obtained. Virtually without argument empiricists followed the Cartesian skeptic and assumed that knowledge must be certain or incorrigible, but they differed with the Cartesians in assuming that for a posteriori knowledge, that certainty must be provided by experience. Thus the key epistemological problem for empiricism was to show how experience could yield incorrigible knowledge of contingent matters of fact.

The first step was to show how observation or sensory experience could yield singular knowledge of the world. This task was complicated by the fact that the senses can deceive us into thinking that the world is other than it is—as in cases of illusion and hallucination. Thus sensation alone does not invariably provide incorrigible singular knowledge of the world. However, according to these empiricists it is impossible to be mistaken as to the nature of our sensory experiences; thus we do have incorrigible knowledge of the *content* of our experiences, even though this content may or may not represent the way the world actually is. In this way, knowledge of the content of our experiences provides a basic stock of incorrigible experiential knowledge which can be exploited, through the operation of human reason or understanding, to obtain additional a posteriori knowledge.

The problem remained how such base knowledge of the contents of sensation could be exploited so as to obtain knowledge of material objects and how it could be exploited to obtain general knowledge via induction. Various attempts by Locke and others to show how knowledge of material objects was possible proved defective, and so we find Hume (expanding some arguments of Berkeley's) maintaining the skeptical view that knowledge of material (and also spiritual) substances is impossible, and thus we are limited to experiential knowledge of our sensations.

Although the operations of human understanding did enable us to associate together ideas obtained from experience and to discern various relations holding between such ideas, thereby obtaining new (singular) knowledge based on experience, Hume argued that induction was incapable of yielding a posteriori knowledge; and so *general* a posteriori knowledge was impossible. In essence, his argument was that the available singular a posteriori knowledge could not guarantee the truth of a generalization unless it was augmented by some known *principle of uniformity* or *induction hypothesis.* But such an induction hypothesis was itself an a posteriori generalization about the world of experience, and so must be known via experience; however, to know such an induction hypothesis on the basis of experience, recourse would have to be made to some other induction hypothesis, and so on into an infinite regress—which precludes the possibility of inductively obtained general knowledge.

According to Hume, this problem precludes knowledge of cause and effect. Thus the seventeenth- and eighteenth-century empiricist attempts to show how the observational/inductive procedures allegedly employed by science enabled science to yield knowledge of the world collapsed into a Humean skepticism wherein only singular knowledge of one's sensory experience was possible, and knowledge—either singular or general—of the material world was impossible. As a philosophy of science, British empiricism was a total failure—which was no small factor in the subsequent nineteenth-century rejection of empiricism in favor of subjective idealisms such as Kant's and Hegel's.

Implicit in these early empiricist views of knowledge was the thesis that our sensory experiences are passively received and that they are in no way conditioned or determined by the understanding, or mind. Being convinced that the physics of his time did, indeed, yield knowledge, Kant took the failure of both empiricism and rationalism to explain how such knowledge is possible as indicating that both approaches were inadequate.[5] Rather, he maintained that experience can yield knowledge of objects only if "filtered through" a synthetic a priori conceptual apparatus which is partially constitutive of our experiences: The objects we experience, and about which science yields knowledge, depend for their existence on both experience and the conceptual apparatus of the understanding. Thus, the world science seeks to investigate and obtain systematic general knowledge about is a world of *intentional particulars.*

Moreover, the conceptual apparatus (the categories) determinative of these experienced objects is governed by various *synthetic a priori principles,* such as the principle of causation.[6] The noninductive establishment of such synthetic a priori principles enabled Kant to sharply downgrade the importance of induction in science. He viewed science, instead, as a deductive systematization: In accordance with various heuristic *regulative rules of reason,* these synthetic a priori generalizations could be exploited deductively to obtain other empirical generalizations or laws, and so general knowledge could be obtained by science. Thus Kant's subjective idealism (wherein the world investigated by science is comprised of intentional particulars) enabled Kant to evade Humean skepticism with respect to both singular and general knowledge of material objects.

Although Kant's subjective idealism, or modifications of it, such as Hegel's, tended to dominate epistemology well into the nineteenth century, during the middle third of that century we find a new empiricist tradition emerging in the work of Hershel, Whewell, and Mill. Unlike the earlier seventeenth- and eighteenth-century empiricism, these nineteenth-century developments were concerned in large part with obtaining a "logic of discovery" and tended to be based on an examination of scientific discoveries as revealed in contemporary scientific practice or in the history of modern science. In general, these empiricists saw scientific discoveries as occurring inductively in manners that can be construed as more sophisticated versions of one or another of Bacon's two methods of induction. They attempted to show that, contrary to what Hume claimed, such inductive methods of discovery also provided for the justifiction of scientific knowledge. However, since these nineteenth-century empiricisms apparently exerted minimal influence on the emergence of logical positivism's brand of twentieth-century empiricism, they will not be considered further. Indeed, with the exception of Mill, in some respects they have more in common with the views of Kant, Kuhn, and Feyerabend than they do with the views of logical positivism.[7]

The next resurgence of empiricism resulted in the emergence of logical positivism in the 1920s. Positivism occurred as the culmination of a reaction, begun by Ernst Mach, against the Marburg-variety neo-Kantian views which dominated nineteenth-century German philosophy of science from the 1870s on, and it looked back to the eighteenth century empiricism of Hume for its inspiration rather than to the nineteenth-century empiricisms of Hershel, Whewell, and Mill. By 1886, Ernst Mach had rejected the view that a priori elements had any legitimate place in the constitution of our knowledge of things, maintaining instead that the principles of science should be construed as abbreviated descriptions of sensations—a view having much in common with Berkeley's phenomenalism and Hume's skeptical conclusions about the impossibility of obtaining knowledge of material or spiritual substances (as opposed to bundles of ideas derived from sensation). Such a view, however, could not provide for the use of mathematics in the formulation of scientific theories; to avoid this defect, under the influence of Clifford, Pearson, Hertz, and Poincaré, this view was loosened gradually so as to allow the inclusion of an a priori mathematical conceptual element in science, so long as it added no factual content to the theory. That is, a priori mathematical constructions could be used in science as a means of providing economical, shorthand descriptions of sensations or phenomena. Logical positivism emerged out of the combination of this modified Machean view, recent developments in mathematical logic, and a number of crucial developments in physics.[8]

Logical positivism offers the following basic picture of scientific knowledge: Certain entities or attributes in the world can be directly observed, and so knowledge of them is nonproblematic. Initially, such direct observational knowledge was construed as the knowledge of sense data (the modern replacement for Hume's sensory impressions and ideas) and so yielded incorrigible knowledge; gradually, however, this view gave way to the thesis of *physicalism* wherein direct observation yielded knowledge of physical objects and their attributes. Although not incorrigible, this knowledge was nonproblematic in the sense that there would be intersubjective agreement among normal observers as to what the facts were.[9] In its early versions, following Mach, logical positivism restricted empirical knowledge to just knowledge of what was amenable to direct observation and maintained that such knowledge must be *conclusively verifiable* on the basis of direct observation. It was soon realized, however, that the most impressive achievements of modern physical science, including relativity and quantum theory, failed to meet this condition. Convinced that such achievements of science did yield knowledge, logical positivists gradually loosened their position.

By 1928 it was maintained that the descriptive language of science could be bifurcated into two parts: an observational language and a theoretical language. The descriptive terms in the observation language referred to entities and attributes which were amenable to direct observation, and the "descriptive" terms in the theoretical language were those which did not refer to entities and attributes which were amenable to direct observation. Whereas observation provided the means for directly ascertaining the truth of singular assertions in the observation language, this was not so for assertions in the theoretical language. The only way the truth of assertions in the theoretical language could be ascertained was if such assertions were construed realistically and had implications expressible in the observation language, which could be verified or falsified via direct observation. Thus theoretical knowledge was possible only to the extent that assertions in the theoretical language had observation language implications—and this was so only if the meanings of terms in the theoretical language had been specified via definitions or meaning postulates (called *correspondence rules)* in terms of observation language conditions. By 1937 these meaning specifications were not required to specify *completely* the meanings of theoretical language terms, but were required to at least *partially define* or specify the meanings of theoretical assertions in terms of conditions specifiable in the observation language. This is the Received View on Theories discussed in chapter 2.

It further was postulated that a single observation language could be used for *all* science and that the meanings of all theoretical assertions could be (partially) specified in terms of that single observation language. Thus all theories had observable consequences, specifiable in the same language, which could be used to test—hence confirm or disconfirm— the theory. This is the thesis of a *neutral observation language.*

In the late nineteenth and early twentieth centuries, physical science had suffered the indignity of discovering that some of its widely accepted theories had postulated the existence of fictitious theoretical entities— such as luminiferous aether—which could not be directly observed. Two different reactions to such occurrences emerged within logical positivism. On the one hand, some positivists (following Mach) embraced an *instrumentalism,* maintaining that theoretical assertions did not purport to describe anything real, but rather were just convenient means of specifying correlations between directly observable phenomena; thus, following Mach, science was restricted to providing knowledge of what could be directly experienced via sensation.[10] Other positivists rejected such instrumentalist tendencies, maintaining instead a *realistic* interpretation of the theoretical language wherein it did make assertions about such postulated entities as electrons. It was further maintained that—provided that the meanings of such assertions were partially defined or specified in terms of *testable* observation language consequences—one could confirm or disconfirm such theoretical assertions about hypothetical entities; thus one could come to know whether such postulated entities do exist and have the attributes attributed to them by the theories which postulate them.

Whether an instrumentalistic or a realistic construal of theoretical assertions in science is opted for, it will be characteristic of theoretical assertions that they provide generalized descriptions of phenomena (putative empirical laws). And if such generalizations are to be knowable—hence if science can yield general knowledge—it must be possible to justify such generalizations on the basis of singular knowledge obtained via direct observation. According to logical positivism, such justification is provided by a process of *inductive confirmation,* for the most part via probabilistic inductive logics which, if successful, could confer nonzero probabilities on generalizations.[11] Although not stressed by positivists, such an approach required giving up the classical empiricist demand that the evidence justifying knowledge render it incorrigible or certain—but this is no more than making the same concession for generalized knowledge that positivism already had made for singular knowledge when it adopted physicalism.[12]

Although logical positivism's empiricist doctrines deviate significantly from the eighteenth-century empiricism of Hume and others, it is illuminating to notice how similar these two empiricist views are. Both begin by postulating a body of *base knowledge* which can be obtained via observation, maintaining that all other a posteriori knowledge must be based upon this base knowledge. In both cases *nonbasic a posteriori knowledge* is obtained via cognitive operations. For Hume these operations are those of associating ideas and discerning relations which hold between them; for the positivists these operations are those of defining or otherwise partially specifying the meanings of nonbasic assertions in terms of observation language assertions which give expression to such basic knowledge.[13] Also, in both cases the base knowledge provided by experience was logically prior to the formation of theories or other operations of human understanding, and thus is not conditioned by one's theoretical beliefs or scientific prejudices. Finally, both versions of empiricism are committed to the view that only induction can yield general knowledge of the sort science purports to provide.

For present purposes, the most significant differences between eighteenth-century empiricism and the empiricism of logical positivism are three: First, the former requires that experience yield evidence justifying knowledge sufficiently strong to render such knowledge incorrigible (hence certain), whereas the latter only requires that knowledge be corrigibly justified with high probability. Second, eighteenth-century empiricism construes base knowledge as knowledge of sensory experiences, whereas positivism construes it as knowledge of directly observable objects and attributes. Third, Hume denies that induction can yield knowledge, whereas logical positivism is committed to the possibility that induction is sufficient to justify knowledge. This latter difference of opinion is a reflection of the positivists' differing views on how strongly knowledge must be justified by evidence.

Both the earlier empiricism's and logical positivism's versions allow a limited amount of epistemic relativity. Depending on the circumstances of life, a person will observe different things, hence will come to know different facts observationally. However, in principle, all normal observers *could* observe the same things and so come to know the same facts regardless of their scientific or other theoretical beliefs. With respect to nonbasic knowledge obtained through reasoning, or the exercise of human understanding, people are not equally creative, or insightful, and so different people will come to know different things as a result of reasoning from premises provided by observation. However, in principle, all rational persons possessing the same base knowledge could come to have the same a posteriori base knowledge. Thus the sum total of a posteriori knowledge possessed by humans ultimately proves consistent and accessible in principle to all rational observers.

To this general empiricist view, logical positivism adds the postulation of a neutral observation language adequate for expressing all observational base knowledge. It also requires that all theoretical language be partially definable in terms of that neutral observation language. Thus regardless of theoretical persuasion, all assertions of putative a posteriori knowledge can be compared and assessed using the neutral observation language. Thus the epistemic relativity allowed by positivism is quite benign, amounting to limited differences in what is known resulting from differences in sensory and cognitive experience.

II. FEYERABEND'S VIEWS

During the 1960s, positivism's views on scientific observation came under heavy attack on two fronts: First, a number of authors (most notably Achinstein and Putnam) argued that the observational/theoretical term distinction was untenable, since the descriptive terms of science generally could be used to refer to both directly observable and nondirectly observable entities and attributes (recall ch. 2). Second, Henson, Feyerabend, and Kuhn developed philosophical theories of observation wherein it was claimed that "observation is theory-laden"; this view, inter alia, entails denials of the observational/theoretical distinction, of a neutral observation language, and of sense-data theories of perception.[14]

Feyerabend mounted his attack against positivistic (and earlier empiricist) treatments of observation in his work entitled "An Attempt at a Realistic Interpretation of Experience."[15] He used this article to develop his own views on observation, and only they concern us here. According to him, science does distinguish (roughly) theory and observation, and thus an observation language is one which is acceptable as a means for describing the results of observations and experiments. Observation languages are characterized relative to a class C of observers: An atomic *sentence* (not statement) a belongs to the observation language A of a class C of observers if and only if (1) there exists a situation S such that any member of C, when presented with S and a, quickly will run through a series of states and operations which terminates in the acceptance or rejection of a; (2) if a is accepted (or rejected) by any member of C when confronted with S, it will be accepted (or rejected) by virtually every C; (3) the acceptance or rejection of a must be causally dependent upon S. The class of such a is a class of observable sentences for C. Thus observable sentences are those where there are phenomena which cause a consensus of members of C to assent to or reject the sentence. But, according to Feyerabend, such assent or dissent is to *uninterpreted* sentences, and such assent or dissent leaves open the question of the interpretation of the sentence and is compatible with different members of C assigning different interpretations to the sentence. Such interpretations endow the sentences with *ontological consequences;* that is, the interpretation of a language postulates the existence of particulars which the interpreted sentences "fit" or describe.[16]

How do we determine which interpretation is appropriate for the sentences of the observation language? Feyerabend's view is that experience can play no decisive role in such a determination: "No set of observations is ever sufficient for us to infer (*logically*) any one of those interpretations (problem of induction)."[17] Intuitively, a correct interpretation would be one where the accepted interpreted sentences correctly describe the phenomena which caused their acceptance. Although Feyerabend is rather unclear as to what these phenomena are (sensations or objects which are experienced), it is clear that correctness of interpretation here is being construed as some sort of *correspondence* notion, where a correct interpretation will be one in which all and only the true interpreted sentences are accepted, and truth is construed in terms of correspondence with (or "fitting") the phenomena.[18]

However, according to Feyerabend, there is no way experience can show that such a correspondence obtains, hence no way experience can reveal that an interpretation is correct or that the accepted interpreted sentences are true. Essentially, his arguments are that experience could not supply the interpretation, because this would require that the experience contain the entertainment and acceptance of the sentence, the phenomenon, and the "fitting relationship"—but this "fitting" would itself be the "fitting" of his assertion that the first sentence fit the first phenomenon. Thus in order to be accepted, this fitting assertion must also fit the second fitting phenomenon—which would require a third fitting phenomenon, and so on, into an infinite regress.[19] Thus there is no way the experience of phenomena can reveal the correctness of an interpretation of an observation language. Furthermore, if the interpretation is supplied prior to the experience of a phenomenon, there is no way that the truth of the interpreted sentence assented to can be revealed or displayed as a result of experiencing the phenomenon.

It follows, then, that there is no way sensory experience can be used to determine the truth or falsity of interpreted observation sentences, although the experience of the phenomena determines the acceptance or rejection of such interpreted sentences.[20] Since it cannot be supplied by experience, "the interpretation of an observation-language is determined by the theories which we use to explain what we observe, and it changes as soon as those theories change." Thus "the terms of a theory and the terms of an observation-langauge used for the tests of that theory give rise to exactly the same logical (ontological) problems. *There is no special 'problem of theoretical entities'.*"[21] That is, one can no more be sure of the existence of the entities described by observation language statements than one can about the existence of theoretical entities. To put the point in a way Feyerabend never does (but which is highly revealing of his position), experience is incapable of playing any significant role in ascertaining the truth of either theoretical or observational assertions.

A number of comments about this view need to be made. First, it is highly reminiscent of Berkeley's view on material objects. Berkeley uses similar considerations to argue that experience is insufficient to guarantee the existence of external physical objects described by language. But whereas he goes on to maintain that it is illegitimate to postulate their existence, Feyerabend is willing to continue *assuming*

their existence but denies they can play any significant role in epistemology. This is why Feyerabend is a Pickwickian realist, while Berkeley
is an idealist.

Second, it now is clear that Feyerabend is a realist only in the ontological sense that he is willing to grant the existence of physical objects.
But he denies any *epistemological realism* in which *the way physical
objects are* plays *any* significant role in knowledge (other than possibly
causing the assent or rejection of observation language sentences, and
whether it does can only be a matter of conjecture on his view). His
position seems to be that since experience cannot determine whether
an interpreted sentence correctly describes or "fits" physical objects,
such a correspondence notion of truth can play *no* role in epistemology.
This is reflected in his practice of referring to the accepted observation
reports as knowledge;[22] thus he is rejecting what usually is a central
ingredient to a realistic epistemology.

Third, as with Berkeley, the sorts of arguments he offers in defense
of his position lend support to the contention that truth via correspondence can play no significant role in an account of knowledge,
only if one accepts the K-K Thesis ('S knows that P' entails 'S knows
that he knows that P'). For if this thesis is accepted, then from the fact
that experience cannot show that such a correspondence holds and from
the vaguely plausible assumption (tacit in his discussion) that such a
correspondence could not be known except if displayed in experience,
it would follow that one cannot know that P is true; hence one cannot
know that he knows that P; hence via the K-K Thesis, one cannot know
that P. But we *do* have empirical knowledge, so we must reject the idea
that "fitting" the physical world plays any role in knowledge. But this
argument (and I can think of no other one compatible with what he
says that will serve his purposes) depends *essentially* on the K-K Thesis,
for if it is denied, the requirement of truth by correspondence is totally
compatible with Feyerabend's other claims: One can experientially *know*
that P, where P "fitting" or corresponding to the physical world is a
condition of knowledge, but one cannot *know that one knows* that P.[23]
We will see later that the fact that correspondence plays no role in his
epistemology is a key source of the extreme epistemic relativism characteristic of his position; and if, as I am willing to concede, he is correct
that experience cannot *display* the truth of observation reports, then
his tacit acceptance of the K-K thesis is a crucial source of his extreme
epistemic relativism.

Fourth, the comparison of Feyerabend and Berkeley can be pushed
even further, for in his treatment of observation, Feyerabend essentially
is presenting Berkeley's view (as modified by his espousal of meta-

physical realism), except that he in effect is maintaining that Berkeley's arguments that correspondences between ideas (interpreted sentences) and physical objects can play no role in epistemology also apply to sensory phenomena as well: Correspondence between ideas (interpreted sentences) and sensory experience is just as problematic, hence has no legitimate place in an epistemology of perception. Thus no a posteriori knowledge is incorrigible, not even knowledge of experience.[24]

Fifth, there are important similarities and differences between Feyerabend's views and those of physicalistic logical positivism. The latter postulates a neutral observation language, interpreted realistically as making assertions about the "external world," although such assertions are nonproblematic in that a consensus could be reached among proponents of competing theories. This consensus makes such observation language assertions neither incorrigible nor certain in the sense required by eighteenth-century British empiricism, nor does acceptance guarantee that the accepted assertions correspond with the "external world" (though realistically inclined physicalists such as Carnap tacitly assumed they always did so correspond). Further, physicalistic logical positivism postulates that all persons speaking the neutral observation language supply the same interpretations to its sentences. Similarly, Feyerabend accepts the idea that observation languages characteristically enjoy intersubjective agreement as to which sentences are to be accepted or rejected, but that such agreement is restricted to limited groups—different "social" groups will accept different bodies of sentences, and within a group the members need not give the same interpretation to the accepted and rejected sentences. Thus both an uninterpreted and an interpreted neutral observation language are impossible. In addition, although the interpretation of the accepted sentences entails ontological commitments, different members of the same or different groups will be making different ontological commitments, and there is no guarantee these commitments correspond to the actual world.

Since Feyerabend accords the accepted (interpreted) sentences the status of knowledge, his position commits him to an extensive epistemological relativism; and since such differential knowledge clearly yields differential knowledge claims, he also is committed to an epistemic-avowal relativism. However, this does not commit him to a metaphysical relativism unless he also is committed to the view that to know that ϕ, ϕ must be true *in a correspondence* sense—a view he has *not* committed himself to and which he apparently would deny. Although this leaves us with a very unclear, completely unspecified idea of what he understands knowledge to be, it does not commit him to anything like the subjective idealism he has been accused of by some of his critics, including myself.[25] In short, Feyerabend's views on observation amount to an extreme skeptical extension of eighteenth-century empiricism coupled with an epistemically gratuitous espousal of metaphysical realism.

We have seen that, according to Feyerabend, observation is theory-laden in the sense that the theories we use to explain what we observe determine the interpretation of observation sentences. How does such interpretation occur? Interpretation is the specification or determination of meaning, and so we must turn to Feyerabend's views on meaning. We explore the issue chronologically. His initial view was as follows:

> The meaning of *every* term we use depends upon the theoretical context in which it occurs. Words do not 'mean' something in isolation; they obtain their meanings by being part of a theoretical system. Hence if we consider two contexts with basic principles that either contradict each other or lead to inconsistent consequences in certain domains, it is to be expected that some terms of the first context will not occur in the second with exactly the same meaning.[26]

But this understates his view, for by 'theory' he means *global theories,* and "to express it more radically, each theory will possess its own experience, and there will be no overlap between these experiences. Clearly a crucial experience now is impossible . . . because there is no universally accepted *statement* capable of expressing whatever emerges from observation."[27] Such theories are *incommensurable* in the sense that the meanings of their descriptive terms depend upon mutually inconsistent principles.[28] Thus Feyerabend is committed to the view that *any* change in a (global) theory changes *all* the meanings of its terms, hence alters the interpretation of the observation language. But as Achinstein has noted, this makes science analytic: Every statement of a theory is constitutive of the meanings of the terms of the theory and of the observation language.[29]

Such a consequence of Feyerabend's meanings doctrines is prima facie incompatible with his views on the growth of scientific knowledge. Following Hume and Popper, he denies that induction is capable of providing general knowledge or of establishing the truth of theories or generalizations;[30] this denial is a reflection of the fact (noted earlier) that theories are logically prior to the interpretation of the observation language, hence are presuppositions of any observational evidence which induction could exploit. Differently put, if induction were capable of establishing the truth of theories on the basis of experience, then (since the theory provides the interpretation of observation language reports) experience would be capable of establishing the correctness of interpretations of observation language statements—something he denies. This view, together with his meaning and observation doctrines, seems to lead to the position that theories are self-certifying and thus any global theory is as acceptable as any other. That is, Feyerabend's views appear to commit him to the view that there is no objective way to decide on the basis of experience between competing theories. Thus, rather than dogmatically asserting a single theory, science ought to encourage the *proliferation of theories,* and these theories will be pitted against experience and against each other in the attempt to "falsify them." Out of such competition some theories will survive, but their survival does nothing to establish their truth; hence it is essential that science continue to proliferate theories and develop new alternatives in the effort to falsify those theories which have withstood the trials of experience and testing.[31]

But such a doctrine seems incompatible with his meaning and observation doctrines: Achinstein charges that since theories provide the interpretation of the observation language and are analytically true, any observation report which would possibly falsify the theory will be analytically false; thus he concludes that experiential falsification of (global) theories is impossible on Feyerabend's view.[32] In the end, this charge is unwarranted, however, for Feyerabend's theory of observation allows the possibility that an observer may be caused by experience to reject an observation sentence which is a logical consequence of the theory, where the interpretation of the sentence provided by that theory makes the rejected statement analytically true. Thus Feyerabend's view does allow for conflict between theory and observation, hence for the observational test of theories; but such conflicts must take the form of rejecting analytically true assertions on the basis of experience under circumstances where one knows that the rejected assertion is a logical consequence of the theory. One who did this while accepting Feyerabend's meaning doctrines (and their consequences) would have to be rejecting *on the basis of experience* a proposition which one *knew* to be analytically true. Experiential falsification thus is possible on Feyerabend's view but involves *fundamentally irrational behavior.*

Feyerabend's proliferation and falsification views also require the testing of competing theories against each other as a means of assessing their comparative merits—for example, by finding experiential circumstances where the predictions of one theory are upheld by experience, whereas the predictions of another are denied by the same experience. Several commentators have charged that Feyerabend's meaning doctrines preclude this possibility, for how can the competing predictions of the theory be assessed against the same observation report, if that observation report would have to assign the same meanings to its constituent terms as the two theories have done? This is impossible since, according to the meaning doctrines, two different (global) theories must assign different meanings to each term they have in common.[33] Feyerabend has protested (rightly, I believe) that this objection is misguided, that the sort of comparability his view requires does not require that the predictions of a theory be compared against an observation *statement* that is neutral with respect to the two theories.[34] For on his view of observation it is possible that advocates of different theories may possess the same observation language (the same stock of *uninterpreted* sentences) and give or withhold assent to the same observation sentences on the basis of the same experiences.

And this is wholly compatible with these observers subscribing to different theories which provide different interpretations for the observation sentences. For example, suppose that S_1 and S_2 subscribe to incommensurable theories T_1 and T_2 respectively. Suppose that T_1 entails the observation *sentence* O and T_2 entails not-O. S_1 and S_2 now can have the same experience which causes them *both* to accept the sentence O. And they can do this despite the fact that in rejecting not-O, as interpreted by T_2, S_2 is not affirming what O asserts, as interpreted by T_1. Thus S_1 and S_2 can both agree that their experience requires the acceptance of O, hence that T_1 is preferable to T_2, since T_1 (but not T_2) entails sentence O which their experience has caused both S_1 and S_2 to accept; and they can do so without having to attach the same meanings to the terms in O.

Thus it is not surprising to find Feyerabend (1965) defending his comparability views as follows:

> T and T' are still incommensurable. Yet it is possible, to a high degree of approximation, to establish an isomorphism between certain selected semantical properties of some (not all) descriptive statements of T' and some (not all) descriptive statements of T (let the corresponding classes be C and C', respectively [*sic*]). . . . Considering that meanings are dependent on structure and not on the particular ways in which the structure is realized, we may say that, within the restrictions given, C and C' have a common core of meaning. We may even identify C and C'. (As $C \neq T$ and $C' \neq T'$, this does not affect the relation between T and $T' \dots$). . . . But the very method of rigging indicates that the demand is superfluous: when making a comparative evaluation of classical physics and of general relativity we do not compare meanings; we investigate the

conditions under which a structural similarity can be obtained. If these conditions are contrary to fact, then the theory that does not contain them supersedes the theory whose structure can be mimicked only if the conditions hold (it is now quite irrelevant in what theory and, therefore, in what terms the conditions are formed). ... [T]he fact that argument proceeded even through the most fundamental upheavals, that it was undisputed and that it led to results shows the meanings cannot be that essential. [Reprinted in Grandy 1973, 182–83]

Such a defense of comparability is allowed by Feyerabend's original positions on observation, meaning, and incommensurability only because his position allows the irrational rejection of propositions known to be analytically true discussed above. Thus, the comparability of competing theories allowed by his view is equally irrational.

In granting Feyerabend the above interpretation of the foregoing passage in response to objections against his "comparability" doctrines, I have been most charitable—and in the estimation of some, excessively charitable. For essential to the defense just offered of Feyerabend's position is granting him the supposition that every observer "has an inbuilt syntactic machinery that *imitates* (but does not describe) certain features of our experience."[35] This concession is weighty, since to suppose that no interpretation is involved in the syntactic decomposition into phonemes, let alone sentences, is to concede very much indeed. In effect, it is to grant to Feyerabend that, although there is no neutral "interpreted" observation language, there is a *common* syntactical language which can be presupposed in the comparison of theories. Although such a supposition is weaker than that of the positivist's "neutral observation language," it is not that much weaker. As Shapere (1966, 59–62) argues (albeit not as clearly as he could have), this not only concedes to the positivist most of what Feyerabend wants to take back, but also is incompatible with his general doctrines on incommensurability. Thus my defense of Feyerabend here, at best, is an exegetical one which, although circumventing some specific criticisms based on exegetical mistakes, does nothing to vindicate Feyerabend's overall program.

Something more needs to be said about the passage quoted above. I have interpreted this passage as involving no retreat from Feyerabend's early extreme meaning doctrines. Other commentators (e.g., Achinstein and Shapere) interpret this and other passages as involving a change in his views on meaning. His new view is asserted to be that different theories can have some meanings in common, where such commonality of meaning is determined by isomorphism conditions. So interpreted, Feyerabend's view is liable to the objection that given the principles of a theory, there will be a number of ways to collect items discussed by principles into classes; thus a wide variety of isomorphism conditions is possible. Hence, Feyerabend's isomorphism conditions do not enable us to determine the sameness or difference of meanings between theories, since they do not enable us to distinguish trivial cases, where meanings are constant, from interesting ones where they are not.[36] The middle portion of the quotation does lend some credence to this interpretation of Feyerabend,[37] and if it is correct, the objections are weighty indeed.

However, as I have already suggested, to defend his comparability doctrines, Feyerabend *need not* retreat from his early extreme meaning doctrines. This realization suggests that in the disputed passage Feyerabend may not be committing himself to a change in his meaning doctrines, for what he concedes about the possibility of common meanings in the middle of the passage he tends to take back toward the end. His point seems to be that sameness or difference of meaning is *irrelevant* to the comparability of theories—as I have suggested in my defense of his comparability claims. Thus I am inclined to interpret the quoted passage, and other similar passages elsewhere, as not involving any significant retreat from, or attenuation of, his original extreme meaning doctrines. Whatever the correct interpretation, I think it should be clear that his general view is somewhat more plausible if he does not retreat from his original position.[38]

It is true that Feyerabend recently has modified and extended his views about how science *ought* to proceed in proliferating theories, attempting to show how it is "reasonable" for proponents of a theory to persist in the acceptance of a theory in the face of falsifying or incompatible experience and adopting a position which he says is a reinterpretation of Lenin's political views.[39] These changes and extensions seem to involve only one significant retreat from his earlier doctrines: Whereas his earlier views followed Popper in stressing the falsification of theories on the basis of conflicts between a theory's predictions and accepted observation reports, Feyerabend now denies that the acceptance of observation reports enjoys such a privileged place. Rather, he asserts, when theory and an accepted observation report are in conflict, one may either reject the theory, reject the accepted observation report, or resort to ad hoc hypotheses which erase the conflict; all are equally legitimate prima facie. Although these changes signal significant revisions of Feyerabend's methodological views (propelling him toward dialectical materialism), they do not involve any significant revisions of his basic epistemological doctrines. Hence we may ignore his later methodological views here.

Feyerabend's views lead to an extreme epistemic-avowal relativism, and since he tacitly equates knowledge with knowledge claims, this epistemic-avowal relativism is an epistemological relativism as well. Knowledge claims are in the form of statements (interpreted sentences). Although experience can cause perceivers to accept or reject statements, experience cannot supply the interpretations of sentences contained in such statements; rather, such interpretations must be supplied by logically prior theories which completely determine the meanings, hence the interpretations, of observation sentences. Thus possessors of different theories cannot give expression to the same observational facts; and there is no way that experience can evidence the truth of observation statements, since experience cannot indicate the appropriate interpretation of the accepted and rejected sentences of an observation language. Induction is denied, and so experience cannot provide evidence which supports or evidences the truth of general assertions such as scientific theories.

In short, empirical truth can play no significant role in epistemology, and experience is utterly irrelevant to the assessment of the truth of empirical assertions. Only in a Pickwickian sense is a posteriori knowledge possible at all. The result is that epistemology reduces to *belief* in theories and obervations which never can be supported by experience. Acceptance of such beliefs should not be uncritical, since there can be conflicts between the observation sentences entailed by a theory and the observation sentences that experience causes an observer to accept. And under at least some circumstances, such conflicts should result in the rejection of a theory (one's system of beliefs) in favor of some alternative. Through such a process of proliferation and rejection of theories it is possible that a theory eventually may be obtained which entails all and only those observation sentences which the observer accepts on the basis of experience. But even if such a theory were obtained, nothing would follow from it as to whether the theory correctly described reality; nothing could be concluded about the factual truth either of the theory or of the accepted observation sentences as interpreted by the theory.[40] For it is entirely possible that different persons will be caused to accept and reject different classes of observation sentences on the basis of their experiences; and so nothing follows as to the truth of theories from their complete agreement with the accepted observation sentences. In short, the most that it is possible to conclude from Feyerabend's views is that from the process of "pitting" theories against observational experience, one ultimately may come to accept a theory which is in perfect coherence with the observation sentences one accepts on the basis of experience. But alternative such coherent systems of belief legitimately can be called knowledge, so an open-ended variety of knowledge is possible wherein different people can know theories which cannot be true of one and the same world. Such is the extreme epistemic relativism that results from Feyerabend's position. Finally, it should be noted that this extreme relativism is a rather straightforward corollary to his theory of observation and that his defense of that theory depends essentially on his tacit acceptance of the K-K thesis.

III. KUHN'S VIEWS

Qua philosopher of science, Thomas Kuhn has focused on the development and defense of a historically based analysis of the growth of scientific knowledge. On this analysis, science for the most part qualifies as *normal science:* a *scientific community* sharing the same theory (which Kuhn variously calls a *paradigm* or a *disciplinary matrix*) focuses its attention on further articulating the theory and solving various puzzles raised by it. Occasionally, the puzzles concerning the theory prove to be intractable anomalies, and this causes the scientific community to call the theory into question, consider alternatives to it, and so on. At this point, where normal science ceases and a *scientific revolution* is in progress, workers in the field do not share, or give allegiance to, the same theory; rather, different practitioners are working with and advocating a variety of "incommensurable" alternative theories as candidates for replacing the previously held theory. This revolutionary proliferation of theories continues until one of them begins to emerge as victor and a new scientific community coalesces around, and gives allegiance to, that theory. Normal science then reemerges, with the scientific community again attempting to further articulate the successor theory and to solve various puzzles it raises.[41] Underlying Kuhn's account of the growth of scientific knowledge is a view of scientific knowledge remarkably like Feyerabend's—despite the fact that their views on the growth of scientific knowledge are radically different.[42]

However, whereas Feyerabend's views on the nature of scientific knowledge have been formulated fairly explicitly, Kuhn's views are, for the most part, only implicit in *The Structure of Scientific Revolutions* and must be extrapolated from that work with the aid of his various more recent attempts to clarify his position.[43] For the most part, his views on the nature of scientific knowledge are to be found in his characterization of normal science, and the extent to which these views lead to epistemic and metaphysical relativity is to be found in his discussion of scientific revolutions.

From an epistemological perspective, a major task of Kuhn's discussion of normal science is developing an analysis of theory and observation, for Kuhn denies both the positivistic analysis of theories (the Received View) and the observational/theoretical distinctions it embodies. Recall from section I that according to the positivists, there is a neutral observation language which can express all observation reports. Theories are attached to nature via *correspondence rules* which specify the observational consequences of the theory and (partially) define the meanings of the theoretical terms showing up in the formulas of *symbolic generalizations* of the theory. Kuhn denies that theories attach to nature in such a way. For it is characteristic of normal science that theories are attached to nature in an open-ended variety of ways, employing new versions of symbolic generalizations which immediately are recognized by members of the scientific community as appropriate. In principle, no set of rules is adequate to specify the allowed variety of attachments of symbolic generalizations to nature. Rather, such attachments are modeled on similar *exemplars* (archetypal applications of theory to phenomena, a stock of which is the common possession of a scientific community), where such similarity is assessed not by rules but by a learned *resemblance relation;* this resemblance relation is acquired during one's scientific training and apprenticeship from the study of exemplars.

This resemblance relation also determines the meanings of the terms in, hence the interpretation of, the symbolic generalizations of the theory; and it also provides a means for classifying experiences by grouping shared experiences together on the basis of their resemblance as determined by the resemblance relationship. Such experiences include those of observation, so the theory determines the organization of one's observations—determines what it is that one observes or sees. Theories (or as he now tends to call them, *disciplinary matrixes*) are construed as comprising the organized combination of symbolic generalizations, values, beliefs in particular models (the most basic of which constitute ontological commitments such as, e.g., "heat is the kinetic energy of constituent parts of bodies"), a stock of exemplars, and, presumably, the resemblance relationship or the meanings it determines.[44] Thus "observation is theory-laden" in a way that entails the denial of the positivistic neutral observation language and also its observational/theoretical distinctions.

Kuhn's most sustained attempt to specify his views on observation is in Kuhn 1974. There he asks us to consider an admittedly oversimplified case where a boy, Johnny, and his father are at the zoo, and his father points out various ducks, geese, swans, and other birds to him, giving their names; gradually, with some mistakes, Johnny learns reliably to call various large white birds by their correct names when confronted with sensory stimuli of ducks, geese, and so on. Kuhn characterizes this as the acquisition of a *learned resemblance relation* by virtue of which Johnny comes to group certain stimuli of birds together and with the appropriate name, and he does so as a result of being exposed to various exemplars (Johnny's father pointing out birds and giving their names). According to Kuhn, the same general process will work in learning how to apply sentences or previously uninterpreted symbolic generalizations to nature (sensory stimuli?), and thus it explains how the study of exemplars teaches one to apply uninterpreted symbolic generalizations to sensory stimuli and to nature.[45] Throughout this discussion Kuhn explicitly construes symbolic generalizations as *uninterpreted*—that is, as sentences in Feyerabend's sense.[46]

Kuhn's analysis here is remarkably similar to Feyerabend's treatment of observation, for Kuhn is maintaining that as one comes to belong to a scientific community, one's sensory stimuli cause one to give assent to, or dissent from, the same characteristic uninterpreted sentences of symbolic generalizations as others in the community do. The class of sentences to which such assent or dissent normally is given is what Feyerabend calls an observation language. However, Kuhn and Feyerabend apparently disagree over how such sentences (as well as others) in a language are interpreted—how meanings are assigned to the sentences and their constituent terms. Whereas on Feyerabend's view these interpretations cannot be supplied by one's sensory experiences, Kuhn's learned resemblance relation, obtained at least in part from experience via the study of exemplars, plays an essential role in associating phenomena together and providing meanings or interpretations for symbolic generalizations.

The difference here, though, may be more apparent than real, for acquiring a resemblance relationship, on Kuhn's account, does not seem to fall under *any* of the ways experience could supply interpretations that Feyerabend considers; thus the available evidence does not enable us to determine the extent of agreement or disagreement between the two. Even though Kuhn is more explicit than Feyerabend (though not very) in specifying what he understands theories to be (his "disciplinary matrixes"), since he does construe exemplars, symbolic generalizations, and apparently the learned resemblance relations as constituents of theories, it is the case that both Kuhn and Feyerabend are committed to the view that theories supply the interpretation of observation language sentences, although they most probably do not agree on how this is accomplished.[47]

Another possible point of disagreement, which also turns out to be moot, concerns Kuhn's apparent view that the resemblance relation provides a "psychological set" which organizes one's sensory experiences (not sensory stimuli) of the world and thus determines what one sees or what one sees things as.[48] To my knowledge, Feyerabend never takes a position on whether the theory-supplied interpretation of the observation language in any way conceptually organizes sensory experiences into something akin to *Gestalten.* Minimally then, Kuhn and Feyerabend hold similar views on observation and the interpretation of (observation language) sentences, and Kuhn's view even may be a more specific elaboration of Feyerabend's view; but the evidence is inadequate to determine whether the latter possibility in fact is the case.

Kuhn clearly is committed to the view that observation yields knowledge and that in coming to learn to apply symbolic generalizations to nature, a person thereby acquires knowledge.[49] He asks, "How, then, do we acquire the knowledge of nature that is built into language? For the most part by the same techniques and at the same time as we acquire language itself, whether everyday or scientific."[50] Commenting on his use of 'knowledge', he says:

> Perhaps 'knowledge' is the wrong word, but there are reasons for employing it here. What is built into the neural process that transforms stimuli to sensations has the following characteristics: It has been transmitted through education; it has, by trial, been found more effective than its historical competitors in a group's current environment; and, finally, it is subject to change both through further education and through the discovery of misfits with the environment. Those are characteristics of knowledge, and they explain why I use the term. But it is strange usage, for one other characteristic is missing. We have no direct access to what it is we know, no rules or generalizations with which to express this knowledge. Rules which could supply that access would refer to stimuli not sensations, and stimuli we can know only through elaborate theory. In its absence, the knowledge embedded in the stimulus-to-sensation route remains tacit.[51]

What Kuhn offers as the characteristics of *knowledge* instead strikes me as being more characteristic of *knowledge claims,* or what is accepted as knowledge by groups of persons—even though authors who accept the K-K thesis typically identify claims to know justified by adequate evidence with knowledge per se. Kuhn apparently makes this identification and construes "justification by adequate evidence" as meaning "accepted by a social group sharing a common language and global theory," for he says, "I regard scientific knowledge as intrinsically a product of a congeries of specialists' communities."[52]

It is not entirely clear whether Kuhn understands knowledge to involve anything more than the collective belief of groups as reflected in commonality of linguistic usage, because there is good reason to interpret him as being committed to the view that knowledge is justified true belief. For one thing, Kuhn clearly views knowledge as belief, and his view that learning to use language is a source of knowledge can be construed as a doctrine on justification for observational knowledge. Clearly, he is committed to the view that observational knowledge is true: "Members of a given scientific community will generally agree which consequences of a shared theory sustain the test of experiment and are therefore true." Yet he understands truth in a special way here: " 'Truth' may, like 'proof', be a term with only intra-theoretic applications."[53] His is a coherence view of truth, wherein truth is a matter of coherence with the theory-interpreted observation-language reports accepted by members of a scientific community. In addition, Kuhn is quite explicit that this is not a correspondence notion of truth wherein truth involves correctly representing nature, or "what is really out there." His reason for rejecting a correspondence notion of truth is that "there is, I think, no theory-independent way to reconstruct phrases like 'really there'; the notion of a match between the ontology of a theory and its 'real' counterpart in nature seems to me illusive in principle."[54] His arguments in defense of his rejection of a correspondence notion of truth focus on showing that such correspondence cannot be ascertained. But nothing follows from these arguments about whether knowledge must be true in the correspondence sense—unless one takes recourse to the K-K thesis. Thus my earlier discussion of Feyerabend's rejection of a correspondence notion of truth for knowledge also applies to Kuhn. Kuhn's and Feyerabend's views on the nature of knowledge and truth thus are remarkably similar.

By contrast, their views on how relativistic this knowledge is are somewhat different, ultimately reflecting their differing views on how theory-laden they think meanings are. Kuhn's views on the relativism of knowledge emerge most clearly in his treatment of revolutionary science. Although he characterizes a scientific revolution as those periods in science when members of a scientific discipline or "community" are not working within a shared theory, it is equally legitimate to construe this notion as including various practitioners working from within different theories, none of which is widely accepted by the discipline.[55]

The latter way of putting the matter has the advantage of pointing out the extent to which the epistemology of normal science carries over to revolutionary science. It also serves to make the important point that revolutionary scientists *do* engage in many of the characteristic activities of normal science (solving puzzles concerning the replacement theory they advocate, further articulating the proffered theory, etc.) in the process of pushing the proposed replacement theories they are developing or helping to develop. Such a perspective does not mislead us about Kuhn's epistemological views, provided that we keep in mind that according to Kuhn, revolutionary scientists *also* engage in a variety of activities not usually encountered in normal science—for example, debate over the relative merits of competing theories, with a fair amount of miscommunication between partisans of different proposed replacement theories resulting from the "incommensurability" of those theories. The important point here is that to the extent that revolutionary scientists are committed to, or are propounding, a proposed alternative theory, the epistemology of Kuhn's normal science account applies to them; and viewed from the epistemological perspective, his treatment of scientific revolutions reveals the extent of epistemic and metaphysical relativism which results from his normal-science epistemological views.

Suppose we have two scientists working in the same revolutionary area of science, each propounding alternative theories T_1 and T_2. How might they (or an outsider committed to neither) compare the competing merits of their respective theories and thus come to decide which theory is correct? Kuhn rules out the possibility that any body of agreed-upon evidence could establish the truth or falsity of either theory; for he apparently denies the possibility of inductive confirmation, although he never says why.[56] He also denies that any theory can be decisively falsified by evidence, since in any conflict of a global theory and experiment, both theory and experiment can be challenged, and so an experimental "refutation" of a global theory cannot be a decisive refutation.[57] Nevertheless, to the extent that proponents of the two competing theories accept a common body of evidence (known interpreted observation language sentences), they can compare the respective abilities of the two theories to accommodate this body of evidence (though they may disagree as to which of this shared evidence an adequate theory should accommodate, which Kuhn construes as a conflict of values).

To what extent can proponents of the two theories share such a common body of evidence (have a shared stock of "facts")? In *The Structure of Scientific Revolutions*, Kuhn sometimes seems to be saying that this never is possible; for on occasion he appears to be maintaining Feyerabend's extreme meaning doctrines, hence that proponents of two competing global theories cannot attach the same meanings to any terms they have in common. Thus any (uninterpreted) observation language sentences they agree on will be given different interpretations by their respective theories, hence express different facts. Evidently, there is no shared body of evidence ("facts") they can resort to.

However, as I have argued elsewhere, I think this interpretation distorts Kuhn's views. He maintains, instead, a weaker thesis to the effect that global theories determine meanings in such a way that at least some of the terms they may have in common are given different interpretations.[58] In any case, he subsequently has adopted this latter position on meaning change.[59] Thus some provision exists for shared interpretation of terms in the observation language, hence for a common body of facts expressible in these terms. These shared meanings for terms also provide a common vocabulary for exploring the different meanings scientists respectively attach to other terms, which allows for the possibility that they may come to find there are further facts they can agree upon.[60] Accordingly, evidence *can* be used to compare the relative merits of competing alternative global theories in revolutionary science. Nevertheless, because his more recent position on meaning change is quite similar to the one Achinstein and Shapere interpret Feyerabend as retreating to, it is liable to the same sorts of objections they raise against Feyerabend. In the absence of a theory of sameness and difference of meaning, then, it does not appear that such objections can be answered satisfactorily.

Since Kuhn's epistemological views are quite similar to Feyerabend's, many, but not all, of the epistemic and metaphysical relativities characteristic of Kuhn's position are similar to those previously outlined in section II: Since Kuhn's views commit him to the K-K thesis, the resulting range of epistemic relativism and the range of epistemic-avowal relativism will be much the same as for Feyerabend. The epistemic relativism allowed here is indeed great and is in no way restricted by how the world really is. Members of a scientific community doing normal research or members of a revolutionary cell pushing the same proposed theory will be caused (via study of exemplars) to give assent to or dissent from various observation language sentences; these patterns of assent and dissent determine the meanings of observation language terms (whereas they do not for Feyerabend). To the extent that different patterns of assent and dissent are possible with respect to different vocabularies which classify experiences differently, a wide range of epistemic relativity is possible. The range of such relativity will be somewhat less than its range on Feyerabend's view, since the interpretation of the observation language provided by the theory (which includes the learned resemblance relation) is not completely independent of the pattern of assent and dissent. In addition, although it is possible, and usual, for adherents of theories to agree on the same experiential facts, this does not restrict the range of epistemic relativity since (through Kuhn's doctrines denying inductive confirmation and decisive falsification) a scientist may reject evidence that was once previously accepted. Thus evidence imposes no necessary restrictions on the acceptance of—hence the knowledge provided by—a theory. Most importantly, the epistemic relativity involved is such that knowledge is in no way restricted by the requirement that it must correspond to the way the world is.

Although Kuhn has been accused of being committed to an extreme metaphysical relativism which is a subjective idealism, this charge is unwarranted. While a Husserlian idealism *is* compatible with his position, just as it is for Feyerabend's (see n. 25), it is very unclear whether he in fact is committed to such an idealism and its attendant metaphysical relativity. For on the one hand, he persists in saying things such as "our world is populated in the first instance not by stimuli but by the objects of our sensations, and these need not be the same, individual to individual, or group to group," which tend to suggest such an idealism. But on the other hand, in the same discussion he postulates the immutability of stimuli between observers in such a way as to require that stimuli have objective existence in the sense of a metaphysical realism—which would seem to preclude an idealism.[61] His position on metaphysical relativity is impossible to discern from the evidence; but it turns out not to be terribly important, since he rejects the possibility that correspondence with the way the world is can play any role in knowledge, thus rendering both a metaphysical realism and a metaphysical idealism gratuitous and epistemically irrelevant.

Finally, I observe (without supporting argument) that Kuhn and Feyerabend both are committed to the denial of a logic of discovery, and this denial is intimately connected to their rejection of inductive confirmation and decisive falsification.

IV. KUHN AND FEYERABEND AS THE LAST DEFENDERS OF MORIBUND EMPIRICISM

Despite the fact that they differ radically on how the growth of scientific knowledge does and should proceed, Kuhn and Feyerabend hold remarkably similar views about scientific knowledge, and these views result in extreme epistemic and epistemic-avowal relativisms. Additionally, because of their doctrines on truth, nothing interesting in the way of a metaphysical relativism follows. The epistemic relativism which does result from their views is sufficient, I maintain, to render their views unacceptable. For it seems to me that science *is* an enterprise concerned with obtaining knowledge *about the world,* where this involves *correctly* describing how the world *is;* and their analyses of knowledge preclude this possibility. In short, I am maintaining that an adequate epistemology of science must restrict the relativism that scientific knowledge enjoys to types compatible with a correspondence notion of truth, where the correspondence is to a world construed realistically — a world of nonintentional particulars.

It is not my intention in this chapter to defend or argue these deeply held philosophical convictions about scientific knowledge which prompt me to reject their treatments of knowledge and embrace a scientific quasi-realism. Rather, my focus here is to explore what the failures of Kuhn's and Feyerabend's epistemologies can tell us about what a viable epistemology (embodying the philosophical prejudices just stated) would look like. The most effective way of doing so is, I think, to construe Kuhn and Feyerabend as being empiricism's last bastion of defense. The following scenario (most of which can be filled in by the preceding discussions) makes such a construal quite plausible: Empiricism is an attempt to show how science is capable of yielding knowledge of the world; knowledge is construed as belief justified by experience so as to escape Cartesian skeptical doubts, where those skeptical doubts invariably focus on showing that the person S who claims to know P does not know that the available evidence is sufficient to preclude the falsity of P, from which it is concluded that S does not really know that P. This attack by the skeptics presupposes two requirements conceded by British empiricism: (1) a justified true belief analysis of knowledge wherein the justification must *guarantee* the truth of P and (2) the K-K thesis, which is required to make the inference that S does not know that P from the fact that S does not know that the evidence S has constitutes such a justification.

British empiricism attempted to show that science could not only yield knowledge consistent with these two epistemic strictures, but could do so in such a way that it made knowledge representative of the world (via a correspondence or representative view of truth). It was maintained that an incorrigible base knowledge of sensations existed which could be exploited by the operations of human understanding to obtain the sort of knowledge science provides. But given empiricism's basic assumptions about knowledge mentioned earlier, via the K-K thesis, the thesis that knowledge is justified true belief, and the correspondence view of truth, it followed that in order to know that P, one had to know with certainty that P corresponded with the way the world was. A succession of arguments followed, advanced most notably by Berkeley and Hume, to the effect that for various classes of P, one could not know with certainty that P corresponded with the way the world was: This could not be done for any P descriptive of the physical world (as opposed to sensations), and it could not be done for any contingent generalizations (the impossibility of justifying induction). Thus on Hume's view, empiricism can only accommodate the singular knowledge of particular sensations.

In later logical positivism, realistic tendencies reasserted themselves by attempting to show that a modified empiricism could allow for knowledge of the physical world: If one allowed the justification for knowledge to confer merely high probability on P, and P was true in a correspondence sense, *that* would allow general scientific knowledge. Under the doctrine of physicalism, observation could yield base knowledge (rendered sufficiently justified by intersubjective agreement to qualify as knowledge), and recourse to an appropriate inductive-probability logic of confirmation would suffice to confer sufficiently high probability on true a posteriori generalizations so as to yield general knowledge, including (via the Received View on theories) theoretical knowledge. In effect, positivism accepted the correspondence notion of truth and the K-K thesis, but rejected the demand that the justifiction for knowledge that P be sufficient to guarantee the truth of P.

Subsequently, two connected sorts of criticisms were advanced against positivism which were designed to show that weakened justification would not be sufficient to circumvent the skeptic and allow for the possibility that science can yield the sort of knowledge it claims to produce.[62] Popper argued that inductive confirmation is impossible, hence that the positivistic approach cannot yield general knowledge. Kuhn and Feyerabend accepted this Popperian view and they further argued that consensus of opinion over which observation language assertions to accept or reject can differ from community to community, and so the acceptance and rejection of observation language sentences is not indicative of any correspondence holding between the accepted sentences and the way the world is. Thus, if a pervasive skepticism is to be avoided with respect to scientific knowledge, even the "high probability" criterion for justification is too strong. The most that can be insisted on is consistency between the accepted observation language sentences and one's other beliefs (including theoretical ones), and even this is not invariably insisted on.

Via the K-K thesis, to know that P one must know that P is true, which is to say, one must know that P corresponds with the way the world actually is—if one accepts a correspondence view of truth. Berkeley and Hume had argued that this could happen only with *P* descriptive of sensations, if certainty is insisted on. Having argued that these findings cannot be reversed by positivism's high-probability view of justification, Feyerabend goes on to argue (and Kuhn tacitly agrees) that regardless of the stance taken on how strong the justification must be, one cannot know that *P* descriptive of one's sensory experiences corresponds to one's experiences. Hence if a correspondence notion of truth is insisted on, a total skepticism results.

Refusing to accept such a skepticism, Kuhn and Feyerabend reject the correspondence notion of truth, instead adopting a coherence view of truth and justification for knowledge. (We have seen that these various critical arguments require recourse to the K-K thesis, as did the original skeptic's challenge and Berkeley's and Hume's earlier arguments restricting the scope of possible knowledge on the empiricist view). They thereby escape the Cartesian skeptical doubts about knowledge and come to a position whereby science *can* yield knowledge. But the knowledge allowed is highly relativistic and very Pickwickian, since such knowledge amounts to nothing other than coherent systems of belief, where a wide variety of ad hoc defense mechanisms are allowed in order to preserve consistency. This knowledge is also virtually independent of how the world actually is (the only control being how the world might influence one's beliefs involved in accepting and rejecting observation language assertions, and on their views it is impossible to ever show that the physical world exists, let alone exerts any such influence). In short, Kuhn and Feyerabend have worked from within the empiricist framework, gradually giving up more and more of the classical empiricist demands on knowledge in an attempt to allow science to be an epistemic enterprise; but in doing so, their key weapon is recourse to the K-K thesis, and so they are involved in a last-ditch effort to preserve a watered-down empiricism. Kuhn's and Feyerabend's highly unacceptable epistemic relativism is what empiricism reduces to in its most attenuated version. Their epistemologies are what a consistent eighteenth-century British empiricism ultimately reduces to—the last gasp of a moribund epistemology which, if one shares my philosophical instincts about what an adequate epistemology should be like, mercifully should be put to sleep.

V. TOWARD A VIABLE EPISTEMOLOGY OF SCIENCE

The foregoing empiricist scenario is overly sketchy, but I would maintain that the story it tells basically is true; and the first three sections of this chapter have attempted to sketch key portions of the evidence in favor of it. But this scenario also indicates that the empiricists were mistaken in accepting the K-K thesis: Had they not accepted it, the Cartesian skeptic's challenges could have been rejected as illegitimate, since these challenges depend essentially on the K-K thesis. Thus the various concessions as to what we cannot know (in a non-Pickwickian sense) granted to the skeptic by Berkeley, Hume, Kuhn, and Feyerabend need not have been made. All that the arguments supporting such concessions succeed in showing, if the K-K thesis is denied, is that we cannot establish that the correspondence conditions for truth are met in such cases; but nothing follows from this about whether the correspondence holds, hence nothing follows about whether one does in fact know. In short, the K-K thesis has showed up at virtually every crucial juncture as empiricism has proceeded toward complete capitulation to the skeptic; if the K-K thesis had not been granted, such capitulation need not have occurred. Empiricists surely are correct that our experience *does* play an important and essential epistemic role in obtaining scientific knowledge, but what our scenario indicates is that experience can make no contribution to scientific knowledge so long as the K-K thesis is accepted.

What I conclude from all this is that a viable epistemology of science, where experience plays an essential role in knowledge, must begin by denying the K-K thesis, thereby rendering the Cartesian skeptic's challenges question-begging; having done this, one next must reassess all the various concessions to the skeptic that empiricism has made. When such a reassessment has been made, I strongly suspect we will want to take back most of them (including relaxation of the requirement that the justification for knowledge must render the belief certain) and that in doing so, a viable epistemology of science can be developed. But such an epistemology will not be an empiricism since it denies the K-K thesis and thereby refuses to take the skeptic very seriously. And such an epistemology will be, I predict, fully consistent with the philosophical prejudices advanced in my rejection of Kuhn's and Feyerabend's views. The next three chapters will further explore the development of such a realistic epistemology for science.

NOTES

1. For a comprehensive critical discussion of them, see Suppe, 1977, 3–241, 617–49.

2. Cf. Suppe 1975, sec. IV, as well as Laudan 1977. Inter alia, the former indicates why positivism and the "subjective" views of Kuhn and Feyerabend

most appropriately are construed as belonging to the history of the philosophy of science rather than to contemporary philosophy of science.

3. Of course, the logic of discovery is claimed to be a logic of justification as well; nevertheless, it proves useful to distinguish these two views of induction in the manner that I have done.

4. Thus, e.g., in his *Essay Concerning Human Understanding,* Locke is fairly explicit that this is a key motive for developing his empiricist epistemology (see Locke's "The Epistle to the Reader," 1959, 14). It should be noted that this motive required misconstruing actual scientific practice of the time, treating it as being more inductivist than it actually was. Such empiricalization of science was common during this period and on occasion led to the falsification of texts. Cf., e.g., Cohen 1974 and Shapere 1974 for discussions of such revisionist history of science by philosophers.

5. Kant began his philosophical career more or less accepting the neo-Leibnizian rationalism of Christian Wolff; progressively, however, and largely in response to scientific considerations such as the Leibniz-Clarke dispute over absolute vs. relative space, he became increasingly critical of Wolffian rationalism and its ability to provide for the knowledge yielded by science. The "Transcendental Aesthetic" of his *Critique of Pure Reason* (1781, 1961) is largely shaped by the defects he found in rationalism's treatment of space. His rejection of empiricism was occasioned by Hume's arguments against induction.

6. Synthetic a priori principles are ones whose denials are not logical contradictions but yet must be true if we are to experience objects *as objects;* arguments establishing that they are presuppositions of the experience of objects as objects, hence true because we *do* experience objects as objects, are known as transcendental arguments.

7. Thus, e.g., Whewell maintained that even the simplest facts involve something of the nature of theory, which seems to anticipate Kuhn's and Feyerabend's view that observation is theory-laden; and like Kant he viewed ideas as conditioning sensory experience and allowed that Newton's laws of motion have the status of necessary truths.

8. The emergence of logical positivism is discussed in more detail in sec. I of Suppe 1974b. Subsequent developments in logical positivism discussed here appear in more detail in sec. II of the same work. A convenient but elementary dicussion of aspects of the various developments in the history of the philosophy of science discussed in the present chapter is provided by Losee 1980; unfortunately, no more comprehensive or advanced history of the philosophy of science presently exists.

9. Although positivists debated the relative merits of the sense-data and physicalistic construals of direct observation (see, e.g., Carnap 1932), they tended to view them as equivalent theses (cf. Carnap's comments in Carnap 1963a, 50–51). So far as I have been able to discern, they did not give any significant consideration to the question whether observational knowledge was incorrigible or not, though early on they were quite concerned with avoiding relativistic epistemological views. Physicalism clearly requires treating obser-

vation as corrigible. In general, the positivists concentrated on "logical" issues and devoted very little time to analyzing the nature of the knowledge yielded by direct observation. Cf. Suppe 1974b, 45–49, for a survey of what they do say on the issue.

10. For a helpful discussion of the instrumental tendencies in logical positivism and their influence on the emergence of the so-called Copenhagen interpretation of quantum theory, see Gardner n.d. Hempel 1958 provides the classical critical attack on the instrumentalistic version of logical positivism. More contemporary attacks are found in chs. 3 above and 11 below.

11. For a dissenting view, however, see Carnap 1945. His position there still has an epistemic role for induction in science.

12. For a detailed description of these various developments in the positivistic views about theoretical assertions in science (many of which are ignored here), cf. Suppe 1974b, sec. II, 1977a, 619–32. A convenient nonhistorical elementary source of information about various positivistic treatments of induction is B. Skyrms 1975.

13. The differences between Hume and the positivists in this respect are less significant than it may appear initially; during the eighteenth century, linguistic meanings were identified with ideas which either were obtained from experience or else constructed out of experience via the operations of human understanding. Thus there was a definitional component to the association of ideas.

14. For detailed discussion of these two lines of attack, cf. Suppe 1974b, secs. IV and V-B-1, and Suppe 1975.

15. Feyerabend 1958. The attacks essentially are his well-known ones on positivistic treatments of reduction (cf. Suppe 1974b, 1975).

16. Feyerabend 1958, 144–46, 148–49 et passim.

17. Ibid., 150; italics added. But notice that Feyerabend, in commenting later on his "pragmatic theory of observation" presented in the article under consideration, tends to identify the acceptance and rejection of observation sentences with "human experience" (cf. Feyerabend 1965a). For a discussion of this tension in Feyerabend's views, cf. Shapere 1966, 59–61.

18. Cf. Feyerabend 1958, esp. sec. 4.

19. Ibid., 155.

20. Ibid., sec. 5 et passim. It should be noted that Feyerabend does not explicitly discuss truth, though the views on the determination of truth for observation sentences attributed to him clearly are tacit in his discussion and follow from what he does say. For the purposes of this chapter it is important that these tacit views be made explicit.

21. Ibid., 163, 164; original italics.

22. Feyerabend 1970, 21–29, 47, 99 n. 21.

23. For further development of this possibility, see chs. 12 and 13. For additional arguments against the K-K thesis, see Suppe 1977a, 717–27.

24. Feyerabend 1958, 169.

25. Cf., e.g., Scheffler 1967, 19. Although he does not specifically level this charge against Feyerabend here, it is clear that Scheffler is making a general

charge against "subjectivist" views of science and that he does count Feyerabend as being among the "subjectivists."

If Feyerabend were to accept the common thesis that *knowledge is justified true belief,* where truth is interpreted in terms of some correspondence, a metaphysical relativism *would* result, where proponents of different theories are concerned with different worlds inhabited by different particulars. Such a metaphysical relativism would be compatible with his espousal of ontological realism, the result being a view not unlike Husserl's, where the world is not created out of "whole conceptual cloth," but the "essences" of particulars, or their kinds, would be conceptually organized.

26. Feyerabend 1965a, 180; italics added.

27. Ibid., 214. The interpretation which follows of the foregoing, and related, passages is the most standard one and is supported by the general thrust of Feyerabend's discussion. There is, however, contravening text: See Shapere 1966, 53–57, for a sensitive discussion of the exegetical problems, and a criticism of the various plausible exegetical positions. The primary alternative reading of Feyerabend's position, which Kuhn has embraced recently, is considered later in my discussion. Rather than attempt to sift all the exegetical evidence, I attribute the position discussed here to Feyerabend and the weaker position discussed below to Kuhn, the justification for this expedience being that whichever (problematic) exegesis of either is adopted, at least some of the objections apply.

28. Feyerabend 1965a, 227 n. 19.

29. See Achinstein 1968, 96.

30. Achinstein 1962, 63.

31. Ibid., 29–30. Later Feyerabend abandons this falsification view, maintaining that one should continue to proliferate and use "falsified" theories as well as those that have withstood empirical testing (Feyerabend 1970, 43 et passim).

32. Achinstein 1968, 96–97.

33. Ibid. Such counterarguments require interpreting (contra Feyerabend) the observation reports as *statements* rather than *uninterpreted sentences.* Shapere (1966, 57–58) raises criticisms which presuppose this interpretation; however, he also considers the "uninterpreted sentence" construal of observation reports and presents devastating criticisms against it (59–62). Thus the criticisms raised here focus on Achinstein's discussion, not Shapere's.

34. Cf. Feyerabend 1965 and 1965b.

35. Feyerabend 1965a, 214–15.

36. Achinstein 1968, 94–95; Shapere 1966, 62–65.

37. As Shapere (1966, 53–57) indicates, there is other textual evidence that supports this reading, although it does not cohere with the dominant themes in the Feyerabend corpus.

38. This is not to suggest, however, that his "original position" meaning doctrines are that plausible, for quite decisive objections have been raised against them by Shapere 1966, 59–62 et passim.

39. Feyerabend 1970b, and esp. 1970.

40. However, if one adopts a Husserlian sort of idealism (cf. n. 25 above), which is compatible with Feyerabend's views, this will not be so; but the relativistic conclusions which follow in the text below would not be affected.

41. The basic articulation of this view is to be found in Kuhn's 1962 book, *The Structure of Scientific Revolutions*. It is further developed in his "Postscript" to the revised edition of this book (1970b) and in other works of his (1970, 1970a, 1974). For a discussion of his 1974 work, see Suppe 1974, 500–17. For convenient detailed summaries of his views and the main criticisms of them, see Suppe 1974b, 135–51, 191–221. The identification of paradigms or disciplinary matrixes with theories here is based on Kuhn's comments in Suppe 1974, 500–01.

42. Whereas Kuhn sees science as being basically normal science punctuated by occasional scientific revolutions, Feyerabend deplores the dogmatically held allegiance to theoretical ideologies characteristic of normal science. He doubts that normal science actually occurs in science and maintains that even if it does, it should not; and to the extent it does occur, science should reform itself by driving out normal science and promoting the wholesale proliferation of theories we have seen him advocate. For a discussion of the differences between Feyerabend's and Kuhn's views, see Feyerabend 1970a; for a discussion of similarities in their underlying epistemological views, see Shapere 1966.

43. These recent attempts are his four articles cited in note 41 above. My discussion does not take into account his recent Thalheimer lectures on "Scientific Development and Lexical Change," given at Johns Hopkins University, November 12–19, 1984, since they have not been published and my access to them has been subject to the condition that I not quote from, or comment on, the presentation draft version.

44. See, e.g., Kuhn's postscript, sec. 2, to his 1970 book and also the discussion of his 1974 paper in Suppe (1974, 500–17).

45. For an explicit statement of the generalizability of his bird-naming case to whole sentences and the symbolic generalizations of science, see Kuhn's discussion in my 1974 book (503–04, passim). This discussion is part of his "reply" to my commentary (1974a) therein on his paper. In my commentary I criticize this generalization from terms to sentences, which is only implicit in his paper. There I also criticize Kuhn's instinct to reify this ability to discern resemblances as a "learned resemblance relation." Criticisms of similar reifying instincts are found in Shapere 1966, 70–71. Kuhn is in the process of working on these ideas again and gave his latest thoughts in his Thalheimer lectures, which have not been published (see n. 43 above).

46. Kuhn 1974, 464.

47. It is important to note that the foregoing comparison has been restricted to the interpretation of observation language sentences (in Feyerabend's sense). This is because neither Kuhn nor Feyerabend has much to say about the interpretation of nonobservation language sentences found in a theory. Indeed, it is unclear whether they think there *are* any such sentences; since they allow observation language sentences to contain "theoretical" terms, it very well

may be the case that except for generalizations, etc., of these, they deny that there are any a posteriori nonobservation sentences. Their extreme incorrigibility views suggest, but do not establish, that this might be the case.

48. It is not clear which of these options Kuhn is committed to, but it is clear from the following that he is committed to at least one of them. See Kuhn 1970b, "Postscript," 192, 194, 195, 197–98, and Kuhn 1970a, 274–76, for the evidence. The extent to which Feyerabend is committed to such a view is unclear. However, Shapere (1966, 59–60) offers evidence to the effect that at least some such commitment has been incurred by Feyerabend.

49. Cf. Kuhn 1970b, 175, 196, and Kuhn 1970a, 253, 265, 272, 275.

50. Kuhn 1970a, 270.

51. Kuhn 1970b, 196. Discussion surrounding this and the previously quoted passage makes it clear that both are concerned with the same sense of 'knowledge'.

52. Kuhn 1970a, 253.

53. Ibid., 264; ibid., 266.

54. Kuhn 1970b, 206. His most sustained defense of this view is found in Kuhn 1970a, 264–66.

55. This is not to say that all practitioners are working from within some theory.

56. Certain passages suggest he is accepting Popper's arguments against inductive confirmation (see Kuhn 1970, 12, 13, et passim, for the suggestive evidence).

57. Kuhn, 1970, sec. III, esp. 13.

58. See Suppe 1974b, sec. V-B-2-a.

59. See Kuhn 1970b, 198. Cf., however, n. 27 above.

60. Cf. Kuhn 1970b, 201–04, and Kuhn 1970a, 238, 261–62, 268–69, 277.

61. Kuhn 1970b, 192–93.

62. A third line of criticism is provided by the Gettier (1963) paradox. See Suppe 1977a, 720–23, for a discussion of the Gettier paradox and its implications for the epistemology of science.

11

Scientific Realism

Despite a rich history of debate that stretches back to at least ancient Greece,[1] our consideration of the problem of scientific realism conveniently can begin with Carl G. Hempel's treatment of it in his "Theoretician's Dilemma" (1958). In this work he formulates, and attempts to refute, a very strong defense of instrumentalism—one which concludes not only that theoretical entities are unnecessary for doing science, but therefore that it is illegitimate to postulate their existence. Despite generally dominant positivistic proclivities for instrumentalism,[2] Hempel's basic instincts long have been realistic and even hostile to instrumentalism, and his article appropriately can be construed as championing a realistic construal of scientific theories.

Although Hempel's championing of a theoretical realism borrows heavily from the positivistic construal of theories as partially interpreted axiomatic systems, it deviates from prior versions of that account by replacing dependence on the observational/theoretical term distinction with the acceptance of a theoretical/basic vocabulary distinction—a move far more significant than many recognized when his article first appeared. Underlying this change was an acceptance of Quine's argument against the analytic/synthetic distinction, the feeling that the classical positivistic observational/theoretical distinction presupposed the former, and the attendant desire to avoid dependence on either suspect bifurcation.

Nevertheless, few contemporary observers noticed this shift in position, and his basic vocabulary was generally conflated with the positivistic observational vocabulary. Yet one does find in philosophy of science a subsequent loosening of the vocabulary being contrasted with the theoretical—for example, Sellars' opposition of the manifest versus the scientific image. What one finds is a gradual reworking of the instrumentalism-versus-realism dispute from something grounded in the positivistic observational-versus-theoretical term distinction into a descendant issue grounded in a common sense–versus–theoretical science distinction—of which Sellars' manifest-versus-scientific image contrast is illustrative.[3]

And with these one finds a proliferation of views—including not only Sellars' view that what is real is what the ultimately successful scientific theory posits (and that only those commonsense entities and properties which are reducible to them are likewise real), but also Cornman's attempt to defend his compatible commonsense scientific realism which allows the ontic reality of nonreducible commonsense entities and attributes as well.[4] To grossly oversimplify matters, they both agree that ultimate scientific theories do reveal the correct ontic commitments of theories, but they disagree as to what ontic implications such scientific realism has for common garden ("observational") knowledge claims. Sellars believes few if any of the latter are conjunctively reducible to entities of the ultimately correct theoretical claims, and so are ultimately incorrect: The manifest image supports few defensible ontological commitments. Cornman, by contrast, believes that commonsense and ultimately correct theoretical assertions both make defensible ontological commitments.

However, despite these disagreements, both grant the observational/manifest image a privileged epistemic status which enables one to obtain the ultimately correct knowledge revelatory of what ontologically is real—they only disagree as to what those ontological commitments are. Indeed, I would maintain that other than disagreement over (roughly) what in the manifest image is reducible to the ultimately correct theoretical scientific entities and attributes, what the ontological significance of such reducibility is, and hence what of the manifest image is real, the two were far closer than their protestations and disputes would suggest.[5]

The point I have been working toward here is that despite Hempel's attempt to escape the positivistic observational/theoretical distinction, despite Sellars' attempt to get beyond the manifest image toward the scientific image, despite Cornman's attempt to rework a nonbifurcative observational/theoretical distinction that escapes objections to the strict bifurcative positivistic observational/theoretical distinction, all these authors work within some revised observational/theoretical distinction that attempts to reflect some intuitive distinction between the domains of "ordinary experience" and theoretical excursions beyond. Hempel and Cornman tacitly concede a primacy to the former and view the burden of proof as accruing to any ontic commitments beyond. Sellars reverses things and seeks aggressively to establish simultaneously the ontic primacy of the ultimate theoretical, and this at the cost of the ontic illegitimacy of the manifest image. In quite different ways, then, all these authors ascribe an epistemic primacy to the observational (or "manifest image")—Hempel and Cornman construing the manifest image as being sufficiently privileged ontologically and epistemologically as to be the minimal standard which any theoretical ontological and/ or epistemological extensions must meet to be legitimate, and Sellars viewing the manifest image and our cognitive, and other, operations thereupon, while epistemically ultimately inadequate, as providing nevertheless the only, and indispensable, basis for evolving to a body of knowledge (and corollary ontic reading) that can prove correct.

I. EPISTEMOLOGY AND SCIENTIFIC REALISM

It is my contention that according such primacy to the manifest image is anachronistic, unwarranted, and ultimately leads to a significant misconstrual of the problems of scientific realism. To see this, we need to review certain positivistic developments concerning the nature of observational knowledge.

Recall from chapter 10, section I, that initially the positivists adopted a sense-datum theory of the observational, with an implicit incorrigibility view of the epistemic access to it. Then without serious argument, and believing it was just an alternative way of "saying the same thing,"[6] the positivists equivocated this with, and adopted, a "thing-language" construal of the observable, with an attendant thing ontology. This move, which initially was tied to physicalism, concomitantly involved replacement of an incorrigibility justificatory condition for knowledge by a "high-likelihood" evidential requirement. Although positivists generally did not take this move as all that significant, it is of major import. For epistemologically it is to reject long-standing basic empiricist doctrines on knowledge and ultimately undercuts the basis for recent instrumentalist/realist disputes.

Going back to at least Locke, a key premise of the empiricist enterprise has been the view that there is a kind of "direct acquaintance" with the content of "direct perceptual experiences" which renders beliefs about those contents incorrigible and incapable of error. Moreover, such incorrigibility provided an essential basis for a posteriori knowledge, since (following Descartes) the requirement was imposed that to know that ϕ one must have known evidence that guarantees the truth of ϕ (i.e., precludes the possibility that ϕ might be false). Incorrigible knowledge of the content of direct perceptual experiences enjoyed that guarantee and was the only evidential basis on which additional a posteriori knowledge could be obtained. Further arguments purported to establish that the contents of direct perceptual experiences had to be nonphysical particulars (e.g., sense data). If the observational is identified with what can be experienced via direct perception, this yields a plausible basis for the epistemic primacy of (direct) observational knowledge.

But with the move to physicalism, the positivists gave up that basis while still maintaining the epistemic primacy of direct observational knowledge. Subsequent developments have vindicated positivistic rejection of a sense data/incorrigibility view of observational knowledge—Gettier-paradox and other associated "red herrings" notwithstanding.[7] For one can find in the literature enough evidence to refute both (a) the postulation of sense data as the constituents of basic perceptual experiences and (b) the doctrine of some privileged incorrigible epistemic access to the contents of those experiences. As to the latter, I am convinced that Wilfrid Sellars' (1956) arguments against "the given" adequately undercut claims of incorrigible privileged access to the contents of such experiences in ways that are strongly reinforced by private language arguments and rendered decisive by suitable refinements of them.[8] And as to the postulation of sense data as the constituents of such experiences, I think Cornman (1975, ch. 2) has shown that metaphysically there is no reason to postulate the existence of such "phenomenological" entities as opposed to postulating sensing states of perceivers; moreover, when coupled with denial of incorrigible privileged access to the contents of basic perceptual experiences, epistemic analogues to Cornman's arguments establish that there is no epistemic reason to postulate sense data, as opposed to sensory states. Thus there is no justification, either metaphysically or epistemologically, for postulating either sense data or any sort of infallible or incorrigible knowledge of the contents of basic perceptual episodes. In at least these respects the above-mentioned radical epistemic changes positivism made in the move to physicalism have been adequately vindicated. What the positivists, as well as subsequent authors such as Cornman and Sellars, failed to realize is that such moves undercut any straightforward attribution of epistemic primacy to direct observation.

Let me begin to show why this is so by establishing a crucial lemma: that knowledge of our sensations, of the contents of our sensory experience, is not essential to empirical knowledge of physical objects—whether "directly observable" or not. On one reading, Chisholm's (1957) and (1965) adverbial theory of perception serves as a useful argumentative foil for doing so—though, as I will briefly discuss below, this reading is a questionable exegesis of Chisholm's more recent views (e.g., Chisholm 1974 and 1982). Roughly speaking, his perceptual theory is as follows: Sense data are rejected in favor of adverbial sensory states of a perceiver; that is, basic perceptual episodes consist in a person "being appeared to ϕ-ishly." (For example, when I think I see a pink elephant, I am appeared to pink-pachyderm-ishly.) And one obtains knowledge of how one is appeared to which, while not being incorrigible in the earlier empiricist sense, nonetheless is in a sense impregnable. Such knowledge how one is appeared to is essential to other perception-based knowledge, for obtaining the latter requires exploitation of the former. Thus without such knowledge how one is appeared to, perceptual knowledge is impossible.

But this surely is incorrect for several reasons. First, as Chisholm (1957) himself argues, such knowledge will have to be expressed in noncomparative terms. And not only can arguments be mounted to show that such noncomparative uses are impossible, but Sellars (1956) has shown that noncomparative appearance descriptions cannot be epistemically prior to (comparative) physical language uses of, for example, "red"—and such priority is precisely what Chisholm's position requires.

Second, even if one could have the required sort of epistemically prior knowledge how one is appeared to, such knowledge is not essential to perceptual knowledge. In defense of what he calls the percept theory of perception, Roderick Firth (1965) has detailed the sort of perceptual reduction necessary to come up with the pure phenomenological experience and its description required by sense-data theories, and a straightforwardly analogous "perceptual reduction" is required for Chisholm's adverbial theory of sensing. The essential point is the same in both cases: it is exceedingly difficult, and a learned art, to perform the sort of perceptual reduction necessary to come to the sort of knowledge of our sensory experience either position requires. Indeed, it is a talent that many perceivers lack. (So far as I can tell, all my attempts to perform such a perceptual reduction have failed.) It would seem, then, that a consequence of Chisholm's view is that many perceivers (myself included) have no perceptual knowledge, since we are incapable of performing the required perceptual reduction and so have never come to the requisite knowledge of how we are appeared to. The only "out" seems to be to posit that whenever we obtain perceptual knowledge, we do the perceptual reduction, hence obtain the required base knowledge how we are appeared to, subliminally and in ways that involve beliefs, conceptual operations, and so on, that generally may be nonelicitable. Then on Chisholm's epistemology, it will need to be further postulated that we employ such hidden knowledge in subliminal inferences to come to the often conscious beliefs and knowledge we have of, for example, observable physical objects. But the postulations of such ephemeral analogues to conscious processes seem to me unsupported by anything other than the need to preserve an implausible theory, and so they are basically repugnant.

In the absence of any evidence in support of such postulations, I prefer to turn to an alternative theory, especially since I do believe that a more plausible theory is forthcoming which enjoys far greater evidential support. Thus I think it is reasonable to reject any theory of perceptual knowledge that requires epistemically prior knowledge how one is appeared to, or for that matter *any* phenomenological knowledge of our sensations or sensory experiences. (As we shall see later, I am not denying there is a crucial role to be played by sensory states in obtaining perceptual knowledge. And while I am not denying that sometimes phenomenological knowledge of sensations is possible, I am denying that such knowledge is essential to perceptual knowledge of physical objects.)

It may be challenged, plausibly, that I've misinterpreted Chisholm's theory of the directly evident and its role in perception-based knowledge. For increasingly over the years, Chisholm has reduced the role of elicitable directly evident beliefs and inferences in his epistemology in favor of conditions which, roughly, either (a) make subliminal crucial cognitive, doxastic, and other inferential operations needed to obtain knowledge, or else (b) reduce the base knowledge of the directly evident to a weakened sort of knowledge that may be completely nonelicitable, but does not require inferences to establish knowledge that is not directly evident (cf., e.g., Chisholm 1957, 1966, 1974, and 1982). In either case, his view involves subliminal cognitive acts of the sort I have objected to. And further, the concessions to the subliminal directly evident knowledge tend to undercut any basis for showing that such knowledge how one is appeared to is epistemically crucial. Certainly none of Chisholm's arguments for the role of "being appeared to" propositions in obtaining perceptual knowledge establish a role for sensory states stronger than I will argue for below. Thus I do not think that questions of the proper exegesis of Chisholsm's epistemology of perception seriously affect the correctness of these conclusions I have drawn from a consideration of his views.

The situation I am urging, then, is this: Perceptual knowledge generally is of physical particulars, their interrelations, and the attributes thereof. These are distinct from, and are not contained within, our sensations or their phenomenological contents.[9] Baldly put, our ordinary perceptual knowledge of physical objects occurs without knowledge (epistemically prior or otherwise) of the phenomenological contents of our sensing experiences, though it does involve the *having of sensations* construed as being in a sensory state, where such states may even be described phenomenologically as how one is appeared to; and the subjects of such perceptual knowledge (e.g., physical objects) are not constituents of our sensations.

If, as is plausible, we grant that what we "directly experience" are our sensations, it follows that our perceptual knowledge generally is of what we do not "directly experience"—namely, physical objects and their attributes. But then, virtually all our perceptual knowledge is of what we do not directly experience, and further, it requires no prior knowledge of what we do directly experience (sensations). What seems to follow is that we are in the rather peculiar situation that all nonintrospective perceptual knowledge, whether of the "observable" or the "theoretical," is equally problematic, since the subject matter of neither is "directly experienced" in any epistemologically (as opposed to phenomenologically) significant manner. Thus in one respect the early empiricists and sense-datists are both correct: All knowledge of physical objects is equally problematic. On the other hand, they are wrong in supposing there is a less problematic direct "perceptual" knowledge available and necessary to exploit evidentially in the attempt to obtain perceptual knowledge of physical objects.

A sketch of what, to my mind, are key ingredients of a viable theory of perceptual knowledge may help clarify matters. When I perceptually come to know that ϕ, I employ various detectors (e.g., eyes, ears, etc.) that are causally stimulated mediately or immediately by characteristics of the perceived object. Such stimulation then triggers off causal chains that (i) produce a sensation I experience (i.e., cause me to go into a particular sensory state), (ii) cause me to think a thought about some physical object(s) and its (their) attributes, and (iii) cause me to assume a propositional attitude (e.g., belief, disbelief, musing about, etc.) with respect to that thought. When the propositional attitude toward that thought is one of acceptance or belief, when the thought refers to and correctly describes a configuration of physical objects and their attributes, and when the referred-to objects and their attributes enter into the appropriate causal relationships with the sensory state I assume, the thought I think, and the propositional attitude I assume toward that thought—then I *know that* the physical objects in question have the characteristics my thought(s) ascribes to them and I accept.[10] The process is noninferential, being mediated in part by what Sellars (1975) has termed the "brute organization" and much exploiting the processes involved in knowing how to use a language (in which one thinks); and it does not involve knowledge of the phenomenological characteristics of one's sensations, though one's sensations (qua sensory states) are causally or empirically essential. Further, it does not necessarily involve one's detectors being directed upon the object(s) of perceptual knowledge; all it requires is that the detectors focus on objects suitably interconnected causally or empirically with the objects known perceptually.[11] Further, on pain of denying perceptual knowledge to the relatively unsophisticated, it cannot require epistemically prior knowledge of these empirical regularities as a precondition for the most basic perceptual knowledge, or its expansion.

It should be stressed that what I have been sketching is a theory of perceptual knowledge, not a general theory of perception or perceptual experience. Indeed, it is concerned with the latter sorts of issues only insofar as perception or perceptual experiences are crucial to perceptual knowledge, and I am urging that much that has traditionally concerned philosophical accounts of perception is not epistemically crucial or essential. Much of what is characteristic of the phenomenon of perception is not particularly crucial to an understanding of perceptual knowledge.

But rather than getting embroiled in such issues of perception and perceptual knowledge or even in defending the view of perceptual knowledge I have sketched and favor, for the moment I wish to sidestep these issues indicating that my only motive *here* is to sketch enough of a perceptual knowledge theory as is necessary to make plausible a key claim of mine: that *all* ordinary objects of perceptual knowledge are causally (or empirically) remote from the contents of sensation and hence, in a sense, equally problematic—be they tables and chairs or electrons. If I am correct about this, any attempt to divide the physical objects amenable to perceptual knowledge into the observational and the theoretical ultimately is artificial; for in both cases they must remain causally (or empirically) related to our sensations via essentially similar causal (or empirical) regularities. (This is not to deny, however, that there may be other important differences.) That is, fundamentally, all perceptual knowledge of physical objects is epistemically remote from the phenomenological contents of our sensations. This, I suggest, is what ultimately underlies the correct claim that "observation is theory-laden" and indicates what some (but definitely not all) of the epistemic basis and import of that slogan is.

Notice what happens to the classic instrumentalism-versus-realism dispute with respect to theories if we grant the correctness of these epistemological claims: *Only* a realism with respect to theories is tenable, if one views realism as minimally involving the claim that statements referring to entities other than the contents of one's sensory experiences can be (and are) known. For granting the knowledge of any physical objects or their attributes, such knowledge is "theoretical" in an important sense. And thus the issue is not whether "theoretical" knowledge is possible—for it clearly is—but what are the *limits* of "theoretical" knowledge.

At this point in my argument, then, I have argued that (a) all perceptual knowledge of physical objects importantly goes beyond the phenomenological contents of our sensory experiences; (b) such knowledge does not essentially rest upon phenomenological knowledge of any such experiences; (c) perceptual knowledge exploits causal or empirical regularities between attributes of physical objects and the sensory, doxastic, and other cognitive states of perceivers; and (d) this makes perceptual knowledge of all physical objects depend upon features of such causal and cognitive regularities. Thus, (e) in certain respects, all (nonintrospective) perceptual knowledge is equally problematic in ways that make all perception-based knowledge of physical objects similarly problematic, hence in a sense "theoretical." Consequently, (f) the issue of scientific realism is not whether theoretical knowledge is possible, but rather what its limits are.

Differently put, as I partially argued earlier in chapter 3, the issue of instrumentalism versus realism collapses in that an instrumentalism which acknowledges knowledge of "observable" physical objects is just a restricted realism, and the operative question is whether there is any epistemic basis for drawing the line limiting perception-based knowledge to the directly observable limits that instrumentalists have insisted on. The same comments apply *mutatis mutandis* to antirealisms such as van Fraassen's, and thus they complete the argument against van Fraassen's observational/nonobservational distinction set forth in chapter 1, hence his constructive empiricism, by fulfilling the obligation I incurred in chapter 1. The "causal" account of perceptual knowledge sketched above strongly suggests there is not such an epistemic basis. In any case, the question of scientific realism now importantly involves a question of line drawing quite unlike prior disputes. The manifest image enjoys no peculiar epistemic priority.

II. CONCEPTUAL DEVICES

We now turn to another flaw in classic disputes over scientific realism. Traditionally, debates over instrumentalism versus realism have presumed that all the nonobservational terms in a theory were interpreted as referring to real nonobservable entities or else none were (e.g., they were eliminable). But such a construal is radically at odds with actual scientific practice. In a given theory formulation some terms may be construed as literally referring, while others function as various *conceptual devices* such as approximations, idealizations, simplifications, and so on.[12] That is, various "nonobservational" terms in a theory formulation may enjoy different cognitive statuses, and those statuses may change as a theory develops.[13] This in turn reflects and closely relates to the fact that theories undergoing active development frequently are not put forward as literally or even counterfactually true, but rather as "promising," "worth pursuing," "approximately correct," "being on to something," "being in a certain respect importantly true, but in other respects profoundly wrong as well," and so on. And in their developmental states, such theories typically are importantly incomplete in their accounts of phenomena.[14]

Such truth statuses are not merely presumed but rather are assessed and defended on the basis of observational, experimental, theoretical, and other considerations and evidence. Moreover, neither the incorporation of conceptual devices into theories nor the use of the more qualified truth statuses with which theories sometimes are advanced automatically constitutes an instrumentalism. For it is quite consistent with such practices to assert that conceptual devices refer to actual entities but describe them in ways that are not literally true; and the ways in which a theory can be promising or approximately true (but importantly wrong or incomplete) may include the postulation of "theoretical entities" which are not described or characterized in a fully adequate way by the theory. In short, a defensible realistic construal of theories need not be committed to either the literal truth of theories or to the absence of conceptual devices in established theories.

If by a *fully realistic construal of theories* we mean one where every theoretical term is interpreted as referring to actual entities and the characterization of such entities provided by such theories must be literally true, then few theories actually produced by science are fully realistic. The way to accommodate this fact is, I believe, to view fully realistic accounts of theories as being a limiting case, one from which the quasi-realism of the Semantic Conception, the employment of conceptual devices, and such partial or approximate truth assessments deviate. The functioning as a conceptual device, or being promising, approximately true, and so on, tacitly involve employing the literal truth of theories as a limiting benchmark against which theoretical deviation is to be assessed and characterized.

An important question thus is raised whether that literally true benchmark ever is knowable. Crucial here is the question whether theories *ever* can be true under a fully realistic construal. Although I do not have decisive arguments to the effect that the answer is negative, I am convinced that no such literally true theory ever has been advanced by science. Indeed, in earlier chapters (especially 3 and 4) I have defended the view that theories can be empirically true but that this does not involve their typical linguistic formulations being literally true. That is, I have advocated a quasi-realistic construal of theories.

Roughly speaking, my view is that theories centrally contain theory structures indicating admissible state transitions which stand in some mapping relationship to real phenomena with suitable semantic relationships between such linguistic formulations of theories and these theory structures, phenomenal systems, and the mapping relationships. Thus far, my view of theories closely resembles van Fraassen's semantic view of theories (van Fraassen 1970; 1980, ch. 3), in ways that we previously have acknowledged (see, e.g., his 1970 article and Suppe 1974b, 221–30, as well as ch. 1 above). Further, I agree with van Fraassen that the linguistic formulations of theories do *not* provide literally true descriptions of the phenomena described by theories— where we do disagree is on why this is so. While I maintain that, in the limiting case at least, theoretical statements are intended to be true, and the language in which such statements are made is not to be construed literally, by contrast, van Fraassen (1980) maintains that the language of theoretical statements should be literally construed but that theories need not be true to be good. Thus while we share a denial that theoretical descriptions are literally true, we differ on why this is so in ways that lead me to be a quasi-realist and van Fraassen to defend an idiosyncratic antirealism. Since Edward MacKinnon (1979) recently has shown that what is joint to van Fraassen's and my semantic views of theories does not require accepting van Fraassen's antirealism,[15] and since my concern here is what the limits of realistic theoretical knowledge are, I will not examine van Fraassen's antirealism here (see instead ch. 1, sec. II) but rather merely will concentrate on why I think theories are not literally true but yet support a quasi-realism.

Basically, my position is that while theories do not offer literal descriptions of how the real world behaves, they do purport to describe how it *would* behave if the world *were* "nice and clean." By this I mean, how it *would be* if the parameters used to specify states were orthogonal to, or independent of, all neglected parameters not definable in terms of the incorporated theoretical parameters. Thus theories provide a counterfactual description how the world *would be if* neglected parameters *did not* influence the phenomena the theory purports to describe. But typically, neglected parameters at least sometimes do influence the phenomena, and so the characterizations offered by theories are not literally true, but at best counterfactually true, of the phenomena within their scopes. This is the quasi-realistic construal of theories I have long advocated.

I have already argued that a central issue of scientific realism is what are the limits of what can be perceptually known. Thus it is incumbent upon me to raise the question whether such a quasi-realism is an epistemic limit, or whether theories are knowable under a fully realistic construal. The answer to this question centrally involves a factual issue: What are the orthogonality characteristics of real-world attributes? If the world is so organized that the crucial attributes of some phenomenal natural kind constitute a manageably small class of attributes of entities where such attributes are orthogonal from all other attributes that ever occur in conjunction with such phenomena, then literally true theories are possible. But if no such manageably small sets of crucial orthogonal attributes occur, then the quasi-realistic construal of theories is the best we can do. Which is the case depends upon how the world is constituted and thus cannot be settled on the basis of abstract philosophical considerations. Further, even if literally true theories sometimes are possible, we must face the prospect that different kinds of phenomena may differ radically in their orthogonality characteristics—that is, even if some kinds of phenomena in principle admit of literally true theoretical characterizations, others may not.

Two implications follow, I think, from this discussion: First, that it is wise to retain a literally true, fully realistic construal of theories as our limiting case; for although no such theories have ever been produced and we may have suspicions they never will be, we cannot establish the correctness of such suspicions. Second, and much more important, it should give us pause to question seriously whether even the limiting construal of the instrumentalism-versus-realism issue urged earlier is a serious philosophical problem worth pursuing. For while the truth statuses the world might allow for theories is an important part of the scientific realism issue, questions of scientific realism ultimately are epistemic—Cornman's (1975) attempt to view it as a mere metaphysical issue notwithstanding.

The basic issues concern what kinds of entities can we come to know the world contains and what characteristics of them can we come to know. Where the entities of concern include both those of the manifest image as well as "theoretical" ones which extend beyond that image, the literal or other nonliteral truth statuses of theories are important to the issue primarily because theories are a vehicle for putative knowledge of the world, and to constitute knowledge, our beliefs, whether common garden or scientifically theoretical, must be true. To be sure, the interpretative status of true theories is a limit on such knowledge, but it is only one of many. If anything like the account of perception-based knowledge I sketched earlier is correct, then the sorts of exploitable empirical regularities between the characteristics of physical objects and other "real" entities, the sensory detectors of perceivers, sensory states, the "brute organization," and other cognitive processes importantly determine the ontological limits of what can be known. And what empirical regularities of the epistemically requisite sort do exist thus are absolutely crucial to establishing the ontological limits of the empirically (i.e., perceptually based) knowable. And frankly, I do not see any reason to suppose that philosophical analysis *alone* is capable of determining those limits, although we will see that philosophical considerations do have important contributions to make in any viable attempt to delineate such limits or establish such epistemic capacities.

III. IS THERE A PHILOSOPHICAL PROBLEM OF SCIENTIFIC REALISM?

Earlier I argued that the problem of scientific realism basically is one of delimiting what is knowable in a perception-based manner. Now I have just concluded arguing that such limits depend not only on the orthogonality characteristics of the entities and their attributes which constitute possible real phenomena for investigation, but also on the sorts of empirical regularities that obtain between such entities and their attributes, on the one hand, and on the other hand, the various cognitive and other perceptual apparatus employed in obtaining perceptually based a posteriori knowledge. Further, I have urged that determining these characteristics, hence determining the limits of perceptually based knowledge (and thus resolving the scientific realism problem) is a sufficiently empirical issue as to be undecidable by mere philosophical analysis. It would seem, then, that if successful, my arguments have established that the problem of scientific realism is a philosophical pseudoproblem.

I prefer to view it otherwise. For to dismiss "the problem of scientific realism" as a philosophical pseudoproblem is to lose sight of what the genuinely problematic and legitimate issue raised by the scientific realism issue is. To see this let us return to the earlier claim that, in an important sense, all knowledge of physical objects and their attributes is equally problematic and "theoretical." If we take this idea seriously, we are faced with some very serious philosophical problems, ones whose solution ultimately must be philosophical, although significantly informed by what we do in fact know empirically. Specifically, we must seek answers to such questions as the following:

(1) What is it for a knowledge claim to be true?
(2) How can and how do we employ our sensory and cognitive resources to reliably assess the truth of putative a posteriori knowledge claims?
(3) Given that the assessment of a knowledge claim sanctions a knowledge claim as correct, hence likely to be true, what ontological conclusions legitimately can be drawn as to what sorts of entities do exist, and with what confidence can we assert the existence of such entities?

The answers to such questions clearly will have to be informed by empirical knowledge about perception, the world, and our epistemic interactions with that world. But such empirical findings are not sufficient; for our issues are fundamentally epistemic, and any adequate epistemological account, inter alia, must legitimize such epistemic claims as it draws upon. That is, the task of philosophical analysis here is to indicate what empirically must be true if perception is to be a basis of a posteriori (including scientific) knowledge and at the same time not deny what (by any plausible standards) we do know empirically about perception. If this is successfully done, we have established much. For manifestly we do have empirical knowledge — not only of the world of the manifest image, but also of electrons, protons, quarks, DNA, and the like.

I hope the foregoing discussion displays that there are genuine, fundamental, and terribly important philosophical problems of scientific realism. At the same time, however, I hope I have displayed how far removed those genuine problems are from the focal concerns that have occupied either earlier twentieth-century debates over instrumentalism versus realism or what MacKinnon (1979) terms the "new debates" over scientific realism. For I have argued, first, that such debates, at most, reduce to issues over what limits there are on the range of physical objects and their attributes which are knowable on the basis of perception. And second, I have argued that the determination of such limits is fundamentally an empirical, not a purely philosophical, issue. Nevertheless, I have urged that empirically informed philosophical accounts of knowledge, truth, truth assessment, perception, and the ontological consequences thereof—that is, answers to questions such as (1) through (3) listed earlier—are crucial to establishing what we can know, including what ontologically we can come to know. What I deny is that such findings will enable us to establish the sort of epistemological and ontological iron curtain both instrumentalists and scientific realists have haggled over.

If the problem of scientific realism is to be the irrevocable drawing of such a curtain, it is a philosophical pseudoproblem. But if it is to be a means of addressing, and making progress toward understanding, the nature of scientific knowledge and its unrestrained potential, then problems of scientific realism are among the most central problems not only in philosophy of science, but also in epistemology and probably metaphysics. Further, the genuine problems are ones recent debates over scientific realism leave largely untouched. I do believe—and hopefully have made a convincing case for—the contention that, appropriately understood, within the scientific realism debates reside crucially important philosophical problems of such central and fundamental importance. Herein lies the explanation for my belief that the scientific realism issues are best joined by developing the epistemology underlying the stance one wishes to take (cf. ch. 1, sec. III). At the same time I hope I have shed some light on the sort of role the sensations or perception are to play in any epistemology that proves viable in solving these problems of scientific realism.[16] The views taken here on the role of sensations and perception in a posteriori knowledge together with the rejection of the K-K thesis in chapter 10 will strongly inform and condition the epistemological analysis given in the next chapter.

NOTES

1. See the editor's introduction (3–71) to MacKinnon 1972 for a useful but selective survey of the history of scientific realism controversies. More recent developments are critically surveyed in his 1979 article.

2. I interpret Carnap as being another major dissident on this issue, dating his implicit commitments to some form of theoretical realism to around 1939, if not before (cf. ch. 2, sec. I above for the arguments). However, his 1950 work, superficially at least, raises a basis for challenging my construal. While I think that latter article is extremely difficult to reconcile with the overall Carnap corpus and its intellectual development, my present belief is that it can be reconciled with my interpretation in ch. 2 of his views on the reality of theoretical entities.

3. Cf. Sellars 1963a and 1965.

4. See Cornman 1975, esp. ch. 8.

5. The basis of this claim rests on my conviction that Cornman (1975, ch. 7) misinterprets Sellars as an indirect realist; rather, they both maintain

sensing theories. That Sellars does is made clear by, e.g., sec. 61 of Sellars 1956.

6. See Carnap 1963a, 50–51. See also ch. 10, n. 9, above.

7. For these paradoxes see, e.g., Gettier 1963; Ackerman 1972, ch. 4; Chisholm 1974; Clark 1965; Harman 1968, 1970, 1970a; Lehrer 1965; Lehrer and Paxson 1969; Skyrms 1967; Sosa 1965, 1969; Turk-Saunders and Champawat 1964; and the numerous other such articles subsequently published.

8. For a survey and critical evaluation of private language arguments, see Turk-Sanders and Henze 1967.

9. I am glossing over many issues here—including the intentionality of such experiences, the possibility that physical objects (as opposed to sense data) might be constituents of sensory experiences (which I deny), etc. These issues will be discussed at length in my *Facts, Theories, and Scientific Observation* (in progress).

10. What the appropriate causal relationships are is problematic. See ch. 12, sec. IV, for what I presently believe are the appropriate causal relationships. For present purposes, the precise nature of the causal relationship is not crucial.

11. Thus the account encompasses what Dretske (1969) calls the objects of primary and secondary epistemic seeing (*seeing that*). His views will be discussed in ch. 12.

12. See Shapere, "On the Role of Conceptual Devices in Science," unpublished manuscript, n.d., and Suppe 1977a, 706–12, which, inter alia, summarizes Shapere's paper. For characterizations of abstractions and idealizations, see ch. 3, sec. IV, above.

13. And this is so regardless of what simplifying, approximative, etc., assumptions not mandated by the theory may be employed in using the theory in various calculative applications. In his 1969 work, Shapere conflates these two cases (see n. 29 in ch. 3 above for criticisms to this effect). In his unpublished "Conceptual Devices" paper, he carefully marks the distinction and clarifies matters considerably.

14. Cf. Suppe 1977a, 706–16, and Boyd 1976.

15. It should be noted that in this article MacKinnon discusses only van Fraassen's development; however, those features he does discuss for the most part constitute areas of joint agreement.

16. The positions on observation and perceptual knowledge sketched (or previewed) in this chapter are developed and defended in detail in my *Facts, Theories, and Scientific Observation* (in progress).

─────── 12 ───────
Conclusive Reasons and
Scientific Knowledge

The rejection of positivism's neutral observation language and the recognition that Kuhn's and Feyerabend's portraits of science are those of an irrational enterprise have made understanding and accounting for the objectivity of science a crucial philosophical problem—as Scheffler, Shapere, and others have made so very clear.[1] Neither the epistemic rigidity and conservatism of positivism nor the extreme subjectivity of the *Weltanshauungen* analyses seems to have a grip on the objectivity of scientific knowledge. In chapter 10 I made the case that the common ingredient of these failures is the uncritical acceptance of long-standing epistemological doctrines such as the *K-K thesis:*

> '*S* knows that *P*' entails '*S* knows that he knows that *P*'.

And as I have argued elsewhere,[2] more recent investigations of, and developments concerning, the role of rationality in the growth of scientific knowledge strongly favor epistemologies which reject the K-K thesis. The implications of such a rejection are far more profound than has been widely recognized: An adequate epistemology of science not only must part company with many dominant trends in epistemology this century if it simultaneously is to account for the extent of scientific knowledge, cohere with what we know of rationality and the growth of scientific knowledge, and also preserve for science the sort of objectivity that widely is presumed and expected; such an epistemology ultimately must also squarely challenge standard philosophical intuitions about what constitutes knowledge (intuitions which, as I maintain later, are conditioned less by actual epistemic achievements than by theory-laden philosophical prejudices and allegiances).

My purposes in this chapter are (a) to illustrate and give evidence for the above charges by examining the controversy surrounding an earlier attempt to work out the sort of epistemology denying the K-K thesis that adequately coheres with actual scientific practice—namely, Dretske's *Seeing and Knowing*;[3] (b) to argue that while Dretske's (1969) epistemology is seriously flawed, his most basic intuitions and insights generally are sound and can be reworked into a defensible epistemology of science;[4] (c) to develop such an epistemology; and (d) to sketch how it can be joined with recent work on the growth of scientific knowledge so as to make simultaneous sense of the objectivity and the fallibility of science's epistemic efforts. An underlying theme will be that what distinguishes scientific knowledge from "common garden" knowledge is not an epistemic difference but, rather, standards for the defensibility of knowledge claims. I begin by looking at Dretske's *Seeing and Knowing* epistemology and prominent objections to it.

I. DRETSKE'S ANALYSIS OF CONCLUSIVE REASONS

The heart of Dretske's analysis of knowledge is his notion of a conclusive reason. According to him, we call R a *conclusive reason* for P if and only if

(1) R would not be the case unless P were the case.[5]

He understands (1) as expressing "the relationship between states similar to R and P *under a fixed set of circumstances* . . . where the circumstances C are defined in terms of those circumstances which actually prevail on the occasion of R and P."[6] But the circumstances C do not include *all* the circumstances that prevail on the occasion of R and P; rather they are restricted to "just those prevailing circumstances which are logically and causally independent of the state of affairs expressed by P."[7] Moreover, he tells us that (1) can be expressed as

$$\sim\!\diamondsuit(R \ \& \ C \ \& \ \sim\!P)$$

where '$\diamondsuit$' is some unspecified empirical or causal possibility operator.[8] Dretske nowhere indicates what he means by either logical or causal independence. However, the notion of the logical independence $[(\phi \bigcirc \psi)]$ of two propositions ϕ and ψ is a well-defined standard notion:

$$(\phi \bigcirc \psi) = \text{df.} \diamondsuit(\phi \ \& \ \psi) \ \& \ \diamondsuit(\phi \ \& \ \sim\!\psi) \ \& \ \diamondsuit(\sim\!\phi \ \& \ \psi)$$
$$\& \ \diamondsuit(\sim\!\phi \ \& \ \sim\!\psi),$$

where '$\diamondsuit$' is the logical possibility operator. Derivatively we can say that the states of affairs described by ϕ and ψ are logically independent if and only if $(\phi \bigcirc \psi)$. The notion of causal independence is not a standard notion, but it seems natural to define analogously what it is for two propositions ϕ and ψ to be causally independent $[(\phi \copyright \psi)]$:

$$(\phi \text{ © } \psi) = \text{df.} \Diamond(\phi \text{ \& } \psi) \text{ \& } \Diamond(\phi \text{ \& } \sim\psi) \text{ \& } \Diamond(\sim\phi \text{ \& } \psi)$$
$$\text{\& } \Diamond(\sim\phi \text{ \& } \sim\psi);$$

and derivatively, we say that the states of affairs referred to by ϕ and ψ are causally independent if and only if $(\phi \text{ © } \psi)$. These definitions are such that '$(\phi \text{ © } \psi)$' entails '$(\phi \text{ O } \psi)$', '$(\phi \text{ © } \psi)$' is true if and only if '$(\phi \text{ © } \sim\psi)$' is true, '$(\phi \text{ O } \psi)$' is true if and only if '$(\phi \text{ O } \sim\psi)$' is, and 'O' and '©' are symmetric operators. Subsequently I will interpret logical and causal independence in terms of 'O' and '©'.

The analyses of logical and causal independence enable us to display an ambiguity in Dretske's characterization of the circumstances C relative to which the conclusiveness of reasons are assessed. Let F_i be atomic sentences describing the occurrence of various attributes in some situation; then the circumstances C can be construed as a conjunction $\underset{i \in \Gamma}{\&} F_i$, where Γ is the index set of all those attributes or factors which meet Dretske's independence requirements mentioned above—namely, that C is "restricted to just those prevailing circumstances which are logically and causally independent of the state of affairs expressed by P." This could mean that for every conjunct F_i of C, it must be the case that $(F_i \text{ O } P)$ and $(F_i \text{ © } P)$; or it might mean that C is to be the maximal conjunction of actually obtaining factors F_i such that $(C \text{ O } P)$ and $(C \text{ © } P)$. These two restrictions are *not* equivalent. Dretske gives us no hint as to which of these conditions is the intent of his logical and causal independence conditions. However, the first interpretation is stronger than the second; and since one of my objections to Dretske's account of conclusive reasons is that his independence conditions are too strong, the charitable move seems to be to interpret Dretske as imposing the weaker of the two possible independence conditions. Thus I am interpreting Dretske in such a way that (1) is satisfied if and only if

(2) C is a true description of the maximal set of actually obtaining attributes characteristic of the situation in question such that
   (i) $(C \text{ © } P) \text{ \& } (C \text{ O } P)$
   (ii) $\sim\Diamond(R \text{ \& } C \text{ \& } \sim P)$.

Thus (2) specifies what it is to be a conclusive reason.[9]

Exploiting his analysis of conclusive reasons, Dretske introduces the following definition:

(3) *S has conclusive reasons, R, for believing P* if and only if
   (A) R is a conclusive reason for P . . . ,
   (B) S believes, without doubt, reservation, or question that P is the case and he believes this on the basis of R,

(C) (i) S knows that R is the case or

    (ii) R is some experiential state of S (about which it may not make sense to suppose that S *knows* that R is the case; at least it no longer makes sense to ask *how* he knows).[10]

And he maintains that having conclusive reasons for believing P is a necessary and sufficient condition for knowing that P is the case.[11]

Certain features of Dretske's analysis deserve emphasis. First, although presented differently, this analysis of *having conclusive reasons* is a version of the traditional thesis that

(4) S knows that P if and only if

    (i) P is true;

    (ii) S believes that P;

    (iii) S's belief that P is justified,

wherein clauses (A), (B), and (C) specify when (iii) is satisfied in such a way that satisfying (iii) guarantees that (i) and (ii) are also satisfied. Second, unlike most versions of (4), it avoids Gettier- and Lehrer-type paradoxes.[12] Third, when a conclusive reason R is an experiential state of S, it is possible that S may not know that R. In general, to know that P in virtue of having conclusive reason R under circumstances C, S need not know that C obtains. Hence Dretske's analysis entails the denial of the K-K thesis ('S knows that P' entails that 'S knows that he knows that P'). Fourth, R, C, and P are distinguished largely on epistemic grounds: R is either an experiential state of S (e.g., having a sensation) or else a proposition known by S. 'C' designates a set of occurrent circumstances, where the conditions may be comprised of a finite or an infinite number of conditions; as such, there is no guarantee that C can be fully described propositionally except in a language involving infinitely long conjunctions; hence there is no guarantee that S could have full knowledge of the circumstances C. P must be a proposition S believes on the basis of R; however, Dretske nowhere indicates what it is to believe P *on the basis* of R.

There is one respect in which Dretske's formulation of his analysis obviously is unsatisfactory. Nowhere does he indicate what he means by an experiential state. The fact that the only experiential states he mentions are sensory states suggests that the former be identified with the latter. Such an identification will not work, however. For suppose that I am shown for the first time into a room about which I had no prior knowledge or information. Throughout my stay in the room I am in a succession of experiential states (i.e., having sensations) without break such that each of the states qualifies as a conclusive reason for 'The room is painted green', and I believe that the room is painted green on the basis of these states. Thus I know that the room is painted green so long as I am in the room. Then I leave the room, continuing to believe that it is painted green. When I leave the room do I know that the room is painted green? I clearly do; yet according to Dretske's analysis, if experiential states are identified with sensory states, it seems not. For having left the room, I no longer am in a sensory state which qualifies as a conclusive reason for 'The room is painted green'; and so I do not now know that the room is painted green by virtue of satisfying clause (C-ii) of his analysis (3). So if I am to still know that the room is painted green, it must be by virtue of something satisfying clause (C-i); that is, by virtue of knowing some conclusive reason R. But under the circumstances of the case, the only R which could serve this function are R I had come to know by virtue of my experiencing the room (i.e., on the basis of experiential [sensory] states qualifying as conclusive reasons) and being outside the room, I am no longer in such states, hence no longer have conclusive reasons for R and no longer know that R.

The problem here is that the knowledge we obtain via our sensory states often does persist after we cease to be in such states, yet on the present interpretation of experiential states, Dretske's analysis provides no means for such knowledge to so endure. This strongly suggests that experiential states must be interpreted so as to include not only sensory states, but also memory states and probably other cognitive states such as doxastic and epistemic states, inferential states, and so on. Moreover, the postulation of such non-sensory states seems to be required generally by "causal" analyses of knowledge;[13] so I will assume this broader notion of experiential states is correct. So construed, (3) obviously can allow for the preservation of knowledge via memory and also for inference as a source of knowledge.

II. WHETHER CONCLUSIVE REASONS ARE NECESSARY FOR KNOWING THAT

Pappas and Swain argue that Dretske's requirement of having conclusive reasons is too strong to serve as a necessary condition for knowing that P.[14] Formulating Dretske's conclusive reason analysis (1) as

(5) In circumstances C, R would not be the case unless P were the case, where C is as in (2-i),

they argue that having conclusive reasons is not a necessary condition for knowing that P by presenting two counterexamples.

Their *first counterexample* concerns a case where we clearly would say that someone, *S*, knows that there is only a cup on the table (*P*) because he is having a visual experience of the cup under normal conditions *C*. Yet (5) fails to be satisfied: For suppose the situation were exactly the same except that there is no cup, but only a 3-D image of a cup projected at the same place by a hidden holograph apparatus such that *S* has the same visual experience (*R*) he would have if only a cup were on the table. Since 'There is only a cup on the table' (*P*), is not logically independent of a statement to the effect that such a holograph apparatus is present and projecting a cup image, and so on, the presence or absence of such an apparatus cannot be included among the conditions *C*. As such, the appropriate instance of (5) is not true, and so in this paradigm case of knowing that there is only a cup on the table, *S* fails to have the conclusive reason required by Dretske's analysis.[15]

Commenting on this counterexample, Pappas and Swain offer a more restricted reading of (5) which not only blocks this counterexample, but is such that "there is also some reason to think that this restricted way of reading the conditional is what Dretske has in mind, although his remarks are far from clear on this and related matters" (1973, 74):

> (6) In circumstances *C*, *R* would not have been the case if the circumstances other than *C* had been different in only the following way: *P* is false, and whatever other changes in truth values are required logically or causally by the falsity of *P*.

Although this interpretation (6) of (5) (which differs from [2] above, as we shall see) escapes their previous criticisms, they claim it is liable to their *second counterexample:* An employee, *S*, of the local electric company, having the requisite knowledge about the local generating and distribution system, goes to a friend's, notes on the way that the street lights are on, sees the lights are on at his friend's, and concludes his company's generators are working. Under these circumstances, they claim we would want to say *S* knew that the company's generators were the cause of his friend's lights being on (*P*). But suppose that, unbeknown to *S*, his friend had his own emergency generating system which automatically came on whenever (and only when) the power supply fails; so his lights would be on even if the power company's generators had failed. "This aspect of the situation is not one of those that is to be included in the circumstances, *C*, for it is not causally independent of *P* (if *P* were false, then that would be causally sufficient for the generator to begin producing electricity)" (75). As such, the relevant instance of (6) is not satisfied, hence S does not know that the company's generators are operating under Dretske's analysis. Yet according to Pappas and Swain, "Surely, we do not want to say that the fact that his friend has a generator in his basement *prevents S* from having knowledge that the company's generators are causing the lights to be on" (76). And they take this case as illustrating "that a person can know something even though they might be mistaken" (76).

This counterexample should be unconvincing to many philosophers: For the acceptability of Pappas and Swain's second counterexample depends on whether one agrees with them "that a person can know something even though they might be mistaken" *in the circumstances.* For anyone who denies this (as I do), their counterexample will be unconvincing; and in Dretske's case, since he explicitly denies this,[16] their "counterexample" is question begging as well. Moreover, contrary to what they suggest, (6) cannot be what Dretske intends, since it in effect makes the satisfaction of (1) depend on a set of circumstances *only some of which actually obtain,* and in the passages already quoted (in sec. I) it is completely clear that Dretske requires that the satisfaction of (1) be relative to some set C of circumstances *all of which actually obtain.* Thus (2) still is our most plausible candidate for interpreting the causal and logical independence conditions imposed on (1).

Dretske does not find Pappas and Swain's two counterexamples convincing and proposes to dispense with them in accordance with the following suggestion from Raymond Martin:[17] Regardless whether we accept their claim that "we do not want to say that the fact that his friend *has* a generator in his basement *prevents S* from having knowledge that the company's generators are causing the light to be on," we *do* want to say that such an auxiliary generator *being on* prevents S from seeing that the company's generators are supplying electricity for the lights, but that such an auxiliary generator *being off* does not prevent S from having such knowledge. That is, Pappas and Swain's second counterexample can be blocked if C can include the fact that the auxiliary generator is off ($\sim G$), but that if it were on (G) that factor would prevent R from being a conclusive reason. But this move cannot be made if (2) captures the intent of Dretske's independence conditions. For the generator system is such that $\sim P$ if and only if G, which fact is causally independent of whether P; hence, when the generator is off there is no set C' of actually obtaining circumstances containing ($\sim P$ if and only if G), such that '$\Diamond(C' \And \sim G \And \sim P)$' is true. That is, there is no set of actually obtaining circumstances containing $\sim G$ and ($\sim P$ if and only if G) such that '$\Diamond(C \And \sim P)$' is true; hence, by the definition of '©', ~(C © P) for any C containing ~G and (~P if and only if G). However, Dretske's line of reply does work for the holograph case.[18]

Despite the failure of this attempt to escape Pappas and Swain's second counterexample, I think the attempt is basically sound and is precisely the sort of reply that must be given if one wishes to maintain (as Dretske 1969 and I do) that it is impossible for one to know something if one could be mistaken under the circumstances. But as our discussion of Dretske's reply indicates, this sort of response is possible only if one allows C to include circumstances such that C is not causally independent of P and (2) prohibits this. These observations strongly suggest that Dretske is mistaken in requiring that the fixed circumstances C actually prevailing be restricted to just those circumstances which are logically and causally independent of P. This suggestion will be explored and defended in sec. IV.

From the foregoing discussion of Pappas and Swain's "counterexamples," I conclude that Dretske's analysis *is* defective, but that the defects in his analysis do not automatically lend support to Pappas and Swain's contention that a person can know something even though they might be mistaken. However, I do not intend to debate the merits of their suggestion here, except to offer the following observations: Traditionally, epistemologists have insisted that in order to know that P one must have evidence which makes one's belief that P certain; and since Descartes, if not before, such certainty has been construed as incorrigibility. But the price of incorrigibility historically has been a pervasive skepticism. Dretske's (1969 and 1971) insight has been that certainty does not require incorrigibility, and his attempt has been to evade skepticism by analyzing knowledge in terms of certain but corrigible beliefs.[19] In this respect, his analysis is faithful to the traditional demand that one's knowledge that P be certain;[20] as such, his break with traditional epistemology is relatively minimal. Pappas and Swain urge a wholesale rejection of this traditional philosophical intuition about the role of evidence in knowledge; in doing so they join ranks with a number of other contemporary epistemologists. Such a break may be necessary—as a last resort. But such last-resort moves seem to me plausible only if there are overwhelming indications that the demand that knowledge be certain is unworkable. While there are such indications if certainty is construed as incorrigibility, they do not exist for corrigible certainty. Accordingly, it seems to me preferable to attempt to analyze knowledge under the supposition that knowledge must be certain but not incorrigible. And in what follows I will assume this is so without further argument.[21]

III. WHETHER HAVING A CONCLUSIVE REASON IS SUFFICIENT FOR KNOWING THAT

Raymond Martin has argued that satisfying Dretske's conditions for having a conclusive reason is not a sufficient condition for knowing that.[22] He does so by presenting the following counterexample: S is at the racetrack and places a bet that Gumshoe will win the first race and/or Tagalong will win the second. He then leaves the track, returns after the second race without gaining any information about the outcome of either race—which was that Gumshoe won the first and Tagalong lost the second. Upon returning, he goes to the pay-off window and hands in his betting ticket, whereupon the usher pays him off; nothing is said during this transaction. On the basis of seeing the usher's actions (R), he believes that Gumshoe won the first race (P). Since Tagalong's losing the second is logically and causally independent of P (under any plausible analyses of logical and causal independence), it is to be included among the circumstances C; and so it is the case that under circumstances C, R would not be the case unless P were the case.[23] So via (2) and (3), S has a conclusive reason for believing that P, hence knows that P. But, says Martin, these results of Dretske's analysis "are surely unacceptable. It is seriously counterintuitive to claim that R is a conclusive reason for P, or if R is S's only reason for believing that P, that S has a conclusive reason for believing that P."[24] As such, having a conclusive reason is not a sufficient condition for knowing that P.

According to Martin, the reason we find it counterintuitive that S would know that P in this situation is that it is physically possible that R and not P. What makes P necessary given R is the fact that, unbeknown to S, Tagalong lost the second race (together with other circumstantial facts); and our intuitions are that S could know that P in this situation only if he possessed knowledge that Tagalong lost as well as R. Martin sees this counterexample as a direct challenge to Dretske's whole approach to analyzing knowledge without succumbing to skepticism; for key to Dretske's avoidance of skepticism is the move of not requiring that S know the circumstances C, only requiring that he possess the conclusive reason R. And Martin sees this counterexample as strongly suggesting that this move will not work (1975, 216–17).

At first blush, Martin's counterexample seems compelling, as does his discussion of its consequences. As such, it poses a serious threat not only to Dretske's analysis of knowing that, but also to any other analyses along similar lines. Nevertheless, I think these are important *theoretical reasons* for accepting Martin's case as a genuine case of knowing that, and rejecting the counterintuitive character of the case as not being decisive. This line of defense against Martin's charges will be developed below in terms of our modified Dretskian analysis.

IV. A MODIFIED DRETSKIAN ANALYSIS

We now have considered and evaluated a number of putative defects in Dretske's conclusive reasons analysis; and for some of these we have proposed interpretations which assuage the difficulties. But there still remain three main difficulties with his analysis which must be resolved if anything like his position is to prove viable as an account of knowledge: First, it is necessary to provide an account of what it is to believe that *P on the basis* of a conclusive reason *R;* second, restrictions on the circumstances to which conclusive reasons are to be relativized must be weaker than his causal and logical independence requirements; third, the analysis must be able to dispense with Martin's racetrack case. Since I am convinced that Dretske's intuitions about conclusive reasons and the role they play in knowledge are essentially rightheaded, it seems to me desirable to focus on the second problem. My approach will be the dialectical development of an alternative to Dretske's analysis which is similar in its basic intuitions yet resolves the difficulties just listed; Dretske's own analysis frequently will serve as my argumentative foil.

The examples we have considered thus far are ones where the conclusive reasons *R* are experiential states of *S;* in such cases *R* is a conclusive reason by virtue of some sanctioning generalization of form (2-ii) which is empirically true. Let us call such conclusive reasons *basic conclusive reasons.* Dretske does not require that the sanctioning generalizations for basic conclusive reasons be causal generalizations,[25] and so denies that his analysis is a *causal* analysis of knowledge. But he would allow that any causal generalization satisfying the conditions of (2) will qualify as the sanctioning generalization for a conclusive reason *R.* For the present I want to confine my attention initially to *basic causal conclusive reasons*—that is, basic conclusive reasons whose sanctioning generalizations are causal generalizations.

For such basic causal conclusive reasons we can discover a possible underlying rationale for Dretske's analysis of conclusive reasons. To begin, consider the simple case of a normal observer *S* looking at a cup on a bare table under ordinary circumstances, having a sensation of the cup, and thereby knowing there is a cup on the table. Under such circumstances, (α), the cup being on the table reasonably might be construed as *the* or *a cause* of *S* having the sensation; (β) the circumstances (including S's being a normal observer looking at the table under normal circumstances) are such that of all the factors present, S could be having that sensation only if there were a cup on the table. It is plausible to suppose that under the circumstances, failure of either of these two conditions would preclude S from having a basic causal conclusive reason for believing that there is a cup on the table, which reason guaranteed the truth of that belief. What do these two conditions amount to? Condition (β) can be rendered as

(7) $\sim\Diamond(R \ \& \ C \ \& \ \sim P),$

where R is the sensation (experiential state), C are the prevailing circumstances, and P is the state of there being a cup on the table. If the supposition is made that C meets condition (2-i), then (7) is just a way of formulating Dretske's analysis of conclusive reasons. Thus (7) also admits of the following formulation:

(8) Whenever C, R would not be the case unless P were the case.

Condition (α) is automatically satisfied by our supposition that R is a basic causal conclusive reason. But what is involved in condition (α) being satisfied? What conditions must be met in order for P to be *the* or *a cause* of R under the circumstances? It is well known that what counts as "the cause" of an event or state of affairs in a particular situation is some factor(s) selected on pragmatic grounds from the causally relevant factors operant in the situation.[26] Gorovitz (1965, 1969) provides a helpful analysis of the pragmatic basis for making such a selection; according to him, the pragmatic selection must be from among factors c meeting the following condition with respect to the event or state of affairs e:

(9) (a) e would not have occurred if c had not occurred (i.e., all conditions simultaneous to c but not including c [or e] do not constitute a jointly sufficient set for e), or else

(b) c is a member of a minimal set of conditions such that e would not have occurred unless some member of that set had been fulfilled.[27]

In addition, all of the conditions simultaneous to c (including c) must constitute a jointly sufficient set for e. Condition (9-a) is just a special case of (9-b)—namely, that case where the minimal set of conditions is the singleton set whose only member is c. Since (9-b) concerns cases of causal overdetermination, and the duplication of causes there clearly prevents any of them from qualifying as a conclusive reason (since [7] will not be satisfied), we shall confine our attention to just (9-a). Any causally relevant factor c satisfying condition (9) which belongs to a set of factors jointly sufficient for e is *a cause of* e. On Gorovitz' analysis, which of these factors are to be selected is done on the basis of some standard of comparison (roughly a set of rational expectations not unlike Toulmin's ideals of natural order or explanatory ideals).[28] For the purposes of basic causal conclusive reasons, it is not so important that P be correctly cited as being *the* cause of R; what is important is that the causal influence of P under the circumstances be such that given an appropriate standard of comparison, it could be cited as the cause of R[29]—which is to say that under the circumstances, P must be *a cause of* R. Thus if Gorovitz' analysis is adequate, satsifying condition (9) and his sufficiency condition—where P is c and R is e— is the essence of meeting condition (α).

Although approximately correct, Gorovitz' analysis (9) unfortunately is not fully adequate for two reasons. First, the parenthetical gloss of 'e would not have occurred if c had not occurred' is incorrect. For the joint occurrence of all conditions simultaneous to c but not including c *and* the occurrence of e is compatible with all conditions simultaneous to c but not including c or e not being jointly sufficient for e; but 'e would not have occurred if c had not occurred' precludes this possibility. The appropriate gloss is that the occurrence of just some of those factors simultaneous to c, but excluding c and e, and no *others* is sufficient for the *nonoccurrence* of e—which is very close to what (7) expresses.[30] Second, consider a case where c and e are widely separated in time—as when c is a particular star exploding at time t, and e is the visual sensation a perceiver S has at some later time t' as a result of light from the exploding star stimulating his retina and so on. For the explosion to be a cause of that visual sensation, various regularities concerning light transmission, episodes in S's life, and so on, *must* obtain in the interval between t and t'. But (9) only takes into account those conditions which are *simultaneous* to c, and so excludes from consideration all these other *subsequent* factors occurring in the interval from t up to and including t' which play a role in the explosion of the star (c) being a cause of S being in the visual state (e). And the same difficulty occurs whenever there is any gap (however small) between the time c occurs and the time e occurs.

Of course, this difficulty can be gotten around by assuming some thesis of total causal determinism, but in presenting an analysis of knowledge I prefer to avoid making such strong and questionable metaphysical commitments. Another way out of the difficulty would be to construe 'simultaneous' in (9) as meaning "occurring in the closed time interval $[t, t']$"; this relativizes the causal regularity holding between *c* and *e* to the set *C* of all conditions actually occurring in the time interval [*t*, *t'*] with the exception of *c* and *e*. This will not work, however, since among the standing conditions allowed in the time interval [*t*, *t'*] will be various intermediate effects of *c*, which in turn qualify as causes of *e*; and if these are not excluded, it will be the case that the standing conditions *C* will be sufficient for *e*, and so *c* generally will fail to qualify as a cause of *e*. Obviously, then, these intermediate effects which also are causes of *e* must be excluded from *C*. Replacing (9) by the following definition eliminates these two objections while preserving the sound insights of Gorovitz' (9):

> (10) Let *c* be a factor obtaining at time *t*, let *e* be an event or state of affairs obtaining at time *t'*, where $t \leq t'$. Let *C* be all those factors which actually obtain in the closed time interval [*t*, *t'*] with the exception of *e*. Then *c* is a cause of *e* if and only if there is some set *F* of factors and there is some minimal set *M* of factors containing *c* such that
> (i) $F \subseteq C$; $M \subseteq C$; and $F \cap M = \varnothing$;
> (ii) $F \cup M$ is sufficient for *e*;
> (iii) *e* would not have occurred given *F* if *M* had not occurred (i.e., the occurrence of *F* and the nonoccurrence of *M* or any other *M'* — not necessarily contained in *C* — such that (ii) holds when *M* is replaced are jointly sufficient for the nonoccurrence of *e*).

As before, we are only concerned with the case where $M = \{c\}$, since otherwise the elements in *M* fail to qualify as conclusive reasons; subsequently we will tacitly assume (10) is so restricted to singleton *M* containing *c*.

Although Gorovitz offered his original analysis as a general treatment of the pragmatics of causal ascriptions or explanations, my claims for the revised account (10) are far more modest. I offer (10) only as a foil for presenting and motivating a satisfactory account of conclusive reasons. Specifically, the function of (10) is to lead to an analysis of a (noncausal) contextual necessity condition adequate for the purposes of improving upon Dretske's conclusive reasons analysis. I make no claims as to the adequacy of Gorovitz' (9) (beyond my criticisms above) or of my (10) as a general account of causality. Indeed, such concerns are irrelevant to my epistemological concerns here. For issues of causality (including whether [9] or [10] are adequate analyses of causality notions) ultimately are irrelevant to the problem of presenting a satisfactory analysis of conclusive reasons.

What is required for such an analysis is that there be circumstances under which the experiential state R of a person S be a reliable indicator that some (external) state of affairs P is the case. Such reliability *may* be due to P causing (being a cause of) S being in experiential state R, but it need not be. It would be sufficient if P and R were correlated tightly enough that R was a reliable indicator that P. (Such could be the case, for example, if P and R were linked effects of a common cause.) The contextual necessity condition (12) introduced below and erected upon a generalization of (10) is the reliable indicator condition I offer as central to my epistemology, and it does not require that P be a cause of R. Whether or not it provides an analysis of any causality notion is irrelevent to its adequacy for my purposes—notwithstanding the fact that I am using a critique of Gorovitz' causality analysis and an examination of basic causal conclusive reasons as vehicles for obtaining and motivating my more general contextual necessity condition.

With these caveats made, let us return to the analysis of basic causal conclusive reasons. Letting P be c and R be e (10-iii) provides us with an important feature of meeting condition (α): Among the circumstances in the closed time interval from c to e there must be a subset F (excluding P and R but including the nonoccurrence of certain factors) such that

(11) Whenever F, R would not be the case unless P were the case.[31]

But (11) differs from (8) only in the choice of actually operant conditions used to relativize the sanctioning generalization: Whereas C in (8) must exclude any condition in the time interval which is not causally or logically independent of P, F can contain some factors which are not causally or logically independent of P. Since by hypothesis, R is a basic causal conclusive reason for P, (8) must be a causal generalization. But (11) indicates that such causal generalizations are to be relativized to some F, not C; hence the correct set of conditions for (8) should be such an F, not C. Our discussion thus far has provided an underlying rationale for Dretske's analysis of conclusive reasons, where they are restricted to basic causal conclusive reasons, and also has provided reasons for rejecting Dretske's restriction of the relativizing conditions to just those conditions present that are logically and causally independent of P. And if we are to reject such a restriction for basic causal conclusive reasons, there seems to be no reason not to reject it for basic conclusive reasons in general or conclusive reasons in general.

The expansion of our proposed treatment of basic causal conclusive reasons to conclusive reasons in general is not entirely straightforward. For the former requires that a conclusive reason c be *a cause of* the experiential state *e,* but such a requirement cannot be imposed on conclusive reasons. To see this, consider the following case: My secretary Rose Merrywoods was transcribing one of my dictating tapes when the phone rang; reaching for the stop button, she accidentally hit the erase button and erased a portion of the tape. Later, seeing what she had done, she believed (correctly) that the tape had been partially erased. However, unbeknown to her, earlier I secretly had erased *exactly* the same portion of the tape, since it contained a confidential efficiency report on her performance (which she was not supposed to know about) that I absentmindedly had dicated on the tape. Under the circumstances, what Rose did was sufficient to guarantee that part of the tape was erased, and so her experiential state of seeing the machine running with the erase button depressed was sufficient to guarantee that part of the tape was erased; thus (along Dretske's line) she has a conclusive reason for believing that the tape had been partially erased. However, the tape being erased was not a cause of her experiential state, since what she saw—the machine running in the erase mode—was not a factor in the erasure of the tape. This indicates that there can be conclusive reasons R for believing that P under circumstances where P is *not a cause* of $R,$ provided that R would not have occurred under the circumstances unless P were the case. That is, clause (iii) of (10) captures an important truth about what it is to be a conclusive reason, whereas clause (10-ii) expresses a condition which, per accident, is characteristic of basic causal conclusive reasons but fails to be met by conclusive reasons in general. Dretske's own conclusive reasons analysis reflects this fact, and so his insistence that a conclusive reasons analysis should not be *causal* (strictly speaking) is vindicated. But even (10-iii) is not sufficiently general, since it limits P to descriptions of the circumstances S is in, whereas a posteriori knowledge includes other form propositions as well. The following condition generalizes (10-iii) to cover any form a posteriori proposition which can be known:

> (12) R is a conclusive reason for P under the circumstances if and only if there is a C descriptive of the actual circumstances (including both the presence and absence of various factors) such that '$\sim\!\Diamond(C$ & $\sim\!P$ & $R)$ & $\Diamond(C$ & $\sim\!P)$ & $\Diamond R$' is true.

Whenever (12) is satisfied by P and R we shall say that P is *contextually necessary* for $R.$

Several comments on (12) are in order. First, the second conjunct is our replacement condition for Dretske's independence conditions and is a generalization of what is implicit in (10-iii). Without this restriction, C could include circumstances which necessitate the truth of P regardless whether R occurred; under these circumstances C would be sufficient to guarantee the truth of $\sim\lozenge(C \,\&\, \sim P \,\&\, R)$ regardless whether R was true or false, and so R would not be indicative of the truth of P. Moreover, since '$\lozenge\phi$' implies '$\lozenge\phi$', this condition also imposes the requirement that $\lozenge(C \,\&\, \sim P)$. Second, the requirement that $\lozenge R$ simply says that $\sim\lozenge(C \,\&\, \sim P \,\&\, R)$ is not true by virtue of $\sim R$ being causally necessary. This is implicit in the very notion of an experiential state. Third, our interpretation of experiential states allowed epistemic states such as the state of S knowing that Q (K_sQ). Suppose that Q logically entails P; since K_sQ entails Q, it follows that K_sQ entails P. Hence for any C such that $\lozenge(C \,\&\, \sim P)$, $\sim \lozenge(C \,\&\, \sim P \,\&\, K_sQ)$; so via (12), knowing that Q is a conclusive reason for any P entailed by Q. Fourth, C may not always be finitely expressible, in which case (12) would require recourse to a nonstandard language (e.g., one containing infinite conjunctions, etc.).

It is my contention that (12), as elaborated by the foregoing comments, is an adequate analysis of conclusive reasons. In further support of this contention I note that when conclusive reasons are interpreted in accordance with (12), Dretske's analysis of knowledge can evade Pappas and Swain's "counterexamples" in precisely the way Dretske has suggested (see sec. II); for the generator or the holograph *being off* can be included among the factors C in such a way that (12) is satisfied, but (12) will not be satisfied if the generator or holograph *is on*. Since the two cases are parallel, it will suffice to consider just the generator case. Letting the circumstances be as specified in section II, let C' include the information about S's experiences, knowledge of the power distribution situation, and only one fact about his friend's backup system, namely that S seeing his friend's lights on (R) implies that either the generator is on (G) or that the power company's generators are causing the lights to be on (P). Suppose further that $\sim G$, and let the C in (12) be $C' \,\&\, \sim G$. Now clearly, $\lozenge R$; and $\lozenge(C' \,\&\, \sim G \,\&\, \sim P)$, since it is possible that $\sim R$—in which case nothing follows from C' as to whether G or P. Assume now that $\lozenge(C' \,\&\, \sim G \,\&\, \sim P \,\&\, R)$, and suppose this possibility obtains; hence C', $\sim G$, $\sim P$, and R are supposed true. From $\sim G$ and $\sim P$ we obtain $\sim(G \vee P)$; hence by the fact that C' contains (if R then $(G \vee P)$) it follows that $\sim R$. But this is a contradiction, so $\sim\lozenge(C' \,\&\, \sim G \,\&\, \sim P \,\&\, R)$. Hence (12) is satisfied, and R is a conclusive reason for P. By contrast, suppose the actually obtaining circumstances are as originally given except that $\sim P$ & G. Since R, for *any* actually obtaining circumstances C it will be the case that $(C \,\&\, G \,\&\, \sim P \,\&\, R)$; hence $\lozenge(C \,\&\, G \,\&\, \sim P \,\&\, R)$ for any such C. Therefore, there is no actual C such that $\sim\lozenge(C \,\&\, G \,\&\,$

$\sim P$ & R); so (12) cannot be satisified, and R is not a conclusive reason for P.

The ability to handle the generator case serves to add teeth to our earlier suggestion that Dretske's requirement that C be causally and logically independent of P was too strong. The way in which our replacement analysis (12) uses the causal possibility operators enables us to explain why logical and causal independence of P and C is too strong. Typically, modal operators such as '$\Diamond$' are interpreted in terms of possible worlds alternative to the real world. In the case of conclusive reasons, these alternative worlds must be like the actual world in that some circumstances C, which obtain in the actual world, obtain in that possible world. But in contrast to the actual world, P is false of that alternative world. As is well known, such an alternative world must deviate from the actual world in more than just the nonobtaining of P;[32] in particular, the nonobtaining of P will require further deviations in that alternative world with respect to some factors in the real world that are not causally and logically independent of P. Dretske apparently thinks that this requires restricting the C common to the actual world and this alternative possible one to *just* those circumstances logically and causally independent of P. But this is much stronger than is needed—all that is needed is that the circumstances C which carry over to the alternative possible world be such as to be compatible with the falsity of P. All this requires is that the alternative possible world be such that 'C & $\sim P$' is true of it, which requirement is imposed by $\Diamond(C$ & $\sim P)$ in (12); and this is much weaker than Dretske's causal and logical independence requirement.

Although it is not clear that confusions about what conditions alternative causally possible worlds must meet is the source of Dretske's logical and causal independence conditions, such a conjecture is reinforced by consideration of issues raised in those passages of *Seeing and Knowing* where Dretske discusses *background conditions*.[33] For cases of seeing that b is P, Dretske gives the following characterization:

> B is a *background condition* if and only if (a) B is logically and causally independent of the (nonrelational) features and properties of b itself (and, in particular, of b's being P) and (b) there are variations in B which affect the way b looks to S. The distance between S and b, the lighting conditions (*not* the reflected light—this is causally dependent on the properties of b itself), the angle from which S sees b, the medium through which S sees b, the state of S's eyes, nervous system, and brain (insofar as these are not causally dependent on his seeing b), what lies between S's

eyes and *b*—all are, generally speaking, background conditions. *Normally any one of these can be varied to produce a corresponding alteration in the way b looks to S without altering the fact that b is P.*[34]

Thus background conditions are just the *C* of (2-ii). This passage is the closest Dretske comes in *Seeing and Knowing* to defending his independence condition for background conditions.[35]

The passage does make it clear that Dretske sees dangers in allowing causal interactions between *b* and the background conditions; two such dangers are hinted at. First, his parenthetical glosses on examples of background conditions indicate that one function of the independence condition is to eliminate factors which are intermediate effects of *b*'s being *P* which also are causes of *b*'s looking the way it does to *S*. The danger here is genuine—being exactly the problem we discussed above with respect to (9), which prompted us to replace it by (10). Thus our proposed analysis of basic causal conclusive reasons does not succumb to this danger even though it rejects Dretske's independence conditions; similarly (12) avoids such problems. Second, the italicized sentence at the end of the passage indicates that Dretske also sees a danger in allowing *b*'s being *P* to be an effect of background conditions. For if is were allowed, then the background conditions would be such that $\sim\diamondsuit(C \& \sim P \& R)$ was vacuously satisfied since $\sim\diamondsuit(C \& \sim P)$. But this possibility can be avoided by imposing the requirement that $\diamondsuit(C \& \sim P)$—which is a much weaker restriction than $(C © P)$. Thus we see that Dretske is correct in thinking that some restrictions on *C* are necessary to eliminate these two dangers. But the imposition of the causal and logical independence condition is an overreaction; for it imposes restrictions on *C* far in excess of what is needed.

A possible line of objection to (12) concerns Dretske's claim that if he did not impose his independence restrictions on *C,* the result would be a trivialization of (1). In support of this claim he considers the case of two mountains *M* and *N* with lava distributed between them. Although the lava is there as a result of the eruption of *M,* the geology of the area is such that at the time when *M* erupted, *N* would have erupted if *M* had not; and had *N* erupted, the lava it deposited would have had the same distribution as the present lava deposit. According to Dretske, the lava distribution is not sufficient to enable one to know that *M* erupted; so to avoid sanctioning the lava distribution (or rather the experiential state resulting from it) as a conclusive reason for '*M* eruped' (*P*), Dretske argues that the second mountain not erupting ($\sim N$) must be excluded from the relativizing circumstances *C,* and he invokes the causal independence condition to exclude $\sim N$ from *C.*[36]

However, the lava case has essentially the same form as the generator case, and so his differential treatment of the two cases seems to me highly unwarranted. My own intuitions are that (in analogy to his reply to Pappas and Swain) the appropriate treatment of the lava case is to say that S has a conclusive reason for 'M erupted' if N did not erupt, but that he does not have a conclusive reason if N did erupt. Moreover, this is precisely what (12) determines to be the case, as can be shown using the same general arguments as were used in the generator case earlier in this section. My discussion of Martin's racetrack case below, inter alia, provides further evidence in support of my contention that the lava and generator cases should be handled precisely as (12) does. However, before considering Martin's case, further development of our revision of Dretske's position is required.

According to Dretske, S knows that P if and only if S has a conclusive reason R for believing P; and the latter notion is analyzed via (3). Clause (B) of (3) requires that S believe, without doubt, reservation, or question, that P is the case and that he believes this *on the basis of R*. What is it to *believe P on the basis of R?* Certainly the requirement is not that R be a sufficient condition for S's belief that P; rather, the condition seems to be that R plays some *essential* role, under the circumstances, in S coming to believe that P. If one allows that being in experiential state R can be *a cause of* S's coming to believe that P, then our condition (10) is an analysis of what it is for a factor to play such an essential role—which suggests that S believes that P on the basis of R if and only if (10) is satisfied, where c is R, and e is 'S believes that P'.[37] And in accordance with our discussion above and in section I, the experiential state R can be any of a number of kinds of states including sensory states, memory states, and epistemic states. Thus we obtain the following as our modified Dretskian analysis of a posteriori knowledge that P:

> (13) S knows that P if and only if
>   (i) S is in an experiential state R;
>   (ii) S believes that P, and being in the experiential state R is a cause of that belief;
>   (iii) the circumstances are such that R is a conclusive reason for P in accordance with (12).

In case R is an epistemic state of knowing that Q, we understand this as meaning that S previously knew that Q and has continued to do so in such a way that (13) continues to be satisfied with respect to Q. This could be achieved, for example, by being in a memory state such that later being in the memory state qualifies as a conclusive reason for Q and is a cause of S's later belief that Q. Although we leave the notion of belief as an unanalyzed primitive notion, we do assume that beliefs may be unconsciously held.[38]

Prefatory to our consideration of Martin's racetrack case, we will need to display certain corollaries to (13). As with Dretske's original analysis, our modified analysis (13) entails the denial of the K-K thesis. This denial results in conclusive reasons R playing quite different evidential roles in knowledge that P and in the defense of claims to know that P.[39] If S knows that P, then S has a conclusive reason R for believing that P; and that conclusive reason R makes S's belief that P *certain* in the following very strong truth-evaluating sense: Whenever S has a conclusive reason for believing that P, P *must be true*. As such, conclusive reasons provide *all* the justification for knowledge that one *reasonably* could want. On the other hand, having conclusive reasons R for believing that P may leave S very *ill-equipped* to *defend* his true claim to know that P: First, S in general will not know all the relevant circumstances C operant by virtue of which R is a conclusive reason for believing that P; and he might not know which of the operant circumstances belong to C. So S may be quite unable to defend his claim against skeptical challenges to the effect that perhaps the circumstances are such that P might be false despite R being the case. Second, it may be the case that S is unable to describe the experiential state R, may not even know that he is in state R, and may not even know that R is evidence for his belief; if so, these difficulties, combined with the first sort indicated, may leave him even less able to defend his knowledge claim against the skeptic. Third, although being in the experiential state R is *a cause of S* believing that P, R alone may greatly underdetermine his belief that P. For example, if S is the sort of person who is fairly daring in playing his hunches, it may be the case that R will satisfy condition (10) with respect to believing that P under circumstances where it would be just as reasonable (for all S is aware of) to believe some Q which is incompatible with P. As such, his beliefs may be capriciously but firmly held on the basis of R; but whenever R is a cause of his capricious belief that P and R is a conclusive reason for P, he will know that P. However, unless he is extremely lucky in his hunches, his knowledge claims will be highly unreliable, and he probably will be quite ill-equipped to defend them against the skeptic.

From this perspective, the skeptic is reduced to being a bully or a gadfly: The thrust of his attack is to get S to *withdraw* his knowledge claims; and even if he does succeed in showing that S *cannot defend* his knowledge claim, it does not follow that he has shown that S does not know that P. Of course, if the skeptic succeeds in getting S to withdraw his knowledge claim, it may have the effect of causing S to abandon his belief that P; and if he does, it will be the case that S does not *now* know that P. But it does not follow that S did not know that P at the time when he claimed to know that P and still believed that P on the basis of a conclusive reason R.

We are now in a position to reconsider Martin's racetrack case. There, S's conclusive reason for believing that Gumshoe won the first race was the usher's paying off on a bet that either Gumshoe would win the first or Tagalong would win the second or both. Since this payoff was equally compatible with either Gumshoe or Tagalong winning, and S had no additional information which favored one outcome over the other, his belief that Gumshoe won strikes us as highly unreasonable; and so we want to reject his claim to know that Gumshoe won, since the claim is unreasonable despite the fact that by (13) the claim is true. And this is a totally appropriate thing to do, since his claim *is* unreasonable and S is quite incapable of defending it under the circumstances of Martin's case. It is, I suggest, the fact that it would be unreasonable for S to *claim to know* that Gumshoe won that leads Martin to conclude, "It is seriously counterintuitive to *claim* . . . that S has a conclusive reason for believing that P."[40]

But it follows from this neither that S does not have a conclusive reason for believing that P nor that S does not know that P. The *unreasonableness* of such *claims* is totally compatible with S having a conclusive reason for believing that P and knowing that P. As Alan White puts it, "the criteria for judging the making of a claim, that is, whether the claim is reasonable or unreasonable, are those of confidence and good evidence, while the criterion for judging the claim itself, that is whether the claim is valid or not, is that of truth."[41] And in Martin's case the truth of the matter is that S *does know* that Gumshoe won the first, since (via [12]) he has a conclusive reason for believing that he won, and (via [13]) he does know that Gumshoe won: Capricious as it may be, S does believe that Gumshoe won without doubt, question, or reservation; and under the circumstances C (including Tagalong losing) he would not have been paid off unless Gumshoe had won — hence his belief is certain in the very strong sense that under the circumstances, it could not be wrong.

Simply put, Martin's case is one of those where, because of doxastic derring-do, S *does* know that P but is quite unable to defend a claim to know that P; as such, any claim of his to know that Gumshoe won strikes us as unreasonable. But that only shows it sometimes is unreasonable to claim to know what you in fact do know. We thus have theoretical reasons for denying that Martin's case is a counter-example to a Dretskian sort of analysis of knowledge.

To many, I suspect, the foregoing discussion of Martin's racetrack case may appear to degenerate into the mere trading of epistemic intuitions and other philosophic prejudices, for does it not seem to be a case where Martin is urging his sensitive intuitions about 'knowledge' and I am urging my contrary intuitions? Were this the case, then the dispute would be nothing more than an inconclusive clashing of intuitions.[42] But to dismiss the dispute in this way would be, I contend, a mistake; for in this case there is a means for adjudicating this prima facie clash of intuitions. Central to my analysis of 'knows that' is an explicit denial of the K-K thesis; it follows that any purported counter-example to my proferred analysis that depends essentially upon the K-K thesis is question-begging—hence is incapable of serving as a counterexample to my analysis. Thus the only counterexamples which *could* count against my analysis of knowledge must be ones which do not presuppose the K-K thesis. Since my account of knowledge that is one such that to know that ϕ the supporting evidence that ϕ must guarantee that ϕ is true, the only non–question begging counterexamples must be such that one can believe that ϕ, where ϕ has this truth-evaluating certainty, but still one does not know that ϕ.

All the purported counterexamples I have encountered proceed as follows: They attempt to show that the evidence which provides ϕ with truth-warranting certainty is evidence I am *insufficiently aware of* to defend a *claim* to know that ϕ—from which the attempt is made to conclude I do not *know* that ϕ. But such an inference is unwarranted *unless* the evidence I *can* adduce in support of a *claim* to know that ϕ must be *exhaustive* of the evidence by virtue of which I *do* know that ϕ. In the absence of *independent* arguments in support of the K-K thesis (of which I am aware of none which do not implausibly presuppose deductive omniscience, such as Hintikka did in his 1962 book, *Knowledge and Belief*), such recourse to what is needed to adequately defend *claims* to know is question-begging. In short, it is my contention that counterexamples, such as Martin's, which attempt to exploit S's inability to adequately defend claims to know that ϕ so as to show that S doesn't *really* know that ϕ, where my analysis sanctions that S does know that ϕ, must be question-begging by virtue of recourse to either tacit or explicit assumption of the K-K thesis—where such an assumption cannot be defended on sufficiently independent grounds. In short, Martin's racetrack case is an ingenious example of a multiply repeatable class of counterexamples which ultimately are question-begging—hence constitute no significant challenge to the analysis I have offered.

The foregoing observations on Martin's racetrack case provide a theoretical basis for defending the earlier contention that (13)'s handling of the lava and generator cases is correct. Under (13), the lava distribution does qualify as a conclusive reason for 'M erupted', and so one can know that M erupted on the basis of the lava distribution—contrary to Dretske's intuitions. But essentially the same considerations we involved in handling Martin's case apply to this case: The possibility that N might have erupted reduces the reasonableness of a claim to know M erupted, but it in no way affects the truth of such a claim.[43] Essentially the same considerations add to the defensibility of our resolution of Pappas and Swain's generator case.

V. SOME ALTERNATIVE VIEWS BRIEFLY CONSIDERED

My response to Martin's case in effect was to embrace the putative counterexample as a genuine case of knowing, arguing that our philosophically contaminated and question-begging intuitions to the contrary are not to be trusted. I now turn to the brief consideration of certain other strategies for countering Martin's case.

Robert Nozick (1981) offers a causal analysis of knowledge rather similar to both Dretske's and our (13). According to it,

> (14) S knows, via method (or way of believing) M, that P if and only if
>   (i) P is true.
>   (ii) S believes, via method or way of coming to believe M, that P.
>   (iii) If P weren't true and S were to use M to arrive at a belief whether (or not) P, then S wouldn't believe, via M, that P.
>   (iv) If P were true and S were to use M to arrive at a belief whether (or not) P, then S would believe, via M, that P. [179][44]

If only one method M is relevant to one's belief that P, then S knows that P by virtue of satisfying (14). If more than one method M is relevant to one's belief that P, for S to know tht P there must be one method satisfying conditions (i)–(iv) that "outweighs" all other methods (182). He further suggests that the counterfactual conditionals in clauses (iii) and (iv) be interpreted using Lewis-like possible-worlds semantics (Lewis 1973), where the possible worlds relevant to assessing these conditionals are those "closest to" or "in the neighborhood of" the actual world (Nozick 1981, 176, 179, 680–81).

Martin (1983) argues that Nozick's analysis is liable to a version of his racetrack example. Garrett (1983) challenges this claim, questioning whether the racetrack case satisfies clause (iii) of Nozick's analysis. He writes,

> This is true only if the possible worlds in which Gumshoe does not win the first and Tagalong wins the second are sufficiently 'far' from the actual world to be irrelevant to the assessment of the claim that S knows that Gumshoe won the first. [182]
>
> Indeed a Nozickian will argue that it is precisely S's insensitivity in such worlds to the fact that Gumshoe does not win the first (i.e., S's failure to track the fact that not-P) which ensures that S's belief does not constitute knowledge. Hence unless we are told why appeal to such worlds in this context is illegitimate we have no reason to believe that Martin has produced a genuine counterexample to Nozick's thesis. [182]

He goes on to argue that Nozick is liable to other counterexamples.

Garrett's defense suggests we might avoid Martin's racetrack counterexample by interpreting the causal modalities in our analysis (12) of conclusive reasons in accordance with Lewis' possible worlds interpretation[45] in a manner parallel to his defense of Nozick. There are several objections to such an approach. First, a prime motivation for developing my conclusive reasons analysis is to provide the epistemic basis for defending my quasi-realistic interpretation of scientific knowledge. One of van Fraassen's prime reasons for being an antirealist is his belief that realisms require giving possible-world physical interpretations to the causal modalities that are ontologically objectionable. Recourse to Lewis-like causal worlds thus will make defending my scientific realism far more difficult.[46] Second, one of my main objections to, or qualms about, Lewis' treatment of counterfactuals is that it is extremely sensitive to choice of distance or similarity measures for comparing actual and possible worlds, coupled with the fact that he has little to say in the way of detailed instructions on how to choose such measures other than reliance on intuitions for specific examples. Indeed, the disagreement between Martin and Garrett is indicative of how crucially things do depend on the choice of similarity or distance measures and how incapable Lewis' analysis is of settling the issue.

Dretske's own reaction to Martin's racetrack case is instructive. After considerable correspondence with Martin over the case, he eventually abandoned the conclusive reasons analysis of his 1969 and 1971 works and replaced it with a new information content analysis in his *Knowledge and the Flow of Information* (1981).

On this new analysis,

> [Perceptual] knowledge is defined as information caused (or causally sustained) belief. [1983, 58][47]

> Assuming that belief is some kind of internal state with a content expressible as *s* is *F,* this is said to be caused by the information that *s* is *F,* if and only if those physical properties of the signal by virtue which it carries this information are the ones that are causally efficacious in the production of the belief. . . . When it is this pattern of knocks that causes you to believe that your friend has arrived, then . . . the *information* that your friend has arrived causes you to believe that he has arrived. [58–59]

> [When the signal does not produce knowledge] those properties of the signal that carry the information . . . are not the ones that are causally responsible for your belief. [59]

Expanding on the crucial notion of information content, Dretske says,

> A signal *r* carries the information that *s* is *F* = The conditional probability of *S*'s being *F,* given *r* (and [prior knowledge] *k*), is 1 (but, given *k* alone, less than 1). [57]

> The informational content of a signal is a function of the *nomic* (or law-governed) relations it bears to other conditions. Unless these relations are . . . 'counterfactual supporting' relations (a symptom of a background, lawful regularity), the relations in question are not such as to support an assignment of informational content. [58]

Perception is central to this account. He distinguishes between the extensional way of describing our perceptions (seeing) and the intensional way (seeing that) (60), where the information needed to see that is encoded from our sensory-process of seeing (61).

A comparison of his new informational analysis with that of our (13) indicates that what he basically has done is collapse clause (ii) and (iii) together and replace them by the requirement that the beliefs that *P* invoked in knowing that *P* must be caused by the information that *P* in the perceptual experience. Presumably this change enables Dretske to avoid Martin's racetrack case by restricting the belief-forming causal regularities that produce knowledge more than our (13) does.

Does it follow that we should emulate Dretske and revise our analysis to avoid Martin's racetrack case? I think doing so would be unwise for several reasons. The last Dretske quote makes it clear that his account is parasitic upon an account of nomic or counterfactual supporting regularities. Absent such a detailed analysis, we cannot be certain that Dretske's analysis is indeed more restrictive in allowed beliefs than our (13), hence we cannot be certain it successfully avoids Martin's racetrack case. But let us assume that Dretske's informational account in fact does escape the racetrack counterexample.

In his *Seeing and Knowing,* Dretske sharply distinguishes primary from secondary epistemic seeing on the basis of whether one simply sees the object of knowledge or not (1969, chs. 2, 3). In chapter 11 I argued that all perceptual knowledge of physical objects was equally problematic and that the phenomenological properties of sensory experiences had no role to play in an analysis of perceptual knowledge. It follows that the primary and secondary epistemic seeing distinction marks no fundamental epistemic division. It has always seemed to me that Dretske's insistence on distinguishing the two cases was evidence of an inability to break fully with the foundationalist epistemological views he was trying so hard to get beyond. It seems to me that his information content analysis is an even more regressive surrender to foundationalist tendencies—albeit in a way that does deny the K-K thesis. In particular, it is an attempt to ground perceptual knowledge in phenomenological evidence dressed up in information-theoretic terms. My arguments in chapter 11 lead me to reject any such moves as a means of avoiding Martin's racetrack case.

Ruth Millikan (1984) presents an epistemological approach that suggests a means of avoiding Martin's racetrack case. At the heart of her account are two technical notions, *proper functions* and *normal explanations*:

> Very roughly, the proper functions of any body organ or system are those functions which helped account during evolutionary history for survival or proliferation of the species containing the organ or system. Underlining: that an organ or system has certain proper functions is determined by its *history.* It is *not* determined by its present properties, present structure, actual dispositions or actual functions. [316]

> Associated with each of the proper functions that an organ or system has is a Normal explanation for performance of this function which tells us how that organ or system, in that species, historically managed to perform that function. [316]

Exploiting this notion, she suggests "that it is characteristic of those true beliefs that we call 'knowledge' at least that they are true in accordance with a Normal explanation" (317). When a belief fails to constitute knowledge, it is because the "belief matched the world for reasons that completely bypassed evolutionary design" and was "not in accordance with any Normal explanation" (318). She goes on to show that a number of Gettier-like paradoxes can be avoided on this account.

I have no doubt that I can invent any number of evolutionary stories under which the belief that Tagalong won fails to be in accordance with any Normal explanation, thereby avoiding Martin's racetrack counterexample. But I also am fairly confident that I could concoct evolutionary cases in which there were Normal explanations qualifying the belief that Tagalong won as knowledge. The problem is knowing which evolutionary stories are true.

This problem is exacerbated by the fact that, as the Millikan quotes indicate, the correct historical account cannot be determined by the organ or system's present properties or structures, actual positions or functions. How are we to determine, then, what the correct (true) story is, hence what qualifies as a Normal explanation? The problems are essentially the same as those sociobiologists have encountered in the attempt to defend and evaluate their sociobiological explanations of altruistic behavior, homosexuality, and the like.[48] And the seemingly insurmountable difficulties there give faint hope for a satisfactory answer in Millikan's case.

The elimination of present properties or structures, actual positions or functions, raises a further problem: it seems to restrict the knowledge-yielding proper functions to those evolved long ago. Yet in recent years we have seen wide expansions in the sorts of perceptual achievements that yield knowledge—such as those involving infrared photography, thermal sensing, computer-enhanced images, optical and electron microscopic observations, or the use of inferometers, mass spectrometers, and bubble chambers attached to linear accelerators. It seems highly unlikely that the proper functions evolved in the hunting and gathering eras of humankind (or any other eras old enough to have evolved distinctive proper functions) will be sufficiently rich to qualify all these new and distinctive patterns of perception as the paradigmatic cases of observational knowledge they are. For these reasons I do not view Millikan's approach as a promising basis for developing an epistemology that avoids Martin's racetrack case.

One thing that Millikan's, Dretske's, and Nozick's approaches to avoiding counterexamples such as Martin's have in common is that they attempt to restrict the sorts of causal regularities that qualify beliefs as knowledge-yielding. This suggests that our difficulty with

Martin's case is not due to a flawed analysis of conclusive reasons (clause [iii] of [13]), but rather is due to an overly liberal clause (ii) that allows inadequately grounded beliefs to play a role in knowledge. This may prove to be a viable way of avoiding Martin's case, though currently I do not have such an analysis to offer. But even having such a replacement analysis, the considerations just raised suggest another way of challenging Martin's case. It very well may be the case that Martin's racetrack case fails to satisfy clause (13-ii). It seems to me very much an open question whether or not it is psychologically and physiologically possible for the bettor's experiential state to be a cause of him believing that Tagalong won. The realization that Martin's case depends centrally on problematic empirical claims seriously weakens its force as a counterexample.

To summarize, none of the contemporary approaches to avoiding paradoxes and counterexamples we have examined seem as promising as the approach taken in our own conclusive reasons analysis; each of the others seems more fundamentally objectionable than our analysis of possibly having to stand firm against Martin's counterexample, and possibly accepting it as a genuine case of knowing that. But the fact that the case turns on quite problematic empirical claims and has the other defects discussed in the previous section renders the racetrack case sufficiently compromised so as to fail to be a sufficient basis for abandoning the analysis we have presented. Given the alternatives, it seems best to stand by our conclusive reasons analysis. I believe the more detailed and fine-grained development of the analysis being done in my *Facts, Theories, and Scientific Observation* (in progress) will further vindicate this decision.

VI. SCIENTIFIC OBJECTIVITY

Although my ultimate concern is with the objectivity of scientific knowledge, I have concentrated my attention on more basic episte-mological issues in the attempt to lay a sound basis for treating scientific objectivity. Starting from the observation that recent work on the growth of scientific knowledge calls for an epistemology that rejects the K-K thesis,[49] I have attempted to defend such an account of a posteriori knowledge. It remains to sketch how this epistemological analysis can account for objectivity (and rationality) in the growth of scientific knowledge.

The account of a posteriori knowledge defended here is one which acknowledges the possibility (amply realized in routine unsophisticated episodes of, e.g., perceptual knowledge) that one can *know* that P with certainty yet be utterly unequipped to defend *a claim* to know that *P.* It can be shown further that this analysis, suitably and plausibly augmented, allows that one can know universal causal generalizations on the basis of *single* observational or perceptual episodes—hence can know that laws and theories are correct on the basis of singular obervations.[50] Although bordering on philosophical heresy, this finding does cohere with and explain the fact that "respectable" sophisticated branches of science often, and with some reliability, do accept hypotheses, laws, and theories on the basis of single observations or experiments. In short, it does provide an explanation how sophisticated science can and does obtain truths about the world (realistically interpreted) on the basis of highly selected, but limited, observational and experimental expenditures.

Such a possibility for the efficient obtaining of knowledge does not, in itself, shed much light on the objectivity of science. Characteristically, science requires more of its practitioners than that they successfully produce knowledge. Science is a cooperative venture that presupposes that various practitioners can evaluate and act upon others' findings. Individual scientists cannot recreate science for themselves and so must rely on the productions of their colleagues—though such reliance cannot be uncritical, and must be reliable, if science is to have an edge on truth. Science requires that the findings and conclusions reported must be bolstered with sufficient detail about, for example, the experimental design and its execution to enable other practitioners of the discipline to evaluate the claimed results as to their likely veracity. When the findings and their underlying design pass muster, they are accepted and acted upon—or perhaps, if questions remain, they are subjected to additional evaluation, as scientists' initial claims to have discovered charmed quarks were.

Recent work on the growth of scientific knowledge indicates that the canons of rationality for such evaluation that have actually been employed depend upon the content of a particular science, evolve and become increasingly sophisticated as the science is successful, and are such as to render epistemic assessments highly plausible despite the fact that, by ordinary inductive or deductive procedures, they at best enjoy only minimal probabilities.[51] Being dependent upon the content of the science, such canons of rationality for the evaluation of scientific knowledge claims vary and change over the history of science. If these variable and developing evidential bases for the evaluation of knowledge claims in science are identified with the justification required to have knowledge, then radical epistemic relativities—which threaten to undercut scientific objectivity—result. However, if such evidential evaluatory bases are divorced from the justificatory bases for knowledge, both the objectivity of scientific knowledge and the increasingly efficient means employed by successful science for the evaluation of knowledge claims on the basis of limited data (which logically underdetermine the truth of scientific claims) can be reconciled and explained: Scientific objectivity ultimately rests on two factors: (1) The same exploitation of empirical regularities characteristic of interactions between perceivers and their real world environment that all humans exploit in routinely coming to have knowledge of the world—often without being able to say a thing about the nature of such regularities—and (2) the development of increasingly sophisticted means, based on what already is generally or scientifically accepted as true on good grounds, for the evaluation of knowledge claims by those who share the same stock of accepted knowledge claims. In short, scientific objectivity ultimately requires "rock-bottom" abilities to exploit world regularities in obtaining knowledge, whether or not those regularities are known or appreciated; and the spectacular success of science as a cooperative enterprise requires the intellectual abilities to reliably assess the veracity of the products of the former enterprise on the basis of limited but selective knowledge of the circumstances and regularities of those experiences. If the K-K thesis is accepted, the scientific enterprise is impossible; rejecting the K-K thesis allows the scientific enterprise to be objective, successful, and plausible—though, as the analysis presented here suggests, doing so flies in the face of prejudiced philosphical commonsense.[52]

NOTES

1. Scheffler 1967; Shapere 1964, 1966, 1969, 1971, 1982, 1984; Suppe 1974b and 1977a, 617–730; and ch. 10 above.

2. Suppe 1977a, 716–28.

3. Dretske 1969. See also his 1971 article which develops the underlying epistemology of *Seeing and Knowing* in greater detail.

4. I also will give brief consideration to Dretske's more recent epistemological views as presented in his 1981 book and explain why I think these later efforts are wrongheaded.

5. Dretske 1971, 1, 12.

6. Ibid., 7.

7. Ibid., 7–8.

8. Ibid., 9. To facilitate later developments, I have adopted a different notation for the causal or empirical possibility operator than Dretske does.

9. If one were to adopt the stronger interpretation of causal and logical independence, then clauses (i)–(ii) of (2) would be replaced by:

(i') C is a conjunction, each of whose conjuncts is a sentence F describing the occurrence of a single attribute in that set;

(ii') for each conjunct F of C, $(F © P)$ & $(F \bigcirc P)$; and

(iii') $\sim \Diamond (R$ & C & $\sim P)$.

10. Dretske 1971, 12–13, reading 'experiential' for 'experimental', as Dretske intends it to be read (private communication).

11. Dretske 1971, 12.

12. For its avoidance of these, cf. ibid., n. 13, and Pappas and Swain 1973, 73.

13. See Alvin Goldman 1967 for arguments which tend to support this conclusion.

14. Pappas and Swain 1973.

15. Ibid., 74. Minor modifications in Pappas and Swain's presentation of this counterexample have been made to strengthen it. Inter alia, their counterexample raises a more troublesome version of Goldman's (1976) "papier-mâché facsimile of barns" case; our resolution of Pappas and Swain's hologram case automatically provides a solution to Goldman's case. Note, however, that just Goldman's case itself could be handled by pointing out that on it, knowledge is problematic only when the perceiver's viewing perspective is exactly head-on—something that doesn't happen in Goldman's embellishment of the case where one views from a moving car.

16. Cf. Dretske 1971, 13.

17. Martin's proposal and Dretske's acceptance of it occurred in a three-way correspondence between Dretske, Martin, and myself.

18. If one accepts the stronger interpretation of the independence conditions discussed above, the attempted line of defense fails. For $(G © P)$ if and only if $(\sim G © P)$, but the proposed resolution implies the denial of this.

19. The term 'certain' often has been devalued in the recent philosophical literature from a truth-guaranteeing characteristic to one which merely specifies having maximal warrant or being incapable of disproof. On Dretske's analysis, having conclusive reasons for a belief makes one's beliefs be certain in the traditional truth-evaluating sense. Although proponents of these weaker senses of 'certainty' often claim otherwise, these weaker senses of 'certainty' typically are such that one's beliefs can be certain yet mistaken. For detailed discussion see R. Firth 1967.

20. The second through fourth features of his analysis noted earlier in section I are reflections of his requirement that knowledge be certain but not incorrigible.

21. For more extended discussion of these remarks, see chapter 10. For essentially the same reasons just given, I also reject Morillo's (1984) fallibilistic resolution of difficulties with Goldman's (1976) treatment of the barn-facade case discussed in note 15 above.

22. Martin 1975.

23. Notice that Martin (1975) seems to be assuming the stronger interpre-

tation of the independence condition (cf. n. 9) which we rejected in adopting (2). It serves to strengthen, and make more troublesome, his case.

24. Ibid., 216. The example is developed beginning on p. 215.

25. See Dretske 1971, 4–7. At least some of the reasons for this denial will become apparent below.

26. See, e.g., Gorovitz 1969; also note 28 following.

27. Gorovitz 1965, 701. Condition (9) is only one of the conditions Gorovitz imposes on c if it is correctly to be cited as the cause of e. As he presents the analysis, c must precede $e;$ my interpolation allows c and e to be simultaneous. He also imposes the requirement that the characteristic c must be causally relevant to $e;$ in ch. VII, sec. 7, of my *Facts, Theories, and Scientific Observation* (in progress) I argue that this restriction is superfluous.

28. Gorovitz (1969) likens standards of comparison to Kuhn's paradigms; but Kuhn's notion of a paradigm is quite confused, and among the various meanings Kuhn attaches to 'paradigm', that corresponding to Toulmin's ideals seems to be what Gorovitz has in mind.

29. Thus the simplicity of our cup case is somewhat misleading in that P reasonably could be cited as *the* cause of the sensation there.

30. The gloss suggested here incorporates certain findings necessitated by the second objection to Gorovitz' analysis (which follows).

31. In (11), 'F', 'P', and 'R' are construed as standing for propositions or statements describing the occurrence of factors, whereas in (10) they designate the sets of factors so described. The ambiguity in notation here simplifies exposition and should cause no confusion.

32. See the discussion on p. 9 of D. Lewis 1973, for helpful illumination of this point.

33. The relevant passages are on pp. 82–83, 112–113, and n. 1 on p. 187. The need to consider the issues raised in this paragraph was brought to my attention by reading correspondence between Dretske and Martin over Martin's 1975 article. I am grateful to them for access to their correspondence.

34. Dretske 1969, 82–83; italics added.

35. A defense of the independence condition is given in Dretske's 1971 article; however, it will be discussed in conjunction with the line of objection given below.

36. See ibid., p. 5, where the case is developed, and pp. 7–8, where Dretske uses it to motivate the causal independence conditions.

37. Here, for the first time in my discussion, the adequacy of (10) as an analysis of causality becomes germane. Should (10) prove unsatisfactory as an analysis of causality, we would have to interpret (13-ii) below in light of some satisfactory replacement analysis. Doing so does not automatically challenge our earlier heuristic use of (10) in motivating and defending (12).

38. Definition (13) allows the possibility that the actually obtaining circumstances F of (10) include S having various false beliefs that Q which are causes of S believing that P but do not contribute to the satisfaction of (12), hence do not contribute to the satisfaction of (13-iii) but do contribute to the

satisfaction of (13-ii). To many (including Michael Hooker, who pointed this out to me), this is an objectionable feature of my analysis. This line of objection is not compelling to me, since I am not yet convinced that, as a matter of fact, false beliefs cannot play a significant role in obtaining knowledge; for I am inclined to say that the source of one's beliefs is irrelevant to their epistemic status so long as the beliefs are obtained under circumstances which guarantee their truth—though I do admit that when knowledge is so obtained, one will be at a disadvantage in defending one's knowledge claims. As we will see below, I think this is an acceptable feature of an adequate epistemology. For those who remain unconvinced, let me point out that this line of objection easily can be circumvented by adding to (13-ii) the requirement that no false belief of *S*'s be a cause of *S* believing that *P* under the circumstances. Such a modification, which I am not convinced should be made, does not affect subsequent discussion; and the reader demanding such a concession should, in reading what follows, assume the concession has been made in order that the central contentions of this chapter not be obfuscated.

39. For the distinction, and arguments in support of the contention that evidence should play quite different roles in these cases, cf. A. D. Woozley 1952–53 and Alan White 1957. In ch. VIII, sec. 7, of my *Facts, Theories, and Scientific Observation* (in progress), I offer a more sustained and detailed defense of White's general sort of claim here. In ch. 10 of the present book I argue that adherence to the K-K thesis leads Kuhn and Feyerabend to deny that any correspondence notion of truth is relevant to scientific knowledge, and thus (in ways directly attributable to their acceptance of the K-K thesis) leads them to embrace an all-pervasive (and unacceptable) extension of Hume's already unwarranted extreme skepticism; and elsewhere (1977a, sec. III-D) I argue that recent work in philosophy of science on the growth of scientific knowledge not only *strongly* indicates that the K-K thesis should be rejected, but also favors adopting a view like White's wherein "evidence" plays different roles in justifying knowledge than it does in defending knowledge claims—along the lines argued for below. However, for brevity I am willing to embrace White's general position here rather than mounting my own version and defending my own view.

40. Martin 1975, 216; italics added.

41. White 1957 (p. 100 in the Phillips-Griffiths 1967 reprinting).

42. Note that, in analogue to Dretske's solution to the generator case and our proposed treatment of the volcano case, *S* can know that Gumshoe won if Tagalong lost; but if Tagalong had won, *S* could not know that Gumshoe won. The treatment of these cases is strictly analogous—which is at odds with Martin's intuitions, since Dretske's treatment of the generator case was suggested by Martin himself. One of my points here, to be expanded below, is that our intuitions about knowledge are so conditioned by tacit acceptance of the K-K thesis—and the attendant identification of the evidence adequate for defending knowledge claims with that required for knowing—that in cases such as the generator case, the lava case, and Martin's racetrack case our intuitions are sufficiently unreliable as to not be decisive. In such cases,

considerations such as those raised below and alluded to in note 39 above must take precedence over our intuitions in deciding the adequacy of an analysis of knowledge which denies the K-K thesis, hence in deciding what to make of intuition-based putative counterexamples such as Martin's.

43. The last seven pages of Dretske's 1971 article makes heavy use of the distinction between knowing and claiming to know, in much the same way as we have exploited it, to dismiss various putative counterexamples to this analysis. It thus is rather surprising that he did not see that such moves also were applicable to his own mountain case and would have provided the means for avoiding the unfortunate introduction of his independence conditions for C (see also n. 42).

44. Here and in subsequent quotations some notational changes have been made for conformity with my text.

45. Although subjunctive causal conditionals do not occur in (12), $\sim\!\Diamond(C$ & $\sim\!P$ & $R)$ does, and it is equivalent to $\boxed{C}(C$ & $R \supset P)$, which is a causal conditional.

46. In the defense I do make, I have to deal with the interpretation of the causal modalities. In *Facts, Theories, and Scientific Observation* (in progress), I do so in a way that avoids embracing Lewis-like possible worlds—which is incompatible with Garrett's approach. The approach briefly was hinted at in the introduction to part IV of the present book.

47. Dretske 1983, 58. This article is his own précis of his 1981 book; it is followed by a number of critical commentaries on the book together with his replies to critics.

48. See the sociobiology symposium in Suppe and Asquith 1977 for discussion of the problems.

49. Dretske 1971; Suppe 1977a; and ch. 10 above. See also the Epilogue below.

50. This is argued in chs. 6 and 7 of my *Facts, Theories, and Scientific Observation* (in progress). A bare-bones outline of the argument is given below at the beginning of chapter 13.

51. E.g., Shapere 1984. See also Suppe 1977a, 682–704.

52. Further expansion of these themes is found in Suppe 1977a and in *Facts, Theories, and Scientific Observation* (in progress). Hints how this approach relates to more traditional issues in philosophy of science are given in the Epilogue below. See also Shapere 1982.

13

Why Science Is Not Really Inductive

There is a long-standing empiricist philosophical tradition wherein induction is the vehicle for obtaining and providing the requisite justification or evidence for general empirical knowledge that P. Under logical positivism such induction was interpreted probabilistically and tied to the development of inductive logics. Indeed, it was commonplace to claim that probabilistic induction was a good model of actual scientific reasoning. The analysis of the last chapter requires that one have conclusive reasons that guarantee the truth of 'P' if one is to know that P. The evidence in support of P provided by probabilistic induction and inductive logics typically yields evidential weights or probabilities less than one (certainty) and so are incapable of providing conclusive reasons.[1] This raises serious questions whether probabilistic induction has any important role to play in any quasi-realistic analysis of scientific knowledge, and if so, what is that role.

One might wonder whether there can be any knowledge of generalizations on an analysis such as mine which imposes a conclusive reasons requirement so strong that such reasons guarantee the truth of P. For can we ever know open-ended empirical generalizations under such a stringent requirement? I believe the answer is yes. For I believe that we can come to have conclusive reasons for singular causal claims such as "The cracked insulation in the spark plug wires caused the engine to misfire and run ragged." Analysis of such causal claims shows that they *entail* certain open-ended empirical causal generalizations; hence, by the conclusive reasons analysis of chapter 12, if one has conclusive reasons for such singular causal statements, one also has conclusive reasons for the entailed underlying generalizations, hence can know such generalizations are the case. In *Facts, Theories, and Scientific Observation* (in progress) I mount a detailed development and defense of this sort of view. In the present chapter I merely want to assume its conclusion—namely, that on my conclusive reasons analysis of knowledge, we can know that empirical causal generalizations are true.

On my conclusive reasons account, then, probabilistic induction is not needed to obtain knowledge of empirical causal generalizations; indeed, it generally is incapable of providing a sufficiently strong evidential basis for such knowledge. These conclusions are sufficiently radical as to provide a basis for resisting my epistemology. In the present chapter I want to strengthen the plausibility of my position by exploring the question whether science really is inductive. In section I, I will try to show that the standard probabilistic inductive logic account of the confirmation of causal generalizations is implausible, hence that my view gains plausibility by comparison. In sections I and II, I argue that standard inductive logic is not a good model of how science reasons. In sections III and IV, I consider whether there are any other plausible roles for probabilistic inductive logic to play in the scientific enterprise and in philosophy of science.

My approach to considering these issues will be to examine them in the context of a specific incarnation of the view that science reasons in accordance with standard inductive logic under some particular analysis or interpretation of that logic—Arthur W. Burks' treatment in his *Cause, Chance, Reason* (1977).[2] I pick his treatment because I find it a particularly impressive attempt to carry out the inductivist program in fairly fine detail. For example, I know of no better or more sophisticated attempt to develop a probabilistic inductive logic in which generalizations containing the causal modalities can have nonzero probabilities.[3] Further, the criticisms and points I wish to make about inductive science do not turn on features peculiar to his analysis, so no loss of generality occurs by focusing on Burks' particular version of the position.

I. INDUCTION AND THE PRACTICE OF SCIENCE

In his monumental work, *Cause, Chance, Reason*, Arthur Burks attempts to provide a richly detailed account of "the ultimate nature of the knowledge acquired by the empirical sciences" (651). He does so by presenting his presupposition theory of induction, a theory that provides a rich foundational analysis of "standard inductive logic"—which, according to Burks, "is the system of rules of inductive inference actually used and aspired to by the practicing scientist" (654).

Underlying Burks' analysis of the nature of scientific evidence is the view that scientific laws and theories are confirmed on the basis of data acquired via observation and experiment and that such confirmation essentially involves inductive reasoning.[4] Burks really does not argue for this supposition; rather, he takes it as a given. When he began writing *Cause, Chance, Reason* in 1960, the inductive confirmation view was so commonplace it scarcely seemed to warrant defense. But since then, a major revolution has occurred within philosophy of science—one which centrally has involved historical analyses of the place of rationality in the growth of scientific knowledge. Increasingly, one finds philosophers such as Kuhn, Feyerabend, Laudan, Shapere, Lakatos, and others, as well as historians such as Holton, presenting models of scientific reasoning which implicitly or explicitly reject the view that the nature of scientific evidence essentially involves using observational and experimental data to refute or else inductively confirm laws or theories on the basis of repeated observations using the canons of standard inductive logic. Thus it now seems incumbent that the correctness of the inductive confirmation view be defended.

To my mind, the failure to defend that view against its modern-day detractors is a serious weakness of *Cause, Chance, Reason.* To be sure, there are discussions in it which do lay the basis for such a defense. For example, Feyerabend's rejection of the inductive confirmation view rests in part in his agreement with Popper that Hume's arguments against the justification of induction preclude induction being a vehicle of scientific knowledge. In chapters 3 and 10 Burks extensively discusses Hume's problem and presents a neo-Kantian, neo-Keynesian defense of standard inductive logic. And his separation of the logic of empirical inquiry from inductive logic provides the basis for a reply to others such as Lakatos, Laudan, and Shapere: What *they* are investigating through historical analysis is the logic of empirical inquiry, which he acknowledges as legitimate and important; but *he* is investigating something else—inductive logic. Such a reply would not be convincing to me, though, for these authors seem committed to the idea that any separation of discovery and confirmation is artificial—that scientific discovery, experiment, observation, testing, theory development, modification, and evaluation all go hand in hand in ways that ultimately do not fit the inductive testing and confirmation model. This is a serious challenge which, if correct, cuts to the very heart of Burks' enterprise, reducing it to a brilliant piece of technical philosophy which is utterly irrelevant to real science. And in today's philosophy of science that is not only unfortunate, it is a mortal sin.

To sharpen the issue, consider the following passages:

Let us call the system of rules of inductive inference actually used and aspired to by the practicing scientists *standard inductive logic.* This will include the calculus of inductive probability together with rules for analogy, the method of varying causally relevant qualities, and induction by simple enumeration. [103]

Now in fact we all employ standard inductive logic and no one has ever seriously contemplated using any other. [130]

The challenge being offered by recent work on the growth of scientific knowledge is to question whether we in fact *do* employ standard inductive logic in science (second quote), whether in fact there is *a* system of rules of inductive inference actually used and aspired to by practicing scientists which meets Burks' characterization of standard inductive logic (first quote).

Historically, there is reason to doubt whether science is inductive in the ways Burks claims. In section 2.5.4 Burks briefly analyzes several historical episodes—including the Galileo and the Young/Fresnel controversies over light—using Bayes' theorem. Since the calculus of inductive probabilities postdates these episodes, and since the argumentation in these controversies did not invoke inductive probabilities (or any probabilistic precursors), the scientists involved could not have been using standard inductive logic—contrary to what Burks seems to be implying. Now it may be that what Burks means to claim is this: These episodes evidence good scientific reasoning; even though they did not possess an articulate version of standard inductive logic, they behaved in accordance with its dictates and so implicitly employed standard inductive logic.[5] Thus it is not inappropriate to invoke standard inductive logic explicitly in analyzing the reasoning employed in these historical episodes. However, such a reply presupposes that standard inductive logic captures good scientific reasoning, and that is precisely what is being questioned.

We should be suspicious of attempts to read the history of science through inductive eyes. For there is a long history of attempting to reconstruct scientific achievements to make them conform to contemporary inductive canons. The inductive approach to science is a normative philosophical approach for doing science that predates any significant scientific achievements guided by it. That is, it was advanced not as an analysis of how good science has been done, but rather as a program for doing science in a new way. In 1543, Nicholas Copernicus published his *De Revolutionibus* which, while starting a scientific and intellectual revolution, was a work as far removed from the inductive confirmation view of science as one can imagine. Quite likely he borrowed his celestial model from Aristarchus of Samos (fl. ca. 281

B.C.), and his arguments for preferring his heliocentric view rested centrally on the claim it was more faithful to Aristotle in certain crucial respects than was the Ptolemaic geocentric theory. Repeated testing and inductive confirmation did not play any significant role.

Those who were convinced by Copernicus realized that much of the rest of science would fall (especially Aristotelian physics) and saw science as having to start all over again. Descartes' method of doubt was his first step toward developing a rationalistic methodology of science which, it was claimed, would ensure that the new science was accurate and correct. Francis Bacon's *Novum Organum* (1620) offered a different analysis, claiming that the reason ancient science had gone wrong was its reliance on "first principles." To avoid these, and ensure correct scientific theories, one ought to root science in observation and inductive generalization. To this end Bacon developed two new methods of induction which included, in rudimentary form, what Burks calls "the method of varying causally relevant qualities" (102). Although Bacon advocated such an inductive approach to doing science, he did no significant scientific work himself.

During much of the seventeenth century, the most impressive scientific achievements were Cartesian and do not appear at all to fit the inductive confirmation model. Kepler's discovery of the planetary orbits and the development of his three laws in his *Astronomia Nova* (1609), although often cited by inductivists as a paradigm instance of science being done within their model, in fact rather badly fits the model.[6] And while the extent to which Galileo engaged in observation and experimentation is controversial, the consensus seems to be that his work generally does not conform closely to the inductive confirmation model. Indeed, in the *Dialogo* (1629), when asked whether he had actually performed the important experiment of dropping a rock from a moving ship's mast, Salviati (speaking for Galileo) replies, "Without experiment, I am sure the effect will happen as I tell you, because it must happen that way. . . ."[7] Hardly an inductive confirmation view!

Only toward the end of the seventeenth century and the beginning of the eighteenth century do we find important scientists purportedly claiming to work in accordance with the inductive method. For example, Newton in his *Optiks* (1704) writes that "although the arguing from Experiments and Observations by Induction be no Demonstration of General Conclusions, yet it is the best way of arguing which the Nature of Things admits of."[8] But, as the historical controversy over *Hypotheses non fingo* in The General Scholium of the second edition (1713) of his *Principia* (first edition, 1687) shows, it is very unclear how strongly Newton did adhere to an inductivist approach to science. We also find a decline in the influence of rationalism and a growing allegiance to empiricism among philosophers beginning toward the end of the seventeenth century. For example, Locke's *Essay* (1690) is in part an inductivist vindication of the scientific work of his friend Boyle and of Newton. And with this growing championing of empiricism and its inductivism, we find systematic attempts to recast earlier science in an inductivist mold. One of the more scandalous, but not untypical, attempts was the alteration of Galileo's writings by Thomas Salusbury while translating them into the vernacular so as to make Galileo conform (in translation at least) to empiricist and inductivist normative demands; for example, in his 1661 translation of the *Dialogo,* in the passage quoted above Salusbury drops the phrase *senza sperienza* ("without experiment" or "without recourse to experience"), thus defusing the true anti-empiricist thrust of the passage.[9]

With the resurgence of empiricism in the nineteenth century at the hands of Herschel, Mill, and Whewell, we again find attempts to read the history of science through inductive eyes—often distorting that history in the process. Particularly noteworthy here is William Whewell's extensive three-volume *History of the Inductive Sciences* (1837), which, while an impressive historical work still worth consulting, does shape the history of science to conform to the inductivist views he develops (supposedly based on his *History*) in his 1840 *Philosophy of the Inductive Sciences.*

Again, with the rise of logical empiricism this century, we find a new resurgence of inductivism—but it is a very transformed inductivism. Whereas induction in the eighteenth and nineteenth centuries consisted of nonprobabilistic methods of inference from specific instances to causal generalizations, at the hands of Reichenbach, Keynes, and Carnap the enterprise becomes fundamentally probabilistic. Hume's arguments against the possibility of justifying induction no longer applied, although probabilistic analogues did emerge to plague, for example, Reichenbach's self-corrective method for justifying induction. With the logical empiricists, claims abound that scientific laws and theories are inductively confirmed (now in accordance with the probabilistic inductive logics they are developing, not the earlier inductions of the seventeenth through nineteenth centuries). Little attempt is made to defend these claims on historical grounds, although one finds casual references to Kepler, Semmelweiss, and others.

The following points emerge from this sketchy discussion. The inductive view of science initially was promulgated as a prescriptive account about how science ought to be done. That prescriptive account has on occasion taken on some of the trappings of an ideology. Like most other ideologies it has looked to spectacular historical episodes which are seen as exemplifying and vindicating the correctness of the ideology, frequently engaging in revisionist history to make the case for legitimacy. Even when logical empiricism radically altered the nature of induction by making it probabilistic, the old claims that science was in fact inductive survived and were perpetuated without serious reexamination. Thus there are good historical grounds for being suspicious of the claim that standard inductive logic "is the system of rules of inductive inference actually used and aspired to by the practicing scientist" (103, 654).

II. HOW GOOD A MODEL IS STANDARD INDUCTIVE LOGIC?

But grounds for suspicion do not make the suspicions correct, so let us turn to a detailed examination of whether science *does* reason in accordance with standard inductive logic. Immediately we face a problem: Burks' characterization of standard inductive logic quoted above is none too specific, essentially being an ostensive definition ("what is actually used and aspired to by practicing scientists") augmented by a gloss. Nevertheless, piecing together various comments Burks makes, we know it involves using induction by simple enumeration; and since this makes the same probabilistic predictions of future events as Bayes' method for finding unknown probabilities does (126), it involves the use of Bayes' method. It also involves the use of repeated-instance confirmation to inductively confirm laws and other causally necessary generalizations, the use of inductive probabilities in other contexts such as determining empirical probabilities, and rules for analogy.

Outside of natural history, the place where one would most expect to find science proceeding inductively is in the behavioral sciences, especially behavioral psychology and sociology. For much of this century these fields have subscribed to the methodology of operationalism (a particular version of logical empiricism/logical positivism) and inductivism. But even though they subscribe to an inductivist methodology, it does not in fact follow that they proceed in accordance with it. Indeed, the fact that virtually no operational definitions encountered in the behavioral science literature meet the methodological requirements "officially" subscribed to should prompt us to investigate whether in fact the behavioral sciences do employ standard inductive logic.

It certainly is the case that probabilistic inference and reasoning permeate the behavioral science literature. But rarely does one find the use of instance confirmation to confirm generalizations involving causal necessity. More typically one finds investigations of statistically significant measure differences between a subject and a control population, regression and correlational analyses to determine statistical (but not causal) regularities, analyses of variance to explain the sources (but not causes) of differences among subject and control groups, and statistical tests of hypotheses which result in the rejection or acceptance of hypotheses at some confidence level. Occasionally the hypotheses tested are causal, but there is widespread skepticism whether calling them "causal" is appropriate, since the statistics cannot really determine causes. Only with the recent development of path analysis does one find much in the way of attempts to determine causal influence, and then it is a statistical sense of causality they employ (not involving Burks' causal necessity); the same is true of other statistical investigations such as those surrounding the "causes" of cancer.[10] On the surface, then, the behavioral sciences do not seem to exemplify standard inductive logic.

This first-blush assessment surely is incorrect. While Burks stresses the confirmation or rejection of general hypotheses involving causal necessity, other hypotheses not involving causal necessity do come under his conception of standard inductive logic. And these include at least some of the statistical hypothesis testing found in the behavioral sciences. Burks never discusses in *Cause, Chance, Reason* his views about statistical theories of causality, but I am relatively confident that Burks would view the statistical theories of causality developed by, for example, Suppes (1970) and Giere (1980) as being complicated empirical probability claims. More generally, the statistical methods typically found in the behavioral sciences all seem to involve use of statistics to establish (at some level of confidence) empirical probability claims. And since in chapter 8 Burks has analyzed in detail empirical probabilities and how reasoning about them falls within the purview of standard inductive logic, we can conclude that most statistical or probabilistic reasoning in the behavioral sciences does fall within standard inductive logic as analyzed by Burks. To be sure, Burks does not address or attempt to show that this is the case, but this is totally in keeping with his view that "the logic of inductive argument studies the most general, universal, and fundamental types of inductive arguments, leaving the more detailed and specific forms to the individual sciences and statistics" (17), and the resulting enterprise he has set for himself.

Although the behavioral sciences do provide many instances of science proceeding in accordance with standard inductive logic, it provides little evidence that science uses standard inductive logic to obtain instance confirmation of generalizations involving causal necessity. Since for Burks this is a most central part of standard inductive logic (indeed the main thrust of *Cause, Chance, Reason* is to examine, analyze, and explain how this is possible), the behavioral sciences provide an unacceptably weak vindication of his claims for standard inductive logic being the means whereby science reasons about evidence.

Burks' own examples (cited earlier) suggest it is the physical sciences which he takes as best exemplifying standard inductive logic. We now examine this idea. Our starting points are his claims that "the rule of induction by simple enumeration makes the same probabilistic predictions of future events as does Bayes' method" (126) and his Bayesian analysis of instance confirmation (sec. 10.3.2), for these collectively indicate that the Bayesian model is at the very heart of his account of how inductive scientific inference proceeds in the verification of laws and other generalizations involving causal necessity. On the Bayesian model one has a set of *logically possible,* mutually exclusive, and jointly exhaustive hypotheses which one wants to choose among on the basis of repeated testing. One attaches prior probabilities to each (and the assignment may be arbitrary), tests them, then obtains posterior probabilities. Using the latter now as new prior probabilities, one iterates the procedure until one hypothesis emerges as the probabilistic victor — and one hypothesis must, if one repeats the test long enough.

As a first challenge to this Bayesian view of instance confirmation, let us look at Lakatos' research programme model of theory development; in doing so I do not intend to minimize either the serious problems it faces or the historical accuracy challenges besetting it.[11] Lakatos' basic idea is that the unit of scientific assessment is not the theory, but rather a supratheoretical unit which he designates as a *research programme.* Research programmes contain a *problem shift* — a sequence of theories, each successor in the sequence being an augmentation or semantic reinterpretation of its immediate predecessor in the sequence. Allowable modifications in producing the sequence are constrained by what Lakatos terms the positive and negative heuristics. Collectively these heuristics and the problem shift constitute a *research programme.* As indicated elsewhere (in my work cited in n. 11), I have been fairly critical of this supposedly "historically derived" model, and I do not subscribe to its veracity. Nevertheless, despite all its defects in analysis, Lakatos does target an important aspect of theoretical development and the roles of experimentation and testing therein — namely, that when one is developing a theory, one uses experimentation not to refute or confirm a hypothesis, but rather as a crucial ingredient in further defining a crude initial approximation of what is believed to be a promising theory into what, hopefully, will be an ever-increasingly close approximation to an ultimately adequate theory. Initially this perspective (which is roughly right-headed) seems quite at odds with Burks' instance confirmation or refutation view and especially his Bayesian construal of that view.

Is Burks' analysis really so incompatible with such a Lakatosian view? Probably not, for minimally on Lakatos' view, should a current theory in the problem shift prove inadequate (as in neo-Popperian fashion it is supposed to), presumably the positive and negative heuristics are supposed to provide some (unspecified) guidance for the revised next-incarnation successor theory in the problem shift. Thus one might plausibly construe the testing of the current theory in the problem shift as being the choice, on the basis of observation and experiment, between the present incumbent theory in the problem shift and some anticipated alternative replacement.[12] If so, we plausibly can view theory development, seen as involving repeated testing of successive theories in a problem shift, as being a Bayesian decision between the current problem shift incumbent, an anticipated replacement (or a few such), and a "none of the above" alternative.[13] It is my opinion that much of the sort of development of theories Lakatos attempts to capture in his problem shift model at best roughly typifies some roles experiment does play in testing, evaluating, and developing theories. And to the extent that the use of observation and experiment to produce the successor theory in a problem shift is not serendipitous and involves the testing of the current incumbent theory against an anticipated replacement, where some semblance of prior probabilities can be attached to each, I think Burks' Bayesian instance confirmation model is basically applicable (although its specific application could be detailed much more if Burks chose to engage in "the more detailed and specific forms" [17] of inductive argument which he eschews in his search for "the most general, universal, and fundamental types of inductive argument" [17]). Thus, to the extent that Lakatos' research programmes model enjoys legitimacy, it does not appear to be obviously incompatible with Burks' claims for standard inductive logic—at least if we grant Burks the claim that he has defused the Humean anti-inductivist arguments which are at the core of Popper's philosophy of science and which, despite various distancing efforts, do influence Lakatos' view of the roles of observation, experimentation, and testing in science.

A much more important threat to Burks' Bayesian instance confirmation view of science comes from the history of science-based philosophical analyses advanced by Shapere. A key point of Shapere's examination of rationality in the growth of scientific knowledge is the recognition that, contrary to the presuppositions of the Bayesian model, science does not resort to observation and experiment to decide against the *logically possible* alternatives to the favored hypothesis, but rather, it more selectively uses observation and experiment to test among only the favored hypotheses which are plausible.[14] This recognition, which I believe to be essentially correct, seems to me to constitute one of the deepest challenges I know of to the view that science fundamentally does reason and proceed in accordance with standard inductive logic.

To an extent, Burks is aware of the problem I have just raised. In his discussion of the Bayesian method he is aware that the logically possible alternatives to a favored hypothesis are potentially unlimited, but that Bayes' method requires a specific finite set. To this end he engages in the practice of combining the seriously entertained alternatives (the plausible ones, as opposed to the logically possible ones) together with a "none of the above" alternative (with negligible prior probability) as a means of meeting the specific finitary option requirement (85ff, 510). In so doing, he is tacitly acknowledging Shapere's point that we use observation and experiment to decide between the plausible (not the logically possible) alternative hypotheses, laws, or theories.

Such tacit acknowledgment of Shapere's contention does not, however, salvage his claim that science works in accordance with standard inductive logic. Indeed, it is a near-fatal concession which seems to concede his case to the newly arisen anti-inductivists, in the process bringing attention to what is one of the more vexing problems which Burks addresses in *Cause, Chance, Reason* but does not fully resolve: the problem of prior probabilities (90–92, sec. 8.3.4). The Bayesian method gives an excellent account of how, *given prior probabilities,* one can use testing to come up with improved (in the long run at least) estimates of new prior probabilities (viz., use the posterior probabilities from the prior ones in Bayesian iteration), but it tells one absolutely nothing about how to get the enterprise started. If one wishes to start a Bayesian inductive enterprise in a pristine manner, where does one obtain the *initial* prior probabilities? The Bayesian model gives no clue—other than to say that however capricious, uninformed, or misguided, it does not make any difference in the long run. But this does not cohere with Shapere's analysis. The very choice of which alternative hypotheses to treat seriously amounts to a choice of which logically possible alternative hypotheses enjoy significant prior probabilities on Burks model, and in the first instance, the Bayesian model gives no guidance. In short, the Bayesian model says that when we have logically prior plausibility judgments as to which alternative hypotheses are worth pursuing, we can start applying the Bayesian method—which is the heart of standard inductive logic.

But to acknowledge this is to acknowledge that standard inductive logic is a hopelessly impoverished model of actual scientific reasoning in the evaluation of hypotheses. For it is to concede that standard inductive logic presupposes a logically prior sort of reasoning—plausibility assessment. Differently put, we have a *dilemma*: If standard inductive logic is intended to provide an analysis of that plausibility reasoning, then we have a vicious regress where each iteration of the Bayesian method requires a logically prior application; hence it is impossible to ever get the Bayesian method going. Hence standard inductive logic is an inadequate model of scientific reasoning about evidence and the evaluation of hypotheses. If, on the other hand, standard inductive logic does not provide an analysis of that plausibility reasoning, standard inductive logic is a critically incomplete, hence an inadequate, model of scientific reasoning about evidence and the evaluation of hypotheses. Burks is not unaware that there are problems concerning prior probabilities:

> In each application of Bayes' theorem it is fair to ask: What is the source of the prior probabilities? Usually they derive from previous empirical situations. They might be posterior probabilities just renamed. More typically they come from general experience. . . . But this process of tracing back prior probabilities to earlier evidence must finally terminate, since the total available evidence is finite. And when it does terminate the same question arises: What is the epistemological basis of the prior probability assignment? [91]

Burks goes on to suggest that "since prior probabilities are expressed by atomic inductive probability statements, this problem is a special case of our first main question: What is the general nature of an atomic inductive probability statement?" (ibid.).

In section 8.3.4 Burks returns to the issue. There he discusses how his dispositional theory of empirical probabilities and a foil—the positivistic theory of empirical probability—differently treat prior probabilities. His conclusion is: "The dispositional theory . . . holds that prior probabilities are conditional and are subject to the norms of standard inductive logic. These norms are common to all men and are thus intersubjective rather than subjective (pp. 103, 136, 305, 326–327). Consequently, the dispositional theory makes prior probabilities intersubjective, in contrast to the positivistic theory that makes them subjective and relative to the individual" (529). The intersubjectivity of norms, as amplified at the locations Burks cites, consists in the claim that we all employ standard inductive logic and in his analysis of atomic inductive probability statements via his pragmatic theory of inductive probability (summarized on pp. 305–6).

Does Burks' treatment of prior probabilities dissolve the dilemma we posed for standard inductive logic? It is clear from the last quote that Burks is committed to embracing the first horn of our dilemma. Thus standard inductive logic must provide the plausibility assessment means of obtaining the prior probabilities needed to get the Bayesian method going. The most plausible account I can think of allowed by Burks' treatment is the following: Prior probabilities are either empirical or inductive probabilities. Either way, they ultimately are based upon atomic inductive probabilities. Atomic inductive probabilities have action implications. "An atomic inductive probability statement does and should express a disposition to act or 'bet' in certain ways under conditions of uncertainty" (305; italics deleted). The "certain ways of betting" consist in betting rationally in accordance with the canons of Burks' calculus of choice. Then on Burks' account, one's rational beliefs produce betting dispositions which determine a system of atomic probability assessments—and these can be the source of prior probabilities needed to get the Bayesian method going.

This appears to be Burks' intended treatment of the problem of prior probabilities. Is it adequate to dissolve our dilemma? In applying the calculus of choice we are faced with various decisions to be made in the face of uncertainty; rationally making those decisions induces atomic inductive probabilities. The decision making reflects a coherent belief and value structure. It is not unreasonable to interpret those decisions—which are logically prior to the probabilities[15]—as involving nonprobabilistic plausibility assessments. If so, Burks is able to agree with us that the Bayesian method of standard inductive logic does presuppose a logically prior plausibility assessment logic. But his pragmatic theory of inductive probability incorporates such a plausibility assessment via the calculus of choice. And since these are incorporated into his pragmatic theory of inductive probability, and the latter (inter alia) is part of his characterization of standard inductive logic, the first horn of the dilemma is incorrect: Suitably understood, standard inductive logic does incorporate the sorts of pre-probabilistic reasoning needed to avoid the vicious regress.

Technically, this enables Burks to escape the dilemma. But it does not vitiate the points I was trying to make via the dilemma: That there is a form of reasoning involved in hypothesis assessment in science (plausibility assessment) which is more basic and fundamental than inductive probability assessment, and that an adequate model of scientific reasoning about evidence and hypothesis assessment must analyze and address it. Burks has done so only to a limited degree, in effect telling us that when it is done systematically in accordance with his calculus of choice, it will determine a set of atomic inductive probabilities which could be used to characterize what the scientist or other individual actually did. Thus it really is not the case that standard inductive logic constitutes "the system of rules of inductive inference *actually used*" (103), but rather, standard inductive logic is a rational reconstruction of rational scientific inference. While it does allow for plausibility assessment and tells us that it can be reconstructively characterized probabilistically, it tells us nothing about how those plausibility assessments are made or what their logic is (beyond being coherent enough to satisfy the calculus of choice). Thus as a rational reconstruction it is seriously incomplete, since standard inductive logic can reconstruct nothing of the reasoning wherein one obtains the plausibility assessments which are reflected as the atomic inductive probabilities needed to get Bayes' method going.

A closely related difficulty is the following. On a Bayesian model it tacitly is supposed that the prior probabilities initially attached to hypotheses ordinarily are sufficiently far removed from the correct probabilities that a sizable number of observations and iterations of the Bayesian procedure will be needed to determine which hypothesis is the correct one. With surprising frequency this is not what happens; rather, hypotheses, laws, and theories are accepted on the basis of single, or just a few, observations or experiments. For example, general relativity theory has been put to the test only a handful of times, and most of these came after the theory enjoyed general acceptance. (This in part reflects the fact that in the more theoretical portions of physics, observation and experiment, while crucially involved, play a somewhat diminished role which is not reflected in the inductive-confirmation picture.) How can such limited testing as a basis for acceptance be accounted for on Burks' Bayesian model? The only plausible way is to suggest that in such cases the scientists assigned prior probabilities which were so close to correct that one or a few iterations of the procedure were sufficient.

If we make this move, the question immediately arises: How were these prior probability assessments arrived at? As our previous discussion indicates, Burks' answer is to suggest they came from prior applications of the Bayesian method or else from general experience. I seriously doubt that historical analysis will vindicate the former possibility. For example, key tenets of general relativity theory had not been around to obtain prior probabilities via Bayesian means. Thus it appears that the prior probability problem not only comes up at the very beginning of the scientific enterprise (e.g., in the move from pre-science to science), but at very sophisticated stages as well. As to the idea that these prior probabilities come from "general experience," this is so vague that I do not know what to make of it. Given our previous discussion of prior probabilities, the most plausible interpretation seems to be that it involves the nonprobabilistic plausibility assessments which can be reconstructed as atomic prior probabilities. But then, this is just to concede that in such one- or two-experiment/observation cases, it is the plausibility assessment, not the Bayesian-analyzed repeated testing and inductive confirmation, that is at the heart of reasoning about evidence and hypotheses. This increasingly strengthens the contention that scientific research and the evaluation of hypotheses centrally involves plausibility assessments which cannot adequately be captured by the Bayesian method or Burks' account of prior probabilities and thus that Burks' inductive confirmation model inadequately captures or analyzes the role of observation and experiment, and the ways of reasoning about them, that actually characterize the evaluation of hypotheses in science.

Shapere's work lays the basis for one final challenge to Burks' claim that "*the* system of rules of inductive inference actually used and aspired to by the practicing scientists [is] *standard inductive logic*" (103, italics added). This view implies that there is a fixed, stable set of rules for reasoning about evidence and for the evaluation of hypotheses adequate for, and employed by, all of science. One of the more important historical claims resulting from Shapere's work is that as sophisticated science proceeds, it develops improved patterns of reasoning not previously employed in ways that are conditioned by the content of science, and that much of scientific progress consists in such development of increasingly subtle improved patterns of reasoning (e.g., ones which enable us to assess a hypothesis on the basis of one or a few observations or experiments). As he likes to put it, "We learn how to learn as we learn." Further, he sees no good philosophical grounds for supposing that there will be some ultimate fixed set of reasoning canons for science; rather, there is no reason to suppose this process of evolving new, improved canons of reasoning is not open-ended and ongoing. Thus there is good reason to reject the view that there is a fixed system of rules for scientific reasoning. And if we reject that, we must reject Burks' basic contention that standard inductive logic is that fixed system of rules.

Collectively, the above discussions lead me to conclude that (a) plausibility assessment plays a central role in scientific reasoning about evidence which standard inductive logic does not capture; (b) standard inductive logic is not a good descriptive model of actual scientific reasoning about evidence and hypotheses; (c) based on the dilemma discussion given earlier, any inductive confirmation analysis of science must be based on a logically prior theory/model of plausibility assessment which must be nonprobabilistic and noninductive; and (d) there is no good reason to suppose that there is a fixed set of inference canons which will exhaust the range of successful reasoning patterns which science has developed and will continue to develop. Thus standard inductive logic seems to be a seriously defective model of scientific reasoning about evidence and hypotheses.

III. INDUCTION AND METHODOLOGY

Given these defects in the standard inductive model, does it follow that works on probabilistic induction such as Burks' *Chance, Cause, Reason* are beside the point and fail to make significant contributions to philosophy of science? In this and the next section, I consider two other sorts of contributions probabilistic inductive logics might make to philosophy of science.

At the end of the previous section I mentioned approvingly Shapere's dictum that "We learn as we learn to learn." Might it be the case that the processes whereby we do this, whereby we develop improved patterns of reasoning in science, are themselves inductive in ways that suitably could be modeled by probabilistic inductive logics such as Burks'?[16]

For example, we might construe unconditional methodological rules of the form:

(1) You ought to do *y*,

as elliptical versions of

(2) If your central cognitive goal is *x*, then you ought to do *y*,

which is true just in the case where

(3) Doing *y* is more likely to produce *x* than alternatives to *y* are.

Then we might try to establish (3) by using the rule of *induction by simple enumeration*. Burks' statement of the rule is:

If observations show many instances in which property ϕ has been accompanied by property ψ, with no counter instances, then it is quite likely that the next instance of ϕ will be accompanied by ψ. [102]

Here ϕ is "the adoption of a policy," and ψ is "has promoted certain ends in the past." Let "doing y" in (3) be the policy, and let the ends be "producing x." Then the inductive rule becomes:

> (4) If observations show many instances in which doing y has been accompanied by producing x, with no counter instances, then it is quite likely that the next instance of y will produce x.

This inductive rule is not applicable to (3) since it does nothing to establish that doing y is more likely to produce x than any of the alternatives to y. Thus we must construe the end as being "is more likely than any alternative to y to produce x." Then the inductive rule becomes:

> (5) If observations show many instances in which doing y has been more likely to produce x than any alternatives to y, with no counter instances, then it is quite likely that the next instance of doing y will be more likely to produce x than any of the alternatives to y.

This version of the inductive rule clearly applies to statements of form (3), and it is hard to see how any significantly different version of the rule of induction by simple enumeration would be a more plausible construal of it than (5). Subsequently I will assume (5) is the correct version of the inductive rule.

The difference between (4) and (5), and the superiority of (5) as an interpretation of induction by simple enumeration here, make it clear that (3) amounts to the following claim if (a) "is more likely than" plausibly is construed probabilistically and (b) the number of alternatives to y is finite:

> (6) Let $y_1, \ldots, y_n$ be the alternatives to y. Then
>
> $$P(x, y) > P(x, y_1)$$
> $$P(x, y) > P(x, y_2)$$
> $$\vdots$$
> $$P(x, y) > P(x, y_{n-1})$$
> $$P(x, y) > P(x, y_n).$$

If we are unaware of all the logical possible alternatives to y, or if the number of alternatives is infinite, (6) still applies provided that we make

> (7) $y_n \equiv \sim(y \vee y_1 \vee \ldots \vee y_n)$.

When we use empirical evidence to choose among competing hypotheses in science, we do not give serious consideration to all logically possible alternatives. Rather, we only use evidence more selectively to choose among those alternatives which are viewed as plausible (Suppe 1977a, 698–99). Under the present proposal, methodological principles are on a par with scientific hypotheses. Thus at any given stage in science we typically do not have reason to believe we have an exhaustive list of possible means of achieving x. Instead, we often have only one candidate y or, at best, a few that we have thought of. Thus in (6) we typically limit $y_1, \ldots, y_{n-1}$ to those means which are viewed as plausible ways of achieving x, construe y_n in accordance with (7), and let y_n encompass all logically possible means that are not construed as plausible. Although we then can use principle (5) to establish principles of form (3) by showing the inequalities in (6) always have held in examined past cases, we cannot use (5) to establish the correctness of our plausibility assessments that restrict attention to just $y_1, \ldots, y_{n-1}$. If we were to construe (5) as the fundamental principle for building up a complex of other methodological rules (including inductive ones), none of these other methodological principles could be used to justify our plausibility judgments. Thus our methodological assessments must rest on plausibility assessments which cannot be established on the basis of inductive rules such as (5). These plausibility assessments are logically prior to the application of induction by simple enumeration.

The situation here is essentially similar to the problem of prior probability assignments on a Bayesian analysis discussed previously. In both cases it is the plausibility assessment, not the use of the rule of induction by simple enumeration or probabilistic rules, that is at the heart of reasoning about evidence and hypotheses—including those methodological hypotheses having form (5).

IV. INDUCTION AS A PHILOSOPHICAL TOOL

Although induction by simple enumeration, hence standard inductive logic, cannot be *the* basis for the development of methodological principles, this does not preclude the possibility that standard inductive logic might have some other important role to play in the philosophical evaluation of scientific canons of reasoning. Recall that I mentioned earlier that science evolves increasingly efficient canons of reasoning which allow the economical assessment of hypotheses on the basis of data that would be insufficient on Burks' Bayesian inductive confirmation model (unless the prior probabilities were virtually on target). Shapere and others have tried to analyze and present models of actual such reasoning patterns evidenced in science.[17] The generation of such an open-ended variety of reasoning patterns raises some interesting new philosophical problems concerning the evaluation, assessment, and explanation of such reasoning patterns. Specifically, not all reasoning patterns employed by science are, or will be, good reasoning patterns in the sense that hypotheses that they sanction are very likely to be correct. In the evaluation of inference patterns as good or bad, it is not sufficient to just rely upon the intuitive judgments of historically oriented philosophers of science as to what constitutes good reasoning. What we would like to do is to be able to give a philosophical explanation of why particular patterns of reasoning developed by science are good ones (in the sense given above) and others are not. I believe that standard inductive logic, as modeled by Burks, can play an important role in such philosophical assessments and explanations—in ways that are not compromised by the descriptive inadequacy of these models.

To show how this is possible, I am going to assume the conclusive reasons epistemology of chapter 12. My attempt will be to show how Burks' analysis of standard inductive logic could be incorporated into it to provide the sorts of philosophical explanations of reasoning patterns we are concerned with. Even if one rejects the account of chapter 12, my discussion is *illustrative* of the *kinds* of philosophical roles Burks' analysis can perform in K-K thesis–denying epistemologies despite the inadequacy of standard inductive logic as a descriptive model of scientific reasoning.

Although I presume familiarity with the development of chapter 12, as well as with the comments on conclusive reasons for knowledge of causal generalization at the beginning of this chapter, I do need to comment on a few other features of my epistemology. It will be recalled that central to my treatment is the rejection of the K-K thesis.

A corollary to my rejection of the K-K thesis is that the evidence we adduce in defending a claim to know that P generally will be different from that which actually justifies the belief that P (the latter being the complex causal/cognitive/doxastic process S underwent, and the former being the reasons one gives if the claim that P is challenged— e.g., "I saw it under clear observational circumstances"). Indeed, while beliefs always must be justified by conclusive reasons in order to be knowledge, we generally do not demand any justification be *given* for common garden knowledge claims unless we have specific reasons for doubting them; rather, absent such specific doubt, we accept them at face value. I speculate that the reason we do is that, absent duplicity, common garden knowledge claims have a high likelihood of being true—the reasons for this involving the close intertwining of perceptual processes with language acquisition wherein learning a language involves learning to apply it correctly to the world we perceive. That is, learning one's first language and learning to know are inextricably intertwined in ways that make our singular common garden knowledge claims usually correct.

We also develop means for obtaining generalized empirical knowledge. The empiricist view is that we obtain it inductively from our singular knowledge. I have no doubts that induction by simple enumeration or some intuitive precursor ("All crows are black because every crow I've seen—and I've seen a lot of them—has been black") plays an important and frequent role in the *defense* of common garden generalized knowledge claims; and unlike singular common garden knowledge claims, we do not take general ones at face value and typically do demand that some justification be given.[18] However, I seriously doubt that induction by simple enumeration or standard inductive logic constitutes the actual justification which makes the belief of a true generalization be knowledge. Rather, I think that the justification for generalized knowledge rests in the same complex causal/cognitive/doxastic processing that enables singular knowledge.[19] Whatever the means whereby our general beliefs are justified and thus constitute knowledge, standard inductive logic is incapable of supplying that justification. For as our discussion of prior probabilities established, standard inductive logic presupposes a logically prior plausibility assessment, and that is almost certainly rooted in the complex causal/cognitive/doxastic processes of perception and empirical knowledge. Thus it seems to me that standard inductive logic is a suitable means for evaluating or defending knowledge claims but does not provide the justification required for our true beliefs to constitute knowledge.[20]

I would like to suggest further that as we come to learn language and conceptualize about the world, we come to make plausibility assessments without presupposing or otherwise employing any articulable methodological rules or principles; and only modest refinements of these abilities are involved in making the plausibility assessments that underlie the use of standard inductive logic. Such a move will work, however, only if one embraces an epistemology which makes sense of such cognitive acquisitions and allows such plausibility assessments to play an evidential role without having any logically prior adducible justification. These demands can be met by embracing an epistemology of the sort defended in chapter 12.

Let us now turn from common garden knowledge and knowledge claims to scientific ones. Precisely the same epistemic means are involved with such knowledge: perceivers interacting via a complex causal/cognitive/doxastic process with the external world. Only here the causal links between the objects we observe and our receptors are far more complex—for example, photons emitted from the interior of the sun are caught by a satellite photon detector which telemeters signals to earthbound computers, where the signals are computer-enhanced, and printouts, optical displays, and so on, are produced which then are looked at by human eyes which results in sensory experiences, thoughts, and the belief that P about the sun's interior, where the observational circumstances have been so contrived that we could not have had those sensory experiences unless P were true of the sun's interior. Thus we obtain observational knowledge that P about the sun's interior. The knowledge is obtained exactly the same way that I know my dog is sleeping on the sofa—only the subject matter is more remote from me, and the causal processes involved are far more complex and contrived.

Just because what we observe in science usually is so much more remote, and accessible only by contrived, highly complex causal processes, we have good reason not to take individual scientific observational knowledge claims at face value in the way that we do common garden ones. In general we require that scientific knowledge claims—be they singular observational claims or general ones involving causal necessity—be accompanied with some explicit justification: Experimental designs and procedures are to be described, as are statistical, and other, evaluation procedures employed. Precisely what is to be described depends on the scientific discipline and its stage of development, and will vary among these. But the general requirement is that the justification demanded be such that, given the discipline's extant domain of knowledge, the background knowledge (e.g., about instrumentation techniques) it accepts, its methodological standards, and its accepted canons of reasoning, it is highly likely the knowledge claim is correct.

I cannot stress too much the extreme variability in these factors between disciplines and over time which affect what justification is required by a scientific discipline. And the fallibility of these also must be stressed. Given a poor methodology, inaccurate background "knowledge," or bad canons of reasoning, a science may fail to sanction correct knowledge claims or, even worse, it may accept incorrect knowledge claims. Here we need to return to our earlier observation that it is characteristic of sophisticated sciences to develop new and "improved" canons of reasoning which frequently are remarkably efficient in the paucity of data needed for a knowledge claim to pass methodological muster and be accepted—in ways that far exceed the data efficiency of the repeated instance confirmation model of standard inductive logic. Other than these canons and standard inductive logics being alternative means of assessing scientific knowledge claims and deciding which ones to accept, are there any important connections between them?

Burks' statement that "the logic of inductive arguments studies the most general, universal, and fundamental types of inductive arguments, leaving the more detailed and specific forms to the individual sciences and statistics" (17) suggests that there are. Specifically, in light of our foregoing discussion, it suggests that the more efficient canons of reasoning that a science develops (which tend to be highly specific in their applicability) are the more specific forms Burks mentions, and that standard inductive logic augmented with a logic of plausibility assessment constitutes one general, albeit inefficient method, of assessing general knowledge claims involving causal necessity which could, in principle, be used whenever these more specialized canons are used— though such use will require recourse to much more data. *Cause, Chance, Reason* does mount a quite persuasive defense of the latter claim, provided one accepts Burks' presuppositions of induction— which I am willing to do.[21] Thus I am willing to accept the claim that given the unlimited resources and computers capable of making manageable the massive amounts of data that would be required, the knowledge claims for all of science in principle could be assessed by using just standard inductive logic and the Bayesian inference model together with a logic of plausibility assessment.

Does this mean, then, that these special improved canons of reasoning science so frequently develops are just special case applications of standard inductive logic? No, for as I argued above, it is plausibility assessment, not standard inductive logic, which bears the main evaluative burden in many of these canons. Adequate understanding of scientific reasoning about evidence will require investigating, and possibly developing a logic of, nonprobabilistic plausibility reasoning. But absent such a logic, there is a place for Burks' standard inductive logic—in the assessment of canons of scientific reasoning and in explaining why good ones succeed and bad ones do not. Suppose a canon of reasoning says only $H_1, \ldots, H_n$ are plausible. We can set up a Bayesian instance confirmation model with $H_1, \ldots, H_n, \sim(H_1 \vee \ldots \vee H_n)$ as the candidate hypotheses. Then, possibly by computer manipulation, using existing and hypothetical data consistent with available knowledge, we vary the prior probabilities and see whether the instance confirmation model yields the same assessments as the canon of reasoning does. If it does, we have good reason for accepting the canon as a good one and have laid at least part of the basis for explaining why it is a good canon to follow.

If they do not yield the same assessment, several possibilities arise. First, it may be that $\sim(H_1 \vee \ldots \vee H_n)$ wins out. In this case, we know that the plausibility assessments provided by the canon are defective (in the sense of being incompatible with the available background and domain knowledge of the discipline), and this fact lays a basis for explaining why. Second, it may be that different of the $H_1, \ldots, H_n$ pass muster under the Bayesian and the canon evaluations; then we know the canon is incorrect, and we have a starting basis for investigating, and hopefully explaining, why the canon fails. Third, since finitary constraints require truncating the Bayesian process short of the confirmation theorem's "in the limit," we have the possibility that for some prior probability assignments the Bayesian results are compatible with the canon, and for others they are incompatible. In this case we will have to analyze, on other grounds, the reasonableness (plausibility) of the various prior probability assignments. If all goes well, such an assessment will enable us to restrict attention to just the plausible prior probability assignment cases in such a manner that one of the other possibilities already discussed results.

Thus if one accepts the sort of epistemological view I have been defending here and in chapter 12, there is an important philosophical place for standard inductive logic and Burks' analysis of it: It is in evaluating, explaining, and understanding the way general knowledge claims are justified and assessed (but not in the analysis of the role of evidence in obtaining general knowledge), although it is not the method that all of science in fact uses. One does not have to accept the epistemology I have outlined here to grant standard inductive logic, and Burks' analysis of it, these valuable philosophical roles. For the same roles will be available on virtually any epistemology which allows the justifications used to assess knowledge claims to be distinct from what constitutes the justification required for true belief to be knowledge. Of course, standard inductive logic has a different role to play in epistemologies which make induction be the justification required in order for true belief to be general knowledge, but I am convinced that no such epistemology is defensible and compatible with the view that science as we know it is capable of, and routinely does, produce realistic knowledge of the world. Indeed, I am convinced that standard inductive logic will have the valuable philosophical roles I have been urging here on any viable epistemology.

V. CONCLUSION

Is science really inductive? In this chapter I have tried to argue that standard inductive logic is not a good descriptive model of science, although some branches of science (e.g., the behavioral sciences) do reason in accord with it. Thus there is an important sense in which the claim that standard inductive logic is the system of rules of inference actually used and aspired to by practicing scientists is incorrect. Moreover, nonprobabilistic plausibility assessment underlies the applicability of standard inductive logic, is logically prior to and more basic to reasoning about evidence, and it often plays a more important role in scientific reasoning about data than standard inductive logic does. Standard inductive logic cannot be the foundational basis on which the canons of scientific evidence are based or justified. Nevertheless, I believe standard inductive logic (and Burks' analysis of it) provides an important philosophical tool for assessing, analyzing, and explaining the successes and failures of the canons of reasoning which science does employ, and I have tried to show at some length how it can do this and have a valuable and important place in a comprehensive epistemology of science. Indeed, properly understood and deployed, it is congenial with, and has a role to play, in my own epistemological efforts.

NOTES

1. To do so, inter alia, the probabilities would have to be 1. Further, $P(E)$ = 1 would have to entail that $\boxed{C}E$, which is not true on all probabilistic theories.

2. Unless otherwise indicated, all page references in this chapter are to Burks 1977.

3. For discussion why the nonzero probability case is so crucial, see Suppe 1977a, 627–31.

4. 'Inductive' here and throughout this chapter usually is meant not in the looser common sense of "nondeductive," but rather in the stricter, technical sense of inductive logic, wherein probability theory plays a central role; when it does not, context (e.g., the discussion of pre-probabilistic approaches to induction) should make it clear that it does not.

5. Such a construal is especially plausible, since in chapter 5 Burks analyzes inductive probabilities in terms of beliefs and actions—willingness to bet in the face of uncertainty—in such a way that inductive probabilities are manifestations of behavior, not vice versa.

6. For defense of this claim, see Suppe 1977a, 707 n. 241.

7. Galileo Galilei 1970, 145.

8. Isaac Newton 1952, 404.

9. See Cohen 1974, 340. Sec. 5 contains an extended discussion of falsification of texts in translation to make scientists conform to approved philosophies of science.

10. Although path analysis is construed by many behavioral scientists as a means for discovering causal relations statistically, it was originally put forward by Sewell Wright (1921) as a method for exploiting antecedently known causal relations in the correlational analysis of the heritability of traits in animal and breeding contexts. Wright is quite clear that path analysis is incapable of establishing causal relations. See also the warnings on pp. 11–12 of Asher 1976. See also the discussion in my forthcoming paper listed as n.d. in the bibliography.

11. See Lakatos 1970. For a detailed summary and critical evaluation of Lakatos' view, see Suppe 1977a, 659–70 passim.

12. Admittedly, this suggestion leaves no room for insightful new opportunities resulting from "surprising discoveries" in the testing which suggest new moves for designing the next theory to enter the Lakatosian problem shift. However, the positive and negative heuristics Lakatos allows are so constipative that, on his analysis, this seems virtually precluded. In any case, pursuing the line followed below, on Burks' Bayesian analysis this can be handled by construing the "none of the above" clause as gaining an increased probability—and so can be accommodated, provided the "none of the above" hypothesis is given a nonzero prior probability.

13. Meeting the "mutually exclusive and jointly exhaustive competing hypotheses" requirement for Bayes' method typically is feasible only by listing a set of candidate alternatives, together with the nonzero probability denial of the disjunction of these (a "none of the above" clause). Burks himself invokes this gambit in his 1977 book on pp. 85ff.

14. Much of this discussion of Shapere is based upon unpublished work by him. For a comprehensive (but now dated) published account of Shapere's relevant work, see Suppe 1977a, 682–704; my present account is based on works of Shapere discussed therein. See also Shapere 1984.

15. One feature of Burks' pragmatic theory, and the related personalistic theories, is that probabilities are reflections of behavioral dispositions and beliefs, rather than the traditional view that beliefs and decisions are based upon available probability assessments.

16. Larry Laudan explored this idea in a paper presented to the Washington Philosophy Club on December 8, 1984. However, the portion of his manuscript dealing with this possibility does not appear in the published version (Laudan 1986), so I am uncertain whether he still wants to commit himself to the sort of view I discuss here. In any case, the present section of this chapter and a small portion of the next section are adapted from my formal commentary on his proposals which I gave at the same meeting, and so owes much to his way of formulating the proposal then. (Burks does not consider or discuss the proposal which follows.)

17. Cf., e.g., Shapere 1974b, 541, 545–46, 553 and Suppe 1977a, 697.

18. Unless, of course, the generalization is common knowledge. Before it becomes common knowledge, justification would be demanded.

19. See the discussion at the beginning of this chapter.

20. Note that Burks' approach of rooting standard inductive logic in our disposition toward action (willingness to bet in the face of uncertainty) as conditioned and constrained by our innate structure/program complexes is quite congenial to the views I am speculatively propounding here.

21. Returning to my earlier speculations about the intertwined connections between perception, knowledge, and language acquisition, I further speculate that these processes would not be possible unless something akin to Burks' presuppositions of induction were correct. Further, I agree with him that if they were not true, science as we know it would be impossible.

14

Epilogue

In this book I have undertaken to provide the most comprehensive discussion of the Semantic Conception of Theories yet attempted, including its intellectual origins, detailed development, and diverse applications. I have focused mostly on a quasi-realistic version which I believe holds the greatest potential for making explanatory sense of a wide range of scientific practices, conceptual products, and phenomena, as well as for resolving a host of philosophical problems and issues concerning the theoretical side of science. Although the discussions in the various preceding chapters provide, I believe, considerable evidence in support of that version's power and potential in these respects, its viability ultimately turns on whether its quasi-realism can be provided with suitable epistemological underpinnings. In the final section of the book I have attempted to motivate and provide in fair detail a prolegomenon to such an epistemology, to be fully developed (along with its associated metaphysics) in *Facts, Theories, and Scientific Observation* (in progress).

The philosophical problems concerning theories I have focused on here are, of course, only a few of the many that either are important or have garnered considerable attention from philosophers. In this Epilogue I want to survey the larger domain of philosophical issues and problems concerning theories and indicate where I think my efforts here fit into the larger landscape. In the process, I will comment on the promise (or lack of it) I find in various approaches and efforts. Inter alia, my hope is that the discussion will stimulate others to work on these issues, and in ways that complement my own efforts.

I. CHANGING PROBLEMS

As I have detailed at length elsewhere (Suppe 1974b, 1975, 1977a), over the last quarter-century, philosophy of science has undergone a major intellectual revolution, and the nature of theories and theorizing has been a focal issue of debate in that revolution. At the beginning of the 1960s, logical positivism dominated philosophy of science, and its analysis of theories (the so-called Received View on which theories are axiomatic systems wherein theoretical assertions are given a partial observational interpretation via correspondence rules) was routinely assumed in dealing with other problems in philosophy of science.[1] By 1963 that conception of theories and accompanying positivistic views on scientific theorizing and knowledge were coming under increasingly heavy attack by Achinstein, Feyerabend, Kuhn, Putnam, Shapere, Toulmin, and others. These and subsequent attacks were so successful that by 1969 the Received View had been generally discredited. Moreover, the Received View was so central to the entire positivistic program in philosophy of science that its rejection called into question the entire positivistic portrait of science: Its views on discovery and the growth of scientific knowledge, reduction, explanation, observation, induction, and so on, became increasingly suspect and a matter of critical debate. Today virtually every significant part of the positivistic viewpoint has been found wanting and has been rejected by philosophy of science (Suppe 1977a). The dominant thrust of contemporary work in the philosophy of science is the development of new views of science which proceed from, and tend to depend heavily on, close examination of actual scientific practice and products (e.g., theories, explanations) (Suppe 1977a, 650–716).

Among the important impacts of this philosophical revolution has been a radical change in what problems are viewed as crucial in philosophy of science. Whereas positivism was relatively unconcerned with the dynamics of theorizing and discovery—limiting its concern to intertheoretic reduction—today rationality in the growth of scientific knowledge, research methodologies, and the development and improvement of theories and supratheoretical units of science (such as domains, disciplines, research programs, research traditions, and scientific fields) are perceived as being among the most fundamental and basic issues in the philosophy of science.[2] Furthermore, the importance and centrality of a number of traditional problems in philosophy of science have been sharply downgraded, and the nature of these problems has been radically reinterpreted: Positivistic accounts of reduction have little to do with actual reductive phenomena in science; a diverse variety of "reductions" are found in science, and philosophers are concerned with understanding them as they function in the growth of scientific knowledge—recognizing that much of the development of science is nonreductive. Increasingly, philosophers are coming to realize that much of the evaluation of scientific theories and hypotheses is neither deductive nor inductive,[3] and that not only is inductive reasoning only one of an open-ended evolving variety of evaluative reasoning patterns employed by science, but is a relatively crude and inefficient one characteristically employed only at relatively primitive stages of science. Moreover, work on inductive logic increasingly focuses on local induction (inductive strategies appropriate to a given scientific domain) rather than global induction and is expanding to include other statistical strategies employed by science in evaluating hypotheses and theories. Work on explanation, while still concerned with the explanation of events, increasingly is becoming concerned with how theories are explanatory of the underlying unity of, or the interconnection between, items of information associated together by larger units of science such as domains, disciplines, areas, fields, and so on. And as we will see below, problems of theory structure, as well as observation and theory, similarly have been refocused.[4]

Central to the positivistic program was the desire to delimit the borders between science and nonscience in order to provide criteria whereby genuine science could be recognized and pseudoscience exposed as illegitimate metaphysical speculation. And positivists thought this could be done on a priori structural grounds. Thus to be a genuine scientific theory was to possess a specified logical or structural form or else be rephrasable into an account that had the requisite form; and all and only those "theoretical" accounts which met this test qualified as genuinely scientific. Similarly, positivists tried to delimit genuine explanations, confirmations, and so on, on the basis of structural accounts. The urge to delimit on the basis of structure or logical form increasingly is absent from contemporary philosophy of science for several reasons. First, positivistic attempts to delimit scientific entities such as theories and explanations have proven so unsuccessful that there is good reason to doubt that they can be delimited on the basis of structure or logical form. Second, at least some philosophers (e.g., Achinstein and Shapere) are discovering good reasons to conclude that what counts as theory, explanation, or confirmation is (in part at least) an empirical issue whose answer depends on the current state of scientific knowledge and thus cannot be determined on the basis of structure or logical form alone. Third, there is a growing appreciation of the fact that there are a variety of legitimate goals or purposes for philosophical analyses and inquiries—including the discovery of criteria for determining the applicability of metascientific concepts, meaning analyses of metascientific concepts, determining the truth conditions for such concepts, and producing explanatory philosophical accounts of, for example, how the practices and conceptual devices employed by science enable it to yield knowledge. And there is the growing realization that an adequate philosophical account need not embrace or attempt to fulfill all these goals. Thus an adequate philosophical account of theories might satisfy the explanatory goal without providing either a meaning analysis of 'theory' or criteria for determining whether a particular scientific product is or is not a theory. By contrast, the positivists thought otherwise, supposing that structural/meaning analyses would accomplish all these goals[5]—itself a strong "metaphysical" claim substantiated neither by compelling argument nor philosophical accomplishment. With the growing emphasis on the growth of scientific knowledge, the focal goal in philosophy of science has become the production of explanatory philosophical accounts; and the other goals are embraced largely to the extent they are viewed as contributing to such explanatory accounts. The production of delimiting criteria rapidly is ceasing to be an important goal for analyses in the philosophy of science (other than in topical controversies such as whether Creationism is a science), and the importance accorded to meaning analyses is sharply diminishing.

The situation today in philosophy of science, thus, is that a new problem—the growth of scientific knowledge, including the dynamics of theorizing—has emerged as a central problem in philosophy of science and in the process has reoriented, refocused, and made sub-servient many other traditional problems. The focus of these problems now has become, roughly, understanding how reduction, explanation, induction and confirmation, theory structure, and so on, can, do, or could contribute to the growth of scientific knowledge in actual prac-tice—understanding what burdens they bear in this enterprise and explaining how they are able to do so. [The emergence of the Semantic Conception as a replacement for the Received View has further trans-formed these problems. Witness, for example, the changes in the issues of scientific realism, theoretical explanation, and the universality of biological laws documented in earlier chapters.] In short, the names of these problems are the same, but the problems and what counts as solutions to them are radically different from what they were thirty years ago.

It is crucial that we keep this point in mind. For despite the fact that the foregoing is, I claim, an accurate portrait of recent trends in philosophy of science, a number of philosophers of science do not recognize these trends and continue to work on the old problems and seek old types of solutions. This is especially apparent in contemporary European formal philosophy of science which tends to deal with problems and to seek types of solutions that are significant only within a neo-positivistic perspective on science (see, e.g., Przełecki, Szaniawski, and Wójcicki 1976). The important research problems today are not more sophisticated treatments of the old positivistic problems; rather, they are the reinterpreted problems which are formulated in reference to, and potentially can contribute to, the philosophical understanding of the growth and nature of scientific knowledge. It is especially important to note that meaning analyses of concepts such as 'explanation', 'law', and 'theory' have virtually no potential for such a contribution, and so are not critical research problems; rather, what is critical is philosophical accounts that *describe* the roles that explanations, laws, theories, and so forth, play in the scientific enterprise, *describe* their essential features, *explain* how those features enable them to bear the burdens they do in scientific knowledge and its growth, and *explore* how the adequacy of their employment can be rationally evaluated. In developing such analyses, formal, informal, and historical accounts are needed.

An important reason for examining the structure of theories is the fact that understanding the structure of theories can contribute to an improved philosophical understanding of the nature and growth of scientific knowledge. This has been a major concern of this book.

II. RECENT, CURRENT, AND FUTURE RESEARCH EMPHASES

In the wake of the positivistic Received View's rejection, philosophers of science attempted to develop replacement analyses of theories. Of these, *The Semantic Conception of Theories* has been most extensively developed, has proved the most promising, and is the only one to gain significant acceptance.

The Semantic Conception of Theories follows a relatively "formal" approach to analyzing and understanding scientific theories; also valuable is more informal work by Shapere and others concerned with investigating how theories are employed and how they function in actual scientific contexts (historical and contemporary). Such work has focused on the use of theories as cognitive devices such as idealizations and simplifications, on the various types of theories (e.g., compositional and evolutionary) and the rationales for favoring certain types over others, on the relationships between theories and larger units of science (such as scientific domains, areas, fields, and disciplines), and so on (Darden and Maull 1977; Schaffner 1980; Shapere 1984; Suppe 1977a, 706–16). Such informal investigations, and the more formal studies associated with the Semantic Conception, are not, in my opinion, incompatible or in competition. For both approaches share the basic supposition that adequate philosophical analyses of theories must reflect actual scientific practice in the employment and development of theories. Thus the findings of informal studies, such as Shapere's, provide essential data against which the more formal analyses of theories are to be evaluated and tested; they also reveal various aspects of theories and theorizing which not only can be grist for formalistic mills, but also can be suggestive of new aspects of theories and theorizing which ought to be accommodated in attempts to further develop and refine, for example, the Semantic Conception analyses of theories. This is not to say, however, that formal efforts such as the Semantic Conception are merely parasitic attempts to formalize and make precise the findings of such informal studies, for theories do contain theory structures which are mathematical entities that cannot be adequately understood solely through informal analysis. Thus it seems to me a full philosophical understanding of theories will require a judicious mixture of both formal and informal investigation—sometimes by individuals integrating both approaches, other times by workers of each persuasion paying attention to and being influenced by each others' efforts. Kenat 1987 is a particularly nice example of an attempt to combine such historical/informal approaches with the Semantic Conception.

I shall now turn to a consideration of what seems to me the most important recent work on theories, in the process considering both formal and informal approaches and attempting to indicate the connections between their various findings. The most important recent work on theories conveniently can be grouped in four broad areas of investigation: the abstract structure of theories, types of theories, the physical interpretation of theories, and use of theories.

A. The Abstract Structure of Theories

Although there is increasingly widespread agreement that theories are not to be identified with particular linguistic formulations used in propounding them (e.g., sets of sentences or propositions), and that rather they are (or include as a central component) an extralinguistic theory structure, there is considerable disagreement as to the nature of such structures. Some authors (e.g., Sneed, Stegmüller, and Suppes) construe theory structures as set-theoretic entities axiomatizable by a set-theoretic predicate. Others construe theory structures as configurated state spaces (van Fraassen) or suitably connected sets of such spaces or their nonmetrical analogues (Suppe). How significant these differences are is a matter worth investigating; my conjecture is that they reflect more the mathematical preferences of the authors or decisions as to which mathematical approach is most suitable for making progress on other philosophical problems the author is interested in than they do significant philosophical disagreements. Indeed, it seems to me that despite their mathematical differences, there is general agreement among the above authors that theory structures are equivalent to state spaces or the homomorphic images of state spaces. Of particular interest are findings that such abstract structural accounts can be extended to accommodate not only quantitative theories with measurable state parameters, but also qualitative theories with nonmeasurable parameters (ch. 4), provide a useful basis for investigating the structure of theoretical laws construed as state transition relations (chs. 5, 7) and are valuable for approaching questions concerning quantum logic and the logic of theories—especially their relations to, or places in, theories (chs. 3 and 4 and van Fraassen 1972, 1974a). More generally, the Semantic Conception of Theories increasingly is being used by others to make valuable contributions to other issues in the philosophy of science (see ch. 1).

As developed by Suppes, van Fraassen, and myself, the Semantic Conception is not concerned with discovering criteria for delimiting scientific theories or differentiating the theoretical from the nontheoretical, and it is not concerned with giving a meaning analysis of 'theory' or 'theoretical'. Rather, the attempt is to investigate a significant scientific product—theories—of which classical particle mechanics, special and general theory of relativity, quantum theory, plate tectonic theory, various learning theories, population genetics, the genetic theory of natural selection, and so on, are paradigm examples. The foci of the investigations are to determine what epistemic and conceptual burdens science can or does impose on such theories and what characteristics of theories enable them to bear those burdens. Structural accounts, such as those provided by the Semantic Conception, contribute to, but are not exhaustive of, answers to these questions. Other parts of the answer involve accounts of how these structures are physically interpreted and how they are used when so interpreted—as well as accounts of solutions to more fundamental epistemological issues.

Left open is the possibility that there may be *other* notions of 'theory' or kinds of theories found in, and legitimately employed by, science which do not fit the Semantic Conception analysis.[6] Similarly, there is little concern whether theories fitting the Semantic Conception analysis might occur outside of science (as, e.g., a particular version of determinism or near-determinism might).[7] That is, the attempt is not to provide criteria for delimiting theories or the 'theoretical', but rather to provide explanatory philosophical accounts of theories as they are (or can be) employed in science. For Sneed (1971) and Stegmüller (1976), the enterprise is somewhat different: Dominating their account is the desire that it provide criteria for delimiting the theoretical from the nontheoretical and that it provide an account of theory suitable for reworking Kuhn's (1962) account of normal versus revolutionary science. In chapter 1, I have indicated why I do not find this to be a promising effort.

There obviously is need for further work on the structure of theories. For example, the discussions of how natural selection theory is to be treated in chapters 7 and 8 is quite preliminary. Elisabeth Lloyd and Paul Thompson have devoted considerable effort to advancing our understanding of evolutionary theory on the Semantic Conception. See their recent books (Lloyd 1988a; Thompson 1989), as well as their various papers listed in the bibliography. Nevertheless, more work is needed. Similarly, attempts such as Hausman 1981 to use the Semantic Conception to deal with economic theory are only the beginning. Suppes' attempts to apply the Semantic Conception to learning theory in psychology (see, e.g., his 1962) is fairly sophisticated, but its use with other branches of the social sciences is only just beginning—for example, Edelson's (1984) attempt to use it to analyze Freudian psychoanalytic theory. Work on other issues (to be discussed below) will be particularly valuable in assessing the adequacy of the structural accounts already developed—in determining whether they meet the descriptive and explanatory criteria maintained above. To the extent that these future results show these structural accounts to be "right-headed" but defective, refinement and further development of them will be important.

Recent work on the growth of scientific knowledge has revealed the importance of supratheoretical entities such as domains, areas, and fields which frequently contain, or are associated with, one or more theories. Moreover, as Bromberger (1963) has noted, these entities often are referred to in science as theories—for example, 'biological theory' or 'kinship theory'. Thus far their analysis has been largely descriptive and informal, and there is reason to suppose that more formal structural analyses of them could be valuable and important. For example, in discussing scientific domains, Shapere (1974b) indicates that the organization of a domain generates or poses problems that demand solutions but says little about how this occurs. A structural analysis of domains, their organization, and their erotetic properties could substantially advance our understanding of domains. Similarly, it is becoming clear that there are developmental aspects of theories which have not been adequately investigated and understood on which further abstract structural investigations could shed light (see sec. III-B below for related discussion). Thus there also is considerable scope for important abstract structural analyses focusing on aspects of theorizing different from those the Semantic Conception has concentrated on.

B. Types of Theories

It has been commonplace to classify theories on the basis of whether their laws are deterministic or indeterministic and whether those laws are laws of succession, coexistence, or interaction. The adequacy of such classifications increasingly is being challenged on several fronts. First, we saw in chapter 5 that the classification is redundant and that the types of theories provided by the classification are special cases of several more fundamental kinds of laws. Second, work by Shapere (1974a), Schaffner (1980), Darden and Maull (1977), and others on the growth of scientific knowledge has displayed other kinds of theories—for example, compositional theories, evolutionary theories, and interfield theories. What is most striking about these kinds of theories is that not only do their most distinctive features not show up in the traditional classification, but they are features that characteristically link up with particular reasoning patterns employed in the growth of scientific knowledge. This is extremely important, for it is emerging that the content of a science at a given time rationally favors certain types of theories and renders other types implausible (see Darden and Maull 1977; Shapere 1984; and Suppe 1977a, 682–704). Thus investigating the kinds of theories science in fact employs—where kinds are delimited on the basis of both structural characteristics of the constituent laws and the reasoning patterns in terms of which the plausibility of possible theories are evaluated—is called for because of its direct links to understanding the growth of scientific knowledge and its potential for testing the adequacy of the above-mentioned abstract analyses of theory structure. This seems to me to be a particularly important research problem, and it is one that will require a judicious combination of historical research and philosophical analysis.

C. The Physical Interpretation of Theories

The abstract structures discussed above do not become scientific theories until they are provided with physical interpretations (mapping relations between theory structures and phenomena). Further, it is clear that these physical interpretations are not explicitly stated (as the Received View required) but are implicitly or intensionally specified and are liable to alteration, modification, or expansion as a science progresses. There has been substantial research done on the physical interpretation of theories, which conveniently may be viewed from the perspective of controversies over scientific realism involving Sellars, van Fraassen, Boyd, Glymour, and Cornman. (I have discussed these issues in ch. 11 as well as portions of ch. 1 above.) Of course, issues surrounding the physical interpretation of theories are crucial to, but not exhaustive of, the question, What is it for a theory to be adequate?

D. Uses of Theories

As was discussed in chapter 11, work by Shapere and others has revealed that theories often do not even purport to be true but rather are introduced as an "idealization," an "abstraction," a "simplification," a "model," or even as a "fiction," or one may have a theory in a particular stage of development where one does not know which of the statuses the theory has. In the latter case, one's concern with reason, observation, and experiment is to determine whether a theory provides a realistic account of phenomena or whether it is some *conceptual device* falling short of providing a realistic account or how it can be modified to provide a more realistic account. This indicates that theories admit of a variety of different physical interpretations depending on their use, and that the realism controversies just discussed should be construed as debating the limits of descriptive accuracy theories *in principle* can achieve and still be known (see ch. 11). But such descriptive adequacy is only one of a variety of uses of theories, and the adequacy of a theory will be relative to its uses and the aims of a particular scientific enterprise.

Typically, different physical interpretations will be required for different uses of theories. Thus it becomes crucial to approach questions of the physical interpretation of theories from the perspective of different uses, viewing the controversies over scientific realism as being concerned with only one use—albeit an important one, since it is the use against which other uses apparently are to be identified and evaluated. It is important to investigate the variety of uses science typically engages in and to investigate how theory structures are physically interpreted in these uses; Kenat 1987 is a particularly good example of this approach. I would suggest that examining the reasoning patterns science employs in evaluating candidate theories will provide particularly valuable and revealing evidence to be exploited in analyzing the various physical interpretations of theories in diverse uses of them. And when that use is to provide true accounts of phenomena, such evidence—augmented by physical considerations—just might enable us to make some progress on resolving, or at least refining, current disputes over scientific realism. I remain convinced that the best way to defend a scientific realism or quasi-realism is to produce a satisfactory epistemology for science, and that how one physically interprets theories will be an important constraint on the detailed development of such an epistemology. It certainly was for the epistemology developed in chapters 10 through 13 above.

Thus far I have been discussing what I take to be the most important lines of recent and current research on theories, in the process commenting on what I feel ought to be the main emphasis for future research along these lines. In doing so I clearly have ignored a number of areas of recent research that involve theories. These include problems of theory versus observation and the theory-ladenness of observation, as well as a whole range of questions concerning the role of theories in explanation, reduction, observation, and experimentation, and so on. These areas are all important for understanding the nature of theories and their uses in the scientific enterprise. They obviously can be profitably informed by, and contribute to, the lines of research on theories which I have discussed. In some cases, I have ignored some areas of research on theories either on the ground that I do not feel they are very important or else because I think they are fundamentally wrongheaded. These include, in the first instance, attempts to rework or refine Ramsey methods for eliminating or characterizing theoretical terms. In my opinion, such attempts inevitably require incorporating correspondence rules (or other assertions of experimental, measurement, and related procedures) into theories and thus embody a view of theories which is untenable for reasons I have discussed elsewhere (Suppe 1974b, 102–09; ch. 2 above).[8] Second I have excluded the vast body of literature on the meaning of theoretical terms and/or meaning change issues on the ground that it does little to enhance our understanding of theories, since it tends to presuppose untenable views of theory or of meaning. Further, if the Semantic Conception is at all on the right track, its construal of theories as extralinguistic theory structures standing in mapping relations to real phenomena makes such issues largely irrelevant to an understanding of theories—however intrinsically interesting and valuable they might be and whatever relevance they may have to other communicative aspects of the scientific enterprise. Thus for example, while I agree with Thomas Kuhn that "how language fits the world" is a very important philosophical question (1974, esp. 468), I disagree with him that it is of crucial importance to understanding theories and their physical interpretation—largely because I do not share his views on meaning and epistemology which lead him to think they are central to undertanding theories and theorizing (see my 1974a and ch. 10 above). Third, I have ignored attempts to provide a single account of 'simplicity' as employed in scientific reasoning on the ground that a close look at how simplicity considerations are employed in actual science reveals such a diversity of simplicity notions as to render the search for a single account unpromising. [Fourth, van Fraassen 1989 makes a compelling case for work on metaphysical accounts of laws of nature and inference to the best explanation not being promising avenues to pursue.] Finally, there are areas of research or theories which are only just beginning to be explored or have not dominated recent work on theories, which nonetheless are important and ought to be emphasized in the future; these will be discussed in the next section.

III. EMPHASES THAT SHOULD GUIDE FUTURE RESEARCH

The discussion in the previous section indicated not only what lines of current research on theories I think are unpromising, but also what main lines of current research deserve emphasis and the directions in which I feel these lines should be developed in the future. There are several other lines for future research that I feel also warrant serious emphasis.

A. Models versus Theories

It has been commonplace either to view models and theories as quite distinct entities or else to view theories as one type of model which is sharply distinguishable from other kinds of models (Suppe 1967; Suppes 1961). Such a view implicitly supposes that adequate theories provide true general descriptions of "natural" classes of phenomena, whereas models do not.[9] When the diversity of uses of theories in science is recognized, these views immediately become suspect. The differences between theories and models become blurred when, for example, a theory is being used as an "idealization" or "approximation" (see Kenat 1987). Moreover, recent work on modeling and simulation by Burks (1975) and Zeigler (1976, 1976a) strongly suggests that the class of structures of dynamic models substantially overlaps the class of theory structures.

This raises the question whether the primary difference between theories and models rests in the nature of mapping relations between structures and phenomena (physical interpretations of the structures) or perhaps the kinds or classes of phenomena so represented. For example, one might propose that a theory structure is a model whenever it is propounded as something other than an empirically true theory. Thus conceptual devices and theories whose intended scopes were not natural kind sets of phenomenal systems all would be models. For instance, it would allow one to present much the same analysis of optimum design models in evolutionary biology as Beatty (1980) does, without taking recourse to his almost surely false supposition that theories do not make empirical claims (see ch. 1, sec. I). Even if this proposed analysis of models were to be developed and proved viable, it would not obviate the need for a comprehensive reassessment and investigation of the relationships between theories and models of phenomena, though it might play an important role in such a comprehensive study. Wimsatt 1987 is a promising step in that direction.

Wimsatt (1979) discusses the heuristic use of models and notes that gradual refinement of models can lead to microtheories, and he has suggested to me in conversation that theories can be construed as clusters of models. Taking a similar line, Schaffner (1980) has argued that philosophers of biology have presented distorted accounts of theory in the biomedical sciences, because they have concentrated on atypical theories such as population genetics while ignoring what he calls "middle-range theories"; he further maintains that these "middle-range" theories are best characterized as a series of overlapping interlevel temporal models. These suggestions are important because they suggest important relations between models and theories which have not been adequately explored. Schaffner's proposals were considered in chapter 8 with respect to the adequacy of the Semantic Conception — specifically, whether the Semantic Conception can accommodate such theories in its analysis. What that chapter did not consider was the implications of my treatment for understanding the relations between theories and models. And I have not explored what happens when heuristic uses, such as the ones Wimsatt discusses, play an important role in converting models into theories.

B. Individuation of Theories

Work on the growth of scientific knowledge suggests that theories are extended, evolve, change, undergo developments, and so on. This raises serious questions about how theories are to be individuated and ultimately bears heavily on how the growth of scientific knowledge is to be construed. Specifically, do alterations in theories produce new descendant theories, as Lakatos (1970) supposed in his notion of a "problem shift"? If so, then it is not the case that, strictly speaking, theories evolve or change; rather, it is the case that theory development consists in the production of a series of closely related descendant theories. And if this is so, is there some supratheoretical entity such as

Lakatos' "hard core" (ibid., 133) or Shapere's (1974b) "gradual development of an initial vague idea" (553) which is altered and developed in such a way that the closely related descendant theories all are fillings in of that entity? On the other hand, if alterations in theories do not produce new descendant theories, but rather theories are things that can grow, evolve, and change without becoming a different theory, then this suggests that many versions of the Semantic Conception are inadequate by virtue of improperly individuating theories. If so, then perhaps theories are collections of possible models united by virtue of instantiating some core principle or idea, as Stegmüller (1976, sec. 7) maintains. If this approach proves correct, then what most versions of the Semantic Conception have identified as theories become models of the theory or "theory instances"; thus some modifications in the Semantic Conception would be needed, but it is not fundamentally misguided. And of course, what that core would be needs to be investigated much more fully; whether such a core notion is viable presently remains an open question, since all the plausible candidates are either inadequate or else amount to vague suggestions.

[But such radical solutions may not be necessary. Da Costa and French (n.d.) introduce a notion of partial models which suggests another approach to treating evolving theories under the Semantic Conception. Still another approach would be to allow the theory structures to be self-organizing systems with an evolving or changing structure. Such an approach is wholly compatible with construing theory structures as relational systems as we did in chapters 3 through 5 above. Both of these approaches, if successful, would seem able to circumvent individuation problems without requiring significant alteration in my version of the Semantic Conception.]

These individuation issues are fundamental, for they concern what it is to be *a* theory. And it is an issue which has close connections with the question of how one and the same theory can admit the diverse variety of uses mentioned in section II-D above, as well as the various issues concerning the relation between theories and models discussed in section III-A. Kenat (1987) makes useful beginnings at approaching these issues. The individuation problem can be deepened further by linking it to the question whether or not our notion of what counts as a theory is fixed or whether it depends upon the content of science itself.[10]

C. The Relations between Theories, Observation, and Knowledge

We have observed that the adequacy of theories often is evaluated on grounds other than literal truth, and we also have alluded to the fact that the evaluation of theories in advanced areas of science typically is neither inductive nor deductive. Indeed, there are numbers of cases where the adequacy of a theory is settled on the basis of single observations. If science *is* the epistemic enterprise we suppose it to be, then it must be possible to know that theories are adequate. Thus the problems of theory, observation and experiment, and knowledge come together: An adequate philosophy of science, inter alia, must provide integrated accounts of all four which can explain how successful, actual scientific practice can provide knowledge of the adequacy of theories in their diverse uses. Such an account, inter alia, must also be able to explain how a theory can be known to be true or approximately true on the basis of single observations or on the basis of data sufficiently meager as to preclude deductive, inductive, or statistical confirmation under anything like the sorts of models philosophy of science thus far has developed. In addition, it must be able to account for the role of theory in observation without compromising the epistemic objectivity of science. It is precisely at this point that the problem of theories, the growth of scientific knowledge, scientific realism, metaphysics, and epistemology link up and become the fundamental issue in philosophy of science: What is the nature of scientific knowledge? I have explored that issue in chapters 12 and 13 and will pursue it in far greater depth in *Facts, Theories, and Scientific Observation* (in progress).

D. Historical Studies of Earlier Views

Philosophy of science has a rich history. Understanding the strengths and weaknesses of earlier views—why they were put forward, precisely where they went wrong, and where they were righteaded—is an important area of research, not only because it might possibly contribute to the improvement of current research efforts, but more fundamentally, because such research is itself a central part of philosophy. The history of philosophy is our lingua franca, and thus its study and understanding is crucially important.

Philosophy of science has been relatively remiss in studying its own history: No comprehensive history of the philosophy of science has been produced this century, and even the dominant philosophy of science movement this century, logical positivism, has been inadequately researched. More research is needed of the sorts attempted by Coffa (1977, 1987, 1989), Creath (1987, 1987a, n.d.), Friedman (1983b, 1987, 1987a), Demopoulos and Friedman (1985), Proust (1987), and myself (1974b, 1975, 1977a). In this respect, the untimely death of Alberto Coffa at the height of his historical productivity is to be especially mourned. With specific reference to theories, there is a need for substantial research on positivism and positivistic philosophical views on theories. Now that the Schlick, Carnap, Reichenbach, and Hempel archives are becoming accessible to researchers, there is a need for extensive restudy and reevaluation of positivistic contributions to philosophy of science.

IV. WHY RESEARCH ON THESE PROBLEMS IS IMPORTANT

In the foregoing discussion of what I see as the crucial research problems concerning theories, I have tried to indicate how these problems relate to the philosophy of science and thus why I think such research on these problems is important to the discipline as a whole. Underlying my discussion has been a deep conviction that theories are a main vehicle of scientific knowledge and thus become involved in one way or another in the entire scientific enterprise. As I wrote in *The Structure of Scientific Theories* (1974), "A philosophy of science's analysis of the nature of theories, including their roles in the growth of scientific knowledge, thus is its keystone; and should that analysis prove inadequate, that inadequacy is likely to extend to its account of the remaining aspects of the scientific enterprise and the knowledge it provides. At the very least, it calls for a reassessment of its entire account of scientific knowledge" (3). Thus it should be clear that research on the problems I have discussed is important—if research in the philosophy of science is important.

Why is research in the philosophy of science important? Ultimately it is important because knowledge for its own sake is a good thing, but more can be said than just this. Science is a force of major importance in our society which touches virtually every individual's life. Science not only studies our environment but it informs the technology which shapes our environment and influences a wide range of public policy deliberations. Thus, understanding science is especially important, just because science itself is very important. To understand science it is not sufficient to learn and understand the various specific theories and findings produced by science: One needs to know what to make of these results; one needs to know and understand how the procedures and activities that science engages in enable science to produce the sort of knowledge it claims. This is a sort of understanding which the typical scientist has no edge on: One can do good science without possessing such an understanding, and besides, scientific training does not particularly equip one for obtaining such an understanding. For the questions which must be answered en route to such an understanding are philosophical questions—not scientific ones. Thus research in philosophy of science is important.

Whether research in philosophy of science is practically or instrumentally important is less clear. Science is strongly influenced by philosophy at various junctures (see, e.g., Petersen 1968), and so one might urge that science would benefit if scientists had a better philosophical understanding of science. In support of this argument one can find cases where scientists have exploited philosophy in making their scientific contributions. For example, Ernst Mach used his own analysis of the development of Newtonian mechanics as the basis for his criticism of the concepts of mass, space, and motion, and this criticism helped Albert Einstein replace the aether theory with relativity; Niels Bohr was influenced in his solution of some of the paradoxes of quantum theory (the "complementarity principle") by the philosophical writings of Kierkegaard and William James, and so on. But there may be even more truly innovative and creative scientists who have made major contributions while being philosophically illiterate. On the negative side, during this century positivistic philosophy of science has had a profound impact and influence on several of the less advanced branches of science such as behavioral psychology and sociology—with consequences that were arguably disastrous—though a strong case can be made that much of this was due largely to the uncritical and unsophisticated acceptance of outdated philosophical views (e.g., operationalism) that positivists had rejected on good grounds (Suppe 1984, 1984a). While it is unclear whether science would benefit from a high level of sophistication in the philosophy of science by scientists, it *is* clear that a number of scientists do see philosophy of science as relevant and potentially beneficial (see, e.g., Suppe and Jacox 1985), and it is desirable that when science turns to philosophy of science for aid or insight that philosophy of science have something to offer. Because theories are so centrally important to science, philosophical understanding of theories is of particular importance; and since our understanding of theories today is substantial but seriously incomplete (as the previous sections of this Epilogue should make clear), it is particularly important that the philosophical understanding of theories advance.

Another area of instrumental importance for philosophy of science is in providing the understanding whereby nonscientists concerned with legislation can evaluate, understand, and act on the findings of science. And the philosophical understanding of science can be useful to ordinary citizens whether in helping them evaluate, for example, pronouncements about cancer by the media or just to help them understand what this thing called science is. One thing is clear about all these possible instrumental benefits of philosophy of science research: They will not be realized if philosophers of science write only for philosophers. More comprehensible and manageable presentations are needed to make contemporary research in philosophy of science accessible to the philosophical laity—whether scientists, legislators, public policy experts, or ordinary citizens. Hempel's *Philosophy of Natural Science* (1966) and Kuhn's *Structure of Scientific Revolutions* (1962) are read because they are readable, not overly technical, works in the philosophy of science, despite the fact that the portraits of science they present are seriously flawed.

Part of the value of research in philosophy of science does rest on the potential instrumental benefits accruing to the understanding of science that it can provide; but to the extent that such benefits do accrue, they are only fringe benefits. Knowledge for its own sake is a good thing and thereby important. Science is important because it yields knowledge. Philosophy of science is especially important because it yields philosophical knowledge and understanding of science. I hope the present volume makes some contribution to that knowledge and understanding and will inspire others to make more important contributions.

NOTES

1. Theories were also being construed as "a deductively connected collection of laws" in positivistic writings. This typically occurred when structural characteristics of theories played little role in the account being offered. It seems to me that the Received View usually was being tacitly presumed in such cases, and so this formulation should count as a rather vague version of the Received View.

2. Although I think this is an accurate contrast of the dominant positivistic attitudes with more recent ones, the growth of scientific knowledge is not a matter of only quite recent philosophical concern. Many nineteenth- and twentieth-century philosophers of science who influenced, interacted with, or belonged to the positivistic movement were concerned with the growth of scientific knowledge—including Mill, Whewell, Duhem, Popper, and Nagel.

3. The term 'inductive' is used ambiguously in the philosophical literature; sometimes it is used to mean "nondeductive," and other times it is used more narrowly to refer to the sorts of nondeductive patterns of reasoning from the particular to the general that philosophers typically study under the rubric of "inductive logic" or "induction." I use the term in the latter, more restrictive sense. See ch. 13.

4. A number of the above developments are discussed in detail in the various chapters of Asquith and Kyburg 1979. For elaboration and defense of the perspective just presented, see also my 1977a.

5. Post-positivistic Anglo-American analytic, or "ordinary language," philosophy also was dominated by this supposition, though it rejected taking recourse to the artificial languages employed by positivists, preferring "ordinary language" instead.

6. To date, the Semantic Conception has proved quite robust in being able to accommodate newly discovered kinds of theories such as Shapere's (1974a) compositional and evolutionary theories, Darden and Maull's (1977) interfield theories, and Schaffner's (1980) interlevel theories of the middle range (see ch. 8 above). The main senses of 'theory' not accommodated are those of conjecture or supposition and those referring to a larger area, field, or domain of science, as in 'sociological theory'.

7. One reason for this lack of concern, at least on my part, is the fact that specifying the structure and physical interpretation of theories seems to leave open the question whether a particular theory can be established by using typical scientific means and, failing this, whether there are other means by which such a theory could be established or known. Thus whether a particular theory is "scientific" very well may depend upon other epistemological questions, hence need not be settled by one's philosophical analysis of theories. The positivists, of course, so intertwined their epistemology and their analysis of theories that they were of a whole, but this seems to me one of their more serious philosophical errors.

8. Many of these approaches also rely on some sort of observational/ theoretical distinction and thus are liable to the sorts of objections discussed in my 1977 (66–86) and ch. 2 above, or upon some "antecedently available versus theoretical distinction" (where correspondence rules are replaced by "bridge principles") such as Hempel (1969, 1974) presents, and thus are liable to the sorts of objections raised on pp. 255–65 of my 1977. See also ch. 11 above.

9. For example, if theories are construed along the lines of the Semantic Conception, this thesis would take the form of claiming that in theories the theory structures stand in one of the mapping relations discussed in chs. 2, 3, and 4 above to natural kind classes of physically possible phenomena, whereas in models the structures either stand in a different sort of mapping relation to phenomena or else are mapped onto single phenomena or artificial classes of phenomena (i.e., the mapping relation is not "universal" in the sense discussed in ch. 8).

10. It should be noted that Kuhn's and Feyerabend's extreme views on meaning and incommensurability (see ch. 10 above and Suppe 1977, 135–51, 170–80, 199–208, and 636–49) do yield an account of the individuation of theories, and thus much of the recent literature of meaning change (see ibid., 646 for references) is tacitly concerned with linguistic means for the individuation of theories. However, once theories are distinguished from their linguistic formulations (as on the Semantic Conception), it becomes clear that such meaning change issues have little to do with the individuation of theories—especially the sorts of problems we have been considering.

Bibliography

Unpublished manuscripts not in press cited in the chapter endnotes usually have not been included in the bibliography.

Achinstein, P.
  1963   Theoretical Terms and Partial Interpretation. *British Journal for Philosophy of Science* 14:89–105.
  1968   *Concepts of Science.* Baltimore: Johns Hopkins University Press.
  1971   *Law and Explanation.* Oxford: Oxford University Press.
Achinstein, P., and S. Barker, eds.
  1969   *The Legacy of Logical Positivism.* Baltimore: Johns Hopkins University Press.
Ackerman, R. J.
  1972   *Belief and Knowledge.* Garden City, N.Y.: Anchor Books.
Alston, W., and G. Nakhnikian, eds.
  1963   *Readings in Twentieth-Century Philosophy.* Glencoe, Ill.: Free Press.
American Psychiatric Association
  1968   *Diagnostic and Statistical Manual of Mental Disorders* (DSM-II). 2d ed. Washington, D.C.: American Psychiatric Association.
  1980   *Diagnostic and Statistical Manual of Mental Disorders* (DSM-III). 3d ed. Washington, D.C.: American Psychiatric Association.
Aristotle
  1928–52 *Collected Works.* 12 vols. Edited by W. Ross. Oxford: Oxford University Press.
Asher, H. B.
  1976   *Causal Modelling.* Beverly Hills, Calif.: Sage Publications.
Asquith, P., and R. Giere, eds.
  1981   *PSA 1980: Proceedings of the 1980 Biennial Meetings of the Philosophy of Science Association.* Vol. II. East Lansing, Mich.: Philosophy of Science Association.
Asquith, P., and H. Kyburg, Jr., eds.
  1979   *Current Research in Philosophy of Science: Proceedings of the PSA Critical Research Problems Conference.* East Lansing, Mich.: Philosophy of Science Association.

Asquith, P., and T. Nickles, eds.
  1982   *PSA 1982: Proceedings of the 1982 Biennial Meetings of the Philosophy of Science Association.* Vol. I. East Lansing, Mich.: Philosophy of Science Association.

Ayala, F.
  1982   *Population and Evolutionary Genetics: A Primer.* Menlo Park, Calif.: Benjamin-Cummings Publishing Co.

Ayala, F., and T. Dobzhansky, eds.
  1974   *Studies in Philosophy of Biology.* London: Macmillan.

Bacon, F.
  1620   *Novum Organum.* Part 2 of *Instauratio magna.* London: J. Billium. Translated by James Spedding in R. L. Ellis and J. Spedding, eds., *The Philosophical Works of Francis Bacon.* London: n.p., 1861.
  1960   *The New Organum and Relating Writings.* Edited by F. H. Anderson. New York: Liberal Arts Press.

Bambrough, R.
  1966   Universals and Family Resemblances. In *Wittgenstein,* edited by G. Pitcher, 186–204. Garden City, N.Y.: Anchor Books.

Baumrin, B., ed.
  1963   *Philosophy of Science: The Delaware Seminar.* Vol. II. New York: Interscience.

Bayer, R.
  1981   *Homosexuality and American Psychiatry: The Politics of Diagnosis.* New York: Basic Books.

Beatty, J.
  1979   Traditional and Semantic Accounts of Evolutionary Theory. Ph.D. dissertation, Indiana University.
  1980   Optimal Design Models and the Strategy of Model Building in Evolutionary Biology. *Philosophy of Science* 47:532–61.
  1981   What's Wrong with the Received View of Evolutionary Theory? In P. Asquith and R. Giere 1981, 397–426.
  1982   The Insights and Oversights of Molecular Genetics: The Place of Evolutionary Perspective. In Asquith and Nickles 1982, 341–55.
  1987   On Behalf of the Semantic View. *Biology and Philosophy* 2:17–22.

Beckner, M.
  1959   *The Biological Way of Thought.* New York: Columbia University Press. Reprint, Berkeley: University of California Press, 1968.

Belnap, N. D., Jr.
  1963   *An Analysis of Questions: Preliminary Report.* Santa Monica, Calif.: Systems Development Corp.

Belnap, N. D., Jr., and T. B. Steel
  1976   *The Logic of Questions and Answers.* New Haven: Yale University Press.

Beth, E.
  1948   *Natuurphilosophie.* Gorinchem, Neth.: Noorduyn.

1949   Towards an Up-to-Date Philosophy of the Natural Sciences. *Methodos* 1:178–85.

1959   *The Foundations of Mathematics.* Rev. ed. Amsterdam: North Holland, 1964. Reprint, New York: Harper and Row, 1966.

1961   Semantics of Physical Theories. In Freudenthal 1961, 48–51.

1963   Carnap's Views on the Advantages of Constructed Systems over Natural Languages in the Philosophy of Science. In Schilpp 1963, 469–502.

Bieber, I., H. J. Dain, P. R. Dince, M. G. Drellich, H. G. Grand, R. H. Grundlach, M. W. Kremer, A. H. Rifkin, C. B. Wilber, and T. Bieber

1962   *Homosexuality: A Psychoanalytic Study.* New York: Basic Books.

Birkhoff, G., and J. von Neumann

1936   The Logic of Quantum Mechanics. *Annals of Mathematics* 37:823–43. Reprinted in von Neumann 1962, vol. IV, 105–25.

Boyd, R.

1973   Realism, Underdetermination, and a Causal Theory of Evidence. *Nôus* 7:1–12.

1976   Approximate Truth and Natural Necessity. *Journal of Philosophy* 123:633–35.

Braithwaite, R. B.

1953   *Scientific Explanation.* New York: Harper Torchbooks.

Braaten, L. J., and C. D. Darling

1965   Overt and Covert Homosexual Problems Among Male College Students. *Genetic Psychological Monographs* 71:269–310.

Bridgman, P. W.

1927   *The Logic of Modern Physics.* New York: Macmillan.

Bromberger, S.

1963   A Theory about the Theory of Theory and about the Theory of Theories. In Baumrin 1963, 79–106.

1966   Why Questions. In Colodny 1966, 86–111.

Buck, R., and D. Hull

1966   The Logical Structure of the Linnean Hierarchy. *Systematic Zoology* 15:97–111.

Bunge, M.

1959   *Causality—The Place of the Causal Principle in Modern Science.* Cambridge, Mass.: Harvard University Press.

Burks, A. W.

1975   Models of Deterministic Systems. *Mathematical Systems Theory* 8:295–308.

1977   *Chance, Cause, Reason.* Chicago: University of Chicago Press.

Burks, A. W., H. H. Goldstine, and J. Von Neumann

1946   *Preliminary Discussion of the Logical Design of an Electronic Computing Instrument.* Princeton: Institute for Advanced Study. 2d ed., 1947. Reprinted in von Neumann 1962, vol. 5, 34–79.

Campbell, N. R.
1920   *Physics: The Elements.* Cambridge: Cambridge University Press.
        Republished as *Foundations of Science.* New York: Dover, 1957.
        Reprinted in part in Feigl and Brodbeck 1953.

Carnap, R.
1932   Die physikalische Sprache als Universalsprache der Wissenschaft.
        Erkenntnis 2:432–65. A revised English translation can be found
        in Alston and Nakhnikian 1963.

1936-37 Testability and Meaning. *Philosophy of Science* 3:420–68; 4:1–40.
        Reprinted as a monograph. New Haven, Conn.: Whitlock's Inc.,
        1950. Excerpts reprinted in Feigl and Brodbeck 1953.

1939   *Foundations of Logic and Mathematics.* Chicago: University of
        Chicago Press.

1942   *Introducton to Semantics.* Cambridge, Mass.: Harvard University
        Press.

1945   On Inductive Logic. *Philosophy of Science* 12:72–97.

1947   *Meaning and Necessity.* Chicago: University of Chicago Press.
        Enlarged ed., 1956.

1950   Empiricism, Semantics, and Ontology. *Revue internationale de
        philosophie* 11:208–28. Reprinted in Linsky 1952 and the enlarged
        1956 edition of Carnap 1947.

1956   The Methodological Character of Theoretical Concepts. In Feigl
        and Scriven 1956, 33–76.

1959   Beobachtungssprache und theoretische Sprache. In *Logic: Studia
        Paul Bernays Dedicata,* vol. 34 of Bibliothèque Scientifique, 32–44.
        Neuchâtel: Éditiones du Griffon.

1963   Carl G. Hempel on Scientific Theories. In Schilpp 1963, 958–66.
1963a   Intellectual Autobiography. In Schilpp 1963, 3–84.
1966   *Philosophical Foundation of Physics.* New York: Basic Books.

Cartwright, N.
1983   *How the Laws of Physics Lie.* New York: Oxford University Press.

Chandler, H.
1966   Three Kinds of Classes. *American Philosophical Quarterly* 3:1–5.

Chisholm, R.
1957   *Perceiving.* Ithaca, N.Y.: Cornell University Press.
1965   The Theory of Appearing. In Swartz 1965, 168–86.
1966   *Theory of Knowledge.* Englewood Cliffs, N.J.: Prentice-Hall.
1974   On the Nature of Evidence. In Chisholm and Swartz 1974, 224–50.
1982   *The Foundations of Knowing.* Minneapolis: University of Min-
        nesota Press.

Chisholm, R., and R. Swartz, eds.
1974   *Empirical Knowledge.* Englewood Cliffs, N.J.: Prentice-Hall.

Churchland, P. M.
1985   The Ontological Status of Observables: In Praise of the Super-
        empirical Virtues. In Churchland and Hooker 1985, 3–34.

Churchland, P. M., and C. W. Hooker, eds.
1985   *Images of Science: Essays on Realism and Empiricism with a Reply from Bas C. van Fraassen.* Chicago: University of Chicago Press.

Clark, M.
1965   Knowledge and Grounds: A Comment on Mr. Gettier's Paper. *Analysis* 24:46–48.

Coffa, A.
1977   Carnap's *Sprachanschauung* Circa 1932. In Suppe and Asquith 1977, 205–41.
1987   Carnap, Tarski, and the Search for Truth. *Nôus* 21:547–72.
1989   *To the Vienna Station: Semantics, Epistemology and the a priori from Kant to Carnap.* Edited by L. Wessels. Cambridge: Cambridge University Press.

Cohen, I. B.
1974   History and the Philosopher of Science. In Suppe 1974 and 1977, 308–49.

Cohen, L. J.
1975   Comment [on Salmon's Theoretical Explanation]. In *Explanation,* edited by S. Körner, 152–59. Oxford: Blackwell.

Cohen, R. S., and M. W. Wartofsky, eds.
1965   *Boston Studies in the Philosophy of Science.* Vol. II. New York: Humanities Press.

Colodny, R., ed.
1962   *Frontiers of Science and Philosophy.* Pittsburgh: University of Pittsburgh Press.
1965   *Beyond the Edge of Certainty.* Englewood Cliffs, N.J.: Prentice-Hall.
1966   *Mind and Cosmos: Explorations in the Philosophy of Science.* Pittsburgh: University of Pittsburgh Press.
1970   *Nature and Function of Scientific Theories.* Pittsburgh: University of Pittsburgh Press.
1972   *Paradigms and Paradoxes.* Pittsburgh: University of Pittsburgh Press.

Copernicus, N.
1543   *De Revolutionibus orbium coelestium.* Norimbergae: apud Ioh Petreium.
1978   *On the Revolutions.* Translated by Edward Rosen, edited by J. Dobrzycki. Baltimore: Johns Hopkins University Press.

Cornman, J.
1975   *Perception, Common Sense, and Science.* New Haven: Yale University Press.
1977   Sellars on Scientific Realism and Perceiving. In Suppe and Asquith 1977, 344–58.

Creath, R.
1987   Some Remarks on "Protocol Sentences." *Nôus* 21:471–75.

1987a   The Initial Reception of Carnap's Doctrine of Analyticity. *Nôus* 21:477–99.

n.d.   Carnap's Epistemology. Forthcoming.

Cuppy, W.

1983   *How to Become Extinct.* Chicago: University of Chicago Press. Originally published by Farrar & Rinehart, 1941.

da Costa, N. C. A., and S. French

n.d.   The Model-Theoretic Approach in the Philosophy of Science. Forthcoming.

Dalla Chiara, M. L.

1976   A Multiple Sentential Logic for Empirical Theories. In Przełecki, Szaniawski, and Wójcicki 1976, 43–56.

Dalla Chiara Scabia, M. L., and G. Toraldo di Francia

1973   A Logical Analysis of Physical Theories. *Revista del Nuovo Cimento.* 2d ser., vol. 3:1–20.

Darden, L., and N. Maull

1977   Interfield Theories. *Philosophy of Science* 44:43–64.

Demopoulos, W., and M. Friedman

1985   Critical Notice: Bertrand Russell's *The Analysis of Matter:* Its Historical Content and Contemporary Importance. *Philosophy of Science* 52:621–39.

Destouches, J. L.

1942   *Principes fundamentaux de physique théoretique.* Paris: Hermann.

Dretske, F.

1969   *Seeing and Knowing.* Chicago: University of Chicago Press.

1971   Conclusive Reasons. *Australasian Journal of Philosophy* 49:1–22.

1981   *Knowledge and the Flow of Information.* Cambridge, Mass.: MIT Press.

1983   Précis of *Knowledge and the Flow of Information. Behavioral and Brain Research* 6:55–62.

1983a   Author's Response. *Behavioral and Brain Research* 6:82–90.

Duhem, P.

1954   *The Aim and Structure of Physical Theory.* New York: Atheneum. Originally published in French in 1906.

Earman, J.

1986   *A Primer on Determinism.* Dordrecht, Neth.: Reidel.

Edelson, M.

1984   *Hypothesis and Evidence in Psychoanalysis.* Chicago: University of Chicago Press.

Ellis, B.

1966   *Basic Concepts of Measurement.* Cambridge: The University Press.

Feigl, H., and M. Brodbeck, eds.

1953   *Readings in the Philosophy of Science.* New York: Appleton-Century-Crofts.

Feigl, H., and G. Maxwell, eds.
1961   *Current Issues in the Philosophy of Science.* New York: Holt, Rinehart, and Winston.
1962   *Minnesota Studies in the Philosophy of Science.* Vol. III. Minneapolis: University of Minnesota Press.
Feigl, H., and M. Scriven, eds.
1958   *Minnesota Studies in the Philosophy of Science.* Vol. I. Minneapolis: University of Minnesota Press.
Feigl, H., M. Scriven, and G. Maxwell, eds.
1958   *Minnesota Studies in the Philosophy of Science.* Vol. II. Minneapolis: University of Minnesota Press.
Feyerabend, P.
1958   An Attempt at a Realistic Interpretation of Experience. *Proceedings of the Aristotelian Society,* n.s., 58:143–70.
1962   Explanation, Reduction, and Empiricism. In Feigl and Maxwell 1962, 28–97.
1962a   Problems of Microphysics. In Colodny 1962, 189–283.
1965   On the Meaning of Scientific Terms. *Journal of Philosophy* 62:266–74. Reprinted in Grandy 1973, 176–83.
1965a   Problems of Empiricism. In Colodny 1965, 145–260.
1965b   Reply to Criticism. In Cohen and Wartofsky 1965, 223–61.
1970   Against Method: Outline of an Anarchistic Theory of Knowledge. In Radner and Winokur 1970, 17–130.
1970a   Consolations for the Specialist. In Lakatos and Musgrave 1970, 197–230.
1970b   Problems of Empiricism, Part II. In Colodny 1970.
1978   Changing Problems of Reconstruction. *British Journal for the Philosophy of Science* 28:351–69.
Firth, R.
1965   Sense Data and the Percept Theory. In Swartz 1965, 204–70.
1967   The Anatomy of Certainty. *Philosophical Review* 26:3–27. Reprinted in Chisholm and Swartz 1974, 203–23.
Fine, A. and P. Machamer, eds.
1986   *PSA 1986: Proceedings of the 1986 Biennial Meetings of the Philosophy of Science Association.* Vol. II. East Lansing, Mich.: Philosophy of Science Association.
Fisher, Sir R. A.
1958   *The Genetical Theory of Natural Selection.* New York: Dover. Reprint of the 1929 2d ed.
Ford, D. H., and H. B. Urban
1963   *Systems of Psychotherapy: A Comparative Study.* New York: Wiley.
Freudenthal, H., ed.
1961   *The Concept and the Role of the Model in Mathematics and Natural and Social Sciences.* Dordrecht, Neth.: Reidel.

Friedman, M.
    1983a   *Foundations of Space-Time Theories: Relativistic Physics and Philosophy of Science.* Princeton: Princeton University Press.
    1983b   Critical Notice: Moritz Schlick, *Philosophical Papers. Philosophy of Science* 50:498–514.
    1987   Logical Truth and Analyticity in Carnap's *Logical Structure of Language.* In *Essays in the History and Philosophy of Mathematics,* edited by W. Aspray and P. Kitcher. Minneapolis: University of Minnesota Press.
    1987a   Carnap's *Aufbau* Reconsidered. *Nôus* 21:521–46.

Galilei, Galileo
    1629   *Dialogo di Galileo Galilei Linceo Mathematica Sopraodinario.* Florence: Per Gio: Batista Landini.
    1970   *Dialogues Concerning the Two Chief World Systems—Ptolemaic and Copernican.* 2d ed. Translated by Stillman Drake. Berkeley: University of California Press.

Gardner, M.
    1979   Realism and Instrumentalism in 19th Century Atomism. *Philosophy of Science* 46:1–34.
    n.d.   Quantum Mechanics and the Received View of Theories. Presented at the 1974–75 Pittsburgh Colloquium Series in Philosophy of Science.

Garret, B. J.
    1983   Nozick on Knowledge. *Analysis* 43:180–84.

Gasking, D.
    1960   Clusters. *Australasian Review of Psychology* 38:1–36.

Geach, P.
    1962   *Reference and Generality.* Ithaca, N.Y.: Cornell University Press.

Gettier, E., Jr.
    1963   Is Justified True Belief Knowledge? *Analysis* 23:121–23.

Ghiselin, M. J.
    1974   A Radical Solution to the Species Problem. *Systematic Zoology* 23:536–44.

Giere, R.
    1979   *Understanding Scientific Reasoning.* New York: Holt, Rinehart and Winston.
    1980   Causal Systems and Statistical Hypothesis. In *Applications of Inductive Logic,* edited by L. J. Cohen and M. Hesse, 251–70. New York: Oxford, University Press.
    1988   *Explaining Science: A Cognitive Approach.* Chicago: University of Chicago Press.

Gilmour, J. S. L.
    1940   Taxonomy and Philosophy. In *The New Systematics,* edited by J. S. Huxley, 461–74. Oxford: Oxford University Press.

Glymour, C.
    1976   To Save the Noumena. *Journal of Philosophy* 73:635–37.

1980   *Theory and Evidence.* Princeton: Princeton University Press.
1985   Explanation and Realism. In Churchland and Hooker 1985, 99–117.

Goldman, A.
1967   A Causal Theory of Knowledge. *Journal of Philosophy* 64:357–72.
1976   Discrimination and Perceptual Knowledge. *Journal of Philosophy* 73:771–91.

Gorovitz, S.
1965   Causal Judgments and Causal Explanation. *Journal of Philosophy* 62:695–711.
1969   Aspects of the Pragmatics of Explanation. *Nôus,* 3:61–72.

Grandy, R., ed.
1973   *Theories and Observation in Science.* Englewood Cliffs, N.J.: Prentice-Hall.

Grünbaum, A.
1984   *The Foundations of Psychoanalysis: A Philosophical Critique.* Berkeley: University of California Press.

Gutting, G.
1985   Scientific Realism vs. Constructive Empiricism: A Dialogue. In Churchland and Hooker 1985, 118–31.

Hacking, I.
1983   *Representing and Intervening.* Cambridge: Cambridge University Press.
1985   Do We See Through a Microscope? In Churchland and Hooker 1985, 132–52.

Hardegree, G.
1976   The Modal Interpretation of Quantum Mechanics. In Suppe and Asquith 1976, 82–103.

Harman, G.
1968   Knowledge, Inference, and Explanation. *American Philosophical Quarterly* 5:164–73.
1970   Induction: A Discussion of the Relevance of the Theory of Knowledge to the Theory of Induction. In Swain, 1970, 83–100.
1970a   Knowledge, Reasons, and Causes. *Journal of Philosophy* 67:841–55.

Harrah, D.
1963   *Communication: A Logical Model.* Cambridge, Mass.: MIT Press.

Hartkämper, A., and H. J. Schmidt, eds.
1981   *Structure and Approximation in Physical Theories.* New York: Plenum Press.

Hausman, D.
1981   *Capital, Profits, and Prices: An Essay in the Philosophy of Economics.* New York: Columbia University Press.

Heilprin, L., ed.
1985   *Towards Foundations of Information Science.* White Plains, N.Y.: American Society for Information Sciences.

Hempel, C.
1952   *Fundamentals of Concept Formation in Empirical Science*. Chicago: University of Chicago Press.
1954   A Logical Appraisal of Operationalism. *Scientific Monthly* 79:215–20. Reprinted in Hempel 1965, 123–33.
1958   The Theoretician's Dilemma: Studies in the Logic of Theory Construction. In Feigl, Scriven, and Maxwell 1958, 37–98. Reprinted in Hempel 1965, 173–226.
1963   Implications of Carnap's Work for the Philosophy of Science. In Schlipp 1963, 685–709.
1965   *Aspects of Scientific Explanation and Other Essays in the Philosophy of Science*. New York: Free Press.
1965a   Aspects of Scientific Explanation. In Hempel 1965, 331–496.
1965b   Typological Methods in the Natural and Social Sciences. In Hempel 1965, 155–71.
1966   *Philosophy of Natural Science*. Englewood Cliffs, N.J.: Prentice-Hall.
1969   On the Structure of Scientific Theories. In the *Isenberg Memorial Lecture Series, 1965–1966*, 11–39. East Lansing: Michigan State University Press.
1970   On the 'Standard Conception' of Scientific Theories. In Radner and Winokur 1970, 142–63.
1974   Formulation and Formalization of Scientific Theories: A Summary-Abstract. In Suppe 1974, 244–54.
Hempel, C. G., and P. Oppenheim
1948   Studies in the Logic of Explanation. *Philosophy of Science* 15:135–75. Reprinted with a postscript in Hempel 1965, 245–95.
Henkin, L., P. Suppes, and A. Tarski, eds.
1959   *The Axiomatic Method with Special Reference to Geometry and Physics*. Amsterdam: North Holland.
Hesse, M.
1962   *Forces and Fields*. New York: Philosophical Library.
1966   *Models and Analogies in Science*. Notre Dame, Ind.: University of Notre Dame Press.
1977   Truth and the Growth of Scientific Knowledge. In Suppe and Asquith 1977, 261–80.
Hintikka, J.
1962   *Knowledge and Belief*. Ithaca, N.Y.: Cornell University Press.
Hooker, C.
1975   On Global Theories. *Philosophy of Science* 42:152–79.
Hooker, E.
1957   The Adjustment of the Overt Male Homosexual. *Journal of Projective Techniques* 21:18–31.
Hopwood, A.
1950   Animal Classification from the Greeks to Linnaeus. In Linnean Society of London 1950, 24–32.

1950a   Animal Classification from Linnaeus to Darwin. In Linnean Society of London 1950, 46–59.

Horan, B.
1986   Sociobiology and the Semantic View of Theories. In Fine and Machamer, 1986, 322–30.

Hull, D.
1955   The Effect of Essentialism on Taxonomy: Two Thousand Years of Stasis. *British Journal for the Philosophy of Science* 15:314–26; 16:1–18.

1964   The Logic of Philogenetic Taxonomy. Ph.D. dissertation, Indiana University.

1967   Certainty and Circularity in Evolutional Taxonomy. *Evolution* 21:174–89.

1967a   The Metaphysics of Evolution. *British Journal for the History of Science* 3:309–37.

1968   The Operational Imperative: Sense and Nonsense in Operationalism. *Systematic Zoology* 17:438–57.

1976   Are Species Really Individuals? *Systematic Zoology* 25:174–91.

1979   Philosophy of Biology. In Asquith and Kyburg 1979, 421–35.

Jackson, D., and S. Stich, eds.
1979   *The Recombinant DNA Debate.* Englewood Cliffs, N.J.: Prentice-Hall.

Jeffrey, R. C.
1970   Statistical Explanation vs. Statistical Inference. In Salmon 1970, 19–28.

Kant, I.
1781   *Kritik der reinem Vernunft.* n.p.: I. F. Hartknoch. 2d ed., 1787.

1961   *Critique of Pure Reason.* Translated by Norman Kemp Smith. New York: St. Martin's Press.

Kaplan, A.
1964   *The Conduct of Inquiry.* San Francisco: Chandler Publications.

Kemeny, J., and P. Oppenheim
1955   On Systematic Power. *Philosophy of Science* 22:27–33.

Kemeny, J., H. Mirkil, L. J. Snell, and G. L. Thompson
1959   *Finite Mathematical Structures.* Englewood Cliffs, N.J.: Prentice-Hall.

Kenat, R. C., Jr.
1987   Physical Interpretation: Eddington, Idealization, and Stellar Structure Theory. Ph.D. dissertation, University of Maryland.

Kepler, J.
1609   *Astronomia Nova.* Pragae: n.p.; Heidelberg: G. Voegelinus.

1983   Astronomia Nova. Translated by O. Gingerich and W. Donahue. In *The Great Ideas Today,* edited by M. J. Adler and I. Doven, 305–41. Chicago: Encyclopaedia Brittanica.

Kuhn, T. S.
1962 *The Structure of Scientific Revolutions.* Chicago: University of Chicago Press.
1970 Logic of Discovery or Psychology of Research. In Lakatos and Musgrave 1970, 1–24.
1970a Reflections on My Critics. In Lakatos and Musgrave 1970, 231–78.
1970b *The Structure of Scientific Revolutions.* Enlarged ed. Chicago: University of Chicago Press.
1974 Second Thoughts on Paradigms. In Suppe 1974, 459–82.

Lakatos, I.
1970 Falsification and the Methodology of Scientific Research Programmes. In Lakatos and Musgrave 1970, 91–196.

Lakatos, I., and A. Musgrave, eds.
1970 *Criticism and the Growth of Knowledge.* Cambridge: Cambridge University Press.

Lambert, K., and G. Brittan, Jr.
1987 *An Introduction to the Philosophy of Science.* 3d ed. Atascadero, Calif.: Ridgeview Publishing Co.

Laudan, L.
1977 *Progress and Its Problems.* Berkeley: University of California Press.
1981 A Confutation of Convergent Realism. *Philosophy of Science* 48:19–49. Reprinted in Leplin 1984.
1986 Some Problems Facing Intuitionist Meta-Methodologies. *Synthese* 67:115–29.

Lehrer, K.
1965 Knowledge, Truth and Evidence. *Analysis* 25:168–75.

Lehrer, K., and T. Paxson
1969 Knowledge: Undefeated Justified True Belief. *Journal of Philosophy* 66:225–37.

Leplin, J., ed.
1984 *Scientific Realism.* Berkeley: University of California Press.

Lester, D.
1975 *Unusual Sexual Behavior: The Standard Deviations.* Springfield, Ill.: Charles C. Thomas.

Levins, R.
1966 Strategy of Model Building in Population Biology. *American Scientist* 54:421–31.
1968 *Evolution in Changing Environments.* Princeton: Princeton University Press.

Lewis, C. I.
1929 *Mind and the World Order.* New York: Dover.

Lewis, D.
1973 *Counterfactuals.* Cambridge, Mass.: Harvard University Press.

Linnean Society of London
1950   *Lectures on the Development of Taxonomy.* London: Linnean Society.

Linsky, L., ed.
1952   *Semantics and the Philosophy of Language.* Urbana: University of Illinois Press.

Lloyd, E. A.
1984   A Semantic Approach to the Structure of Population Genetics. *Philosophy of Science* 51:242–64.

1984a   A Semantic Approach to the Structure of Evolutionary Theory. Ph.D. dissertation, Princeton University.

1987   Confirmation of Evolutionary and Ecological Models. *Biology and Philosophy* 2:277–93.

1987a   The Semantic View Defended. *Biology and Philosophy* 2:23–26.

1988   A Structural Approach to Defining Units of Selection. *Philosophy of Science* 55.

1988a   *The Structure and Confirmation of Evolutionary Theory.* Westport, Conn.: Greenwood Press.

Locke, J.
1690   *An Essay Concerning Humane Understanding.* London: Printed by Eliz. Holt for Thomas Basset.

1959   *Essay Concerning Human Understanding.* 2 vols. Edited by A. C. Fraser. New York: Dover, 1959.

Losee, J.
1972   *A Historical Introduction to the Philosophy of Science.* New York: Oxford University Press.

1980   *A Historical Introduction to the Philosophy of Science.* 2d ed. New York: Oxford University Press.

Ludwig, G.
1981   Imprecision in Physics. In Hartkämper and Schmidt 1981, 7–20.

Mackey, W.
1963   *Mathematical Foundations of Quantum Mechanics.* New York: Benjamin Co.

MacKinnon, E.
1972   *The Problem of Scientific Realism.* New York: Appleton-Century-Crofts.

1979   Scientific Realism: The New Debates. *Philosophy of Science* 46:501–32.

Macklin, R.
1972   Mental Health and Mental Illness: Some Problems of Definition and Concept Formation. *Philosophy of Science* 39:341–65.

Margenau, H.
1950   *The Nature of Physical Reality.* New York: McGraw-Hill.

Martin, R.
1975   Empirically Conclusive Reasons and Scepticism. *Philosophical Studies.* 28:215–17.

1983   Tracking Nozick's Sceptic: A Better Method. *Analysis* 43 (1):28–33.

Mates, B.
1965   *Elementary Logic.* New York: Oxford University Press.

Maxwell, J. C.
1891   *A Treatise on Electricity and Magnetism.* 3d ed. Oxford: The Clarendon Press. Reprint. 2 vols. New York: Dover, 1954.

Mayr, E.
1964   *Systematics and the Origin of the Species.* New York: Dover.

McKinsey, J. C. C., A. Sugar, and P. Suppes
1953   Axiomatic Foundations of Classical Particle Mechanics. *Journal of Rational Mechanics and Analysis* 2:253–72.

McKinsey, J. C. C., and P. Suppes
1953   Transformations of Systems of Classical Particle Mechanics. *Journal of Rational Mechanics and Analysis* 2:273–89.

Meixner, J.
1979   Homogeneity and Explanatory Depth. *Philosophy of Science* 46:366–81.

Melnick, A.
1974   *Kant's Analogies of Experience.* Chicago: University of Chicago Press.

Merton, R.
1949   *Social Theory and Social Structure.* Glencoe, Ill.: Free Press.

Messiah, A.
1961   *Quantum Mechanics.* 2 vols. New York: John Wiley and Sons.

Mill, J. S.
1965   *A System of Logic.* 8th ed. London: Longmans. 1st ed., 1843.

Millikan, R. G.
1984   Naturalist Reflections on Knowledge. *Pacific Philosophical Quarterly* 65:315–34.

Montague, R.
1962   Deterministic Theories. In *Decisions, Values and Groups.* Vol. 2. Edited by N. F. Washburne. New York: Pergamon Press. Reprinted in *Formal Philosophy and Selected Papers of Richard Montague.* Edited by R. H. Thomason, 303–59. New Haven: Yale University Press, 1974.

Moran, P. A. P.
1962   *The Statistical Processes of Evolutionary Theory.* Oxford: Clarendon Press.

Morgenbesser, S., ed.
1967   *Philosophy of Science Today.* New York: Basic Books.

Morillo, C. R.
1984   Epistemic Luck, Naturalistic Epistemology, and the Ecology of Knowledge—or What the Frog Should Have Told Dretske. *Philosophical Studies* 46:109–29.

Moulines, C. U.
1975   A Logical Reconstruction of Simple Equilibrium Thermody-
        namics. *Erkenntnis* 9:101–30.
Nagel, E.
1961   *The Structure of Science.* New York: Harcourt, Brace.
Nagel, E., P. Suppes, and A. Tarski, eds.
1962   *Logic, Methodology and the Philosophy of Science: Proceedings
        of the 1960 International Congress.* Stanford: Stanford University
        Press.
Newton, I.
1687   *Philosophiae Naturalis Principia Mathematica.* London: Jussu
        Societatis Regiae ac Typis sephi Streater. 2d ed., 1713.
1704   *Opticks: Or A Treatise on the Reflexions, Refractions, Inflexions,
        and Colours of Light.* London: Printed for S. Smith and B. Walford.
1952   *Opticks.* New York: Dover.
1971   *Sir Isaac Newton's Mathematical Principles of Natural Philosophy
        and His System of the World.* Translated by A. Motte and revised
        by F. Cajori. 2 vols. Berkeley: University of California Press,
        1971.
Northrop, F. S. C.
1947   *The Logic of the Sciences and the Humanities.* New York: Mac-
        millan.
Nozick, R.
1981   *Philosophical Explanations.* New York: Oxford University Press.
Pappas, G. S., and M. Swain
1973   Some Conclusive Reasons against Conclusive Reasons. *Austra-
        lasian Journal of Philosophpy* 51:72–76.
Pauling, L. and E. B. Wilson
1935   *Introduction to Quantum Mechanics.* New York: McGraw-Hill.
Petersen, A.
1968   *Quantum Physics and the Philosophical Tradition.* Cambridge,
        Mass.: MIT Press.
Przełecki, M.
1969   *The Logic of Empirical Theories.* London: Routledge and Kegan
        Paul.
1976   Interpretation of Theoretical Terms: In Defense of an Empiricist
        Dogma. In Przełecki, Szaniawski, and Wójcicki 1976, 158–69.
Przełecki, M., K. Szaniawski, and R. Wójcicki, eds.
1976   *Formal Methods of the Methodology of Science.* Wrocław: Osso-
        lineum.
Proust, J.
1987   Formal Logic as Transcendental in Wittgenstein. Translated by
        Jill Buroker. *Nôus* 21:501–20.
Putnam, H.
1962   What Theories Are Not. In Nagel, Suppes, and Tarski 1962,
        240–51.

1971   The 'Corroboration' of Theories. In *The Philosophy of Karl Popper,* Book I, edited by P. Schilpp, 221–40. LaSalle, Ill.: Open Court Publishing Co.

Quine, W. V. O.
1959   *Methods of Logic.* Rev. ed. New York: Holt, Rinehart, and Winston.

Radner, M., and S. Winokur, eds.
1970   *Minnesota Studies in the Philosophy of Science.* Vol. IV. Minneapolis: University of Minnesota Press.

Ramsey, F. P.
1931   *The Foundations of Mathematics and Other Logical Essays.* London: Kegan Paul; New York: Harcourt Brace.

Reichenbach, H.
1962   *Rise of Scientific Philosophy.* Berkeley: University of California Press.

Rubin, H., and P. Suppes
1954   Transformation of Systems of Relativistic Particle Mechanics. *Pacific Journal of Mathematics* 4:563–601.

Rudner, R.
1966   *Philosophy of Social Science.* Englewood Cliffs, N.J.: Prentice-Hall.

Salmon, W.
1970   *Statistical Explanation and Statistical Relevance.* Pittsburgh: University of Pittsburgh Press.

1975   Theoretical Explanation. In *Explanation,* edited by S. Körner, 118–45. Oxford: Blackwell.

1977   An 'At-At' Theory of Causal Influence. *Philosophy of Science* 44:215–24.

1978   Why Ask Why? An Inquiry Concerning Scientific Explanation. *Proceedings and Addresses of the American Philosophical Association* 51:683–705.

1984   *Scientific Explanation and the Causal Structure of the World.* Princeton: Princeton University Press.

Salmon, W., and M. Salmon
1979   Alternative Models of Explanation. *American Anthropologist* 81:69–74.

Schaffner, K.
1980   Theory Structure in the Biomedical Sciences. *Journal of Medicine and Philosophy* 5:331–71.

n.d.   *Discovery and Explanation in the Biomedical Sciences.* Forthcoming.

Scheffler, I.
1967   *Science and Subjectivity.* Indianapolis, Ind.: Bobbs-Merrill.

Schlipp, P., ed.
1963   *The Philosophy of Rudolf Carnap.* LaSalle, Ill.: Open Court Publishing Co.

Scriven, M.
1958   Definitions, Explanations, and Theories. In Feigl, Scriven, and Maxwell 1958, 99–195.
1959   Explanation and Prediction in Evolutionary Theory. *Science* 130:477–82.
1961   The Key Property of Physical Laws—Inaccuracy. In Feigl and Maxwell 1961, 91–101.
1962   Explanations, Predictions and Laws. In Feigl and Maxwell 1962, 170–230.

Sellars, W.
1956   Empiricism and the Philosophy of Mind. In Feigl and Scriven 1956, 253–329.
1959   *Philosophical Perspectives.* Springfield, Ill.: Charles C. Thomas.
1963   *Science, Perception, and Reality.* London: Routledge and Kegan Paul.
1963a   Philosophy and the Scientific Image of Man. In Sellars 1963, 1–40.
1965   Scientific Realism or Irenic Instrumentalism. In Cohen and Wortofsky 1965, 171–204.
1975   The Structure of Knowledge. In *Action, Knowledge, and Reality,* edited by H. Castañeda, 295–348. Indianapolis, Ind.: Bobbs-Merrill.
1977   Is Scientific Realism Tenable? In Suppe and Asquith 1977, 307–34.

Shapere, D.
1964   The Structure of Scientific Revolutions. *Philosophical Review* 73:383–94.
1966   Meaning and Scientific Change. In Colodny 1966, 41–85.
1969   Notes Toward a Post-Positivistic Interpretation of Science. In Achinstein and Barker 1969, 115–60.
1971   The Paradigm Concept. *Science* 172:706–09.
1974   *Galileo: A Philosophical Study.* Chicago: University of Chicago Press.
1974a   On the Relations between Compositional and Evolutionary Theories. In Ayala and Dobzhansky 1974, 187–202.
1974b   Scientific Theories and Their Domains. In Suppe 1974, 518–65.
1982   The Concept of Observation in Science and Philosophy. *Philosophy of Science* 49:485–525.
1984   *Reason and the Search for Knowledge: Investigations in the Philosophy of Science.* Dordrecht, Neth.: Reidel.

Shaw, H. K. A.
1950   Post-Darwinian Development of Taxonomy (Botany). In Linnean Society of London 1950, 60–79.

Shoenfield, J.
  1968   *Mathematical Logic.* New York: Addison-Wesley.

Simpson, G. G.
  1961   *Principles of Animal Taxonomy.* New York: Columbia University Press.

Skyrms, B.
  1967   The Explication of X Knows That P. *Journal of Philosophy* 65:373–89.

  1975   *Choice and Chance.* 2d ed. Belmont, Calif.: Dickenson. 3d ed., 1985.

Sloep, P. B., and W. J. van der Steen
  1987   The Nature of Evolutionary Theory: The Semantic Challenge. *Biology and Philosophy* 2:1–15.

  1987a   Syntacticism *versus* Semanticism: Another Attempt at Dissolution. *Biology and Philosophy* 2:33–41.

Smart, J.
  1950   Post-Darwinian Development of Taxonomy (Zoology). In Linnean Society of London 1950, 80–83.

Smart, J. J. C.
  1963   *Philosophy and Scientific Realism.* London: Routledge and Kegan Paul.

Sneed, J.
  1971   *The Logical Structure of Mathematical Physics.* Dordrecht, Neth.: Reidel.

  1976   Philosophical Problems in the Empirical Science of Science: A Formal Approach. *Erkenntnis* 10:115–46.

Socarides, C.
  1970   Homosexuality and Medicine. *Journal of the American Medical Association* 212:1199–1202.

Sokal, R., and P. H. A. Sneath
  1963   *Principles of Numerical Taxonomy.* San Francisco: W. H. Freeman.

Sosa, E.
  1965   The Analysis of 'Knowledge that P'. *Analysis* 25:1–8.
  1969   Propositional Knowledge. *Philosophical Studies* 20:33–43.

Sprague, T. A.
  1950   The Evolution of Botanical Taxonomy from Theophrastus to Linnaeus. In Linnean Society of London 1950, 1–23.

Stauffer, R. C., ed.
  1949   *Science and Civilization.* Madison: University of Wisconsin Press.

Stegmüller, W.
  1976   *The Structure and Dynamics of Theories.* New York: Springer-Verlag.

Strauss, M.
  1938   Mathematics as Logical Syntax. *Erkenntnis,* vol. 7.

Strawson, P. F.
1964   Truth. In *Truth,* edited by G. Pitcher, 32–53. Englewood Cliffs, N.J.: Prentice-Hall.

Suppe, F.
1967   The Meaning and Use of Models in Mathematics and the Exact Sciences. Ph.D. dissertation, University of Michigan.
1971   On Partial Interpretation. *Journal of Philosophy* 68:57–76.
1973   Facts and Empirical Truth. *Canadian Journal of Philosophy* 3:197–212.
1974   *The Structure of Scientific Theories.* Urbana: University of Illinois Press.
1974a   Exemplars, Theories and Disciplinary Matrixes. In Suppe 1974, 483–99.
1974b   The Search for Philosophic Understanding of Scientific Theories. In Suppe 1974, 3–241.
1974c   Theories and Phenomena. In *Developments in the Methodology of Social Science,* edited by W. Leinfellner and E. Köhler, 45–91. Dordrecht, Neth.: Reidel.
1975   Post–World War II Developments in American Philosophy of Science. *Ruch Filozoficzny* 33:135–68.
1977   *The Structure of Scientific Theories.* 2d ed. Urbana: University of Illinois Press.
1977a   Afterword—1977. In Suppe 1977, 617–730.
1981   The Bell and Weinberg Study: Future Priorities for Research on Homosexuality. In *Nature and Causes of Homosexuality: A Philosophic and Scientific Inquiry,* edited by N. Koertge, 69–97. New York: Haworth Press.
1984   Beyond Skinner and Kuhn. *New Ideas in Psychology* 42:89–104.
1984a   Accepting and Rejecting Behaviorism: A Reply to Critics. *New Ideas in Psychology* 42:119–24.
1984b   Curing Homosexuality. In *Philosophy and Sex,* 2d ed., edited by R. Baker and F. Elliston, 391–420. Buffalo: Prometheus Books.
1985   Towards an Adequate Information Science. In Heilprin 1985, 7–28.
1985a   Information Science, Artificial Intelligence and the Problem of Black Noise. In Heilprin 1985, 63–78.
1986   Grünbaum, Homosexuality and Contemporary Psychoanalysis. *Behavioral and Brain Research* 9(2):261–62.
n.d.   Explaining Homosexuality: Philosophical Issues, and Who Cares Anyhow? To appear in a volume of *Boston Studies in the Philosophy of Science.* Dordrecht, Neth.: Reidel. Forthcoming.

Suppe, F., and P. Asquith, eds.
1976   *PSA 1976: Proceedings of the 1976 Biennial Meetings of the Philosophy of Science Association.* Vol. I. East Lansing, Mich.: Philosophy of Science Association.

1977   *PSA 1976: Proceedings of the 1976 Biennial Meetings of the Philosophy of Science Association.* Vol. II. East Lansing, Mich.: Philosophy of Science Association.

Suppe, F., and A. Jacox
1985   Philosophy of Science and the Development of Nursing Theory. In *Annual Review of Nursing Research,* vol. 3, edited by H. H. Werley and J. J. Fitzpatrick, 241–67. New York: Springer Publishing Co.

Suppes, P.
1957   *Introduction to Logic.* New York: Van Nostrand.
1959   Axioms for Relativistic Kinematics with or without Parity. In Henkin, Suppes, and Tarski 1959, 291–307.
1961   A Comparison of the Meaning and Use of Models in Mathematics and the Empirical Sciences. In Freudenthal 1961, 163–77.
1962   Models of Data. In Nagel, Suppes, and Tarski 1962, 252–61.
1967   What Is Scientific Theory? In Morgenbesser 1967, 55–67.
1970   *A Probabilistic Theory of Causality.* Vol. 24 of *Acta Philosophica Fennica.* Amsterdam: North Holland, 1970.
1979   Patrick Suppes—A Self-Profile. In *Patrick Suppes,* edited by R. J. Bogdon, 3–56. Dordrecht, Neth.: Reidel.

Swain, M., ed.
1970   *Induction, Acceptance and Rational Belief.* New York: Humanities Press.

Swartz, N.
1985   *The Concept of Physical Law.* Cambridge: Cambridge University Press.

Shwartz, R., ed.
1965   *Perceiving, Sensing, and Knowing.* Garden City, N.Y.: Anchor Books.

Szasz, T.
1964   *The Myth of Mental Illness.* N.Y.: Hoeber.
1970   *The Manufacture of Madness.* N.Y.: Harper and Row.

Tarski, A., and R. Vaught
1957   Arithmetic Extensions of Relational Systems. *Composito Mathematicae* 13:81–102.

Theophrastus
1916   *Enquiry into Plants.* Translated by A. Hart. Loeb Classical Library. Cambridge, Mass.: Harvard University Press.

Thompson, P.
1983   The Structure of Evolutionary Theory: A Semantic Approach. *Studies in History and Philosophy of Science* 14:215–29.
1985   Sociobiological Explanation and the Testability of Sociobiological Theory. In *Sociobiology and Epistemology,* edited by J. Fetzer, 201–15. Dordrecht, Neth.: D. Reidel.
1986   The Interaction of Theories and the Semantic Conception of Evolutionary Theory. *Philosophia* 37:28–37.

1987   A Defence of the Semantic Conception of Evolutionary Theory. *Biology and Philosophy* 2:26–32.

1988   The Conceptual Role of Intelligence in Human Sociobiology. In *Intelligence and Evolutionary Biology,* edited by H. J. Jerison and I. L. Jerison. New York: Springer-Verlag.

1988a   Logical and Epistemological Aspects of the "New" Evolutionary Epistemology. *Canadian Journal of Philosophy* 412.

1989   *The Structure of Biological Theories.* New York: State University of New York Press.

n.d.   David Hull's Conception of the Structure of Evolutionary Theory. In *The Philosophy of David Hull,* edited by M. Ruse. Dordrecht, Neth.: D. Reidel. Forthcoming.

Toulmin, S.

1953   *The Philosophy of Science.* London: Hutchinson.

1961   *Foresight and Understanding.* London: Hutchinson; New York: Harper Torchbooks, 1963.

1972   *Human Understanding,* Vol. I. Princeton: Princeton University Press.

Turk-Saunders, J., and N. Champawat

1964   Mr. Clark's Definition of Knowledge. *Analysis* 25:8–9.

Turk-Saunders, J., and D. F. Henze

1967   *The Private Language Problem: A Philosophical Dialogue.* New York: Random House.

van Fraassen, B.

1967   Meaning Relations among Predicates *Nôus* 1:161–79.

1969   Meaning Relations and Modalities, *Nôus* 3:155–67.

1970   On the Extension of Beth's Semantics of Physical Theories. *Philosophy of Science* 37:325–39.

1972   A Formal Approach to the Philosophy of Science. In Colodny 1972, 303–66.

1974   The Formal Representation of Physical Quantities. In *Logical and Empirical Studies in Contemporary Physics,* vol. 13 of *Boston Studies in the Philosophy of Science,* edited by R. S. Cohen and M. Wartofsky, 196–209. Dordrecht, Neth.: Reidel.

1974a   The Labryinth of Quantum Logic. In *Logical and Empirical Studies in Contemporary Physics,* vol. 13 of *Boston Studies in the Philosophy of Science,* edited by R. S. Cohen and M. Wartofsky, 224–54. Dordrecht, Neth.: Reidel.

1975   Wilfrid Sellars on Scientific Realism. *Dialogue* 14:606–16.

1976   To Save the Phenomena. *Journal of Philosophy* 73:623–32.

1977   On the Radical Incompleteness of the Manifest Image. In Suppe and Asquith 1977, 335–43.

1980   *The Scientific Image.* Oxford: Clarendon Press.

1985   Empiricism and the Philosophy of Science. In Churchland and Hooker 1985, 245–308.

1989   *Laws and Symmetry.* New York: Oxford University Press.

von Neumann, J.

1932   *Mathematische Gründlagen der Quantenmechanik.* Berlin: Springer.

1955   *Mathematical Foundations of Quantum Mechanics.* Princeton: Princeton University Press. Translation of von Neumann 1932.

1962   *Collected Works.* 6 vols. New York: Pergamon Press.

1966   *Theory of Self-Reproducing Automata.* Edited and completed by A. W. Burks. Urbana: University of Illinois Press.

von Neumann, J., and O. Morgenstern

1953   *Theory of Games and Economic Behavior.* 3d ed., Princeton: Princeton University Press.

Wessels, L.

1976   Laws and Meaning Postulates [in van Fraassen's View of Theories]. In *PSA 1974,* edited by R. S. Cohen et al., 215–35. Dordrecht, Neth.: Reidel.

Whewell, W.

1837   *History of the Inductive Sciences.* London: J. W. Parker.

1840   *Philosophy of the Inductive Sciences.* London: J. W. Parker.

1859   *History of the Inductive Sciences.* 3d ed., 2 vols. New York: David. Appleton and Co.

1967   *Philosophy of the Inductive Sciences.* 3d ed., London: Cass.

White, A.

1957   On Claiming to Know. *Philosophical Review* 66:180–92. Reprinted in *Knowledge and Belief,* edited by A. Phillips-Griffiths. New York: Oxford University Press, 1967.

Wiener, N.

1949   *Extrapolation, Interpolation, and Smoothing of Stationary Time Series, with Engineering Applications.* Cambridge, Mass.: MIT Press.

1950   *The Human Use of Human Beings.* London: Eyre and Spottsewoode.

1961   *Cybernetics, or Control and Communications in the Animal and the Machine.* 2d ed. New York: John Wiley and Sons.

Wilmott, A. J.

1950   Systematic Botany from Linnaeus to Darwin. In Linnean Society of London 1950, 33–45.

Wilson, M.

1985   What Can Theory Tell Us about Observation? In Churchland and Hooker 1985, 222–44.

Wimsatt, W. C.

1979   Reduction. In Asquith and Kyburg 1979, 352–77.

1987   False Models as Means to Truer Theories. In *Neutral Models in Biology,* edited by N. Nitecki and A. Hoffman, 23–55. Oxford University Press.

Wittgenstein, L.
1953   *Philosophical Investigations.* Translated by E. Anscombe. New York: Macmillan.

Wójcicki, R.
1974   Set Theoretic Representations of Empirical Phenomena. *Journal of Philosophical Logic.* 3:337–43.
1974a   The Semantic Conception of Truth in the Methodology of Empirical Sciences. *Dialectic and Humanism* 1:103–16.
1976   Some Problems of Formal Methodology of Science. In Przełecki, Szianiawski, and Wójcicki 1976, 9–18.

Woozley, A. D.
1952–53 Knowing and Not Knowing. *Proceedings of the Aristotelian Society* 53:151–72.

Wright, S.
1921   Correlation and Causation. *Journal of Agricultural Research.* 20:557–85.

Zeigler, B.
1976   The Hierarchy of System Specifications and the Problem of Structural Influence. In Suppe and Asquith 1976, 227–39.
1976a   *Theory of Simulation and Modelling.* New York: John Wiley.

Index

A Note on the Author

Frederick Suppe is Professor of Philosophy in the Committee on the History and Philosophy of Science and the Philosophy Department at the University of Maryland at College Park and in the School of Nursing Doctoral Program at the University of Maryland at Baltimore. As a distinguished philosopher of science he is perhaps best known for his work on the structure of scientific theories. His seminal introduction and afterword to *The Structure of Scientific Theories* are classics in the literature. He is one of the main developers of the Semantic Conception of Theories and has published over fifty scholarly articles. He lives on a 165–acre farm in Virginia's Shenandoah Valley.